THE COMPREHENSIVE

HISTORY OF PSYCHOLOGY

THE COMPREHENSIVE
HISTORY OF PSYCHOLOGY

ARUN KUMAR SINGH, Ph.D.
Retd. University Professor &
Former Head
Dept. of Psychology
Patna University, Patna

MOTILALA BANARSIDASS PUBLISHERS
PRIVATE LIMITED • DELHI

Seventh Revised Edition : 2017
First Edition : Delhi, 1991

ISBN: 978-81-208-0804-1 (Cloth)
ISBN: 978-81-208-0859-1 (Paper)

MOTILAL BANARSIDASS
41 U.A. Bungalow Road, Jawahar Nagar, Delhi 110 007
8 Mahalaxmi Chamber, 22 Bhulabhai Desai Road, Mumbai 400 026
203 Royapettah High Road, Mylapore, Chennai 600 004
236, 9th Main III Block, Jayanagar, Bengaluru 560 011
8 Camac Street, Kolkata 700 017
Ashok Rajpath, Patna 800 004
Chowk, Varanasi 221 001

Printed in India
by RP Jain at NAB Printing Unit,
A-44, Naraina Industrial Area, Phase I, New Delhi–110028
and published by JP Jain for Motilal Banarsidass Publishers (P) Ltd,
41 U.A. Bungalow Road, Jawahar Nagar, Delhi-110007

To

My Wife

KUMUD RANI

PREFACE

This book is intended for students of undergraduate and post-graduate classes. My major reason for writing it is my dissatisfaction with other texts available in the field, which I discovered through teaching the course for many years. The texts written in this field by foreign writers don't fully cater the needs of our students of Indian Universities. Moreover, none of these texts mention about the position of psychology in India. Instead, they concentrate only upon Western positions. The students and many teachers, too, remain in dark about the status of psychology in India. With the publication of *The Comprehensive History of Psychology* this darkness will no longer remain in the minds of Indian students and teachers because a separate chapter on *An Overview of Psychology in India* has been added, apart from elsewhere discussion of the works of Indian psychologists. This book differs from others in the field in several ways :

* The text is shorter than many other so it can be easily handled by undergraduate and post-graduate students even in one-semester where so provided.
* I have selected only important systems and theories that are often found in other texts. Therefore, I have gone into the greater depth and detail. The advantage of this will be that students will gain indepth knowledge of those systems and theories rather than a little knowledge of each of the different theories and concepts.
* In discussing each system I have placed much emphasis upon the historical antecedents, which in itself, is unique. This will help the students in understanding those background factors that have led to the emergence of the different system.

The book has been written in twenty chapters. The *first* chapter in introductory and briefly introduces the different systems of psychology. Chapters *second* and *third* examine the status of Psychology before Wilhelm Wundt. The *fourth* chapter is exclusively devoted to the contributions of Wilhelm Wundt, the father of Experimental Psychology. From Chapter *fifth* to *eighteenth* different classical systems and modern psychologies have been lucidly presented. The chapter *nineteenth* intends to predict where the psychology is going and what its position is today. The *last* chapter is exclusively devoted to the work of Indian psychologists in an overall perspective. At the end of each chapter, *Know Yourself* has been appended for healthy mental exercise of the students.

I am grateful to a number of people for their helpful suggestions and constructive criticisms. In fact, some students as well as teachers had shown very enthusiastic interest in reading the manuscript and pointing out the errors. I feel highly indebted to all those people.

Like all textbook writers, I owe a great debt to my wife, Kumud Rani, for extending gracious assistance through all phases of manuscript preparation. I am also indebted to Dr. Alpana Sen Gupta, Research Associate in Psychology for carefully supervising the typing of the manuscript. Finally, I am grateful to Publishers Motilal Banarsidass, Publishers Pvt. Ltd., Delhi, in general and Shri Kamla Shankar Singh, Motilal Banarsidass, Patna in particular who took pains in bringing the book before you at right time. Wherever errors have occurred and brought to my attention, they have been corrected. However, the final responsibility to any such errors remains with me. If you find any such error, provide a feedback for which I am eagerly and earnestly waiting.

January, 1991 **ARUN KUMAR SINGH**

SEVENTH EDITION

In preparing seventh edition of *'The Comprehensive History of Psychology'*, an attempt has been made to broaden and update the basic concepts and theories. I have also kept in view the suggestions of my colleagues and students of different parts of the country. These colleagues and students have taken pains to read carefully the different portions of the previous edition and have sent their enlightened suggestions for improvement. Although it has not been possible for me to incorporate their all types of suggestions into the book, I have tried to honour them maximally. Keeping in view their suggestions, *'Major Events in Psychology'* and *'Glossary'* have been added and updated in this book. I must express my deepest sense of gratitude to all of them. For understanding about psychological development taking place at the international level, a chapter on *International Psychology* has been added. Views of Indian psychology have been duly elaborated so that its contributions could be better understood.

January, 2017 **ARUN KUMAN SINGH**

MAJOR EVENTS IN PSYCHOLOGY

B.C.

2200 Chineses starts Civil Service Examinations.

400 Hippocrates propounds first theory of personality based on constitutional types.

399 Plato anticipates the value of differential psychology in his famous book *The Republic*.

350 Aristotle formulates three laws to account for association of ideas. He is considered as *Father of all Psychologies*.

A.D.

1650 Descrates proposes mind-body relation as on of dualism.

1651 Thomas Hobbes publishes his famous treaties on human nature.

1690 John Locke announces that mind, at birth, is a *tabula rasa*—a blank state.

1749 David Hartley formally establishes '*Associationism*' which is the study of how ideas are formed and connected.

1791 Galvani concludes that the nature of nerve impulse is electrical.

1794 Pinel orders removal of chains from mental patients in France.

1807 Bell and Magedie concludes anatomical and functional discreteness of sensory and motor nerves.

1821 Flourens conducts first significant experiment in localisation of brain functions.

1823 Bessel performs first measurement of individual differences and calculates personal equation in astronomical observations.

1826 Johannes Muller propounds *doctrine of specific nerve energies*.

1834 Gall and Spurzheim propose impetus for intensive study of brain function by incorrectly assuming that the mind's faculties are localized.

1841 Dorothea Dix starts compaign to improve conditions in mental hospitals in America and Europe.

1842 Weber first proposes quantitative law in psychology.

1846 Weber formulates first quantitative law in psychology, popularly known as *Weber's law*.

1850 For the first time Helmholtz measures the rate of conduction of nerve impulse.

1860 Fechner publishes his famous book *Elements of Psychophygics* in which he sets forth various methods of psycholophysical measurement.

1860 Young-Helmholtz *theory of colour vision* comes into being.

1861 Paul Broca formulates location of specific area for speech in brain.

1869 John Stuart Mill formulates theory of *mental chemistry* to account for development of complex ideas.

1869 Francis Galton publishes his famous book *Hereditary Genius* and the study of individual differences rapidly spreads and expands through the work of Galton.

1870 Fritsch and Hitzig discover specific sensory and motor areas in brain.

1872 Charles Darwin gives emphasis upon continuity of mind between animals and men.

1878 Hering develops *theory of colour vision.*

1879 Wilhelm Wundt establishes the first psychological laboratory at Leipzing University (Now Karl-Marx University) and psychology is established as an independent scientific discipline by him.

1879 Galton develops the first projective technique, a word association test.

1882 Comparative psychology is started with publication of Romane's book on animal intelligence.

1883 G. S. Hall establishes the *first* American psychological laboratory at John Hopkin University.

1884 William James formulates his famous theory of emotion.

1885 Sir Francis Galton starts his *first* mental testing centre in London.

1885 Ebbinghaus publishes first significant experimental studies in the field of memory.

1887 First professional journal of Psychology in United States is published by G. S. Hall *(American Journal of Psychology).*

1889 First International congress of psychology was held in Paris.

1890 William James publishes his famous book *The Principles of Psychology.*

1890 J. M. Cattell coins the term *mental test.*

1890 G. S. Hall founds *American Psychological Association* and becomes its first president.

1892 Titchener founds *'Structuralism'* as a part of psychology in America.

1892 G. S. Hall establishes *American Psychological Association* and became its first president.

1894 Lloyd Morgan formulates the law of parsimony.

1895 Freud and Breuer publishes the famous book *Studies in Hysteria.*

1896 Lighter Witmer starts first psychological clinic in Pennyslavania University

1896 Karl Pearson develops statistical theory of correlation.

1896 J. M. Cattell becomes influential in development and use of mental tests in America.

1898 At Columbia University E. L. Thorndike conducts some of the first experiments on animal learning to discover principles of learning.

1898 First experiment in Social psychology is conducted by Norman Triplett, an American researcher.

1900 Sigmund Freud publishes his popular and famous book *The Interpretation of Dreams.*

1904 Spearman describes intelligence in terms of general (g) and specific (s) factors.

1905 Binet and Simon develop first standardized intelligence test for children in France.

1905 Mary Caulkins elected first woman President of APA.

1906 I.P. Pavlov, a Russian physiologist, publishes his classic studies on dog in the field of classical conditioning.

1907 *Psychological clinic,* first clinical journal was founded by Witmer.

1908 William McDougall publishes *first* text in social psychology.

1908 Margaret Foly Washburn becomes the first woman to be awarded Ph. D. in Psychology.

1908 First clinical internship was started at Vineland Training School.

1909 William Healy lays the foundation of first child-guidance center, the *Juvenile Psychopathic Institute* at Chiago.

1910 Goddard's English translation of the 1908 revision of Binet-Simon intelligence scale is published.

1911 Stern develops the concept of *Intelligence quotient* (IQ).

1912 Gestalt Psychology is established in Wertheimer's paper on *Phi phenomenon.*

1912 J. B. Watson publishes his famous book *Psychology as a Behaviourst Views it.*

1913 J. B. Watson establishes the popular school of *Behaviourism* in psychology.

1913 Carl Jung establishes school of *Analytical psychology* after separating himself from Freud.

1916 First Indian Department of Psychology is established at Calcutta University.

1916 In India first Psychology department at Calcutta University comes into being.

1916 At Stanford University Terman revised Binet-Simon test for use in United States. This new test is called as *Stanford-Binet.*

1917 First group tests of intelligence are devised for use in United States army.

1917 Clinical Psychologists break away from APA to form American Association of Clinical Psychology (AACP).

1917 Kohler publishes the results of popular studies conducted on primates in the field of problem solving.

1917 AACP rejoins APA as its clinical section.

1920 Francis Sumner becomes the first blackman to earn a Ph. D.

1920 Watson and his wife Raynor demonstrate that fear in child can be learnt.

1921 J. M. Cattell founds *Psychological Corporation.*

1921-30 Gestalt Psychology attains its peak influences.

1921 Hermann Rorschach, Swiss Psychiatrist, devised a technique of measuring personality through use of unstructured materials like ink blots.

1921 The famous book *Concept of Repression* is published by Prof. Girindar Shekhar Bose. The book was praised for scholarly insight by sigmund Freud.

1922 Edward Tolman proposes *'Purposive Behaviourism'.*

1922 Morton Prince establishes the first major Social psychology Journal *The Journal of Abnormal and Social Psychology.*

1922 Indian Psychoanalytic society is established at Calcutta University by Prof. Girindra Shekhar Bose.

1924 David Levy introduces Rorschach Inkblot test to America.

1924 M. C. Jones employs learning principles to remove children@s fear.

1924 David Levy introduces Rorschach Test in America.

1924 Indian Psychological Association is founded.

1924 Second Indian department of psychology was established at Mysore University.

1926 Indian Journal of Psychology is begun to be published.

1928 The famous book *Intrdocution to Social Psychology* is published by Prof. N. N. Sen Gupta and Prof. R. K. Mukherjee

1929 Lashley expresses his views on brain mechanisms and intelligence.

1931 Clinical Division of APA appoints committee on training standards.

1931 First Black woman Inez Prosser is awarded Ph. D. in Psychology in America.

1933 Inez Prosser becomes the first black woman to earn a Ph. D. in Psychology.

1934 J. L. Moreno develops *Sociometry.*

1935 Thurstone develops the technique of factor analysis in formulating a theory of intelligence.

1935 Muzafer Sherif, using autokinetic effect, performs first laboratory experiments on formation and change of social norms.

1935 Murray's TAT is published.

1936 First clinical Text book *Clinical Psychology* is published by Louttit.

1936 George Gallup develops methods for conducting public opinion polls and surveys.

1937 Neo-Freudians give emphasis upon the importance of social factors in personality development and functioning.

1937 Clinical section of APA breaks away to form American Association for Applied Psychology (AAAP).

1938 B.F. Skinner publishes his famous and popular book *'The Behaviour of Organisms'* which summarizes researches on operant conditioning.

1938 Myers, Jung and Spearman participate in Indian science congress.

1938 First *Mental Measurement Year Book* is published.

1939 Wechsler-Bellevue Intelligence Scale is published.

1939 Clinical division of American Psychological Association breaks its relation from *American Association for Applied Psychology* or AAAP.

1940 Lumbini Park Mental Hospital is established at Calcutta.

1941-45 The field of clinical psychology witenesses rapid expansion due to shocks of the second World War.

1942 Technique of client-centred therapy is developed by Carl Rogers.

1943 C. Hull presents his mathematico-deductive theory of learning in his famous book *Principles of Behaviour*.

1943 Minnesota Multiphasic Personality Inventory (MMPI) is published.

1945 Kurt Lewin establishes a Research Centre for studying group dynamics at M.I.T.

1945 AAAP rejoins APA.

1945 Psychological wing of Defence Research is established in India which became part of the Defence Science Organisation of India in 1949.

1946 National Institute of Mental Health begins supports for training of clinical psychologists.

1946 Third Indian Department of Psychology was established at Patna University.

1947 American Board of Examiners in Professional Psychology was organized.

1947 Akhilanand (London) publishes Hindu Psychology.

1949 Boulder conference on training in clinical psychology was convened.

1949 Hebb introduces Behaviour therapy in his famous book organization of behaviour that narrows down the distance between Psychology and Neurophysiology.

1951 International Union of Psychological Science (IUPSYS) is born at thirteenth International Congress of Psychology in Stockholm.

1952 American Psychiatric Association publishes first *Diagonostic and Statistical Manual* (DSM-I).

1953 APA *Ethical Standards for Psychologists* is published.

1954 Abraham Maslow starts humanistic movement.

1955 National Institute of Mental Health and Neuro-sciences (NIMHANS) is established at Banglore in India

1957 California Psychological Inventory (CPI) is developed to measure dimensions of Normal Personality.

1957 L. Festinger proposes *Theory of cognitive dissonance* for explaining attitude change.

1957 Sanford Training Conference is organized.

1958 Miami Training Conference is organized.

1961 Albert Bandura formulates social learning theory and begins the cognitive revolution.

1962 Mental Hospital is established at Ranchi, India

1965 Chicago Training Conference is organized.

1966 *Indian Academy of Applied Psychology* or IAAP is established

1968 PSY D training programme began at the University of Illinois.

1968 *Indian Association of Clinical Psychology* or IACP is established.

1969 California School of Professional psychology is founded.

1972 First ICSSR Survey of Research in Psychology in India edited by Prof. S. K. Mitra. is pubished.

1973 Vail Colarado Training conference is organized.

1978 Herbert Simon receives Noble prize for its important works in the field of cognition.

1980 Third Edition of DSM (DSM-III) is published.

1981 Roger Sperry receives Noble prize for split-brain research.

1980-81 Second ICSSR's Survey of Research in Psychology edited by Dr. Udai Pareekh is released.

1981 APA publishes its revised *Ethical Principles of Psychologists.* Second ICSSR Survey of Research in Psychology in India edited by Udai Pareekh is released.

1982 Psychological Research Wing of DRDO, India is elevated to a full-fledged organizaiton and named as Defence Institute of Psychological Research or DIPR.

1987 DSM-III Revision is published.

1987 National Academy of Psychology (NAOP) India, is founded.

1988 Third ICSSR Survey of Research in Psychology edited by Prof. Janak Pandey is released in three volumes.

1988 American Psychological Society is formed.

1989 Revised version of MMPI is published and became known as MMPI-2.

1994 DSM-IV is published

2000 Arvid Carlsson, a Swedish scientist, is awarded Nobel Prize jointly with Paul Greengard and Eric Kandel, American scientists, for the discovery of treatment of 'Parkinson' disease and other neurological disorders.

2000 Elizabeth Loftus does pioneering work on false memory and eye witness testimony.

2000 DSM-IV (TR) is published.

2000 Fourth ICSSR Survey of Research in Psychology in India edited by Prof. Janak Pandey is released in three volumes.

2003 Fifth edition of Standard-Binet Intelligence test (SB-5) is released.

2009-11 Fifth ICSSR Survey of Research in Psychology in India edited by Prof. Girishwar Mishra. (Four volumes) is released.

2010 New Subfields such as clinical NeuroPsychology and Evolutionary Psychology develop.

2013 DSM-V is released.

❑

BRIEF CONTENTS

Chapters

1. Systems and Theories *1*
2. Prescientific Psychology : Ancient Greek Philosophical influences. *16*
3. Prescientific Psychology : Modern Philosphical Influences. *26*
4. Beginning of Experimental Psychology. *58*
5. Wilhelm Maximillian Wundt : Beginning of Structuralism. *90*
6. Structuralism. *114*
7. The Psychology of William James and other Pioneer American Psychologist : Forerunners of Functionalism. *128*
8. Functionalism. *145*
9. Modern Associationism. *168*
10. Early Behaviourism. *188*
11. Later Behaviourism. *215*
12. Gestalt Psychology. *259*
13. Psychoanalysis. *284*
14. Heris to Freud. *306*
15. Field Theory. *342*
16. Hormic Psychology and Dynamic Psychology. *359*
17. Humanistic Psychology. *370*
18. Existential Psychology. *384*
19. Cognitive Psychology. *395*
20. Psychology : Today and Tomorrow. *414*
21. An overview of Psychology in India. *418*
22. International Psychology. *449*

Glossary. *467*

References. *485*

Name Index. *503*

Subject Index. *508*

CONTENTS

CHAPTER 1
SYSTEMS AND THEORIES 1

Chapter Preview 1
Systems in Psychology : Meaning and Types 1
Theories and Hypotheses 4
Functions of Psychological Systems and Theories 5
Evaluating Systems of Psychology 6
Some Basic Issues in Psychology 8
Chapter Highlights 14
Review Questions 15

CHAPTER 2
PRESCIENTIFIC PSYCHOLOGY : ANCIENT GREEK PHILOSOPHICAL INFLUENCES 16

Chapter Preview 16
Hellenic Period 17
Socrates 18, Plato 19, Aristotle 20
Decline of Greek Naturalism 22
Science in Renaissance (1400–1600 AD) 23
Chapter Highlights 24
Review Questions 25

CHAPTER 3
PRESCIENTIFIC PSYCHOLOGY : MODERN PHILOSOPHICAL INFLUENCES 26

Chapter Preview 26
Mind-body Problem : 27
Rene Descartes 27, Gottfried Leibnitz 29, Benedict Spinoza 31, Conclusion regarding Mind-body Problem; Monism 31
Empiricism : 32
Tomas Hobbes 32, John Locke 33, George Berkeley 34, David Hume 37
Associationsim : 39
David Hartley 39, The Scottish School (Thomas Reid, Douglas Stewart, Thomas Brown) 41, Back to British Associationism : The

Mills 44, James Mill 44; James Stuart Mill 46; Alexander Bain 47, Herbert Spencer 50

Nativism, that is, German Psychology before 1850 : 51

Immanuel Kant 51, Johann Friedrich Herbart 52, Hermann Lotze 55

Chapter Highlights 56

Review Questions 57

CHAPTER 4

BEGINNING OF EXPERIMENTAL PSYCHOLOGY 58

Chapter Preview 58

Psychophysics : 59

Ernst H. Weber 59, Gustav Theodor Fechner 61

The Development of Neurophysiology : 65

Sensory and motor nerves : Bell and Megendie 65, Specific nerve energies : Johannes Muller 66, Early studies of nerve impulses : Its electrical nature and velocity 68, Phrenology : Franz Joseph Gall 69, Localization of functions in brain : Flourens and Broca 70, Reflex action and Reaction time 72, Sense Physiology : Hermann Von Helmholtz and Edward Hering 75

The Theory of Evolution : 81

Charles Darwin 81, Sir Francis Galton : Psychologist of Genius 83

Chapter Highlights 86

Review Questions 88

CHAPTER 5

WILHELM MAXIMILLIAN WUNDT : BEGINNING OF STRUCTURALISM 90

Chapter Preview 90

Brief Life-sketch of Wilhelm Wundt 90

Antecedent Forces 92

Wundt's Systematic Psychology 93

Work of Leipzig Laboratory 97

Evaluation of Wundt's Contribution 100

Wundt's contemporaries : 101

Franz Brentano : Act Psychology 101, Carl Stumpf 103, George Elias Muller 104, Wurzburg school 106, Oswald Kulpe 106, Karl Marbe 107, Henry Watt 108, Karl Buhler 109

Chapter Highlights 110

Review Questions 112

CHAPTER 6
STRUCTURALISM 114

Chapter Preview 114
Brief Life-sketch of Edward Bradford Titchener 114
Titchener's Structural Psychology 115
Criticisms of Structuralism 122
Wundt and Titchener : A comparative look 123
Fate of Structuralism 125
Chapter Highlights 125
Review Questions 127

CHAPTER 7
THE PSYCHOLOGY OF WILLIAM JAMES AND OTHER PIONEER AMERICAN PSYCHOLOGISTS : FORERUNNERS OF FUNCTIONALISM 128

Chapter Preview 128
Brief Life-sketch of William James 128
William James' Psychology 130
Stream of consciousness 135
Significance of Williâm James 136
Some pioneer American Functionalists 137
G.S. Hall 137, James McKeen Cattell 138
Chapter Highlights 143
Review Questions 144

CHAPTER 8
FUNCTIONALISM 145

Chapter Preview 145
Antecedents of Functionalism 146
Founders : Chicago Functional Psychology : 148
John Dewey 149, James Rowland Angell 150, Harvey A. Carr 152
Functionalism as a System 152
Columbia's Functional Psychology : 157,
James McKeen Cattell 157, Edward Lee Thorndike 157, Robert Sessions Woodworth 158
Criticisms of Functionalism 160
Distinction between Structuralism and Functionalism 161
Fate of Functionalism 163
Chapter Highlights 164

Review Questions 167

CHAPTER 9
MODERN ASSOCIATIONISM 168

Chapter Preview 168
Historical Background of Associationism 169
The Association of Stimulus and Response : 171
Hermann Ebbinghaus 171, Ivan Petrovich Pavlov 173, Vladimir Bekhterev : The Psychology of motor conditioning 175, Edward Lee Thorndike : The Psychology of connectionism 176
Criticisms of Thorndike's System 182
Importance of Thorndike 184
Chapter Highlights 185
Review Questions 187

CHAPTER 10
EARLY BEHAVIOURISM 188

Chapter Preview 188
Antecedents of Early Behaviourism 188
Brief Life-sketch of John Broadus Watson 193
Watsonian Behaviourism as a System 195
Secondary Features of Watsonian Behaviourism 200
Watson's Experimental Formulations 202
Criticisms of Watson's Behaviourism 205
Some other Early Behaviourists : 208
Albert P. Weiss 208, Walter S. Hunter 209, Edwin B. Holt 209, Karl Lashley 210
Chapter Highlights 213
Review Questions 214

CHAPTER 11
LATER BEHAVIOURISM 215

Chapter Preview 215
Edwin R. Guthrie 216
Clark L. Hull 220
Burrhus Frederic Skinner 227
Edward Chace Tolman 238
Tolman's Purposive Behaviourism 239

J. R. Kantor : Interbehaviourism 246
Albert Bandura 251
Distinction between Early Behaviourism and Later Behaviourism 255
Chapter Highlights 256
Review Questions 258

CHAPTER 12
GESTALT PSYCHOLOGY 259

Chapter Preview 259
Antecedent Forces 260
The Founding of Gestalt Psychology : 262
Max Wertheimer 262, Wolfgang Kohler 264, Kurt Koffka 265
Protest of Gestalt Psychology against other systems 266
Basic Experimental contributions of Gestalt Psychology 267
Gestalt Psychology as a System 276
Criticisms of Gestalt Psychology 278
Present Status of Gestalt Psychology 280
Chapter Highlights 281
Review Questions 282

CHAPTER 13
PSYCHOANALYSIS 284

Chapter Preview 284
Brief Life-sketch of Sigmund Freud 285
Antecedent Forces of Psychoanalysis 288
Freudian Psychoanalysis as a system 291
Contributions of Freudian Psychoanalysis 294
Criticisms of Freudian Psychoanalysis 303
Chapter Highlights 304
Review Questions 305

CHAPTER 14
HEIRS TO FREUD 306

Chapter Preview 306
Alfred Adler's Individual Psychology 307
Differences between Freud and Adler 313
Carl Jung's Analytical Psychology 314
Distinction between Freud and Jung 320

Neo-Freudians : 320

Karen Horney 320, Erich Fromm 324, Harry Stack Sullivan 326, Erik Erikson 332

Comparison between Freud and Erikson 338

Distinctions between Freudian and Neo-Freudian 339

Chapter Highlights 340

Review Questions 341

CHAPTER 15

FIELD THEORY 342

Chapter Preview 342

Kurt Lewin's Field Theory 343

Tolman's Cognitive Field Theory 353

Brunswik's Field Theory (or Probabilistic Functionalism) 354

Chapter Highlights 357

Review Questions 358

CHAPTER 16

HORMIC PSYCHOLOGY AND DYNAMIC PSYCHOLOGY 359

Chapter Preview 360

Basic features of McDougall's Hormic Psychology 360

Woodworth's Dynamic Psychology 365

Comparison between Woodworth and McDougall 367

Chapter Highlights 368

Review Questions 369

CHAPTER 17

HUMANISTIC PSYCHOLOGY 370

Chapter Preview 370

Basic Tenets of Humanistic Psychology 371

Antecedent Forces 373

Rogers' Self Theory or Rogers' Person-centered Theory 374

Maslow's Self-actualization Theory 377

Criticisms of Humanistic Psychology 381

Chapter Highlights 382

Review Questions 383

CHAPTER 18
EXISTENTIAL PSYCHOLOGY 384

Chapter Preview 384
Basic Tenets of Existential Psychology 384
Antecedent Forces 385
Major Contributions of Existential Psychology 387
Ludwig Binswanger 388, Medard Boss 389, Roll May 390
Criticisms of Existential Psychology 391
Comparison between Existential Psychology and Humanistic Psychology 392
Chapter Highlights 393
Review Questions 394

CHAPTER 19
COGNITIVE PSYCHOLOGY 395

Chapter Preview 395
Antecedent Forces 396
Major Contributions of Cognitive Psychology : 398
Jean Piaget 399, Noam Chomsky 403
Criticisms of Cognitive Psychology 412
Chapter Highlights 412
Review Questions 413

CHAPTER 20
PSYCHOLOGY : TODAY AND TOMORROW 414

Chapter Preview 414
Psychology Today 414
Psychology Tomorrow 417
Chapter Highlights 418
Review Questions 418

CHAPTER 21
AN OVERVIEW OF PSYCHOLOGY IN INDIA 419

Chapter Preview 419

Psychology in India during Ancient Times 420
Psychology in Modern Times 429
Chapter Highlights 445
Review Questions 446

CHAPTER 22
INTERNATIONAL PSYCHOLOGY 449

Chapter Preview 449
Views of Ancient Greek Philosophers 450
Ancient Chinese Philosophers 451
Ancient Indian Psychlogy 452
Rise of Modern Psychology in Different Countries of the world 452
Psychology in Britain and France 453
Development of Psychology in Undivided Soviet Russia 453
Establishment of Psychological Associaiton around the world 455
Birth of International organization of Psychology, 457
Distribution of Psychologists at International level 458
Distribution of Psychological Organizations at International level 459
Common Characteristics in Development of Psychology 460
Cross-Cultural Psychology 461
Psychology in Cross-disciplinary Interaction 463
Chapter Highlights 464
Review Questions 466

Glossary 467
Reference 485
Name Index 503
Subject Index 508

■

CHAPTER 1

SYSTEMS AND THEORIES

CHAPTER PREVIEW

This chapter introduces the major systems or schools of psychology. These schools have been briefly described.

Each system discusses the different aspects of psychology by framing its own theories and hypotheses. Therefore, this chapter also introduces the distinction between theories and hypotheses. Major characteristics of a good theory have also been incorporated.

What functions are served by the various systems of psychology ? This basic question has also been answered. Psychological system and related hypotheses serve some basic functions like organization function, heuristic function, closure function, morale function and limiting function. Each of these functions has been discussed and their relevance has been emphasized.

How can one evaluate the psychological system ? In this connection, the views of important authorities like McGeoch, Watson, Fuchs and Kawash have been discussed. These psychologists have provided a general framework of some selected dimensions on the basis of which a system can be easily evaluated.

Finally, some basic issues in psychology have also been discussed. Psychology inherited most of these issues from philosophy and physiology. These issues are still widely contested.

SYSTEMS IN PSYCHOLOGY : MEANING AND TYPES

Psychology has a long past but short history. Prior to the establishment of an independent experimental science in 1879, psychology was a part of philosophy. As an independent discipline, psychology thus is about 120 years old. Even in such short period, many changes have taken place. In fact, diverse opinions exist about its subject-matter and methods of investigation.

After 1879 and during the beginning of the present century, many groups of people came forward to express more or less similar viewpoints regarding the subject-matter of psychology and its methods of investigation. One characteristic of these groups was that their members shared similar viewpoints regarding the subject-matter of psychology, its methods as well as regarding the other aspects of psychological phenomena and opposed the viewpoints of others. Such group was called as *Schools* of psychology. In this sense, important types of schools like Structuralism, Functionalism, Behaviourism, Gestalt Psychology, etc. developed—all explaining the subject-matter in their own way and emphasizing upon new method of investigation. Such schools have been identified as *Systems* of Psychology. McGeoch (1933) has defined system in the following way :

"By the term psychological system is implied a coherent and inclusive, yet flexible, organization and interpretation of the facts and special theories of the subject."

Obviously, then, system includes those persons who establish a systematic and coherent framework or orientation within which psychologists work in relating the psychological events. In fact, the term systematic means orderly which distinguishes a system in psychology from haphazard thinking and irregular observations. However, the term school and the term system can be very lightly *distinguished* in one sense. When we pay attention to a group of associated psychologists, it constitutes school of psychology. But when we pay attention to a group of ideas brought together to form a coherent set of belief about psychology, it constitutes a system. Such ideas gradually pave the way for having a group of associated psychologists. The important systems of psychology were six, each emphasizing its own outlook towards how psychology should proceed. These systems are :

1. ***Associationism*** : Although this is not a very important school of psychology, it has a definite and constructive importance upon emergence of modern psychology. This school mainly emphasizes that psychologists should concentrate upon associaation of ideas or of words or of stimulus-response connection. This association is governed by a set of principles. Complex events can be better understood by analyzing it into several smaller and simpler events. Associationism can be broadly grouped into two broad categories—Older associationism and Newer associationism. Older associationism comprises contributons of psychologists who have their basic orientation towards philosophy. David Hartley, Thomas Brown, James Mill, James Stuart Mill, Alexander Bain are some of the important contributors to this. Newer associationism comprises contributions of those psychologists and physiologists who have greater inclination towards modern experimental psychology. Ebbinghaus, Pavlov, Bekhterev, Thorndike and Guthrie are the major contributors.

2. ***Structuralism*** : A system founded by E. B. Titchener, Wilhelm Wundt's pupil, in America. Titchener had learnt about psychology at Leipzig in Germany under Wundt. In this sense Wundt has been regarded as originator of the system. The system stresses that psychology is the study of conscious experience which, through the method of introspection, can be analyzed into its three basic elements—sensations, feelings and images.
3. ***Functionalism*** : Functionalism as a system (and not as a school) was founded by William James, one of the greatest American psychologists. However, as a school, functionalism was founded by John Dewey and James Angell at the University of Chicago and reached the peak of the prominence with Harvey A. Carr. It may be said that John Dewey started functionalism as a school, James Angell fostered it and Harvey Carr brought it up to its fruition. According to this school, psychology is the study of mental activity or adaptive behaviour and its method is that of introspection as well as observation. Like structuralism, this school accepted that psychology was the science of conscious experience no doubt, but it emphasized upon functional utility of consciousness rather than upon its analytical character.
4. ***Behaviourism*** : As a school, behaviourism was founded by J. B. Watson in 1913. According to this school, psychology is the science of behaviour and not of conscious experience. Since psychology is an objective science, it uses empirical methods like observation, conditioning, testing and verbal report. It rejected introspection as method of psychology.
5. ***Gestalt psychology*** : Gestalt psychology is a German school of psychology established by Max Wertheimer in 1912. For this school, psychology is the study of both behaviour and consciousness (Lundin, 1985). This school gave primary emphasis upon the study of wholes. The whole is different from the sum of its parts. Premature analysis of the whole is dangerous. Apart from Wertheirmer, this school came to be closely identified with his colleagues like Kurt Koffka and Wolfgang Kohler. All these psychologists later migrated to United States of America.
6. ***Psychoanalysis*** : Psychoanalysis as a school arose in a very different manner from other schools. While other schools sprang up in academic circles, psychoanalysis sprang up in medical and

clinical tradition with Sigmund Freud as its founder. According to this school, psychology is mainly concerned with the study of unconscious and sexual motivation which are manifested through dreams, psychopathology of everyday life, free associations, etc.

After world war II, various older and tightly organized systems of psychology like Functionalism, Behaviorism and Gestalt school were becoming too limited to deal with all the facts that were emerging and by 1980s they had disappeared from practical usage. In fact, many more people entered the field, did the experiments and developed various theories. As a consequence, the growth of knowledge became tremendous. Hence, psychologists moved towards specialization and preferred to work in limited areas. Consequently, highly specific theories developed in various areas of psychology which produced a narrowly restricted field that did not attempt to explain the entire field. Even today these theories operate within that broader though less tightly framework. Today one can still think within a framework that may be called as a behaviouristic or gestaltist or psychoanalyst.

THEORIES AND HYPOTHESES

As it is obvious from above discussion, a system of psychology tends to explain all aspects of psychology within one general framework. A theory does the same thing but taking any one aspect of psychology. In other words, the scope of a theory is limited and is generally concerned with some particular aspect of psychology like forgetting, perception, learning, thinking, emotion, etc. Then what a theory is. A theory may be defined as a set of related assumptions from which, by reasoning, testable hypotheses can be generated. This definition, obviously, has three important features. *First,* a theory is a set of assumptions. It means not a single assumption can fill the requirement of a theory. This is because a single assumption cann't serve to integrate various facts. *Second,* all concepts of a theory must be stated in such a way that they must permit, with sufficient precision and logical reasoning, deduction of various clearly stated hypotheses. *Third,* the theory must generate such hypotheses which are testable. If the hypothesis is not testable, it is meaningless and worthless.

There are some prerequisites of a good theory. A few of these are as under:

1. A good theory is based upon a number of observations and integrates them into a meaningful relationship. In this sense, a good theory becomes a statement of assumed relationships between events that are observable.

2. A good theory integrates both formal or theoretical propositions as well as empirical proposition. The formal proposition consists of words, sentences and/or symbols which reflect assumed aspects of the theory. The empirical observations are the observations—experimental or non-experimental—upon which the theory is based.
3. A good theory must be testable in terms of specific hypotheses. If the hypotheses are found to be correct one after testing them, the theory stands validated and gains strength. On the other hand, if they are found to be incorrect ones, the theory is weakened and it needs modification or revision.
4. A good theory must also be heuristic in nature. In other words, a theory must generate such researches through which the validity or falsity of the theory may be tested.

Like theories, hypotheses are also assumptions but of a more narrow and restricted nature. Through hypothesis a tentative relationship between cause and event is established. Since a theory is of general nature, one may not be able to test the entire theory. Take an example. A theory of forgetting has many aspects, all of which can't be tested. One may consider how or why forgetting occurs and the various conditions which facilitate or inhibit forgetting. Therefore, some specific hypotheses are set-up. Subsequently, these various hypotheses can be experimentally tested. For example, one aspect of interference theory of forgetting is that similarity of original task and interpolated task produces higher forgetting. This aspect or hypothesis has been experimentally tested by several experimenters and they have found it to be true one. In this way, several hypotheses, one after another, can be tested. When all such hypotheses are tested experimentally and found to be true ones, a basic principle or law is finally established. For example, in the field of learning, after testing several hypotheses through experimentations, Thorndike established a famous law of learning which is called as the *law of effect* that was subsequently reformulated by Skinner as the *principle of positive reinforcement* which states that when a certain response is followed by reward, the strength is increased and such reward is identified as positive reinforcer.

FUNCTIONS OF PSYCHOLOGICAL SYSTEMS AND THEORIES

Why do we emphasize upon systems and related theories in psychology? What purposes are served? Answering these questions, Lichtenstein (1967) has said that various psychological systems and related theories do certain important functions and as such, they have been recognised in psychology. Following are the major functions served by psychological systems and related theories—

1. *Organization function* : A system does the function of organization. It organizes various diverse facts, principles and data into a meaningful whole. In other words, system gives a meaningful shape to the diversified facts by organizing them into a whole.
2. *Heuristic function* : A system and related theories also generate new researches and findings both experimental and non-experimental. This is meant by heuristic function. In absence of it, the system will be ineffective.
3. *Closure function* : Systems also do closure function. Generally all relevant and important facts are not available before the systems. Hence, psychologists proceed to close or fill the gap created by absence of such facts by making theoretical propositions. In absence of closure function, the gap will remain a gap and then, a meaningful whole will not be emerging.
4. *Morale function* : Psychologists either working alone or in group tend to form system or develop theory. As a consequence, these psychologists tend to share some basic convictions, thoughts, feelings, emotions, sentiments of each other and also profit by such interaction.
5. *Limiting function* : There are different systems in psychology and each, according to its basic tenets, determines what should be included or left out in studying different aspects of psychology. For example, behaviourism is a school or system in psychology which includes only behaviour as subject-matter of psychology and completely excludes consciousness from it. Likewise, structuralism is a system which takes consciousness as the subject-matter of psychology, thus completely ignoring behaviour from its purview. Likewise, most of theories in comparative psychology utilizes animal beings as subjects and excludes human beings.

In this way we find that systems serve many functions and due to this, they have got proper recognition.

EVALUATING SYSTEMS OF PSYCHOLOGY

The study of system of psychology has attracted ever-increasing interest. It has now been recognized as a legitimate field of study within psychology. Its study gives us a general idea about how developments took place in psychology and in what ways they have influenced new thinking of the psychologists. For making the study of systems of psychology more meaningful and useful, psychologists have evolved some general guidelines. If a system fulfills the requirements of those guidelines, the system is positively evaluated.

There are three types of guidelines, each mentioning some criteria for evaluation of systems of psychology.

1. McGeoch (1933) has spelled out some criteria for evaluation of a psychological system These criteria, in fact, present some basic issues which must be discussed by a system. These are six : the definition of psychology, general postulates, nature of data, principles of selection, principles of connection and mind-body issue. On the whole, McGeoch meant to say that the system must be clearly described and its all relevant assumptions and assertions must be presented in an organized and systematized manner.
2. R. I. Watson (1967) has also provided us with a set of detailed criteria each relating to some issues in both scientific psychology as well as pre-scientific psychology. After making a careful review of the major issues in both pre-scientific psychology as well as in scientific psychology, he came to the conclusion that there are *eighteen issues* which could be expressed as bipolar dimensions. Those eighteen issues are : conscious mentalism-unconscious mentalism, contentual objectivism-contentual subjectivism, determinism-indeterminism, functionalism-structuralism, empiricism-rationalism, inductism-deductism, mechanism-vitalism, monism-dualism, molecularism-molarism, methodological objectivism-methodological subjectivism, naturalism-supernaturalism, nomotheticism-idiographicism, peripheralism-centralism, rationalism-irrationalism, purism-utilitarianism, quantitativism-qualitativism, staticism-developmentalism, staticism-dynamicism. Although it is difficult as well as problematic to rate the position of each system on each of these eighteen dimensions, Watson's this prescriptive system represents a very thoughtful and useful evaluative technique.
3. Some psychologists like Fuchs and Kawash (1974), Coan (1979) have made factor analytic studies of systems on issues reported by Watson or some similar issues. These psychologists asked respondents or various persons to give their opinions regarding positions of various systems on these selected issues. In Fuchs

and Kawash's study respondents rated each system on thirty-six factors which were obtained by having the names of the ends of Watson's eighteen dimensions. In Coan's study respondents rated each system on thirty-four factors which were similar to those thirty-six factors. Coan's findings were more impressive and revealed six first-order bipolar factors-subjectivism-objectivism, qualitative orientation-quantitative orientation, personal orientation-apersonal orientation, dynamic orientation-static orientation, holism-elementalism, endogenism-exogenism. These sets of factors or dimensions can guide us in making a very useful comparison of various systems in psychology.

Thus evaluation of the different systems of psychology is not a very straight forward and simple task because the criteria are not universal nor equally acceptable to all. However, the criteria reported by recent factor analytic studies have, to a greater extent, minimised the differences among psychologists and have provided a very useful guidelines for meaningful comparisons. For convenience, in this book criteria adopted by McGeoch (1933) would be followed.

SOME BASIC ISSUES IN PSYCHOLOGY

Although psychology has a very brief history, many divergent system and theories exist right form its beginning. Psychologists have discussed in details what is the subject-matter of psychology, what should be its method and how it should present its data, etc. As a consequence, many controversial issues have been born and these issues are still widely contested. Psychology inherited most of these issues or problems from philosophy and physiology. That is why, it is said that philosophy is the mother and physiology is the father of psychology. Some of these issues which are still of interest are as under:

1. *Mind versus Body*

This is one of the oldest issues in psychology. This is also known as *mind-body problem*. The issue very clearly states that in both animals as well as human beings there exist mind and body. Naturally, then, some of the questions that arise in this connection are : how are mind and body related ? How does one get from bodily processes to mental processes ? Is really something like mind exist ? etc. In psychology some systems approve the idea that both mind and body exist. Such systems are called as *dualistic systems*. Structuralism, the important system of psychology, for example, was a dualistic system because it considered that both mind and body existed and their relationship was more or less parallel. Titchener, father of Structuralism, has named this as "doctrine of psychophysical parallelism". According to this doctrine physical processes (body) and mental processes (mind) run along side by side as parallel streams. There is no interaction between them and neither one causes the other. But change in any one is always accompanied by a change in other. Watson, who founded another system called behaviorism, has, however, rejected the concept of mind and, therefore, he has not approved the idea of dualistic system. He has concentrated upon bodily processes only. For Watson, therefore, psychology became the study of bodily responses made towards stimuli present in the environment. One reason why Watson rejected the concept of mind was that it was not observable event and did not exist within the framework of space or time. But system such as psychoanalysis has again accepted the existence of body as well as mind. Freud, father of psycho-analysis, in fact, developed a rather much complicated concept known as 'mental apparatus' from the basic concept of mind and this has proved to be a very important explanatory principle.

2. *Heredity versus Environment*

This is also known of *nature-nurture* issue or *nativism-empiricism* issue in psychology. This issue tries to determine how much of human behaviour is due to hereditary factor and how much of it is due to environmental factor. Among the early psychologies that emphasized the study of experience and perception, issue was how much of experience was inherent or unlearnt and how was the result of direct experience or observation. In seventeenth century. Descartes had opined that some ideas are inherent or in born. Likewise, Kant had also stressed the importance of inborn perceptions of our world. Gestalt psychologists also emphasized the importance of nativistic position by making distinct that certain ways of perceiving the world came to us without any prior training or learning.

In contemporary psychology this issue takes another form, that is, of learned versus unlearned behaviour. In other words today the issue is how much of our behaviour is determined by hereditary factor such as native capacity and talent and how much of our behaviour is determined by pure learning. Behaviorists including Watson laid emphasis upon environmental view. Watson made it clear that in a normal person environment was all important determiner of behaviour. On the other hand, McDougall and also to same extent Woodworth laid emphasis upon the importance of inherited disposition. Very clearly McDougall stated that a person is gregarious because he has instinctive tendency. Learning play little role in determining the direction of that gregarious behaviour.

Today most of the psychologists adopt an *interactionist* position regarding this issue. Human behaviour is viewed as resulting from the interaction of heredity with environment. A given native factor operates differently under different environmental circumstances. In other words, an environmental influence differs in effect depending upon the native factor of the person on whom it is operating.

3. *Molar versus Molecular*

This is another important issue round which most of the events in psychology have revolved. This issue has equal concern for those who emphasize upon objective approach as well as for those who emphasize upon subjective approach to psychology. The issue is related to the kind of unit the psychologist should employ in his study. Should one study the whole (molar) or break it into its separate and independent component (molecular) ? Applying this unit to behaviour, it can be argued whether one should study the reactions of the whole organism (molar) or one should keep limit to simple discrete responses or reflexes? Watson emphasized that psychology studies discrete molecular responses of the persons. Other later behaviourists have also followed the lead of Watson and they, too, have pointed out that by taking small molecular response such as bar pressing response of rat or pecking response by a pigeon, it is possible to quantify them easily and then, the basic relationship can be discovered. Therefore, the best unit of analysis for psychologists, according to them, is molecular analysis.

This molecular analysis of behaviour has, however, been criticised by those who emphasize upon molar analysis. The critics have said that the molecular analysis or description of behaviour is too limiting in operation and does not convey anything meaningful. These critics have called Watson ironically as 'muscle twitch psychologist'. Kantor, for example, has emphasized that psychology studies an entire organism's behaviour at any given time and, therefore, the best scientific unit of analysis is the whole organism as it reacts with environment.

Molar-molecular issue is not the concern of objective aspect only but it is also the concern of subjective aspect. Wundt and Titchner had emphasized that conscious experience should be analyzed into its component parts like sensations, images and feelings. Hence, they had approved the molecular analysis. On the other hand, Gestalt psychology, a very important system in the history of psychology, had vehemently opposed this type of molecular analysis and pointed out that it was impossible to break consciousness into its elementary components. According to Gestaltists, psychologist must deal with perception as a whole and any attempt to analyze it into its different parts would be a meaningfulness. They also reported that whole is not the sum of its parts.

4. *Subjectivism versus Objectivism*

This is closely related to mind-body issue. Objectivism refers to consideration of whatever can be seen or measured directly, accurately and precisely. Most of the bodily activities or responses of human being and animal being are of this type. To be objective, however, is not synonymous with being experimental although most of the experimental psychologists try to be at least objective in their observation and interpretation of data. Objectivity, therefore, means mere interpersonal agreement in observation. Behaviourism has emphasized much upon objectivism in psychology.

Subjectivism has been emphasized by systems like structuralism, Gestalt psychology, existential psychology and humanistic psychology. It refers to explanation of human behaviour in terms of private or inner experiences of person. Psychological facts can be understood in terms of what a person thinks, feels or experiences. Since these events are private to the individual, they can't be known through direct observation. As a system though structuralism has gone out, its impact in terms of recent movement of humanistic psychology and existential psychology is still felt because these two types of psychologies are largely dependent upon the subjective reports of thoughts, ideas, feelings, wishes, motives, etc.

There are psychologists who like to maintain the essence of both subjectivism as well as objectivism in psychology. They consider psychology to be the study of behaviour (objectivism) as well as the study of experience (subjectivism).

5. *Quantification versus Qualification*

Quantification means to report one's findings in terms of numbers. Thus quantification involves measurement which is defined as assignment of numerals to certain observed events according to certain rule. Those psychologists who emphasize upon objective approach prefer quantification of psychological facts. The quantification may be done in terms of different units. For example, a response may be quantified in terms of magnitude, rate as well as latency. In other words, a response may be quantified in terms of its amount (magnitude), in terms of how often it takes place (rate) and in terms of how long it takes before it is manifested (latency). As an example of quantification of response in terms of magnitude, total amount of secretion of saliva of Pavlov's dog after bell may be cited. As an example of rate of response, rat's pressing of lever in Skinner box may be cited. Likewise, in Skinner box how quickly the rat presses the lever after the light is on may be cited as an example of latency. A response may also be quantified in terms of other units.

There are some data in psychology which are called subjective data, which can't properly be quantified. Such data are qualitative in nature. For example, when a person listens to a sound, he describes it as loud or soft. Likewise, when a person sees a light, he describes it as either intense or mild. Such feelings can't be described in terms of numbers. Similarly, a person observes how two dogs fight and how a bird builds a nest. These are behaviours which are being objectively observed no doubt but they are qualitative and not quantitative.

There are theories in psychology which mainly emphasize upon quantification, whereas there are also some theories which wholly emphasize upon qualification. Those theorists who emphasize upon quantification stress that vigorous measurement is necessary for relevance of psychological data. On the other hand, those who put stress upon qualification state that most of the psychological events can be described without such vigorous measurement.

6. *Determinism versus Teleology*

Deterministic view maintain that any behaviour at the present is determined by what has happened in the past. Thus this view very clearly points out that the present behaviour is determined by past history or past causes. Freud and Watson are the great supporters of deterministic viewpoint in psychology. These psychologists have frequently asserted that a person's behaviour is wholly determined by past experiences, even by those experiences which were present at birth, though apparently the person may not experience so. From strict deterministic point of view, a person is not the master of his fate because much is determined by the events of past over which he has no control. Thus determinism, in fact, considers environmental events to be more important. This is widely supported by Watson's claim that a healthy infant, by control of its environment, may be made either a doctor, lawyer, or even a thief or beggerman.

The supporters of teleology, on the other hand, believe that future determines or affects the present behaviour. The idea may apparently look absurd but on close scrutiny it may not appear so absurd. Alder, one of the disciples of Freud and who later on broke with him, is a strong supporter of teleological viewpoint. He is of view that the present behaviour of human is guided by the future goals that he sets up. These goals, in fact, influence how we act at the present time. From this interpretation, it is obvious that teleological viewpoint emphasizes upon purposive nature of behaviour. All behaviours are goal-directed and therefore, have a definite purpose. McDougall and Tolman who differed a lot otherwise, at least share the concept of such purposivism.

7. *Utility versus Purity*

This issue has philosophical roots. The utilitarian point of view suggests that facts and principles discovered by psychologists must be applied to some utility. It should not be mere theoretical and analytical. On the other hand, those who believe in purity point of view do not care for applied or practical side and became fully satisfied with mere discovery and analysis of psychological facts and principles. Structuralism was of this type of system. Structuralists were satisfied with their analytical approach and never emphasized upon what such analysis does for human beings and what purposes are served for human beings, etc. Functionalism, another system which arose as a protest against structuralism, was such which emphasized upon applied or practical aspect. They wanted to develop psychology which can be of useful ends for the person. Thus structuralists wanted to develop a pure psychology, whereas functionalists wanted to make psychology applied.

8. *Reductionism versus Non-reductionism*

This is another issue which involves whether or not the subject-matter of psychology defined in whatever manner, may stand on its own as independent of other disciplines or should it be reduced to some basic level of analysis. Some psychologists favouring reductionist point of view, feel that psychological events should be reduced to the basic level of analysis of biological processes. A very extreme approach of reductionism has been proposed by Weiss who have pointed out that all behaviour could be reduced to the activities of electron and protons. These reductionists have also made it clear that since psychology deals with living organism, its status is reduced to a branch of biology. Psychologists emphasizing internal drives as motivating stimuli and importance of nervous system in memory definitely adopt reductionist's approach in psychology.

Non-reductionists, on the other hand, take opposite view. Guthrie, Skinner and Lewin have adopted non-reductionist view. Guthrie and Skinner have considered psychology to be study of responses emitted by the organism towards stimuli. There responses can be described in quantitative manner no doubt but they cannot be reduced to physiological components. Lewin did not speak of stimulus-response units but he definitely consider a person that existed in life space, to be affected by all the psychological facts that influenced him at any given time. Lewin expressed the view that psychology need not be reduced any more.

Making a comparative study of these two opposing viewpoints, it can be said that the non-reductionists argue that psychology is an independent branch like chemistry, physics and physiology and does not need to be reduced to a more base level. On the other hand, reductionists feel that the causes of psychological events must be found in internal psychological functions. According to reductionists, non-reductionists simply *describe* and not *explain* the basic causes of psychological events.

9. *Theory versus Data*

This is another issue over which systems in psychology differ. Our intention is that a good psychological theory should begin with scientific data. To clarify this issues, it is essential to look at both extremes.

On one extreme there are psychologists like Freud and later analysts who have shown such dependence upon theory. In fact Freud formulated his different theories without any well-collected data. But if we pay attention to Freud's theories, we would came to the conclusion that he was having a kind of data, that is, his observation of what his patients told him. These included their free association and reports and analysis of the dream. However, his opponents have criticised him for these unreliable mode of obtaining data.

On the other extreme, there are psychologists who claim that theory is not necessary and data or results of experiment or observation are all enough for psychology. Thus they are of opinion that we don't need any theoretical propositions and all principles of psychology can be formulated from the data. B.F. Skinner is an example of this viewpoint. In fact he set one such proposition in his famous article, "Are Theories of learning necessary ?". In this article he had finally concluded that theories are not necessary for learning. He expressed the view with certainty that if an experiment is carried with all its proper control and manipulation, results or data are enough and add to the principles of psychology.

These are some of the basic issues towards which systems of psychology had been active. Although the various systems have died today, these issues have been so important ones that they have been vigorously taken up by the modern psychologists.

CHAPTER HIGHLIGHTS

1. Psychology has a long past but short history. Previously it was a branch of philosophy and in 1879 it was established as an independent and experimental science with effort of Wilhelm Wundt in Germany. Thus its real history is of only about 120 years.

2. In such a short period, psychology began to develop through what was called system or school. A system or school means a group of associated psychologists who hold more or less similar ideas or viewpoints towards subject-matter of psychology and its method of investigation but oppose any other viewpoint regarding subject-matter of psychology and its method of investigation. In sense, structuralism, functionalism and behaviourism were all different schools or systems of psychology.
3. Various systems of psychology have proposed different theories and hypotheses in different fields. In reality, a theory takes any one aspect of psychological fact and tries to explain it. Thus a theory is a set of related assumptions from which by reasoning, testable hypotheses can be generated. Like theories, hypotheses are also assumptions but of a more narrow and restricted natured. Through hypothesis a tentative relationship between cause and effect is established.
4. Various systems in psychology like structuralism, functionalism, behaviourism, etc. served certain functions. Therefore, they have been widely recognized and still their impact is felt. They do various functions like organization function, heuristic function, closure function, morale function, and limiting function.
5. There are certain basic issues in psychology towards which various systems in psychology were once very active. Although these systems have met their natural death, these issues are no longer dead and are influencing thinking of modern psychologists. Those issues are mind versus body, nativism versus empiricism (or heredity versus environment), molar versus molecular, subjectivism versus objectivism, quantification versus qualification, determinism versus teleology, utility versus purity, theory vs. data, etc.

REVIEW QUESTIONS

1. "Psychology has a long past but short history." Discuss.
2. Discuss the different criteria for evaluating the various systems of psychology.
3. Discuss the major issues which have been emphasized by different systems of psychology.

■

CHAPTER 2

PRESCIENTIFIC PSYCHOLOGY : ANCIENT GREEK PHILOSOPHICAL INFLUENCES

CHAPTER PREVIEW

Greek naturalism started with the sixth century B.C. It was mainly interested in answering questions about the nature of universe. Directly or indirectly, there were some seeds of emergence and development of psychology in the viewpoints expressed by these early scientists like Thales, Pythagorus, Heaclitus, Democritus, Hippocrates.

Three important scientists of this period whose impact upon later psychology was felt, were Socrates, Plato and Aristotle. Among these, the contributions of Aristotle were directly relevant for later development of psychology.

With the death of Aristotle and the conquests of Persia, India and Egypt by Alexander the Great, there occurred breakdown in Greek naturalism. Four schools of different thoughts emerged in Post-Artistolerian periods—Epicureans, Cynics, Skeptics and Stoics. Of these, Epicureans have probably the greatest relevance for modern psychology.

During the period 1400–1600 AD a scientific movement called renaissance started. Various kinds of discoveries and researches in this field not only affected developments in the field of psychology but also in other fields.

If we pay attention to the thoughts of ancient Greek philosophers, we are bound to find evidences for the fact that psychology existed at that time too. The early Greek thinkers from the Hellenic period (600–322 B.C.) to the time of Aristotle, in fact, believed in a world which they could observe. This is clear from their emphasis upon the study of science including mathematics and astronomy. The Greeks, in fact, wanted to learn about nature in its various aspects and they did not approve of a world of spirit or transspatial soul. Their religion was primitive in nature and for them gods and goddessess were having human qualities. Since Greeks were interested in the study of *naturalism,* the topic of the present chapter can be reasonably called as Greeks' naturalism. Today, scientific psychology takes more or less the square view as it is also concerned with the nature of behaviour and how does an organism react to its environment. There is another point of similarity between ancient Greeks' psychology and modern scientific psychology. Like ancient Greeks, this scientific psychology also disregards spirit, mind or whatever names one uses to attach to this unobservable phenomena.

We shall study the contribution of three important ancient Greek thinkers, namely, Socrates, Plato and Aristotle but prior to this, we shall also have some observation of other thinkers and philosophers of the Hellenic period.

THE HELLENIC PERIOD (600–322 B.C.)

The study of Greek naturalism starts with sixth century B.C. This period is usually called as *cosmological period* because scholars or thinkers of this period were mainly interested in the following types of questions :

What is the nature of this universe ? Is this universe made of one thing or many things ? If it consists of many things, how can they be accounted for ?

To answer these questions one of the earliest scientists of this period was **Thales (600 B.C.)** who provided a scientific explanation of Cosmos that revealed that all things came from water and were ultimately reduced to water. He gave much importance to water probably because it was essential to life. He had also predicted, though accidently, that there were eclipses of the sun.

Pythagorus, a great mathematician of that time, pointed out that the ultimate explanations were found in numbers because numbers were the first principles. He reported that numerical relations of width, length and height used in construction of temples had a definite relation to the beauty of the resulting structure. He had also demonstrated that in tuning the lyre, why the most beautiful chords were those whose construction followed the simple mathematical relations. In nutshell, he believed that soul was at home with numbers and the entire universe was ordered mathematically for providing scientific and beautiful yields.

Heraclitus, another scientist of that time and different in temperament from Pythagorus, believed that the first principle was not number rather the first principle was fire and therefore, strife or conflict is the father of all things in universe.

The most finest example of Greek naturalism or naturalistic psychology was to be found in **Democritus** (460–370 B.C.). His principle is known as *principle of atomism.* He expressed the view that world is made of tiny particles (called atoms) which are constantly in motion. Not only living things, even soul also consisted of atoms. These atoms differed in terms of size, shape, angularity and so on. Since they were constantly in motion, they interact with each other. Memory, perception and thought are all expressions of this interaction in which atoms combine and interact with each other. He was the first Greek philosopher to provide a scientific explanation of sensation. According to him, all sensations involved some immediate contact. For example, seeing involved sending of atoms through air to eye which after making contact, receive a copy of the object seen. Likewise, sensation of task involved all those atoms that were small, angular, thin and winding. He also made it clear that there was no dualism, and no distinction between mind and body.

Another Greek who was physician and had a significant impact upon the later growth of psychology was **Hippocrates** (460–370 B.C.) Based upon four primary elements, namely, earth, air, fire and water, he propounded his theory of humors within the body. These humors were of four types—phlegm (based on earth), blood (based on air), yellow bile (based upon fire) and black bile (based upon water). These four humors accounted for the four basic temperament of human personality. For example, blood was said to produce sanguine temperament (cheerful), yellow bile was said to produce choleric temperament (fiery), phlegm was said to be related to phlegmetic temperament (slow) and black bile was said to be related to melancholic temperament. A normal personality contained these four humors in balance. Due to any reason if humors got out of balance, one might run into the condition of depression. Hippocrates also provided an unique explanation of epilepsy. He was of view that epilepsy was caused by improper actions of those organs that produced and regulated bodily fluids or humors particularly blood and phlegm. Thus he rejected the basic idea of that time that epilepsy was due to any thing other than natural causes.

With this introduction, now we shall examine the contributions of three most important Greeks who influenced the later developments in psychology. Those Greeks were as under :

1. Socrates (469–399 B.C.)
2. Plato (427–347 B.C.)
3. Aristotle (384–322 B.C.)

A discussion of the contributions of these Greeks is presented separately.

SOCRATES (469–399 B.C.)

Socrates was vigorous, generous, humorous person who became a controversial figure in Athens. He strongly believed that there was a genuine rational powers within human beings and these powers pointed human beings not only towards correct ways but to moral realities and socially right living which if needed one could test for itself also. He was also concerned with political behaviour, economics, ethics and aesthetics. So he could be regarded as one of the first social scientists. He also talked about *'Psyche'* which mean soul or spirit, if literally translated. Watson (1978) has suggested that 'Socrates' idea of psychic was similar to the modern conception of an ethereal substance which in form of shadow leaves the body of death and goes to Hades.

As we know, we infer about the above views of Socrates from his dialouges recorded by his pupil Plato. His method was known as conversational critical method. Murphy (1972) has rightly commented that it is extraordinarily difficult to tell how much of these dialouges was of socrates and how much was that of Plato. Two other Athenian youths namely Xenophon and Aristophanes had also a chance to observe Socrates's extraordinary dialouges.

PLATO (427–347 B.C.)

Plato was a disciple of Socrates. He belonged to a well-to-do family of Athens. He also started teaching at the age of forty in an Academy which had attracted many persons of reputes. Most of Plato's views were in form of dialogues in which the main speaker was Socrates.

Plato is well-known for his theory of ideas. In fact, Plato was a dualist who considered idea spearated from matter. Ideas consisted of forms and contents consisted of matter. Therefore, ideas can be thought of as formulas or patterns. For him, the basic reality was idea which had the following characteristics.

(i) Idea was changeless

(ii) Idea was perfect. Of the several types of ideas, only real perfect idea existed.

(iii) Idea was timeless.

(iv) Idea was distinct from matter because former was perfect where as the latter was imperfect. We could perceive the imperfect matter through our imperfect senses.

Like Socrates, Plato also spoke of psyche or soul. His concept of psyche included at least three things, namely, moral qualities of man, thinking and behavioural sources of many types of activity or behaviour.

If pay attention to Plato's dialogues, it would be cleared that he mainly believed in a soul as immaterial and immortal in a more spiritual sense. Such conception of a spiritual soul may be regarded as an exception to the general beliefs of Greek thought of the time. We get evidence for this spiritual interpretation of soul in Plato's doctrine of *reminiscence* which clearly mentioned that knowledge existed in the soul prior to any actual experience. To support this, reference could be made of a famous passage in the dialogue entitled the *'Meno'*. In this dialogue. Plato asked questions from uneducated slave boy in such a manner that the boy appeared to have the knowledge of geometry. From where does this type of knowledge come ? Obviously the boy had never learnt geometry because he was a little slave boy. The direct implication is that the knowledge existed in the soul prior to birth.

ARISTOTLE (384–322 B.C.)

Aristotle was born in Asia Minor. He was pupil of Plato at the Academy in Athens. He remained there until the death of Plato. Later, he had opportunity to be tutor of Alexander the Great. Subsequently, he returned to Athens to found his own school. After death of Alexander, he had to face a very aggressive and hostile attack and due to this he was forced to go to island of Euboea where he died in 322 B.C.

Aristotle was a sort of universal genius. He was the first real psychologist and his natural way of describing events of psychological nature had strong impact upon modern psychologists who generally accept psychology as a natural science of behaviour. Following Keller (1937), Aristotle is regarded as *father of all psychology* because psychology gradually emerged with its roots in thinking of Aristotle. Aristotle's contributions which was relevant for psychology, has been presented in his two works—*De Anima* which was translated to mean *Concerning the Pscyhe or Soul* and *Parvu Naturalia*. The first work is a very systematic work and the second work is, in fact, a series of essays on a variety of both psychological and biological subjects. Parva Naturalia contains accounts of youth and old age of walking, sleeping and dreaming, of the processes of remembering and recollection and of the psychology of men and women.

His contributions can be systematically presented under the following three heads :

(i) Metaphysical position

(ii) De Anima

(iii) Laws of association.

These three may be discussed as under :

(i) *Metaphysical position :*

Aristotle has made his metaphysical position very clear. For him, things were made up of *matter* and *form*. Unlike Plato, these two were inseparable. Form could not exist without matter and there was no matter without form. Therefore, matter and form were always found together, but is only through form that the potentialities inherent in matter could be actualized. Thus matter was what made things possible and form was something actualizing the potentiality. It was form that made us humans and distinct from animals but matter made us the particular individuals that we were. The relationship between matter and form could be explained through an example—for the form bronze, tin and copper were the matter and at the next higher level bronze became matter for actualizing another form like a statue. In this way, for Aristotle, all things could be organized hypothetically from pure form to pure matter.

(ii) *De Anima* :

It is one of the most systematic work of Aristotle. In its first part there was an introduction in which Aristotle expressed his view upon what psychology was and what was its problems. The main part dealt with the psychological action particularly senses and their object. The last part dealt with more complex activities.

In *De Anima* he presented an orderly construction of a system of knowledge in which study of psyche or soul could be brought into relation with the study of living organisms. The psyche, as a form, was never separate from the organism but was merely a function of it. In fact, psyche could be compared to the function of an instrument like cutting was to a knife, vision was to the eye, etc. He also made it clear that psyche was neither physical substance nor mental substance. Therefore, psyche could be thought of as one form of the organism, that is, its function. The organs and tissues were matter of the body but their form constituted the function.

All living organisms had a hierarchy of psyches or functions. At the bottom of the hierarchy there was nutritive and vegetative psyches which are biological functions and psychological functions or psyches lie at the next level. For example, sensing and perceiving functions are the psychological psyches which were common to both man and animals. Through senses, the living organisms gain information about things. He viewed that each sense was associated with a particular organ of the body. For example, hearing for ears and seeing for eyes and so on. Each organ has specific and distinct objects which it sensed. He also recognized the importance of a third factor which connected the sensing organism with the stimulus objects and that was *media of contact*. For sight and hearing, air was the media of contact, for taste and touch, flesh was the medium of contact and for smell, media of contact were both air and water. For coordinating the information coming from different sense at a particular time, he talked about a *common sense* which was different from the general meaning we have today. The common sense, in fact, organized more than one senses. For example, the common sense allowed person to identity a brick through both the sense of touch and sight.

Another class of functions or psyches is the capability of all living organisms for producing motion. Living bodies are thought to be self-moving, that is, they need not move by application of any external force. Quite related to this function was appetite. Both animals and humans had apetite which was directed by an image that was sainstying and leading to immediate pleasure. Because of reasoning capacity, the person could be moved or motivated by what was right and wrong. This type of motivation has been called by Aristotle as *wish*.

At the top of hierarchy of psyches or functions was *reasoning* which was found only in human beings. Reasoning function meaned simply to know and reflect. In fact, reasoning made use of these materials provided and then went beyond it. In fact, reasoning could take the materials provided from the senses and refine it.

(iii) *Laws of associations :*

Aristotle also talked about *association*. In association the person began with the sensation which was immediately encountered and searched for the object. He pointed out that the person remembered things by virtue of contiguity, similarity and contrast. In other words, we thought of Paul because he was with Peter, or because he was like Peter or because he contrasted with Peter. Thus Aristotle arrived at three laws of association—similarity of things, contiguity or togetherness and contrast or opposites. This view of Aristotle later became the doctrine that all operation of mind depended upon associations laid down in experience and became of utmost importance for the psychologies of eighteenth and nineteenth centuries as well as for modern learning theories.

Thus we find that Greek naturalism arose to its peak with the work of Aristotle. With the death of Aristotle, there ocurred a gradual shift of scientific thinking from Greece particularly, Athens to other parts of the world.

DECLINE OF GREEK NATURALISM

With the death of Aristotle and the conquests of Persia, India and Egypt. Alexander the great, the intellectual horizons of Greeks became widened. As a consequence, there followed a breakdown of Greek naturalism into other ways of thinking. Now Greek naturalism yielded to a new interpretation of psyche that was not only subjective but also spiritual. The rise of spiritualism was upheld by the rise of Christianity by gentle efforts of Plotinus (A.D. 205–270), St. Augustine (A.D. 354–430) and St. Thomas Aquinas.

In fact post-Aristoterian thinkers were not much concerned with psychology. Much of what they said about psychology was grossly the dilution of Aristotle's thinking. Thinkers shifted their attention more to political and moral matters. Following four schools were recognized to spread their views in post-Aristoterian eras :

(i) Epicureans : The leader of Epicureans was Epicurus (341–270 B.C.). This school emphasized that man's pursuit should be the search for happiness. Achieving happiness meant to avoid pain and to avoid pain meant withdrawal from the maladies of the outside world. In fact, an active search for pleasure could result in pain when it was withdrawn. Later on, this Epicurean doctrine became important base for Freudian's pleasure principle and principles of reward or reinforcement in the field of learning.

(ii) Cynics : This school held the view that the society was full of hypocrisy, hate, grief and jealsy. So it advocated withdrawal from these activities for maintaining peace and mental calm.

(iii) Skeptics : The leader of this school was Pyrrho of Elis (360–270 B.C.) who pointed out that sensory perception alone, cannot be fully dependent upon. The school did not also fully believe in pure form. Pyrrho of Elis emphasized that what might be concluded from any particular sensory experience, might be wrong in light of later and newer experiences.

(iv) Stoics : Leaders of this school were Epictetus (A.D. 50–120) and the emperor Marcus Aurelius (A.D. 121–180). This school was, in fact, founded earlier by Zeno (333–262 B.C.). The basic psychology of this school was to accept all the things in a spirit of content. Today we regard stoic as that person who accepts misfortune without any complaint. Along with this is the strong belief of determinism that what is to happen, will happen. There was a causal ordering of the world and one must accept his fate as a part of that order.

Of these four schools growing in post-Aristotlerian period the Epicureans probably have the greatest relevance for modern psychology although the most widespread school was that of the stoics.

SCIENCE IN RENAISSANCE : 1400–1600 A.D.

Renaissance was such a movement of scientific and intellectual search which prepared a general atmosphere that might eliminate stereotypes, false beliefs and attitudes from the masses. Such movement started in Italy during fourteenth century and reached its peak in sixteenth century. During this period there occurred such a significant development in agriculture, commerce, education, industry, art and science that Europe played a leading role in the world and its impact was felt on the entire universe. It was the direct result of this movement that some of the coins of spain bore the words **Ne plus ultra** which meant there is *nothing beyond*. Spain and Pillars of Hercules were the edge of the world. Then Columbus discovered America in 1492, one of the great achievements of that time. As a result 'Ne' was removed from the coins and only remained plus ultra which meant there was *'more beyond'*.

During this period of renaissance no name of such important persons could be mentioned that might have significant impact upon the later growth of psychology but definitely due to the various scientific discoveries a new mentality was born which affected not only psychology but also the other allied fields. Some of the important discoveries are as under :

(i) Printing press was invented in 1450. As a consequence publication of books started rapidly.

(ii) Copernicus discovered solar system in 1543. In fact his theory that the earth and the planets moved in circles about the sun was beginning of the modern astronomy.

(iii) Galileo improved the telescope which helped in confirmation of Copernicus theory. Galileo had primarily concerned with the fundamental problems of mechanics and optics.

(iv) Gilbert is England did great work in the field of magnetism. For him, the direct observation was the basic method.

(v) Kepler formulated laws of planetary motion which, among others, made it clear that planets have elliptical rather than circular orbits.

(vi) Newton did extraordinary work in the field of optics. With the help of prism he had demonstrated that white light may be split up so as to produce spectral colours. He had also contributed in space, time, mass, motion, force and so on.

(vii) Harvey had discovered blood circulation.

A direct consequence of all these discoveries and similar others was preparation of such a mental and physical environment where scientific growth could take place. In field of psychology the use of observation, testing, measurement, evaluation and experimentation was much as a function of these scientific discoveries and inventions.

CHAPTER HIGHLIGHTS

1. Greek naturalism was started with the sixth century B.C. In this period the scientists were interested in knowing about the nature of universe. Thales, Pythagorus, Heaclitus, Dermocitus, Hippocrates

expressed their scientific views about the nature of universe that have direct bearing upon the development of psychology later on.

2. Socrates (469–399 B.C.), Plato (427–347 B.C.) and Aristotle (384–322 B.C.) were important contributors. Socrates expressed his view about psyche which meant soul or spirit. Plato who was a disciple of Socrates, had talked about idea and its characteristics in detail. Plato's doctrine of reminiscence had also been very popular. Aristotle expressed his viewpoints about the metaphysical position and laws of association. All the important contributions are mentioned in his two works *De Anima* and *Parva Naturalia*.
3. With the death of Aristotle and the conquests of Persia, India and Egypt by Alexander the Great, the intellactual horizons of Greeks became widened. As a consequence, there followed a breakdown of Greek naturalism into other ways of thinking. In post-Aristotlerian eras four schools of different thoughts emerged—**Epicureans, Cynics, Skeptics,** and **Stoics.** Of these four schools, Epicureans have probably the greatest relevance for modern psychology although the most widespread school was that of the stoics.
4. During the period 1400–1600 A.D. a scientific movement in almost all fields took place. The movement is technically called as renaissance. Important scientific researches and discoveries by Copernicus, Galileo, Gilbert, Kepler, Newton and Harvey created such a horizon that affected developments not only in psychology but also in other fields.

REVIEW QUESTIONS

1. Assess the contributions of Socrates and Plato in scientific development of modern psychology.
2. What is the relevance of Aristotle's contributions for emergence of modern psychology ?
3. Point out the reasons of decline of Greek naturalism. What light is thrown on the nature of psychology by Post-Aristotlerian period.

■

Chapter 3

PRESCIENTIFIC PSYCHOLOGY : MODERN PHILOSOPHICAL INFLUENCES

CHAPTER PREVIEW

As we know, psychology broke away from philosophy in late nineteenth century. In this chapter those philosophical influences that have direct impact upon the emergence of modern psychology have been discussed. Such philosophical influences have been discussed under four headings : mind-body problem, empiricism, associationism and nativism. Although there are a number of philosophers dating back several centuries to Descartes in the history of modern philosophy, they have little or no direct impact upon psychology. Hence, their viewpoints have not been independently discussed. However, their major views have been incorporated where it was felt necessary. In this chapter, discussion has started with Descartes, sometimes known as father of modern psychology.

Philosophers prior to Descartes like St. Thomas and St. Augustine accepted a clear-cut distinction between body and mind. But they never cared for relating them. But continental philosophers like Descartes, Leibnitz and Spinoza, for the first time, proceeded to provide a solution to the existing mind-body problem. The viewpoints of each of these philosophers have been discussed separately.

Empiricism movement began in Britain and it protested against the viewpoint of continental philosophers like Descartes, Leibnitz and Spinoza. This movement represented by John Locke, George Berkeley, David Hume, emphasized that we derive idea of gaining knowledge from sensory experience rather than from intuition or inference. This empiricist movement was a direct forerunner of modern objective psychology.

The movement of associationism grew directly out of the British empiricist movement. The major associationists were : David Hartley, James and John Stuart Mill, Alexander Bain and Herbert Spencer. All these classical associationists tried to explain how the different ideas can be associated together and how many laws of association should be. Such laws or principles have been very important for modern psychology. In fact, these principles have been the base for modern learning theory. Persons like I.P. Pavlov, Edward Thorndike and Vladimir Bekhtrev depended upon these principles of association in explaining learning. This group of persons have been termed as modern associationists. A separate chapter on modern associationism has been added (chapter 8).

Nativism was a reaction against empiricism and was represented by German philosophers like Immanuel Kant, Johann Friedrich Herbert and Hermann Lotzé who were all very active in the first half of the nineteenth century. These philosophers held the view that perception was not necessarily dependent upon experience or learning. The major implication of this principle was found in modern Gestalt psychology.

MIND-BODY PROBLEM

As pointed out in the previous chapter, this is one of the basic issues whose root is philosophical but has very profound impact on modern psychology. Ancient philosophers like St. Augustine and St. Thomas believed that there was a complete division between these two aspects of person, that is, mind and body. These philosophers never thought that these two could be related with each other in any significant way. But philosophers of 17th century for the first time pointed out that mind and body were related in a significant way and we get a very vivid glimpse of this concern in the writing of three important continental rational philosophers like Descartes, Leibnitz and Spinoza whose viewpoints may be presented as under :

1. *Rene Descartes* (1596-1650)

Descartes, born in a rich family in France, was much interested in psychological principles and issues. Therefore, sometimes he is known as *father* of modern psychology. He spent time studying in Paris and Rome. In 1649 he went to Sweden on an invitation of Queen Christian to teach her philosophy. There he wrote a very important book entitled "The Passions of soul". However, as Boring (1950) and Murphy (1949) have pointed out, he was of poor health and he could not tolerate severe northern winters as well as the demands of the Queen to get up at 5.00 A.M. He developed pneumonia in February, 1650 and died.

Historians like Boring (1950) and Murphy (1949) have regarded Descartes as a scientist, a philosopher, a mathematician and a psychologist. In fact, he was a gentleman-intellectual. In considering resolution of mind-body problem given by Descartes, it is essential to consider his viewpoints regarding nature of body, the nature of soul or mind, and dualism of mind and body and their interaction.

In explaining the functions of body Descartes was well aware of the physiological knowledge of the time. He knew well about the action of muscles, nerves and other biological structures. At that time, Harvey had just discovered the circulation of blood. Therefore, he was aware of facts of circulation and of digestion correctly. From the works of other physiologists he easily understood that muscles operate in opposing pairs and considered functioning of nerves to be important for sensation and for movement. But he considered nerves as hollow tubes which carry animal spirits in different directions. By animal spirits he meant material substances which could move very quickly. According to Descartes, human body is like a *machine* when it is considered without its soul. He pointed out that animals are only machines with various kinds of reflexes, instincts and other automatic actions. He held that animals have no soul and therefore, they are *automata*. This mechanical view about the nature of body necessarily assumes that body refers to all that is inanimate.

What's about the nature of soul or mind ? He believed that in each and every person there is a soul or mind which is thinking substance and that has the power to direct and alter the mechanical activities of the body. Soul refers to all that is in us and that cannot be conceived in any manner which pertains to a body.

For Descartes, mind or soul and body consist of two different substances. Body consists of extended matter whereas the soul consists of unextended matter. Although soul and body consist of two different matters, they are connected with each other. In some activities such as sensing and perceiving both are operating. The mind or soul acts upon the body and directs its mechanical activities and is acted upon the body through its modes of sensation, emotion and perception. Thus the relation between mind and body is one of interaction.

How then, does the interaction take place ? Where is the point of connection because the two are different things ? To answer this question Descartes looked into the brain and its different structures. He reported that we have two eyes, two ears, and even two halves of brain but one little organ in the middle of the brain that has no duplicate, that is, pineal gland. For Descartes, the pineal gland became the point of interaction or connection between body and soul. Take one example to see how operation of interaction take place. How do we have sensation of something ? The images from the two eyes set up action in animal spirits which stimulated pineal gland making an impression on it. Through mind we would sense the impression. There are also activities which operated in reversed order. Suppose the mind or soul wishes to remember something. This desire activates the pineal gland which, in turn, sets up animal spirits in pores of brain to find out the traces left by the objects or events encountered previously.

One of the most important teachings of Descartes is that of innate ideas which are not derivable form experience in any way but which come to mind with such certainty that their acceptance is assured. Ideas relating to God and self belong to this category. Some of his critics, however, raised doubt over the existence of innate idea and such stand of Descartes was sharpened by the opposition of the English empiricists (Locke, Berkeley and Hume) as well as by modern empiricist (Lotze, Helmholtz, Wundt, etc.)

Though Descartes' explanation is today regarded as primitive, his psychological interactionism served as a model for several modern psychological schools like psychoanalysis and functionalism.

2. *Gottfried Leibnitz* (1646-1716)

Leibnitz was one of the great mathematicians of his day but he was surpassed by Newton. The publication of Locke's *Essay* in 1690 had stimulating effect upon Leibnitz and encouraged him to write the *Nouveaux essais* which was never printed during life time of Leibnitz because Locke death occurred at the intended year of publication, that is, 1704. However, that *essais* was published after 50 years since Leibnitz's death. Throughout his life, Leibnitz was engaged in political writing which got final intellectual recognition posthumously. The growth of his philosophy was vital to the development of psychology and here we are concerned with his that philosophy.

As compared to Descartes, Leibnitz is less important for experimental psychology but what he has offered, has significant influence upon psychology. Leibnitz's view regarding psychology can be summarized under two heads as under :

(i) ***Monadology*** : The study of monad is called monadology. The monad is the element of all being and a point of force. It is indestructible, uncreatable and immutable but it is not static. According to its own laws, is undergoes continuous process of developmental changes but during such changes neither its identity nor its unity is changed.

Since monads are immutable, uncreatable, indestructible, they don't affect each other. Hence, there is no interaction among them. Thus, for Leibnitz, world is "an infinite pluralism of independent monads" (Boring, 1950). A human individual, for example, is made up of many monads. Leibnitz has also emphasized upon character of individual monads. He pointed out that these individual monads have certain degrees of consciousness. By 'degree of consciousness' he meant that extent of clarity to which things could be reflected in totality. Some monads have poor degree of consciousness and some monads have higher degree of consciousness. Those monads which have poor degree of consciousness are unconscious, although they produce some activities which may be imperceptible. Leibnitz has called such low degree of awareness or consciousness as *petites perceptions* (little perceptions). The petites perception by monad is unconscious. For example, the sound of single falling drop of water may be regarded as petite perception or unconscious perception.

From the above sketch of Leibnitz's monadology, it is obvious that activity lies at the base of his system. Monads having high degree of consciousness produces activities which are obvious and perceptible and monads having very low degree of consciousness produce activities that are vague and imperceptible.

(ii) ***Parallelism*** : Leibnitz formulated the theory of psychological parallelism which attempts to relate spirit or mind monads to body monads, a theory which is usual alternative to the theory of interactionism of Descartes. Leibnitz was of view that since monads don't make interaction, each monad is self-contained. These two (mind monads and body monads) are not causally related. They follow parallel course. The resultant correlation appear as if one has caused the other. To illustrate the view of parallelism, he has himself given the example of two clocks so constructed and set that they run always parallel to each other without making any interaction between them.

The above two concepts of Leibnitz had great impact upon modern psychology. Leibnitz's concept of degree of consciousness and unconsciousness was major source to Freud and Jung who formulated separate theories of unconscious. Thus it was not Freud who has created the concept or idea of unconscious (as most of us think) rather it was Leibnitz who had foretold it. Freud developed it to the most important part of mind and to be the seat of instincts. In it ideas are repressed from consciousness, too. Later on, Jung divided unconscious into personal unconscious and collective or racial unconscious to elaborate it further. Likewise, Leibnitz's idea of parallelism had directly influenced the psychology of Wundt and Titchner in the late 19th and early 20th centuries as well as Gestalt psychology. These schools considered mind and body as two separate and independent entities which always operate parallel to each other.

3. *Benedict Spinoza* (1632-1677)

Spinoza was a contemporary of Descartes and had been author of several popular books of seventeenth century. He advocated a unique stand on mind-body relationship and perhaps, that is, his single important contribution relevant for psychology. He pointed out that mind and body could not be separated from each other. These two are simply different aspects of the same substance. Since these two are simply different aspects of the same substance, bodily activities don't affect or cause changes in mental activities and similarly, mental activities don't cause changes in bodily activities. This was a unique kind of mind-body relationship which was termed as *psychological double-aspectism*. To illustrate this, suppose we cut the brain into different parts horizontally and vertically. Each part may look unique and strange but essentially, they are parts of the same thing, that is, brain.

One of the chief advantages of this Spinoza's parallelism or psychological double-aspectism in psychology has been that it can be easily taken apart from its context and used freely without regard to its metaphysical implications. The mental activities and the physical activities can be treated as two streams of events neither of which acts as a cause of the other but together constitutes a system in which change in one is regularly accompanied by a change in other.

Conclusion regarding mind-body problem : Monism

It is apparent from the above discussion of viewpoints expressed by Descartes, Leibnitz and Spinoza that these persons have tried to recognize the existence of both mind and body and thus, their approaches have been dualistic ones. The problem relating to these two have been solved by way of discovering certain relation between these two. Such dualism in psychology continued for a pretty longer period of time.

Recent attempt to solve the problems relating to mind and body has been to deny the existence of preferably mind and thus the problem is automatically solved. Such approach in psychology has been known as *monism*. The first support in modern period for monism was given by J. B. Watson, founder of behaviourism, who rejected mind or consciousness to be the subject-matter of psychology. Other behaviourists like Skinner, Kantor and Guthrie also provided support to Watson's rejection of dualism. These behaviourists were monistic ones, that is, they maintained complete denial of the concept of mind. These behaviourists have shown that behaviour is the function of living body.

EMPIRICISM : HOBBES, LOCKE, BERKELEY AND HUME

Empiricism began as a movement in Great Britain and as a movement it protested against the viewpoint of continental philosophers like Descartes, Leibnitz and Spinoza, As we know, empirical means gathering ideas from observation rather than from any intuition, conjecture or inference. Accordingly, empiricism lay emphasis upon the fact that we derive idea of gaining knowledge from sensory experience. Thus for empiricists, all knowledge comes from experience which does not necessarily originate in the world of reality. Perhaps, empiricists' major emphasis upon their dependence on experience has kept them united. The whole empiricist movement had a profound effect on the development of psychology. We shall here examine the viewpoints of four important British empiricists, namely Hobbes, Locke Berkeley and Hume.

1. *Thomas Hobbes* (1588-1679)

Hobbes was British, born in Maimesburg, England. His views towards empiricism and also towards associationism were nicely represented in his two books, namely, *Human Nature* published in 1650 and *Leviathan* published in 1651. He was a contemporary of Descartes.

Hobbes was much influenced by Galileo's mechanical experiment and by the concept of motion. Philosophically he was overwhelmed by the desire to reduce everything to motion. According to him, mental activity consisted of motions in the novels system which, in turn, resulted from motions in external environment. Hobbes had rejected Descartes' doctrine of interaction between soul and body. For Hobbes, mental activity was simply the motions of atoms in the brain. Motion and mental activity coexisted but Hobbes never explained how they coexisted.

Hobbes also introduced the concept of association of ideas and rejected Descartes' concept of innate ideas. He believed that the lawful succession of ideas was, in fact, responsible for all kinds of thought and action. He was of view that this succession occurs in terms of association by contiguity. He considered association to be 'trains of thoughts'. He made distinction between uncontrolled association and purposive or directed thinking. The former was unguided, without design and inconstant whereas the latter was orderly and regulated by some desire and design. He paid much attention to regulated type that broadly guides the process and tendency to seek causes for consequences.

Historians generally agree that Hobbes had very little influence upon his successor Locke who did not obtain inspiration form Hobbes. Therefore, we must content with above outlines of Hobbes.

2. *John Locke* (1632-1704)

John Locke was born in a small village in England. He also spent part of his life in politics and in some governmental offices. He wrote a famous book *An Essay Concerning Human Understanding* which was subsequently revised several times and in the fourth edition (1670) of that book he, in fact, had presented his major philosophical ideas that had direct relevance for emergence of psychology as science.

Locke's interest in philosophy emerged by his reading the books of Descartes while he was a student at Oxford University. He vehemently opposed Descartes' doctrine of innate ideas. Locke pointed out that ideas are not inborn rather they came from experience of the person. Like Aristotle, he believed that mind is like a *tabula rasa*, that is, a blank sheet of paper upon which due to experiences of various sort, ideas are born (written !), For Locke, idea is an element and the mind is capable of analysis into ideas. In mind there are two sources of ideas :

(i) *Sensation* : By sensation mind received experiences from external sources. After such experiences, perceptions are made and ideas are also born. Sensation, as Locke pointed out, is the primary source of all knowledge.

(ii) *Reflection* : Mind also reflects upon itself and through this reflection, mind obtains knowledge of its own operations. This is also called 'internal sense' or more appropriately today as introspection. This is the secondary source of ideas.

Locke further pointed out that ideas may be simple or complex and either type may be ideas of sensation or reflection. The simple ideas are pure and unanalyzable and generally came from primary source, that is, sensation. For example, when we see the green colour, it produces a simple idea of 'being greenish'. The complex ideas are made up of combination of simple experiences or ideas. They can be analyzed into simpler ideas. Such ideas are generally formed through what is called reflection. Another difference between simple ideas and complex ideas is that the simple idea is more reliable because it seems to correspond well with the object. For example, idea of 'being greenish' corresponds well with the green colour. But complex idea was not so reliable and dependable because through it we get only a rough approximation to the external world. For example, we are seldom able to get the nature of truth which is obviously a complex idea.

For Locke, ideas have two basic qualities—primary qualities and secondary qualities. Primary qualities are those which are not separable from the object. Qualities like shape, solidity, movement, extension, etc.

are examples of primary qualities. In fact, through primary qualities mind and the external object become directly connected. Secondary qualities are qualities which don't exist in the object in which they are sensed. Such qualities are known apart from the object in which they are sensed. Colour, sound, taste, touch are examples of secondary qualities.

Locke published the fourth edition of his famous book entitled *an Essay Concerning Human Understanding* in 1670 and in this edition he added a new chapter of the "Association of Ideas". In this chapter he propounded *doctrine of association of ideas.* By association of ideas he meant combination or connection of ideas. Those ideas are easily combined or connected with each other which occur frequently. Thus Locke anticipated the law of frequency which became an important law of associationism and even today it is considered to be one of the most important law of association. In association of ideas he included both simultaneous association and successive association. He did not make a clear distinction between these two types of association. However, for him simultaneous association was a complex idea.

Locke believed in dualism but his viewpoints regarding dualism was different from that of Descartes. Locke believed in mind as being separate from body no doubt but mind of each person with different experiences is different from everyother mind with separate experiences. In fact, Locke has nowhere shown concern about the physiological correlates of mind and body as Descartes did. Locke merely assumed that mind and body existed as separate entities. In what ways they are related was not his main concern.

In summary Locke's significance in psychology is due to the following reasons :

(i) Locke rejected the concept of innate ideas and pointed out that ideas are born due to our experiences. For him, mind is like a *tabula rasa.*

(ii) Locke introduced the principle of association of ideas which became the founding stones of associationism.

(iii) Locke believed in mind as separate from body but this dualism was unique in itself and was distinct from Descartes' dualism which emphasized more upon its physiological correlates.

3. *George Berkeley* (1685-1753)

Berkeley was the immediate successor of Locke in British empiricism. He was an Irishman who was educated at Trinity College, Dublin. He was a highly religious man and has presented his philosophy in his two major books *An Essay Towards a New Theory of Vision* published in 1709 and *A Treatise Concerning the Principles of Human Knowledge* published in 1710. In these two books he has outlined his contributions that are directly relevant to psychology. In fact, his contributions can be explained under the following three heads :

(i) *New Principle* :

In his *A Treatise Concerning the Principles of Human Knowledge* Berkeley has outlined what is called 'new principle'. This new principle, in fact, is not wholly new and contains a good deal of what Locke had already said. In this new principle Berkeley had tried to explain the new way or approach to the problem of how one got knowledge of the external world. As Boring (1969) has put it, "This principle consisted essentially in the denial of matter as such and in the affirmation of mind as the immediate reality." Berkeley was of view that perception is reality. The problem before us is not how mind is related to matter (as Descartes had said) nor as to how matter generates mind (as Locke had said) but is how mind generates the matter. For him, *esse is percipi* that is, *to be* consists in *being perceived*. In other words, material substance is not real. The existence of things or objects depends on their being perceived. We know only sensory qualities of the objects. Thus in sharp contrast to Locke, for Berkeley there are only secondary qualities and not primary qualities. External objects have no bodily substance. All we really know of the real physical world is the impressions we had. Berkeley explicitly pointed out that we perceive nothing but our own experiences. Regarding existence of an object all that could be said is that they have been perceived. Therefore, we have only individual minds and the experiences residing in them. The question is : from where do we get experiences if there is no physical world of objects ? Giving the answer, Berkeley pointed out that ideas or experiences do come from God. The existence of things, consists in God's perception. Thus we have minds and their experiences as well as God and his experiences. The belief that the entire reality is nothing but minds and their experiences came to be known as *subjective idealism.* If somehow we all experience the same thing, it means God has given us the same idea. In nutshell, for Berkeley, anything lying outside the experiences of mind must be within the mind's of God.

(ii) *Theory of visual space perception* :

This theory was outlined in his book *an Essay Towards a New Theory of Vision* published in 1709. In this theory Berkeley has tried to explain how we perceive distance or third dimensions with our eyes that experience only two dimensions. In order to explain this, he considered the old explanations in terms of angles of light (that come from the object seen) highly inadequate because a person never sees such angle of light. He, therefore, suggested that a person perceives distance or depth of objects by *association* of certain specific experiences. For example, when certain visual experiences become associated with sensations of touch and movement that usually occur while we make certain eye adjustments in looking at near or far objects, we have an accurate perception of distance. In fact, this was the first application of the principle of association to a strictly psychological problem. Thus in Berkeley's theory of visual space perception we find an extension and application of the principles of association previously introduced by Locke.

In this theory of perception of distance, he outlined three criteria of distance. First criteria is *convergence.* In other words, the distance between the two pupils is altered when we turn our eyes in looking at far or near objects. Second criteria is *blurring of* objects specially when they come too near to us. Third criteria is *straining* of eyes, that is, when objects come too near us, we can temporarily prevent the blurring of objects or appearance getting more confused. This third criteria may be named as *accommodation.* Of these three criteria, the first and the last criteria have been okayed by later empiricists but the second one has not been accepted because they claim that blurring of objects occurs not only when objets come too near to us but it also occurs when they go too far to us. In other words, blurring occurrs when objects go beyond as well as come nearer the focus of eye.

(iii) *Theory of 'meaning'* :

In the empiricism of Berkeley mind generates matter whereas in Locke's empiricism matter generates mind. It was, therefore, essential for Berkeley to find a solution to the problem of 'meaning' among ideas generated by mind. He proposed that meaning emerges when ideas become connected or associated with each other. Due to his emphasis upon metaphysical position, Berkeley had also rejected the existence of abstract ideas which he considered as 'delusions of words'. Locke had accepted the existence of abstract ideas though he had rejected the doctrine of innate idea.

Thus we find that Berkeley was such an empiricist for whom a person knows nothing more than his experiences. Since we don't know about the objects or real world, such experiences do come form God. Berkeley's emphasis upon association in explaining the perception of depth and distance was a step highly appreciated by subsequent empiricists.

4. *David Hume* (1711-1776)

Hume was a Scotsman born in Edinburg. He was another British empiricist who was for most part, a self-educated person. In 1739 he published his famous work *A Treatise on Human Nature*. It has been considered as the most important work of Hume. But this book could not give the anticipated fame to author and hence, he became disappointed and immediately started writing another book entitled *Enquiry Concerning the Human Understanding* which was published in 1748. What is considered as the most important of Hume work and which has directly influenced modern psychology, can be grouped into the following three heads :

(i) *Distinction between Impression and Ideas*

Locke had included both impression and ideas under the term *idea*. But Hume made a distinction between the two. In fact, this is considered as Hume's most important work. Hume opined that both ideas and impressions are a kind of experiences and that way, they are similar. Here it would be desirable to mention the viewpoints of Locke and Berkeley. As we have seen, Locke had accepted objects experiences and minds which received them. Berkeley had accepted experiences, minds and existence of God. For Hume, there were only experiences. He denied the existence of God and mind or soul. Hume said that despite similarity between ideas and impressions, they are distinct experiences not to be defined physiologically. Hume used the term *idea* in general sense of words like image and idea stand today. An idea is a kind of experience we have in absence of objects. An impression is a kind of experiences which carries the modern meaning of sensation or perception. Thus impression may be either sensations or perception.

The chief distinction between idea and impression is in their vivacity. The impression are more vigorous, vivid, lively than the ideas. In other words, impressions are vivid and vigorous whereas ideas are weak, faint and vague. Therefore, Hume has said that ideas are nothing but faint copies of impressions. According to Hume, both ideas and impressions can be simple or complex. A simple idea resembles a simple impression. Hence, there is on-to-one relationship between simple idea and simple impression. A complex idea consists of so many simple ideas and therefore, has little or no resemblance with an impression.

Hume established a causal relationship between impression and idea. He was of view that impression causes the corresponding idea. In order to explain this he postulated the following facts :

(a) Simple idea resembles simple impression.

(b) Simple ideas and simple impressions must have occurred previously at some time.
(c) Initially, the impression must have occurred prior to ideas.
(d) Ideas fail to occur when the corresponding impressions don't occur.

Hume went a step ahead in explaining Locke's doctrine of complex ideas. He pointed out that there could be three types of complex ideas. One type may be of relations such as ideas of resemblance, quantity, quality, etc.; second type may be of modes or modalities such as ideas of sounds, colours, light, etc. and the third type may be of substances such as ideas of books, persons, and other objects or substances which are easily named. In fact, through such division of complex ideas, Hume established some kind of mental chemistry as the psychological method.

(ii) *Association*

Like his several predecessors, Hume was concerned with association. For him, association refers to a force or attraction among ideas through which they are united. For Locke and Berkeley, there were two laws of association, that is, law of contiguity and law of similarity. Hume pointed out that there were three laws—law of resemblance or similarity, law of contiguity (or togetherness in space and time), and law of cause and effect. When we see a picture, it may lead to our thoughts relating to objects contained in the picture. This illustrates law of similarity. On seeing a particular book of 'History of Psychology', we may think of other book of history of psychology seen some days back. This illustrates law of contiguity. We may associate a wound with the pain that follows it. This illustrates law of cause and effect. Later on, he reduced cause and effect to contiguity and therefore, only two laws were left.

(iii) *Doctrine of cause and effect*

This is one of the famous doctrine of Hume's psychology which states that causes seem to *act* to produce effect though entire action remain unseen. How does this happen ? Hume analyzed this problem in greater detail and reported that this happens due to the following three conditions.

(a) There is a spatial and temporal immediacy of cause and effect. In other words, causes and their effects are always contiguous in both space and time. If there occurs big time interval and if there is distance, the causes will no longer have their effects.
(b) A cause always occurs prior to its effect.
(c) There must be a necessary connection between cause and its effects.

A look at Hume's psychology makes it clear that by denying existence of mind and consequently, dualism that existed since Locke and Berkeley, he made an outstanding contribution. Thus Hume's psychology was the first psychology without mind as separate from body since ancient Greek philosophers.

ASSOCIATIONISM

The movement of associationism grew directly out of the British empiricist movement. This new movement of associationism was also largely British and continued till the end of nineteenth century. If we pay attention to the basic features of associationism, it becomes obvious that associationism as a movement, in fact, carried the major viewpoints already expressed by Locke, Berkeley and Hume a step ahead. These British empiricists had in fact told much about the association of ideas. The associationists tried further to explain that how the different ideas could be associated together and how many laws of association should be. This viewpoint of associationism had a major impact upon modern psychology in particular upon structuralism and modern theorists like Pavlov, Skinner, Thorndike, etc.

The principal associationists are Hartley, James Mill and John Stuart Mill, Alexander Bain and Herbert Spencer. The history of psychology bears testimony to the fact that as associationism was gaining prominence, a group of psychologists at Scottish Universities revolted against it. This group is known as Scottish School. While discussing associationism, we shall also discuss major features of Scottish School.

1. *David Hartley* (1702-1757)

Hartley was contemporary of Hume and has been regarded as *father* of British associationism. Although Hartley was contemporary of Hume, he had some personal traits in sharp contrast with Hume as it has been pointed out by Hartley's son. Hartley basically belonged to medical profession and practise it throughout his life. He also knew Latin and in 1746 he wrote on association of ideas in Latin. He had been deeply influenced by the philosophical psychologies of Locke on the one hand and Newton's observation that all physical objects were forms of motions (Newton's theory of vibration). In fact, Hartley's psychology was the hybrid of Locke's theory of association of ideas and Newton's theory of vibrations. Hartley's entire psychology was contained in his famous book *Observations of Man* published in 1749. Eight years later, he died.

Hartley's contribution to psychology can be explained under the following two heads :

(i) *Dualistic viewpoint*

Hartley's psychology was dualistic in nature and he was, in fact, much anxious to explain mind-body relationship. Like Descartes, he had a deep interest in physiological explanation of bodily activities. In this sense, he has been regarded as one of the primitive physiological psycholo-gist. As a physiologist, he had carried Newton's idea of motion into physical or bodily activities. He pointed out that sensation and bodily motions are dependent upon the brain, spinal cord and the nerve. After being stimulated by an object, there are produced small vibrations in these nerves. In fact these small vibrations give rise to sensation or motion in person. For example, when light strikes the eyes, the nerves in eyes produce small vibrations due to which we have visual sensation of motions in objects. Hartley postulated that in brain and spinal cord (or in nerves system) there occurs vibrations still smaller than vibrations which occur in nerves. Such exceedingly small vibrations have been called as *vibratinucles* or *miniatures*. According to Hartley, these vibratinucles are the *physiological counterparts* of ideas.

In nutshell, both sensations and ideas are dependent upon vibrations. Vibrations for sensation occur in nerves and vibrations for ideas occur in brain. Vibrations for ideas are always smaller than vibrations for sensations. The fact that sensations are dependent upon vibration in the nerves rests upon Hartley's observation that sensation continues to persist even after removal of stimulus. When light (stimulus) is cut off or removed, we continue to see it for brief period of time. Why ? Obviously because of vibrations produced by light in nerves. Such vibrations gradually become weaker in strength if not repeated by presenting the stimulus.

(ii) *Laws of association*

Hartley pointed out that association may occur among sensations, ideas or motions or among all of them. He further pointed out that the association may be of two types—simultaneous or synchronous association and successive association. Due to simultaneous association there occurs trains of thought and due to successive association there occurs fusion of simple ideas into complex one. Association, since it covers both simultaneous association and successive association, becomes the base for what was then called 'mental compounding'. For Hartley, there is only one law of association, that is, law of contiguity and he has explained how this law works in brain. He pointed out that when two sensations reach the brain either simultaneously or successively, they cause vibrations in such a way that they become connected with each other due to their contiguous nature. When one idea reactivates a vibration, the other vibration would automatically occur. He further argued that the different parts of the brain are so connected that if a first stimulus is presented producing vibrations in the particular region, the second brain region would be automatically aroused without the second stimulus. For example, if a series of associations or sensations such as A, B, C, D occurs in succession *a sufficient number of times*, they leave a trace of vibrations (idea) a, b, c, d. The reoccurrence of A, then, would automatically produce b, c and d vibrations (apart from a). From this example, it becomes obvious that for Hartley *repetition* (a sufficient number of times) was also a favourable condition for association.

Hartley further proceeded to apply these principles of association to various psychological phenomena. For example, he pointed out that relation of perceived visual distance to visual size is a matter of association. Emotions are also associations of various sensations and ideas. When we try to memorize something or to recollect the past, we, in fact, do so by associating the different ideas.

On the whole, we find that Hartley has tried his best to relate mental activities (idea) with physical setting (vibrations) and has presented a physiological explanation of mental activities or idea in terms of vibratory motions of the brain. For him, each mental idea has its physiological correlates or vibration in brain. This view is also known as *psychophysical parallelism*.

2. *The Scottish School*

As pointed out above, with Hartley British Empiricism developed into British associationism in 1749. Subsequently, it was James Mill, another British associationist, with whom associationism flourished in 1829. After that, James Mill's son James Stuart Mill, Alexander Bain and Herbert Spencer took over the lead of associationism. But what happened to psychology in between in intervening 80 years, that is, in between 1749 and 1829. It was in this period that a minor revolt against associationism occurred in Scotland by a group of psychologists. This group has been called the *Scottish School*. Thus for the moment we interrupt our discussion of British associationism and pause to discuss the contribution of the Scottish School. Which arose in protest against the said associationism. The important figures in Scottish School were : Thomas Reid (1710-1796). Douglas Stewart (1753-1828) and Thomas Brown (1778-1820).

Thomas Reid graduated from Aberdeen at the age of 16 and in 1752 was appointed Professor of Philosophy in King's College. He published several books of which two were most influential. One such book was *Inquiry into the Human Mind on the Principles of common sense,* published in 1764 and another book was *Essays on the Intellectual powers of Man* that was published in 1785, that is, four years after his retirement. He died in 1796.

Historians state that Reid has, though accepted the soundness of British associationism, attacked particularly the Hume's psychology. It was, in fact, Hume's skepticism that gave rise to Reid's psychology. He proposed that it is wrong to say that mind knows only about its own processes and can't sense the existence of real objects and other minds. In fact, mind knows more than its own processes and it also senses the real objects. He proposed that mind is an organized entity having powers to perform various psychological activities. In this sense, he has been called a faculty psychologist. He pointed out that there are twenty-four active powers of the mind (such as self-preservation, hunger, self-esteem, imitation, duty, imagination, pity etc.) and six intellectual powers such as perception, judgement, memory, conception, moral taste, and will.

As we known Locke and Berkeley had accepted the existence of real objects and their sense qualities but Hume had denied the existence of real objects. Reid lodged a strong protest against Hume's denial. He pointed out that real objects exist and we do experience sensation from them. Reid has said, "All mankind could not be wrong and go against the wisdom of the ages". Obviously, then since every person knows about the existence of real objects through having sensations from them, it automatically proves that there is the existence of real objects. He has, however, made a *distinction* between sensation and perception. The experiences of sensation when expanded, constitute perception. For any object to be sensed and perceived, it is essential that at least two qualities must be there. First, a general conception about the object and the instantaneous objective existence of the object. Now the question is : how is sensation expanded into perception ? Reid's answer is that we received experiences from real objects (sensation) and with the help of God's wisdom necessary *pluses* are added to turn sensation into perception or man's wisdom about external world. Reid has also objected to Hume's laws of association.

Douglas Stewart was disciple of Reid and was Professor of Moral Philosophy at Edinburgh for nearly thirty-five years. He published his famous book *Element of the Philosophy of the Human mind in* three volumes. First volume of this book was published in 1792 and the second volume was published in 1814 and third volume in 1827. In fact, Stewart merely popularized Reid's philosophy by lectures before businessmen, ;lawyers, professional persons, etc. and contributed nothing original. Particularly, Reid's doctrine of faculties was much popularized and listners welcome the viewpoints expressed by Stewart. Thus Stewart gave us nothing which can be considered important for psychology.

Thomas Brown was a disciple of Stewart. In academic life he was a very close associate of Stewart and in fact, when Stewart's health started failing day-by-day in 1810, he virtually used to do all this major academic works and ultimately, he appointed him as his coadjutant. Thus both worked in partnership and one day there occurred a big jolt to the enthusiasm of Stewart when he found that Brown was ready to make a compromise with British associationism. The partnership continued for 10 years and in 1820 Brown died. Brown's lectures were collected and immediately published after his death in the same year. The name of this collection was *Lectures on the philosophy of the Human Mind*. In fact by this time Brown's philosophy came to reinforce British associationistic empiricism. Thus Brown brought Scottish Psychology back to the association movement.

Not daring to use the term 'association', Brown instead used the term *suggestion*. He proposed that mind or soul was unitary and had suggested that there were certain principles through which mind functions, For Brown the primary laws of suggestion were contiguity, resemblance (similarity) and contrast. In fact, there were also secondary laws of suggestions which explained the possible variations that occurred in the suggestibility (or associatedness) of the ideas. The variations may be in terms of duration of original sensations, their relative liveliness, their relative frequency of degree of coexistence with other suggestions and constitutional differences of mind or temperament.

Despite the open support to the associationists, Brown did not completely revert to become another associationist. In fact, he maintained the distinction. For solving the objection of the existence of real things as proposed by Berkeley and Hume, Brown appealed to muscular sensation (today called kinesthetic or proprioceptive sensation). In fact, Brown took sensations from real objects and then added the muscle sense. We came to know about the existence of real objects because of our feeling of muscular excitations. For example, we have pure sensation of rose from sight and sense. When we know that the sensed rose requires some muscular effort to move it, then the sensed rose begins to suggest some resistance. By such suggestion, the rose is turned into the perception of real object. If we pay attention to this explanation, it becomes obvious that there is little distinction between Berkeley's use of association for explaining our belief in the existence of real object and Brown's attempt brought the Scottish school more close to the British empiricism. Boring (1950, p. 208) has very nicely worded the situation :

"Brown's philosophy in this way came to reinforce associationistic empiricism; and Brown to the modern reader, it must be said, seems to belong more with Berkeley, Lotze and Wundt than with Reid and Stewart."

In this way we find that associationism which grew out of British empiricism was temporarily interrupted by the Scottish School. But towards the close of this school, once against supporters of the Scottish school started expressing themselves more in favour of associationism. In this way, the Scottish school which started in protest against associationism became friendly to this movement.

3. *Back to British Associationism : The Mills*

In fact associationism reached its culmination in eighteenth century with the efforts of James Mill and his son John Stuart Mill. Alexander Bain was also no less important. The two Mills and Bain were instrumental in bringing philosophical psychology to the point from where Wundt took it and gave it the status of scientific psychology.

James Mill (1773-1836), by birth, was a Scot. In 1802 he went to London along with Sir John Stuart who was a Member of Parliament of London. In London he started writings about psychology and for various journals. Such writings were his sole source of income. In 1805 he was married and was blessed with a son named John Stuart Mill who became more popular than his father later on. Among the books which had brought fame to him were *An Analysis of the Phenomenon of Human Mind* published in 1829 and *The History of India* published in 1817. The latter book, in fact, changed his fortune because it brought a good revenue as well as a high salaries appointment to the East India Company.

In *An Analysis of the Phenomenon of the Human Mind* he presented his basic viewpoints of simple-minded associationism. In describing elements of mind he was very close to Hartley and Hume. Like them, he pointed out that mind is composed of *sensations* and *ideas*, that is, sensations and ideas are the basic classes of elements of mind. Both ideas and sensations are the primary states of consciousness. In fact, he used *idea* in the modern sense of image. Thus for him ideas are copy (or image) of sensation. Thus ideas and sensations are highly similar.

Despite this similarity, the two differs. Idea occurs only when sensations have previously occurred. In this way ideas are derived from sensations. Another point of distinction is that law of associations applies only to ideas and not to sensations like Hartley, for Mill there was only one law of association, that is, law of contiguity. He further pointed out that contiguity works in two ways—successively and simultaneously. In other words association of ideas can be successive or simultaneous. Of these two ways, successive associations are more frequent and numerous. To use illustration from James Mill, *seeing the horse* is the example of sensation but *thinking of its master* is the example of idea. The idea of master may make one think of his office that *he is a minister of state.* This is another idea. This new idea may force one think of *public affairs.* Thus we see that various ideas become successively associated with other through contiguity.

Simultaneous or synchroneous associations help in building perception of objects. For example, when idea of colour, hardness, shape, size and weight of a stone simultaneously occur together, we have perception of this object, that is, stone.

Mill also pointed out that the strength of associations of ideas varies and he has proposed *three criteria* for measuring the strength of association. These three criteria are as under :

(i) ***Permanence*** : Association may be temporary or permanent. A permanent association is always stronger than a temporary association.

(ii) ***Certainty*** : A correct idea occurs with more certainty than an incorrect idea and therefore, former is always stronger than the latter.

(iii) ***Facility*** : It means spontaneity or lack of effort in the formation of ideas. Spontaneous associations are more stronger than associations of ideas formed with greater effort.

Besides these observational criteria of measuring strength of association, he has also proceeded to explain those *factors* which produce change in the differences of associations. Such factors are called *conditions of associations.* Vividness and frequency are two such factors which do make difference.

James Mill believed in what is called principle of 'mental mechanics'. According to this principle complex idea of any real object is nothing but an addition of the original simple ideas put together by association. Thus he emphasized upon the fact that any complete (or complex) idea consists of so many simpler ideas. For example, the idea of an elephant is made up of so many simpler ideas like idea of four legs, of trunk, idea of big ears, etc.

John Stuart Mill (1806-1873) son of James Mill was another important man during which associationism flourished. In fact, he was more able than his father and had much greater effect upon the history of human thought. He had been, for the most part, privately taught by his father. His psychology is contained mainly in three books—*Logic* published in 1843, *Examination of Sir William Hamilton's Philosophy* published in 1865 and in the edited and annotated edition of his father's book, *An Analysis of the Phenomenon of the Human Mind.* John Mill's contribution to psychology may be grouped into the following three headings :

(i) *Doctrine of association*

Like his father, John Stuart Mill said that sensations and ideas are the basic elements of mind. On the basis of Hume's view, James Mill had opined that ideas are distinguishable from sensations in that they are weaker. John Mill rejected this view of his father since John Mill had further little to say about sensation, the matter remains no larger worth discussing here.

He also accepted the laws of association propounded by his father but made a fruitful addition. James Mill had recognized only one law of association, that is, contiguity. But in 1843 John Mill announced three laws of association—*similarity, contiguity* and *intensity*. Contiguity also includes *frequency*. In 1865 he announced a revision and now for him, the important laws of associations were—*similarity, contiguity, frequency and inseparability* omitting *intensity*. Ideas may coalesce according to any of these laws.

(ii) *Mental Chemistry*

James Mill had propounded the principles of mental mechanics according to which any complex idea consists of simpler ideas, that is, when so many simple ideas are added together, they constitute a complex idea. John Stuart Mill differed from his father. He substituted the principle of mental chemistry for the principle of mental mechanics. According to the principle of mental chemistry, the additive process has been rejected. Any complex idea is not the sum of simple ideas. In fact, when many simple ideas fuse together, a complex idea is born. Thus a complex idea is generated by the simple ideas and not *consists* of them. The resulting complex idea or associative whole is not only the sum of its parts (or simple ideas) rather it contains something new just as water is not merely oxygen plus hydrogen and nor is all of hydrogen or all of oxygen. Thus laws of phenomena of mind are similar to chemical laws. When many ideas operate in mind together, a process similar to chemical combination takes place there. These several ideas, like a chemical combination, melt and coalesce into one another and finally appear as on whole idea (called complex idea). John Stuart Mill has explained this with an analogy that as when seven colours rapidly follow each other, it *generates* white but not that they are actually white. So also when simple ideas occur in contiguous with each other, it generates the complex idea. This is what is known as 'mental chemistry'.

(iii) *Theory of Perception*

The theory of perception or more appropriately called *psychological theory of matter* has been outlined more clearly in his *Examination of Sir William Hamilton's Philosophy* published in 1865. As we know, the problem of making distinction between perception and sensation has been essentially the problem of belief in existence of objects or matter as lying behind experience. John Stuart Mill pointed out that human mind is capable of making *expectations* and therefore, after having experiences or sensations, we become capable of forming *possible sensations* which might be felt though they are not being felt at the moment. Making a distinction between sensation and matter, John Stuart Mill pointed out that sensations are fugitive as well as transitory whereas matter is permanent and fixed. He further pointed out that though sensations are not permanent like matter but *possibilities of sensations* are permanent. Matter or object is nothing but simply the *permanent possibilities of sensations.* Perception of matter or object is nothing but simply a belief in those possibilities. In nutshell, we can say that for John Stuart Mill sensation is fugitive and transitory whereas perception is permanent because it is based upon possibilities of sensation.

John Stuart Mill's psychology has been, on the whole, very influential one. His doctrine of association proved very important in making psychology as experimental one. His theory of matter of object as the permanent possibilities of sensation has also proved very crucial for modern view of perception.

4. *Alexander Bain* (1818-1903)

Bain was a Scotsman and belonged to a poor family. He spent his whole life in Aberdeen. Due to poverty, his education was irregular. He had also difficulty in getting professorship in Scottish universities. Therefore, he moved into London where he came in close contact with John Stuart Mill, his 12 years senior and derived inspiration for writing. He helped a lot in the final revision of the *Logic* written and published by John Stuart Mill. He stated writing for systematic psychology in 1851 and the whole work, for convenience of publication, was divided into two volumes published in different years. In fact, these two volumes were his principal works which concern us most in psychology. The first volume was *The Senses and the Intellect* published in 1855 and the second volume was *The Emotions and the Will* published in 1859. The first volume was revised and the revised editions were published in 1864, 1868 and 1894. Likewise, revised editions of the second volume were published in 1865, 1875 and 1899. In 1872, he also published his famous book *Mind and Body*. In 1876 he founded *Mind*, the first psychological journal in any country. He gave it financial support until 1892. *Mind* is still being published.

Historians wrote that though Bain was not a great man in the sense Descartes, Johannes Muller and Wundt were because no system or school had been derived from his works. However, due to his able work associationism reached its culmination and it also started being absorbed into physiological psychology. Because of his emphasis upon physiological explanations of mental events, Boring (1969) has recognised him as the first modern physiological psychologist. Since Bain's physiological explanation has been more sophisticated than that of Hartley and Descartes, the justification of Boring appears to be more correct.

The entire works of Bain which is relevant to psychology, can be presented under the following four heads :

(i) *Psychophysical parallelism*

In fact Bain was not the first to discuss parallelism in psychology. We may recall from the work of Leibnitz and Hartely that they had mentioned and discussed the phenomenon in greater detail. Bain pointed out that every human activity has two sides—the physical side and the mental side. The physical side works as such a system in which cause and effect are more or less quantitatively equivalent whereas the mental side tends to run in parallel with the physical side. In mental side there does not occur any quantitative equivalence as we find in case of physical side. However, he was not himself much clear about this parallelism and was therefore, not sure whether he was dealing with two different substances or two aspects of the same substance.

(ii) *Physiological psychology*

Prior to Bain, Descartes as well as Hartley had made physiological psychology popular. But Descartes' physiological psychology was primitive whereas Hartley's physiological psychology was the speculative physiology of Newton. It was Bain who put physiological psychology on scientific track. Therefore, Boring (1969) has very rightly considered him as the *first modern physiological psychologist*. As a physiological psychologist, he described the sense organs and their functioning. He also discussed reflex arc. To Aristotle's five senses, he added the 'organic sense' which is directly involved in hunger, thirst, or other internal conditions. He has also described the functioning of muscles in opposing pairs.

(iii) *Doctrine of associationism*

Bain pointed out two fundamental laws of association—contiguity and similarity. Contiguity explains *retentiveness* of activities or sensations. By contiguity sensations cohere in such a way that subsequent occurrence of any one may lead to recurrence of another. The effectiveness of contiguity, as Bain has argued, depends upon *repetition* of contiguities, as well as upon attention of the individual. Since individual differs in terms of aptitude for retaining something, *individual difference* in aptitude, therefore, also makes a difference. Bain also pointed out that associations which are individually too weak to revive the past idea or sensation get a success in doing so by acting together. This is called as *compound association*. Through law of similarity, Bain has explained constructive association which takes place in thinking, memory, and constructive imagination. Thus Bain also dealt with the principle of creativity which states that by means of associations mind develops power to form new combinations or aggregates, different from those already experienced. But unfortunately, the law of similarity could not be popular nor taken over by later psychologists who thought that law of similarity can best be accommodated with law of contiguity.

(iv) *Doctrine of Will*

Bain pointed out that action may be spontaneous or deliberate. An action is said to be spontaneous when it occurs independently of any external stimulation. *Relex action* as well as *instinctive action* are its example. Such actions are, however, controlled by nervous system. Bain further pointed out that all actions involve actual movement and therefore, give rise to muscular sensations or sensations of innervation. Thus in all movement there is definite sensory experience or experience of effort. Such experience is known as *will*. This will ultimately pervades our mental life.

In this way we find that Bain had anticipated much about what we today know as modern psychology. It was during this period that associationism reached its culmination and was ready to be absorbed by the experimental context. In nutshell, he completed the transformation of philosophical empiricism into psychological associationism.

5. ***Herbert Spencer*** **(1820-1903)**

Spencer's real influence upon psychology started with publication of his *Principles of Psychology* in 1855 which was revised in 1870. In this book he has considered association to be a very significant binding principle. Conscious apprehension of sensations was termed as *feeling* by Spencer and he made a distinction between centrally initiated fellings (called emotions) and peripherally initiated feelings (called organic and external sensations). Among these feelings he added a new element called *relations,* that is, among different feelings there may be relations of coexistence, of sequence and even of difference. He pointed out that through *association* both feeling and relations are held together. He recognized *similarity* as the only law of association because, for him, any association to occur, similarity among feelings must be there.

The most important and novel thing in Spencer's psychology was application of his evolutionary doctrine to association. He had developed this doctrine in the years prior to the publication of Darwin's theory of evolution in 1859. Spencer's associationism is known as *evolutionary associationism.* According to evolutionary associationism, association contains hereditary quality which in successive generations becomes cumulative. He was of view that when particular association occurs often enough in an individual, this is safely passed on to his offspring. These associations, after several generations, are transformed into *instinct*. Gradually, from these instincts, cognition and memory are carved out. In this way we find that there is an evolutionary hierarchy where simpler states produce more complex ones.

After Spencer, British associationism came to an end. It remained for the later experimental psychologist to take over the principles and apply them to the various field. In fact, many of the principles outlined by British associationism were directly taken by the experimental psychologists like Wundt and Titchner. The experimentations based upon stimulus-response psychology were also directly encouraged. As Marx & Hillix (1987, p. 50) have said, "British empiricism left a legacy of the utmost significance to the newly developing experimental science of psychology. A major part of this significance lay in the methodological point of view which associationism developed and refined. The stimulus-response type of thinking and experimenting grew out of it."

NATIVISM, THAT IS, GERMAN PSYCHOLOGY BEFORE 1850 : I. KANT, JOHANN HERBART, HERMANN LOTZE

Nativism was a reactions against empiricism. In fact, German philosophers of the first half of the nineteenth century were very active and their viewpoints influenced the emergence of scientific psychology not lesser than the British empiricism and associationism. Those German philosophers who influenced the emergence of modern psychology were Immanuel Kant, Johann Friedrich Herbat and Herman Lotze. These German nativists held the view that perception was not necessarily dependent upon experience of learning. Its major implications are today seen in modern Gestalt psychology that started as protest against structuralism.

1. *Immanuel Kant* (1724-1804)

I. Kant was born in Konigsberg in 1724. He wanted to be one of the great philosophers of his time. He never travelled more than forty miles from his birthplace in whole of his eighty years of life. In 1755 he obtained his Ph. D. degree from the University of Konigsberg and in 1770 he got a chair in the department of logic and metaphysics at Konigsberg University. Kant became famous and influential philosopher with the publication of his book *Critique of Pure Reason* in 1781. This book was revised in 1787. He also published two more books—*Critique of Practical Reason* published in 1788 and *Critique of judgment* in 1790. In fact, these books had vary profound influence upon the academic growth of Kant. He died in 1804.

Although Kant was a great philosopher, he was not a psychologist. In fact, he held anti-attitude towards psychology when he pointed out that psychology could never be a science (Lundin, 1985). Despite this, Kant is remembered because his viewpoints had important impact upon emergence of modern psychology. His viewpoints which had much impact upon psychology can be presented under following two heads :

(i) *Views on subjectivism*

Kant's insistence on subjectivism clearly indicate his strong faith in the importance of those mental activities that can't reduced to brain or bodily processes. He made it clear that mind cannot be reduced to brain or bodily processes nor its reality can be shown by using any deductive methods. He provided a compromise between empiricists and his stand on subjectivism. He pointed out that empiricists were right in claiming that knowledge could come through experience only but their explanation was inadequate in the sense that they never showed how experience itself was born. He further pointed out that mind could not be the blank sheet (or *tabula rasa*) as it was thought by empiricists. There must be some organizing principles which are learnt by the persons. Thus Kant's compromise formula was such in which the experience remains a teacher but it also needs students who have the ability to organize those experiences. For Kant, experience was a unitary phenomenon that can't be broken down. This viewpoint of Kant had directly influenced modern psychology. For example, Gestalt psychology, being influenced by this viewpoint, directly made the presupposition that perception could not be broken into different parts. Hence, we perceive something as whole. By such insistence on unity of perception, Kant gave a hard blow to the associationism of British empiricists.

(ii) *Views of nativism*

Explaining his theory of nativism, Kant said that our tendency to preceive space and time was not wholly dependent upon experience rather this tendency was native or inborn. In other words, we can say that according to nativists, individuals have some inherent ways of knowing about the world and these ways are in no way dependent upon experience or learning. Kant's this theory of nativism influenced a lot to viewpoints of early twentieth century of Gestalt psychology which accepting this theory with a slight modification, pointed out that we perceive something in natural ways that did not in any was depend upon learning or experience. This was termed by Gestalt psychology as "primitive organization of experience.' One recent application of Kant's theory of nativism is also seen in studies of depth perception in human infants. Today there are sufficient evidences to indicate that human infants have native depth perception by the age they are able to crawl. In several instances it has been shown that such infants should tend to avoid crawling over "visual cliffs" even though their mothers might be attracting them from opposite side.

In this way we find that Kant's viewpoints have direct impact upon thinking of modern psychology, particularly upon the thinking of Gestalt psychologists. Perhaps, due to this reason, Kant is remembered as being one of the important German philosophers.

2. *Johann Friedrich Herbart* (1776-1841)

Johann Herbart is the next important German philosopher who is popularly known as father of scientific pedagogy. His schooling was poor and he had been taught by his mother at home. At the age of sixteen, he was deeply influenced by the philosophy of Kant. At the age of thirty-one, he became Kant's successor at Konigsberg University in 1809. He accepted some of Kant's philosophical ideas yet he was not a wholly nativist. In 1833, he went to Gottingen as Professor of philosophy and he held this appointment till his death in 1841. After his death, his chair was occupied by Lotze.

For Herbart, psychology is a science which is based upon experience, metaphysics and mathematics. Since psychology is based upon experience, it is empirical observation (not experiment) that is the appropriate method of psychology. Observation grows out of experience. Psychology is metaphysical and it is this nature of psychology that distinguishes it from physics which is experimental. Psychology is mathematical and that is another way in which it is distinct from physics. Physics uses both methods, that is, experiment and calculation. Psychology uses only method of calculation. Thus Herbart made use of mathematics in psychology to a greater extent and in that perspective, we can easily see that Fechner's original idea of mental measurement was not really original and has been derived from the combination of Herbart's use of mathematics with Weber's experiments.

For Herbart, what psychology is *not*. He pointed out that psychology is not experimental, not descriptive and not physiological. For Herbart, psychology is not physiological because the study of physiology does not provide any solution to the problem of mind. Despite this, he has recognized a definite relation between mind and body. He pointed out that bodily conditions sometimes might facilitate the arousal of an idea (as it is found in case of intoxication) and sometimes they might interfere in the arousal of an idea. The former is known as *principle of reinforcement* and the latter is known as the *principle of repression.*

Although Herbart accepted Kant's notion of unitary mind or soul, he later allowed that the mind could be a composite of smaller units or ideas. For Herbart, ideas have two important dimensions, that is, intensity as well as quality and every idea is distinguishable from one another in terms of intensity and quality. He pointed out that mind could be analyzed into separate ideas which vary independently in terms of quality and intensity. The dimension of intensity or force is more or less equivalent to clearness.

According to Herbart, each idea has a tendency of *self-preservation,* that is, each idea has a tendency to maintain itself as it comes into contact with other ideas. It also tends to drive out those ideas with which it is incompatible (or in a state of inhibition). By so driving out the incompatible ideas, each idea reverts to the state of complete liberty (or absence of inhibition). Thus Herbart made inhibition rather than *association* as the key point in his system. He further pointed out that when as idea is met with incompatible ideas or a group of stronger ideas, it is thrown below the *limen of consciousness*. Such thrown idea does not die but for some time, become unconscious where it persists. In unconsicious, ideąs have forces of various intensities. If these forces were strong enough to counter the forces already present in the consciousness, they enter into consciousness. Such interaction of forces within and outside consciousness is called *psychic dynamics* by Herbart. Herbart's this idea about unconscious influenced Freud to a greater extent in formulating theory of unconscious. An idea that is inherently weak may get admission into consciousness and maintain itself there, if ideas lying above the limen of threshold are compatible and/or congenial with the weak idea. Thus ideas already in consciousness always repel the entry of uncongenial idea and make entry of the congenial idea. However, all uninhibited ideas go to the consciousness and are assimilated to ideas already there. This process is named as *apperception* and the group of ideas into which the new idea is accommodated is called *apperception mass*. Herbart had also mathematically calculated conditions which tended to determine what could and could not enter consciousness.

Herbart also spelled out about union of ideas specially when there is little or no conflict. He pointed out that when two ideas belong to the same sense modality and are not in conflict with each other, they immediately unite. This is called *fusion*. For example, red colour and blue colour (both belonging to the same sense modality) unite with each other to give the new idea of violet. Two ideas may belong to the different sense modalities (as with a colour and a sound) and if there is no opposition or conflict between them, they still may unite with each other. Such unity has been called as *complication*. Later on Wilhelm Wundt adopted these two terms, namely, complication and fusion to widen his system.

In nutshell, it can be said that although Herbart was not a supporter of psychology being an experimental science, his influence upon modern psychology was great. His view of conscious and unconscious directly influenced Freud in formulating the theory of unconscious. Therefore, it becomes clear by now that Freud did not invent the concept of unconscious. Not only this, the entire idea of measurement and quantification laid down by Herbart provided a straight basis for development of modern experimental psychology.

3. *Herman Lotze* (1817-1881)

Lotze was a son of physician and following father's step, he matriculated under the faculty of medicine in 1834 at the University of Leipzig. At this university, he came into contact with important and influential persons like Weber, Volkman and Fechner. He took his degree in medicine from University of Leipzig. Still he was half a philosopher and his dissertation was entitled as *The future biology according to philosophical principles*. In 1839 he was appointed as *Dozent* in both the faculty of philosophy as well as in the faculty of medicine. In 1844 he took over Herbart's chair at Gottingen (Herbart had died in 1841) where he remained almost until his death, being finally succeeded by G. E. Muller. Thus he spent about thirty-seven years at Gottingen and during this longest stay, his interest changed from physiology to philosophy. Brentano, Stumpf and G. E. Muller were all deeply influenced by the viewpoints of Lotze.

Historian like Boring (1950) wrote that Lotze exerted some influence upon the experimental psychology no doubt but that influence was not great. His influence in psychology was due to his books *Medical Psychology* or *The Physiology of the Soul*. Lotze's theory of space perception was the single most important contribution that influenced modern psychology to a greater extent and perhaps due to that reason, he finds a place in the history of psychology. Lotze's theory of space includes perception of space of touch and vision. His theory of space states that on a native or innate capacity to perceive space, persons build up their perceptions of space through experience. The raw data are of non-spatial characteristics that consists of specific aggregation or complex of intensities which accompany the stimulation of the skin and muscles in case of space perception of touch and in case of space perception of vision, the complex of intensities is aroused by eye movements. Such aggregations or complexes of intensities are called as *local signs* by Lotze. Such local signs have the basic purpose of distinguishing the stimulation of the particular point.

It is apparent from discussion of the theory of space that it can fit either in the interpretation of nativists or in the interpretation of empiricists. His emphasis upon native capacity of mind for spatial perception definitely places him in nativists quarter. On the other hand, his explanation that perception of space is generated by experiences gained from non-spatial objects or materials, easily puts him in empiricists' quarter.

On the whole, it appears that German psychology under the leadership of Kant, Herbart and Lotze made significant impact upon the development of modern scientific psychology.

CHAPTER HIGHLIGHTS

1. Psychology is considered as hybrid of philosophy and physiology. So far as the philosophical impacts are concerned, they have preceded the physiological impacts. The philosophical impacts upon psychology can be categorized under four main headings—mind-body problem, empiricism, associations and German nativism.
2. Ancient philosophers like St. Augustine and St. Thomas had strong faith in complete division of two aspects of man, that is, *mind* and *body*. These philosophers, however, never cared about the fact that these two aspects could be even related in some significant way. But continental philosophers of 17th century like Descartes, Lebinitz and Spinoza tried to show that these two aspects of person could be related to each other though each had proposed a different solution to the question of mind and body. Among these three explanations, Descartes explanation through mind-body interactionism, was most psychological. Due to this reason, he is sometimes called as the *father of modern psychology*.
3. As a revolt against the viewpoints of continental philosophers like Descartes, Leibnitz and Spinoza, a new movement named empiricism was born. This movement was led by three British philosophers—John Locke, George Berkeley and David Hume. Empiricism, as emphasized by these British philosophers rejected the popular notion held by Descartes which claimed that ideas are inherited or inborn. They said that all knowledge including idea came from learning or experience. The whole empiricist movement had a profound effect on development of not only many brands of psychology but also upon development of psychology as science in general.
4. The movement of associationsim grew directly out of the British empiricist movement. This new movement was also largely British and continued till the end of nineteenth century. The major associationists who carried this movement were David Harley, James Mill, John Stuart Mill, Alexnder Bain and Herbert Spencer. The primary concern of these associationists were how ideas could be hooked together and through what principles or laws ideas become associated together. In fact, the major facts of associationism had profound impact upon the formulation of principles of structuralism and modern learning theory. The most influential persons like I. P. Pavlov and Edward Thorndike depended upon those principles of association while formulating their theories of learning.

5. At the Scottish Universities some teachers like Thomas Reid, Douglas Stewart and Thomas Brown revolted against British associationism. This group of men became known as the Scottish school which temporarily interrupted the development of British associationism. They had substituted the word 'suggestion' for 'association'. But towards the close of this school, once again supporters of Scottish school started expressing themselves more in favour of associationism. In this way, the Scottish school which started in protest against associationism became friendly to this movement.
6. Another philosophical moment which had a direct impact upon modern psychology was nativism that flourished in Germany before 1850. In fact, nativism was reaction against empiricism. Those German philosophers who were most active as nativists were Immanuel Kant, Johann Herbart and Hermann Lotze. These nativists, in general, were of view that perceptual experience was not necessarily dependent upon learning. Its major implication today is upon modern Gestalt psychology which claimed that perceptual organization is not governed by learning.

REVIEW QUESTIONS

1. Discuss the ways through which mind-body problem was dealt with by various continental philosopher psychologists.
2. Discuss the salient features of Cartesian psychology.
3. "The whole empiricists movement had significant impacts not only upon different brands of psychology but also upon the emergence of psychology as a science." Discuss.
4. Discuss the contributions of John Locke and George Berkeley in development of psychology.
5. "The movement of associationism grew out of the British empiricists movement." Justify the statement.
6. In what ways the various principles of associationism proved boon for the modern learning theorists. Explain with illustrative examples.
7. What were the causes of revolt of Scottish psychologists against the British associationism ? Who was the main psychologist that became instrumental in brining the Scottish psychology back into the British fold ?
8. "German nativists based their psychologies upon the pillars different from those of empiricists". Justify the statement.

■

CHAPTER 4

BEGINNING OF EXPERIMENTAL PSYCHOLOGY

CHAPTER PREVIEW

In this chapter focus has been given on all those issues which are related to the body and have direct impact upon emergence of the scientific psychology. Most of these issues have emerged from scientific developments in the field of physiology, physics and biology in between 1800–1850, that is, during the first half of the nineteenth century. Such physiological impacts upon modern scientific psychology have been examined under three headings, namely, psychophysics, the development of neuro-physiology and the theory of evolution.

Psychophysics mainly covers the contribution of two important figures—E.H. Weber and G.T. Fechner who were not psychologists. Weber was a physiologist and Fechner was a physicist. They had done exceptional work in the area of measurement of sensation. They had also developed some methods to measure sensations. Those methods popularly known as psychophysical methods, historically, led to the development of modern experimental psychology.

The development of neurophysiology, among others, basically includes the physiology of brain, contribution of Johannes Muller and specific nerve energies, contribution of Hermann Von Helmholtz and Edward Herring. As a whole, the development of neurophysiology explained the functioning of nerves and muscles, theories that tend to explain the functioning of brain as well as the theories relating to the functioning of hearing and vision.

The chapter also focuses upon theory of evolution that has too a direct impact upon development of modern psychology. Charles Darwin and Francis Galton were two most important figures whose evolutionary theories provided a strong impetus to the emergence of modern psychology. The psychology of Willian James, functionalism particularly Chicago school, Freudian Psychoanalysis and Willian McDougall's hormic psychology have great obligations to the evolutionary theories of Darwin and Galton.

A note of caution ! If we pay attention to the philosophical sources which were instrumental in making psychology an experimental science, it is obvious that during those philosophical studies some efforts were made to study these physiological processes although not with so much of emphasis. For example,

Descartes tried to explain the mind-body interactionism through physiology. David Hartley also tried to explain associations in terms of brain motions or vibrations. Alexander Bain also emphasized upon the physiological correlates of mental functioning. Hence, physiological sources were also being examined during philosophical regime but not with an emphatic effort.

PSYCHOPHYSICS

Psychophysics is the science which tries to investigate the quantitative relationship between physical stimulus and resulting psychological experience. We have seen that the philosophers had made senses, the channels of information coming from objective world and the resulting field of consciousness as the central topics in psychology. It remained for physiologists, however, to suggest empirical and experimental methods for studying psychological data relating to that consciousness. Two German scientists have made unparallel contribution in the field of psychophysics. They are E. H. Weber, a reputed physiologist, and G. T. Fechner, a reputed physicist. Their contributions and their impact upon emergence of psychology may be outlined as under :

1. *Ernst H. Weber* (1795–1878)

Weber was an important German physiologist. He taught physiology at Leipzig University in the capacity of Professor of physiology from about 1818 to 1860. There he conducted his well-known researches on touch. Those researches provided breeding ground for the development of psychophysics. In fact, psychophysics had started with Weber's experimentations. Weber's entire work on experimentation relating to psychophysics can be divided under the following *three* categories :

(i) The first category of Weber's experimentations was related to temperature sense. On the basis of his several experiments on temperature sense, Weber concluded that sensation of warm and cold did not directly result from actual temperature stimulation rather it resulted from change in the temperature of skin. For example, if we place our hand in a moderately warm water, we will no longer feel a sensation of warmth because our hand will adapt to the warm water. But if there is increase in the temperature of water, a feeling of warmth will be produced (because there also occurs a change in the temperature of skin).

(ii) Another category of Weber's experimentations was related to touch sense. He held the view that the sense of touch produces three distinct types of sensations, namely, sensation of pressure, temperature and locality. In fact his these varied experimentations became a starting point for any research in touch sensation. His these experimentations also led to the discovery of what is popularly known as the *two-point threshold or limen* which attracted a series of experiments conducted by different persons. In his experiments on touch sense, Weber demonstrated that when two separate pin-points of stimuli stimulate the skin of the subject, he tends to report the feeling of two separate stimuli. If the distance between these two stimuli is gradually reduced, a point comes where the subject reports the feeling of only one pin-point although his skin is being touched with two pin-points. This distance between two points is known as two-point threshold. If distance of two stimuli with which skin is to be touched, is below this threshold, the subject would report only one point. A distance greater than this threshold would be reported as two separate points. After conducting a series of experiments, Weber concluded that two-point threshold was not constant for different parts of the body. Some parts of the body are sensitive while other parts are not sensitive to that extent. In sensitive parts, the two-points threshold was small whereas in less sensitive parts it was large. That is the reason why, it was very small for the tips of fingers and large for the back of the body. Surprisingly, the two-point threshold also varied from one person to another and sometimes within the same person due to changes in the situation.

(iii) Perhaps the most important contribution for which Weber could become popular in psychology, was his experimentations on muscle sense, although with regard to its importance Thomas Brown already had expressed his viewpoints. In fact, Weber demonstrated that there is no single sense of touch. Instead, there are many senses of touch. The muscles, the skin and the internal organs of the body all make separate and special contributions.

Weber was mainly interested in knowing how well one can discriminate differences in the weights of objects by lifting and comparing them with each other. In other words, to what extent muscle sense contributes in discrimination of weight. Therefore, in Weber's experiments the basic problem was whether differences in weight could be determined better by subjects if they lifted the weights or when the weights are simply placed upon his hand by the investigator (that is, when active manipulation of objects is not allowed). For doing such experiments, Weber took two series of weights—a standard weight and some complarable weights. Results of such experiments conducted by Weber revealed two basic points. *First,* the subjects made correct discrimination when they were allwed to lift the wight. It means that the sensitivity to weight is increased when muscular sense is also included or added to the senses that merely perceived the touch of weights. Hence, the more sences were used, the more precise was the sensation. *Second,* it was reported that the ability to discriminate small differences in stimuli depends not only on the intensity of stimulus alone but on a *ratio of difference to the standard weight.* The smallest differnce between the two physical stimuli which can be detected was called *just noticeable difference* or *jnd* or the *difference threshold*. Therefore, a jnd is the smallest difference between two stimuli that is detetable 50% of time. This was really a very important discovery, which later came to be known as *Weber's laws* and attracted a series of experiments by later psychologists. Weber had made it clear that there was not a one-to-one relationship between magnitude of differnce and the subject's ability to detect the discrimination. As research proceeded ahead, Weber found that the *jnd* between the two weights was a constant ratio, that is, 1:40 of the standard weight. In other words, a weight of 41 grams was perceived to be just noticeable different from a standard weight of 40 grams and maintaining the same ratio, an 82 gram weight was just noticeable different from a standard weight of 80 grams. Obviously, it meant, then, that in case of standard weight of 40 gram, the given weights less than 41 but greater than 40 would be below the threshold or would not be a noticeable difference but weights greater than 41 gr. could be discriminated as heavier than 40 gram. Thus ability to perceive a discrimination is not dependent upon the absolute size of the difference but on the ratio between the difference and the standard weight. Weber not only investigated the muscle sensation but he also investigated visual discrimination and found the similar results.

On the whole, it is said that Weber's experimentations were milestones in the experimental research on sensation and perception because those experimentations very clearly demonstratd that the quantitative methods can be applied the the psychological problems. His guidelines are even today a great source of further psychological researches.

2. *Gustav Theodor Fechner* (1801-1887)

Gusatv Fechner was born in a little village in Germany. His father died when he was only five years old. Despite his poverty, he went to Leipzig University in 1817 to study medicine. After he had qualified in

1822, his interest turned to physics and mathematics. He was much attracted to the new discovery of Ohm who had formulated his laws stating relationship between current, resistançe and electromotive force in an electice circuit. He lived by translating several French scientific handbooks into German. It was chiefly in physics that he made his reputation due to his varius demonstrations and researches relating to how quantitative measurements of direct currents were possible. In fact, during 1830s he enjoyed a period of sharpened intellectual activities. His major interest and various researches in physics were highly instrumental in finally being appointed as professor of physics at Leipzig University. There, he had a circle of able associates including E. H. Weber, A. W. Volkmann and even young Lotze who had come as a student in 1834. This golden period, however, tempted Fechner too much and a consequence of heavy mental works, he had a serious nervous breakdown. Besides this, he had also injured his eyes by looking at sun through shaded glass in a bid to study after-images. He remained surrounded by his illness until 1850 during which there was a complete withdrawal from academic activities. After this protracted illness, he became religious, turned to metaphysical philosophy and became interested in spiritualism. However, there was nothing very new in his philosophy.

What did Fechner do for psychology ? His basic goal was to measure 'subjective' sensation and for doing so, he started with the work of his Leipzig colleague E. H. Weber. Weber had experimented on weight discriminations, pitch discriminations and visual discriminations. From all these experimentations, he had formulated a basic law—that the ability to discriminate or perceive small difference in a stimulus depends not on the intensity of the stimulus alone but on a certain ratio between the difference and standard stimulus used. Fechner named this as Weber's law. According to Fechner, this Weber's law, however, did not provide a basis for a sensory scale. In fact, Fechner was interested in providing such sensory scale which could demonstrate a parallel between physical events (stimulus) and mental events (sensation). He wanted to measure by how many degrees one sensation was greater or lesser than other sensation. Fechner postulated that the intensity of sensation such as intensity of brightness, loudness, etc. increases not in a direct proportion to the increase in the intensity of the stimulus but more slowly. For making measurement of sensation precise, he aided by Volkmann who was Professor of physiology at Leipzig University, took a massive project of experimental research in 1850. After about ten years of massive researches, his famous book *The Elements of Psychophysics* was published in 1860. In this book he explained his view and work which proved very influential in the development of modern psychology. In a bid to measure differences between sensations, he outlined three experimental methods. These methods are called *psychophysical methods* which are still today being used as popular methods of studying sensations in laboratory. A description of these three methods are as under :

(i) ***Methods of limits*** : This method is also known as *method of smallest perceptible differences or method of just noticeable difference.* In this method Fechner increased the intensity of stimulus in measured steps until his subject reported a change in the intensity of his sensation. First, he started by presenting so weak a stimulus that the subject did not respond. Then, he gradually increased the intensity of stimulus until the subject reported a clear sensation being produced by that stimulus. Next, he started with adequate stimulus intensity and gradually decreased its intensity until the subject reported to sensation. Averaging the results of trials taken in this way produced absolute threshold or *Reiz limen* (RL). For calculating DL, he took two stimuli, one a standard stimulus and another a set of comparison stimuli and then varied the comparison until the subject reported of difference changed to 'no difference'. Conversely, it is also possible to begin with a situation in which the subject reports 'no difference' until a difference is noted after the comparison stimulus has been changed by a specific degree. Averaging the results thus obtained, we get *differential limen or DL.* In using this method to calculate DL, Fechner noted carefully the number of just noticeable difference in order to construct a sensory scale for measuring each sensation being produced by changes in the intensity of stimulus. Considering all just noticeable differences to be equal, Fechner constructed his sensory scale.

(ii) ***Method of constant stimuli*** : This method is also known as *method of right and wrong cases.* In this method Fechner presented stimuli or stimulus differences in some random order. Taking each stimulus difference as constant, he calculated the relative frequency with which a specific judgment was made for each stimulus. By plotting those judgments, he derived the value of RL and DL.

(iii) ***Method of average error*** : This method is also known as *method of adjustment* or *method of reproduction.* In this method Fechner presented his subjects a standard stimulus and also instructed them to manipulate the comparison stimulus till they perceived no difference between the comparison stimulus and the standard stimulus. Sometimes their adjustments or manipulations fell short and sometimes they were too large. After many trials, these errors were averaged and the degree of error became the estimate of threshold or limen.

Using these various methods in his extensive programme of experiments, Fechner formulated from the results a law that was applicable to all sense modalities such as sight, hearing, touch, etc. According to Fechner's this formulation, if the intensity of the physical magnitude of the stimulus increases in geometrical order 1, 2, 4, 8, 16, etc., the resulting increase in the sensation magnitude of just noticeable differences takes place in arithmetical order like 1,2, 3, 4, 5, etc. In this way Fechner announced that there was a logarithmic relationship between the intensity of stimulus and the resulting intensity of sensation. This formulation is today known as *Fechner's law* which certainly placed the study of sensation on a quantitative basis and developed experimental psychology. In fact, due to such important discovery and formulations, Fechner has been called as *Father of psychophysics.*

As said in the beginning, Fechner, later on, had become interested in philosophy, too. As such, he believed that everything has a soul or mind. He tried to provide a solution of the existing mind-body problem which has been much discussed by philosophers. Providing a solution to this mind-body problem, he said that the soul or mind and the body are related to each other in the same way as the inside and outside of a circle, which are the opposite sides of the same line. Such solution of mind-body problem was called *identity hypothesis* because the inside and outside connotate to the same identical circle. Fechner's law, as stated above, denoted clearly that sensation is proportionate to the logarithm of the magnitude to the physical stimulus. Fechner held that this law proved the solution of mind-body in terms of identity hypothesis. Mind was, accordingly, the logarithm of body ! Although this relationship was accepted by psychology, Fechner could not have much influence in philosophy and the identity hypothesis today in psychology is not regarded as a healthy solution to the mind-body problem.

In the history of psychology there was one great critic of Fechner, namely, William James who thought that the entire enterprise of Fechner was useless and without any "proper psychological outcome" (William James, 1890 : 534). He felt that Fechner's psychophysical methods were arid and futile.

Despite these criticisms by William James, one can't forget that it was Fechner who first introduced quantitative method in the study and measurement of sensation and was instrumental in developing a system of experimentation is psychology.

THE DEVELOPMENT OF NEUROPHYSIOLOGY

Not only the work done in the field of psychophysics by Weber and Fechner but also researches done in the field of neuropysiology specially those relating to how nerves and muscles work, the various theories about functioning of brain as well as the physiology of hearing and vision in the first half of the nineteenth century had a great impact upon emergence of modern experimental psychology. Hence, to ignore these researches would be a great unfair omission. Among the various researches relating to different neurphysiological developments in between 1800 and 1850, the following were the seven most important ones that have direct bearing upon the emergence of modern psychology :

(1) *Sensory and motor nerves : Bell and Megendie*

Sir Charles Bell (1774-1842) was one of the brilliant and most talented Scottish physiologists. He was also a good anatomist and surgeon. Although born in Edinburg, he achieved great prominence first in Great Britain and then in France also. He is well-known for his discovery of making distinction between sensory nerves and motor nerves although such distinction had already been announced by Galen but that was lost for centuries. Bell discovered that sensory nerves and motor nerves are anatomically and functionally discrete and distinct. Sensory nerves communicate signals from external and internal environment to spinal cord. Such fibers enter into spinal cord through posterior or dorsal root. Motor nerves carry signals from spinal cord to muscles initiating responses. Such nerves leave spinal cord through anterior or ventral root. The distinction between sensory nerves and motor nerves was named as *Bell's law* and was later called as the *Bell-Magendie Law* because Francois Magendie (1783-1855), a French physiologist, made the discovery independently by performing more convincing experiments. Having established the fundamental distinction between sensory nerves and motor nerves, Bell formulated what is called *law of forward direction* in the nervous system. This law stated that condition in nerve occurs in one direction only. This law proved very helpful in later studies of reflex action and reflex arc. Bell also studied in detail the trace of pathways of nerves in the entire body.

In 1811 Bell also formulated the doctrine of the specific energies of nerves that later received a precise and detailed formulation in the work of Johannes Muller. Bell pointed out that since nerves intervene between events in environment and our consciousness, they also influence the character of our experiences. Thus each nerve imposes its own specific energies or characteristics on what we experience. Specific nerves, Bell argued, are stimulated by appropriate stimuli and not to any other stimulus. From the doctrine of specific energies of nerves as formulated by Bell, the following two things emerged :

(i) The same stimulus may produce different sensations according to the nerves it stimulates. Thus a blow to head may stimulate nerves in eyes, ears and skin of head producing sensation of flash of light, ringing noise and pain respectively.

(ii) If the different stimuli impinge upon the same nerve, same sensation will occur in each stimulation. Thus the same visual sensation occurs if light impinges our eye or if eyeball is mildly pressed.

In nutshell, the doctrine of specific energies stated that every nerve produces its own characteristic quality of sensation and these qualities depend upon the structure and function of nerve rather than upon characteristics of stimulus. In 1826 Bell also added a *sixth* sense of muscle sense to already known five senses. He also demonstrated that sensation from muscles was necessary for better motor control. This was named as *nervous circle.*

(ii) *Specific nerve energies : Johannes Muller*

Johannes Muller (1801-1858) took his Ph. D. degree from the University of Bonn in 1822 and remain as professor until 1932. In 1933, he became professor of physiology at the University of Berlin. This was the post of great distinction and honor. He is best known for his book *Handbuch der physiologie der Menschen* (Handbook of the physiology of Man) that was the exhaustive work of more than three quarters. This was one of the standard books presenting the exhaustive summary of what was known on the subject at that time.

In *Handbuch* he set forth the most famous doctrine of specific energy of nerves which was considered as the most fundamental law in sense physiology. A look at the history reveals that the formulation of this doctrine had already been done by Bell and there was nothing new that Muller added to this doctrine. Hence, as some persons have reasoned, it should be called as Bell's doctrine rather than Muller's doctrine. A well-known historian like Boring (1950-81) has said :

"Careful study shows, however, that there is in this doctrine not one single principle that was new with Muller, everything of importance had already been started by Sir Charles Bell, and there is no doubt that Bell himself thought as clearly in these matters as did Muller."

Despite this, Muller's name has been more well associated with the doctrine of specific energies of nerve because of two major reasons. *First*, the publication of the formulation of the doctrine by Bell was done privately either in lectures or in privately printed papers "for the observations of his friends". Naturally such publications were not much credited by persons. *Second*, Muller insisted upon the doctrine more emphatically and gave it appropriate, explicit and precise formulation.

Muller's this doctrine very clearly stated that each sensory nerve yields a specific kind of sensation irrespective of how it might be stimulated. The sensation produced is not affectd by the characteristics of stimulus rather it is directly affected by the nerve connected to the sense organs and the brain center where the nerve is finally terminated. Muller has formulated this doctrine in terms of six separate laws which can be briefly mentioned after Boring (1950) as under :

(i) We are directly not aware of objects but of our nerves. In other words, the nerves serve as intermediaries between perceived objects and the mind, thus imposing their own characteristcs on what is experienced in perception.

(ii) There are five types of nerves, each imposing its own specific quality upon the mind.

(iii) The same stimulus influencing different types of nerves gives rise to the qualities specific to that set of nerves. Conversely, the different stimuli affecting the same nerve always produce the same quality unique to that nerve.

(iv) Since mind is located in the brain, there is an equivalence of internal and external stimuli. Thus there Muller tried to make the psychic or mind equivalent to the external event.

(v) The nerves have some definite relations to external objects. The external objects stimulate the nerve only when they possess some definite characteristics. If these definite characteristics are not possessed by the object, it does not affect the nerve at all or only exceptionally.

(vi) The mind has selective power over the specific energies of nerves. As a consequence, it has direct influence upon sensations. Hence, we can attend to some parts of the stimulus excluding attention to other parts. This is true in case of all five senses. Muller's this last law subsequently gave rise to host of researches in 'higher mental processes'.

Muller's doctrine has been criticised.Muller's doctrine of specific energy was wrong in the sense that sensory nerves do not have specific energies. Lotze pointed out that all sensory nerves are alike there is no qualitative specificity. It is well-known today that we have different sensations not because of any specificity of nerves but because of their terminations in central nervous system particularly in the brain. In fact, if anything really good came out from Muller's doctrine, it was that it provided a good scientific basis for later theories of hearing and vision.

(3) *Early studies of nerve impulses : Its electrical nature and velocity*

It was towards the end of eighteenth century that Luigi Galvani (1737-1798) began his experiments on the stimulation of frog's legs in a bid to show the nature of nerve impulse. He demonstrated that it is possible to produce a kick in forg's leg by attaching the cut end of the nerve to two rods of different metals. In 1791 he also discovered 'wet-cell batteries' out of frogs' leg. From several experiments on forgs, he finally concluded that animal tissue produce electricity. In 1800 Alessandro Volta (1745-1827) demonstrated that elctricity was due to the use of two different metals and frogs muscle simply acted as a detector of electrical potential. This controversy was finally resolved by Alexnder Humboldt (1769-1859). He demonstrated that there were two types of related phenomena—*intrinsic animal electricity* and *bimetallic electricity.*

Scientists including Johannes Muller had faith that the transmission of nerve impulse was unmeasurable because it was very rapid or instantaneous. Muller had also thought that velocity of nerve impulse was definitely equivalent to the speed of light. But in 1850 Hermann Helmholtz measured the velocity and found it to be much slower, that is, it was 50 meters per second in forg's motor nerve. In sensory nerve of the man he reported that the nerve impulse has a velocity between 50 and 100 meters per second. All these measurements provided a great impetus for later scientists in making important discoveries like *refractory phase* and *all-or-none principle.* A refractory phase of nerve indicates that a nerve remains in inexcitable state for a brief period of time immediately after an impulse has passed through it. During the rest period, recovery takes place. All-or-none principle states that after being excited, a nerve fiber or muscle stands completely discharged.

(4) *Phrenology : Franz Joseph Gall*

The doctrine of phernology was bornwith Franz Joseph Gall (1758-1828). A german by birth, he got high prominence in Paris. He was an anatomist whose major interest was in the study of localisation of various psychological functions in the brain. Broing (1950) has written that even as a schoolboy, Gall used to find a relationship between the psychological charateristics of his friend and his shape or bump of the head. As a schoolboy, he was convinced, for example, that those who had prominent and outstanding eyes had good memories.

In fact Gall was much impressed by the viewpoints of faculty psychology as earlier announced by the Scottish School and in that tune, he tried to locate the various faculties in the different specialised parts of the brain. More or less the same interest was carried out in adulthood. This interest gave rise to phernology. The doctrine of phrenology,as propounded by Gall, states that every psychological function or faculty is dependent upon specific region of the brain and if the particular function is well developed in person, the concerned region in the brain will expand and push out the brain and hence, a part of the skull. Such push caused a bump that could be easily measured at the surface of the head. This doctrine attracted the attention of several scientists of the day and they enquire further into the nature of brain localisations being studied in this way.

Gall's phrenology was later on modified and expanded by his pupil, Spurzheim (1776-1832). There were three fundamental propositions of this modified and expanded phrenology : They were as under :

(i) The exterior of the skull corresponds to the configurations in the interior part or brain.

(ii) Gall accepted the analysis of mind into several faculties as propounded by the scottish school, particularly by Thomas Reid and Dauglas Stewart. Accordingly, the phrenology of Gall and Spurzheim proposed that mind can be meaningfully and satisfactorily analysed into thirtyseven faculties or functions or powers.

(iii) These thirty-seven faculties or functions are disctinctly located in thirty-seven specific part of the brain. The superior functioning of any faculty or function thus can be easily correlated with the enlargement of the corresponding place in the brain.

Phrenology in its modified from had a termendous poularity. Any common man or woman could easily find out his or her special developed talents by measurements of the shape and bumps on the skull.

But later investigators working on the localisations of brain functions demonstrated that the propositions of phrenology were worng. Today and even during those days any person working according to the propositions of phrenology were considered as fraud and deceiver. Despite these, one of the biggest benefits of phrenology was that it encourged a lot of important and serious researches on functioning of brain in later nineteenth century.

(5) *Localization of functions in brain : Flourens and Broca*

The study of physiology of brain and its various functions received a strong impetus from the phrenology of Gall and Spurzheim. Although Flourens is the most popular figure who carried the research on physiology of brain, Luigi Rolando (1770-1831), prior to him, had made a comprehensive anatomical study of brain and also carried out elementary and crude experiments in 1809. On this basis, he concluded that cerebral hemispheres are the principal centre for 'higher mental processes'. Sensations, for him, was localized in *medulla oblongata.* To support all these vague generalizations, Orlando had provided pathological data and postmortem examples.

Fierre Flourens (1794-1867) was, however, a physiologist who was "precise in his technique, clear and trenchant in his writing, and essentially right in his conclusions". (Boring, 1950 : 63). He worked as professor of physiology at Paris and published a collected edition of his papers in 1842. His major interest was in knowing about the functions of the brain. He used mainly pigeons as subjects and his method of experimentation was that of extirpation in which a part of the brain was removed as a whole without any mutilation and subsequent behavioural changes were observed. His anatomical studies enabled to isolate some distinctive regions of brain for investigation such as the *cerebral hemisphere, cerebellum, coropora quadrigemina, medulla oblongata, spinal cord* and *nerves.* His findings revealed that removal of *cerebral lobes* resulted in abolition of thought and voluntray activities. Hence, thought and voluntary activities were located in cereburm. The removal of *cerebellum,* prevented efficient or controlled movements. When such pigeons attempted to walk or fly, they fell over. Therefore, he concluded that cerebellum was the seat for coordination and control of movement. The *medulla oblongata* was taken to be the centre of nervous system, ordering the sensations before they are accurately preceived. The *corpora quadrigemina* was related to seeing because after removal of it, the animal became blind despite the cereburm was intact. The *spinal cord* was responsible for conduction of nerve impulse and the functions of nerve were excitation of central processes and muscles.

Thus Flourencs, on the basis of his experimentations, came to the conclusion that the various parts of brain have specific properties, proper functions and distinct effects. Despite these diversities or localisation of functions, he said that the nervous system operates as a whole. There is overall integration. Such generalisation was made by Flourens on the basis of one of his observations that the functions of the removed organ of the brain were again recovered after some time, that is, the lost functions were soon taken over by other organs of brain. In fact, this particular generalisation proved very helpful to Franz and Lashley in the twentieth century in propounding their theories relating to the brain functions. With advancement of Flourens' researches, the popular 'phrenology' movement of the day gradually vanished.

On the whole, Flourens empirically established the brain as the seat of the mind and physiology as essential background for understanding psychology (or psychological functions). His researches also demonstrated that the experimental method rather than armchair speculation done by Hartley is the valid and scientific method of investigating problems in physiological psychology.

After Flourens, the physiology of brain made slow progress till Paul Broca (1824-1880) made important announcement regarding the speech area in 1861. Before this announcement and after Flouren's demonstrations, Stilling in 1842 provided a method of cutting a continuous series of sections of brain tissue that provided a fresh impetus to anatomical studies. Lister, in 1833, had already shown the existance of cell structure in blood and in animal tissues. By 1850s, it was well established that grey matter of human brain was cellular in structure and human brain consisted of millions of such cells.

In 1861 Paul Broca announced that the location of centre for speech was in the side of the left cerebral hemisphere. This area became later known as *Broca's area.* This discovery of Broca was based not on experimentation but on a clinical observation of a patient whose only trouble was that he was unable to talk although he communciated intelligently and successfully through signs. On examination Broca found that his vocal appratus was perfectly in good condtion. When the patient died five days after his examination, he conducted an autopsy which revealed a lesion in the third forntal convolution of the left cerebral hemisphere. Thus Broca's discovery favour an exact localisation of functions.

Broca's this outlook also got support from the studies of two German physiologists, Fritsch and Hitzig, who in 1870s announced that they had discovered the localization of motor areas in the brain. They conducted experiment on a dog whose cortex was electrically stimulated. They reported that when specific region of the cortex was stimulated with strong current, the dog went into generalized convulsions. On the other hand, when weak current was given, they could discover different centres for five different groups of muscles from neck to foreleg. Ferrier in London had also reported similar results by similar technique of electrical stimulation of dogs, cats and rats. Thus by 1870s, a clear picture of motor centres in brain emerged.

By the end of the nineteenth century, the sensory centres were also located. The visual sensation was found to locate in occipital lobe (rear) of the cortex; the auditory sensation was located in temporal lobe (side) of the cortex and the somesthetic sensation was located in the post-central region.

Thus the studies of brain revealed so many important physiological descriptions and analysis of psychological functions. These descriptions and analyses proved of monumental importance for emergence of psychology as on experimental science.

(6) *Reflex action and Reaction time*

The concept of reflex action, as it is known today, refers to the automatic and involuntary action or response towards a stimulus. In fact, people were aware of such response since 1650 when Descartain philosophy was at its peak of prominence. Howerver, the first important experimental study on reflex action was done by Robert Whytt in 1751. In first part of the nineteenth century Marshall Hall (1790-1857) conducted a very convincing experiment on reflex action. Johannes Muller also made significant contribution to the concept of reflex action. Hall conducted experiment in 1832 and published it in 1833. Johannes Muller published his own work on reflex action in *Handbuch* in 1834, acknowledging Hall's priority. Hall pointed out that reflex action depends only upon spinal cord and not at all on brain. Such actions are always unconscious. Muller held similar views except that such actions were also mediated by the brain. In fact, Hall's this conclusion regarding reflex action was based upon one experiment on a snake. In this experiment he severed the spinal cord of snake between the second and third vertebrae. He observed that the animal remained motionless with the exception of occasional gaspings and slight movements of the head, and continued indefinitely in such motionless condition. Howerver, the stimulation to the parts of the body produced vigorous movements in the snake. This clearly showed that actions or movements can be mediated by the spinal cord disconnected from brain. As a matter of fact, on the basis of such conclusion, Hall tried to make a clear-cut distinctioon among four kinds of bodily movements as under—

(i) ***Voluntary movements*** : Such moventnts depend upon consicousness and the action of the cerebrum.

(ii) ***Respiratory movements*** : Such movements depend upon *medulla oblongata* and are involuntary in nature.

(iii) ***Involuntary movements*** : These movements depend upon muscular irritability produced by direct stimulation.

(iv) ***Reflex movements*** : Such movements were dependent upon spinal cord and were independent of brain and consciousness. Hence, reflex actions were unconscious.

Hall's this viewpoint that reflex actions are governed by spinal cord only and are unconscious was attacked by Plfluger in 1853. He pointed out that it was very diffcult to make a distinction between the function of spinal cord and brain. In fact, reflex actions are governed by both these organs. Since brain also controls the reflex actions, they are conscious and not unconscious. Such responses or actions are also purposive and useful to the organism in making adaptation. To show this, Plfluger conducted experiment on a frog in which it was observed that forg's leg scratches exactly at that point where it was stimulated by acid. On the other hand, Lotze, one of the important philosopher-psychologists of the day, opposed Plfuger and supporting Hall said that brain is the primary organ of consciousness. Since reflex actions go only up to the spinal cord, they can't be regarded as conscious. Hence, they must be unconscious activities.

The primary interest on the 'response' side of the physiological psychology of this period was centred on the study of reaction times. The study of reaction time origniated in Astronomy and has a brief history. As every psychologist knows, in 1796, the astronomer Royal, Maskelyne, dismissed his assistant, Kinnebrook, because he found that the latter's observation of the star movements differed by a second from his own. Later, Bessel (1784-1846), a German astronomer under whose supervision a new observatory had been erected in 1813, demonstrated that the difference between any two observers might be due to innate personal differences in ability to make perceptual discrimination. He experimentally tested this by comparing the times taken by various trained observers in reacting to a star movement. He found that even with trained observers, there were big differences. These differences, for example, between observer A and observer B, were called *personal equations*. Later, various methods of dealing with or determining perrsonal equation were discovered. One such method was the use of chronograph developed in USA in 1850. In fact, chronograph was nothing but the forerunner of modern kymograph. The chronograph consisted of a revolving drum with a paper fitted to the curved surface. Two markers drew two parallel lines on the surface of the paper. An electromagnet connected to one marker produced a jerk at every second and therefore, it produced a regular wave-like line measured off in seconds. Another marker produced a jag in line whenerver the observer pressed a key after being certain that he has noticed a star crossing the line. One of the biggest advantages of this instrument was that it became now possible for astronomers to measure how much any one of the observers deviated himself from the truth—a fact known as *absolute personal equation*. Before the chronographic method, they had to keep themselves satisfied with the measurement of relative personal differences for pairs of observers. Such astronomical observations led to two types of experiment in new experimental psychology—the *complication experiment* and *the reaction experiment*. In complication experiment the individual reaction times were involved in a peculiar mixture of a series of auditory impressions and visual impressions. The experiments were called 'complication' because they involved processes from more than one sense organ. In reation experiment there was involved the measurement of absolute personal equation. The investigator who took over the reaction experiment from the astronomers in 1865 was a Dutch physiologist, F. C. Donders. He reported that as the stimuli were made complex, the reaction time increased. Not only this, as the way of responding was made complex so that the subjects had to make both discrimination and choice, the reaction time also increased. Since Donders, many important persons like Hermann Helmholtz and Wilhelm Wundt conducted a series of investigations in the late nineteenth century. Due to these investigations this period is also known as *mental chronometry*. Helmholtz very clearly demonstrated that nerve impulse takes time to travel.

From reaction experiments, two things were obvious. *First*, given a stimulus it takes time to register the same within the nervous system. *Second*, given an impulse, it takes time to form a response. Some questions also arose due to these delays (or lapse of time) which later on became important fields of study in physiological psychology. For example, what delays occur between sense organs and peripheral nerve, between brain reaction and muscle reaction ? What time the person takes in recognizing, deciding, choosing, judging or executing the response ?

(7) *Sense physiology : Hermann Von Helmholtz (1821–1894) and Edward Hering (1834-1918)*

Hermann Ludwig Ferdinand Von Helmholtz (popularly known as Hermann Von Helmholtz) was the son of school master. He was a very weak child and did not do better in school life. In 1838, at the age of 17, he could realise that he wanted to be physicist specializing in optics but as that time pure science offered little opportunity for career development, he chose medicine and on successful completion, he was appointed as surgeon in the Prussian Army in 1842 and remained there till 1849. He kept his academic interest alive while acing as surgeon. Due to this, he became soon attached to academic circle at Berlin University. Here he came in close contact with Magnus, professor of physics and with Johannes Muller, professor of physiology. Boring (1950 : 299) writes, "It was his natural bent for physics that took him to Magnus and his training in medicine that threw him into physiology with the great Muller." Due to his strong interest in physiological study of optics and acoustics, he worked as a physiologist and it was as a physiologist that he did researches which could be classified as experimental psychology. In fact, as physiologist his reputation grew very rapidly and he was appointed professor of physiology at Konigsherg in 1849. Magnus died in 1871 and he was called to Berlin as professor of physics. He remained here until his death in 1894. Recognizing his natural genius as physicist and physiologist, he has been considered as one of the greatest scientists of the nineteenth century.

Major contributions of Helmholtz which had a direct impact upon emergence of modern scientific psychology may be summarized under the following heads :

(i) *Reaction time : Speed of the nerve Impulse*

Helmholtz's work established his reputation in 1850 when he successfully measured the speed of nerve impulse. Prior to Helmholtz, it was believed that speed of the nerve impulse could not be measured due to its rapidity. It was also assumed that its speed was many times the speed of light. He has invented a myograph, a revolving drum for recording muscular contractions. He took a motor nerve of a frog's leg that was attached to a muscle and set the apparatus (myograph) at the designated speed in such a way that both the momemnt of stimulation and the twitch could be recorded. In this way he was successful in measuring the time elapsed between the stimulation and the twitch for nerves of different lengths. Subsequently, it became easier for him to calculate the speed of the nerve impulse because all relevant data like speed of myograph, the time interval between stimulation and movement and the length of the nerve were all available. Finally, he came to the conclusion that the speed of the nerve impulse was much slower than ever thought—it was only *ninety feet per second.* Later researches for measuring speed of the nerve impulse were conducted with the help of more sophisticated instrument and it was revealed that there occurs considereable variation in the speed of impulse and there are also a number of variables that affect the speed.

(i) *Reaction time : Speed of the nerve impulse*

Later Donders (1868), a Dutch physiologist, also realized the importance of Helmholtz's work in reaction time study. He realized that the method of presentation of stimulus and the nature of the task required from the subject was of paramount importance—a fact not given much weight by Helmholtz. Donders used three methods for studying reaction line—*a* method, *b* method and *c* method. In a method subject responded as quaickly as possible the moment the stimulus was presented. This is called *simple reaction time.* In *b* method subject was to respond in one way if the first stimulus was presented and to respond in another way if the second stimulus was présented. This is called *choice reaction time.* In *c* method the subject was again presented two stimuli with the instruction to respend if he saw one and not to respend if he saw the other. This is called *discrimination reaction time.* Donders observation was that time in *c* method was longer than that in a method. This happened because *c* method not only involves reaction but also discrimination between two stimuli.

(ii) *Theory of vision and Theory of audition*

Having measured the speed of the nerve impulse, Helmholtz advanced his theory of vision and theory of hearing. His greatest contribution to the experimental psychology of vision was publication of *Handbuch der physiologischen Optik* that appeared in three valumes or parts in 1856, 1860 and 1866. In 1867, it was published together as a whole. These three volumes were physical, physiological and psychological respectively in explanation of vision. In fact, in 1851 Helmholtz had invented an instrument called *opthalmoscope* through which he could directly look into the eye's of the subject. With the help of this instrument, he conducted several important investigations into physiology of vision. In 1851 he also undertook to develop a theory of colour vision which was originally propounded by Thomas Young (1773-1829). All beginners are well aquanited with this theory which is popularly known as *Young-Helmholtz theory of colour vision.* Helmholtz incorporated his discovery of speed of nerve impulse to support his theory of specific fibre energies which, in fact, was an outgrowth of Johannes Muller's doctrine of specific energies of nerves. Young had earlier proposed that there were three types of sustances in the eye, each of which was sensitive to a particular wavelength mainly, red, green and blue. Extending this simple theory of Young, Helmholtz said that there are three kinds of specific fibres within optic nerve which are responsive to wavelength of three pure colours—red, green and blue. Each fibre is maximally stimulated to a particular wavelength and to a lesser extent by wavelength of immediately next on the spectrum. Despite this, the nearby wavelength also stimulate the other two fibers and therefore, we see mixed colour. For example, we see yellow because of mixture of stimulation of red and green. When these three primary colours are properly balanced, we get white or grey. A proper mixture of these three colours may produce other colours. The theory also implied that there must be areas in brain which are specialized in producing the sensation of three primary colours or their mixtures.

In 1863 he published a similar but less extensive work on hearing in his book *Tonempfindungen*. He propounded a theory of hearing called *resonance or harp theory* of hearing. The theory implied that in inner ear there is a mechanism called basilar membrane. This is a very minute structure whose shape resembles to a harp or piano, that is, smaller at the top and wider at the bottom. Helmholtz proposed that this minute structure responds to all kinds of variations in pitch and loudness that a person is usually capable of making discriminations. The basilar memberane is attached to several nerve fibers which go to and terminate in the auditory area of brain. Helmholtz proposed that each fibre is capable of responding to a specific tone producing a certain pitch and loudness.

Another of Helmholtz's discoveries in the field of audition was the way in which we are able to know the timbre or quality of a tone. It is known to all that vibration rate, middle C on the violin was the same as that of middle C on the piano but there occurs differnce in quality not a commonly understood phenomen. Helmholtz tried to explain this difference by referring to the fact that different musical instrument produced the same fundametal frequency, that is about 256 cycles per second for middle C but in addition, they also produced different overtones, that is, higher multiples of the fundamentl frequency. By varying the intensity of the overtones he could synthetically produce the tonal qualities of various musical instrument.

Finally from his theory of audition he proceeded to formulate his *theory of discord or distonance and harmony or consonance.* Discard is caused by what is known as beating—a kind of throbbing or waxing and waning of sounds resulting from the simultaneous presentation of two tones of nearly the same vibration rate. Thus discard was due to the presence of beats which could be either between fundamentals or between the overtores of the two tones under consideration. Consobance or harmony results from absence of beating or discord.

Thus Helmholtz's contributions in the field of hearing and vision as outlined in his two books mentioned above, very vividly showed that how research techniques in physics and physiology might be applied in studying problems of visual and auditory perception.

(iii) *Empiricism*

While working as professor of physiology at Konigsberg, Helmholtz became a bit interested in Kant's philosophy which summarily stressed that ideas are inborn or innate. A person's judgements about various objects and their relations to each other are made in terms of innate inclinations. Obviously, such philosophical principles were opposed to British empiricists who believed in Locke's doctrine that mind at birth is *tabula rasa* upon which eveything is written with various kinds of experiences that a person gains in his life. Thus British empiricists had faith in the doctrine of genesis of the mind through individual experience. Rejecting Kant's philosophy, Helmholtz stood for psychological empiricism and accepted it as a basis for a scientific philosophy. As a consequence, the British empiricists' philosophy of mind was promptly incorporated into Helmholtz's theory of perception. Joining of Helmholtz in empiricists' camp also produced the famous controversy of geneticism and nativism in perception. Lotze, Helmholtz and Wundt represented geneticism whereas Muller, Hering and Stumpf represented nativism.

(iv) *Unconscious Inference*

Helmholtz propounded the doctrine of unconscious inference which was mainly derived due to his strong faith in empiricism. The doctrine very simply stated that when we perceive, our resulting perceptual experience contains something which is neither contributed by stimulus nor by the receptor. Our past experiences do contribute to this something in quite unconscious way. Hence, it is called the doctrine of unconscious inference. Boring's example (1950 : 308) of stereoscopic vision nicely illustrates this doctrine : a geometer with all date of retinal disparity and binocular parallax could easily estimate the depth of other distant objects in his visual perception. Yet, in actual perceptual experience, he makes the valid calculation of the disatance instantly by unconscious inference. From the explanation of this doctrine, it is obvious that we never have 'pure perception'. Objects known in perceptual experiences are never simply the effect of external stimuli nor the reactions of receptors but are aggregate of sensations which are themselves product of so many learning experiences. Helmholtz, in this way, fully incorporated the approach of empiricist philosophies. He outlined three major characteristics of unconscious inference as under :

(a) ***Unconscious inferences are irresistible*** : It means that when we perceive, the resulting perceptual experiences do come immediately. We can't readily modify or correct them by conscious processes. Hence, they are 'irresistible'. Since they are unconscious, they can't be resisted or corrected by any conscious reasoning.

(b) ***Unconscious inferences are developed by experience*** : Helmholtz proposed that unconscious inferences remain at first conscious and with the help of principles of association and repetition, they readily develop into unconscious inference. Since due to experiences gained out of association and repetitions in daily life these inferences can be corrected or developed, their degree of irresistibililty as explained in the first point is not perfect. For example, some varieties of optical illusion can be corrected or even abolished by having a certain attitude toward the stimulus situation.

(c) ***Like conscious inference, unconsicous inference is inductive*** : As in conscious inference after making certain analogy, we reach to a certain conclusion so also in unconscious inference by making similar analogy we immediately jump to a definite conclusion. For example, all men are mortal, Mohan is a man. Therefore, he is mortal. The unconscious induction is that all men are already known to be mortal and since Mohan which is a new perceptual experience, also turns out to be a man, our brain immediately and automatically infer that he must also be mortal.

(v) *Theory of Perception*

Helmholtz's theory of perception (or perzption) is very simple and strightforward. He was of new that sensory pattern was dependent upon the characteristics of the stimulus object. Such sensory pattern is called *perzeption*. The characteristics or properties of object imply their effect upon the sense, that is, the relations of objects to the sense organ. Thus for Helmholtz, object is aggreagate of sensations. However, he has continued that a pure perception rarely occurs. This is because perception is always attended by imagination, memory and unconscions inference.

In this way we find that Helmholtz, the physiologist turned physicist, laid down the foundations for all future physiological and psychological researches. Frequently, he drew attention of the scientists to the possibility of new development within experimental science, that is, towards the possibility of applying scientific methods to the problems in psychology. He could not be called as father of experimental psychology although he dealt with those problems and issues which were definitely forerunners of modern sense psysiology. His procederes definitely today serve as a model of modern experimental design.

Another person who did investigations in the field of sense physiology is **Ewald Hering** (1834-1918). He is mainly known for formulating an alternate theory of colour vision in opposition to that of trichromatic theory of Young-Helmholtz. His theory is popularly known as Hering theory of *opponent-colour theory* or *opponent-process theory*. He proposed that there were set of receptors like black-white, red-green and blue-yellow. He thus felt that four primary colours, namely, red, green, blue and yellow (instead of three as proposed by Helmhotz) were necessary for an adequate theory of colour vision. Each colour tended to produce a chemical change in the eye. Each receptor of the pair tended to function in two ways. One colour was produced when receptor was in anabolic or assimilative or building-up phase and the other appeared when the receptor was in a tearing-down phase or catabolic phase. For example, blue, when used at stimulus, would tend to produce an anabolic or assimilative function. Its opposite, yellow, would tend to produce a catabolic function. In the same way, red-green or black-white would upset the chemical equilibrium in opposite directions, depending on the type of colour used. If any two of these opposed functions take place simultaneosly, the person has the perception of grey colour. The major difficulty of the Young-Helmholtz theory that in a red-green colour blind person still sees yellow which is not a primary colour has been solved by Hering theory which takes into account yellow as one of the four primary colours.

The major sketch of the features of the neurophysiological developments under seven independent headings definitely show that the experimental psychology was in fact growing up spontaneously within the physiology. Many of the problems, techniques and methods of new modern psychology were, in fact, formulated and tested within the development of experimental physiology.

THE THEORY OF EVOLUTION

The evolutionary thinking of nineteenth century had much influenced the modern psychological theories. Although we generally associate evolutionary theory with Charles Darwin, the emergence of this theory has a long history before Darwin. For example, Lamarck, a famous botanist and zoologist, in 1744, had studied so many plants and animals and put forward a theory explaining why characteristics of these organism differed from one generation to another. But this theory failed to answer other pertinent evolutionary questions. Likewise, Spencer had also developed evolutionary doctrine prior to 1859 the year in which Darwin's most famous book *Origin of Species* containing his theory of evolution was published.

Despite these evolutionary developments, it remained for **Charles Darwin** (1809-1882) who put the evolutionary doctrine to the notice of all itellectuals and scientists by providing empirical evidence in support of it. His this theory was published in 1859 which is considered as very important data in the history of psychology. *The Origin of Species by Natural Selection* briefly known as *The Origin of Species* presented his theory of evolution in whose formulation Darwin had been influenced by reading two books : Lyell's *Principles of Geology* (1830) and Malthus's *Essay on the Principles of Population* (1798). During his trip to south seas (1831-1836), he had chance to observe a tremendous number of plants and animals. After returning to England, he was persistently troubled by one question : Why do certain plants and animals seem so perfectly adapted to their present environment ? After careful thought he came to the conclusion that in every generation some individuals or species survive and produce while others die before they can produce. In other words, there is a process of selection, that is, those best suited to the available environment survived and the remaining die out. From Malthus's *Essay*, Darwin was also convinced that the number of offspring in any one generation is always greater than the number able to subsist on the available resources for maintaining existence. Therefore, there must be some struggle for existence among individuals from which the strongers survive at the expenses of weakers.

All these led Darwin to formulate his theory which can be berifly outlined under the following three heads :

(i) ***Variation*** : Darwin postulated that members of single species vary among themselves. This variation occurs because some members are well-adapted to their environment. Thus environment influence variation occurring either in the whole organism or only in some part of it.

(ii) *Survival of the fittest* : Darwin also postulated that those best suited or adapted to the environment on the basis of struggle for the existence, survive. Thus only the fittest survive in an envirnment. In order to be fit, the organism, must properly nourish itself and make proper protection from enemies. A particular organism may survive in one environment but not in another. If the environment is changed, those will be considered fit that survive on the basis of struggle in the new environment.

(iii) *Natural selection* : Natural selection occurs due to variation that constantly occurs in a given species. As the environment is changed, those fitting the new environment will be naturally selected and gradually this natural selection would result in the evolution of a new species.

Darwin was, howerver, not satisfied by mere formulation of this evolutionary doctrine in support of which he persented mass data. In 1871 he published another book *Descent of Man* in which he emphasized the similarity between human characteristics and those of higher animals from which the popular belief emerged that human beings are descended from an ape-like ancester. Man's intellectual abilities differ from those of certain verterbrates like apes only in degree and not in kind. His theory provoked a big controversy and protest. In order to defend his viewpoints, he turned towards psychological studies of emotional behaviour of human beings and animal beings. He demonstrated that human beings resembled animal beings in facial and postural expressions during emotional activities. Based on all such researches, he published a book *The Expressions of Emotions in Man and Animals* in 1872.

Darwin's influence on psychology was great. Some of the major implications of Darwin's theory for psychology may be outlined as under :

(i) Darwin's viewpoints made the study of animal behaviour a very important part of psychology. This led to development of a separate branch of psychology named *comparative psychology* where animals were regarded as worth studying for their behavioural as well as their biological aspects. Thus with his initiative, animals behaviours were started being compared to human behaviour. This also led to some methodological revolutions. It was being realized that psychology might adopt some of the basic methods of biology in solving its own problem. As a consequence of this initiativeness and subsequent similar researches, many theories in psychology are self-consciously biological.

(ii) Darwin's approach to explain his data was both genetic as well as developmental. In other words, he prefers to explain any characteristic behaviour by demonstrating how it origniated in the organism and to trace how it developed under environmental influences. Thus Darwin believed that both influences, that is, genetic influence as well as environmental influences were important in determining behaviour. This led to the famous *nature-nature controversy* in mdern psychology. How much of genetic factors (nature) are responsible for a behaviour and how much of the enviornmental factors (nurture) are important for the given behaviour ?

(iii) Darwin had accepted a mind-body dualism and has applied his theory of evolution to both mind and body. He propounded that both animals and humans have mind and body. However, he also proposed that animals' mind is less active than human's mind and therefore, it engaged in thought processes no doubt but to a lesser degree than humans. This stand of Darwin gave a big jolt to current philosophical tradition that held that animals have no mind or soul like human beings.

(iv) The evolutionary theory of Darwin had more profound influence upon Fredudian psychoanalytic movement, and the functionalism including the psychology of William James, Freud was very much influenced by Darwinian theory in formulating his theory of instinct which very clearly stressed the animal nature of man. The death instinct in man is manifestation of such animal nature. The functionalists very much stressed the significance of the concept of psychological 'adaptation' or 'adjustment' that Darwin gave to psychology. These psychologists considered the whole concept of psychological adjustment as a necessary tool for explanation of good psychological survival and sound mental health.

In this way we find that Darwin's theory of evolution brought a sort of revolution in psychology. Due to his impact, the scope of psychology became wide and it justified for being called as psychological science.

Sir Francis Galton* (1822-1911) : *Psychologist of Genius

Sir Francis Galton, Darwin's causin, was a scientist of eminence who had profound impact upon the emergence of modern psychology. He started his academic life as a geographer and explorer. He was much interested in meteorology and this interest led him to construct first weather map of the British Isles. During his extensive tours, he observed that there existed a lot of differences between people both in terms of socio-cultural group as well as in terms of individuals within a group. This observation became a root for his interest in studying human nature.

In fact, Galton applied the evolutionary thinking of Darwin very strictly and specifically to psychology. In 1869 he published his book *Hereditary Genius* in which he summarized data on 997 eminent persons in a total of 300 British families. In this book he made it clear that eminence or individual's greatness tend to follow family lines with such certainty that it is simply absurd to look into any environmental influences. He had collected data from families of jurists, scientists, engineers, and authors. He became convinced that powerful mental functions were easily passed from one generation to another. Like Darwin, he also believed that in these families in past there must existed a great variations of mental abilities and the outstanding ones were able to survive and pass on to the next generation. Thus Galton finally concluded that the outstanding abilities or powerful mental functions are inherited. Galton's this conclusion, however, suffers from one major limitation. The crux of the study was the selection of sample. He selected individuals who belong to families of 'recognized eminence'. Individuals from working class or lower-middle class were not included. Obviously, the criterion of the selection of sample was biased and in such situation it was natural for Galton to get that type of result.

Galton was also much impressed by the concept of 'variation' of Darwin. He became a staunch supporter of the fact that a *constant variation* from one generation to another existed. As such, despite hereditary transmission there would be some *individual differences*—a concept which was highly emphasized by Galton and that later on generated a lot of researches which laid the foundations for the branch of psychology popularly known as *psychometrics*. This concept of individual differences emphasized that one individual differs from another individual in terms of physical traits as well as mental traits. Interest in this concept led him into the areas of psychological statistics and the measurement of mental abilities. In 1884 at the International Health Exhibition in London he established an 'Anthropometric Laboratory'. At this laboratory, for payment of small fee, a person could take several tests designed to assess basic human attributes. Apart from physical mesurement such a bodily mesurement or measurement of muscular strength, psychological variables like sensory capacities, reaction times, associative processes involved in imagery as well as formation of habits were investigated.

It was in course of these investigations that Galton made significant contributions to psychological statistics. These included the method of ranking, percentile ranking and the correlation. With the help of method of ranking, it was possible to rank individuals from highest to lowest according to their performance on some specific aspects of the psychological measurement; with the help of percentile ranking it was possible to group them in order of merit and with the help of correlation it was possible to compare one group of individuals with that of others to see degree of high or low relationship. He used the numeral 1 to indicate perfect correlation and + (plus), – (minus) and 0 (zero) to indicate positive, negative and no relationship respectively.

Galton's psychological researches were by no means limited to these psychometric measurement through statistics. In 1883, he published his book *Inquiries into Human Faculty and its Development*. In this book he has very nicely demonstrated use of questionnaire for assessing the use of mental imagery. His investigations revealed a considerable range of individual difference in the use of mental imagery. Some individuals had no experience of visual imagery whereas some individuals were vivid and clear visualizers having clear image of early perception and their details. In history of psychology Galton's this attempt to study mental imagery with the help of a questionnaire was the first attempt to use the questionnire as a means of collecting psychological data.

In devising the basic concept of correlation, he did useful researches that were valuable not only to psychology but also to cirminology. He reported that for nearly all physical mesurements of human body, correlations were highly positve. Since correlations were high and positve, after kniwing about only the part of the body, we can predict about basic bodily dimensions with greater accuracy. In this connection he discovered that 'fingerprints' could be regarded as a foolproof way of identification. His this view led others to adopt the fingerprinting as an important means of conducing investigations and researches in criminology.

Thus we see that Galton was really a genius showing diversity of interests both within psychology and in other fields like geography, anthropology, criminology, statistics as well as in biology. In fact, this deversity of interest prevented him from completing any major project. In view of this, Boring (1950) has rightly suggested that Galton was genius who never quite attained greatness. Despite this, the technique that he developed, proved very useful for later psychological researches. Among these techinques, the rating scales, the coefficients of correlation, questionnaires, were notable.

With the presentation of these historical instroduction including both the philosophical introductions as well as development of psychology within psychophysics, neurophysiology and evolutionary doctrine, we are now ready to study the beginnings of modern experimental psychology with the start of formal systems of psychology.

CHAPTER HIGHLIGHTS

1. During the first half of the nineteenth century some important developments took place within three fields, namely, psychophysics, neurophysiology and the evolutionary theories, which had a direct bearing upon the emergence of modern experimental psychology.
2. In the field of psychophysics W. H. Weber, a reputed physiologist, and G. T. Fechner, a reputed physicist, made notable contribution. In fact, psychophysics had started with Weber's experimentatioins but flourished with Fechner's efforts. Weber's experimentations on temperature sense, touch sense and muscle sense were highly commendable. Of these, his experimentations with muscle sense was the most important and for this, he could became highly popular in psychology. His experimentation on muscle sense led him to arrive at a conclusion that ability to dicriminate small differences in stimuli depended not only on the intensity of stimulus alone but on a ratio of difference to standard stimulus. This statement later came to be known as *Weber's law.* According to Fechner, however, this Weber's law did not provide a sensory scale for demonstrating a parallel between physical events (stimulus) and mental events (sensation). In fact, he wanted to measure by how many degrees one sensation was greater or lesser than other sensation. In a bid to measure differences between sensations, he propounded three methods, popularly known as *psychophysical methods.* Those were method of limits, method of constant stimuli and method of average error. Using these various methods, Fechner's basic formulation was that if the intensity of the physical magnitude of the stimulus increases in geometrical progression, the resulting increase in the sensation magnitude of just noticeable differences takes place in arithmetical progression. This formulation came to be known as Fechner's law.
3. Developments taking place within neurophysiology in between 1800 to 1850 were no less important ones. Seven such developments were

highly important for emergence of modern experimental psychology. Bell-Magendie law had established a clear-cut distinction between sensory nerves and motor nerves. Charles Bell had also anticipated the doctrine of specific energies of nerves that later received a precise and scientific formulation in the works of Johannes Muller. Expanding this doctrine in his *Handbuch,* Johannes Muller said that each sensory fibre yields a specific kind of sensation irrespective of how it might be stimulated. The sensation thus produced is not affected by the characteristics of stimulus rather it is directly affected by the nerve connected to the sense organ and brain centres where the nerve terminates. Muller had, however, thought that the transmission of nerve impulse was unmeasurable due to its high rapidity. But in 1850 Hermann Helmholtz demonstrated that the conduction of nerve impulse could be measured and that its velocity was for less than that of light. He reported that it was 90 feet per second.

4. The concept of phrenology was another important doctrine originally practised by Franz Gall and later on modified and expanded by Spurzheim. The doctrine recognized that there are thirty-seven faculties or functions of mind and the superior functioning of any faculty is manifested by the enlargement of the corresponding area in the brain. Although this doctrine later on could not survive on scientific footing, it gave rise to interest in the study of localization of function in the brain. Fierre Flourens conducted anatomical studies that enabled him to isolate some distinctive regions of brain for investigation such as the cerebral hemisphere, cerebellum, corpora quadrigemina, medulla oblongata, spinal cord and nerves. In each of these parts of brain a specific function was found to localize, Later on, in 1861, Paul Broca announced the discovery of location of centre for speech in the side of left cerebral hemisphere. This area was known as Broca's area. These studies of brain revealed so many important physiological descriptions and analysis of psychological functions which proved very beneficial in helping psychology in being experimental one.

5. Studies of reflex action and reaction time gave important revelations. Studies of reflex actions indicated that such movements were dependent upon the functioning of spinal cord and were independent of brain and consciousness. This viewpoint was based upon the findings of Marshall Hall. Reaction time experiments conducted by Bessel gave rise to *personal equations* and later *absolute*

personal equation. These experimentations confirmed that nerve impulse takes time in travelling and producing a response.

6. Lastly, Helmholtz's work done in the field of sense physiology was the greatest impetus for development of modern experimental psychology within physiology. His theory of colour vision, popularly known as Young-Helmholtz theory had very obviously established that there are three kinds of specific fibres within optic nerves which are responsive to wavelength of three pure colours—red, green and blue. Each fibre is maximally stimulated to a particular wavelength and to a lesser extent by wavelength of immediately next on the spectrum. A propoer mixture of these three pure colours produced different colours. Helmholtz's doctrine of unconscious inference was also important. The doctrine very simply stated that when we perceive, our resulting perceptual experience contains something that is neither contributed by stimulus nor by the receptor but by our past experiences in unconscious way.
7. The evolutionary doctrine of Charles Darwin was also an important movement which was instrumental in emergence of modern experimental psychology. Darwin's concept of variation, survival of the fittest and natural selction proved very attractive and invited the attention of several scientists. One of the most influential of such scientists was Darwin's cousin, Francis Galton. Directly impressed by the concept of variation and natural selection, he propounded the concept of individual difference—a concept which laid the foundation for a branch of psychology popularly known as *psychometrics*. Through the concept of individual difference, he emphasized that one individual differs from another individual both in terms of physical traits as well as mental traits. His establishment of Anthropometric laboratory at London in 1884 became a centre for studying the individual differences in basic human qualities like sensory capacities, reaction times, as well as associative processes. During these investigations, he made important contributions to psychological statistics that included the method of ranking, percentile ranking, and the correlation. All these techniques proved very useful in not only emergence of the experimental psychology but also in carrying researches into different fields even today.

REVIEW QUESTIONS

1. "Psychophysics had started with Weber's experimentsations but flourished with Fechner's efforts." Justify the statement in light of the experimental evidences.

2. Discuss the contributions of E. H. Weber in the fields of temperature sense, muscle sense and touch sense.
3. Discuss the major contributions of G. T. Fechner. How do those contributions become instrumental in establishing psychology as a science ?
4. Outline the major neurophysiological developments in between 1800-1850 that provided a base for establishing modern scientific psychology.
5. Did phrenology influence the functioning of later faculty psychologists ? Illustrate your answer with typical examples.
6. Discuss the contributions of Hermann Helmholtz in development of psychology.
7. In what ways Hermann Helmholtz's doctrine of unconscious inference became an important inspiration for Sigmund Freud ?
8. Discuss the contributions of Charles Darwin and Francis Galton in development of modern psychology.
9. "Francis Galton was a forerunner of testing movement in psychology." Justify the statement by relating his contributions to modern field of psychological testing.

■

CHAPTER 5

WILHELM MAXIMILIAN WUNDT : BEGINNING OF STRUCTURALISM

CHAPTER PREVIEW

This chapter focuses briefly on the life-sketch of Wilhelm Maximilian Wundt and those antecedent forces that led Wundt to formulate his psychology. Among the major antecedent forces were the philosophy of John Locke and John Stuart Mill. Mill's view regarding mental chemistry in explaining the association of ideas was a great impetus for Wundt in pointing out that the immediate experience can be analyzed into elements.

In examining Wundt's systematic psychology, Wundt's definition of psychology and its subject-matter have been examined. Wundt's defined psychology as the study of immediate experience or consciousness which could be analyzed into the psychical elements or atoms—sensations and feelings. Here focus has also been given upon introspection method and his viewpoints regarding mind-body problem. Wundt had pointed out that mind and body were parallel but not interacting systems.

As important works of first psychological laboratory established by Wilhelm Wundt at Leipzig University (now Karl Marx University) in 1879, his experimental findings regarding sensation, perception, reaction time, attention, feelings, word associations have been discussed. All these revealed his experimental greatness by attracting students from different corners of the world. Finally, evaluation of Wundt's experimental psychology has been done with the intent to reveal strength and weaknesses of his system.

In the last section focus has been given on the work of Wundt's major contemporaries like Franz Brentano, Carl Stumpf, and on the work of Wurzburg school which is famous for its contribution towards 'imageless thought'.

BRIEF LIFE-SKETCH OF WILHELM WUNDT (1832-192)

Wundt was born as the fourth child of his parents in Germany in 1832. His family never had much money. The financial condition further worsened when his father suffered a stroke and had to pay his assistant, out of his poor salary, for doing major work. His father's assistant, Friedrich Muller, tutored him at home but from this tutoring he could not profit much due to his habit of daydreaming. When Wundt joined high school, he failed in the first year due to his poor study habits and daydreaming. As a consequence, he had to change his school and his elder brother tried hard to prod him out of daydreaming and into study. Since the financial condition of the family was not strong, Wundt could not afford to go to the University for higher studies and so he chose medical school from where he topped the list of successful candidates in 1855. Such course created an interest in the study of science including anatomy and physiology. Soon after, Wundt started teaching courses (but without any salary) at the University of Heidelberg. Hardly after a few months, he developed tuberculosis and he had to take an extended vacation. It was during this vacation that he wrote his first book *Contributions to the Theory of Sensory Perception* that was published in 1862. In 1858 he began a 7-year career as the assistant of Hermann Helmholtz on the basis of a small salary. But as his assistant he was not pleased because of constant drilling of Helmholtz' students. After completion of 7 years, he resigned. His interest in physiology also began to go down and perhaps, this was the major turning point in his career because he began to think about those psychological problems that were earlier left by several philosophers.

In 1871 Wundt was appointed to a salaried post at the University of Heidelberg but the salary was poor. Therefore, he had to accept extra teaching assignments for receiving more money. With some improvement in his financial position, he married Stophie Man in 1872 at the age of 40 years and had three children.

In 1875 Wundt was appointed to chair in philosophy at the more prestigious University of Leipzig (now Karl Marx University) and held this position till his retirement in 1917. Here at this University, he founded the first psychological laboratory which became popular as *Psychological Institute*. In 1879 this laboratory was shifted to his own building that was later destroyed during World War II. He published his book *Principles of Physiological Psychology* during 1873–74 and in this book he strongly pleaded for establishment of psychology as an independent experimental science.

With establishment of psychological laboratory at the Leipzig, he became a very popular teacher. While lecturing for psychology, he frequently used demonstrations. This novelty attracted many students both from within Germany and from foreign countries. Leipzig, thus, rapidly became the centre for experimental researches in psychology. Kraepelin, Lehmann and Kulpe were his important German students who studied under Wundt. From U.S.A., James Mckeen Cattell, G. Stanley

Hall, Edward Scriptures and Charles Judd came to Leipzig and studied under him. All these psychologists later became founders of psychology in U.S.A. Edward Bradford Titchener and C. Spearman were Wundt's British Pupils. Of these, Titchener became one of Wundt's distinguished disciple who finally took Wundt's psychology to the Cornell University in U.S.A., to refine it, popularize it and named it as *Structuralism* (See chapter 6). During the period 1875-1919 Wundt produced 186 doctoral candidates. Some of these doctoral dissertations were purely philosophical. However, majority of them were experimental.

As Wundt's experimental researches increased, he naturally needed an appropriate plateform for publication of its results. As a consequence, he founded a journal *Philosophische Studien* in 1881. This journal published both experimental researches as well as theoretical papers in psychology. In 1896 his another book *Outline of Psychology* was published. In this book he undermined the earlier emphasis upon physiological and anatomical processes and made it a complete psychological treatise in strict sense by outlining his systems in detail. Much earlier, he had also shown some interest in social psychology. As a consequence, his book *Volkerpsychologie* (Folk Psychology) appeared in 1900. But it could not be as popular as his other books.

Wundt died in 1920, three years after his retirement. He had guided and supervised only 14 Ph.D. dissertations from U.S.A. (Tinker, 1980). Despite this, about half of American psychologists still trace their academic linkage to the psychology of Wilhelm Wundt at Leipzig (Weigel & Gottfurcht, 1972; Hillix & Broyles, 1980).

On the whole, Wundt's impact on psychology was tremendous. He initiated experimental researches in psychology and supervised the first generation of experimental psychologists. Hence, he has been popular as *father of experimental psychology*. One of his students, Weyer (1921), nicely commenting upon Wundt's work says, "... We psychologists in America, his followers, might say he contributed *us* and our psychological laboratories."

ANTECEDENT FORCES

Wilhelm Wundt is credited with starting experimental psychology as an independent science. In other words, he made psychology independent of other sciences like physiology, biology as well as from clutches of philosophy. He rediculed the philosophical armchair analysis of mental processes and the physiologists' attempt to study psychological phenomena by emphasizing upon anatomical analysis. What antecedent forces led Wundt to constitute experimental psychological researches ?

Wilhelm Wundt was a philosopher turned psychologist. As a philosopher, he was much impressed by John Locke's view that all knowledge came from experience. Wundt, accepting this, defined psychology as the study of immediate experience. John Stuart Mill had already propounded the concept of mental chemistry. Deriving inspiration from it, Wundt analyzed the immediate experience of conscious experience into its two primary elements—sensations and feelings. Alexander Bain and Herbert Spencer had also talked about association of ideas and they had also propounded some basic principles of associations. Similarly, Wundt also talked about synthesis of elements of consciousness and used association as the basic principles of connecting elements of consciousness. Apart from this, he also studied associations in the experimental laboratory. Johann Herbart's doctrine of apperception was also important one which encouraged him to pay more attention to this phenomenon both experimentally and systematically.

Wundt was not only a philosopher but also a physiologist who had received a degree in a medicine. For some time he was also assistant to Hermann Helmholtz, a greatest physiologist of the times. All these created sharp interest in physiological explanation of psychological phenomena. His book *Principles of Physiological Psychology* was directly the product of his interest in physiology and anatomy. Wundt was also much influenced by Fechner's psychophysical methods and held that these methods were very fruitful in studying element of conscious experience such as sensation.

Thus we see that Wundt in formulating his systematic approach to this new science of psychology was influenced by several antecedent forces. Today his primary importance is due to the fact that he separated psychology from philosophy and took it into laboratory where experiments could be easily performed.

Wundt's work could be discussed by dividing them into two categories, namely, *Wundt's systematic psychology* and the *experimental work of Leipzig laboratory*.

WUNDT'S SYSTEMATIC PSYCHOLOGY

Wundt proposed his 'systematic psychology' in his famous book *Outline of Psychology*. In this book he spelled out the fundamentals of his systematic psychology that may be presented under the following five categories :

1. ***Definition and subject-matter of psychology***

For Wundt, psychology is broadly the science of experience. He divided experience into two parts—the immediate experience and the mediate experience. By mediate experience Wundt refers to the experience that is used as a way to locate about something other than experience itself. By immediate experience Wundt meant the experience as such. For example, suppose we describe directly the experience of toothache, it is our immediate experience. But when we use this experience in locating cavity (that produced toothache experience) to be checked up by a dentist, this constitutes our mediate experience. Wundt defined psychology as the study of immediate experience or conscious experience and *not* of mediate experience.

Wundt emphasized upon the atomistic nature of consciousness or conscious experience. Accordingly, he pointed out that the conscious experience could be analyzed in terms of two psychical elements or atoms—*sensations* and *feelings*. The sensations were regarded as the objective contents of consciousness and the feelings were regarded as the subjective contents of consciousness. The sensory elements (or the element of sensation) chiefly come through functioning of sense organs like hearing, seeing, touching, smelling, tasting and so on. When sensations are blended together, it gives rise to *images*. Thus images were not regarded as an independent component of consciousness by Wundt. The feeling component, however, does not come from any sense organ. They had three dimensions—excitement-clam, tension-relaxation and pleasure-displeasure. Wundt pointed out that every conscious feeling could be located in three-dimensional space. This is popularly known as *tridimensional theory of feeling*.

Sensations and feelings, the two primary elements of conscious experience, have two basic attributes—quality and intensity. The sensation elements are easily recognized in terms of their quality and intensity. The feeling elements are also very easily recognized in terms of intensity as when we say that we have no feeling or extreme feeling of pleasure or extreme feeling of displeasure. However, in terms of quality the feeling elements are harder to recognize and distinguish.

The elements of sensations and feelings are combined to yield what is called *psychical compound*. One characteristic of this compound is that it consists of a group of simple sensations or feelings or a combination of both. Ideas and emotions are good examples of psychical compound. The compound idea of a flower may consist of various sensations such as sensation of the particular colour of the flavour, its softness, its smell as well as a feeling of pleasantness. Emotions are the compounds of different types of feelings. Will is some sort of feeling that leads to overt action. Volition, hardly distinguishable from feeling, represents tendency of the organism to behave in purposive manner. Wundt maintained that psychology studies the processes of sensation, feeling and violation, the unity of which constitute consciousness.

2. ***Principles of connection***

How do the elements of conscious experience combine ? What principles do govern their combination ? Wundt paid special attention to these basic questions and pointed out that elements of consciousness were combined by means of *association*. The fusion of elements into consciousness may be simultaneous or it may be successive. In other words, elements may fuse into complexes so that one simultaneously arouses the other or it may fuse together in such a way that whenever one idea appears, another idea immediately follows. Association also involves *assimilation and complication*. Assimilation refers to association of elements by similarity or by contrast. Several optical illusions do occur due to such assimilation. A short person standing between two tall persons looks still more shorter due to assimilation of visual sensations by contrast. The process of complication, partly derived from the complication experiment of Herbart, refers to association of the sensations from two sense modalities such as eye and ear.

In explaining the combination of elements by association, Wundt formulated the *principle of creative synthesis*. In fact, the root of this principles lies in John Stuart Mill's doctrine of mental chemistry. Based on the analogy of a chemical compound, the principle of creative synthesis explained that the elements of consciousness might form such a complex or compound, whose characteristics were different form the characteristics of the component elements. This principle was later on taken over by the Gestalt psychologists who pointed out that the perception of whole is not the sum of the perception of its part. Wundt has also talked about the *law of psychic relations* which was concerned with the problem of meaning of a particular event. But Wundt never developed this law in scientific way and it remained for his pupil, Titchener, to expand the significance of meaning in his *context theory*.

3. ***Method of Psychology***

Wundt pointed out that the methods of studying conscious or immediate experience were experimentation and *introspection* or in a rough German translation, *Selbstbeobachtung* (self-observation). Introspection was the method through which a person could analyze the conscious process for finding out how its elements were synthesized.

However, Wundt sounded a strong caution that his version of introspection was not a mere self-observation. By introspection he meant controlled observation of the elements of consciousness which were made under experimental conditions (Marx and Hillix, 1987). Therefore, nonexperimental introspection was excluded from Wundt's purview. Wundt suggested that his method of introspection was such that for it, there must be a trained introspectionist. He must follow certain rules for making good introspection. Some of these rules were as under :

(i) The introspectionist should be able to locate from where the process starts.

(ii) He must be capable of maintaining "strained attention".

(iii) The entire observation must be capable of being repeated.

(iv) The conditions must allow for introduction or elimination of some stimuli. In other words, possibility for variations in the strength or quality of the stimulus must be there.

From these rules it was obvious that for Wundt, introspection was not mere self-observation. It had to be followed by experimentation because the experimenter produced variations in the conditions of the stimulus and the resulting changes in the experiences are observed by the introspectionist. Thus for Wundt, *introspection* and *experimentation* were not separable. That is why, it is said that his introspection was experimental introspection.

4. *Apperception*

The doctrine of apperception formulated by Wundt has been derived from Herbart's concept of apperception and *apperceptive mass* (see discussion on Herbart's psychology done in chapter 3). Boring (1950) has made it clear that for Wundt, the term apperception has *three* aspects—apperception as phenomenon, apperception as cognition and apperception as activity. As phenomenon, apperception refers to the focus of consciousness. It, therefore, amounts to a focusing of particular element into consciousness. This is today known as *attention*. Thus through apperception certain elements are focused and made dominant in the consciousness. The entire organisation that follows a apperceptive reaction may be outlined in this scheme : Stimulation—Perception (Presentation of sensation in consciousness)—Apperception (focusing of the sensation in consciousness)—Will (feeling to produce a certain drive for action). As a cognitioin, apperception is the unifying factor in mental processes or consciousness. The processes of sensations, feeling and volition are united into consciousness through apperception.

Apperception is the synthesis of elements into the totality of consciousness. Apperception may also be analytical. Judgement is a kind of analytic apperception because it isolates the content. As an activity, apperception is an active process. Apperception is always accompanied by a feeling of activity. So, it is an active current in the stream of consciousness.

5. *Mind-Body problems*

Wundt pointed out that mind and body were parallel but not interacting systems. This was known as *psychophysical parallelism*. Thus mind and body existed side-by-side without making any interaction between them. Therefore, for Wundt mind did not depend upon body. It could be studied directly. This stand of Wundt have led Van Hoorn and Verhave (1980) to classify him as a parallelist whereas Boring (1950) has classified him as dualist. Blumenthal (1980) and Richards (1980) have termed Wundt as an *identity theorist*, accepting mind and body as *two* aspects of the same reality. Whatever may be the brand, it is obvious that for Wundt, mind could be studied directly without showing any dependence upon body. Perhaps, that was the reason, he made distinction between mediate experience and immediate experience, the former being physical and the latter being mental.

On the whole, Wundt's system was an attempt to spell out the subject-matter and method of psychology, basic principles as well as his stand regarding mind and body issue. In fact, the methods used by Wundt were not original in the sense that they had been borrowed from experimental physiology of Helmholtz and the psychophysics of Weber and Fechner.

WORK OF LEIPZIG LABORATORY

Although the experimental works of Leipzig laboratory done by Wundt and his students was simply developing and systematizing the empirical work already done by Helmholtz, Weber and Fechner, it was significant in demonstrating that the experimental psychology could study something in laboratory and it could produce a certain result. All laboratory works done at Leipzig was published in the *Philosophische Studien*—a journal founded by Wundt in 1881. In between 1881 and 1903 this journal published 100 research articles from Leipzig laboratory.

Wundt's experimental work done in Leipzig laboratory could be summarized in the following five headings :

1. *Sensation and Perception experiments*

Wundt and his students investigated visual perception more than other sensory modes. In the field of visual perception, experiments on colour discrimination, colour mixing, colour blindness, visual contrast, after-images, perception of form, binocular vision and optical illusions were highly popular. In auditory perception the experiments on beats, tonal fusion and analysis of intervals were common. In the field of touch perception, the perceptual problems of tactual localization and the two-point threshold (first studied by Weber) were common. Some studies on perception of time were also reported. Among these, experiments on estimation of various time intervals were common. Thus sensation and perception were the major topics of experimental researches done at Leipzig laboratory. According to Tinker (1980), about 70 per cent of 186 doctoral dissertations produced by Wundt's laboratory had sensation and perception as their focal theme.

2. ***Reaction time experiments.***

Reaction time experimentations were partly derived from Helmholtz and Donder's studies and partly from personal equation problems in the astronomical observations. Wundt had regarded reaction time experimentations to be the most important ones because he hoped to discover through these experimental designs the three postulated stages between stimulus and response (perception-apperception-will). Thus with the experimental studies of reaction time, it was hoped to develop a way of studying various stages that existed in complex perceptual situation. Experiments on three types of reaction time were conducted. In simple reaction time experiment a subject reacted by pressing a key as quickly as possible to one stimulus. In discrimination reaction time experiment a subject reacted to one stimulus (towards a green light) by pressing a key but not to a second stimulus (towards red light). In choice reaction time experiment a subject reacted with the right hand to one stimulus (green light) but with left hand to another stimulus (red light). Wundt demonstrated that in the complex perceptual situation like complex reaction time, the person first perceived the stimulus (first stage), then he apperceived it (that is, made distinction as red or green : second stage) and finally, he responded according to the instruction (third stage). But later experiments revealed that these three stages proved hard to be discriminated by even trained subjects. Later reaction time experiments compared the time taken by subjects in responding when they were instructed to pay attention to stimulus (sensorial reaction time) and when they were instructed to pay attention to finger movements (muscular reaction time). It was found that the reaction times were shorter in the latter case than in the former case. Wundt hypothesized that this was due to the process of apperception. He also proceeded to measure the time taken for apperception to occur. But his this programme received a strong set back by Kulpe, one of his students, who demonstrated in 1891 that when conditions of reaction were made complex, the whole task was changed from beginning to end. It was not the case that one process is changed, while other processes remain the same. Despite this, reaction time experiments were highly useful in showing individual differences in the ability to reproduce various time intervals on request or in estimating an interval of time when the beginning and the end were indexed by the different stimuli.

3. *Association experiments*

Wundt was heavily impressed by the concept of association and he conducted a series of experiments on word association. In these experiments he presented a stimulus word to the subject with the instruction to reply with the first word that comes to his mind. He also measured the time required in responding with this first word. On the basis of these experiments, he came to the conclusion that there were two types of association—inner association and outer association. Inner association referred to intrinsic connection between words. For example, table-chair, student-teacher, man-woman, etc. are illustrations of intrinsic connection. Outer associations are associations which are accidental in nature and such associations are established through habits. For example, king-palace, guest-house and so on constitutes outer associations.

4. *Attention experiments*

For Wundt, attention was vivid perception of a narrow region of consciousness. This narrow region was separate from the rest of consciousness. Wundt studied range of attention and fluctuation of attention. For Wundt, attention was bidimensional because it embraces not only simultaneous but also successive events. James McKeen Cattell, student of Wundt, conducted one classic study on span or range of attention by demonstrating that how many units (words, letters, dots) could be attended in short exposure of time. Marbe, another Wundt's pupil, demonstrated fluctuation of weak stimuli which was obviously interpreted by Wundt that attention fluctuated.

5. *Feeling experiments*

The experimental studies of feeling at Leipzig culminated into the formulation of tridimensional theory of feeling by Wundt. At the Leipzig laboratory, the feeling was studied by the method of paired comparison. In this method the subjects were required to compare every stimulus with every other one in the given series. For example, if one was required to compare the sweetness of a variety of tones, one would compare tone A with tone B, C, D, E, and so on to the every tone given in the set. Each time the subject would be presented with two tones and would be required to state which of these two given tones was more pleasing to him. In this way, an order of sweetness would be eventually established.

Thus we find that at Leipzig laboratory a variety of experimental works was undertaken by Wundt and his students. If we pay close attention to these experimental works, they were in many ways unadventurous and over-indebted to the methods and viewpoints already established by Helmholtz, Weber and Fechner. Despite this, his thoroughness and fresh initiativeness in concentrating experimentally on some selected fields, gave valuable impetus to the new experimental psychology. Nobody can underestimate Wundt's achievement in making the Leipzig laboratory work instrumental in establishing the status of psychology as experimental science.

EVALUATION OF WUNDT'S CONTRIBUTION

Wundt's overall contribution to the psychology was that he made psychology independent of philosophy and established it as an independent experimental science—one that even remains today. In this sense, he should more properly be called as grandfather rather than father of experimental psychology. Despite this greatness, he has been criticised. His major criticisms may be outlined as under :

(i) Critics state that Wundt treated psychology in somewhat narrow sense by concentrating upon some selected topics for experimental researches and by giving emphasis upon analytical character of conscious experience. Although this criticism may be regarded as true one, in fact, there has been shown greater narrowness in modern psychologists' attempt to understand the Wundt's psychology. Since he was German and belonged to the first of the first line of experiment psychologists, he has been regarded as old fashioned by modern psychologists who seldom appreciate him to the extent he deserves. Anderson (1971) has presented an empirical evidence to such lack of appreciation given to Wundt. He gave a list of Wundt's statements to a group of graduate students of psychology. The students were required to match these statements with the names of a group of outstanding psychologists including Wundt in the history of psychology. Results revealed that none of the Wundt's statements was attributed to him by most students. Perhaps, they thought that these statements were too experimental or too modern or too statistical to belong to 'old-fashioned' Wundt.

(ii) The critics of Wundtian psychology have said that Wundt regarded the contents or elements of conscious experience as something stationary and structural in nature. They were thought to exist as physical objects exist. Perhaps, due to this reason, the name *existentialism* was attached to Wundtian psychology. Critics were of view that elements such as sensations and feelings did not exist in reality like a physical object. Wundt provided no obvious evidence in support of his claim.

Despite these criticisms, Wundt's greatness in establishing psychology as an experimental science was unparallel. Although today the experimental psychologists use different methods, have different theories and they don't indulge in the introspection of Wundtian type, the basic spirit has remained unchanged. Psychology now no longer belongs to philosophy and it exists as an independent experimental science. Had there been more than one Wundt in the history of psychology, we would have been blessed with something more for psychology as an experimental science. Murphy (1949 : 159) has very nicely compared the status of psychology before and after Wundt as such:

"Before Wundt... established his laboratory, psychology was little more than a waif knocking now at the door of physiology, now at the door of ethics, now at the door of epistemology. In 1879, it set itself up as an experimental science with a local habitation and a name."

WUNDT'S CONTEMPORARIES

Wilhelm Wundt was undoubtedly one of the greatest psychologists of the late nineteenth century. In his time, Wundt was hard to be criticised. In fact, he was such a writer that by the time a critic might raise his objection, he would change his position meeting the anticipated objection of the critics (Schultz, 1969). Despite this, there were psychologists who expressed different viewpoints from Wundt and had important influences upon modern psychology. At any cost, they should not be ignored. They were Franz Brentano and Carl Stumpf who opposed and criticised Wundt vigorously and Oswald Kulpe who did not oppose Wundt to that extent but tried to improve and expand upon Wundt's ideas. G.E. Muller was also important psychologist of that time who different with Wundt.

Franz Brentano (1838–1917) : Act Psychology

Brentano was trained for priesthood since the age of 16 years. At

Berlin, he was taught philosophy by Trendelenburg who made him aware about the philosophy of Aristotle. Aristotle remained a major force throughout his life and he was a great Aristotelian. He resigned priesthood because he did not like to accept the doctrine of the infallibility of the Pope. He took his Ph. D. degree in philosophy and taught this subject on salaried appointment first at Wurzburg and later at Vienna. About a year, Carl Stumpf, was Brentano's pupil at Wurzburg. In 1874, Brentano published one of his most famous book *Psychologie vom empiricshen Standpunkt (psychology from an empirical Standpoint)*. In the same year Wundt had published his famous book *Principles of Physiological Psychology*.

Brentano was recognized as a great competitor to Wundt. Some historians have also regarded him as Wundt's most important critic (Lundin, 1985). Brentano lodged a protest to Wundt's psychology of content, which gave birth to analytical character of consciousness. Wundt had vehemently pointed out that consciousness, the subject-matter of psychology, could be better understood in terms of analyzing it into its contents like sensations and feelings. Brentano, instead, set forth *act psychology*, according to which psychology studied *mental acts* or *processes* rather than mental contents. The psychologist should study mental acts or processes of mind and not its contents. For Brentano, act always *refer* to objects. For example, in seeing a colour, seeing is an act or process which always refer to something seen. Likewise, hearing is a mental act which always refers to something heard. For Brentano, seeing and hearing are acts and colours and sounds are contents. Psychology studies these mental acts and not these contents. However, for Wundt, psychology studies these contents only. Thus a sharp distinction between Brentano and Wundt developed, that is, a sharp distinction between acts and content developed.

Brentano divided mental acts into three types—*ideating, judging,* and *feeling*. Ideting refers to having an idea whether real or imagined, present or past, it does not matter. Sensing and imagining are examples of ideating act. Judging refers to determining affirmation or denial of objects. Acknowledging, rejecting, perceiving and so on are the examples of judging. Feeling refers to having certain attitude towards the object. Loving and hating are examples.

Brentano is popular for having his influence upon structural psychology (Wundt and Titchener), phenomenology, Gestalt, psychology and psychoanalysis. Of these influences, his influence upon structural psychology is the most important. In fact, his influence upon Wundt is more by opposition than by any positive contribution. He sharply differed from Wundt on several points. Some of these points may be summarized as under :

(i) Brentano was an empiricist whereas Wundt was an experimentalist. Brentano's psychology was based upon observation and not upon experimentation. He established no laboratory and never manipulated any variable.

(ii) Brentano built his psychology around mental act whereas Wundt built his psychology around sensory contents.

(iii) Brentano's approach to psychological problems was argumentative whereas Wundt's approach to psychological problems were descriptive and explanatory.

(iv) Brentano was not a professional psychologists. Boring (1950) has called him as *courageous idealist* who believed in untrammelled research. Wundt was a professional psychologist.

(v) Lastly, Brentano was only an individual whereas Wundt could be regarded as an institution in which experimental psychology was established and flourished.

Carl Stumpf (1848–1936)

Stumpf was Brentano's student at Wurzburg for a year (1866–1867). He was, therefore, very much influenced by Brentano and could be considered as one supporter of act psychology. By native endowment, he was interested in music. But at that time, since no university gave formal degree in music, he turned to philosophy and took his doctorate degree from Gottingen University in 1868. He wrote many books on the psychology of tone and music. Lotze, at Gottingen, gave a fatherly treatment to Stumpf and taught him thoroughly the theory of knowledge. He also encouraged his interest in taking courses in physics and physiology. Stumpf also succeeded Brentano as professor in 1873 at Wurzburg University and after six years he started his academic trip to Prague, Halle, Munich and finally Berlin (1894). In 1894 he was made professor in German psychology at the University of Berlin where he established a laboratory. This post was considered a prize post at that time and it might have gone to Wilhelm Wundt but as historians pointed out, Wundt could not get this appointment due to opposition of Hermann Helmholtz (Boring, 1950).

Stumpf became interested in the study of experimental psychology via his philosophical pursuits. He was important basically for the following two reasons :

(i) Stumpf was a great musician and his strong interest in music led him to the study of psychological problems of tone. His researches were published in his famous book *Tonpsychologie (Tone Psychology)* in two volumes in 1883 and 1890. At that time, it was considered as the most celebrated research on sense of hearing since Helmholtz. He studied tonal fusion both acoustically and from the point view of musical theory. He also formulates several laws for explaining tonal fusion. For example, his one law stated that degree of fusion was not affected by timbre, that is, by the qualities of the instrument producing the tones. Another important law was that degree of tonal fusion was the function of the vibration ratio of the different components. Apart from all these, he also studied attributes of tones such as pitch, loudness, volume and brightness.

(ii) Another reason of his importance was that like Brentano, he opposed Wundt's analysis of consciousness into sensations and feelings. Thus he became a supporter of Brentano's act psychology. He pointed out that the mental acts are the fundamental subject-matter of psychology. The activity of mind in judging, imagining, sensing, hating, etc. are true activities for psychological studies. Therefore, like Brentano, Stumpf pointed out that psychology studies 'functions' or 'acts' such as perceiving, desiring, willing and also 'relations' among objects and events. No doubt we experience sensations, Stumpf argued, but the basis is the activity that produces such experience. For example, we cannot hear without *hearing* something.

Stumpf's laboratory at Berlin had also attracted several persons who later became very important and influential psychologists. Kohler, Koffka and Wertheimer were Stumpf's students at Berlin University. However, neither Kohler nor Koffka felt much loyalty to Stumpf and the real inspiration came to them at Frankfurt in 1910 from Wertheimer's experiment on apparent movement. Later, Kohler succeeded Stumpf in 1921 at Berlin University. Wertheimer was also made professor in 1922. These persons founded new school of psychology called Gestalt psychology. Thus the idea of foundations of Gestalt psychology was born at Frankfurt but subsequently was fully established at Berlin after retirement of Stumpf.

Georg Elias Muller **(1850–1934)**

Muller was born the same year (1850) as another famous German psychologist, Ebbinghaus was born. He was born in Saxony, nearer to Leipzig. He studied philosophy and history at Leipzig. In 1869 he went to Berlin to study history but that was interrupted by service in army during Franco-Prussian war. In fact, Muller did not like this service and become interested in the study of philosophy. He, therefore, returned to Leipzig in 1871 and in 1872 he went to Gottingen to meet Lotze who became his close personal friend. Muller completed the training in philosophy and received his doctorate degree. After receiving this degree, he became a tutor. Then he suffered a severe illness which forced him to come back to his parent's home. During this period, he studied psychophysics in detail and had also made several correspondence with Fechner. As a consequence, psychophysical methodology was extended and revised by him. Muller's work made many innovations in psychophysical methodology. Apart from his short period as professor of philosophy at Gzernowitz (1880–81), he remained at Gottingen where he succeeded Lotze as Professor of philosophy (Lotze had been persuaded to go to Berlin in 1881 where he died after a few months). At Gottingen, Muller retired after completing forty years of continuous service. During this forty years, he made Gottingen such a centre for experimental psychology that rivalled against Wundt's Leipzig laboratory. For these forty years, he had considerable impact upon German Psychology and was reported by an American visitor in 1892 as having one of the *finest research laboratories* in Germany. In this laboratory he had trained many experimental psychologists who later become very influential and powerful. F. Schumann, Oswald Kulpe, Alfons Pilzcker, David Katz and Edgar Rubin were some of the most distinguishable assistants to Muller.

Muller was purely an experimental psychologists. His chief areas of interest were : psychophysics which he inherited from Fechner and visual perception that he inherited from Hering and memory from Ebbinghaus. In 1896–97, he published influential articles on colour vision in which he tried to remove the deficiencies of Hering's theory. He pointed out that the three basic dimensions of colour vision (black-white, yellow-blue and red-green), in fact, depended upon reversible photochemical substances. He argued that in Hering's theory when red-green, blue-yellow and black-white excitations are all in equilibrium, a person should see a 'visual silence' but actually he sees a grey colour. Why ? Muller postulated that this happens because the molecular action of cortex arouses a constant grey which serves as base. For this, Hering had proposed a complicated compound of sensations, the elements of which completely neutralise each other. Muller also presented some experimental evidences in support of this theory.

Muller's work on memory was the greatest one. By having inspiration from Ebbinghaus' work, he did impressive researches in the field of memory. He devised a method for constructing nonsense syllables of equal difficulty. Muller developed method of hits and method of paired associates. In method of hits, after presentation of syllable the subject was required to recall that syllable which followed it in a list he had already learned. This method enabled Muller to measure the speed of recall. With the help of method of paired associates, Muller studied the role of recency and frequency in forming associations. Through this method, pairs of syllable near top and bottom of the list were contrasted with pairs lying at middle. Likewise, pairs of syllables presented frequently were contrasted with pairs of syllables presented less frequently. He also showed from his studies that middle syllables in the list were difficult to learn than those lying in the beginning or in the end. He also demonstrated that intentional repetitions were better than incidental repetition. It was Muller who had demonstrated that to learn whole (that is, learning materials from beginning to end without any interruption) was efficient than learning parts (that is, by dividing the materials into separate bits and learning each bit separately). Through these various methods, Muller quantitatively studied the different aspects of memory. Finally, Muller along with Pilzecker, developed, the *interference theory* which is still very popular and investigated theory in psychology. They named interference of new learning as *retroactive inhibition.* Not only this, Muller had also advanced the idea of *consolidation* in memory, a concept which later become important in passive avoidance learning experiments in explaining forgetting.

All these experimental studies in memory and visual perception did not mean that he had altogether dropped his interest in psychophysical methods. He refined Fechner's psychophysical methods and he also published book on psychophysics of lifted weights. His researches concentrated mainly on the error of localization and the two-point limen on the skin. In 1903 Muller published a handbook of psychophysics.

In nutshell, we can say that Muller was purely an experimental psychologists with no inclination towards philosophical theories. Within the field of experimental psychology, he demonstrated a broad interest and fertile mind. That is the reason why Boring (1950) has considered Muller as second only to Wundt.

The Wurzberg School : Kulpe, Marbe, Watt and Bhuler

Oswald Kulpe (1862–1915) studied at Leipzig in 1881 and did specialization in history. However, he was attracted by Wundt's programme of experimental researches being conducted in psychology. In 1883 he went to Gottingen to study under G.E. Muller and completed his doctoral dissertation in experimental psychology working for three years. In 1887 he took his doctoral degree. In 1886 he had returned to Leipzig to work as Wundt's assistant until 1894. Here he did important research work and published two books. At the Leipzig laboratory, he came into contact with Tithener who later became his close friends. Kulpe's first book was *Grundriss der Psychologie (Outlines of Psychology)* which was translated into English by Titchener. His second book was a sort of *Manual* of experimental psychology that reported in detail about Leipzig's experimental work. In 1894 he was appointed as professor at Wurzburg University and two years later he founded a laboratory which attracted a number of students both from Germany itself as well as from foreign countries. James Angell was one of such American students who later founded school of functionalism at the University of Chicago.

In this way we find that Kulpe had started his career as a student and assistant of Wundt at Leipzig and in the first part of his career, he remained devoted to Wundt's system. But later on he broke with Wundt's system because he considered Wundt's psychology too narrow. Regarding his experimental work at the laboratory of Wurzberg University, he became convinced that *thought processes* was the major part of the study of psychology which was entirely ignored by Wundt. He pointed out that Wundt did a great mistake by omitting higher mental processes' from the purview of the study of psychology. Accepting Wundt's view regarding conscious experience and the introspection method, he pointed out that thinking was such a higher mental process which occurred even in absence of sensations and images. This was termed by him as *'imageless thought'*. Several subjects participating in the study of thinking at the Wurzberg laboratory clearly pointed out that while they were thinking about the solution of a definite problem, no mental content like images occurred to them. This led Kulpe to conclude that thinking could occur without images.

There were also other persons who were closely associated with the Wurzberg school and experimented with the new phenomena called imageless thought. They were Karl Marbe, Henry Watt and Karl Buhler.

Karl Marbe (1869–1935) who was to succeed Kulpe in the Wurzberg University, published his experimental studies of judgement of weights. Marbe asked his subjects to tell which of the two weights was heavier. Usually, the subjects made correct judgement except when they were too difficult. Subsequently, the subjects were asked to introspect as to what was going on in their conscious experience when they were judging. Results revealed that no subject ever reported about the presence of any sensory or imaginal content while they were making judgement, However, Marbe found that various 'conscious attitude' (or *Bewusstseinslagen* in German) like hesitation, doubt, etc. passed through consciousness. These were interpreted as the *new imageless element of mind*.

The next important person in the series at Wurzberg group was **Henry Watt** (1879-1935). Watt was a student of Kulpe at Wurzberg University and he experimented extensively with word associations. He presented a stimulus word to the subject who was required to produce a response word under various situations which formulated a specific task (or Aufgabe) such as naming a word of subordinate relationship, naming a species word, etc. He divided his method into four stages :

(i) instruction regarding the nature of task,

(ii) presentation of the stimulus word,

(iii) researching for reaction word,

(iv) occurrence of the reaction.

In each step the subjects were asked to introspect regarding their conscious processes. Watt demonstrated that it was the first phase only which alone determined the reaction. Once the 'Aufgabe' or task was well-conceived, the subject readily responded with an appropriate word without any conscious effort. Thoughts occurred spontaneously on the presentation of the stimulus. The thought itself was imageless and could not be described introspectively. In this way, the final conclusion to which Watt arrived was that with proper preparation or instructions or task (or Aufgabe) a set or readiness was established which controlled the thought process that occurred without any conscious content. Such finding was definitely shocking to those who had accepted the basic assumptions of systematic psychology of Wundt. Later on, the findings of Watt were confirmed independently by Binet in France and Woodworth in America.

Another important person at Wurzberg was **Ach** who, among other things, introduced the concept of *determining tendency*. It is a kind of tendency which links associations into an orderly sequence from the 'Aufgabe' established in the beginning to the conclusion of task requiring some thinking. Thus determining tendency tends to reinforce associative tendencies. This tendency operates unconsciously which makes it a physiological process. In 1905 he performed experiments in which conflicts were introduced between strongly established associations and determining tendency and it was gradually found that such associations were overcome by the unconscious working of the determining tendency. Such experimentations of Ach opened a new field of investigations in psychology. Ach also verified many of the older work on reaction time with the help of Hipp chronoscope.

In 1907 **Karl Buhler** (1879–1963) reached Wurzberg and conducted several experiments. He gave his subjects some problems for solution. After the solutions were reached, they were asked to introspect about those steps through which they reached the particular solution. He reported that there were non-sensory thought processes—a new thought element that did not belong to the same category as sensations or images.

In 1909 Kulpe left Wurzberg for Bonn. In 1912 he presented the summary of the work done at Wurzberg school and in 1913 he died, leaving the entire programme unfinished one. In fact, with his untimely death, the Wurzberg school ceased to function and its members started thinking in other directions.

What was the overall achievement of the Wurzberg school which was a short-lived organization ? Most of the historians have agreed that the overall achievement is negative in the sense that the findings of Wurzberg school revealed that conscious experience as the field for description, analysis and measurement of human behaviour provided no relevant data for understanding behaviour. It obviously meant that factors which influence our behaviour in thinking about solution of a problem were not to be found in consciousness. This was definitely a negative and shocking hypothesis to the psychologists in Germany who were actively engaged in analysing and describing the contents of consciousness. Not only this, the introspection, though used by Wurzberg school, was considered as a less useful technique by this school. Wundt also criticised Wurzberg experiment and considered them as *mock experiments.* He objected to the study of the higher mental processes in the way Wurzbergers did. All experiments conducted by Wurzberg school, Wundt emphatically said, disregarded the fundamental principles of scientific observation and therefore, were invalid. Titchener, one of the pupils of Wundt, attacked the 'imageless thought' of Wurzberg school in his famous book, *The Experimental Psychology of Thought Processes* published in 1909. He suspected that such results of Wurzbergers were due to their faulty or incomplete introspection. Results of all these criticisms was that finally, Wurzberg school lost its prominence in favour of Wundtian psychology and later it was Wundt's pupils who were recognized as leaders of new experimental psychology in German universities. With Titchener this new psychology also went to U.S.A. at Cornell in 1892 from where it spread into whole of America.

In nutshell, we can say that British laid foundations for modern psychology partly in their philosophy and partly in physiology, and Germans took much of their physiological researches for converting one branch of it into independent experimental psychology. However, it remained for Americans to advance this new discipline to the status of what we know today about psychology. Thus modern experimental psychology is the product of British, Germans and Americans painstaking efforts.

CHAPTER HIGHLIGHTS

1. Wilhelm Wundt established the first psychological laboratory in 1879 at Leipzig University. His contribution towards psychology did not lie mere in this fact. He made psychology independent of sciences like physiology, biology and from the clutches of philosophy. In fact, he was a philosopher turned psychologist. As a philosopher, he was much influenced by the views of John Locke which stipulated that all knowledge came from experience. John Stuart Mill's concept of mental chemistry was also a big source of impetus for Wundt. Wundt, apart from being a philosopher, was also a physiologist. He had occasioned to work as assistant in Helmholtz's laboratory. All these also equipped him to advance the physiological explanation of psychological phenomena. His book *Principles of Physiological psychology* was directly a product of all such interests.
2. Wundt's contribution to psychology has been explained under two general heads—his systematic psychology and his work of Leipzig laboratory. As a systematic psychologists, Wundt proceeded to explain definition and subject-matter of psychology, principles of connection, method of psychology, apperception, mind-body problems, etc. He made a distinction between mediate experience and immediate experience. Having the experience of toothache was the immediate experience but by means of such experience if one tries to locate the cavity in tooth, this becomes mediate experience. Psychology, for Wundt, was the science of immediate experience or conscious experience. He analyzed the conscious experience or consciousness into two major elements—sensations and feeling, sensations were the objective elements whereas the feeling were subjective elements. To explain feelings, he propounded *tridimensional theory of feeling*. For him, the method of studying consciousness was introspection. He also explained the doctrine of

apperception. He explained apperception as a phenomena, as a cognition and as an activity. For solving mind-body problem, he pointed out that mind and body were parallel and not interacting systems.

3. Experimental works done at Leipzig laboratory were another major contribution of Wundt to psychology. His experimental works have been divided into five separate categories—sensation and perception experiments, reaction time experiments, association experiments, attention experiments, and feeling experiments. In *sensation and perception*, Wundt investigated visual perception, colour discrimination, colour mixing, colour blindness, perception of form, binocular vision and optical illusions. According to Tinker (1980) about 70 per cent of 186 doctoral dissertations produced by Wundt's laboratory had sensation and perception as their focal theme. *Reaction time experiments* were taken by Wundt to be the most important ones because through these experimentations he hoped to discover the three postulated stages between stimulus and response, that is, perception-apperception-will. Wundt's experiments on *Word associations* were also highly important ones. These association experiments had revealed that there were two types of association—inner association and outer association. Inner associations reflect intrinsic connection between words and outer associations reflect associations learnt through our habits. *Attention experiments* revealed the nature of attention which, for Wundt, was bidimensional, fluctuating and having specific range or span. *Feeling experiments* studied feeling with the help of method of paired comparison and such researches led Wundt to formulate the tridimensional theory of feeling.
4. Making a fair evaluation of Wundt's psychology on the whole, it has been said that critics, in general, have regarded Wundtian psychology to be narrow in its scope. Due to this he has not been appreciated to the extent he should. Even an empirical evidence is available to support this lack of appreciation (Anderson, 1971). It is also said that Wundt's contention that the elements or contents of conscious experience exist in the same way as some physical object exists, was not correct. Wundt provided no empirical evidence in support of his claim.
5. Some Wundt contemporaries like Brentano, Stumpf and G.E. Muller had also important impact upon psychology. Hence, they have not been ignored. Brentano is popularly associated with *act psychology*. Brentano has been recognised as a great competitor to Wundt and in

fact, his greatness lie more in opposition to Wundt than for making any positive contribution. Brentano, lodging a protest against the analytical character of Wundt, pointed out that psychology studied *mental acts* or *processes* rather than *mental contents*. He studied mental acts by dividing them into three categories—ideating, judging and feeling. Stumpf, by native endowment, was interested in music but was formally trained in philosophy. His great interest in music led him to conduct experimental studies in psychology of tone and music. He was opposed to Wundt's psychology and was a supporter to Brentano's act psychology. He had established a psychological laboratory at Berlin that had later attracted very important and influential psychologists like Kohler, Koffka and Wertheimer. G.E. Muller was another German contemporary of Wundt. He was purely an experimental psychologist. His chief areas of interest were psychophysics, visual perception and memory that he inherited from Fechner, Hering and Ebbinghaus, respectively. Muller, along with Pilzecker, developed the interference theory which is still very popular.

Wurzberg school in Germany under the leadership of Kulpe also started as a very important rival organization to Wundt's Leipzig group of psychologists. He along with other Wurzbergers like Marbe, Watt, Ach and Buhler conducted several experiments and jointly came to the conclusion that the content of consciousness was nonsensory as well as imageless. By introspection when their subjects explored consciousness, nothing like images were found in thinking. This gave rise to an important concept, that is *imageless thought* in psychology. But with untimely death of Kulpe in 1913, the programme of the Wurzberg school received a severe jolt and for ever, remained unfinished and unfulfilled. Later Wundtian group of psychologists strongly criticized Wurzberg school. Wundt lodged a strong protest to the study of higher mental processes in the way Wurzbergers attempted to study. As a consequence, the impact of this short-lived organization upon psychology soon vanished and like before, Wundtian psychology remained a powerful ancestor to modern psychology.

REVIEW QUESTIONS

1. Discuss the importance of Wilhelm Wundt in establishing psychology as an experimental science.
2. Discuss the contributions of Wilhelm Wundt as a systematic psychologist.

3. Assess the contributions made by Wilhelm Wundt's laboratory at Leipzig University.
4. "Wilhelm Wundt was not an individual but an institution". Comment.
5. "Psychology needed many more Wilhelm Wundt and not one." Comment.
6. Discuss the contributions of Franz Brentano and Carl Stumpf as rebels of Wilhelm Wundt.
7. Assess the contributions of Wurzberg School in highlighting the importance of imageless thinking.
8. Assess the contributions of G.E. Muller in establishing modern experimental psychology.

■

CHAPTER 6

STRUCTURALISM

CHAPTER PREVIEW

This chapter focuses upon a very important system of psychology called structuralism or introspection psychology or existentialism. This school was founded at Cornell University in America by E.B. Titchener, Wundt's pupil at Leipzig University. Titchener was a British psychologist who after taking his Ph. D. degree from Leipzig University in Germany, established this system of psychology at Cornell University rather than at Oxford University in Britain.

Structuralism as established by Titchener clearly spelled out that the psychology deals with experience as dependent upon the experiencing individual. Thus, like Wundt, Titchener defined psychology as the study of consciousness which was distinct from mind. This chapter also makes clear how Titchener tried to improve upon Wundt. For Titchener, there were three elements of consciousness—sensations, images and affections. Wundt had not regarded images as an independent element. Titchener's method of introspection along with the several rules for making introspection method more effective have also been discussed. His viewpoints regarding perception, attention, association and emotion have also been discussed. Titchener's most famous theory called context theory of meaning has also been nicely incorporated.

A lucid comparison of Wundt and Titchener has also been done for knowing about the point of similarities and dissimilarities between the two.

Finally, the system of structuralism has been evaluated and its fate has been outlined.

BRIEF LIFE-SKETCH OF EDWARD BRADFORD TITCHENER (1867–1927)

Titchener was born in the English town of Chichester. His family had little money. With the help of scholarship, he got admitted into Malvern College and then entered into Oxford University from where he took his Bachelor's degree. This also completed his training as a physiologist. But he was dissatisfied with what he had learnt till now. Therefore, he went to Germany at Leipzig University to get training with famous psychologist, Wilhelm Wundt. He studied with Wundt for 2 years, that is, from 1890 to 1892 and obtained his doctorate degree in 1892. His dissertation was on binocular effects of monocular stimulation. Although Titchener spent only two years with Wundt, he (Wundt) made a great impression upon him—an impression which was never obliterated.

After returning from Leipzig, Titchener became an extension lecturer of Oxford. He would have liked to remain at Oxford but the English were not ready to show any sympathy or even were not ready to accept the 'new' psychology of Titchener. Therefore, he decided to immigrate to America at Cornell University where he remained for rest of his life, that is, for nearly thirty-five years. There he taught psychology and did many experimental demonstrations in the laboratory which had been established by James Angell just a year before. During his thirty-five years brilliant career at Cornell University, he established his system, wrote articles and books and guided research students. During this thirty-five years, he guided and supervised *fifty* doctoral dissertations in psychology. Some of the important textbooks of Titchener were : *An outline of Psychology* (1896), *The Primer of Psychology* (1898), *Experimental Psychology* (1901–1905) in four volumes, *Lectures in the Elementary Psychology of Feeling and Attention* (1908), *Experimental Psychology of Thought Process* (1909), and *Textbook of Psychology* (1910). He was also editor of the *American Journal of Psychology*, succeeding G.S. Hall.

In 1904 Titchener organized a group of *experimentalists* meeting annually at various laboratories. E.G. Boring, one of Titchener's student and influential historian of Psychology, was an active member of this group. During last years of his life, the interest of Titchener turned from psychology to numismatics or coin collecting. He died in 1927 probably due to brain tumor.

Although Titchener was such an Englishman who never gave up his British citizenship, he was very Germanic and much like his teacher, Wundt, even in having a beard. He never became Americanized and throughout his life, expanded the new and basic psychology that he learnt from Wundt. In this sense, he was *more Wundtian than Wundt himself*.

TITCHENER'S STRUCTURAL PSYCHOLOGY

Titchener established structural psychology as a system in America in 1898 in his paper "The postulates of a structural psychology'. The basic features of this structural psychology may be enumerated as under :

1. *Subject-matter of psychology*

Titchener made it explicit that all science had its starting point in experience. He did not accept Wundt's idea that psychology studies immediate experience and physics studies mediate experience. In fact, he objected to distinction of experience into immediate experience and mediate experience. For Titchener, all experiences were immediate. Psychology and physics differed from each other not because they dealt with different subjects but because of the fact that they treated their common subject-matter from different point of view. Psychology studies experience with reference to the person who experiences it whereas physics studies the experience without reference to the experiencing person. Thus the physicist studies the experience as independent of the experiencing person whereas the psychologist studies the experience as dependent upon the experiencing person. Accordingly, Titchener's formal definition of the subject-matter of psychology was "experience dependent on an experiencing person". By the experiencing person, Titchener meant the living body.

Titchener further made distinction between mind and consciousness. For him, mind consists of the sum total of a person's experiences *summed from birth to death*. Consciousness consists of the sum total of a person's experiences *at any given time*.

For Titchener, there were three basic problems of psychology —the *'what'*, the *'how'* and the *'why'* of psychology. The *'what'* refers to the analysis of mental experience into its simplest components. The *'how'* refers to discovering how these components are combined and the laws which govern the combination. The *'why'* refers to the ways mental events correlate with their physiological conditions, namely, brain and nervous system events. Titchener's formulation of these three basic problems of psychology was similar to Wundt's formulation.

Like Wundt, Titchener analyzed the elements of consciousness. For Titchener, there were *three* basic elements of consciousness—*sensations, images* and *affections*. Wundt had not regarded images as an independent element of consciousness. Sensations were regarded as the elements of perceptions. In his *outline of Psychology* Titchener pointed out that there were more than 42,415 different types of sensations. Images were elements of ideas and represented those patterns which were not actually present. Affections were the elements of emotion. Titchener had rejected Wundt's tridimensional theory of feeling. Of Wundt's three dimensions, namely, pleasant-unpleasant, strained-relaxed, and excited-calm, Titchener accepted only the first dimension. He reduced the last two dimensions to sensations and images. Later on, Titchener even rejected the pleasant-unpleasant dimension of feeling (Henle, 1974) because for him affect had no independent characteristics. Towards the last years of his life, he further simplified his system by accepting the likelihood that there was no clear-cut distinction between sensations and images and finally, considered sensations to be more dominant. In Titchener's posthumous book *Systematic Psychology : Prolegomena* it was made clear that psychology dealt primarily with sensory materials or sensation.

For Titchener, these elements of consciousness had some basic attributes. Wundt had pointed out two basic attributes—*quality and intensity*. Titchener expanded the list to four—*quality, intensity, clarity* and *duration*. Sometimes one more additional attribute *extensity* also was found to occur. Quality referred to difference in kind such as green, hot, etc. Intensity referred to strength such as strong-weak, bright-dim etc. Clarity referred to the experience that was dominant and outstanding and therefore, varied with attention rather than objective characteristics of the stimulus. Affections did not possess the characteristics of clarity. Sensations and images, however, have had that. By duration was meant temporal attribute of experience, such as long and short interval. Extensity referred to the experience of scatteredness or spread in space. This attribute applied only to vision and touch. Later, Stevens (1934) showed that this attribute also applied to tones because loud tones produced more extended experience than soft tones. For Titchener, sensations and images have all the four attributes, namely, quality, intensity, duration and clearness. Affection had the first three attributes but lacked the attribute of clearness. In his various texts, Titchener devoted much space to sensations and images. He made it clear that it was not easy to make distinction between sensation and image. However, in terms of intensity, an quantitative difference could be made. A point may easily be located along the intensity dimension where image might become strong enough to be called as sensation or where sensation might become weak enough to be called as image. He had also rejected Wurzberger's claim for imageless thought and pointed out that they got that type of result because of *faulty or incomplete introspection*.

In this way, Titchener made explicit about the whole structure of consciousness in terms of its elements and their basic attributes. In this way, he answered the first basic problem of psychology, that is, 'what' psychology is about.

2. *Methodology of Psychology*

Much like Wundt, Titchener considered introspection and experimentation to be the primary methods of investigation. In fact, for Titchener, the method of introspection was even more formalized and practiced procedure than it was for Wundt. He further pointed out that introspection could be scientifically carried out only by well-trained observers. Titchener had outlined several important rules for making introspection more effective. Some of these rules were as follows :

- (i) The observer must be completely impartial and unprejudiced.
- (ii) He must have proper control over his attention and must not allow it to vary to and fro.
- (iii) The mind and the body of the observer must be fresh, that is, the observer must not have fatigue or exhaustion because these things would prevent from having sustained concentration.
- (iv) The observer must have a positive attitude towards the introspection. In fact, he must be interested in the process.

Keeping these rules in view, a trained observer ignoring objects and events as such, concentrates upon pure conscious experience. Such observers are interested only in the direct contents of experience rather than in the inferences made on the basis of those contents. Like Wundt, Titchener considered introspection, as a part of experimentation. It was this experimentation that made psychology scientific. An experiment, for Titchener, was an observation that could be repeated, isolated and varied.

One of the biggest problems that Titchener encountered in introspection was what he called as *'stimulus error'*. By stimulus error was meant to see thing or object rather than the conscious experience generated by the concerned object or thing. The common example used by Titchener to illustrate the stimulus error was to see a 'table' and call it a 'table'. If an observer or introspectionist saw a table while making his scientific observation of table, he was committing 'stimulus error' because he was attending to the stimulus (table) rather than the conscious process that the stimulus was producing in him. Thus Titchener was not interested in the statement 'I see a table' because table was a 'meaning word' based upon aggregation of previsual and tactile sensations by which table was identified. In fact, Titchener was interested in aggregate of sensations (a meaningless aggregate) produced by the 'table' acted as stimulus. Such emphasis by Titchener required that the observer or introspectionist must be exceptionally trained so that he might not commit any stimulus error.

3. *Principles of Selection*

One of the basic problems with which Titchener was seriously concerned was why certain stimuli were selected in consciousness. He solved this problem by use of the concept of attention. In attention the conscious elements are arranged and thus, it becomes the focus of consciousness. Hence, the concept of attention, for Titchener, was reduced to sensory clarity. He outlined three general stages of attention—(a) native or involuntary or primary attention (b) voluntary or secondary attention, and (c) derived primary or habitual attention. In involuntary or primary attention native factors like quality and intensity of the sensory experience tend to determine attention. We generally pay attention to sudden noise or a flash of light due to such native factors. Voluntary or secondary attention refers to purposeful focusing on elements in consciousness. This is a difficult stage because one has to maintain attention at a high level of clarity. Derived attention or habitual attention arises due to repetition of similar circumstances. Here again attention is involuntary but this is due to some learnt habits rather than due to some unlearned or native-factors. A nurse attends habitually to the signals of patients.

Titchener regarded these three stages as continuous rather than separate ones. According to him, reaching the last stage of derived involuntary attention was the basic objective of education. A student fixated at the second stage of attention (where he has difficulty to keep the sensory content or materials in consciousness) may have several types of academic difficulty. An example of continuity in these three stages may be student's interest in reading a particular course book. In the beginning, his attention may be held by several native factors like novelty and expectations regarding the probable benefits from reading the book. As reading progresses, he may have some difficulties due to difficult explanations and terminology. He may find difficult to maintain his attention. This is the second stage. Frequent exposure to such explanations and terminology will come to maintain a certain level of attention and this marks the beginning of third stage.

4. *Principles of Connection*

Although Titchener did not gave much importance to the principle of connection or association, he held the law of contiguity to be the fundamental law of association for sensations and images. The feeling was dropped to be an independent element of experience. He pointed out that whenever a sensory or imaginal content occurs in our conscious experience, all those sensory or imaginal contents are likely to appear which in past have occurred in contiguous with that. Thus law of contiguity was his main law of association. For Titchener, elements of consciousness was not 'things' rather 'processes' that did not fit together 'side-by-side and angle-to-angle'. The various elements overlap, modify and arrest one another which create difficulty in synthesis. Titchener was not a static elementalist whereas Wundt was. For Wundt, these elements are like 'things' and possess the property of physical object. Despite this, he (Titchener) considered the laws of synthesis to be important one.

Titchener also proceeded to explain the problem of meaning with the help of principle of connection. The problem was : how does meaning become connected to sensation and images ? In order to answer this, Titchener in 1915 formulated his famous *context theory of meaning,* a theory which though touched by Wundt but had never been fully explained by him. According to this theory, meaning of sensation or image was determined by the *context* in which it occurred in consciousness. The context of sensation was the result of the past experiences with the sensation. Thus meaning was the result of connection between past associations and images. A simple sensation had no meaning because it had only cover or immediate raw experience having no context. Perceptions and ideas which were more than simple sensation and images had core as well as context. Context gives meaning to core. Hence, they were meaningful. Sometimes, core was separated from context. for example, repeating a word time and again makes context disappear and the word also becomes meaningless. By repeating the word, the context became separated from the core. Sometimes, context might be added to the core. For example, when we learn the meaning of a foreign word, we add context to the core or raw experience produced by the native word.

5. *Emotion*

For Titchener, emotions are nothing but intensified feelings arising from sensations within the body. Therefore, the important core of emotion is feeling or affective aspect of conscious experience. He pointed out two methods to study emotion—method of impression and method of expression. When we want to make comparison of the different affective characteristics, the method of impression is used. For example, to study the affective characteristics of the different colours, we may, through the comparison arrange them in order from pleasantness to unpleasantness. In expression method the emotion is studied on the basis of bodily changes such as breathing, blood pressure, heart rate, changes in gastrointestinal activities, etc.

6. *Thinking*

Titchener's work on thought was, at first, simply the criticism of Wurzbergers who held that the process of thought was imageless. He emphasized upon the sensory and imaginal nature of thought process in contrast to the viewpoints of Wurzbergers who emphasized upon the 'imageless thought'. His subjects did not confirm the imageless content of thought process. Titchener suspected that the overall results of Wurzbergers were caused by the faulty or incomplete introspection. His viewpoint was that the so-called element of thought was probably an unanalyzed blend of kinesthetic sensations and images that were difficult to find in consciousness. Titchener also rejected the 'will' element, which had been regarded as fundamental by Wundt. He held that will was nothing but simply complex of images through which ideas were formed in advance of action. But Titchener also accepted some of the viewpoints of Wurzbergers. For example, he accepted the determining tendency of Ach and also the viewpoint of Wurzbergers that the thought may be unconscious. Introducing his context theory of meaning in the explanation of thought process, he further said that it is the context which makes conscious sensory and imaginal content meaningful ones. This was particularly true for new perceptions and ideas (new thinking). But for old and accustomed ones, the sensory or imaginal core or experience occurs without conscious context and the meaning is carried unconsciously. Due to this reason Wurzbergers, perhaps, reported lack of conscious content in thought process.

7. *Mind-body problem*

Regarding mind-body problem, Titchener adopted the position of *psychophysical parallelism* from Wundt. Like Wundt, he believed that mind (or mental activities) and body the (the bodily or physical activities) are different from each other. No interaction takes place between them and neither causes the other. However, a change in one is followed by change in other. Thus, Titchener, like his teacher Wundt, was a *psychophysical parallelist*.

On the whole, we find that Titchener's structuralism was more neat and well-defined than that of Wilhelm Wundt. It was also self-contained. It recognized the basic problems of psychology—the 'what' and the 'how' and the 'why' of psychology. Its biggest impact on modern psychology was that it initiated the importance of experimental vigour in psychology.

CRITICISMS OF STRUCTURALISM

Although structuralism as a system had many positive contributions towards psychology, its opponents termed it as 'orthodox' and criticised vehemently as under :

1. Critics have said that Titchener's structuralism was too self-contained and it was limited to the analytical framework of conscious experience. What is the utility or function of conscious experience ? The question was simply turned down by Titchener because its purview had nothing to do with psychology. In fact, Titchener had no interest in practical applications of psychology. This was one of his serious limitations. Titchener had no interest in applied branches of psychology which were emerging at that time. Therefore, he excluded child psychology, animal psychology, social psychology and abnormal psychology from main body of psychology. Likewise, when Watson started his behavioural studies, Titchener also ignored them by saying that they were *not* psychology.

2. The biggest objection was made towards the use of method of introspection. Critics were of view that method of introspection was inadequate on several grounds given as under :

(i) In true sense, introspection no longer remains introspection rather it is changed into retrospection because it naturally takes some time to report about the contents of conscious experience. Due to this lapse of time, some of the contents are forgotten. Titchener did not agree with this criticism and pointed out that the so-called above danger may easily be avoided by having a trained introspectionist who would make perfect report about the conscious element within that lapse of time.

(ii) Another criticism of method of introspection was that act of introspecting might change the experience itself. For example, if one starts inspecting the experience in anger, the state of anger might disintegrate and finally disappear. Again, Titchener answers that in case of trained introspectionist it would not occur because they became unconscious of the act of introspection after practice.

(iii) Another criticism of introspection method was that psychologists working with this method in different laboratories were getting different results. Boring (1950) in an article entitled *The History of Introspection* has provided several examples of contradictory results coming from different laboratories that were relying on introspection. Titchener's suggestion to overcome this difficulty was to develop an adequate language or set or procedures to describe the introspective experiences. However, for this, even trained introspectionist needed practice.

(iv) Critics also pointed out that there were some data in psychology which could not be obtained by method of introspection : For example, unconscious influences which play an important role in maladjustment could not be studied by introspection. Moreover, several interesting psychological facts were being revealed even though animals can not introspect.

All these criticisms revealed that the introspection method of structural psychology was inadequate and was providing unreliable and subjective data.

3. The Gestalt psychologists lodged a strong protest against the elementalistic analysis of structuralism. They pointed out that the psychological phenomena must be studied as a whole. This whole is not the sum of its parts or elements. Hence, the whole should not be divided into its parts.

Despite these criticisms, structuralism, as a system of psychology was instrumental in establishing psychology as an independent experimental science. Wilhelm Wundt was the real source of inspiration for establishing structuralism by Titchener who, as one of his faithful students, tried to improve upon his viewpoints.

WUNDT AND TITCHENER : A COMPARATIVE LOOK

Wundt was the teacher of Tichener at Leipzig University in Germany. Titchener had come from Britain (Oxford University) to learn new psychology from Wundt. After returning to Oxford, he came to Cornell University in America where he founded structuralism, the very first formal system in psychology. In this system he modified and expanded Wundt's view regarding psychology. In fact, he was *more Wundtian than Wundt himself*. It was natural, therefore, that Titchener would have possessed many similarities with his teacher, Wundt. Some of the major *similarities* are as under :

1. Like Wundt, Titchener pointed out that psychology was the study of conscious experience. Thus the subject-matter of psychology was consciousness for both these psychologists.

2. Both these psychologists considered introspection, experimentation and observation to be the primary methods of psychology. Like Wundt, Titchener also made it explicit that introspection or self-observation was the part of the experimentation. Both emphasized upon the necessity of having trained introspectionists.

3. Like Wundt, Titchener believed in psychophysical parallelism. Therefore, regarding mind-body issue both these psychologists opined that there was clear distinction between mental events and physical events. Neither caused the other and there was no interaction between them. Both were running parallel to each other and changes in one were accompanied by changes in other.

Despite these similarities, there were some points of dissimilarities between Titchener and Wundt. Following were the major points of *dissimilarities* :

1. Wundt held that there were two elements of conscious experience—sensations and affections. Titchener pointed out that there were three elements of conscious experience—sensations, affections and images. In fact, images were not regarded as an independent category of conscious element by Wundt rather he considered it to be occurring due to blend in sensations.

2. Wundt held that there were two primary attributes of conscious experience—quality and intensity. Titchener extended the number of attributes to four by adding duration and clearness or clarity. One more attribute, that is, extensity had also been later added by Titchener. The attribute of extensity, however, applied only to vision and touch. Titchener also made it clear that the attribute of clarity did not apply to affection or feeling.

3. Titchener rejected the tridimensional theory of feeling of Wundt. Of the three dimensions of feeling, namely, pleasant-unpleasant, strained-relaxed, excited-calm, Titchener rejected the last two dimensions because they were not feeling at all rather they were kinesthetic experience. Later, Titchener rejected even the pleasant-unpleasant attribute of feeling (Henle, 1974).

4. Titchener criticised the applied aspects of psychology. He held that psychology is pure and general science, having no practical aims. Therefore, the applied aspects of psychology such as child psychology, animal psychology and abnormal psychology which were springing up at that time, were ignored by Titchener saying that they would not yield any *psychological information*. Wundt, on the other hand, did not do so and he insisted upon the fact that the behaviour of children and abnormals yielded valuable psychological information.

5. Wundt was an institution providing training to a vast number of psychologists and expanding the scope of psychology from armchair speculation to experimental laboratories. Titchener was basically an individual who did the same thing but in a very limited way.

Thus we find that despite some similarities, differences exist between Titchener and Wundt.

FATE OF STRUCTURALISM

Structuralism was especially significant because it was the first comprehensive system spelling out the goals and methods of psychology as a science. However, structuralism as a system is dead today. For us, today it is simply the dim memory of the psychological past at Leipzig University as wèll as at Cornell University. It met its natural death because it had nowhere to go, it had rejected objective data and it had totally ignored practical application. As an ardent student of Titchener and in some way his most likely successor, Boring in his book *The Physical Dimensions of Consciousness* (1933) tried hard to salvage what was left of structuralism by defending conscious experience to be the legitimate study of psychology. At this stage, Boring, in fact, intended to wed structuralism to the increasing scientific sophistication by chiefly correlating conscious experience and the physiological processes particularly with the characteristics of nerve impulses in the brain. But four years later, that is, in 1937, he announced that the study of consciousness and private experience was no longer useful to psychology and therefore, it should be derived out of scientific psychology. This gave a big jolt to dying structuralism and resulted in its immediate death.

CHAPTER HIGHLIGHTS

1. Titchener was an English psychologist who went Germany to study psychology from Wilhelm Wundt at Leipzig University. After returning from Germany, he perferred to settle in America rather than in Britain. He established a system at Cornell University in America which was called as structuralism.
2. Titchener's structural psychology or structuralism emphasized that psychology was the study of experience dependent upon the experiencing person. In other words, for him, psychology was the study of conscious experience. He held that there were three elements of consciousness—sensations, images and feelings or affection. Later on, he dropped feeling as an independent category of element. He also rejected Wundt's tridimensional theory of feeling. Towards his last years, he urther simplified his system by concentrating upon the sensory experience or sensation to be the only primary element of conscious experience. He recognized four basic attributes of conscious experience. They were : quality, intensity, clarity and duration. Apart from these four, he also held

extensity to be an attribute of experience but this applied only to vision and touch. He also made it clear that affection or feeling did not possess the attribute of clarity.

3. For Titchener, introspection and experimentations were the primary methods of psychology. Her also stressed the fact that introspection can be scientifically carried out only by well-trained observers. He also drew attention towards a common error called stimulus error made by introspectionist. By stimulus error he meant to concentrate upon stimulus or object rather than upon conscious experience generated by that stimulus. A trained observer is always aware of such error and therefore, he tries to avoid such error.
4. Titchener's viewpoints regarding thinking was also highly important. He criticised the experimental findings of Wurzbergers by emphasizing that thought was not imageless as they had reported. Their findings that thinking was imageless was due to their faulty or incomplete introspection. Therefore, he emphasized upon sensory and imaginal nature of thought process.
5. Like Wundt, Titchener believed in principle of psychophysical parallelism. Regarding the mind-body issue, he stated that the physical events and mental events ran parallel to each other and the change in one was followed by change in other. But there were no interactions because they were completely different from each other.
6. The biggest criticism of structuralism was regarding its method of introspection. Critics held that the method of introspection or self-observation was inadequate on at least *four* grounds. Likewise, they also held that structuralism was too self-contained system keeping itself limited to the analysis of conscious experience. After all, what was the utility or function of such conscious experience ? Never explained by structuralism.
7. The two giant originators of structuralism, namely, Wundt and Titchener, were having many points of similarities and dissimilarities. Both held that the subject-matter of psychology was conscious experience, its method was introspection and mind-body were parallel to each other without having any interaction. Despite these similarities, there were dissimilarities. Wundt held that there were two independent categories of element of conscious experience (sensations and feelings) whereas Titchener held that they were three, namely, sensations, feelings and images. Where as Wundt made his tridimensional theory of feeling a central one, Titchener outright rejected this theory. Wundt had some inclination towards

practical applications of psychology whereas Titchener completely rejected applied aspects of psychology.

8. Although structuralism gave psychology an independent status as an experimental science, its fate was not bright. Today, it is no longer alive. For us, it is simply the dim memory of psychological past at Leipzig University as well as at Cornell University.

REVIEW QUESTIONS

1. Discuss the major contributions of structuralism as outlined by Titchener.
2. "Titchener was more Wundtian than Wundt himself". Comment.
3. Make a comparative study of Titchener and Wundt.
4. Define structuralism. Discuss the fate of structuralism.

■

CHAPTER 7

THE PSYCHOLOGY OF WILLIAM JAMES AND OTHER PIONEER AMERICAN PSYCHOLOGISTS : FORERUNNERS OF FUNCTIONALISM

CHAPTER PREVIEW

In this chapter focus has been given upon the viewpoints of one of the major American psychologists, William James as well as upon some other pioneer American psychologists. William James lodged objections to Wundt and the growing structuralism of Titchener. Chronologically William James was between Wundt and Titchener. Thus in American psychology James both precedes and follow Titchener.

How James has opposed the concept of consciousness as expressed by Wundt and other structuralists have also been discussed. Rejecting the structuralists' view that consciousness is something that is static and that can be broken down into its separate elements, he pointed out some major characteristics of consciousness. He emphasized more upon the functional utility of studying consciousness rather than upon its analytical character by pointing out some basic characteristics of consciousness. His this new approach was in a sense anticipation of the functionalism movement that later started at the University of Chicago.

James viewpoints regarding other important phenomena like emotion, memory, instinct, the self, etc. have also been elaborated. An evaluation of James psychology has also been presented.

Lastly, the viewpoints of some early American psychologists like G. S. Hall and J. M. Cattell who were important parts of the functional traditions have been presented and their relation to later founding of functionalism has been elucidated.

Thus in this chapter the viewpoints of the important forrunners of functionalism, namely, William James, G. S. Hall and J. M. Cattell have been lucidly discussed.

BRIEF LIFE-SKETCH OF WILLIAM JAMES (1842-1910)

William James was born in a wealthy and highly gifted family in New York city. Henry James, the famous novelist, was his brother who was born fourteen months later. William James' early education took place both in America as well as in Europe. Since he belonged to a wealthy family, he traveled a lot and had scattered education in England, France, Switzerland and Germany. He started as an art student showing strong inclination towards painting. At the age of nineteen, he entered Harvard University to study sciences and in 1869, he received his degree in medicine. Subsequently, he was appointed instructor to teach anatomy and physiology at Harvard University. In fact, during this period he became interested in experimental psychology. Watson (1978) has pointed out that William James established the first psychological laboratory in 1875 for presenting undergraduate students a course entitled 'The Relations between physiology and psychology.' In the same year he also got about 300 dollars for purchasing physiological and psychological apparatus for the laboratory. Despite this, we credit Wundt for establishing the first psychological laboratory at Leipzig in 1879. Why ? Although the history is vague, it is said that the laboratory of William James was not a real laboratory. It was simply a room with some brass instruments having a very poor scope for full demonstration of what was taught to undergraduate students. The arguement which goes against William James is that he really did not 'found' a psychological laboratoy. Boring (1950) has pointed out that there were many demonstration laboratories known to exist prior to 1879, but such laboratories were, in fact, not founded; they simply occurred and existed. Apart from this, William James apparently never considered himself as an experimental psychologist and even disliked the tedium of laboratory pursuits (Bringmann, 1979, Jacobson, 1979). Therefore, William James laboratory might be considered merely as an "anticipation" of laboratory that was formally "founded" by Wilhelm Wundt and from which energed a scientific psychology (Boring, 1950). During 1880s, he published several article in *Mind*—a British journal that was devoted more to philosophy than to psychology. In 1890 he published his most famous book *The Principles of psychology* in which he set down his basic viewpoints towards psychology. In 1889 he became professor of psychology at Harvard University. Soon afterwards, his interest shifted to philosophical problems and this marked his greatest period of productivity. In 1897 he became professor of philosophy and published six major books on philosophy. Thus academic position of William James varied from a psychologist to a philosopher. During his psychology years, he taught some students who later on became eminent psychologists. E. L. Thorndike, R. S. Woodworth and James Angel were among those. Despite all these, he was not a great experimentalist and left few original results. His major contribution in psychology was his effort to combine various psychological principles suggested by the experiment of others, to make appropriate conjecture from those principles and present the results in attractive and comprehensive verbal package.

However, in the field of modern psychology he is well-known for his *Pragmatism* (1909). This became a very popular movement which implies that validation of any knowledge must be in terms of its utilitarian consequences. Underlying this was the important assumption that psychology must study *functions.*

Chronologically, William James belonged between Wundt (10 years his senior) and Titchener (25 years his junior). Although he had obvious opportunity to be guided by Wundt, he did not find experimentalism of Wundt much inspiring. His psychology was also not systematic. It is said that in his career most of the time he was a philosopher and "sometime" psychologist. In 1907 he resigned his active service at Harvard University. He died at age of sixty-eight, that is, in 1910 leaving behind a tradition, an influence, a style and a thought which was much more effective than a formal school of psychology could have.

WILLIAM JAMES' PSYCHOLOGY

William James has been considered as one of the greatest American Psychologists to date (Becker, 1959). He exerted his influence on latest trends in psychology in unparalleled way. He strongly criticized elementalism and Wundtian introspectionism. Not only this, he placed an extensive positive programme before his psychology. In his programme he had emphasized upon what was called *pragmatism* which stated that validation of any knowledge in psychology must be done in terms of its values or utilities. In that sense, he has been considered as a *pragmatist.*

Although James' psychology was not systematic nor experimental like that of Wundt's psychology, his approach giving much emphasis upon applied or functional aspects of psychology, gave birth to later functionalists' movement at the University of Chicago. In this sense, he has been considered as a *forerunner* of functionalism—a system which was founded by John Dewey and James Angell at the University of Chicago. In fact, William James founded the functionalism as a system but not as a school (Marx & Cronan-Hillix, 1987).

William James' pragmatic psychology has been set down mainly in his two-volumed *Principles of Psychology* that was published in 1890. In 1892 he published a condensed book called *Psychology : Briefer Course* that served as a textbook for beginners in psychology. People, however, considered it to be a 'money-maker' and it was really so. His entire psychology may be broadly explained as under:

1. *Definition and subject-mater of psychology*

According to James, psychology is "the science of mental life, both of its phenomena and of their conditions". By 'mental life' he meant consciousness. By 'phenomena' he meant the subject-matter that was found in experience. However, this experience should not be interpreted in a way as Wundt and Titchener had. Like Wundt and Tichener, for James psychology was also concerned with conscious experience or consciousness but he emphasized not upon its analytical character rather than upon its functional utility. For James, consciousness was a continuous and dynamic complex and not something composed of discrete bits joined together. Its main concern was adaptation to the changing stimulation of the environment. To study consciousness as it was given in immediate and actual experience was the main concern of the psychologists. This has also been termed as *Stream of Consciousness* which is so important and popular that author thinks it proper to devote a separate section (next section) for it. By 'condition' James meant that the bases for mental life or consciousness could be found in the body. Thus James psychology was also concerned with physical beings.

2. *Methods and Snares*

According to James, psychology was a part of natural science and therefore, the study of human beings must be considered in their adaptation and readaptation to the environment. James considered the following methods to be important and useful for psychology.

(i) ***Method of introspection*** : James defined psychology as the science of mental life or consciousness and further, he pointed out that introspection was one important method to study consciousness. He considered introspection to be the 'natural gift' of a person and for this training was not needed. Thus James' introspection was different from introspection of trained observer of Wundt and Titchner. For James, introspection was merely catching the moment of consciousness as it passed through it. It was a form of observation that is neither infallible nor impossible. Although introspection was beset with some difficulties, it could be verified by using appropriate checks and by marking comparison of the various reports.

(ii) ***Experimentation*** : James was never an experimentalist. He himself preferred not to conduct experiment. Still he recognized the importance of the experimental method. Although he made little use of the experiments done by Germans like Weber, Fechner and Wundt, he believed that some kind of experimentation could yield valuable information regarding psychology.

(iii) *Comparative method* : The comparative method was not a primary method of psychology and it was merely a subsidiary to the method of introspection and experimentation. Through this method, the mental life of animals, children, defective and even insane could be studied. But he considered this method to be inexact and investigator was left with his own common sense in handling this method.

James was also aware of the difficulties and problems encountered in execution of these methods. He called them as *snares*. For him, in general, introspection was inaccurate, experiment was futile and comparative method was 'wild work'. Apart from these, there were *two* common difficulties in executing these methods of psychology. First difficulty was related to language. James was of view that facts of consciousness could be conveyed through words and there was not a reliable relationship between words and facts of consciousness. If we had no word for a fact of consciousness, we simply tend to ignore them. Second difficulty was what has been called as *psychologist's fallacy* by James. By this, he meant, that we generally tend to read our perceptions more than what is really present there. In fact, in such fallacy the person remains outside the mental state he really observes. For example, suppose one observes a tree. He already knows may things about a tree and he may suppose that all those things (that he knows) are in the present perception of tree. If we pay attention to James' 'psychologist's fallacy', it becomes obvious that it is similar to Titchener's stimulus error although James was opposed to structuralists' this term.

3. *Emotion*

In explaining emotions, James developed a theory which had been very popular and a single most important contribution to psychology. At about the same time C. G. Lange, a Danish physiologist, published a similar theory. So today this theory is popularly known as *James-Lange theory of emotion.* Prior to this theory, the popular explanation which is based upon commonsense view was that we perceive an object, experience emotion and then, make appropriate emotional behaviour. In other words, we see a bear, became afraid of it and subsequently, we run away. This paradigm was like : Stimulus (bear)—Experience (emotion)—Response (running) Reversing this order, James said that after perception of emotion provoking stimulus, emotional behaviour occurs and this is followed by emotional experience. Thus we see a bear, run away and therefore, we become afraid. Thus the paradigm becomes : Stimulus—Response—Experience. James also made it clear that such emotional behaviour or response includes both the external reactions (such as running) as well as internal reactions such as changes in blood pressure, heart rate, flow of adrenalin etc. James' this theory very clearly outlined his position regarding interaction of mind and body. Perception of bear produced a mental impression that led to bodily activities and physiological changes (emotional behaviour). Subsequently, a feedback regarding all such activities and changes was sent to brain that helped in experiencing emotion.

Today James-Lange theory of emotion is important mainly in the historical context because it has been replaced by Cannon-Bard theory which stated that emotional behaviour did not precede emotional experience rather occur simultaneously.

4. *Instinct*

By instinct James meant unlearnt patterns of reacting. In advocating the doctrine of instinct he was influenced by Darwin and other animal psychologists of his time. He pointed out that these instincts facilitate both human beings as well as animal beings in doing things in natural way. He also made it clear that human beings, as compared to other species, have the largest number of instincts. Among human infants crying, biting, moving and vocalizing are some of the major instincts. In adults imitation, pugnacity, hunting, play, love, fear and jealousy are the major instincts. For James, instincts were self-preservative as well as unlearned. Despite this, he did not consider instincts to be blind and invariable rather they were modifiable by habit. With changes in the conditions antecedent to the onset of the instinctive act, the instinct may itself stand changed or modified. Therefore, for James, instincts were non-rational.

5. *The Self*

For James, self was equivalent to what we today call as 'personality'. By the term self, James meant 'me' or empirical self which consisted of a hierarchy of three aspects. At the bottom of hierarchy was *material self,* next on the hierarchy was the *social self* or social selves and at the top of hierarchy was the *spiritual self*. Material self consisted of our body and personal possessions like money, property, home, clothes, furniture, etc. Social self was one which was formed on the basis of recognition of a person by others who also held some opinion about him. An individual may have different self for his friend, mother, father, his sister, wife etc.

Thus to the extent we make different interactions with different persons, we develop different social selves. Thus social selves reflect different aspects of personality. Spiritual self referred to the various psychological functions or what James called, "all the psychic faculties or dispositions taken together". Thinking, intellectual capacities, willing, etc. were a few examples of the spiritual self. He also made it clear that he never intended to use this term in the sense of soul.

Apart from these three aspects of empirical self or the self as known, James considered the concept of 'pure ego' or 'I' or self as a *knower* that did the functioning of knowing.

6. *Memory*

James considered ability to memorize something as the special characteristic of the brain structure. Earlier faculty psychologists had pointed out that memory is a unitary function and can be improved with training. If a person strengthens his memory in one area, his memory in other area is also strengthened. The only experiment James ever did in this connection was that in which he and some of his students acted as subjects. First, he learnt 158 lines of Victor Hugo's *Satyr* and noted down the total time taken. Then, he spent about a month committing to memory Milton's *Paradise lost.* After this, he returned to the *Satyr* and memorized another 158 lines. Results revealed that these 158 lines actually took longer than the first 158 lines and thus, all the work on *Paradise lost* was lost because it failed to improve his ability to memorize. Thus no support to faculty psychologists was provided to their general mind-training idea. Later, he divided memory into two parts—primary memory and secondary memory. *Primary memory* was short-term memory and *secondary memory* was long-term memory.

7. *Mind-body problem*

James believed in the existence of both mind and body and to this extent, he was having a position similar to Wundt. But he was in *interactionist* and not a *parallelist* like Wundt. He believed that mind and body interact with each other and not that they run simply parallel to each other. In his book *Principles of Psychology* some chapters exclusively dealt with neurological and physiological processes of the body and some chapters exclusively dealt with mental processes. He has made it clear that sometimes mind operated to serve the body and at some other time body took over more automatically leaving the mind to do some other important works.

In this way we find that James' psychology was more broad though less experimental than that of Wundt and Titchener. Specially his emphasis upon pragmatism, that is, upon the view that validation of any knowledge must be done in terms of its values and utilities, has been very influential one and also the one that later led to the foundation of functionalism.

STREAM OF CONSCIOUSNESS

Perhaps the crux of William James' psychology is to be found in his 'Stream of Consciousness'—one of the most important chapters of his book *Principles of Psychology*. What is stream of consciousness ? For James, psychology is the study of consciousness as we know it at first hand. In other words, the starting point of psychology is immediately felt experience (not mind or soul which is manifested through consciousness). This is what he meant by the 'Stream of Consciousness'. While formulating his view on stream of consciousness, he opposed the concept of consciousness as expressed by Wundt and Titchener who had taken it to be a static state that can be analyzed or broken down into several elements.

James explained consciousness by its five major characteristics as under :

(1) ***Consciousness is personal*** : He pointed out that consciousness is personal and individualistic and every thought belongs to some one.

(2) ***Consciousness is always changing*** : This is a vital characteristic which distinguishes him from Wundt. Through this characteristics James wanted to emphasize that we have never exactly same idea or thought twice. No state once gone can ever *recur and be identical*. This is, in fact, a physical impossibility. Objects can reoccur no doubt but not thoughts or ideas. Therefore, consciousness is like a constantly flowing stream which sometimes proceed very rapidly and sometimes very slowly.

(3) ***Consciousness is continuous*** : James pointed out that consciousness is sensibly continuous. There is no break in stream of consciousness although there may be temporary inter-ruptions in continuity as we find in case of sleep. But after sleep, Peter is still Peter and Paul is still Paul. They never mix with each other.

(4) ***Consciousness deals with objects other than itself*** : He pointed out that thoughts are unitary, no matter how complex they are. The objects may be complex but thoughts produced by those objects still be continuous and of unitary character. Through this characteristics he has stated his dualism between the mind and object it deals with.

(5) ***Consciousness is always choosing or selective*** : At any moment we are bombarded by several stimuli that produce several sensations. We actively choose a few to attend and bring it to consciousness. Likewise, preception is also a selective process.

In expressing his view on stream of consciousness, (apart from these major characteristics), he also proceeded to explain the *purpose* or *function* of consciousness. It has twofold purposes for the organism :

(i) It makes the human being as a better-adapted organism. It helps the persons in making conscious choice that helps in better adaptation with the environment.

(ii) Whenever the person is faced with any new problem requiring new adjustment, consciousness, by making appropriate relationship with the nervous system, helps the person a lot.

The entire stream of consciousness or thought, for James is the subject-matter of psychology and it is clearly reflected by adults, children, insane, animals, etc.

SIGNIFICANCE OF WILLIAM JAMES

Everyone has accepted the greatness of William James, yet it is difficult to point out to specific achievements in psychology as the basis of his greatness or reputation. He did not invent any technique or method as did Fechner and Helmholtz; he did not conduct any experiment except in his earliest phase; he did not systematize the various experimental results to formulate a theory as did Wundt; he did not formulate any original theory like Freud and Darwin nor did he define any new area of investigation as Galton did. What then is in James which earned him a place to be recognized as one of the distinguished founders of psychology ?

Boring (1950) has suggested three reasons for his greatness. Those reasons are as under :

(1) The first reason was personal. His personality was highly charming and magnetic. He had also an elegant writing style which were considered unparallel by many psychologists of his time.

(2) The second reason was negative. He, in fact, opposed to the elementalism of structuralism of Titchener and Wundt. He also opposed the psychology of Kulpe. Not only he opposed these dominant and influential psychologists but also offered an alternative approach about the nature of psychology in the time when psychology was being independent from philosophy.

(3) The third reason was positive. He has been considered as a

pioneer American psychologist who directed others to go where they already wanted to go. In this sense, he allowed psychology to come into being in America. He was one of the major antecedent forces in movements like functionalism, mental testing and behaviorism.

Apart from these three reasons, some other reasons have also been suggested by contemporary psychologists for James' eminence. Some of these reasons may be cited as under :

(4) James was such a psychologist who could be considered as a *pragmatist*. As a pragmatist, he had emphasized upon usefulness of a psychological study. Today the days of pure researches' in psychology are going to wane and psychologists as well as the common people are asking question : What useful purpose can the psychological investigations be put to ? In answering this question, James' pragmatism has been one of the guiding principles.

(5) Recent movements like existential psychology and humanistic psychology have also been one of the reasons of James' popularity. In these movements psychologists are basically doing, nothing except that they are rediscovering James' stream of consciousness.

(6) James launched and popularized psychology and made the scholars of the day realized that this new branch had ample scope and therefore it must be contended with.

Thus, we find that there were several reasons of James' greatness. Despite the fact that he could be considered as a half-hearted experimentalist, he brought many problems on surface which made the psychologists of the day to owe their indebtedness. Stream of consciousness was one of such problems.

SOME PIONEER AMERICAN FUNCTIONALISTS: G. S. HALL (1844–1924) AND J. M. CATTELL (1860–1944)

There were some pioneer American functionalists whose viewpoints were important for later development of functionalism. Among them, G. S. Hall and J. M. Cattell were leading ones.

Granville Stanley Hall was born in a farming family although his father was in his early days a school teacher (Ross, 1972). After studying at Williams College, he went to the Union Theological Seminary, New York, to study for the ministry. Soon, he realized that this was not a correct vocation for him and by borrowing money from others, he left for Germany to study philosophy at the University of Berlin and Bonn. After returning from Germany, he got a temporary tutorship (1876-79) at Harvard University and this enabled him to study under William James and he obtained his Ph.D. degree in Psychology under James in 1878 on 'muscular perception of space'. After Harvard, he left again for Germany where he studied with Wundt at Leipzig University, lived next door to Fechner and also studied physiology under Ludwig. He was the first American student of Wundt. Thus Hall was a *hybrid psychologist* having features of both James and Wundt.

After staying for two years in Germany, he returned to America and in 1882 he was offered lectureship and in 1884 he became the Chairman of the department of psychology at the newly constituted John Hopkins University. In 1883 he opened the first psychological laboratory in U.S.A. At this University he had John Dewey and James McKeen Cattell as his students. In 1887, he founded the *American Journal of Psychology*. In 1891 he founded the *Pedagogical Seminary* (now named as *Journal of Genetic Psychology*). In 1892 he founded the *American Psychological Association* and became its first president.

In 1888 when Hall was only 44, he was asked to became the first president of the new Clark University. The post of president was an administrative post. He combined the presidency with the chair of psychology and later founded an active graduate school for doing research work to undergraduate students. At Clark University he was not only a successful administrator but also a good organizer. The American Psychological Association founded by him regularly met to discuss the various research papers and Hall was also instrumental in bringing here Freud, Jung and Ferenczi in 1909 when Clark University was celebrating its twentieth anniversary. These popular psychoanalysts introduced the technique of psychoanalysis to American psychologists. This illustrious gathering helped Hall in shifting the interests of American psychologists away from the German model. Hall produced eighty-one Ph. D.s at Clark University although only fewer of them could became popular in psychology. Lewis Terman, a porminent psychologist in the field of mental testing and individual differences, was one of them.

Hall had first turned to child psychology. He used the questionnaire, originated by Galton, in studying children's display of anger, fear, play, cry, etc. Results of such studies were published in the journal *Pedagogical Seminary* that had been founded in 1891. At Clark University he had also conducted several researches on children behaviours which were published in his two-volumed *Adolescence : Its Psychology* in 1904. His this publication had great heuristic value in the sense that it stimulated so many new psychological studies of children's problems. He also worked in the fields of applied psychology, educational psychology,

psychology of sex, psychology of religion, and even elimentary sensations. In his old age, he also became interested in the psychology of old age and published a book *Senescence* in 1922.

Thus we find that Hall who was the first American to study at Leipzig under Wundt, after returning to America deviated widely from the practice of the Leipzig approach. His this way of looking at the psychology resulted in development of psychology in many diverse directions. Particularly, the applied aspects of psychology greatly flourished.

James McKeen Cattell was the son of William Cattell who was president of Lafayette College. He completed his undergraduate course at Lafayette College and subsequently went to England and Germany in 1880 for two years. Then returned to America for a year and studied at John Hopkins University under G. S. Hall. In 1883 he went to Leipzig and served as pupil-assistant to Wundt for three years. He obtained his Ph. D. in 1886 under Wundt. In 1887 he was appointed lecturer in Psychology at the University of Pennsylvania. In 1888 he became lecturer at Cambridge University where he came first into contact with Sir Francis Galton whom he described as 'the greatest man I have ever known'. Then, Cattel became Professor of Psychology at Pennsylvania in 1888 and remained there till 1891. He had also established a psychological laboratory. The most important outcome of this short period of professorship was his publication on the *perception of small differences* in 1892. From Pennsylvania, Cattell went to Columbia University in 1891 where he formed a second laboratory. Here he remained for twenty-six years (1891-1917). Here on the invitation as well as the financial help from Cattell, E. L. Thorndike reached with his two best trained chikens. At Columbia, Thorndike experimented with different kinds of animals like cats, dogs, etc. in different kinds of puzzle boxes. During his stay at Columbia for twenty-six years (1891-1917) Cattell supervised 344 doctoral dissertations leading to Ph. D. degrees. Among them, Thorndike, Woodworth, Strong and Dashiell were the most distinguished ones who obtained the degree. In 1917 when America entered into the First World War, Cattell was dismissed by Columbia University due to his pacifistic stand which was fearlessly and frankly expressed by him. However, he sued the university for the order and was awarded 40,000 Dollars as compensations. But he was never reinstated.

In his post dismissal years, he was actively engaged in editorships and establishing new organization. In 1921 he founded the *Psychological Corporation* that acted as an institute for researches in applied psychology as well as an advisory body for industry, education and other practical problems. This institute became highly successful both financially as well as in terms of getting scientific prominence. He also became the president of Ninth International Congress of Psychology in 1929. He died in 1944.

Cattell's work is scattered among many topics published in several books and journals. They were brought, together by six of his students under the following six categories:

1. ***Reaction time*** : Cattell had started work on reaction time at John Hopkins University and took them to the Leipzig University. He did various experiments in different fields of reaction times and by 1902, his work was almost finished. He also developed some new apparatus to be used in reaction time experiments and modified the existing ones. He thus invented lip-key and voice-key to be used in the study of vocal reaction times and modified and improved the chronoscope. He studied reaction time as it was dependent upon sense organ and peripheral location of tactual stimuli. On the basis of the results of his own experiments, he became convinced that the subtractive procedure was not a valid procedure to study time for the process of choice and the time for the process of discrimination—the former being greater than the latter. This subtractive procedure had already lost its importance at Leipzig due to frequent criticisms by Kulpe. He also studied muscular time and sensorial time and took muscular time as the subcortical reflex. He reported that the sensory type of subjects gave sensorial reaction time more quickly than the muscular reaction time. However, he was not ready to accept Lange's classical distinction between the sensorial reaction time and muscular reaction time and that the sensorial reaction time takes 1/10 of a second less than muscular reaction time.

2. ***Association*** : Cattell also conducted several researches on association times. An association time was one which elapses between presentation of a word by the experimenter and its related associated word told by the subject. He studied two types of association—first, constrained associations and second, free associations. In constrained association the subjects were required to give word having specific association such as supraordinate association or superordinate association with the word presented by the experimenter. In free association, no such restriction or constrain was imposed and he was left to say any word that he thinks to be associated in any way. His findings revealed that constrained association took shorter time than free association. Likewise, supraordinate association took shorter time than subordinate association. 'Goat—Animal' and 'Fruit—Apple' are

examples of supraordinate association and subordinate association respectively.

3. *Perception and Reading* : In the field of perception he was mostly interested in visual perception particularly the retinal time of visual perception. Subsequently, he also studied the time that a person takes in perceiving and naming the objects such as letters, words, sentences, colours, forms, etc. In these studies he used tachistoscope for presenting the objects for brief period of time. His findings revealed that time for each item decreases up to simultaneous presentation of five objects. These experiments are today regarded as classical experiments on *span or range of attention.* Through these experiments he was interested in studying the relation of times to similarity. His findings revealed that the subjects perceived more letters when they (letters) formed a word and they also perceived more words when they formed a sentence. This happened because the combination became familiar to the subjects.

He also studied reading time in relation to familiarity of language. His results were that reading times for different languages varied with degree of familiarity without awareness of the subjects. The reading time of the familiar language was shorter than the reading time of less familiar language. He also used this technique in the legibility of different letters of alphabet. Such innovations by Cattell inspired the subsequent psychologists to do some more studies leading to some practical results.

4. *Psychophysics* : Cattell had no sympathy with the work of Germans like Fechner, Muller and Wundt in the field of psychophysics simply because they were based upon introspection. He did work with Fullerton in the field of psychophysics. They criticized the psychophysical methods of Fechner. About the method of average error they said that in this method time given to the subjects for equating the stimulus was not controlled and therefore, many unwanted factors related to this came into force. Likewise, they also criticized the method of limits on the ground that the judgement *'equal'* that applied to the range of stimuli, was dependent purely upon introspective experiences which produced greater variability in practice. They were, however, sympathetic to the method of constant stimuli because this method, according to Cattell, made use of the normal law of error. Although in this method, subjects also gave judgement *'equal'*, but Cattell easily avoided this source of error by dividing such judgements equally between the other two categories of judgements, namely, heavier and lighter (in case of weight discriminatiion experiment).

Cattell, in collaboration with Fullerton, also substituted Weber-Fechner law by a law of the square root. In other words, $S = K \log R$ was substituted by $S = K \quad R$. This substitution was based upon both theoretical rationale as well as upon the empirical results. Apart from this substitution, Cattell also discovered a new psychophysical method in which amount of sensory difference was measured inversely by reaction time.

5. ***Order of merit or ranking method*** : This method was discovered by him in 1902 in his study of placing of shades of grey in order. He selected 200 shades of grey and the subjects were required to order those shades in degree of brightness. Errors were determined by reference to an objective scale for measuring difference in colour stimuli. After getting success in this method, he extended this method to the field of study of value judgements. He prepared a list of important scientific researchers in a particular discipline. He selected 10 distinguished scientists in a particular discipline to act as judges who ranked all the names in the list quite independently in order of scientific merit. These rankings were combined and a central tendency or average rank was computed. This average rank was approximation to 'actual order of merit'. This average rank served two purposes. First, the accuracy of each judge's rank was estimated by comparing it with average rank order. Second, the average rank when combined with other data helped Cattell in studying scientists in relation to place of birth, social status of parents, religion, education, etc. In order to know change in the trend of the background and training of scientists he repeated this study every seven years. Later, this method was widely applied in study of personalities and psychometric fields.

6. ***Individual difference*** : Cattell was also interested in the study of individual difference. As a consequence, he published in 1890 a research paper on mental tests and measurements. In 1893 he published another paper on tests of senses and faculties. E. L. Thorndike, one of the students of Cattell, also did a lot of researches in mental tests for animals by placing them into various puzzle boxes. Throndike was also encouraged by Cattell to plan similar mental tests for students studying at Teachers' College founded at Columbia.

On the whole, Cattell's psychology can be broadly said to be a psychology of human capacity. It is not concerned with analysis of human capacity into some conscious causes rather it is concerned with description of human nature in terms of its range and variability. That is why, Boring (1950) has considered this psychology of human capacity of Cattell as a functional psychology.

CHAPTER HIGHLIGHTS

1. Chronologically, William James belonged between Wundt (10 years his senior) and Titchener (25 years his junior). He was one of the greatest American psychologists. He strongly criticized elementarism and Wundtian introspectionism. He placed an extensive positive programme for development of psychology. In this massive programme for development, he emphasized upon what was called *pragmatism* which stated that validation of any knowledge in psychology must be done in terms of its values or utilities. In that sense, he has been considered as a pragmatist.
2. Williams James' psychology has been set down in his two-volumed *The Principles of Psychology* published in 1890. He defined psychology as the science of mental life both of its phenomena and of their conditions. By mental life, he meant consciousness. He pointed out that the starting point of psychology is immediately felt experience. This is what he referred to as *stream of consciousness* Explaining his view on stream of consciouseness, James pointed out five major characteristics of consciousness : it is *personal, always changing, continuous, deals with objects other than itself,* and *selective.* The *purpose* of consciousness is to help the persons in better adaptation to their environment. For studying mental life, James considered three methods—method of introspection, experimentation, and comparative method. Another of his very popular contribution to psychology has been in the field of emotion—the well-known James-Lange theory of emotion. According to this theory, the popular paradigm for explaining emotion that is stimulus (bear)—Experience (emotion)—Response (running) was replaced by Stimulus—Response—Experience. In other words, we see the stimulus such as bear, run away and therefore, afraid. Thus according to this theory, emotional behaviour precedes emotional experience His contribution in other fields like instinct, self and memory was no less important. Regarding the solution of mind-body problem, his position was that of an *interactionist.*
3. Although William James has been considered as one of the greatest American psychologists, yet it is difficult to point out to his specific achievements in psychology as the basis of his greatness. Boring (1950) has, however, pointed out *three* such reasons. First reason was *personal.* His personality was highly charming and magnetic. Second reason was *negative.* He opposed to the elementarism of Titchener and Wundt. Third reason was *positive.* He directed others to go where they already wanted to go.

4. Some other American psychologists' contributions were also important. These psychologists were contemporaries of William James and have been regarded as pioneer American functionalists. G. S. Hall and J. M. Cattell were two such psychologists. G. S. Hall was the first American to reach at leipzig University to study under Wundt. He obtained his Ph. D. degree under William James in 1878. Thus Hall was a hybrid psychologist having features of both James and Wundt. In 1883 the opened first psychological laboratory at John Hopkins University. In 1892 he founded *American Psychological Association* and he became its first president. In 1888 when Hall was only 44, he was asked to become the first president of Clark University. This was an administrative post. In 1909 he invited Freud, Jung and Ferenczi to participate in the twentieth anniversary of Clark University. Through their lectures these ditinguished guests introduced the technique of psychoanalysis to American psychologists. This has been considered as one the major achievements of Hall.
5. J. M. Cattell has been another distinguished American psychologist who had obtained Ph. D. degree under Wundt at Leipzig University. He was also pupil-assistant to Wundt. His work is scattered among many topics published in different books and journals. His students have made painstaking effort to summarize them under *six* major categories—reaction time, association, perception and reading, psychophysics, order-of-merit ranking method, and individual difference.

REVIEW QUESTIONS

1. "William James was a half-hearted experimentalist but still more popular than a whole-hearted experimentalist". Comment.
2. If you were William James, which of the two—Titchener or Wundt—you have preferred most ? Give reasons.
3. What do you mean by James' stream of consciousness ? In what ways it made him a very prominent psychologist.
4. What, in you opinion, were the major causes of eminence of William James ?
5. Discuss the major contributions of william James that helped in elevating the status of scientific psychology.
6. "G. S. Hall was hybrid psychologist having features of both William James and Wilhelm Wundt". Elucidate.

■

CHAPTER 8
FUNCTIONALISM

CHAPTER PREVIEW

Several antecedent forces were active in final shaping of functionalism as a system. Of these, evolutional principles enunciated by Spencer, Darwin and Galton were important ones. Hence, they have been emphasized. Another major antecedent force was the psychology of William James who has been one of the greatest American psychologists of the nineteenth century and has been regarded as a forerunner of functionalism.

Functionalism was formally founded by the psychologists of Chicago University. As founders, the names of John Dewey and James Angell are frequently taken. Harvey Carr has been the developer of functionalism. The contributions of these pioneer psychologists of functionalism have been discussed separately. The widest coverage has been given to the viewpoints of Harvey Carr under whose regime functionalism reached the peak of its popularity.

As a system, functionalists' viewpoint regarding the subject-matter of psychology, methods of psychology, its basic postulates, mind-body problems, principles of connection, principles of selection, nature of data, etc. have been adequately explained.

R. S. Woodworth has been held responsible for bringing functional psychology to Columbia University although he departed enough from functionalist's programme to develop what he named as dynamic psychology. James McKeen Cattell and Edward Lee Thorndike also contributed to the development of Columbia's functional psychology. In fact, Cattell and Thorndike's contributions in education and mental testing were the leading ones.

A separate section has been added to recognize the major lapses and weakness of the functional psychology. Four major weaknesses of the system have been recognized. First is related to the use of the term of function; second is related to the subject-matter of psychology; third is related to their failure to make a clear-cut distinction between applied psychology and pure psychology and fourth is related to its teleological character.

Structuralism and functionalism were the earlier schools of psychology and each make attack and counterattack over the other. This happened because of some fundamental differences between the general outlook of these two schools. Four such differences have been discussed. These differences relate to the subject-matter, methodology, mind-body problem, etc.

Lastly, as a system, what is he fate of functionalism ? has been discussed. No doubt as a system it is a no longer alived today but its ideas are still carried out by many learning psychologists as well as by those actively engaged in mental testing movement. In this sense, we can say that functionalism has taken rebirth. Therefore, like structuralism, functionalism was never rejected by the psychologists. The only thing that can be said is that it was absorbed into the mainstream of modern psychology having its obvious impact into some applied fields.

ANTECEDENTS OF FUNCTIONALISM

Functionalism as a school arose as a protest against structuralism. It was one of the most flexible schools of American psychologists. Many antecedent forces were said to be working behind the birth of this system. Those antecedent forces can be divided into two classes—*evolutionary theory* and *the psychology of William James.*

1. *Evolutionary theory*

Spencer, Darwin and Galton were the three primary evolutionary sources that affected the formulation of functionalism. In 1885 Spencer published his famous book *Principles of Psychology.* For Spencer, evolution involved a change from indefinite homogeneity to definite heterogeneity having a continuous process of integration and differentiation. Such changes are nothing but a continuous process of *adjustment* and adaptations to external conditions or environments. Every animal responds in a certain way to his environment. The higher an organism was on the evolutionary ladder, the more complex and differentiated were its responses. The simplest responses are inflexible and represent a total adjustment to environment. These are called *reflexes.* Higher animals show complex reflex actions which are called *instincts.* The higher animals generally show more complex and flexible behaviours which evolve out of simple and undifferentiated ones through the process of adjustment. All higher mental functions are part of this process. Spencer also pointed out that the more useful a function is, the more pleasant it is. Such useful functions are transmitted by heredity to the offsprings. According to Spencer, since the mind evolved along with the body, with greater differentiation, the more *useful* experiences were born. In this way, we find that for Spencer continuity between species particularly between animals and humans was the key factor in evolution. Spencer took it to be a fundamental factor in the development of consciousness out of living materials and the fundamental to the development of living materials out of inanimate nature. In fact, this represented a transfer of biological problem into the field of psychology and made Spencer's psychology the first functional psychology.

Charles Darwin was another important person who could be regarded as evolutionary forerunner of functionalism. He published his *Origin of Species* in 1859 and *Expressions of the Emotions in Man and Animals* in 1872. Darwin, appreciating the stand of Spencer, pointed out that life is struggle for existence. Only better-equipped or fit individuals have more chance for survival and for reproduction through the process of natural selection. In other words, the better an animal or individual adapts to his environment, the more likely he is to survive and reproduce. Those who fail to adapt, die. Psychology studies those various ways of adjustment. All mental activities, Darwin argued, should be interpreted as adjustive functions of the individual. Darwin also believed that the whole process of adjustment and adaptation applies to the psychological as well as physical functions because mind evolved along with the body. Darwin also considered emotions to be biologically useful functions and their expression served definite functions. For example, showing teeth in anger indicates readiness to fight, desire to overcome one's enemy and survive. On the whole, Darwin's theory was instrumental in establishing continuity between human beings and animals that was later considered important for the extended study of animal psychology and widened the scope for functional psychology.

Sir Francis Galton was much inspired by his cousin Darwin in studying the role of hereditary factors in human beings. Galton placed great emphasis upon the study of individual differences. His book *Hereditary Genius* was published in 1869 and contained the studied of individual differences in intelligence. He applied statistical methods to the study of problems of genetics and his study of individual differences led to the utilitarian point of view in psychology by emphasizing upon development of mental traits. Such utilitarian viewpoint had a considerable impact upon later foundation of functionalism.

2. *William James*

William James has been regarded as one important forerunner of functionalism. It is said that he founded functionalism as a system (but not as a school) in his two volume work ***Principles of Psychology*** published in 1890 (Marx & Cronan Hillix, 1987). Jame's view was that behaviour is *adaptable* and in order to survive psychologically, an organism must be able to *adjust* to its environment. This view became the central theme of functionalism. Sometimes such adaptation was having more of a bodily process and at other times, it became more of the domain of the mind. Thus in any behaviour both mind and body were involved. Jamės also held the view that consciousness is the product of evolution. Like other functions, it has been evolved for a particular use. Jame's view on *pragmatism* had also a direct influence on functionalism. James was a psychologist, a biologist, an expert in physiology and above all, a philosopher. As a pragmatists, he pointed out that the validation of any knowledge is to be done in terms of its consequences or its usefulness. The functional psychologists carried James' pragmatism into their psychology to broaden the base.

Thus evolutionary theories of Spencer, Darwin and Galton were major forces that influenced functionalism. William James had also been influenced by such evolutionary theories and his psychology, in turn, influenced functionalism to a greater extent.

FOUNDERS OF CHICAGO'S FUNCTIONAL PSYCHOLOGY: JOHN DEWEY, JAMES ROWLAND ANGELL AND HARVEY CARR

Functionalism was the first American school in true sense of the term. Although William James had set the stage, this school was founded by John Dewey and James Rowland Angell at the University of Chicago in 1894 when they came to teach psychology at this University. Harvey Carr may be more appropriately considered as its *developer* rather than *founder*. Functionalism reached the peak of its popularity under the leadership of Carr. Later, Robert Sessions Woodworth brought functionalism to Columbia University although his psychology departed enough from the functionalists' position to develop a new system called *dynamic psychology*.

Although functionalism was never a highly differentiated system, some psychologists have tried to define it in loose language. For example Woodworth (1948) had pointed out : "A psychology that attempts to give an accurate and systematic answer to the question 'what do men do ?' and 'why they do it ?' is called a *functional psychology*." But Woodworth's this definition was not wholly adequate because a true functional psychology is also concerned with the uses or utilities of person's behaviour and consciousness in making adaptation to the environment. Thus a functional psychologist also studies functional relationship between antecedent forces and behaviour or consciousness. To have a clear understanding of functional psychology, it is essential to examine the contributions of important functionalists. We shall first consider the contributions of founders, then of its developer.

***John Dewey* (1859-1952)**

Dewey was prominent philosopher, educator and psychologist of his time. He studied under G. S. Hall at John Hopkins University from where he took Ph. D. in Philosophy. Before coming to the University of Chicago in 1894, he taught at Minnesota as well as Michigan. At Michigan, it was Dewey who had sent James Angell to study with William James at Harvard University. Later, Angell rejoined him at Chicago University and founded the functionalism.

Dewey published a book *Psychology* in 1886 and was much pleased with its popularity. But its popularity was soon shadowed by William James' book *Principles of Psychology* that appeared in 1890. Ten years later, that is, in 1896 Dewey published a short research paper entitled *The Reflex-arc concept in Psychology*. This paper marks the starting-point of functionalism as a definite movement. In fact, through this paper he attacked the psychological elementalism of the structuralists. He emphasized that the psychological activity should not be broken down into elements or parts rather they should be considered as a whole. Thus he tried to replace the molecular analysis of structuralism by molar analysis of psychological activity. In this paper he lodged a strong protest against the traditional analysis of reflex-arc concept that broke behaviour into stimulus and response units and also emphasized that sensory nerves and motor nerves that participate in reflexes behave separately. Dewey's view was that such distinctions between stimulus and response were not based upon actual differences in existing reality rather that were purely functional and were based upon different roles that they play in the total co-ordination of behaviour in maintaining to goal. Thus the stimulus-response distinction was artificial and it persisted because of old mind-body dualism. He used a familiar example to show inadequacy of explanation of behaviour in terms of reflexes. He gave an example of child who saw a flame, reached there and burnt his fingers. This act or behaviour was not a simple sequence of three discrete events—seeing, reaching and being burnt. It could be said that seeing was the stimulus and reaching was the response and that the sensation for seeing come first and then motor act, that is, reaching followed. In fact, sensation does not precede movement or motor activities because the two can't be separated from each other. Thus there is no partition or division between the activities of the organism. Dewey viewed behaviour as *total co-ordination* that helped the organism in making adaptation to the situation. Thus the total co-ordination of behaviour and not the part of it, should be the unit of study of psychologists. On the whole, it can be said that Dewey's concern was with the act as a function, particularly adaptive function.

Thus from Dewey's research paper two fundamental points were derived :

(i) In studying behaviour molar approach rather than molecular approach should be adopted. This stand of Dewey was appreciated by Gestalt psychology that came into being 20 years later.

(ii) The behaviour should be studied in context of its function particularly adaptive function.

Dewey's above research paper may be regarded as the last contribution to psychology. During the remaining days of stay at Chicago, he became interested in education and philosophy. He launched *progressive education movement* and applied pragmatism in education. He emphasized the notion that the education is life, learning is doing and teaching should be student-oriented rather then subject-oriented. In 1904, he left Chicago to join Columbia University as professor of philosophy. He remained there for the rest of his career. As a social philosopher, Dewey was extremely concerned with man's welfare. He maintained that knowledge played a vital role in person's survival and adjustment. His this view has also been regarded as one of the contributions in augmenting the scope of functionalism.

James Rowland Angell (1867-1949)

Angell belonged to a well-educated family. His father was president of the University of Vermont and later of the University of Michigan. His grandfather was also president of Brown University. At Michigan University, Angell had studied under John Dewey who later sent him to William James at Harvard University from where he took his M. A. degree. He had also occasioned to study with Wundt and was a lifelong friend of Titchener with whom he met in Germany. He never received Ph. D. degree in his hectic career though he was awarded twenty-three honorary doctorates in whole of his career. He joined the University of Chicago as professor of psychology in 1894 where his beloved teacher, John Dewey, was already working. At Chicago, Angell separated the department of psychology from the department of philosophy and became its Chairman after Dewey went to Columbia as a professor of philosophy. He made the department a centre for research and teaching. J. B. Watson and Harvey Carr were among the distinguished students.

After joining Chicago University, Angell published a paper with A. W. Moore. This paper appeared in the same volume of *psychological Review* (1896) in which Dewey's paper on reflex arc had been published. In this paper he published the results of the experiments on reaction time. In 1903 he published a research paper showing the relationship between the functional psychology and the structural psychology and in 1904 he published a textbook. However, his clearest exposition of the functionalism position was found in his presidential address in 1906 to the American Psychological Association entitled "The Province of Functional Psychology" that was published in 1907. In this address he outlined *three* separate conceptions of functional psychology. Finally, he left Chicago University in 1921 to join Yale University as its president. He remained there until his retirement in 1937. It was natural that during days of presidency his interest in psychology declined due to heavy administrative pressure.

The three separate conceptions of Angell's viewpoint towards the functional psychology had been outlined in 1906 presidential address to American Psychological Association. Those three separate conceptions were as under :

1. Functionalism was contrasted with structuralism. The structuralists addressed themselves to contents of consciousness whereas the functionalists addressed themselves to the operations of a mental process. In other words, the major task of structuralism was to analyse the consciousness into its different contents or elements whereas the major task of functionalists was to discover how a mental process operates, what it accomplishes for the person and under what conditions it appears. A mental function studied by the functionalists was an enduring function and not a glimpse of momentary consciousness as studied by the structuralists.
2. Functional psychology was the "psychology of the fundamental utilities of consciousness". The mind is always engaged in mediating between the environment and the needs of the organism. Any psychological function, therefore, can be considered as accommodation one or as adaptive process. Since these functions are not isolated events rather parts of a larger functioning organism, they help the organism in making better adaptations to the environment. Such adaptations help the organism in its survival.

3. Functional psychology may be regarded as a typical method of dealing with the mind-body problem. Thus it may be regarded as the psychology of psychophysical relations. It was concerned with the entire psychophysical relationship between the organism and its environment. Thus functionalism dealt with the totality of relationship of organism to environment including mind-body functions. Therefore, the study of non-conscious and habitual behaviour were also included in functional psychology. According to this third view, mind and body could not be separated but belonged to the same whole. There occurred constant interplay between these two.

Angell also made it clear that these three conceptions of the functional psychology were not independent rather interrelated. The first two conceptions of the functional psychology restricted it to the study of conscious experience. The third conception widened the scope of the functional psychology by including study of non-conscious and habitual behaviour (Marx and Cronan-Hillix, 1987).

Harvey A. Carr (1873-1954)

Harvey, A. Carr is another important representative of the functional psychology. He obtained his Bachelor degree and Master degree from the University of Calorado. Then he went to the University of Chicago to study experimental psychology and obtained his Ph. D. degree in 1905. In 1921 when Angell left Chicago University to take presidency at Yale University, he took Angell's position as head of the psychology department although this appointment was not formalized for two additional years. By this time, functionalism had completely settled down as one of the dominant and recognized school. However, it was under the leadership of Carr that Chicago functionalism flourished and reached the peak of its popularity. He published his famous book *Psychology : A Study of Mental Activity* in 1925. In this book he expressed functionalism as complete and developed system. Accordingly, we shall now consider Chicago functionalism as a system as developed by Carr who pointed out adjustment or adaptation as the main tenets of functional psychology.

FUNCTIONALISM AS A SYSTEM

As we know, functionalism as a system rose to its peak of popularity during Carr's tenure as chairman of the department of psychology at Chicago University. Consequently, we shall discuss it in Carr's perspective as outlined in his book *Psychology : A Study of Mental Activity* published in 1925. The main tenets are as under :

1. *Definition and Subject-matter of Psychology*

Psychology, according to Carr, is the study of mental activity or adaptive behaviour. Thus adaptive behaviour or act is the key concept in psychology. It involves processes like perception, memory, feeling, judgment and will. These processes help us in making adjustment to the environment. Thus psychology does not deal with elements or contents but with processes. Carr regarded consciousness as an abstract concept like intelligence. Being an abstract concept, it can't play an important role in adapting the organism to the environment. It can't accent for our adaptive behaviour which is main concern. From this emphasis, it becomes obvious that Carr was bringing functional psychology nearer to behaviourism.

According to Carr, adaptive behaviour has three characteristics : (i) a motivating stimulus, (ii) a sensory stimulus, and (iii) a response that modifies the situation in a way that satisfy the motivating stimulus. When a thirsty person reaches the water, drinks it to the point of satiation, he is showing an adaptive act or behaviour. In this example, thirst is a motivating stimulus, water is sensory stimulus and drinking is an adaptive act. The motive as stimulus goes on dominating our behaviour until organism acts in such a why that the stimulus is no longer effective. Thus motive arouses and directs our activity. There are *three* ways in which adaptive act may brought the motive to an end. *First* way is that the adaptive act may directly remove the motive. For example, eating may remove hunger. *Second*, the actual continuance of the act may disrupt motive by introducing a still more stronger stimulus. For example, a person cutting a tree in sun may quit due to sheer exhaustion. *Third*, the adaptive act may produce some sensory consequences that may resolve the motive. For example, a servant reaching for a hot kettle on oven may drop it because of the feeling of pain to his fingers.

In higher organisms like man, Carr divided adaptive act into two parts. The first part consists of making attentive adjustments in which desired motor behaviours and appropriate sensory adjustments take place. In the second part the consummation of acts after achieving the goal takes place. Carr also recognized two kinds of consequences of an adaptive act. One type of consequence of any adaptive act is its satisfaction due to resolution of motivating stimulus and second type of consequence involves some auxiliary effect. For example, eating not only resolves our hunger motive (first type of consequence) but it also gives nourishment to our body (second type of consequence). Carr made it clear that a behaviour should not be explained in terms of this auxiliary or ulterior consequence rather it should be explained only in terms of the motive itself. We eat primarily because we are driven by hunger (and not by nourishment).

2. *Postulates*

Although there were not any clearly stated postulates of functionalism, it had certain assumption about psychological activities. Marx & Cronan-Hillix (1987) have stated those postulates as under :

(i) All activities are initiated by some sort of sensory stimulus. In absence of such stimulus, no response can occur.

(ii) All sensory stimuli affect not only motives but also behaviour.

(iii) Behaviour is intrinsically adaptive as well as purposive.

(iv) Behaviour is a continuous and co-ordinated process and it tends to modify the stimulus situation.

3. *Methodology*

Carr accepted different methods for studying mental activity. Functionalism accepted the method of structuralism, that is, introspection but added observation. He also accepted experimentation to be the most desirable method of gathering data but he also cautioned that in human studies complete controls were highly difficult to achieve with experimental method. He also recognized method of common observation as a means of gaining knowledge about an event. Thus we see that functionalism did not adhere to anyone particular method. The best method depended upon the nature of the problem being investigated.

4. *Mind-body problem*

Carr explained mind-body problem in a very simple and uncontroversial way. He described mental activity as being psychophysical one. It is psychical in the sense that individual has some knowledge of the activity being done. He does not perceive, reason or will without being aware of it. A mental activity is physical in the sense that it is a reaction of the physical organism. He made no effort to explain the connection between the physical and psychical aspect. The relationship was simply accepted as it appeared in our experience. Thus for functionalists, the mental activity did not exist as a separate entity as it existed for structuralism. Angell in his article "The Province of Functional Psychology" had also made it clear that mind and body could not be separated and they, in effect, belonged to the same whole. However, the two interacted. *Any adaptive act or mental act involves the totality of both psychical and physical events.* Thus early functionalists like

Angell took an *interactionist* position like William James. The later functionalists like Carr while talking about a psychophysical process, incorporated a definite *dualism* though the solution for him seemed to be one of doubled-aspectism. In nutshell, it can be said that the functionalists were dualistic in the sense of recognizing both psychical and physical aspects of experience but it was not dualistic in the sense of separating them in structuralist-manner.

5. *Nature of data*

Functionalism stressed more on the adjustment or adaptation of the organism to the environment. By emphasizing upon adjustment, functionalism stressed upon the objective data and by accepting introspection, it also showed its adherence to the subjective data. However, as functionalism aged, it laid increasing emphasis upon the objective data.

There are sample evidences to support the use of objective data in functionalism. Carr studied processes like perception, emotion and thinking. He defined *perception* as the cognition of something present in relation to some act of adjustment. He considered perception to be an adaptive act. For him, it was also a selective process because the organism responded to only certain aspect of incoming sensory stimuli. Perception was different from sensation in the sense that it also added meaning to the sensory experiences. He also believed that perception was influenced by variables other than past experiences. Important variables influencing perception were needs and attitudes of the perceiver as well as his purpose and goal. This view of Carr opened the subsequent venue for research in the influence of personality variables in the field of perception. Carr also studied *emotion* and considered it as *organic adjustment*. Emotions occurs where there does not seem to be scope for adjustment. In emotion the extra energy that the person gets to meet the external situation is from internal activities like greater heart rate, increase in blood pressure and respiration, etc. He considered *thinking* as an apprehension of the situations or objects that were not immediately present in the environment. He pointed out that ideas or thoughts were readily substituted for previously responded stimuli through perception. These ideas or thoughts produced such responses that had adaptive significance. For example, thought of catching fire in home may lead a person to another safest place. Carr also made it clear that such thoughts could be a sound basis for showing creativity because it might result in creative adaptive behaviour. More or less similar explanation for *reasoning* was provided by Carr. Like thinking, reasoning had also adaptive significance. In study of perception, thinking and emotion introspective data were considered relevant.

6. *Principles of Connection*

The principles of connection were nothing but the principles of learning and hence, were the central point of focus for functionalists' research programme. Carr adopted the principles of association directly from associationistic tradition. He distinguished between *descriptive laws of association* and *explanatory laws of association*. The law of similarity could be placed under the former category and the law of contiguity could be placed in the latter category. He divided the explanatory laws into two categories—*origin or functions of association* and *fundamental strength of associations*. Contiguity may be placed into the first category because it threw light upon origin of association. Functional strength explained why some associations are stronger than others. The law of frequency or repetition comes under this category. Greater repetition of association results in increased associative strength.

Hilgard and Bower (1975) have summarized functionalists' position on learning in a nice way. According to them, the basic functionalists principles involved in learning process were as under :

(i) There are individual differences in the capacity of learner.

(ii) Differential practice leads to different forms of learning curves.

(iii) Motivation is essential for learning.

(iv) The degree of meaning is a dimension over which material can be scaled from the most meaningful to the most nonsensical.

7. *Principles of selection*

Carr also concentrated upon mechanisms of behavior selection. He regarded *attention, motives* and *learning's* to be the three primary agents of behaviour selection. He considered attention as nothing more than sensory-motor adjustment. It tended to facilitate perception. Motives were defined as a relatively persistent stimulus that directed actions. Hunger is motive in the sense that it directs our behaviour in a certain way. Learning was regarded as the basic agent of behaviour selection and it operates in the three ways :

(i) Some adaptative mechanisms or associations are acquired through experience.

(ii) As associations or adaptative mechanisms are acquired, other aspects of stimulating situation somehow come to he associated with the response (as it happens in conditioning) and in future, becomes capable of eliciting it.

(iii) Some adaptative mechanisms or associations are learnt because they are imposed by society. For example, we learn to have or to show affection towards certain caste and class of people.

In this way we find that Carr laid down the basic tenets of functionalism. In fact, in his time as a system functionalism appeared to be the most fundamental American psychology making concentration upon applied aspects of psychology in a coherent way.

COLUMBIA'S FUNCTIONAL PSYCHOLOGY

The functional psychology at Columbia University enjoyed more freedom from dualistic restriction and descriptive explanation. A glimpse of this freedom is clearly seen in the contributions of three most influential psychologists, namely, James McKeen Cattell, Edward Lee Thorndike and Robert Sessions Woodworth.

Jame McKeen Cattell's contribution as a functionalist had already been examined in chapter 6. He had studied with Wundt and obtained Ph. D. degree under him. After returning to America from Germany, he had worked for twenty-six years (1891-1917) at Columbia University. Later, he had been dismissed by Columbia University for his pacifistic stand towards America's entry into Second World War. His contributions particularly in the field of individual differences, reaction time and psychophysics were the most notable one and his functionalists' position was most obvious one. The reader is reffered to chapter 6 for detailed study of his contributions in these fields.

Edward Lee Thorndike (1874-1949) has been another most influential Columbia psychologist who can be regarded as an important functionalist, though he preferred to be called as a *connectionist*. Unlike many of his predecessors, he had received all his training in America. After graduating from Wesleyan University he went to Harvard to study English literature and philosophy. He worked under William James. At Harvard, his first research was conducted in the field of animal learning. This involved baby chicks and the experiment was conducted under primitive conditions as there was no room for such study in laboratory of Harvard University. Thorndike's landlady objected to his keeping of chicks in his room and James tried to find space in the laboratory and museum at Harvard but remained unsuccessful. This problem was finally solved by placing the chicks in the cellar of William James' house—a research project which was also enjoying to Jame's children. Later, at the invitation and the financial help rendered by James McKeen Cattell, Thorndike went to Columbia along with two of his best trained chicks. At Columbia, Cattell encouraged his work on animal intelligence.

Therefore, he studied with cats, dogs and monkeys in different kinds of puzzle boxes. He had constructed fifteen puzzle boxes for cats, nine boxes for dogs and three for chicks. He finished off his animal researches, and took his Ph. D. on the thesis *Animal Intelligence : An experimental study of associative processes in animals*. This thesis was published in 1898 and is now considered as one of the classic treatises on animal learning. This thesis was republished with further papers on various animal experiments in 1911. Heidbreder (1961) had pointed out two major reasons of the popularity of Thorndike's this book. *First*, it presented the first systematic study of animal intelligence by means of laboratory experiments and *second*, it led to the formulation of a theory of learning that attracted a number of psychologists for fruitful researches. His theory of learning will be discussed in *chapter 8* when we shall be considering him as an associationist or connectionist.

Cattell requested Thorndike to extend his interest from animal learning to the problems of human learning. From 1902 and onwards, Thorndike became more interested in educational psychology. In 1903 he published *Educational Psychology* and his status was raised from instructor to a full professor. In 1904 he published *Introduction to the Theory of Mental and Social Measurements*. This was the year when Dewey had come from Chicago University to Teachers College, Columbia where Thorndike was a professor. Like Dewey, Thorndike also became interested in measurement in education and studied problems relating to education in laboratory. He had no faith in minute introspection's of the trained observers like Wundt and Titchener. Therefore, he intensively studied the performances of several subjects and analyzed the results statistically.

In this way due to influence of Thorndike's work, psychological experiments stepped aside from the old and beaten path and there was brought greater flexibility in the design of the laboratory experiments in psychology. Thorndike's experimental designs used with animal subjects were soon extended to human subjects.

Robert Sessions Woodworth (1869-1962) was another leading Columbia functionalist. Boring (1950), Schultz (1969) and Marx and Cronan-Hillix (1987) have termed him as a functionalists' although he departed enough from the established functionalists' tradition to develop a new system often called as *dynamic psychology*. However, we shall here consider Woodworth more as a functionalist rather than as formulator of dynamic psychology although it is a bit difficult to separate these two aspects of Woodworth.

Woodworth studied psychology and philosophy with William James and Royce at Harvard University. He took his Ph. D. degree under Cattell in 1899 from Columbia University where he met Thorndike who also obtained his Ph. D. under Cattell. After that Woodworth taught physiology for three years in NewYork hospitals and one year with Sherington, the famous physiologist, at Liverpool. In 1903 he came back to Columbia University as instructor and was elevated to the rank of professor in 1909. He succeeds Cattell as head of the department of psychology in 1917 (when Cattell retired). He retired in 1942.

Woodworth's professional career started at about time when Thorndike had started working over animal intelligence and had ended in modern period. He published six most important books : *Le Movement* (1903), his revision of Ladd's *Physiological Psychology* (1911), *Dynamic Psychology* (1917), *Psychology* (1921), *Contemporary Schools of Psychology* (1931), and *Experimental Psychology* (1938). His last three books have been very popular and therefore, have been revised several times. *Psychology* was revised several times and had firth edition in 1947. *Experimental Psychology* was later revised by Harold Schlosberg in 1954 and was one of the major handbook in the field of experimental psychology. In 1956 he was awarded the first Gold Medal from the American Psychological Foundation. He revised his *Contemporary Schools of Psychology* in 1948 and 1964.

In fact, Woodworth was first a functional psychologist and then, a dynamic psychologist. He bears many resemblance's with Cicago functionalists. Still he wanted to develop a functionalism independent of the Chicago functionalists. Like his Chicago counterparts, he was not fascinated to conduct experiments with nonsense syllables. In formulating his system he was more truly devoted to evolutionary principles than his Chicago counterparts. He laid emphasis upon the study of cause-effect relationship. In other words, he emphasized upon the *response* and *factors* that caused it to occur. In this way, he was one of the earliest S-R (Stimulus-response) psychologist. But later he also considered those things to be very important that went inside the organism. Thus for S-R formula, he substituted S-O-R (stimulus-organism-response) formula. Woodworth liked to begin with the response and then, investigated the antecedent conditions, of which stimulus was one part. Other factor of the conditions was organism with its store of energy called *drive* as well as other physiological events. In fact, the crux of Woodworth's system lay in his account of *drive* and *mechanism*. Drive answered *why* of behaviour and *mechanism* answered *how* of behaviour. Applying this distinction to Thorndike's Cat in puzzle box in early days at Columbia, Woodworth pointed out that animal's biting, pushing, scratching, constituted mechanisms and hunger was the drive. In this example, we see a clear distinction between mechanism and drive. However, Woodworth pointed out that it was also possible for a mechanism to acquire its own drive function. What was previously only a mechanism may also involve drive or become a drive for other acts and run under their own power. G. W. Allport (1937) later developed a similar idea in his famous motivational concept called *functional autonomy*. Thus Woodworth's idea of mechanism was very similar to Carr's *adaptive act* because behaviours included under mechanism were purposive responses. In defining psychology Woodworth included both behaviour and consciousness and did not completely excluded introspection. His functionalism represented a true eclecticism because he tried to take the best from all different systems. Boring (1950 : 565) has very nicely commented, "Half of what he says about freedom from constraint, about using causal relations, about employing introspection and physiology and the study of movements as the occasion requires is good functionalism."

CRITICISMS OF FUNCTIONALISM

Functionalism had to face many objections. Some of the vital objections may be enumerated as under :

1. Some critics have pointed out that functionalism used its basic concept 'function" in vague and vacillating sense. The concept of 'Function' has many different meanings. For example, a function may mean activity much as perceiving, breathing, digesting, etc. It may also mean utility of an activity for the organism. For example, the function of breathing is to purify the blood. Still, there is a third meaning of function (familiar in mathematics) to denote dependence of one variable upon another. We may, for example, say that breathing is a function of lungs' activities. Functionalists tried to use the term function in both mathematical sense as well as utilitarian sense. This created a vague impression about functionalism. Such vague, use of the term has been cited as a sign of confusion and inconsistency in functionalism. Carr, however, has argued in a different vein. He has pointed out that these dual usage of the term is not inconsistent and the similar uses of the term are also found in biology.

2. Functionalism was also attacked by structuralists who preferred contents to functions. They further pointed out that the study of functions, utilities and values was such that none could be observed

introspectively. Therefore, none ·could from the subject-matter of psychology. Although this criticism is not considered valid today, but in its day, it was of utmost importance because similar attack was made by functionsalists towards structuralism. Functionalists had attacked by claiming that psychology could not be the study of elements of static consciousness.

3. The functionalists had wider interest in applied aspects and made valuable contributions towards making it still more applied. Critics pointed out that functionalists failed to make a clear-cut distinction between pure science and applied science. Their position as applied scientists would have been more clear had they been pointed an obvious stand distinct from the pure scientists. Modern psychologists, however, don't give much weight to this criticism because both pure and applied scientists today use same scientific methods and procedures. The distinction, if any, between the two depends upon the purpose of the investigation.

4. Functionalism emphasized upon the goals and utilitarian concepts and in doing so, it has been accused of being teleological (the future governs the present). This was, of course, a serious criticism for determinists but could not be regarded as a very uncommon position. McDougall, Tolman, Adler and Jung were also teleological. Moreover, this criticism becomes useless in the present context because functionalism used only teleological concepts in describing its data but never provided teleological explanation (Heidbreder, 1961). It used teleological concepts whenever it emphasized upon utility of process or function.

5. Henle (1957) has criticized functionalism on the ground of being *too* eclectic. In fact, they have been vapid and nondescript eclectics (Marx & Cronan-Hillix, 1987). Eclecticism means patching together something best taken from different systems. The tendency of the functionalists to pick and choose various kinds of techniques and problems for widening the scope of his system and making it more scientific and compact has created a lot of difficulty and problems. Despite this tendency, functionalism never developed as a strict and compact system like structuralism, behavioursism and Gestalt psychology. It always evolved like a flexible system that maintained its existence by adhering to some basic tenets.

DISTINCTION BETWEEN STRUCTURALISM AND FUNCTIONALISM

As we know, structuralism is the name of the system developed by

Titchener in America and by Wundt in Germany. In fact, Titchener had studied under Wundt and popularized his psychology with some modification under general banner of structuralism. Functionalism was founded by Chicago psychologists like John Dewey, James Angell and Harvey Carr and it arose as a protest against structuralism. Woodworth had carried functionalism to Columbia University. These two schools, namely, structuralism and functionalism criticized each other and had many attacks and counterattacks due to some basic points of difference which may be enumerated as under :

1. Structuralism studied elements of static consciousness whereas functionalism studied mental processes or functions as activities leading to practical consequences. In so doing functionalism showed its adherence to Brentano and his act psychology.

2. The leaders of the structuralism like Wundt and Titchener were concerned with 'pure analysis' of mind or consciousness. Thus they, at all costs, wanted to maintain psychology as a pure science avoiding all possible attempts to apply their findings. Functionalism, on the other hand, was more concerned with the utilitarian and commonsense issues in psychology. The leaders of functionslism were more interested in practical applications and applied areas like educational psychology, animal psychology, mental testing, etc. For them the basic question was : what do mental processes accomplish in the world ? Whereas for structuralists the basic question was : How can consciousness be analyzed to locate its contents ?

3. According to structuralists, functions could not directly appear in consciousness and hence, that could not be the object of introspective analysis. Functionalists accepted the method of introspection no doubt but they maintained that introspection was not the only method. They did not has the same attitude towards 'trained introspectionist' as structuralists had.

4. Structuralists and functionalists also differ on the mind-body problem. As we know, the functionalists started with mental activity that was itself dualistic. In other words, it was *psychophysical*. The psychic part was consciousness of one's activity and the physical part was the reactions of the organism. They maintained that in any adaptive act or mental act we had the totality of both physical and psychical events. Thus functionalists' dualism was different from structuralists' dualism in which there was a clear distinction between the mental and the physical events. For structuralists, mental activity could be completely separated from physical activity and could be studied independently. These two types of events, according to them, never interact with each other.

FATE OF FUNCTIONALISM

In the beginning functionalism was a very popular and distinct school in American psychology. William James' pragmatics had set the stage for the beginning of functionalism. At the University of Chicago, John Dewey and James Angell started it and fostered it where as Harvey Carr brought it to its peak of popularity by nursing it. Rober S. Woodworth brought it to Columbia University. Despite all these, functionalism could no longer exist as a formal and popular system in psychology. Several reasons can be given for its poor popularity.

(i) Several important systems like behavioursim and Gestalt psychology emerged at that time. These systems, in fact, attracted the attention of psychologists more than the older functionalism.

(ii) The practice and thinking of functionalists departed from the common people's mode of thinking. At that time, common people somehow became accustomed to think about their experience in terms of its elements. As such, functionalism was not easily popularized.

(iii) The outlook of the functionalists towards one of the vital problems of the day, that is, towards mind-body problem was somewhat obscured and not appealing and convincing to common people. Although functionalists recognized both psychical as well as physical aspect of experience and therefore, they were dualistic but they were not ready to accept these two aspects as separate. This appeared to be contradictory to the thinking of common people of that time.

Despite the fact that functionalism due to the various reasons mentioned above, did not exist longer, its impact upon modern psychology has been broad and unlimited. In fact, it was such American psychology which led to the further developments and refinements. In this sense, *rebirth* of functionalism has taken place. The following two impacts of functionalism are ever felt :

(i) The impact of functionalism in the area of learning has been most obvious. John McGeoch, a Chicago graduate and student of Carr, A. W. Melton, A. L. Irion and Benton J. Underwood made extensive use of the principles and ideas of functionalism in their human verbal learning and retention studies. After obtaining degree from Chicago University and working on forgetting, Fred McKinney conducted researchs in mental helth and counselling. These psychologists have undertaken various research programmes for isolating variables active in the process of learning and forgetting. The emphasis given by these psychologists on the association in the processes of learning memory was nothing but reflextion of the earlier functionalist position.

(ii) Another area in which a clear-cut impact of functionalism is found, is the psychological testing particularly intelligence testing. The first individual intelligence test was develpped in France by Alfred Binet. This test was adapted in English language and revised by L. M. Terman at Stanford University in 1916, 1937 and 1960. D. Wechsler developed an individual intelligence test for adults in 1941, and revised in 1955 and 1981. He also developped intelligence scale for children in 1949 and revised in 1974. For pre-school children he also developed an intelligence sale in 1967. Group intelligence test has also been developed. Without the initiativeness and lead of the functionalism, intelligence testing movement would not have been so popular today.

In nutshell, we can conclude that functionalism, lile structuralism, was not rejected by psychologists. It was rather absorbed into the mainstream of psychology. Today studies being conducted in the field of animal as well as human learning, in meantal testing, in educationl psychology and in abnormal psychology are found to be consistent with functionalists' idea.

CHAPTER HIGHLIGHTS

1. The development of functionalism as a system has several antecedent forces. Out of these forces, the evolutionary principles of Spencer, Darwin and Galton on the one hand and the psychology of William James on the other, have been the primary ones. For Spencer evolution involved a continuous process of integration and differentiation. Such processes are nothing but another from of adaptation and adjustment to external environments. Appreciating the stand of Spencer, Darwin pointed out that life is a struggle for existence and only better-equipped or fit individuals have more chance for survival and for reproduction through natural selection. Galton placed much emphasis upon the study of individual differences. All these evolutionary principles were a direct inspiration for psychologists to study the concept of adaptive act and individual difference (enough for them to be called functionalists !) William James has been the forerunner of functionalism. His

pragmatism has been a major source of inspiration for functionalist's emphasis upon utilitarian aspects.

2. Functionalism was founded at the University of Chicago by John Dewey and his student, James Angell. Harvey Carr of the same University was its developer. In 1896 John Dewey published a short paper entitled *The Reflex-arc concept in Psychology* which marked the starting-point of functionalism as a definite movement. In this paper he made an attack on the elementalism of structuralists and emphasized that psychological activity should be studied as a whole. Thus he advocated the molar approach rather than molecular approach to understanding the adaptive function. James Angell became the chairman of the department of psychology when Dewey left for Columbia University to join department of philosophy as professor. In 1906 presidential address to American Psychological Association he outlined *three* conceptions of functional psychology. *First,* functionalism was contrasted with structuralism. *Second,* functional psychology was the psychology of fundamental utilities or consciousness. *Third,* functional psychology was regarded as the typical method of dealing with the mind-body problem. During the regime of Harvey Carr who later became chairman of the department of psychology at Chicago, the functionalism reached the peak of its popularity. He emphasized that adjustment or adaptations were the main tenets of functional psychology. In fact, his viewpoints fully established functionalism as a system.

3. As a system, functionalism made its position clear on several aspects of psychology. Regarding *definition and the subject-matter,* it outlined that psychology was the study of mental activity or adaptive behaviour. In other words, psychology did not deal with elements or contents but with process. As to its *postulates,* functionalism's basic assertion was that behaviour, initiated by some sensory stimulus, is continuous adaptive and purposive one. Regarding *mind-body problem,* functionalism regarded a mental activity as being psychophysical, that is, partly psychical and partly physical. Obviously, functionalist's stand was dualisitsc but still different from structuralists' dualism. Regarding the *nature of data,* functionalism accepted both objective data as well as subjective date. However, as functionalism advanced in age, it leaned more towards objective data. For functionalists, *the principles of connection* were nothing but the principles of learning which they explained with the various laws of association. Regarding *principles of selection* the functionalists

depended upon attention, motives and learning which were regarded as three primary *agents* of behaviour selection.

4. Apart from Chicago functionalism, there was another functionalism at Columbia University. In fact, R. S. Woodworth had brought functionalism at Columbia University although two other names such as J. M. Cattell, and E. L. Thorndike are also frequently mentioned as Columbia contributors. Although there were many similarities between Chicago functionalists and Columbia functionalists, the latter were different in the sense that they did not show much adherence to the analytical practice of associationists nor did they show any inclination towards nonsense syllable experiment. Columbia functionalists were also more honest to their evolutionary foundations than their Chicago functionalists. Columbia functionalists also made S-O-R formula (and not simply S-R formula) very popular in psychology.
5. Functionalism has also been criticized for its certain lapses. There have been five important criticisms. First criticism was related to the diverse uses of the term 'function'. Second criticism was related to the fact that the study of functions, utilities and values (emphasized by functionalism) could not be the subject-matter of psychology becuase none could be observed introspectively. Third criticism was due to functionalists' failure to make a clear-cut distinction between applied aspect and pure aspect of psychology. As we know, they had given more emphasis upon applied aspect without making it distinct from pure science. Fourth criticism was that functionalism in emphasizing upon the goals and utilitarian concepts had became teleological. Fifth criticism has been provided by Henle (1957) who had pointed out that the functionalism had become too eclectic.
6. Functionalism lodged protest against the structuralism and hence, it differed from the latter. Four basic differences have been outlined. First distinction was that structuralism studies the elements of static consciousness whereas functionalism studies mental processes or activities leading to practical consequences. Second distinction was that structuralism restricted itself to the pure analysis of mind or consciousness whereas functionlism was onccerned with utilitarian and common sense issues in psychology. Third distinction was that structuralism mainly adopted introspection as its chief method to study elements of consciousness whereas functionalism accepted introspection no doubt but it maintained that introspection was not the only method. Fourth point of distinction was related to the

different stand taken by the leaders of the two schools on the issue of mind-body problem. Structuralists believed in doctrine of psychophysical parallelism whereas functionalists considered an adaptive or adjustive act to be psychophysical, that is, partly physical and partly psychical and the two could not be separated from each other because the adaptive act involves the totality of both psychical and physical events.

7. Today functionalism as a formal and distinct school does not exist. It has been absorbed into the mainstream of psychology. Out of many reasons for losing its prominence, the rise of other dominant schools such as behavioursim and Gestalt psychology is frequently cited as one important reason. Although functionalism does not exist, its impact has been clearly felt in at least two areas, namely, in the field of learning and memory as well as in the field of mental testing. In this sense, we can say that functionalism has taken rebirth.

REVIEW QUESTIONS

1. Discuss the major antecedent forces that led to the development of functionalism as a system of psychology.
2. "John Dewey and James Angell were the founders of functionalism but Harvey Carr was its developer". Elucidate it.
3. Discuss the contributions of functionalism as a system of psychology.
4. What were the major points of objections of functionalism against structualism ? What is the fate of functionalism today ?
5. Discuss the major points of distinction between functionalism and structuralism.
6. Assess the contributions of R. S. woodworth as a Columbia functionalist.
7. Discuss the contributions of J. M. Cattell and E. L. Thorndike as Columbia functionalists.

■

CHAPTER 9

MODERN ASSOCIATIONISM

CHAPTER PREVIEW

Associationism was never a formal and distinct school of psychology. It existed as a movement both prior and subsequent to the emergence of the experimental psychology of Wundt. As a movement, it arose from British empiricism. Older associationism and modern associationism were the two forms of associationism. In a formal sense, associationism started with David Hartley, a British philosopher. Later on, philosophers like James Mill, John S. Mill, Alexander Bain and Herbert Spencer developed and elaborated it. From these older associationists, the experimental psychologists took over their various principles like contiguity, similarity, etc., and applied in their fields of investigation like learning, remembering, forgetting, etc.

Modern associationists like Ebbinghaus, Pavlov, Bekheterev and Thorndike emphasized upon the association of stimulus and response that they considered as the fundamental principle of learning. Ebbinghaus invented nonsense syllables and forgetting curve. Pavlov and Bekhterev emphasized upon such association by formulating theory of conditioned reflex and motor conditioning respectively. Thorndike's emphasis upon such association led to what was called connectionism.

Thorndike was both an associationist as well as functionalist. As an associationist, he established his theory of learning of stimulus and response. This was popularly called as connectionism. Connectionism, as a system, defined psychology as the study of stimulus-response connections or bonds held together by associations. Thorndike's early experimentations were on animals and on this basis, he propounded a theory of learning called the law of effect theory. Later his interest switched over to human learning and this also led to the revision of his earlier theory of learning.

Thorndikle's system has been criticized on four grounds—trial-and-error learning, law of exercise, law of effect and elementalism.

Thorndike's role as an educational psychologist was also important. Rejecting the then popular doctrine of formal discipline, he enunciated a new theory of transfer based upon identical elements. He also rejected the idea that intelligence consisted of general mental ability. He divided intelligence into three categories—abstract intelligence, social intelligence and mechanical or concrete intelligence.

HISTORICAL BACKGROUND OF ASSOCIATIONISM

Associationism was never a formal and distinct school of psychology like structuralism, functionalism, behaviourism, Gestalt psychology, etc. In fact, it existed as a principle (rather than as a school) which formed the basis of conducting researches and making explanation by several psychologists independently.

As we know, Wundt founded the first psychological laboratory in 1879. Many principles of associationism were used in those laboratory investigations. Even the leaders of the other schools formed after 1879 have used the principles of associationism in explaining their psychological facts. Immediately, the question arises : from where were the principles of associationism derived ? The answer is from epistemological questions (in philosophy) like : How do we know ? from where do we get a complex idea ? The answer to this second question directly gave birth to a principle of association. The answer was : complex idea is born through the association of simple ideas. Here originates the well-known principles of similarity, contiguity, contrast, etc.

Thus associationism existed prior as well as subsequent to Wundt's psychology. Can then we not trace the historical root of associationism? Certainly, we can. Associationism as a movement can be conveniently be divided into two parts—*Older associationism* and *Modern associationism* with a strong antecedent forces (See Table 8.1) . We have mentioned in this Table Aristotle at the top among the antecedent forces. We start with Aristotle because he was the first philosopher to talk about association through prior to him Plato (427-347 B.C.) had pointed out similarity and contiguity without elaborating them properly. In addition to similarity and contiguity, contrast was also a principle for Aristotle. However, the matter was not seriously considered by later philosopher until British empiricists again took it up on war-footing. John Locke, one of the leading British empiricists, seriously introduced it in the fourth edition of his *Essay concerning Human Understanding* although prior to him Thomas Hobbes another important British empiricist, had lightly talked about 'association' of ideas which he considered to be 'train of thought'. Locke's major concern was to show how experiences could be formed into ideas. He emphasized upon *contiguity* and *similarity* to be the major principles of association. George Berkeley judged perception of depth or distance of objects by associating two dimensions. For him too, *contiguity* and *similarity* were major principles. David Hume, the last of the British empircist, was also no less influential. He pointed out that ideas become associated not only due to similarity and contiguity but also due to *causality*. Thus he went a step ahead than his immediate predecessors in postulating cause and effect as a third principle.

Table 8.1

Associationism and its antecedent influences at a glance

	Associationism	
	Older Associationism	*Modern Associationism*
Antecedent Influences	David Hartley (1705-1557)	Hermann Ebbinghaus (1850-1909)
Aristotle (384-322 B.C.)	Thomas Brown (1778-1820)	Ivan P. Pavlov (1849-1936)
Thomas Hobbes (1588-1679)	James Mill (1773-1836)	V. M. Bekhterev (1857-1927)
John Locke (1632-1704)	John S. Mill (1806-1873)	Deward L. Thorndike (1874-1949)
George Berkeley (1685-1753)	Alexander Bain (1818-1903)	Edwin R. Guthrie (1886-1959)
David Hume (1711-1776)	Herbert Spencer (1820-1903)	William K. Estes (1919-)

From these British empiricism*, a new movement called *associationism** was developed. Today, it may appropriately be termed as *older associationism* that too consisted of British men. What today we call older associationism was founded by David Hertley. He developed his entire psychology around associations and his this effort made associationism for the first time, a formal doctrine. He gave a physiological explanation in terms of brain vibrations. He postulated only one principle or law of association, that is, of contiguity and only with this law he proceeded to explain association of ideas in brain. Although Scottish school was a temporary obstruction in development of British associationism, the last leader of the school, that is, Thomas Brown brought Scottish psychology back to associationistic movement. He had used the word suggestion in place of association. James Mill later proposed his doctrine of *mental mechanics.* According to this doctrine, any idea that we have in our mind is nothing but the addition of its

* A discussion of British empiricism and British associationism has already been done in chapter 2.

original components put together by the principle of contiguity. John Stuart Mill, James Mill's son, did not accept the additive nature of mental mechanics and replaced it by the concept of *mental chemistry*. According to this doctrine, ideas simply fused together to give birth to a new idea with properties different from the properties of constituent ideas. Thus sum was different from its part. In this way association was the adhesive process rather than additive process. He considered contiguity and similarity to be the fundamental principles of association. His father, James Mill, had, however, postulated only one principle, that is, principle of contiguity. Alexander Bain also offered contiguity and similarity as important principles of association and provided physiological correlates of mental activities. Thus, he, in reality, offered nothing new. Herbert Spencer considered contiguity and similarity to be the fundamental binding principles of psychology. His associationism was, however, had Darwinian flavour and hence, termed as *theory of evolutionary association*. Like Bain, Spencer offered nothing new to the psychology. For detailed description of older associationism the reader is referred to chapter 2.

From the older associationism the experimental psychologists took over their various principles and applied in their fields of investigation like learning, remembering, forgetting, etc. These experimental psychologists have been termed as *modern associationists*. We can conveniently take Ebbinghaus as our starting-point of modern associationism. Others who followed Ebbinghaus were Pavlov, Bekhterev, Thorndike, Guthrie and Estes. Of these, associationists, we shall concentrate upon the prominent ones only—Ebbinghaus, Pavlov, Bekhterev and Thorndike. These scientists gave associationism an experimental look under the general rubric of association of stimulus and response.

THE ASSOCIATION OF STIMULUS AND RESPONSE

Those experimental psychologists who have emphasized upon the association of stimulus and response to be the fundamental principle of learning are, Hermann Ebbinghaus, I. P. Pavlov, V. Bekhterev and E. L. Thorndike. The contributions of each of them may by presented as under :

Hermann Ebbinghaus (1850-1909)

Ebbinghaus, one of the prominent German psychologists, studied history and philosophy between 1867 and 1870 at Bonn, Berlin and Halle. He also served in Franco-Prussian war and graduated in 1873. He also visited France where he came across Fechner's famous book *Element* which considerably excited him. In England he extensively studied the work of British associationists. It was this study that inspired him to undertake experimental study of higher mental function such as memory and see how the various principles of associations do work there. In 1880 Ebbinghaus went to Berlin as Dozent and in 1885 he published his famous book *On Memory* which has been considered as the first systematic laboratory investigation of memory involving empirical studies of association. In 1886 he was appointed a full professor and he remained at Berlin until 1894. Then he went to Breslau as the chairman of philosophy department. He died in 1909 at the age of 59 only.

He made two chief technical innovations in experiments on learning and memory. *First,* he adopted one statistical method from physics in which accuracy of observation could easily be estimated through the variations of the several repeated observations about a mean. He postulated that by repeating observations the errors in one direction were roughly canceled by those in opposite direction. *Second,* he also tried to eliminate the qualitative variable error by controlling meaning in the task to be learnt in the experiment. He did this by inventing non-sense syllables which consisted of two consonants separated by a vowel such a ZEK, KAX etc. He invented over 2,000 nonsense syllables to be used in place of words in experiment on learning.

Taking these nonsense syllables, he conducted several experiments in which he was himself subject. He estimated 'memory span' by averaging the number of repetitions of lists of nonsense syllables of varying length before one errorless reproduction. He reported that he could recall syllables up to 7 at one attempt. Hence, his memory span was seven.

In another set of experiments he proceeded to study forgetting quantitatively. He pointed out that the frequency of presentation of the task was an important process for 'stamping in' of associations. He prepared a list of nonsense syllables and read them at uniform speed which he controlled by ticking of his watch. After each reading he paused and then, again started reading that. After a few such readings he recited them from memory and kept a record of his errors. The entire procedure was repeated until he attained the 'complete mastery', that is, reproduced the whole list without any error. He took repeated recall of the list of nonsense syllables learnt at various time intervals. From this, he derived *Ebbinghaus Curve* or *forgetting curve* which indicated that the rate of forgetting during the first hours after the original learning was high and then, it became very slow. During such experimentations, he had also discovered the *'saving method'* by which amount of effort needed to recall previously learnt task was easily estimated.

Ebbinghaus had also studied the impact of different strategies of practice upon association or learning. He conducted several experiments using nonsense syllables as task. He designed two modes of practice. In one mode continuous repetition was done and in other mode, spaced repetition was done in which practice was splitted into various shorter sessions with intervening rest periods. It was found that in rote learning of nonsense syllables spaced repetition was more efficient than continuous repetition.

Although Ebbinghaus did not have high output score like Wundt, what he did was important and fruitful for psychology. His experiments have served as models for procedures in verbal learning studies even today. Before Ebbinghaus, associationists had only talked about principles of associations. Ebbinghaus put those principles of associations on experimental test and also measured the resistance of associations by taking various subsequent recalls.

***Ivan Petrovich Pavlov* (1849-1936)**

Pavlov was born in central Russia. He obtained a degree in animal physiology in 1875 at the University of St. Petersburg and a medical degree in 1883. Then he went to Germany to study with Ludwig at Leipzig University where he also came into contact with Wundt. He came back to St. Petersburg in 1890 as a professor of pharmacology at the Military Medical Institute. In 1895 he became professor of physiology and throughout his life he was an ardent researcher in the field of physiology. He remained here till his death in 1936. In 1924 he was given the title of *Director* of the Physiological Institute for the Russian Academy of Science. In 1904 he was also awarded *Noble Prize* for his brilliant work relating to glandular and neural factors in digestion.

Pavlov's research in the area of psychology came somewhat by accident in 1902. He had developed a surgical technique through which it was possible to measure the amount of saliva secreted by a dog. This particular technique enabled secretion of the particular gland to be diverted through a tube outside the body where the exact amount of secretion could be easily measured without any damage to the nerves. Pavlov found that when meat or bread was placed, the dog salivated. This was quite a natural case. But his most striking discovery was that the stimuli previously associated with the feeding of the animal such as food dish, attendant, etc., also initiated salivary flow in dog after some trials. This *anticipatory salivary flow or reflexes* was psychological or psychic secretion which seemed unimportant for Pavlov but he later became interested in it because its basis was physiological. Pavlov's greatness lay not in recognizing such reflex (because this was known to scientists prior to Pavlov) but in the fact that he scientifically explored it and brought it under close laboratory control. Fearing (1930) reported that such reflexes were known two hundred years before Pavlov. The work of I. M. Sechenov (1829-1905) was also known to Pavlov. Sechenov had clearly established that there was a neurological basis for all psychological activities. Therefore, 'psyche' was not independent of the body rather seated in brain. These psychical processes could be explained as reflexive activity.

Pavlov discovered that a variety of other stimuli associated with food elicited salivation. Buzzer, light, metronome could all elicit salivation. Response to such associated stimuli were termed as conditioned response or reflex (CR). Response of salivation when elicited by a natural stimulus like meat or bread was termed as unconditioned response (UCR), Likewise, on the stimulus side there were two stimuli—unconditioned stimulus (US) and conditioned stimulus (CS). Food was UCS and bell, light etc. were CS. Pavlov pointed out that the conditioned response or reflex was due to higher nerve activity in brain or activities of cerebral cortex. Thus being a physiologist, he gave a physiological explanation of this obvious psychological phenomena which expressed the acquired nature of the stimulus-response relationship. Pavlov coined a special term for this physiological explanation—*irradiation*. By irradiation, he meant "presumed spreading excitatory brain function" (Marx & Cronan-Hillix, 1987 : 52). The major reason of undertaking the study of this type of conditioned reflex learning was the probability to know more about the physiological basis of other related higher central processes.

Pavlov made several variations in presenting CS (bell) and UCS (food) and examined their impact upon learnt behaviour. He reported that when CS was presented without being followed by UCS repeatedly, the strength of the established CR tended to be extinguished. This he termed as the phenomenon of experimental extinction. However, after a lapse a day or two, when CS was again presented, the dog salivated though the amount of flow of saliva was not much. This was termed as the phenomenon of *spontaneous recovery*. Pavlov also observed that the dog tended to salivate to all those stimuli which were similar to original conditioned stimulus. This was termed as *generalization*. In fact, to explain this phenomena in terms of brain functions he had assumed a spread of cortical excitations to several other parts of brain—a fact which was called irradiation. He also observed that with the help of the process of selective reinforcement, he could easily produce a state of *discrimination* which was *opposite* to that of generalizaion. (He had introduced the term reinforcement and the law of reinforcement in 1902). He reinforced a particular tone and did not gave reinforcement to other tone for several trials. After this it was reported that the dog easily discriminated between the exact reinforced tone and similar non-reinforced tones. It salivated to the exact reinforced tone but did not salivate to other such tones. Sometimes Pavlov made the exact reinforced stimulus and other nonreinforced stimuli very similar thus stressing the discrimination too far. In such cases the dog failed to give evidence of any discrimination and not only that, it also demonstrated complete disorganization in behaviour. This was named by him as the phenomenon of *experimental neurosis* because through experimental set-up the dog was made to be neurotic.

On the whole we can say that Pavlov's experimental work (which he claimed to be physiological and not psychological) represented a complete shift ot the concept of association from its philosophical application to idea to the relations between stimuli and glandular responses. From this emphasis later psychologists like J. B. Watson derived a lot to support his system called behaviourism. In this sense, Pavlov should not be regarded as mere an associationist but also one of the antecedent forces that influenced behavioursim. Pavlov's physiological explanation of the phenomenon of the conditioned reflex learning represented a good case of *psychopohysical parallelism* as an explanation of mind-body problem. In Pavlov's work for each stimulus or stimulus pattern there was a corresponding brain patterns of excitations and inhibitions. Today Modern learning psychologists have boldly recognized the kind of learning advocated by Pavlov by naming it as classical, Pavlovian or respondent conditioning as opposed to instrumental or operant conditioning.

Vladimir Bekhterev* (1887-1927) : *The Psychology of motor conditioning

Bekhterev, a Russian contemporary and rival of Pavlov, was a physiologist who was also instrumental in shifting associationism from ideas to overt responses. He pointed out that Pavlov's work was limited to glandular secretions whose direct influence upon overt behaviour was somewhat obscured. Therefore, he turned his attention towards conditioning of motor responses of men as well as animal beings. In fact he was interest in establishing what is called *human reflexology*. The experiment for which he is best known involved the procedure of applying shock to the paw of a dog or goat or hand of the person following some neutral stimulus such as bell or buzzer (CS). The shock was unconditioned stimulus (UCS) and withdrawal of finger or shocked paw was the unconditioned response (UCR). After some pairings of bell with shock, the withdrawal response was elicited by mere sound of the bell. Such withdrawal was the conditioned response (CR). In this way we find that Bekhterev's principles of conditioning were similar to the principles of conditioning reported by Pavlov. However, there was one difference in the outlooks of Bekhterev. He had studied psychology under Wundt at Leipzig and therefore, his concern was more with psychology whereas Pavlov had outright rejected psychology considering its field as "completely hopeless". Like Pavlov, however, he welcomed the idea of physiology-based psychology but outright rejected the subjective approach of Wundt and Titchener towards psychology. His most important book was orginally written in 1907 in Russian language and was translated into English by Teubner in 1928 under the title *General Principles of human Reflexology*. Later, Bekhterev's psychology became a forerunner of behaviourism because it rejected the subjective explanation. It also became an important user of associationistic principles in objective way.

Edward Lee Thorndike* (1874-1949) : *The Psychology of Connectionism

We have already discussed E. L. Thorndike as one of the Columbia functionalists. Thorndike, like Ebbinghaus and Pavlov, brought the associationistic principles out of the philosophers' "ideas" and started experimenting with them. As we have seen, his celebrated work was his Ph. D. dissertation : *Animal Intelligence : An Experimental Study of the Associative Process in Animals* published in 1898. In this dissertation he formulated his theory of learning based upon principles of association. This theory was named as the *law of effect theory of learning*. Thorndike's this dissertation was republished in 1911 with added materials on associative learning in fish, monkeys and chicks. His interest later had shifted from animal learning to human learning partly because this had been suggested to him by his teacher, J. M. Cattell at Columbia University where he spent exactly four decades to finally retire in 1939. He died in 1949. During his post-retirement period of 10 years he remained an active contributor to psychology.

So far as Thorndike's system of connectionism is concerned, it is, in fact, no system like structuralism, functionalism, behaviourism and Gestalt psychology. Thorndike himself reported that he was not a systematist, thinking and contributing to a particular school. However, his viewpoints regarding his own system of connectionism have been collected from his different books and published in *Selected writings from a connectionist's psychology* in 1949. Keeping in view the facts of his *Selected Writings* his system may be enumerated as under :

1. *Definition of psychology*

As we know, Thorndike was not a conscious systematist. Therefore, his viewpoints regarding definition of psychology were implicit in his writings. He can be classied as a functionalist as well as an associationist. As .a functionalist, he emphasized upon the utilitarian aspects of psychology. As an associationist, he considered psychology to be the study of stimulus-response connections or bonds. The bond that held stimulus and response together was *association*. Thorndike gave a broad meaning to connections. Connections may originate from parts or elements of a situation or from the situation as a whole. Connections may also be determined by attitude of a person or by immediately preceding stimuli. They may also occur in long series wherein the response to one stimulus becomes a stimulus for producing another response and so on. They also lead to responses like readiness, attention, awareness, etc. Thus for Thorndike, psychology was the study of S-R connections or bonds held together by associations.

2. *Postulates*

Like Thorndike's view regarding definition of psychology, his statements of postulates were also implicit his writings. However, certain important postulates could be derived from his writings as under :

(i) All behaviour could be analyzed in terms of S-R connections or bonds.

(ii) All behavioural processes are quantifiable.

(iii) The stimulus and response are held together by association.

3. *Mind-body problem*

Thorndike was associationist-cum-functionalist. As such, he was interested in utilitarian aspects of psychology to be explained in terms of S-R bonds.. Therefore, he adopted no formal mind-body position because he considered it a purely philosophical issue with which he was not concerned. As he has opined (1949) : "Under no circumstances, probably, could I have been able or willing to make philosophy my business". He has commonly used words like *mind* and *mental* but never in a philosophical sense. He categorically avoided use of such words which were common in psychology in philosophical context. Therefore, the most legitimate and fairest view about Thorndike's mind-body position is that he liked to remain *unaware* of it.

4. *Principles of connection*

For Thorndike, the principles of connection were nothing but the principles of learning. He enunciated various laws or principles of learning which he, in his later writings, modified substantially. It is, therefore, essential first to consider his principles as they were enunciated in his early writings (before 1930) and subsequently, the changes or modifications introduced by him in his later writings (after 1930).

Thorndike's early experiments were on a hungry cats placed in the puzzle box which was of different kinds. In some boxes the experimental cats were required to press a button for opening the door of the box to come outside for taking food and in some boxes the cats were required to pull a rope or string for opening the door of the box. In some other boxes still complicated procedure for opening the box was operative. Thorndike measured the process of learning in terms of time taken by cat after having been placed in the box, in making the appropriate response that would lead to coming out of the box and receiving the food. Thorndike's observation was that time for trial was somewhat erratic and unpredictable, but gradually with practice, the latency was reduced to a minimum so that as soon as the cat was placed in the box, it immediately freed itself from the box and took the food.

Thorndike reported that in the puzzle box the cat did so many responses like clawing, biting, jumping before the appropriate response (pressing or latching) was done. Gradually, the right response was established and wrong responses were eliminated. He further pointed out that it was the correct response (and not the errors) that eventually led to the fixation of the response to be learned. For Thorndike, learning tended to be blind rather than insightful. Hence, he called it as trial-and-error learning or, as he preferred to call it later, *learning by selecting and connecting*.

From his early series of experimentations he formulated three laws of learning—law of readiness, law of exercise and law of effect. These may be discussed as under :

(i) ***The law of readiness*** : This law was not a very important law and he considered it as mere an accessory principle involving a kind of physiological substratum specifying the circumstances under which a learner would be satisfied or annoyed. He stated these physiological conditions as *conduction units* which could be interpreted as action tendencies. He pointed out three conditions under which the learner would be satisfied or annoyed :

(a) When a conduction unit is ready to conduct, conduction by it is always satisfying.

(b) When a conduction unit is not ready to conduct, forceful conduction is annoying.

(c) When a conduction unit is ready to conduct, not to conduct is always annoying.

Later Thorndike became more interested in educational psychology and propounded what was called 'reading readiness' that referred to the child's level of maturity which is helpful to his ability to start learning to read.

(ii) *Law of exercise* : The law of exercise referred to the strengthening of connections or S-R bonds with practice (law of use) and to the weakening of connections or forgetting by discounting the practice (law of disuse). From this law it became obvious that the more one did practice, the stronger the bonds or connections became. This law applied well to habits and rote memorization.

(iii) *Law of effect* : This is the most significant aspect of Thorndike's connectionism. It stated a weakening or strengthening of a connection as a result of its consequence. A response that produced satisfying effect in the person, was 'stamped in' and a response that produced annoying effect in the person, was 'stamped out'.

It remained, however, for Skinner to develop this law in a more scientific way in his *principles of reinforcement*.

Thorndike's these laws attracted the attention of several psychologists who later came up with several suggestions and criticisms. He himself also conducted several experiments in a bid to extend and test these laws. All these led him to come before the International congress of psychology in New Haven in September 1929 with the statement, "I was wrong". Therefore, he revised his system and published a number of articles and books dating from 1930. Hence, Thorndkie's system after 1930 had a very different radical outlook.

After major revision in 1930 the law of exercise was practically renounced. He pointed out that mere practice was not enough. Practice worked only when it was combined with other factors. For examples, if one were blind-folded and asked to draw lines of four inches for several trials, one would not improve his performance at the end of session. However, if along with this practice, he was given knowledge of result, his performance tended to improve. Thus he did not completely repeal the law of exercise in his revision but made it quite obvious that the amount of strengthening of connections through mere practice was negligible. Another major revision was in the law of effect. Prior to 1930 this law stated that effect of reward was positive, that is, strengthened the connection or bond and the effect of punishment was negative, that is, weakened a connection. In this way, the effects of reward and punishment were opposite. But several experiments gave data contradictory to this formulation. Thorndike himself conducted one experiment on chicks that were placed in simple maze that had three pathways, one of which led to freedom, food and as well as company of other chicks. However, a wrong choice led to the confinement for thirty seconds. His results revealed that rewarding a connection always strengthened it no doubt but punishment (such as confinement) did not weaken the connection. Thus law of effect remained only half true and it was now called as the *truncated law of effect*.

In 1933 he discovered a new phenomenon called the *spread of effect* in support of his truncated law of effect. The spread of effect denoted that the influence of reward in strengthening the S-R connection was not limited to that particular connection (to which reward belonged) but spreaded also to adjacent connections both before and after the rewarded connection. Thus for Thorndike the spread of effect meant spread of effect of reward to the neighbouring punished connections. The degree of effect of reward tended to diminish with distance (both before and after) from rewarded connection. This conclusion was again based upon one experiment conducted by Thorndike himself (1933).

5. *Nature of data*

Thorndike has strong experimental bases behind his formulations. Therefore, his data, unlike Wundt's and Titchener's, were objective and quantified. We have seen that he had collected a lot of objective data obtained from the experimentations conducted by others as well as by himself in support of his various laws of learning and their subsequent modifications. Thus we have sufficient evidence to support that nature of Thorndike's data was objective and experimental.

6. *Principles of selection*

Thorndike was of view that all of a organism's behaviour is *selective*. Stimulus-response associations tend to account for not only acquisition of behaviour but also for selection of behaviour. Thorndike did not consider person as *tabula rasa* on which external events wrote something or as a sensitive plate which tended to duplicate something to which it was exposed. A person behaves in such a way that he has inherent power to attend to something in an exceptional way. In this way, he shows evidence for a selective behaviour. Thorndike did not postulate a separate set of principles to explain the problems of selective behaviour rather considered laws of readiness, exercise and effect sufficient for explaining those problems such as creativity in thinking, etc.

7. *Thorndike's Educational Psychology*

Thorndike was also concerned with problems of education and their applications to human learning and teaching. In the field of educational psychology, prior to the studies conducted by Thorndike, a very popular theory of transfer of training in learning existed. This was well-known as the *doctrine of formal discipline.* The salient feature of this doctrine was that the study of certain hard subjects like Mathematics, Latin and Greek was very worthwhile because it tended to *train the mind.* As a consequence of this training, the mind would be sharpened and other quite unrelated materials would be soon learnt. Hence, there will be a positive transfer in further learning.

Thorndike proposed a theory alternative to the *doctrine of formal discipline.* He proposed this theory in an experiment conducted in collaboration with R. S. Woodworth in 1901 and published formally in his *Educational Psychology* in 1903. According to Thorndike's theory, the degree of transfer from old situation to new situation depended upon identical elements. In other words, if the original situation and the later situation contained more common or identical elements, the degree of transfer from the first situation (original situation) to the second situation (the subsequent situation) would be high. In this way we find that Thorndike rejected the doctrine of formal discipline and enunciated his own theory. He also made it clear that if there were any advantages in studying certain subjects, it was not because of the fact that they trained the mind but because of the common elements among the different subjects.

As an educational psychologist, Thorndike was also concerned with mental testing movement, particularly with the intelligence testing. He objected to the existing theory of intelligence which regarded intelligence as consisting of general mental ability. He outright rejected the idea of this general mental ability and pointed out that intelligence, in fact depended upon a 'number of connections in person's brain'. He criticized Binet's test of intelligence (later revised and named as Standard-Binet Scale) because it assumed a general mental ability. As a substitute of Stanford-Binet Scale, he developed his own test called CAVD (Completion, Arithmetic Reasoning, Vocabulary, Directions) test that measured unrelated abilities which together might be called as *abstract intelligence.* He recognized three distinct types of intelligence—*abstract intelligence, social intelligence and mechanical intelligence.* Abstract intelligence refers to ability to deal with abstract materials like symbols, words and concepts. Social intelligence refers to ability to deal with social relations. Mechanical intelligence refers to ability to manipulate objects, tools and equipment's.

Thus in the field of educational psychology Thorndike's contribution was no less important.

CRITICISMS OF THORNDIKE'S SYSTEM

Thorndike's system had profound impact upon modern learning theory. In fact, he initiated systematic experimental studies in the field of both human as well as animal learning. Despite these, his system has been criticized on the following points :

1. *Trial-and-error learning*

Thorndike emphasized upon randomness in learning because he considered it as a trial-and-error process. Critics particularly Kohler (1947) and other Gestalt psychologists have said that Thorndike considered animals as stupid (in puzzle boxes) making random and undirected responses. But the reality was that they were made to be stupid—because they were put in such a situation that did not give an overall view of the whole situation. Therefore, animals, critics said, were not stupid rather the situation was stupid and forced them to behave in random way. Kohler pointed out that if animals would have been put in an open situation (like his Sultan), clear evidences for insightful learning rather than trial-and-error learning would have been found. However, there are psychologists who may defend Thorndike by claiming that even in open and less controlled situation (that permits overview of the whole situation) there may be random and trial-and-error behaviour though observed less frequently than the intelligent behaviour. (Marx & Cronan-Hillix, 1987).

2. *Law of exercise*

Gestalt psychologists also criticized Thorndike's emphasis upon sufficiency of exercise principle. On the basis of their experimental findings they provided such evidences which forced Thorndike to revise his emphasis upon exercise principle and add a new principle called belongingness. According to the principle of belongingness, a connection between two units or ideas is more readily established if the person somehow perceived the two as belonging together. For example, if the person repeatedly hears—Mohan is doctor; Ram is engineer and Shyam is professor—the association 'doctor-Mohan' will be more stronger than 'doctor-Ram' despite the fact 'doctor' occurs closer in time to 'Ram' than to 'Mohan'. Obviously, this was due to the fact that the person perceives 'Mohan' and 'doctor' as belonging together. The evidences collected from such experiments in which contiguous terms were not necessarily found to be associated in ordinary learning situation build case against exercise principle. Mere repetition of the contiguous terms was not enough for establishing association rather something more was needed and the concept of belonging was that something. Apart from these observations, in Thorndike's own experiments in which the subjects who drew lines of certain length when blind-folded, did not improve with practice. Such experiments also provided evidence against the law of exercise.

3. *Law of effect*

Thorndike's system was also criticized for interpretation of the law of effect. Behaviourists pointed out that Thorndike included mentalistic or subjective concepts like 'satisfaction' or 'annoyance' in his law of effect. Thorndike met this criticism by defining satisfaction and annoyance in objective and quantifiable manner. He pointed out that by the satisfying state of affairs is meant one which the animal does nothing to avoid, other doing things that maintain or renew it. Likewise, by annoying state of affairs is meant one which the animals do nothing to preserve rather often do things to end. These definitions were not circular because state of affairs characterized as satisfying and as annoying were spelled out independently of their influence upon modifiable connections.

Another criticism of the law of effect was regarding its backward effect. The question was : Since the stimulus-response sequence occurs prior to the reward (or punishment), how can the latter have an impact upon sequence that is already gone in time ? The past is gone and effect of something can be felt in present. But this criticism, like first one, is not correct. The effect can be revealed in the probability of occurrence of the response when similar situation next comes. Hull (1952) has also made it explicit that the reinforcement acts upon the persisting traces from stimulus-response sequence that come prior to the satisfaction or annoyance.

Critics have also raised some doubt regarding the automatic of strengthening of a connection due to effect of reward. This position of Thorndike was strengthened due to his discovery of the spread-of-effect phenomenon. However, the safest side is to say that to what extent Thorndike was correct in his emphasis upon automaticality is still a matter to settle. Sufficient evidences exist at both sides.

4. *Elementalism*

Thorndike was an associationist and being an associationist, he adopted elementarism and analytical attitude of British empiricists. Some psychologists immediately took notice of such stand of Thorndike and accused him for bringing narrowness in psychology. Thorndike's theory of transfer of training is one nice example of his elementatrism. His this theory pointed out that the improved efficiency at one task had 'identical elements'. The greater the number of identical elements, grater is the amount of transfer. Such transfer based on identical elements', critics say, definitely narrows down the scope of transfer of S-R connections. Gates (1942) has, however, defended Thorndike's elementarism by pointing out that his elements (Thorndike's element) were broad and should not be interpreted in the narrowest stimulus-response connections. He further pointed out that the term 'identical', in broadest sense, included the degree of similarity. Thus his transfer theory was, in reality, more flexible, and board then was assumed by Thorndike's critics.

In this ways we find that Thorndike's system has been criticized on several grounds by Gestalt psychologists and behaviourists. In past 25 years or so, that importance of Thorndike's system has decreased and some psychologists have preferred to substitute the term 'association" by 'contiguity' or 'functional relationship'.

IMPORTANCE OF THORNDIKE

Thorndike had a record of 50 years of professional career at Columbia University. In fact this period was a highly productive period in which he obtained wide accomplishment in different areas. His importance was due to the following accomplishment :

1. He conducted first systematic laboratory investigation in the field of animal learning.
2. He presented the first complete associationistic learning theory. Hilgard and Bower (1981) have pointed out that Thorndike's connectionism was, in fact, the first theory of learning. Tolman (1938) had similarly judged Thorndike's associationistic theory of learning as standard one and considered it a starting point. To quote him (Tolman, 1932 : 11) "The psychology of animal learning—not to mention that of child learning—has been and still is primarily a matter of agreeing or disagreeing with Thorndike or trying in minor ways to improve upon him...all of us here in America seem to have taken Thorndike, overtly or covertly, as a starting point."
3. He made exhaustive analysis of human learning which forced him to revise his earlier theory of learning.

4. He became an important leader in the field of mental testing by propounding a new theory of intelligence.
5. He also contributed a lot in the field of educational psychology. He was bold enough to reject the then established doctrine of formal discipline and in its place, he propounded his new theory of transfer based upon these concept of identical elements.

CHAPTER HIGHLIGHTS

1. Associationism was never a formal and distinct school of psychology like structuralism, functionalism, behaviourism, Gestalt psychology, etc. In fact, it existed as a principle rather than as a school. As a principle, it existed in the psychology of philosopher like Aristotle, Thomas Hobbes, John Locke, George Berkeley, and David Hume. In Wundt's experimental psychology various principles of association were also used. For convenience, the movement of associationism was divided into two parts—older associationism and modern associationism. In fact, from British empiricism this movement had developed. Older associationism was mainly gauged by Britishmen. It formally started with the work of David Hartely and was temporarily interrupted by the Scottish school. Thomas Brown, though belonged to the Scottish school, brought this school back to associationism. James Mill, John S. Mill, Alexander Bain and Herbert Spencer were all active contributors.

   From older associationism the experimental psychologists took over their various principles such as principle of contiguity, similarity, etc. and applied in their fields of investigation like learning, remembering, forgetting, etc. These psychologists were called as modern associationists. Ebbinghaus, Pavlov, Bekhterev, Thorndike were important modern associationists.

2. Modern associationists like Ebbinghaus, Pavlov, Bekhterev and Thorndike were the pioneer experimental psychologists who emphasized the association of stimulus and response that was considered to be the fundamental principle of learning. Ebbinghaus one of the prominent German psychologists, conducted the first systematic laboratory investigation on memory. He invented *non-sense syllables* that are still very popular materials used in the study of memory. His investigations led him to plot a curve of forgetting popularly known as *Ebbinghaus curve* or *forgetting curve* which indicated that the rate of forgetting immediately after learning was high and then, it became very slow. He is also known for his *saving method* by which amount of effort needed to recall previously learnt

task was easily estimated. Pavlov, a Russian physiologist, had been another important person who had been awarded *Nobel Prize* for his brilliant work relating to glandular and neural factors in digestion. However, his research in the area of psychology came somewhat by accident in 1902. His research in psychology came to be known as *conditioned reflex*. He explored it and brought it under close laboratory control. He reported four major components of such conditioning—Unconditioned stimulus (US), Conditioned stimulus (CS), Unconditioned response (UCR) and Conditioned response (CR). He also repoted that several psychological phenomena like experimental extinction, spontaneous recovery, generalization, discrimination, etc. were important in conditioning. Bekhterev, a Russian comtemporary and rival of Pavlov, was also a physiologist and became instrumental in shifting associationism from ideas to overt responses. In his human reflexology he emphasized more upon conditioning of motor responses of men as well as animal beings rather than upon glandular responses that was somewhat obscured.

3. Perhaps the most important figure in the modern associationism was Edward Lee Thorndike, a Columbia psychologist. His celebrated work was his Ph. D. dissertation briefly called *Animal intelligence* in which he formulated his theory of learning based upon principles of association. His system is more popularly called as *Connectionism*. although he was not a systematist, thinking and contributing to a particular school. His viewipoints published in his book *Selected Writings* threw a lot of light on his system. In this book he outlined definition of psychology, explained important postulates and mind-body problem, and discussed the principles of connection and selection. In discussing his principles of connection, he included the famous *law of effect theory*. His system has, howerver, been criticized on four major grounds—trial-and error learning, law of exercise, law of effect and elementarism. Despite these criticisms, Thorndike's improtance has been unparallel due to four or five major reasons.

4. As an educational psychologist, Thorndike's role was no less important. He was concerned with problems of education and their application to human learning and teaching. In field of educational psychology he discarded the popular theory of transfer called *doctrine of formal discipline* and in its place, advanced his own theory of transfer based upon *identical elements*. His explanation of intelligence was also highly attractive. He divided intelligence into

three types : *abstract intelligence, social intelligence* and *mechanical intelligence*. He rejected the existing theory of intelligence which had regarded intelligence as consisting of general mental ability and instead, pointed out that intelligence, in fact, depended upon "a number of connections in peron's behaviour".

REVIEW QUESTIONS

1. Discuss the historical background of associationism as a movement in psychology.
2. Discuss the imortant contributions of Hermann Ebbinghaus.
3. Discuss the major contributions of I. P. Pavlov and Vladimir Bekhterev.
4. How did Thorndike formulate the base for the development of associationism in his theory of connectionism ? What were the important reasons for his prominence ?

■

Chapter 10

EARLY BEHAVIOURISM

CHAPTER PREVIEW

Behaviourism was established by J. B. Watson not all on a sudden, It had its antecedent roots. Four such roots of early behaviorism have been emphasized—early philosophical trends, animal psychology, Pavlovian conditioned reflex, and functionalism.

A view on Watson's brief-sketch explains how Watson became interested in psychology, what was his academic brilliancy during his life and what forces brought a change in his personality. How did his romance with Miss Raynor virtually led to his academic death.

Watson's primary system mainly emphasized upon giving a concrete, scientific and methodological shape to psychology. To what extent he got success, has been explained in this section.

Watson's behaviourism had also some secondary features. In this section author has emphasized Watson's view regarding language development, thinking, environmentalism and determinism. Of these, his view regarding environmentalism has made him highly popular because he had claimed that he would turn a child either into a doctor, an engineer and any socially accepted personality or into a thief or robber irrespective of his potentialities.

Apart from his effort to organize psychology into a system, he also carried out some experimental programme in fields like learning, emotion and memory. In collaboration with Raynor, he conducted famous experiment on conditioning of fear responses on Albert. In this section his experimental formulations have been given due coverage.

Lastly, the author has outlined the contributions of those psychologists who provided a support to Watson's stand but at the same time tried to improve upon him. Albert P. Weiss, Karl Lashley, Walter S. Hunter and Edwin B. Holt were such major behaviourists.

ANTECEDENTS OF EARLY BEHAVIOURISM

Although we generally credit J. B. Watson as the founder of behaviourism (in 1913),. this school, like others, has a strong antecedent influences. Some of these influences are direct and some of these influences are indirect. But both of them have been exerting powerful influences upon emergence of behaviourism. These antecedent forces may be grouped into four categories—*early philosophical trend emphasizing objectivism, animal psychology, Pavlovian conditioned reflex* and *functionalism*. These may be discussed as under :

1. ***Early philosophical trend emphasizing objectivism***

Watson had studied philosophy in his early years and he knew well about philosophy of Aristotle and ancient Greeks. In his book *De Anima (Concerning the Psyche)* Aristotle had shown his concern with the body and its functions like movement, digestion, sensation, reason etc. He considered these functions as acts of body and in no way separate from it. In this sense, Aristotle may be considered as the first behaviourist who emphasized objective and observable phenomena in psychology. Watson also maintained the same outlook to psychology.

Apart from these Greek philosophers, some French philosophers like Julien de La Mettrie (1709-1751) Pierre Cabanis (1757-1805) and August Comte (1798-1857) were also important forces. La Mettrie emphasized upon *materialism* as opposed to *spiritualism*. In other words, he was of view that man was really a machine. He, therefore, emphasized that there could be physical interpretation of every mental act. Descartes, too, had considered both animals and human body to be machines but he had not given up the idea of concept of soul separate from the body. In this way La Mettrie and Descartes continued their effort towards *psychological objectivism* in which objective data and direct observation were substituted for subjective data and introspection. Cabanis went ahead in providing more objective data by defining mind in terms of objective factors particularly in terms of physiological or brain functions. He pointed out that brain was the organ of consciousness in the same sense as the stomach was the organ of digestion. In this way, Cabanis maintained a mechanistic position and showed fondness for physiological explanations. In doing so, he approached towards psychological objectivism. *August Comte* was perhaps another most important Frenchmen who found, beyond materialism, a movement called *positivism*. According to this point of view, only positive (that is not debatable) knowledge was valid. Such positive knowledge came from only objective observation. Naturally, then, all varieties of positivism rejected the method of introspection and criticized the mentalistic and subjective approaches to psychology. Watson was much influenced by positivism of Comte and accordingly, in formulation of behaviorism as a system, he gave his approach high importance.

2. *Animal Psychology*

As we know, evolutionary theory of Charles Darwin stimulated the study of animal psychology a lot. He did several observations on animals and published the results in his famous book *Expression of emotion in Man and Animals* (1872). He confidently demonstrated a close relationship between expressed emotions in human beings and lower animals. For example, in state of anger human beings as well as some lower animals show grinding of teeth.

George John Romanes (1848-1894) was one of the personal friends of Darwin and was interested in finding out several things about behaviour of animals from whatever sources and methods he could gather them. He collected all kinds of possible literature from stories—both popular and scientific—regarding animal behaviour. He published them in this book *Animal Intelligence* (1886). He popularized a method of collecting data called *anecdotal method*. Despite the fact that he had used some objective and explicit rules for using stories, he was unable to avoid using some inadequate and unscientific observations. Another limitation of Romanes studies was his *anthropomorphism* which meant attributing human traits, motives and abilities to animal behaviour. Romances had used anthropomorphism in order to provide a continuity between human beings and animals. Despite these limitations, Romances was credited with stimulating initial study of animal behaviour and paved the way for conducting more objective and experimental studies later.

Another important figure in study of animal behaviour is C. Lloyd Morgan (1852-1936). He published several books on animal behaviour. Of these books, *Introduction to Comparative Psychology* was the most popular one. He conducted several studies in which a comparison was done between behaviour of human beings with that of lower animal beings. His studies utilized semi-experimental type of observation which was half way between naturalistic observation of animals in their natural habitat and the controlled conditions of the laboratory. He is best remembered by psychologists for what is known as *Llyod Morgan's Canon*. In fact Morgan's Canon was a reaction against the anthropomorphism of Romanes and was application of the *law of parsimony* or *Occam's* Razor in comparative psychology. The law of parsimony stated that when two hypotheses are consistent with the observed data, the simpler hypothesis should be preferred. Thus he pointed out that we should not interpret an action as necessarily demonstrating higher mental process if it can be interpreted as one being lower in the psychological scale. Therefore, rather than talking about intelligence, thinking and memory of animals, we should talk about their habits. Morgan, in fact, wanted to show continuity between humans and animals through his *Canon* that appealed to simplicity and rejection of Romanes anthropomorphism. Romanes had also tried to find out continuity between humans and animals by his anthropomorphism through which he wished to apply mind everywhere. Morgan did so by rejecting anthropomorphism and introducing his Canon that embraced simplicity. Morgan's rejection of anthropomorphism and his Canon's simplicity were the direct antecedent forces of behaviourism.

Having full confidence in his Canon that emphasized upon the simpler of the two hypotheses, Morgan took habit rather than intelligence as explanatory until. He emphasized trial-and-error learning that was characteristics of both animals and humans. His this emphasis had a direct impact upon Thorndike's formulation of theory of learning. Watson was also much stimulated by Morgan's enterprise. He also tried to explain learning by adopting simpler principles (which were enunciated by Morgan) to both human as well as animals. Some psychologists have criticized Morgan's Canon by saying that sometimes it is not the simpler but the complex of the alternative hypothesis seems more correct and scientific. But this does not put his Canon in wrong box. The investigator must account for why the complex hypothesis should be accepted over the simpler hypothesis. If he fails to provide adequate reason, again the simple one should be preferred.

Jacques Loeb (1859-1924) is another major figure in animal psychology. He was a German biologist who came to America in 1891. He is well-known for his acceptance of the concept of *tropism* or *forced movement* as the major explanatory factor in animal behaviour. In tropism the behaviour of an animal is *forced* in the sense that it is direct function of a stimulus. He believed that all the behaviour of lower animals as well as major proportion of behaviour of higher animals was tropistic or forced. The irresistible and mechanical movements of moths towards light is an example of tropistic behaviour. Despite his emphasis upon tropism to explain animal behaviour, he was not concerned with the explanation of human behaviour. However, he studied the human problem of consciousness. He became interested in locating the point in evolutionary scale at which animals had consciousness. The criterion for determining consciousness was presence of associative memory. If associative memory was present in animal, it meant that it had consciousness. Watson had studied under Loeb at the University of Chicago and therefore, he was much influenced by Loeb's tropism in his formulation of behaviouristic principles.

E. L. Thorndike, W. S. Small and Robert M. Yerkes (1876-1956) were other psychologists who contributed a lot in the field of animal psychology. We have already examined the systematic work of Thorndike in the study of animal behavior. Watson for making some studies on animals kept a close touch with Thorndike. It was, therefore, natural that Thorndike might have influenced Watson. W. S. Small introduced first rat maze in 1900 which served as an important apparatus for animal research. Watson made use of Small's maze for studying rats' behaviour. Yerkes had also began his animal research the same year, that is, 1900. He studied varieties of animals—crabs, turtles, rats, birds, pigs, monkeys and finally humans. His researches on monkeys and apes were highly important and this was summarized in *Chimpanzees : A laboratory Colony* (1943). He collaborated with Watson in developing a technique for testing colour vision in animals. Despite this collaboration, he was an admirer of Titchener and pointed out that the study of experience was one of the major task of psychologist. Therefore, Yerkes could not be regarded as a *behaviouist*. Yerkes, however, strengthened the field of comparative psychology and that might be regarded as his basic inspiration for behaviourism. He also strengthened the field of applied psychology by acting as chief of psychological services and testing of intelligence of army recruits during World War I.

3. *Pavlovian Conditioned reflex*

We have examined the details of Pavlovian conditioning and Bekhterev motor conditioning in chapter 8. The significance of these conditioning experiments for behaviourism was twofold. *First,* conditioning experiments served as an objective and scientific method for development and modification of behaviour. *Second,* Watson was much impressed with Pavlov's experimental paradigm of learning and incorporated it into his own explanation for all kinds of human learning.

4. *Functionalism*

Functionalism had a direct influence upon Watson. As we know, Watson completed his Ph. D. dissertation under Angell (at Chicago) who was founder of functionalism. As such, Watson was thoroughly engrossed in functionalistic movement. Since Watson founded his behaviourism as a reaction against functionalism, the impact of functionalism upon behaviourism was said to be negative. The impact of functionalism upon behaviourism can be seen in *two* primary ways. *First,* behaviourism, taking inspiration from functionalism, emphasized upon more objectivity in psychology and rejected the study of conscious experience that was a subjective and mentalistic concept. *Second*, seeing the success of functionalism, behaviourism also showed a strong concern with wider application of psychology in the fields of animal psychology, child psychology and abnormal psychology.

Thus we see that behaviourism, like other systems, in psychology has strong antecedent forces. It was formally founded by Watson no doubt but not in a day. It had its historical roots.

BRIEF LIFE-SKETCH OF JOHN BROADUS WATSON (1878-1958)

J. B. Watson was born on a farm in Greenville, South Carolina. His mother was religious and father was not religious. Watson's personality may have been shaped by this conflicting parental stand (Cohen, 1979). According to his own account, he was not a brilliant student in his early days. He was also arrested twice by police. He attended Furman University in Greenville and studied subjects like Latin, Greek, Mathematics and Philosophy. In 1900 he got his master's degree. Then he entered the University of Chicago to study philosophy under John Dewey. But it was Angell who moulded his interest and steered him into the field of experimental psychology. At Chicago, he also studied physiology and neurology under H. H. Donaldson, a neurologist, and Jacques Loeb. Angell and Donaldson discouraged Watson from doing Ph. D. dissertation under Loeb and they jointly supervised his Ph. D. dissertation that used both neurological and psychological techniques. In this dissertation he tried to correlate the behaviour with the growth of modullation in the central nervous system in white rat. The title of his Ph. D. dissertation was : *Animal Education : The Psychical Development of the White rat*. This thesis was completed in just three years in 1903. He was the youngest man to receive Ph. D. from Chicago University at that time. Historians ascribe one reason for this was that Watson had no extra money for entertainment and therefore, he worked sincerely all through (Marx & Cronan-Hillix, 1987). After earning his Ph. D. he remained at Chicago working with rats in maze. In 1907 he published a paper on *Kinesthetic and Organic sensations of the white rat* in which he showed that kinesthetic cues were basic and frequently used cues by rats in maze learning.

In 1908 Watson went to John Hopkins University to chair the department of psychology (Cohen, 1979). From 1908 to 1920 was his most productive periods. He continued his experimental laboratory researches on animals and established various research programmes with children in collaboration with famous psychiatrist, Adolf Meyer.

According to his own account, his animal researches at Chicago led him to his first formulation for behaviouristic principles in 1903 but his teacher, Angell, discouraged such move saying that such formulations may well apply to animals but not to humans. In 1908 he gave first public speech of his views in form a lecture at Yale University. But he was again badly criticized by his listeners who claimed that his formulations were descriptive and not explanatory. However, in 1913 he gave a mere elaborate and definitive expression to his views in lectures at Columbia University, the contents of which was published in *Psychological Review* in 1913 under the title *Psychology as the Behaviourist view it.* This marked the official launching of behaviourism as a school and became known as behaviourists's manifesto. The chief charateristics of behaviourism as outlined in this manifesto were as under :

(i) Psychology, for behaviourists, is a purely objective experimental branch of natural science.

(ii) Introspection forms no essential part of the methodology of psychology.

(iii) The study of consciousness does not yield any data of scientific importance. Hence, it should be eliminated as the proper subject for investigation.

(iv) The proper subject-matter of psychology is both simple and complex behaviour.

In 1914 Watson's another book *Behaviour : A introduction to Comparative Psychology* appeared. In this book he reported about his experimental work on animals and demonstrated with ample success that animal or comparative psychology could have an independent place among the sciences. In 1915 he became President of American Psychological Association at the young and amazing age of 37. He had also a brief assignment in World War I for testing and selecting pilots. In 1919 his another book, *Psychology from the Standpoint of a behaviourist,* appeared and revised in 1924 and in 1929. In this book the principles of animals psychology were extended into human behavioural problems. The book also gave details of his studies on infantile emotions and emotional conditions. Watson stressed upon verbal behaviour to provide adequate data but at the same time he had rejected introspection. He was criticized by psychologists for such inconsistency. In 1925 he wrote a third book *Behaviourism* which was revised in 1930. This book gave a detailed account of environmentalist position and a programme for improvement of human beings.

In 1920 Watson resigned from faculty of John Hopkins University and the academic world. On November 20, 1920 Watson's wife, Mary Ickes Watson, sued him for divorce and this became so sensationalized that he was asked to resign from the University. None of Watson's friends inside or outside the University came publically to defend him. After divorce, he married Rosalie Raynor, with whom Watson did famous experiment of conditioned fear on an infant named Albert. After resigning the academic field at the 'Young' age of 42, he entered the advertising firm of J. Walter Thompson in New York. He did so well that his annual earning became 70,000 Dollars much more than what he drew last at John Hopkins University. He openly popularized the view that psychology could be broadly applied in the fields like advertising and child rearing. He wrote a book *The Psychological care of the infant and Child* in 1928.

During his non-academic life, E. B. Titchener was the most loyal of all his friends. He kept contact with Watson for several years by writing letters. Watson had no offers of academic positions until the Second World War ended. But it was far too late and he was too old (over 65) to lecture.

On the whole, we can say that Watson's career between 1908 and 1920 was the most productive one, in between 1920 and 1930 he remained active in nonacademic field and after 1930 his career as a contributor to psychology had almost ended.

WATSONIAN BEHAVIOURISM AS A SYSTEM

Watson founded behaviourism in 1913 at John Hopkins University where he was chairman of the department of psychology. This school was founded as a protest against structuralism and functionalism. Due to its dominant position, it earned the nick-name of being *second force* in psychology, the *first force* being psychoanalysis and *third force* was humanistic, phenomenological and existential psychology.

Watsonian behaviourism had two subsystems—primary and secondary.* Watsonian primary behaviourism had two major aspects—*positive aspect* and *negative aspect*. Watson's positive aspect was his emphasis upon objective psychology. He wanted to apply the techniques and principles of animal psychology to human psychology. For him, the study of behaviour rather than consciousness was the major source of data for psychologists. Such aspect of behaviourism was termed as *empirical behaviourism* or *methodological behaviourism*. The negative aspect

* The secondary characteristics of Watson system will be discussed in a separate section.

of Watsonian behaviourism was his rejection of introspective psychology of Titchener and Wundt as well as Angell's functionalism. He rejected introspective data of Titchener and lodged a strong protest against Angell's functionalism because it had accepted introspective data by maintaining an interactionistic role. In 1919 Watson adopted a metaphysical position that denied the existence of mind or consciousness. This was called as *metaphysical or radical behaviourism.*

Watsonian behaviourism as a primary system may be discussed as under :

1. *Definition of Psychology*

For Watson, psychology is a branch of natural science that studies human behaviour. The term behaviour is a broad term that includes verbalization, too. Therefore, 'saying' is also a behaviour. He also made it clear that subject-matter of psychology is not consciousness, not mental functions nor psychophysical processes of any sort.

In a very clearest sense Watson's system was an S–R (stimulus-response) psychology. By stimulus, he meant, any object in the environment or any change in bodily tissues themselves. Stimulus may be simple or complex. If a stimulus is complex, it represents a stimulus situation that can be broken down into smaller units. By response, he meant, anything done by the organism. Responses may be learned and unlearned, overt and covert. Talking, walking, playing are examples of *overt learned responses.* Thinking and perception are examples of *covert learned responses.* All natural reflexes such as eye-blinking, tearing, knee jerk and breathing are examples of *overt unlearned responses.* Blood pressure , digestion, heart beating are examples of *covert unlearned responses.* Watson's behaviourism had two specific objectives—to make prediction about response after knowing the stimulus and to make prediction about the stimulus after knowing the response.

2. *Methods of Psychology*

Watson rejected introspection as scientific method of psychology. Since psychology was the objective science of behaviour, its method must be empirical ones. Watson recognized basically the following methods :

(i) ***Observation*** : Watson had a set of experimental programme. As an experimentalist, he considered experimental method to be indispensable. But at the same time he also accepted naturalistic observations of stimulus-response relationship in the field outside the laboratory. He opined that scientific observation could be made with or without any instrument.

(ii) ***Conditioned-reflex technique*** : Watson adopted the conditioned reflex technique from Pavlov and Bekhterev. He considered conditioning as one scientific method that provided an objective way of analyzing behaviour. This method has two obvious aims. First, by conditioning it is possible to study those processes through which a complex behaviour is built up and torn down. Second, through conditioning even those problems which appear to be highly subjective and stronghold of introspection (such as sensation), can be easily studied. But in practice, the conditioned-reflex technique has not been fully able to fulfil these aims because of some inherent methodological problems.

(iii) ***Testing*** : Psychological testing was also recognized. When a behaviourist used a psychological test, he used it as measure of behaviour or responses (of the person being tested) to the objective situations that test represent. Watson also made it clear that psychological tests are not mental test because they don't measure special abilities as aspects of mind.

(iv) ***Method of Verbal report*** : Watson accepted in case of human subjects verbal report as one method of investigation. In this method the subject gives a report about his own condition or performance. In the hands of behaviourist, such report about own condition or performance is given exactly the same treatment that other overt responses are given. It is never accepted as a report or comment on a 'mental' condition. For example, when a person says, "I am happy", behaviourist considers it not as a report on his 'mental' condition but as a condition or aspect of his total reaction system. Thus Watson considered 'verbal report' as a sort of motor response to the stimuli. He pointed out that like any other motor responses this should be considered at its face value. So the method of verbal report registers the stimulus in as objective way as the thermometer registers the temperature of our body. Structuralists, have, however criticized Watson and said that he has included their method of introspection in his system by a changed name—verbal report.

3. *Postulates of psychology*

Watson made certain basic assun ptions called postulates for the psychology outlined in his behaviourism. The major postulates were as under :

(i) Behaviour consists of glandular secretions and muscular movements and therefore, it is reducible to some physio-chemical processes.

(ii) Behaviour consists of response elements and it can be analyzed by the appropriate scientific methods.

(iii) Every effective stimulus produces an immediate response. Therefore, there is a definite cause-and-effect determinism in behaviour.

(iv) The study of conscious processes must be ignored at all cost because they can't be studied scientifically.

4. ***Nature of the data***

Watson always emphasized upon objective data. He rejected subjective data collected from the study of consciousness by introspection. Behaviours that occur in time and space, objective reports of muscular movements and glandular movements, etc. are the primary data that should be analyzed by psychologists. The nature of these data is such that they can be quantitatively analyzed and meaningful generalization can be easily made.

5. ***Principles of connection***

The laws of frequency and recency were accepted as the major principles of connection. Later, he also included the principle of conditioning as demonstrated in the laboratory by Pavlov. He opined that conditioning is a fundamental principle of learning and in fact, all types of learning can be explained in terms of conditioning. However, he excluded Thorndike's law of effect from the list. He objected to this "effect" principle on the ground that it contained subjectivism which was not tolerable for a behaviourist.

6. ***Principles of selection***

As it has been stated above, one of the two basic objectives of behaviourism was to make prediction about the response. This is done through selectivity of stimulus. A vast range of stimuli stimulates the individual who responds. But at anyone moment some stimuli stimulate the individuals and produce a response while some other stimuli don't stimulate. How are they selected ? Watson assumed that they are selected on the basis of a large number of inherited tendencies. Both selectivity of response as well as appropriate stimulus depends upon some innate and acquired stimulus-response connections as well as upon immediate modifications of these connections through the principle of conditioning.

7. *Mind-body problem.*

The stand taken by Watson on the mind-body problem was the hallmark of behaviourism. Watson as well as other behaviourists denied the existence of mind or consciousness. They pointed out—one body and no mind. Watson made it clear that consciousness is never seen, touched, tasted or smelled. It is a plain unprovable assumption. Thus Watson was clearly monist. History bears testimony to the fact that from the time of Aristotle and the ancient Greeks, psychology, in one way or the other, had accepted the dualism of mind and body. But with advent of Watsonian behaviourism mind was denied its existence. With denial of mind, the mind-body problem remained no longer a problem for behaviourist. All that remained and attracted psychologist was a behaving organism. Watson also made it clear that the brain processes were no longer important for a behaviourist because he considered brain as "mystery box". According to his stand, psychology was concerned only with bodily responses—responses of muscles and glands to stimuli. Thus Watson's behaviourism was a 'mind-less' psychology.

Watsonian solution of mind-body problem by denial of mind and accepting only the body fitted best to epiphenomenal approach as well as to approach of complete physical monism. The epiphenomenal approach maintained that consciousness itself had no importance for science and had no causal role to play.

Watson along with other behaviourists provided some arguments against the existence of mind or consciousness. Some of those may be enumerated as under :

(i) Those who accept consciousness or mind, consider it as continuous process. Behaviourists said that in sleep there occurs gap in consciousness. How could this gap be explained by those who argue for the existence of mind ?

(ii) Structuralists have tried to prove the existence of consciousness on the basis of introspective data. Behaviourists arguing against this stand have said that in introspection the important thing is stimulus and not the so-called conscious experience.

(iii) Behaviourists argued that if existence of mind is accepted, then it must also be accepted that it affects behaviour. But the assumption of nonphysical events (mind) making interaction with the physical events (body) clearly violates the principle of conservation-of-energy. This principle (from physics) states that physical energy is not created nor destroyed but is only transformed. All such energy must be accumulated within physical system. They are not related to nonphysical system. If conscious experiences affect bodily processes, they would have to do so by subtracting or releasing energy to nonphysical system. But according to the principle of conservation-of-energy this can't happen. Therefore, the conclusion is that any mental process or idea can't affect our body (muscles and glands). If any idea affects our body, it means that idea must itself be physical events in nervous system. If it is really so, it is also proved that the idea or mental experience is really physical or monumental.

Thus Watson along with other behaviourists turned to be a strict physical monism by denying the existence of mind or consciousness. "Mental", if it exists, is nothing but simply is the way the physical events function.

Watsonian behaviourism thus was a formally established system, that defined psychology as science of behaviour, accepted objective observation as its primary method and maintained a strict physical monism by denying the existence of mind or consciousness.

SECONDARY FEATURES OF WATSONIAN BEHAVIOURISM

Apart from critical or primary characteristics which were basic and widely accepted, there were also some secondary characteristics of Watsonian behaviourism. In order to have well-integrated knowledge of behaviourism, it is essential to a look upon these secondary characteristics. Such characteristics are also important to know because most of the criticisms of Watson's behaviourism are based upon them. Some of these characteristics are as under :

1. ***Language development***

Watson considered development of language as a learned activity out of infant's random vocalizations and babblings. In such learning the principle of conditioning plays a significant role in three ways. *First,* a small child produces many separate syllables like 'da' 'ba' by the normal vocimotor organs. When he speaks the syllable 'da' and listens it, he again repeats it. Listening the syllable 'da' becomes a conditioned stimulus that evoke further repetition. In this way gradually *circular conditioned response* is established and the child speaks 'dada' or 'baba'—a kind of babbling. This is circular in the sense that it is *self-perpetuating. Second,* the adult members such as mother, father, grandmother, etc. repeat the babbling sound in presence of the child. Such repetition or sounds became a conditioned stimulus and causes the child to repeat them. In this way, child learns to speak the word frequently thus repeated by adult members of the family. *Third*, adult members such as mother may put the object before the child and may repeat the appropriate syllable. For example, mother may show a 'doll of a male boy' and repeat the appropriate concerning syllable. With several repetition a connection between stimuli (doll) and the spoken syllable is established in the mind of the child.

In this way Watson explained language development on the basis of application of principle of conditioning. The physically handicapped children specially the deaf-mute children remain unable to have a normal level of language development due to the fact that these various phases of conditioning don't work properly in them.

2. *Thinking*

For Watson, thinking is an implicit or covert behaviour that consists of tendencies of muscular movements or glandular secretions which are, of course, not directly observable. However, they exert important influence upon overt behaviour. As the child learns to speak since $2\frac{1}{2}$ years of age, he talks out loudly to himself. But frequently parents and other adults in the environment would tell him to be quiet. As a consequence, his overt speech is reduced to silent speech involving only minute muscle movements in the vocal apparatus. This results in thinking which, for Watson, is a *subvocal talking*. However, not all thinking involves muscular movement of vocal apparatus. Watson considered that other parts of the body are also involved in thinking. The deaf mute, for example, think with his fingers because during his thinking, muscles of fingers are seen producing movements. Thus Watson's view was that we thought with our whole body though vocal apparatus such as mouth, lips, tongue and larynx was most actively engaged. In nutshell, we can say that for Watson the basis of thinking was bodily muscular reactions and tendencies—a theory popularly called *peripheral theory of thinking*. Later investigators like Jacobson (1932) and Max (1937) have substantiated the Watsonian view of thinking. Jacobson reported that muscular movements in tongue were active during silent speech and Max reported similar muscular movements in arms and hands of deaf mutes while they were thinking.

3. *Watson's environmentalism*

In 1914 Watson in his book *Behaviour : An introduction to Comparative Psychology* recognized the importance of instinctive behaviours which were hereditary tendencies. By 1925 in his book *Behviourism* he completely rejected the concept of instinct at human level and became an ardent supporter of environmental factors. He pointed out that human performances were dependent upon the way in which the environmental forces acted upon them. For him, every normal human infant has within itself some essential potentialities. It is the environment that moulds these potentialities to make him either a doctor, an artist, a lawyer or a thief. He openly challenged, *who has any evidence to the contrary ?* In 1925 in his book *Behaviourism* he made an extreme position on the importance of environment (which has became famous quotation) :

"Give me a dozen healthy infants... I will guarantee to take anyone at random and train him to become any type of specialist. I might select—a doctor, lawyer, artist, merchant-chief, and yes, even into a beggerman and thief regardless of his talents, penchants, tendencies, abilities, vocations and race of his ancestors."

From his various studies, Watson was also convinced that adult personality disturbances were due to earlier infant and childhood training. The behaviour of a person could better be improved by putting him into a better environment. On this basis he suggested a programme for social improvement called *environmental ethics.* This programme aimed at re-education and rehabilitation based upon Watsonian behaviouristic principles.

4. *Determinism* :

Watson advocated against the principle that individuals are personally responsible for their actions because they possess their own free will. Instead, he pointed out that human behaviour is determined and is not the product of free will. The implication of Watson's this view was specially important in the study of criminal behaviour. Such behaviour, through reconditioning, can be redetermined and re-educated so that criminality may became a part of the system of social control.

We shall see in next section that Watson has been criticized more for these secondary characteristics rather than for his primary ones that were included in discussion of Watsonian system.

WATSON'S EXPERIMENTAL FORMULATIONS

Watson may also be considered as a person who conducted experiment and semi-experiment in different fields of psychology to make his stand of objectivity more experimental and explicit. We can, for example, take *three* such areas in which Watson had launched his experimental programmes—*learning, emotion and memory.*

1. *Learning*

Watson considerably emphasized upon learning. For him, all habits were nothing but the products of learning and were formed on the basis of two major principles—*frequency* and *recency*. With the help of these two principles he proceeded to explain simple maze learning as well as complex human learning. He also lodged a strong *protest* against the *Thorndike's law of effect* and described it to be highly subjective one because it incorporated terms like *satisfying state of affairs* and *annoying state of affairs*.

By 1915, Watson was very much impressed by Pavlov's experiments on conditioned reflexes. Making it to be the fundamental base, Watson claimed that with the help of conditioned responses not only learning but also thinking and emotions could be explained easily. One of the best experiments in psychology was conducted by Watson and Raynor in 1920 that involved conditioning of fear response in young child named *Albert*. At the time of experimentation Albert was only eleven-month old. As a conditioned stimulus, they used white rat and as unconditioned stimulus a loud noise. In several trials the presentation of white rat was almost immediately followed by loud noise evoking responses like falling forward and crying that gave evidences of fear. Eventually, these responses occurred the moment only white rat (without being followed by a loud noise) was presented. Such learnt responses were also found to generalize because on any further trials, Albert also demonstrated similar reactions towards white fur coat, white dog, rabbit etc.

2. *Emotion*

Another major experimental programme of Watson was in the field of emotion where he conducted several studies on children below 3 years age. Some of his studies were experimental or quasi-experimental whereas some of his studies were genetic (or longitudinal) ones. His longitudinal studies with emotional life of the infants and children were particularly famous. He observed a large number of children over a considerable length of time and concluded that there were three clear-cut identifiable emotions present at birth—fear, rage and love. Thus for Watson, these emotions are inborn. He further pointed out that in fear there is a sudden catching of the breath, sudden closing of the eyes, puckering of lips, etc. In rage response the body stiffens and striking movements of the hands and arms are found. In love the infants smile and attempts at gurgling and cooing. On the basis of his semi-experimental observations, Watson also recognized the basic stimuli or conditions that may produce fear, rage and love in infants. His conclusion was that fear was produced by loud noise and loss of bodily support, rage was produced by restraining bodily movement and love was produced by tickling, patting, stroking or manipulating various areas of the body. Thus Watson finally concluded that stimuli that produce emotions (before any type of learning occurs) were very limited. Later on, Bridges (1932) elaborating Watson's this particular experimental programme, found no evidences for his stand and she said that infants did not show any clear-cut evidence of differentiation of various emotions at birth except for general excitation. Despite, this criticism, Watson's basic stand that infants demonstrate only limited innate emotional behaviour has still been popular and widely acceptable to most of the psychologists.

Towards the end of his experimental programme, he also showed some concern towards the acquisition and elimination of the emotional responses. For explaining acquisition of emotional response, he conducted experiment on Albert an eleven-month old child through the technique of Pavlov's conditioning (we have already discussed this experiment above). For showing how a conditioned emotional response is eliminated, he tried out several methods such as verbal appeal, disuse, presentation of unafraid model, etc. But none of these methods were found to be effective. Then he proceeded in collaboration with Mary Cover Jones to undertake an experiment on an infant named *Peter* in which he used technique of reconditioning for eliminating the conditioned emotional response of fear. While Peter was eating, the conditioned fear stimulus (rabbit) was placed at such distance that it might not produce any such response. Gradually, as trials proceeded ahead, that stimulus was progressively brought at closer points while he was continuing eating. At last, it was found that Peter was continuing eating the meal and at the same time handling the rabbit without any fear. Today this original technique of Watson has been renamed as *behaviour modification therapy*. Thus Watson was able to show how the conditioned emotional response of fear, through reconditioning be eliminated.

3. *Memory*

Watson lodged strong protests to all those psychologists who considered memory as a faculty of mind. In fact, he presented a tri-process explanation of memory on the basis of his semi-experimental observations. First, there must be learning of some skill or habit. Second, there occurs forgetting of learnt habits due to disuse. Finally, there could be relearning involving the effort and amount of time taken in regaining the task. When a person remains unable to recall something, it means that certain motor systems that had been developed during original learning stood broken. Watson's this trifold explanation is applied to both motor memory and verbal memory.

In this way we find that Watson was also an experimentalist though not like a modern experimentalist nor like that of Wundtian type. His experimental endeavour was a great source of inspiration to later experimentalists.

CRITICISMS OF WATSON'S BEHAVIOURISM

Psychologists have criticized both primary system and secondary system of Watsonian behaviourism. We have seen that this primary system includes definition of psychology, methods of psychology, mind-body problems, etc. In other words, his primary system includes both methodological or empirical behaviourism and metaphysical behaviourism. Some of the major criticisms of his primary system may be outlined as under :

1. William McDougall was one of the major critics of Watson system. As we know, by 1925 Watson had completely rejected theory of instinct that was the base of McDougall's psychology. Attacking Watson, McDougall pointed out that denial of consciousness and mind as well as total rejection of method of introspection eliminated a great deal of valuable and legitimate data in psychology. For example, when consciousness is denied. the functional relations of conscious experiences, that is, their dependence upon external or bodily conditions could not be studied. Thus Watson was charged with narrowing the scope of psychology and limiting it to the study of overt behaviour.

R. S. Woodworth (who always showed a disliking for Watson from beginning) also criticized Watson's denial of consciousness and his overemphasis upon the study of objective behaviour. Woodworth (1948) pointed out that such emphasis upon objectivity, in fact, will block future researches in the area of sensation and perception. He also criticized Watson's effort to study afterimages. He also criticized Watson' substitution of method of verbal report for method of introspection. He has rightly concluded, "We may conclude that verbal report is not a behaviouristic method and that Watson's use of it is practically a confession of defeat for methodological behaviourism." (Woodworth, 1948, p. 84). Boring (1950), giving a somewhat different level of argument, has also criticized method of verbal report.

This criticism has been replied by Watson and some other behaviourists. We have already dealt with Watson's reply.

2. Watson has also been criticized for his attempt to translate some mentalistic concepts like wishes, meaning, thoughts, etc. into

behaviouristic language. Such mentalistic concepts, in fact, weakens the methodological behaviourism in its emphasis upon objectivity. Heidbreder (1961) has very rightly commented that verbal translations of mentalistic concepts such as wish which is an organic set, meaning of which is nothing but bodily attitude, and thoughts which are simply language mechanisms, etc. create an impression of scientific and objective explanation where as the reality is that they have been simply defined in behaviouristic language and made workable.

Although this criticism is held to be more appropriate one, it has also been replied. This is true that Watson could not do much with these translations in scientific way, it could certainly be regarded as one of his basic efforts to objectify the psychological problems. In later years Watson allowed the mentalistic concepts disappear from psychological scene rather than translate them into behaviouristic language.

3. Another criticism of Watson has been that in his various explanations he used implicit behaviour tendencies that were not directly observable. Thus he was charged with providing a contradictory framework in the sense that on the one hand he himself emphasized upon studying only objectively observed behaviour while on the other hand, he included implicit behaviour tendencies not observable directly. For example, in studying implicit speech he has tried to concentrate on implicit responses like tongue, mouth and larynx movements, etc. not observable directly albeit they were observable in Watson's view. Thus Watson was, in fact, backtracking the restriction upon psychology put by himself.

This criticism has also been replied. In fact there is no inconsistency in assuming implicit behaviour tendencies while attempting to study something in objectively observable frame-work. When Watson based his data on the study of observable responses, the assumed implicit responses no longer remained unobserved. Moreover, Watson was not the psychologist to include assumed implicit behaviour tendencies. Freud's explanation of subconscious processes, Hull's and Tolman's use of various intervening variable in explanation of learning are also examples of such assumed implicit entities.

4. Some psychologists like Tolman (1932) has criticized Watson for either completely excluding purpose from his explanation of behaviour or treating it as a highly unimportant concept in such explanation. Tolman further said that Watson provided a *molecular definition* of behaviour in terms of its physiological details. Tolman rejected this molecular definition and instead, provided a molar definition with

emphasis upon purposiveness without which nobody can do full justice to any psychological explanation.

Later Watson, in principle, agreed with Tolman that behaviour could be defined in molar behavioural terms because it is an 'emergent' phenomenon having its own defining properties. Watson also accepted, in principle, that such molar behaviour could be analyzed in terms of its physiological details.

5. Watson's stand on metaphysical behaviourism has also been criticized. We have seen (first point of criticism) that Watson rejected introspection but accepted verbal report—a point which in the eyes of many psychologists presented a contradictory stand and for which he was vehemently criticized.

The most severe attack upon Watson's metaphysical behaviourism was due to his argument against interactionism and outright rejection of mind. This stand on mind was criticized by both behaviourists like Hunter (1924) and non-behaviourists like Angell (1913), Bergmann (1956), Heidbreder (1961). Hunter opined that denial of consciousness or mind could never be a popular stand among psychologists. Heidbreder, likewise, opined that if Watson outright reject the existence of mind or consciousness, his psychology will not be able to explain terms like thinking and emotion. Bergmann, even making a more bitter attack, pointed out that in order to establish no interacting minds, Watson asserted that there was no mind at all which was, of course, *not only false* but also *silly*.

Watson's stand on his *secondary system* that included environmentalism and determinism among others has also been criticized as under :

6. Critics pointed out that Watson "went overboard" in his position on extreme environmentalism. He altogether rejected hereditary and instinctive factors. He explained differences in behaviours of the persons as solely occurring due to environmental factors. Now-a-days with renewed interest in ethology and sociobiology, most of the psychologists have also started the explanation of behavioural differences in hereditary and instinctual factors. Thus the pendulum has started swinging back.

Despite these criticisms, it can be said with reasonable confidence that Watson established psychology on a firm footing and shown the way for later experimental psychologists to expand their line of experimental researches. However, as structuralism is today *no more*, so also no great system like behaviourism does exist in its original form today.

SOME OTHER EARLY BEHAVIOURISTS

Watson was having a number of ardent supporters who expanded his system and tried to improve upon his psychology. Among such supporters four names are frequently cited—*Albert P. Weiss, Karl Lashley, Walter S. Hunter* and *Edwin B. Holt*. The significant contributions of these persons may be presented as under :

Albert P. Weiss (1879–1931)

Weiss was born in Germany and came to America at a very early age. He took his Ph.D. Degree working under Max Meyer (who had himself come from Berlin) at Missouri in 1916. The remainder of his career was spent at Olio State University. His major work *A Theoretical Basis for Human Behaviour* was published in 1925. In this book he discussed his major experimental programme for what he termed as a *biosocial behaviourism.*

Weiss was an ardent supporter of Watson. Like him, he also proposed a highly objective behaviourism that completely denied consciousness, mind and introspection. He regarded psychology as a biosocial discipline and accordingly, he explained the activity of the organism as a physiological processes making interaction with the environment. He further pointed out that all physiological processes could be reduced to the same elements (electrons and protons) that physics dealt with. In a similar tune, he considered the whole organism to be made up of relatively permanent organization of atoms, molecules and tissues. Changes taking place within the organism were said to be related with electron-and proton changes in the environment. Growth, nutrition and metabolism of the organism are nothing but manifestation of interaction between the organism and the environment.

Weiss analyzed human behaviour into biophysical and biosocial stimuli and reactions. A biophysical stimulus referred to the energy releasing its function in the sense organ. A bio-physical response was one that ended in muscular or glandular activities. A biosocial stimulus (also a biophysical one) was one that had been established as a socialized substitute for other forms of further stimulation. A biosocial response (also a biophysical one) was one in which the muscular response produced a socialized stimulus. It is, thus, clear that, for Weiss, behaviour was both biological and social. Whenever new responses occurred to some changing situations, learning occurred. He also explained group behaviour, social organization and civilization. For him, civilization was nothing but the cumulative effect of the behaviour of the individual in the society towards achieving successful goals. In this way

Weiss had a lot of progressive programme to deal with. But due to his untimely death in 1931, nothing significant was done and his ideas remained unestablished.

***Walter S. Hunter* (1889–1953)**

Like Watson, Hunter was trained under Chicago functionalists. He took his Ph. D. degree working under Angell and Carr in 1912. He taught at various Universities like Texas, Kansas and Clark and finally went to Brown University where he remained for his life. At Brown University, he became interested in experimental research particularly laboratory research rather than in formulating theories. In a bid to abandon psychology's heritage to philosophy, he strongly emphasized the fact that psychology was the science of behaviour and that is nothing to do with dualism. He also brought a technological innovation by attempting to give new name to science of behaviour—*anthroponomy*. 'Anthro' means man and 'nomey' means study of laws of man. But his this technological innovations remained unsuccessful.

At the University of Brown he established a small department for carrying out laboratory researches. He is well-known for his experimental studies of delayed-response and double alternation tasks through which it was possible to study the process of remembering in animals. In such experiments animal was first given a visual stimulus as indicator of food in appropriate box (out of so many food boxes). When in this way a discrimination learning was established, the light for the appropriate box was presented and then switched off. Meanwhile, the animal was restrained, the purpose of which was to determine how long the animal could remember the right door leading to the box. On the basis of several studies, he concluded that animals maintained a bodily posture that helped them in going towards the right direction. It meant that animals remember something by maintain appropriate bodily posture.

***Edwin B. Holt* (1873–1946)**

Holt was a great admirer of William James. He was awarded Ph. D. by Harvard University in 1901. He also taught at this University until 1918 and at Princeton University from 1926 to 1936. In the intervening eight years period he retired to write. After 1936, he again retired to write. His writings had a mixed tone of philosophy and experimental psychology. Boring (1950) has rightly said that he was half a philosopher, a realist and half a good experimentalist. Among his publications important were : *The Concept of Consciousness* (1914), *The Freudian wish and its Place in Ethics* (1915), *Animal Drive and the Learning process* (1931).

Like Watson, he also believed that psychology was the study of behaviour, or what he called ' the specific response relationship'. But at the same time he was different from Watson in the sense that he considered the response not in molecular perspective but in molar perspective. For Holt, response involved the whole unit of activity. This is molar explanation. As we know, Watson had preferred another contrasting explanation called molecular explanation. Watson would explain the walking of a person to a shop in terms of his each step only but Holt would explain the walking this person not in terms of the steps but walking to a shop. For him, the entire event from the first step of walking to coming to shop was one event and should be considered as a whole. Thus, for Holt, behaviour was purposive and in this sense, he had anticipated Tolman's *purposive behaviourism*. For Holt, behaviour was molar, purposive and cognitive. The last aspect of behaviour involved meaning.

Holt also took up Watson's view that thinking was merely a matter of language mechanisms. For him, our language habit or the response to words is nothing but conditioning. In considering the problem of language he opened the way for further studies in the field of verbal conditioning. One basic point of similarity of Holt to Watson was that he had also rejected heredity to be a factor in determining human behaviour. He emphasized that our behaviours are learnt and even the unconditioned reflexes were learnt either in prenatal life or immediatly after birth. For Holt, behaviour is learnt when the person is exposed to either outer motivation or inner motivation. Reinforcements in Pavlov and Watson experiments on conditioning represented outer motivation or stimulation. Inner motivation like hunger, thirst, etc. also forces the person to learn. Holt's emphasis upon the role of these inner motives paved the way for development of learning theory of Hull that explained learning on the basis of drive reduction.

***Karl Lashley* (1989–1958)**

Lashley was a student of Watson at John Hopkins University from where he received his Ph. D. degree in psychology in 1914. His many distinguished teaching appointments were at the Universities of Minnesota (1917-1926), Chicago (1929-1935), and at Harvard (1935-1952). Along with his professorship at Harvard, in 1942, he also took the additional charge of director of the Yerkes Laboratory of Primate Biology, a world-fame Chimpanzee research laboratory.

Lashley was an ardent supporter of Watson. In fact, he provided a strong support to Watsonian behaviourism through his researches in the field of physiological psychology. He rejected consciousness or mind as the study of psychology and introspection as method of psychology. He pointed out that introspection was "an example of pathology of scientific methods" (1923). Despite his support to Watson, he differed from Watson on many important issues.

Lashley is best known for his extensive research in the field of physiological psychology. Like Watson, he did not consider brain as 'mystery box". In fact, he wanted to study localization of different functions in brain and to see what happens to behaviour when parts of the brain are removed. He formulated two major principles as under :

1. *Principle of Mass Action*

Prior to Lashley, theories of specific localization of functions in the brain were prevalent. His experimental findings enabled him to oppose such localization by postulating what he termed as *principle of mass action.* According to this principle, learnt behaviour did not depend on specific neural connections in the brain but on the brain as a whole. In other words, learning depends upon the total mass of brain tissue. Greater the amount of brain tissue, better was the learning and retention of learnt behaviour. Lashley, collaborating with one of his former professor, Shepard I. Franz, conducted several experiments on cats, rats and monkeys. In their experiment on cats and monkeys they placed these animals in puzzle box similar to that used by Thorndike. After animals has learnt to escape from the box, some parts of the brain of these animals were damaged. When animals recovered from the wounds, they were again put into the box. Experimenters observed that now animals were unable to perform the learnt task. However, with further training they were able to relearn. Similarly, Lashley trained white rats to make light-dark discrimination. After such learning, one part of the brain of such experimental rats was removed. It was found that rats did not lose what have been gained earlier.

From these experiments Lashley concluded that brain functions as a whole. The functioning of damaged or removed parts of the brain is taken over by the remaining or undamaged parts. Greater the amount of total mass of the undestroyed tissue in brain, better was the learning and retention. Thus the earlier observation relating to theories of specific localization of functions in the brain was disproved by Lashley's principle of mass action.

2. *Principle of Equipotentiality*

This principle states that all parts of brain are as important as the other and therefore, they are equally potential. If some parts of the brain are damaged or missed, other parts have equipotentiality to carry on the functions of those damaged parts. For example, Lashley reported that when visual areas of rats were removed, its function relating to making discrimination in light intensity remained intact because it was taken over by other equipotential parts of the brain although patterning was definitely lost. Such findings merely confirmed the view that brain functions as a whole and its different parts are equally potential. From such conclusions some psychologists like Wolman (1960), Marx & Hillix (1963) pointed out that Lashley's experimental findings tended to support gestalt theory of wholes and configuration (though he was a behaviourirt). However, by providing experimental evidence, Lashley criticized the isomorphic principle of Gestalt psychology. This principle stated that there was correspondence of parallelism between what we perceive and what appeared in the brain fields. Lastly, Chow and Semmes (1951) conducted experiment in which they placed silver foil in animal cortex, thus shortcircuiting the supposed brain fields. Such placement did not destroy the discrimination which, according to gestalt theory, depended solely upon those fields. How is it possible ?

Psychologist like Krech (1962) while making a review of the problem of cortical localization, has, however, criticized these two principles of Lashley and he has said that these principles (principle of equipotentiality and principle of mass action) are vague and circular.

Apart from his neurological contributions, Lashley has been honoured for his obvious psychological contributions maintaining his behaviouristic outlook. In fact, he was a psychologist who rejected some of Watson's secondary beliefs while continuing to support his methodological behaviorism. He attempted to combine his behaviourism with a field orientation that made him very popular in psychology. One example of Lashley's interest in such orientation was his support for a relational or pattern explanation of transposition learning. Rejecting the traditional S-R interpretation of generalization and discrimination learning, he presented an alternative view. In collaboration with Wade, he formulated a hypothesis called *Lashley-Wade hypothesis* which emphasized that generalization gradient depended upon the opportunity given to the organism to learn about the various properties of stimulus dimension along which generalization was to take place. This automatically rejects the classical S-R interpretation that reinforcement of any single stimulus value produces generalization gradient. Later on psychologists like Terrace (1966) and Kalish (1969) also supported Lashley and Wade. Needless to say, Lashley's famous apparatus called

Lashley's jumping stand has also been very important contribution to the field of discrimination learning.

CHAPTER HIGHLIGHTS

1. Behaviourism, as established by Watson, did not spring up suddenly. It had, like other systems, a strong antecedent forces—that may be grouped into four categories—early philosophical trend empasizing objectivism, animal psychology, Pavlovian conditioned reflex and functionalism.
2. Watsonian behaviourism had two subsystems—primary and secondary. His primary system had two major aspects—positve and negative. His positive aspect was his emphasis upon objective psychology. This aspect of behaviourism was termed as *empirical or methodological behaviourism*. His negative aspect emphasized upon his rejection of introspective psychology of Titchener and Wundt as well as that of Angell's. This aspect was called as *metaphysical or radical behaviourism*. Watson's primary system spelled out clearly the definition of psychology, methods of psychology and emphasized the major postulates of psychology, principles of connection, principles of selection as well as took special interest in mind-body problem by adopting monism.
3. Watson's secondary system mainly emphasized upon language development, thinking, environmentalism and determinism. All these features made his secondary system unique.
4. Apart from his formulation of primary and secondary system, Watson's experimental programme was no less fascinating to psychologists. His experimental studies in the field of learning, emotion and memory were highly appealing. With the help of two basic principles, namely, frequency and recency, he explained simple maze learning and complex human learning. He rejected Thorndike's law of effect describing it a highly subjective one. His experimental studies of development of emotion in children and infants have established that there were three clear-cut identifiable emotions (fear, rage and love) present at birth. He further described the nature of reactions in each of these emotions and the various stimuli that caused it. In the field of memory he made many semi-experimental observations and on that basis, he concluded that memory has a tri-process explanation.
5. Watsonian behaviourism has been criticized on six different grounds. *First*, McDougall and Woodworth criticized Watson for his denial of consciousness, mind as well as total rejection of mehtod of

introspection. *Second,* Watson's efforts to translate some mentalistic concepts like wishes, meaning, thoughts, etc., into behavioursitic language has also been criticized. *Third,* Watson has also been criticized for using implicit behaviour tendencies that were not directly observable. *Fourth,* Tolman (1932) has criticized Watson for either completely excluding purpose from his explanation of behaviour or treating it as a highly unimportant concept in such explanation. *Fifth,* Watson rejected introspection but accepted verbal report which was obviously a contradictory stand and vehemently criticized by several psychologists. *Sixth,* Watson's extreme position on environmentalism has also been criticized.

6. Watson was having a number of ardent supporters. Some of them were Albert P. Weiss, Karl Lashley, Walter S. Hunter and Edwin B. Holt. Weiss is well-known for his biosocial behaviourism. Hunter's anthroponomy is also no less important. Holt emphasized upon molar and purposeful behaviour thus anticipating Tolman's purposive behaviourism. Lashley is well-known for his principles of mass action and principle of equipotentiality.

REVIEW QUESTIONS

1. Discuss the major antecedent forces that led to the emergence of behaviourism.
2. Examine Watsonian behaviorism as a system of psychology.
3. Critically examine the major secondary features of Watsonian behaviourism.
4. Assess the importance of Watsonian experimental programme in emergence of modern experimental psychology.
5. What were, in you opinion, the major points of weaknesses of Watsonian behaviourism.
6. Do you agree with the view that Watson's psychology was a 'mind-less psychology' ? If so, prove this.
7. Discuss the contributions of Albert P. Weiss and Walter S. Hunter in improving the position of Watsoninan behaviourism.
8. Assess the contributions of Karl Lashley and Edwin B. Holt in strengthening the behaviouristic position of Watson.

■

CHAPTER 11

LATER BEHAVIOURISM

CHAPTER PREVIEW

In the present chapter the contributions of six later behaviorists, namely, E. R. Guthrie, C. L. Hull, B. F. Skinner, E. C. Tolman, J. R. Kantor and A. Bandura have been discussed.

Guthrie emphasized upon learning by contiguity. In fact his deemphasis upon motivation and reinforcement has been lucidly presented. His various methods of breaking habits have also been discussed.

Hull formulated a strong system that pushed behaviorism to its place of prominence. Hull's major postulates have been discussed separately. His system was also supported by some experimental evidences. Finally, his system has been criticized on some obvious grounds.

During thirties Skinner actively studied various principles of learning using rats and pigeons as subjects in skinner box and pigeon box respectively. Skinner adopted a descriptive approach in explaining his behaviouristic outlook. That is why his system has also been named as descriptive behaviorism. His system has been sketched under nine subheadings, namely, the psychology of conditioning, drive, emotion, shaping and superstitious behaviour, verbal behaviour, teaching machines and programmed learning, behaviour modification and beyond freedom and dignity.

Tolman's purposive behaviourism was another hallmark in the history of behaviourism. As a purposive behaviourist, he made it clear that learnt behaviour is always directed and oriented toward some end or goal. His system gave emphasis upon four parts, namely, independent variables, dependent variables, intervening variables and theory of learning. Finally, his system has also been criticized.

Kantor's interbehavioural psychology or his interbehavioursim emphasized that the subject-matter of psychology should be the interaction of organism and stimulus objects. For explanation of behaviour he emphasized upon construct rather then intervening variables. His system includes discussion on concepts like psychological interactions, interactional setting, contact medium, interbehaviour history, implicit interactions, affective interactions, emotion and memorial interactions.

Bandura emphasized that human behaviour can be easily understood as a function of reciprocal interaction of behavioural, cognitive and environmental determinants. His behaviourism has been called as soft behaviourism in contrast to hard behaviourism of Skinner and Watson. His emphasis upon modelling technique or technique of observational learning has been a very valuable contribution to psychology.

As we know, by 1930 Watson had completely withdrawn himself from academic circle and stopped writing and theorizing about psychology. Despite this, his impact was widely felt, among the academic psychologists. As a consequence, a group of such psychologists evolved who tried to develop their own theories keeping themselves basically within the general frame-work of Watsonian behaviourism. Such group of psychologists has been recognized as neobehaviourists or later behaviourists. Most historians agree that there were six such important behavioursists—Edwin R. Guthrie, Clark L. Hull, B. F. Skinner, E. C. Tolamn, J. R. Kantor and A. Bandura. In the present chapter, we shall discuss the contributions of each of them separately.

EDWIN R GUTHRIE (1886-1959)

Guthrie obtained his Ph. D. degree from the University of Pennsylvania in 1912. After that he joined University of Washington where he remained till his retirement in 1956. In 1958 he was awarded Gold Medal from the American Psychological Foundation for his important and outstanding contribution to psychology. He wrote several books.

His important books were : *The Psychology of Learning* (1938), *The Psychology of Human conflict* (1938). In collaboration with A. L. Edwards he wrote another elementary book : *Psychology : A First course in Human Behaviour* (1949). Guthrie's major contributions may be outlined under following important headings :

1. *Learning by continuity*

Like Watson, Guthrie also stated that psychology should study only those behaviours that are observable and measurable. He is popularly known for his theory of *contiguous conditioning*. Rejecting Pavlovian conditioning he pointed out that association by contiguity in time or also called as simultaneous conditioning is the most general law in psychology. He stated, "A combination of stimuli which has accompanied a movement will on its recurrence tend to be followed by that movement." (Guthrie, 1938 : 26). In explaining learning Guthrie followed Thorndike but without the law of effect. His viewpoint was that any stimulus pattern gains its full associative strength on the very first occasion of being paired with a response. This is called *single-trial learning*. From this it is obvious that he undermined the importance of practice in learning. His position regarding single-trial learning was in apparent contradiction to the view of S-R theorists who had regarded practice to be one of the fundamental pillars in learning. In order to solve this apparent contradiction, he made *distinction* between act and movement. Movement is a pattern of muscular or glandular responses. An act is a series of movement that brings end results. When he claimed that learning is complete in single trial, he meant learning of movement and not of act. Thus for Guthrie learning is concerned with movements and not with acts and contiguity alone explains association of stimuli and response movements. He further claimed that Thorndike's law of effect was concerned with acts and not movements. Thus, according to Guthrie, Thorndike did not deal with the basic laws of learning.

Despite this, Guthrie agreed to the view that practice or repetition improves learning and practice is needed in learning of act or complex function that is composed of several movements. Learning of simple movement does not require practice but learning of act or any complex function that consists of several movements is learnt through repetitions which, in fact, became separate movements to be associated with exteroceptive, proprioceptive and interoceptive elements of the stimulus situation.

2. *Motivation, reward and punishment*

Unlike Thorndike, Hull and Skinner, Guthrie undermined the importance of motivation. For him, the only significance of motivation (food deprivation) was that it tended to increase the number and vigor of movement that may obtain associative connections with the stimuli.

Guthrie also believed that Thorndike's concept of reward and punishment could also be easily replaced by the *principle* of the last response. Thus with the help of this principle, he also undermined the importance of reinforcement in learning—a concept which is highly important in learning according to Thorndike. Guthrie pointed out that the last response is usually the *lasting response*. Guthrie and Horton (1946) conducted several experiments on cats in puzzle box and it was found that the last response made by cat in box is always repeated when she is placed in the box next. Voeks (1954) also confirmed their conclusion by conducting experiment on human beings. Thus various results indicated a very repetitious and stereotyped response in different subjects. When the animal is put in learning situation, it is the last successful response that either removes the animal from the problematic situation (puzzle box learning) or changes the situation to such extent that no new association related to that stimulus can be learnt (maze learning). In puzzle box situation the last successful response means escape from the box (after which no response occurs) and in maze learning the last successful response is feeding that reduces the drive-produced stimuli substantially. In either case, Guthrie argues, it is not the feelings produced by reward but the last overt specific action caused by reward that becomes conditioned or learnt. Guthrie also made it clear that the learnt response is not strengthened by reward. Reinforcement (reward), however, becomes important because it protects the response from being unlearnt since it brings a change in the stimulus situation by removing the organism from that situation (in which learning had taken place). When the organism is removed from that situation, no question of weakening the original response by associative interference arises (because no learning can take place when organism is himself removed).

So far as the punishment is concerned, it is much similar to motivation for Guthrie. For him, if punishment is to be effective, it must (a) produce behaviour that is incompatible with the punished behaviour (b) be given in presence of stimuli that produced the punished behaviour.

3. *Extinction and Forgetting*

Guthrie had also no difficulty in explaining extinction and forgetting. Pavlov had explained forgetting and extinction as occurring due to removal of reinforcement or unconditioned stimulus. Guthrie explained these phenomena in other terms. For him, when a particular S-R connection is made, it remains in the organism's repertoire in full strength for a period unless some new responses occurs to destroy or replace it. To explain extinction he introduced the concept of *associative inhibition* which meant learning of some incompatible responses that interferes with the previous or original response. Learning of new associative connection, in fact, replaces the previously learnt one and interferes with it. As a consequence, the previously learnt response is extinguished. He explained forgetting in much similar tone. For him, forgetting can't take place without the interference by the succeeding responses.

4. *Breaking habits*

For Guthrie, a habit is an established set of movements that is associated with a large number of stimuli. In general he postulated a principle that the greater number of stimuli that have caused the responses, the stronger will be the habit. Some people have a strong habit of drinking wine because it has been associated with several stimuli—in a party, after meal, before going to enjoy the wife, and thus in the presence of so many conditions. He had outlined *three* methods of breaking a habit. They are as under :

(a) ***Threshold method*** : In this method the stimuli presented are so weak or faint that the undesirable response does not occur. In fact, the intensity of the stimulus is said to be below the threshold for the response to occur. Hence, the name. Gradually the stimuli are increased in strength on successive trials in such a way that the response never occurs. These repeated experiences with the faint or weak stimuli raise the threshold so that even stronger stimuli will be below that threshold. The method is used mainly for eliminating emotional responses like fear, anger, etc.

(b) ***Method of fatigue*** : In this method response to be eliminated is elicited time and again until the person is so tired that he becomes willing to stop making further response and does something else instead. This something else or the other response thus becomes established and the old response becomes extinguished.

(c) ***Method of incompatible stimuli*** : As its name implies, in this method the stimuli which produced an undesired response are presented with the stimuli that evoke a different but incompatible response. Gradually the original stimuli became attached to the new response, thus eliminating the old undesirable response.

5. *Prediction and control*

Like Watson, Guthrie pointed out that aims of psychology should be the prediction and control of behaviour. The aim of any scientific research is the discovery of scientific laws and the validity of scientific laws including psychological laws is assessed by their ability to make effective prediction. These scientific laws deal with only those phenomena which are observable. In this way we find that Guthrie's methodological position was one of radical empiricist who was not ready to accept anything beyond our sensory perception.

Some psychologists have *criticized* Guthrie's contribution on the following grounds :

(i) Psychologists like Thorndike, Skinner, Hull have maintained that Guthrie had tried to sidetrack the major issue like impact of reward or reinforcement in learning. They have shown surprise over how did Guthrie maintain a theory of learning that completely ignored reinforcement. They have claimed that since majority of experimental studies support the role of reinforcement in learning, it is difficult to accept Guthrie's theory that ignores reinforcement.

(ii) On the basis of a few experimental evidences Guthrie had calculated that animals show repetitious and stereotyped responses in learning situation. (Remember Guthrie and Horton's cat in the puzzle box !) Critics have said that by giving emphasis upon such behaviour, he has ignored the role of individual differences. They maintain that due to past experiences and a variety of previous conditioning, the learning organism does not always behave in the same way in learning situation. In fact, each organism has its own characteristic way of behaving in learning situation.

(iii) Some psychologists have maintained that Guthrie had tried to explain too much on the basis of too few facts and principles. Muller and Schoenfeld (1954) have pointed out that Guthrie had also failed to be clear and explicit on too many basic issues. They further maintained that Guthrie touched the issue no doubt but remained unable to give a clear exposition of his stand.

(iv) Guthrie had also failed to provide adequate experimental support in favour of his theory. For example, when we compare the theories of learning of Skinner, Hull and Thorndike with that of Guthrie we find that the experimental evidences in favour of Guthrie are too meagre. In fact, he depended much on anecdotes. Psychologists further pointed out that although his anecdotes were interesting no doubt, but they could not be regarded as substitute for experimental facts.

Despite these criticisms, Guthrie has maintained a position as one of the major learning theorists because much of Guthrie's theory is still hard to disprove.

CLARK L. HULL (1884-1952)

Hull obtained his Ph. D. degree in psychology in 1918 at the University of Wisconsin where he remained till 1928. His doctoral dissertation was in the area of concept formation which was considered by most psychologists of that time to be a masterpiece in experimental design. As Valentine and Wiggins (1949) have pointed out one of Hull's early experiments was conducted to examine the impact of tobacco smoking on efficiency in performing some psychological tasks. Hull's next major area of work was in the field of aptitude testing and he also wrote a text book *Aptitude Testing* which was published in 1928. But later on he dropped this area of work apprehending no future. Next, he turned to work in the area of suggestibility and hypnosis and he devoted several years to these areas. He conducted several experiments in these areas and published *Hypnosis and Suggestibility* in 1933. This book remained an important text for many years.

In 1929 he joined as research professor at Yale University and remained there for the rest of his career. It was here that he along with several colleagues and students developed a theory of learning. He published this in a book *A Mathematico-Deductive Theory of Role Learning* in 1921. The theory was framed in mathematical language and hence most people could not understand it and therefore, it could not be much popular. However, it was simplified in understandable language and reappeared in 1943 in *Principles of behaviour.* Its revisions were done in *Essential of behaviour* (1951) and *A Behaviour System* (1952).

Hull's System : Some antecedent forces

Hull's system, like many others, did not come up suddenly. In fact, in formulating his system he was influenced by the work of many persons of whom Darwin, Pavlov, Watson, Thorndike and Woodworth are frequently named.

Hull was much influenced by Darwin's emphasis upon an individual's biological adaptation to the environment. Organisms develop need that represent a deviation from the optimal biological conditions necessary for existence. For Hull, learning took place when these needs were fulfilled and a biological equilibrium was established. He was also deeply influenced by Pavlov's works on the conditioned reflex. He considered this one simple form of learning through which a complex of learning could also be explained. He also liked Pavlov's concept of reinforcement which he held to be the fundamental base for learning. Much on the same pattern, Hull was also influenced by Thorndike who held reinforcement to be one of the important variables in learning. Hull, however, made a distinction in interpretation of the effects of reinforcement. For Thorndike, reinforcement was effective because it produced *satisfaction* in the organism but for Hull reinforcement was effective because it led to the *reduction of drives* in the organism. Thus Hull's system was very much a drive theory.

Watson was a behaviourist and therefore, his influence upon Hull was that of a behaviourist. In this broad sense, Hull's system may be considered as S-R psychology. At this juncture, Woodworth's influence upon Hull is also worth mentioning. Woodworth is well-known for his S-O-R formula. S is the stimulus which affects organism (O) and the resulting response (R) depends upon both stimulus and response. Hull immediately understood the significance of this formula and incorporated the variables related to organism in his theory to explain learnt behaviour. Such variables were called as *intervening variables* in Hull's system. These variables are inferred or internal states of the organism. However, other behaviourists have lodged a protest against inclusion of such subjective variables by Hull in his system. They claimed that by including such variables Hull's system lost the basic criteria of objectivity. Thus they branded Hull to be a dualist and not a true bnehaviourist like Watson. As this objection is not only with Hull but is also equally shared by other neobehaviourists like Tolman, we can consider it not to be a major deviation.

Hull's Contributions

Hull enjoys a very distinguished position in modern psychological theory. He applied the language of mathematics and logic to the psychological theory in an unique manner done by no other psychologists. Hull had strong belief that whatever exists, exists in some quantity and relationship among them could be discovered by mathematical equations.

Hull's contribution is limited to the field of learning. He began to develop a theory of learning in 1915 and by 1943 it was published in his *Principles of behaviour* and in its later revisions *Essentials of behaviour* (1951) and *A Behaviour System* (1952). Hull had set his theory of learning in terms of 17 postulates and 15 corollaries (Hill, 1980). Keeping in view the purpose of the present book, it is not possible to deal his theory postulatewise and therefore, we will try to avoid becoming entangled in the immense complexity. The interested readers are, however, suggested to consult *Theories of learning* by Hilgard and Bower (1981).

Hull developed *four* methods of discovering scientific truth. *First* is the method of *unplanned observation*. This is a very simple method in which we can discover a truth by simply making the observation of facts in a way that is a most convenient to us. *Second* is the method of *planned observation*. This method differs from the first method in the sense that it is systematic and planned. Its operation is not arranged according to our convenience. *Third* is *experimental testing method* in which the validity of hypothesis is tested by a carefully planned experimentation. *Fourth* is the most important and fruitful method called *hypotheticodeductive method*. It is, in fact, a three-step method. At first step, a system of definitions is set in order. At the second step, on the basis of those definitions of the concepts, some postulates (tentative statements about behaviour) are formulated. At final step, from those definitions and postulates several theorems and corollaries are deduced. On the basis of the entire set of definitions, postulates and theorems a systematic, scientific and integrated theory emerges.

Hull extensively used hypotheticodeductive method in formulating his theory. He defined his theory as systematic deductive derivation of the secondary principles of observable events from some limited number of postulates. For Hull, psychology does not start with some basic principles based on observation but observation and theory go together. In fact, observation provides a kind of check on the validity of the postulates formalized by deduction.

As stated above, Hull's system was stated in several postulates and corollaries. They may be briefly discussed as under :

1. The postulate *first* and *second* dealt with the neural activities in the brain following a sensory input. These postulates state that there occurs a gradual decay in the neural excitation and in the process of interaction specially caused by occurrence of several sensory impulses at a time, one impulse tends to modify the other.

2. *Third* postulate deals with the role of reinforcement in learning. Both Guthrie and Hull were similar in emphasizing a contiguous S-R connections in learning. For Guthrie such connection became established because it occurred in contiguity of stimulus and response and for Hull this became fixed because that was associated with reinforcement. Hull has pointed out that when a response (R) is closely associated with the stimulus trace (S) and when such S-R connections are closely related with a rapid decrease in the drive-produced stimuli (S_D), there occurs an increment (Δ) in the tendency for that S to evoke that R. He also pointed out that the rapid decrease in goal stimulus (S_G) is also reinforcing. This third postulate also contains two vital corollaries that are directly related to learning. One corollary is concerned with secondary drive and another corollary is concerned with secondary reinforcement. When a neutral stimulus is consistently associated with the primary drive, such stimulus gradually acquires the capacity to produce a state like that produced by a primary drive. This is called *secondary drive.* An example of secondary drive is fear. A dog placed in one compartment of a two-compartment box and shocked would readily go to the other compartment box, which is safe. After a few repetitions, the dog when placed in the original compartment would readily go to the second compartment even though

no shock was given to original compartment. This happened due to what is called secondary drive. The secondary reinforcement is a stimulus that acquires the property of reinforcing a reponse due to its association with the primary reinforcement.

3. *Fourth* postulate was again very important for learning and it dealt with habit formation of what Hull called as *habit strength.* It is a kind of intervening variable and refers to the tendency for a stimulus trace to produce an associated response. As Hull pointed out in this postulate, habit strength depended upon the number of reinforced trails. It is also affected by several other variables such as the strength of the drive, delay between response and reinforcement and the time interval between stimulus and response.

4. *Fifth* postulate dealt with primary drive (D). Primary drive is also a kind of intervening variable which was very important in Hull's theory. Drive is a temporary state of the organism that is produced by something our body needs or by painful stimulation. It had three distinct functions as under :

(i) Drive makes the primary reinforcement more effective because such reinforcement always requires the rapid decrement in some drive.

(ii) Drive also produces response because—it activates habit strength into reaction potential (sER). He postulated that drive multiplies with habit strength to produce reaction potential. Thus sER=D × sHR (habit strength). This equation automatically suggest that if the organism has zero drive or no drive, then in that case sER will be zero or there will be no response.

(iii) Some drives also produce action habits set up on the basis of different drive conditions. It means drive also provides distinctiveness among the various internal stimuli (the so-called drive stimuli).

5. *Sixth* and *Seventh* postulates were also important in explanation of learning. The sixth postulate is concerned with stimulus intensity (V) and the seventh postulate is concerned with incentive motivation (K). The stimulus intensity (V) refers to the fact that the probability of a response to occur increases as the intensity of the stimulus increases. Put in other words, the organism responds more readily to intense stimuli than to less intense ones. Incentive motivation (K) is a 'pull' factor and refers to the motivating effect of the incentive provided for making a response (Hill, 1980). It is measured in terms of both quality and quantity of goal (Houston, 1976).

6. *Eighth* postulate dealt with a still more important concept, that is, reactional potential ($_sE_R$). Reaction potential or excitatory potential refers to the tendency to make a given response towards a given stimulus. In fact, postulate relating to this is combination of previous three postulates relating to drive, habit strength, stimulus intensity and incentive motivation. When the conditions have been constant through-out learning situation, the reaction potential ($_sE_R$) becomes equal to the multiplicative product of habit strength ($_sH_R$), drive (D), stimulus intensity dynamism (V) and incentive motivation (K) minus inhibitory potential (I). The postulate relating to inhibition will be discuss shortly. The general equation to get net reaction potential ($_sE_R$) thus becomes :

$$_sE_R = {}_sH_R \times D \times K \times V - I$$

7. The *ninth* postulate dealt with inhibition (I) or inhibitory potential. Hull divided inhibition into two parts—reactive inhibition (I_R) and conditioned inhibition ($_sI_R$). Reactive inhibition refers to a tendency of not repeating a response that has just been made. Therefore, it is a kind of negative drive. The amount of reactive inhibition is dependent upon the amount of efforts required to make the response. As such, it is similar to fatigue, pain or tissue injury. Reactive inhibition dissipates with the time interval. Conditioned inhibition ($_sI_R$) is a kind of habit of nonresponding produced by reactive inhibition. Since both I_R and $_sE_R$ tend to cancel the effects of excitatory potential ($_sE_R$), they are subtracted from $_sE_R$ to arrive at net value of $_sE_R$.

8. The above nine postulates give a substantial understanding of his system relating to the theory of learning. Other postulates dealt with those phenomena which are related to the learning phenomena. For example, *tenth* postulate was concerned with stimulus generalization, *eleventh* with stimulus interaction, *twelvth* with behavioural oscillation (SOR),. *thirteenth* with reception potential as it was related to reaction threshold, *fourteenth* with reaction potential as it was related to reaction latency, *fifteenth* with reaction potential as it was related to reaction amplitude and *sixteenth* with reaction potential as it was related to total response to extinction.

Postulate *seventeenth* dealt with the problem of individual differences. This postulate stated that the constant numerical values appearing in different equations in various postulates and corollaries tend to vary from individual to individual and sometimes from one physiological state to other in the same individual at different times.

In nutshell, it can be said the Hull's system comprises a series of postulates and corollaries that mainly centred around drive, reinforcement and response strength. For him, reinforcement becomes effective because it reduces drive. Mere repetition of stimulus response sequence produces inhibition. The central idea regarding learning in Hull's system is, then, that learning is assumed to increase in a gradual fashion as reinforced practice advances. That is why, his theory of learning is also known as *incremental theory of learning*.

Hull's system : Some experimental support

Hull was constantly modifying his theory in order to keep it in line with the experimental evidences obtained in the field. Hull (1934a) tested experimentally the corollary that was related to delay in reinforcement. This corollary was obviously related to what is popularly called as *goal-gradient hypothesis*. In this experiment. Hull trained some rats to run for food in specially structured runway. His results indicated that the rate of running was one of *positive acceleration*, that is, when they reached closer to the goals, they ran faster. In another experiment Hull (1934b) experimentally studied the order in which rats eliminated the blind alleys in runway or maze. It was found that those blind alleys that were nearer to goal were eliminated sooner than those blind alleys that were away from the goal. Likewise, it was also observed that longer blind alleys were eliminated sooner than shorter blind alleys in learning the maze. Hull (1939) conducted another experiment in order to find out quantitative relationship between alternation of right and wrong responses. For this he constructed a special box that was modification of Skinner box. There were two types of bars in this box—horizontal bar and vertical bar. Both these bars were reinforced in the earlier stages. However, in the latter part of the experiment reinforcement was offered only after pressing the vertical bar. It was found that despite this, animals demonstrated alternation cycles. On the basis of such alternation cycles he also drew curves which were similar to the curves derived by him from his theoretical postulates. Arnold (1947) conducted experiments in which he trained rats in a special push-button apparatus with food reward. Prior to the experiment proper, when animals pushed anyone of the four buttons, reinforcement was delivered. Later, rats were required to press all the four buttons to obtain reinforcement. It was found that as each button was presented, animals' speed of pushing the button increased with an obvious gain in the last button, the one that was immediately followed by reinforcement. This experiment also confirmed the goal-gradient hypothesis. Hovland (1937) has also conducted several experiments on human beings for testing stimulus generalization of galvanic skin reaction to different auditory tones. The experiment yielded generalization gradient similar to those expected by Hull's theoretical and experimental formulations.

The above examples of experimental results demonstrate that how Hull and their associates tried to test their hypotheses experimentally. For examining the other experimental evidences in detail, the interested readers are advised to consult the above references as well as the references cited earlier in connection with Hull's system.

Hull's criticisms

Hull's system has been criticized by many psychologists. Some of the major criticisms are as under :

(1) Critics stated that Hull was obsessed with mathematics in explaining the key-points of his system. They further claimed that his explanation was too complex to understand and too mathematical* to follow. In general, critics were of view that his system could have been very nicely explained by omitting mathematical concepts.

(2) Critics stated that Hull claimed himself to be a behaviourist but at the same time he depended upon inferred states and intervening variables. Thus he maintained a dualistic position. His dependence upon inferred states and wider use of interven-ing variables have been criticized because they can't be subjected to observable operations. For example, his concept of secondary drive can't be objectively studied. Likewise, his idea about stimulus trace was purely subjective. How can its existence be demonstrated ?

(3) Hull's system was though highly logical one, contains many logical flaws. Koch (1959) has observed that Hull's system contains so many logical difficulties due to which we remain at a loss to arrive at a particular conclusion in a logical way.

(4) It is also said that Hull tried to apply his principles to the behaviour of all mammals but he did not take much pains for it. He mainly kept his experimentation and researches limited to white rats with a few exceptions to studies conducted on human beings. In such situation Hull's desire to apply his principles to all mammalian behaviour could not be taken on the scientific footing.

Despite these criticisms, Hull's contributions have been a primary source of inspiration for modern experimental psychologists working in the area of motivation and learning.

BURRHUS FREDERIC SKINNER (1904-1989)

Skinner was born on March 20, 1904. He took his M. A. degree in

---

* In discussing the Hullian postulates, the mathematical aspects have been intentionally omitted by the author.

1930 and his Ph. D. in 1931 from Harvard University. For about 5 years he enjoyed post-doctoral fellowships. Subsequently, he taught at the Universities of Michigan and Minnesota from 1936-1945. In 1945 he took over as the chairman of the department of psychology at Indiana University and remained there till 1948. After that he returned to Harvard and remained there ever since.

During thirties, Skinner was mainly interested in studying various principles of learning using rats as subjects. In this connection he developed an instrument which became popular in the name of 'Skinner Box', although Skinner himself preferred to call it as an *operant conditioning chamber*. This skinner box became so popular in psychology that it is still considered as one of the important contributions of Skinner and till now, has attracted thousands of researches and experimentation's. In forties, he shifted his attention from white rats to pigeons partly because of the fact that faster response rates could easily be established and partly because pigeons lived longer than white rats. Accordingly, he modified his apparatus to suit pigeons as subjects and became now interested in pecking response of pigeons in the pigeon box rather than in lever pressing response done by white rat in the skinner box. During this period skinner also invented an air-conditioned box called *baby tender* to be used with human infants. In fact this box acted as a crib in which infants could be reared and their behaviour could be studied. Skinner reared his one of the daughters in this box for about first two and one-half years. But this apparatus could not be popular like skinner box and some psychologists also pointed out that Skinner's daughter reared in the bay tender actually became neurotic although this was always refuted by Skinner.

During fifties, Skinner invented teaching machine and became interested in programmed learning. His first major book was *The Behaviour of Organisms* published in 1938. In this book he outlined details of his experimental programme and researches. In 1948 he wrote Utopian novel, *Walden Two*, which is nothing but an exemplification of Skinnerian theory in a sort of behaviouristic utopia. In 1953 he published another introductory text called *Science and Human Behaviour* in which he extended the psychological principles outside laboratory to education, law, religion and various other social issues. In 1957 he published *Verbal behaviour* that exclusively dealt with analysis of language from psychological pointview. But such analysis was not liked by linguists. In collaboration with C. B. Ferster, he published another book *Schedules of Reinforcement* the same year. In 1971 he published *Beyond Freedom and Dignity*. His most latest publication was *Enjoy Old Age* that was released in 1983. These were his important publications.

Apart from these publications, Skinner was also honored by various psychological association for his distinguished work. In 1948 he received *Distinguished Contribution Award* by the American Psychological Association. In 1968 he was awarded the *National Medal of Science* for his distinguished achievement. He also got Gold Medal Award in 1971 by the American Psychological Foundation. He died in 1989.

Skinner's Contributions

In describing his system Skinner is very close to the influence of Watson but opposed to Hull. Like Watson, he isolated a bit of behaviour such as lever pressing response or packing response and studied it under a carefully controlled situation. He then manipulated the selected independent variables and examined what happened to the dependent variable. Finally, he established a functional relationship between independent variables and dependent variables. Throughout his whole system, Skinner's approach has been descriptive. That is the reason why his behaviourism is called as *descriptive behaviourism.* As we have seen, Hull prefers a deductive method in psychological researches. He starts with a postulated theory and finally deduces some corollaries and theorems on the basis of some experimental evidences. Hence, his behaviourism was *deductive behavioursim.* Quite opposed to this, Skinner prefers inductive method because he starts with empirical data and gradually proceeds towards some sound generalization. Therefore, Skinner's behaviorism is often called *inductive behaviourism.* Another contrast of Skinner with Hull is that Hull regarded organism as full of variables relevant for psychological researches and expeimentations (cf. his intervening variables). Due to this reason, Hull was branded as dualist. Skinner was a true behaviourist and took organism as 'empty' one. He is least concerned with what goes on inside the organism. Therefore, his approach to psychology may be called as *empty organism approach* that legitimately took objectively observable aspect (behaviour) of the organism to be the subject-matter of psychology. For Skinner, psychology is the scientific study of behaviour of the living organism.

The major contributions of Skinner may be outlined under the following *eight* headings :

1. ***The psychology of conditioning***

Skinner is popularly associated with operant conditioning or instrumental conditioning. In his earlier writing Skinner pointed out distinction between two types of conditioning—*Type S* conditioning and *Type R* conditioning. As a matter of fact, he divided responses into two categories—respondent response and operant response. Respondent response is one that is elicited by a given stimulus. In operant response there is no specific stimulus which can be identified. Such behvaiour is operated on the environment. The conditioning of respondent behaviour is called Type S conditioning because reinforcement in such case is correlated with stimuli. Pavlovian conditioning or classical conditioning represents Type S conditioning. In such conditioning the conditioned stimulus (bell) is presented together with the unconditioned stimulus (food) and gradually it (conditioned stimulus) comes to evoke the response (salivation). Skinner has definitely praised this form of conditioning but at the same time he expressed the view that it is limited in scope and nature. Therefore, Skinner made his concern with operant response that was more wider. It is so named because it is not elicited by a specific stimulus rather in it organism operates upon the environment. Rat's bar pressing and pigeon's pecking are the experimental examples of operant response. The conditioning of operant response was called as Type R conditioning because not the *stimulus* of lever but the *response* of depressing it is correlated with the reinforcement. In this way Skinner drew attention towards the importance of the consequences of the response, that is, the reinforcement that *follows* the response.

Skinner emphasized upon reinforcement as being a central factor in learning. In giving such emphasis he feels indebted to Thorndike who had earlier recognized the importance of reinforcement by formulating his famous *law of effect*. Skinner did not accept this law and reformulated it in a different way. According to Skinner (1938), "If the occurrence of an operant is followed by the presentation of a reinforcing stimulus, the strength is increased." Skinner gave a different account regarding the effectiveness of reinforcement. For Thorndike, reinforcement becomes effective because it produces a satisfying state of affairs. For Hull, reinforcement was effective because it led to the reduction of drives. For Skinner, reinforcement becomes effective because it is presented in the situation as a consequence of certain response.

Apart from the role of positive reinforcer discussed above, Skinner also recognized the importance of *negative reinforcer* in conditioning. Negative reinforcers are stimuli that strengthen the behaviour of the organism when they are withdrawn from the situation. Thus negative reinforcement results from the removal of a negative reinforcer. Electric shock is one example of negative reinforcer. Negative reinforcement is obviously related to punishment but the exact relationship between the two has not been known because punishment involves *presentation* and *not* withdrawal or removal of negative reinforcer. In Skinner box some experiments have been conducted in which animals have learnt lever pressing response on the basis of negative reinforcer. A rat after being placed in the Skinner box was given electric shock through grid floor. When the rat pressed the lever, the shock was terminated. On successive trials the latency of this particular response was greatly reduced which in itself was indication of the fact that response was being strengthened.

One of the most important aspects of Skinner's operant conditioning was *Schedules of reinforcement.* This term refers to a pattern followed in presenting reinforcers after response have been emitted by the organism during experimentation. The Schedule of reinforcement may be broadly divided as *continuous reinforcement and intermittent or partial reinforcement.* Continuous reinforcement is simple and here, reinforcement is given after each response. This is used generally during the beginning part of the training. After the response has been learnt, the schedule is shifted to intermittent one in which some responses are followed by reinforcementand some go without being followed by reinforcement. Ferster and Skinner (1957) wrote a book, *Schedules of reinforcement* in which they gave a detailed account of the different types of intermittent schedule. In such schedule there were two basic patterns—*ratio* and *interval.* Ratio schedule is one in which presentation of reinforcement is depended upon the rate of response. In interval schedule the presentation of reinforcement is depended not upon rate of responses but simply upon passage of time. Ratio schedule and interval schedule may be either fixed or variable. In *fixed ratio schedule* (FR schedule) the subject is reinforced after every fixed number of responses which may be every five, every ten, etc. In *variable ratio schedule* (VR schedule) no number of responses is fixed for presentation of reinforcement. Likewise, in *fixed interval schedule* (FI schedule) the subject is reinforced after a fixed lapse of time. It may be 2 minutes, 3 minutes or 5 minutes or any number of minutes as fixed by the experimenter. In variable interval schedule (VI schedule) no such fixed interval is allowed for giving reinforcement. These four main types of schedules of reinforcement tend to produce a differential rate of responding. In general, ratio schedules produce higher rate of responding than interval schedules. It has also been observed that on both of fixed schedules the subjects demonstrate tendency to respond slowly immediately after responding.

In Skinner's operant conditioning other phenomena like secondary reinforcement, extinction, discrimination, differentiation and aversive conditioning have also been examined. An operant response is extinguished if reinforcer is withdrawn after its occurrence. In discrimination learning animal is trained to make a discrimination between two stimuli and respond accordingly. In one such experiment Skinner trained pigeon to peck at red disc and not to peck at green disc. This was established by giving reinforcement after pecking to red disc. In differentiation, the response side and not the stimulus side is emphasized. In training the pigeon to peck at disc, the experimenter may begin by reinforcing those packing responses that are made near the disc, then reinforcing only those pecking respones that are made near the periphery of the disc and finally to those that are made at the center of the disc. If we pay attention to Skinner's concept of differentiation, it wail be obvious that it in a way denounces Thorndike's law of exercise. In fact, it is not the practice through which correct pecking response is learnt but it is the use of selective reinforcement that helps in learning. In secondary reinforcement those stimuli that somehow became associated with primary ones such as food, water, etc., acquire the property of reinforcing a stimulus. Thus, for Skinner, a stimulus to be a secondary reinforcer first becomes a discriminative stimulus and then, it reinforces a stimulus. For example, if a rat is regularly rewarded after pressing lever in presence of red light, it will continue to press the lever in presence of red light even when such response is not followed by primary reinforcement for some trials. In aversive conditioning, the responses are learnt on the basis of aversive stimuli such as punishment, avoidance and escape. Skinner experimentally demonstrated that aversive conditioning in Skinner box is a reality.

2. *Drive*

Skinner was out and out a behaviorist. Therefore, he did not explain drive in way of inferred states or intervening variables as it was done by Hull. As we have seen, he always preferred an objective criteria. In explaining the concept of drive he again did so. He explained drive operationaliy in terms of hours of deprivation for food, water, etc., or in terms of the percentage of animal's normal body weight. In this way we find that Skinner explained drive in spirit of operationism and made it clear that it could be measured objectively like anything, We should not bother for inferred states as to be its one of the explanations.

3. *Emotion*

Like drive, emotions were also explained by Skinner in a completely objective way. He explained emotional behaviour with respect to the situations or circumstances that affect the probability of a particular response to occur. For example, what happens in emotion of depression or sorrow. All of us have experience such emotion. When conditioned positive reinforcer is removed such emotion is experienced. For example, when death of father who has been the major source of positive reinforcer in the family occurs, a person generally experiences a strong emotion. Likewise, when we meet with our old friend, we have emotion of joy and happiness. This is because the secondary positive reinforcer is represented before us. Likewise, anxiety is the result of conditioning. When a stimulus or warning signal proceeds an aversive stimulus from which the organism can't escape, some behavioral changes are induced. These changes are called anxiety'. Estes and Skinner (1941) conducted one experiment in which they demonstrated that among rats such anxiety was introduced when they were exposed to the presentation of continuous tone followed several minutes later by electric shock. In actual life situation we too experience anxiety whenever a stimulus in form of working signal is given and it is followed by some kind of aversive stimulus from which escape is not possible. Thus, for Skinner, anxiety is not something like inner state of the organism but it is a set of some predisposition's to act in a certain way towards a circumstance of situation.

4. *Shaping and Superstitious Behaviour*

Generally those who dislike Skinner pointed out that Skinner's explanation suits only to simple learning or learning limited to lever pressing in Skinner box. But Skinner invariably demonstrated that animals can be trained to perform complex tasks that ate ordinarily outside their normal range. This is done through *shaping* in which the behaviour of the organism is gradually shaped or molded through a series of successive approximations by selectively reinforcing certain responses and not reinforcing the other. Not all demonstrations of shaping have been done on animals. Human behaviours have also been shaped by the automatic effect of reinforcement (Greenspoon, 1955). Such use has been called as *verbal conditioning*. Ordinarily in operant conditioning experiment the response is contingent upon or related to reinforcement. For example, when a rat makes lever pressing response in the Skinner box, it is followed by reinforcement. But suppose the experimental situation is so redesigned that reinforcement is delivered after some time irrespective of what the rat does in the box. In such situation the reinforcement, in fact, would be independent (or noncontingent) of rat's responses and still that response will be learnt. This is what Skinner meant by superstitious behaviour. In other words, superstitious behaviour is one that is developed due to *accidental reinforcement*. In superstitious behaviour the subject acts as though a certain response produced reinforcement whereas the reality is that there is no necessary connection between that response and reinforcement.

The response is commonly followed by reinforcement merely due to the fact that both response and reinforcement occur frequently. Skinner has experimentally demonstrated such superstitious behaviour in pigeons although examples from human beings are also plentiful. Suppose a student before leaving his room for examination takes curd in hope of good luck in the examination. If he really does well in examination, this experience will produce a superstitious behaviour of taking curd on each day of the examination although the reality is that taking curd is in no way related to doing well in the examination and he might have equally done well even without taking curd.

5. *Verbal behaviour*

Skinner was of view that speech, like other forms of behaviours, also develops due to contingencies of reinforcement. He has presented a detailed analysis of language behaviour in his book *Verbal behaviour* (1957). He has recognized several forms of verbal behaviour among which *autoclitic behaviour*, *echoic behaviour* and *textual behaviour* are common. Autoclitic behaviour is the verbal behaviour that is based upon other verbal behaviour. The speaker may for example, state that "I don't think that ...", "I was about to say...", etc. In all these autoclitics are occurring. In echoic behaviour responses are reinforced when another individual's responses are repeated verbatim. In early stages of speech development children frequently engage in such echoic utterances Textual behaviour refers to verbal behaviour involved in reading aloud or silently from a book or any written material.

Skinner further pointed out that there were two major functions of language—*mand* (from demand or command) *function* and *tact function*. Mand function is one in which a particular speech utterance make certain request or demand upon the another person and get reinforced as another person complies. A child utterance, "Mother, Milk" is reinforced when mother complies and gives milk. Thus mand function appears early in language development of child. Tact function is one that is concerned with naming discriminative objects or stimuli. For example, when one says, "This is a beautiful car", his language obviously is serving tact function.

Despite all these, Skinner's linguistic analysis could not be popular one partly because it was not much praised by professional linguists and partly because it was given a strong negative assessment by Chomsky* (1959).

* For Chomsky's criticisms of Skinner theory of language development, the reader is referred to consult chapter 18.

6. *Teaching machines and programmed learning*

Skinner's principles were greatly applied in education. The idea of programmed learning through teaching machines is example of one such application. A programmed learning is defined as learning through a programme or a series of instructions with the help of a teaching machine or computer. In fact, Skinner's observation was that the traditional classroom teaching by a teacher is not an entirely satisfactory step because of several reasons. For example, in classroom situation each child does not get opportunity to make required responses and rate of learning for anyone student may be either too fast or too slow. Above all, reinforcement in classroom situation is always delayed. To avoid all these difficulties, Skinner proposed programmed learning through teaching machine although he was not the first to suggest this approach. (Sidney L. Pressey at Ohio State University had already suggested the use of teaching machines in 1926-27).

Skinner's method of programmed learning involves the basic principles of shaping and continuous reinforcement. In his method, an item is presented to the student or learner who is required to write his own response in the space provided and then as tap moved forward, the correct answer appeared for comparison. In this way, the student emits his own response to be reinforced by the comparison response. If his answer agrees with exposed answer, this constitutes a reinforcement. If it does not agree, he gets an opportunity to study the correct answer so as to increase his chance of being reinforced next time. In this way one after the another all items (items are called frames) of the programme are gradually exposed and his behaviour is shaped. According to Skinner, this programmed learning through teaching machines has obvious advantages in speeding up reinforcement and reducing the probability of cheating, if any, by students. Recently different programmes have been developed in various areas ranging from simple subjects like english and arithmetic to other complex subjects like physics, electronics, music, etc. Holland and Skinner (1961) also developed their own programme for teaching the basic principles of Skinner's system. Likewise, Geis, Stebbins and Lundin ((1965) have developed another programme for teaching basic principles of classical conditioning and operant conditioning. In modern days due to rapid increase in use of computer, computer-aided instruction (CAI) is rapidly replacing Skinnerian programmed instruction or learning.

7. *Behaviour modification*

Behavior modification or also known as behaviour therapy refers to make desirable changes in behaviour by eliminating or modifying the undesirable ones through shaping, selective use of positive reinforcement and extinction. The field of behaviour modification has witnessed the most recent application of Skinnerian principles. The behaviour modification techniques based upon Skinnerian principles have been applied to different kinds of behaviour problems ranging from mild through neurosis to severe psychosis. Whatever may be the forms of behaviour problems, Skinner's technique is to note down the undesirable behaviours that are to be extinguished and the desirable behaviours that are to be established. Subsequently, undesirable bahaviours are not reinforced and desirable bahaviours are reinforced. Ultimately, this leads to the establishment of desirable behaviour and elimination of undesirable one. Skinner's techniques of behaviour modification have led to fruitful results. For example, thumb sucking in children has been eliminated by Baer (1962). Autistic children have been taught to speak, schizophrenic symptoms have been eliminated and the behaviour of mental defectives have been improved. In fact the literature is so vast that one journal completely devotes itself to researchers conducted on the basis of Skinnerian techniques of behaviour modifications. The journal has been named as *The Journal of Applied Behaviour analysis.*

8. *Beyond freedom and dignity*

Skinner (1971) published a book *Beyond Freedom and Dignity* in which he outlined a social philosophy to go beyond the laboratory and apply his ideas to various social problems. He pointed out that for effective solution of human problems, one must apply a technology of behaviour. The key to a technology of behaviour is found in the contingencies of reinforcement. The aims of these contingencies are found in three types of values (a) in those things that have biological importance, (b) in those things that help others, and (c) in those things that help a cultural survival. He made it fully explicit that in the evolution of culture those aspects that survive are ones which bring us under the fullest consequences of his behaviour. He considered man as 'autonomous', that is, as one who is self-composed persons free to do whatever he likes. His idea about 'autonomous man' has important implications for modern concept of 'self' as incorporated in humanistic psychology. In this book he also made a strong suggestion to refine the earlier idea of freedom and dignity. He believed that an individual is much influenced by the forces in the environment. Some of these forces are aversive. Freedom, according to Skinner, means to get oneself free from aversive controls in our environment. The classical meaning of dignity is what a person attributes to oneself. However, he maintains that when aversive controls are eliminated, the idea of dignity no longer remains meaningful.

Skinner's system, on the whole, contains a set of psychological principles and is based upon rigorous and carefully controlled experimentation's. Despite this, his system has been criticized on the following grounds :

(i) The most frequently cited criticism of Skinner's system is that Skinner has chosen a limited nature of the behaviour for study. For example, he has kept himself limited to lever pressing and/or pecking response. By studying such simple bits of the response of the organism he has tried to make a broad generalization which has been considered by critics as a gross oversimplification of facts. Some critics like Kantor (19709) has also pointed out that Skinner's system makes no attempt to study other important aspects of behaviour like thinking, creativity, problem solving, reasoning, etc. which may be regarded as important omissions from his system.

(ii) Some critics maintain that Skinner took a strict position of descriptive observation of functional relationship in his system and completely ignored the theoretical side. In fact, he felt no need for a 'theory' that could provide more sufficient explanations. But this criticism does not appear to be wholly justified in the sense that he in his book *Science and Human Habaviour* has provided several theoretical explanations for the principles discovered in the laboratory.

(iii) Some critics have said that Skinner's concept of empty organsism is not correct nor appealing. According to critics Skinner deliberately avoided any reference to physiological principles or organism. They, however, maintain that one can't get a true picture of psychology of the individual by ignoring individual himself. When Skinner adopted 'empty organism' approach, it was obvious that for him, behaviour is a product of environmental conditions. Critics said that in so doing Skinner has ignored many organismic conditions such as fatigue, glandular imbalances, etc., that can provide strong base for important psychological explanations.

(iv) Chomsky (1959) has criticized Skinner for his inadequate analysis of verbal behaviour and for his design for culture. He has attacked Skinner's analysis on several grounds. For details the reader is referred to consult Bower and Hilgard's *Theories of Learning* (1981) or Chapter 18 of this book.

Despite these criticisms, Skinner is perhaps second to none in psychology. His contributions to psychology such as Skinner box and schedule of reinforcement have still been regarded as of vital heuristic value. His idea of programmed learning and teaching machines have in fact, shaken up the traditional methods of teaching. Needless to say, application of Skinner's principles in the field of behaviour modifications have brought a revolution in the field of psychotherapy.

EDWARD CHACE TOLMAN (1886-1959)

Tolman started his academic career as engineering student at the Massachusetts Institute of Technology. But later he changed to psychology and obtained his Ph. D. in psychology in 1915 at Harvard University. At this University he was deeply influenced by Holt. For a few years he taught at North-Western University and then in 1918 he joined University of California at Berkeley and taught here for major portion of his career. He also served as psychologist in the Office of Strategic Services (OSS) during World War II. Tolaman's major book, *Purposive Bahaviour in Animals and Men* was published in 1932 in which he has outlined his behaviouristic stand in detail. In formulating his system Tolman was much influenced by Watson's experimental formulation, McDougall's concept of purpose (while rejecting his concept of instinct) as well as by Woodworth's S-O-R-formula.

Tolman's system has characteristics of both the behaviourism as well as the field theory. Therefore, we can classify him both as a *behaviourist* or more particularly as a *purposive behaviourist* as well as a *field theorists.* In fact, the basis for such classification is that during the early part of his career he was deeply influenced by Watson's behaviourism and Watson's announcement regarding psychology as the science of behaviour (and not of consciousness) and his (Watson's) rejection of introspection came to him as a great "relief" to psychology. He adhered to Wastonian principles and also tried to modify them in explaining psychological phenomena with a molar perspective. In this sense, he considered himself as a *purposive behaviourist*. But as he developed his system, he felt inclined to include *cognition* (that is, how a person perceives the field or situation) in his explanation by departing from traditional behaviouristic principles of Watson. Then from a purposive behaviourist, he became a field theorist. In this chapter, we shall discuss Tolman's system as purposive behaviourism. Tolman as a field theorist would be discussed in chapter 15.

Is Tolman a behaviourist ?

.Whether a psychologist is behavioursit or structuralist or functionalist can be easily judged by what he expresses about the different aspects of psychology and how he interprets himself in that particular context. Tolman is well-known in psychology for his theory of learning. According to Spence (1951), there can be two broad categories of theories of learning—stimulus-response theories that include those of Thorndike, Skinner, Pavlov, Hull, Miller, Dollard and Spence and stimulus-stimulus or stimulus-sign theories that include those of Kohler, Koffka, Tolman, Adams and Zener. As we know, S-R theories are strict behaviourists ones and explain learning by giving emphasis upon association. The S-S-theories tries to explain learning by associating it with the psychology of perception.

In fact, Tolman's work defines this classification. His theory and system may be regarded as unique in the sense that he has tried to combine best of the both approaches. He tried to formulate a theory of learning that closely resembles to stimulus-response theory no doubt but at the same time he explained it by non-observable set of intervening variables. The use of such intervening variables definitely goes against the main dogma of behaviourism. Still he regarded his interpretation as behaviouristic one. In fact by providing a molar analysis of behaviour he has distinguished himself from other behaviourists like Watson, Guthrie and Hull. His molar interpretation helped him in establishing as a purposive behaviourist. He is regarded as a behaviourist because he ultimately favored stimulus-response interpretation by defining stimulus and response in his own way. For Tolman, stimulus is a kind of perception of environmental events which are processed and influenced by organism's past history. Likewise, for Tolman response is not collections of muscle twitches or glandular secretions but is behaviour defined in terms of end results or goal. For example, in Skinner box a rat may try to depress the bar by nose or by paws, or by rear ends. For Tolman, all these are the same performance or one response because they all produce the same end results. For Watson and Guthrie they represent different responses because they represent different muscular movements.

In nutshell we can say that Tolman is not an empty behaviourist rather a purposive behaviourist who makes it explicit that learnt bahaviour is always directed and oriented toward some end or goal.

TOLMAN'S PURPOSIVE BEHAVIOURISM

Tolamn has outlined his system in his book *Purposive Behaviour in*

Animals and Men published in 1932. Throughout his programme he stressed psychology as the *study of behaviour and* accepted the definition of behaviour as a stimulus-response affair but he rejected Watson's ways of interpreting behaviour by what he (Tolman) called "premature neurologizing". He also rejected introspection as a method of psychology and even rejected popular Watsonian method of verbal report. He considered behaviour in terms of *mean-end relationship.* In other words, behaviour, for him, is goal-directed, that is, purposive. Due to this reason he has named his system as "an objective behaviouristic purposivism". In addition to this name of his system, his theory is also variously known as *sign-gestalt, sign-significate, cognitive* or *expectancy* theory. He derived idea of purposive behaviour from McDougall's Hormic Psychology but at the same he rejected McDougall's theory of instinct. He also related his theory to gestalt theory because he felt that behaviour was *molar* and *meaningful.* However, he did not accept the Gestalt's principle of psychophysical parallelism or isomorphism. As pointed out above, his theory was not related only to gestalt theory but was also coloured by Lewin's field theory. In this way we find that Tolman tried to incorporate the best of the different theories to make his own system and theory highly unique one. He got success in this direction. Tolman's system is purposive behavioursim because it emphasizes upon the study of observable behaviour which is purposive. It is gestaltic in the interpretation of learning. Wolman (1979 : 155) has nicely commented, "Tolman has combined Watsonian behaviourism and Pavlov's conditioning with Thorndike's law of effect and McDougall's purposivism and the Gestalt theory of perception coloured by Lewin's field theory."

After considering the basic tenets that Tolman held throughout his career, his system can best be explained by dividing it into four parts—*Independent variables, dependent variables, intervening variables and theory of learning.* A discussion of these four parts may be outlined as under :

1. *Independent Variables*

Tomlan in his system has recognized as set of independent variables to be the major causative factors of behaviour. These variables are manipulated and measured by the experimenter. Initially, he recognized *five* such variables and behaviour was considered to be the function of these five variables. In terms of equation, it may be said :

$$B = f\,(S, D, H, T, A)$$

where, S = environmental stimulus

D = Physiological drive

H = Heredity
T = Previous Training
A = Age
B = Behaviour

S and D variables were called as *releasing variables* because they start the behaviour of the organism. H, T and A variables were called as *guiding variables* because ultimately they determine final shape of the behaviour initiated by releasing variables. Later, Tolman revised this list of independent variables and categorized them as *individual difference variables* and *maintenance variables*. Important individual difference variables were H, A, T, and E, popularly known as HATE variables. E variable includes organs factors such as endocrine and vitamin conditions. Important maintenance variables were goal object (G), the stimuli (S), motor response required by the experimental design (R), pattern of preceding and succeeding maze units (P) that represent the experimental tools. Tolman's concern with these various variables demonstrate that for him there were several determinants of behaviour.

2. *Dependent Variables*

Tolman defined dependent variables as those behaviours which are observable. For him, the behaviour of the organism is not passive rather active and selective. Tolman's observation was that a rat in the maze did not passively receive the stimuli rather actively look for and select the significant stimuli. He considered observable behaviour as nothing but a stimulus-response affair and not a mechanistic stimulus-response relationship as it was said by Watson, Hull etc. He divided such behaviour into two types—*simple reflex or tropism* and *docile behaviour*. Tolman was exclusively concerned with docile behaviour. The docility of behaviour simply means that a behaviour is adaptable to changing circumstances and that the way a goal or end will be achieved tends to vary depending upon the means available before the organism. Docile behaviour has many characteristics. It is *molar, purposive, cognitive* and *plastic*.

3. *Intervening Variables*

Tolman's is credited as the first psychologist who introduced the concept of intervening variables in psychology. They are a set of inferred and non-observed variables that intervene between the observable independent variables and observable dependent variables. In fact such variables can't be directly observed but they can be inferred from the behaviour. In 1938 Tolman gave a list of six intervening variables. They were *demand* (for food), *appetite, differentiation, motor skill, hypotheses* and *biases.* In 1952 he revised this list and reduced it to three : *need system, belief value matrix* and *behaviour space.* The need system referred to some kind of inferred state of physiological or psychological drive. The belief value matrix refers to the preference for a particular motive or in other words some inferred motives. The behaviour space is like Lewin's life space. It is a space in which behaviour of the organism takes place. When the person moves in this space, some objects attract him and some repel him. The former is said to have positive valence and the latter is said to have negative valence.

4. *Theory of learning : Experimental Approach*

Tolman is well-known for his theory of sign learning. His this theory was presented as an alternative to S-R theory of learning. In fact, his entire theory of learning can be divided into two parts—the "1932 version" and the "1949 version". The "1932 version" proposed that the organism learns by signs. What it learnt was not a series of muscular or glandular movements rather meanings, that is, it learnt *sign-significates, relations* or *sign-gestalts.* Still in simpler language, we can say that it learns a behavioural route to goal or end. Gradually, it learns a relationship between clues or stimuli in the environment and own expectations. Tolman explained this with observation made in maze learning. In a maze there are several choice points. Therefore, there are many stimuli. At each choice point a certain expectancy is built up. If organism takes an appropriate and correct choice at a choice point, its expectancy is strengthened. In this way by strengthening or confirming several choices, it develops a *cognitive map* of the whole maze. For Tolman, learning is nothing but development of this cognitive map which is a kind of field in the brain that enables the rat (or animal) to run from one place to another in the environment without depending upon a set of bodily movements. In interpretation of learning presented by Tolman, reinforcement or reward was not regarded as significant variable as we find in case of Skinner, Hull, Pavlov and Thorndike. The only significance of goal object was to strengthen or confirm the expectancy of the animal. When these expectations are confirmed, learning is also said to be complete.

In later article (that is, in '1949 version') Tolman added six types of new learning or connections in his theory. In explaining these six types of learning, he took the help of concepts enunciated by Freud and Lewin. These may be outlined as under :

(i) ***Cathexis*** : This concept has been taken from Freudian terminology and is somewhat equivalent to Lewin's conception of valence. For Tolman, cathexis is a tendency to seek particular goal rather then some other goals when experiencing a particular drive. Whenever a particular goal object satisfies a particular drive, a cathexis of that particular drive on that particular goal object is formed or learnt. It is perhaps due to this reason a child develops a relationship (cathexis) between his hunger and biscuits.

(ii) *Equivalence beliefs* : This is a kind of belief that not only reward or punishment will be given in a particular situation but also the belief that the situation itself is equivalent to that particular reward or punishment. Obviously, then this is a kind of secondary reinforcement. For example, a student receiving gold medal from the University thinks it to be equivalent to receiving special honour and prestige for his merit.

(iii) *Field expectancies* : These are cognitions about what leads to what. This is exactly what Tolman earlier called *sign-gestalt expectations.* When the organism learns route from one place to another or learns what tools can be used for what purposes, field expectancies are said to be formed. Cognitive maps are said to be formed of field expectancies.

(iv) *Field cognition modes* : These are higher order modes or expectancy and refer to inclination to learn certain things more readily than others.. Such inclination is partly innate and partly learnt. The best example of field cognition mode is our ability to use language in a variety of learning situations.

(v) *Drive discrimination* : This refers to our ability to distinguish among different types of drives. However, this is not a very important type of learning and is related to the learning of cathexis. In fact, Tolman had derived this concept from the work of Hull (1933) and Leeper (1935).

(vi) *Motor patterns* : Although the motor patterns or muscular skills by which one gets to the goal has never been the major concern of Tolman, he definitely recognized this to be an important aspect of learning theory. Accordingly, he suggested that analysis of such skills by Guthrie in terms of stimulus-response connections was certainly important ones.

Tolman's theory of learning has been so important and provocative that it generated several researches which were conducted either by their followers or by himself. Three lines of experimental evidences are frequently cited in support of Tolman's '1932 version'. These evidences, however, don't provide contradiction to his '1949 version'. These experimental evidence may be briefly outlined as under :

a. ***Reward expectancy experiments***

Expectancy has been one of the important intervening variables in Tolman's theory of learning. During learning, Tolman claims, the organism comes to build certain expectation, the confirmation of which forms the base for development of cognitive map. Tinklepaugh (1928) conducted one experiment to show the phenomenon of expectancy in learning. He placed banana under one of the two containers while the monkey was watching. After a brief delay, the monkey was let loose and it was found that he readily chose the container having banana.

Later, the experimenter placed a lettuce leaf (less preferred food) under the same container. It was found that monkey rejected lettuce leaf and showed a disruption of behaviour. All these happened because he had *expected* banana and not lettuce leaf.

b. ***Place or Goal learning experiments***

One of the major points in Tolman's theory of learning is that animals learn cognitions or they learn by insight and not that they learn

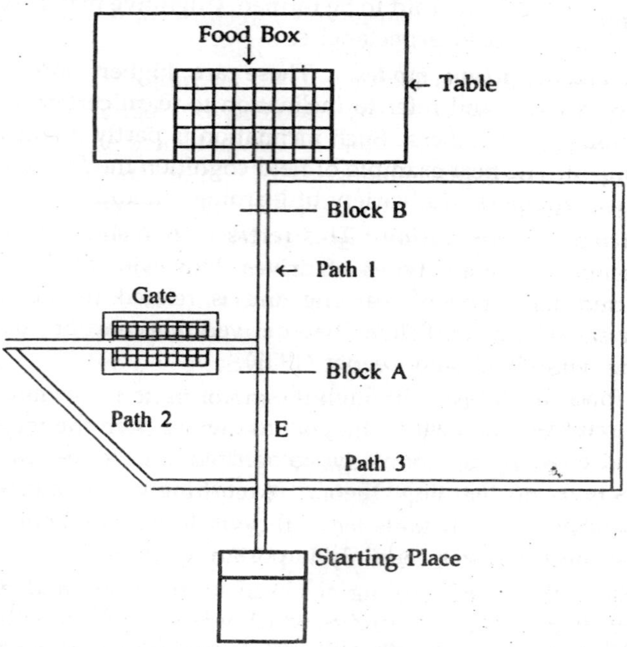

Figure 10·1 : A sketch of maze used in blocked-path experiment conducted by Honzik and Tolman (1936)

the fixed sequence of movements as claimed by Hull. Honzik and Tolman (1936) conducted an experiment to demonstrate this. They constructed a special maze for the purpose that may, for convenience, be called as *blacked-path maze* (cf. Figure 10·1). As it is obvious, in this maze there were three paths 1, 2 and 3 from start box to goal box. Path 1 was the shortest and path 3 was the longest. Path 2 was intermediate. As Figure reveals, there ware two Blocks—A and B. When Block A was imposed, it blocked only Path 1. When Block B was imposed, it blocked both path 1 and 2 because these paths had a common segment leading to the goal box. After giving some preliminary trials to rats for getting them acquainted with the details of the maze, a preference in order of path 1, 2 and 3 was established depending upon which paths were blocked. Results revealed that when Block B was made active, rats rather than going to path 2 and be further frustrated took a direct recourse to path 3 without committing any error. The experiments obviously confirmed the hypothesis of 'cognitive map' of Tolman because rats were behaving according to the insight that they had developed into the whole situation.

c. ***Latent learning experiments***

In Tolman's theory of learning the expectation that animals develop was important and not that the reinforcement or reward was important. We have seen that Hull, Thorndike, Skinner, etc., would argue that it is reinforcement that is important in learning. No reinforcement no learning. Tolman made a distinction between learning and performance. He pointed out that for learning no reinforcement or reward was needed. Learning also took place in absence of reinforcement. Such learning was obviously *latent learning*. To translate such learning into performance, reinforcement was, however, needed. Performance is the overt expression of what has been learnt. Tolman and Honzik (1930) conducted one experiment to demonstrate this. In this experiment rats ran the same maze in three different groups separately. One group, after running, was given no reward at all in the goal box. Another group was given food in the goal box after completion of each run. Still another group ran the maze without food for the first ten days. From eleventh day and onwards they were given food in the goal box after each run. Results revealed that nonrewarded group showed little improvement in its performance. The continuously rewarded group demonstrated gradual improvement. Both the errors and the total running time reduced considerably. The delayed rewarded group did not show appreciable improvement in the first ten days. But on the eleventh day its performance suddenly improved and in a few days became equivalent to the performance of the continuously rewarded group.

According to Tolman and Honzik, in absence of reward or reinforcement delayed rewarded group had learnt the spatial relations but those were latent. When food was given on the eleventh day, rats expressed those learnt relations by using their cognitive maps. The stimulus-response reinforcement theorists find it difficult to explain such results.

In this way we find that Tolman stood in a behaviouristic group that made him distinct from others. His molar interpretation of behaviour, many varieties of latent learning experiments and place learning experiments had made him very popular and a distinguished psychologist. Although Tolman did not introduce rats in psychology, he definitely made them popular and dependable because his rats were very 'hard-worked'.

Tolman's purposive behaviourism has been criticized on the following grounds :

(i) Tolman claimed to be a behaviouirist. But he used so many types of intervening variables like expectancy, cognitive map, etc., which could neither be objectively observed nor be experimentally studied. They could only be inferred. Critics stated that Tolman's system thus represented a bitter dualism that could not be accepted with any scientific grace.

(ii) Marx and Hillix (1963) have pointed out that Tolman has remained unable to present a logically integrated theory. In his theory too many variables were introduced and too many questions remained unanswered. On the whole, this theory gave a fragmented look having little coherence within it.

(iii) Tolman had emphasized upon overt behaviour and at the same time he also talked about so many covert variables. How were these covert variables related to those overt behaviour ? Not explained by Tolman in a comprehensible language.

Despite these criticisms, Tolman's impact upon psychology has been tremendous. Although Tolman clashed with other behaviourists in his denial of presentation of reinforcing state as necessary condition for learning, his stand got a strong experimental support. Tolman's impact in thirties had also one major impact upon other behaviourists. Other behaviourists accepted his viewpoints that intervening variables were very useful variables in explaining learning. Perhaps due to this, Hull made extensive use of intervening variables in his theory of learning.

J. R KANTOR (1888-1984) : INTERBEHAVIOURISM

Kantor got his Ph. D. from the University of Chicago in 1917.

Subsequently, he taught for a short period at the Universities of Minnesota and Chicago. Then he went to Indiana University in 1920 and remained there till his retirement in 1959. Subsequent to his retirement, he taught at several universities including University of Maryland, University of New York and the University of New York and the University of Chicago by holding part-time teaching assignments. He wrote several books : *Principles of Psychology* (1924-26), *Outline of a Social Psychology* (1929), *Problems of Physiological Psychology* (1947), *Interbehavioural Psychology* (1958), *The Scientific Evolution of Psychology* (1963-1969), *Cultural Psychology* (1982).

Kantor's Interbehavioural Psychology

Kantor has developed system* that falls within the general framework of behaviourism but at the same time, it maintains its own distinctiveness. He prefers to call his system as *interbehaviourism.* He has pointed out that psychology, like any other natural science, deals with the events that exist in space and time. He feels that other behaviourists have given much emphasis upon studying the response of the organism but have neglected equally important side, that is, the stimulus object. Therefore, he has made it obvious that the subject-matter of psychology should be the *interaction of organism and stimulus objects.* For explaining behaviour, he has rejected intervening variables and has used constructs instead. Throughout his system he has emphasized that constructs should be related to observable stimulus events.

Kantor's interbehaviourism may be outlined under the following headings :

1. *Psychololgical Interactions*

For Kantor, the basic unit of analysis is the behaviour segment. In a behaviour segment one organism makes interaction with a stimulus object. Therefore, in any such segment both stimulus object and organism are of equal importance. The stimulus may be a person, and object, or some event. Any complex psychological activity involves a succession of such behavioural segments. In any behavioural segment the relationship between an organism and the stimulus event is reciprocal, that is, both affect each other. Therefore, both constitute the *element* of interaction. There are *three* types of functions that are served by the stimulus. Those are *universal stimulus functions, individual stimulus functions* and *cultural stimulus functions.* Some stimulus functions are *universal* because they serve the same functions for all members of a

* His system has also been called by some psychologists as **Field Theory.**

given species. Such functions are generally related to the biolgical make-up of the individual. For example, an extremely heated object stimulates our finger to keep it away. *Individual stimulus functions* are unique and individual to the perosn concerned. These functions are much dependent upon the previous interactions or experiences that the preson has with that particular object. For example, seeing a beggar on the road one person may simply stop to have a look over his condition, another may approach him to talk with him and still another may approach him and give him some money and clothes. How a person will make interastion with a beggar depends upon his previous experiences. *Cultural stimulus functions* are those functions which produce similar reactions in a particular group of persons. These are shared by members of a particular community but they are not universal. For example, in a particular Indian community beef has the stimulus function of an object to be eaten but among members of other community it may merely be a flesh of an animal having some religious sentiments with it. It is also obvious then that like individual stimulus functions, cultural stimulus functions also depend upon the previous interactions or experiences of the individual.

Kantor has supported molar approach to the interpretation of behaviour because he emphasized the fact that the psychological response which is function of the organism, involves the activity of the whole organism.

2. ***Interactional Setting (S)***

Kantor emphasized that the interaction between stimulus and organism takes place in a ceratin setting and not that in vaccum. These setting factors in a way constitute a background against which interaction takes place. Such factors constitute a general circumstances in which a particular interaction may be facilitated or thwarted. Drive, age, etc., may be some examples of setting factors. Kantor also made it clear that they are only setting factors which either facilitate or inhibit the interaction and should not be taken as intervening variables.

3. ***Contact Medium (M)***

Any psychological interaction needs some contact medium (M). In absence of such medium, organism can't make any interaction. For example, if there is no light, the person can't see the stimulus and hence, the qeustion of interaction with that stimulus does not arise. Thus light in itself, for Kantor, is not stimulus rather it is one medium of contact through which interactions take place.

4. ***Interbehaviour History (H)***

Interbehaviour history consists of two subconcepts—reactional biography (RB) and the stimulus evolution (SE). Reactional biography, a very popular concept of Kantor, refres to sum of previous interactions that a person had with different stimulus objects. It is gradually built up and therefore, takes a form of history of interactions and has been named by Kantor as *behaviour equipment*. The stimulus evolution (SE) refers to the process of development of stimulus-function of the objects. On the response side, it simply refers to the development of reactional biography.

On the basis of the various concepts as explained above, Kantor pointed out that :

Psychological event= *f SF*, (stimuls function), *RF* (response function), *H* (interbehaviour history), *S* (Setting factors) and *M* (Contact medium)

5. *Implicit Interaction*

Kantor defined implicit interactions as behaviours like imagining, thinking, judging, reasoning, etc. All such implicit behaviours have at least one stimulus and one organism. The only thing is that the stimulus involved in such implicit behaviour is substitute stimulus—substitute because original stimulus remains no longer present. Pictures, diagrams, maps, a person narrating the scènes seen by him during his journey are nothing but examples of substitute stimulus. Implicit behaviours have some characteristics as undr :

(i) Implicit behaviours are difficult to be observed. However, if one identifies the substitute stimulus, one can be in a better postion to observe implicit behaviour. But this is rarely done.

(ii) Implicit behaviours tend to originate from direct contact with objects or things. Inventions or creative thinking are the results of previous interactions or contact with objects and principles.

(iii) Implicit behaviour may involve sometimes behaviours very closely related to original overt behaviour or may sometimes involve behaviours unrelated to original overt behaviour.

(iv) In some cases the exact nature of implicit behaviour can only be conjectured while in some other cases its nature may be objectively observed. We often understantd these behaviours through verbal report or by their outcome as we commonly find in problem solving behaviour.

6. *Affective Interactions (Feeling)*

In affective interactions such as in feeling the stimulus is of prime importance and it *acts* upon the organism. In other words, the stimulus produces a change in the organism but the organism does not produce any change in the stimulus. Thus in affective interactions the organism is completely affected by the stimulus and such interactions generally involve internal responses or visceral responses. Such affective interactions involve the whole organism. The examples of common affective interactions are joy, sorrow, hate, anger, fear and so on. For example, when a student sees results of the examination and finds his name in first division, he has the feeling of joy. He may also smile and may also make some vocal responses. On the other hands, if he does not find his name in result sheet, he has the feeling of sorrow and may remain silent one.

7. *Emotion*

For Kantor, emotion is a different kind of interaction that may be designated as *no response behaviour segment*. He analyzed emotion in four segments—the pre-emotional behaviour segment, the emotional segment proper, first post-emotional segment and second post-emotional segment. The pre-emotional behaviour segment includes all those interactions that are done prior to the presentation of emotional stimulus. The emotional segment proper includes those interctions that completely disrupts the organism and throw the organism in the state of *psychological freezing*. For example, a person may be completely so stunned over a remark made by others that he becomes voiceless. In the first post-emotional segment a new stimulus may be presented and this new stimulus may cool down his emotion. For example, one of his friend may console him by telling that this is the go of life. We should not take any comment seriously. In the *second* post-emotional segment the intensity of felt emotion is further lowered down and now he feels near normalized. He may say, "Peculiar fellow ! does not understand me properly".

Kantor also made it clear that emotional activity, like feeling, can't be classified. There is always only one emotional activity that can be described in terms of above four stages.

8. ***Memorial Interactions (Remembering)***

Kantor considers memorial interaction or remembering as a forward-looking reaction. It involves a delay between initial behaviour segment and its final behaviour segment. For example, if in morning a student decides to go to his teacher for consultation at 8 P. M. and he keeps this appointment, it is said that remembering has taken place. On the other hand, if he fails to keep this appointment, it is said that forgetting has taken place. For Kantor, remembering consists of three phases—*initiation, delay* and *consummation.* In the intitial phase interaction occurs such as decideing to meet the teacher. In delay phase, some lapse of time does occur between this intitial phase and some future time till memorial act is completed or consummated. The delay may be shorter or longer one. To ensure proper consummation, the person sets up some *substitute stimulus* which may be used in future time to complete the act. The setting up of such substitute stimulus may be *incidental* or *intentional*. When the student writes about the appointment to meet the teacher in his diary, this is intentional one. But seeing some stimulus or hearning some words from somebody, if the student is reminded about his appointment, this is incidental one.

Kantor's interbehavioursim has been criticized on the following grounds :

(i) Some critics say that Kantor has never been clear in his writings. Actually, what he intends to say has not been clear. His style is too wordy and at the same time too difficult to follow.

(ii) It is also said that he has devoted less time to betterment of his system and more time to tearing down other systems. He has continuously harped on such theories and facts that are of limited importance.

(iii) It is also said that Kantor's system lacks heuristc importance. In other words, his system has failed to generate important experimental researches. A complete review of the works done by him reveals that he has remained completely theory-oriented in his outlook and his bibliography includes only one experimental research.

(iv) Some critics also point out that Kantor's works tend to be more philosophical than psychological. Pronko's book *Psychology from the Standpoint of an Interbehaviourist* (1980) provides a good exposition to this stand of Knator's system.

ALBERT BANDURA (1925-

Albert Bandura was born in Mundare in northern Alberta, Canada in 1925. In 1949 he received his B. A. degree at the University of British Columbia and his Ph. D. degree in clinical psychology in 1952 at the University of Iowa. Since 1953 he taught at Standford University where he has since remained. In 1974 he was awarded David Starr Jordan Professorship of Social Science in psychology and he chaired Standford's psychology department in 1976-1977. He has also served as president of American Psychological Association and the Western Pshychological Association. He has also served on the editorial boards of several journals and has acted as editor on social learning theory for Prentice-

Hall for about 10 years. His. researches have been closely tied with behaviour modificiations particullarly, the modeling one. He formulated a theory that is based upon a behaviouristic position which stresses social learning to be the major basis for behaviour acquisition. In collaboration with Richard Walters, he wrote some books like *Adolescent Aggression* (1959) and *Social learning and Personality Development* (1963). Recently, he has publihsed another book, *Social Learning Thoery* (1977) that presents the most complete form of his theory.

According the Bandura human behaviour can be easily understood as a function of reciprocal intgeraction of behavioural, cognitive and environmental determinants. By a process of reciprocal determinism, persons influence their destinies by controlling environmental forces but at the same time they are also controlled by such forces. He said that our behaviour was influenced by environmental influences. He also believed that there were certain cognitions such as expectations, thoughts, etc., which might be regarded as the important cause of behaviour. Acceptance of cognitive factors like perceptions, thoughts, expectations and other internal processes by Bandura definitely make room for entry of mental factors in behaviourism—a factor which was not tolerated by other behaviourists like Skinner and Watson. Thus Bandura's behavioursism may be regarded as 'soft' behaviourism which is obviously in contrast to radical or 'hard' behaviourism of Skinner and Watson.

Bandura, in fact, postulates the existence of a self-system that makes him different from Skinner's behaviourism. According to him, the self-system, "is not a psychic agent that controls behaviour. Rather it refers to cognitive structures that provide reference mechanism and to a set of subfunctions for the perception, evaluotion and regulation of behaviour". (Bandura, 1978 : 348). The self-system acts upon both behaviour and enviornment. If our behaviour would have been solely influenced by the enviornmental forces, there would have been more variability within a person. Our behaviour would have been less consistent because we are constantly reacting to the great diversity of the environemnt. But the reality is that our behaviour is higly consistent and coherent. We are consistent in self-expression and our behavioural traits. From where do such consistency and coherence come ? Obviously such consistencies cannot be accounted for in terms of mere environmental forces. Cognitive factors like expectations, memory, perceptions, etc., bring unity and consistency to our behaviour.

Bandura is well-known for his *modelling technique or technique of observational learning*. He points out that the vast majority of our behaviour is learnt by copying what others do. Thus he makes a distinction between learning and performance. He clearly stated that person can learn without performing any behaviour. Responses need not occur for learning to take place, that is, we can learn by observation. On this point Bandura differs from Skinner who holds the view that occurrence of response behaviour (operant response) is the base of learning. Bandura further believes that reinforcement is not essential to learning. He agrees that reinforcement facilitates learining but it is not a necessary condition for it. Again, Bandura differs from Skinner on this issue because for the latter reinforcement is essential for learning. Bandura (1977a) claimed that learning has two basic sources—*response consequences* and *modelling*. These two may be discussed as under :

1. *Response consequences*

Every response that the person makes is followed by some consequences which may be either satisfying or dissactisfying. There are some consequences which are not cognitively attended and hence, they have little effect. Any complex human behaviour, however, involves the cognitive mediation of the person so that the consequences of a response may have an impact. In general, any response consequence serves at least three functions. *First,* it gives proper information to the person. *Second,* it motivates future behaviour of the person. *Third,* it reinforces the present behaviour of the person.

2. *Modelling*

For Bandura, learning is not limited to response consequence. He believes that most of our learning is acquired through observation or modelling. In modelling we observe others performing behaviours and retain those behaviours for future use. This model is considered by Bandura to be much more efficient than learning by direct experience. Modelling is, however, not simply mimicry or imitation. Modelling includes the psychological effects of being exposed to a model. In other words, it involves adding and subtracting from the observed behaviour and making generalization from one observation to another. Bandura made it explicit that there are four processes that govern modelling. Those processes are—*attention, retention, motor production* and *motivation.* For modelling, it is essential that we must *attend* to the behaviour of other persons. The observed patterns for behaviour must be symbolically *retained* failing which observaion will not lead to new responses. Motor production refers to conversion of cognitive representations into appropriate actions. Here the person remains fully aware of what he is doing. Performance in observational learning is facilitated by *motivating* persons to enact their behaviour.

Bandura made a clear-cut distinction between *antecedent* determinants of learning and *consequent* determinants of learning. The former activates the person and guides his behaviour whereas the latter maintains behaviour after being activated. Antecedent determinants are as sort of predictive stimuli. Human behaviour, to a greater extent, results from our prediction or expectation that a given response will be followed by satisfying consequences. When the behaviour has been activated, persons try to process and synthetize feedback information and thus, create their own consequences. Three major factors in consequent determinants of learning have been recognized. Those factors are as under :

(i) *External reinforcement*

It refers to any reinforcement obtained through direct experience. The external reinforcement can be material such as money, it can be symbolic such as praise, it can be positive such as any reward, it can be negative such as punishment, it can be intrinsic such as those resulting from natural consequences and it can also be extrinsic resulting from arbitrary consequence.

(ii) *Vicarious reinforcement*

Vicarious reinforcement is based upon vicarious experience. By vicarious experience is meant learning through observation of consequences of others behaviour. In fact, Bandura opines that reinforcement need not be experienced directly. When we observe others receiving reward or punishment, we easily learn that certain behaviours are likely to be followed by positive consequence while certain others are likely to be followed by negative consequence. Bandura, Ross and Ross (1964) conducted one experiment in which they demonstrated the role of vicarious reinforcement in modelling. Three groups of children were shown television films in which they observe other children as showing physical and verbal aggression. One group saw the film in which children's aggressive behaviour was positvively reinforced, another group saw such behaviour as negatively reinforced and the third group saw such aggressive behaviour being neither reinforced nor punished. After witnessing the films, these three groups of children were observed in play situation. Results revealed that the group that saw aggressive behaviour being positively reinforced demonstrated more aggression than group that saw aggression being negatively reinforced.

(iii) *Self-producted reinforcement*

Behaviour is also maintained by self-generated consequences apart from direct reinforcement and vicarious reinfocement. Every people set some standards for themselves and behave accordingly. In such situation they don't need any external reinforcement to maintain their behaviour. These standards maintain their behaviour and explain consistency in it. Thus people tend to regulate their own behaviour through the consequences they themselves have produced.

The emphasis upon reinforcement by Bandura makes his position similar to that of Skinner. But Bandura's system is *different from that of Skinner*. Skinner has emphasized only upon external reinforcement whereas Bandura has, emphasized upon vicarious reinforcement and self-reinfocement in addition to external reinfocerment. Another point of distinction between systems of these two psychologists is that Bandura is comparatively a *soft behaviourist* who has made concession to cognitive processes to enter into behaviouristic principles whereas Skinner is comparatively a *hared behaviourist* who has given no credit to such inner causes. Third distinction is that Skinner places more emphasis upon learning by doing but Bandura gives maximum emphasis upon learning by observation or watching. Bandura also rejected Freudian psychoanalytical approach or other neo-Freudian approaches that make maximum use of different hypothetical constructs like libido, psychic energy, id, ego, superego, etc.

Some psychologists have criticized Bandura for inclusion of mentalistic concepts like cognitions or expectations in behaviourism. Particulalry 'hard behaviourists' point out that by doing so Bandura has deserted the cause of scientific and objective behaviourism in favour of more cognitive approach to psychology. That is the reason why some psychologists are leaned towards calling him as a 'cognitive behaviourist' much on the pattern Tolman has been called.

DISTINCTION BETWEEN EARLY BEHAVIOURSIM AND LATER BEHAVIOURISM

The champion of early behaviourism was Watson. Later behaviourists prefer to retain the general framwork of Watson but at the same time tried to improve upon his system. As later behaviourists the contributions of Hull, Guthrie, Skinner, Tolman, Bandura are worth mentioning. A careful scrutiny of the contributions of these later behaviourists indicates that throughout their writings and research work they have tried to maintain the basic tenets of early behaviourism. However, later behaviourists differ from early behaviourists in their outlook as under :

1. Today we accept only some of the concepts of Watson's

behaviourism but his system as a whole is no longer appreciated. But the concepts and ideas of later behaviourists are up-to-date and are widely appreciated by modern psychologists.

2. The early behaviourists have shown interests in the study of various psychological phenomena such as memory, emotion, thinking, learning, etc. Thus their approach was wider and scattered one. But later behaviorurists tried to concentrate upon some basic fields such as learning and motivation only. Thus the approach of later behaviourists was more pin-pointed as compared to the approach of early behaviourists.

3. The concepts, viewpoints and theories of later behaviourists were based upon controlled evidences and experimental supports whereas this was not the case with early behaviourists. Their viewpoints, concepts and theories were mostly intuitively supported. They had little experimental support.

4. One subtle difference between early behaviourists and later behaviourists was that in considering the issue of how a person may improve himself Watson did not mention any technique of improving the behaviour of the perosn or any techniques of behaviour modifications as we know them today. He simply talked about education in a very general sense to be effective for bringing any improvement in behaviour. But later behaviourists particularly Skinner gave special attention to behaviour modifications and also spelled out the various techniques of behaviour modifications.

Despite these difference, later behaviourists are said to rely mainly upon those principles which were enunciated earlier by Watsonian behavioursim.

CHAPTER HIGHLIGHTS

1. A group of psychologists who tried to develop their own theories remaining basically within the general framework of Wastonian behaviourism was called as neo-behaviourists or later behaviourists, E. R. Guthrie is one such behaviourist. Among other things, he is well-known for his theory of learning by contiguity. Guthrie undermined the importance of movitvation, reward and parctice in learning. He postulated three methods of breaking habits, particularly undesirable habits. Those methods were : threshold method, method of fatigue and method of incompatible stimuli. Although Guthrie's theory, in general, lacks experimetnal support, it has also proved hard to be disporved.
2. C. L. Hull is another later behaviourist who formulated his system

that later became very dominant in psychology. In formulating his system he was influnced by Darwin, Pavlov, Watson, Thorndike and Woodworth. Hull's system consists of 17 postulates and several corollaries. He extensively used hypothetico-deductive method in formulating his theory. He postulated several intervening variables like sHR, D, KL, sER, IR, sIR, etc., in explaining his theory of learning. Hull's system was also supported by several experimental evidences provided either hy Hull himself or by his colleagues. Despite all these, Hull's system was criticized.

3. B. F. Skinner was another important later behaviourist who carried the basic fomulations of early behaviourism on a controlled and experimental footing. He is well-known for his psychology of operant conditioning with several experimentations on rats in Skinner box and on pigeons in pigeons box. His viewpoints about shaping, superstitious behaviour, verbal behaviour, teaching machines and programmed learning were highly important. Despite these valuable contributions Skinner's behavioursim has been criticized.
4. E. C. Tolman well-known for his purposive behaviourism, formulated a system that was based upon a set of intevening variables. In fact, he is credited with being the first psychologist who introduced intervening variables in psychology. He explained learning in terms of cognitive map that is built up by strengthening the expectancy at each choice point in the maze. His theroy of learning was divided into two parts—the "1932 version" and the "1949 version". Three popular and independent lines of experimental evidences were offered in support of Tolman's theory of learning. They were : reward expectancy experiments, place or goal earning experiments and latent learning experiments. In "1949 version" he added six types of new learning : Cathexis, equivalence belief, field expectancies, field cognition modes, drive discrimination and motor patterns.
5. J. R. Knator's interbehaviourism is also very popular among later behavioursits. According to it, the subject-matter of psychology should be interaction of organism and stimulus objects. For explaining behaviour, he has rejected intervening variables and instead used constructs. Throughout his system he has outlined various types of interactions that were important in understanding behaviour.
6. For Albert Bandura, another important neo-behaviourist, behaviour can be easily understood as a function of reciprocal interaction of

behavioural, cognitive, and environmental determinants. He is well-known for his modelling technique or technique of observational learning. He points out that vast majority of our behaviour is learnt by copying what others do.

7. A review of the contributions of later behaviourism reveals that the later behavioursim is obviously distinct from the early behaviourism. There are four basic differences between the early behaviourists and the later behaviourists.

REVIEW QUESTIONS

1. Discuss the contributions of E. R. Guthrie as a behavioutirst.
2. Critically examine the major contributions of Clark L. Hull in the field of learning.
3. Critically examine the major contributions of B. F. Skinner in the field of learning, verbal behaviour, behaviour modification and teaching machines.
4. Was E. C. Tolman a behaviourist ? Assess his major contributions in the field of learning.
5. What do you mean by interbehavioursim ? What significant contributions have been made by J. R. Kantor in this field ?
6. Was Badura a 'soft' behaviourist ? Give arguments in favour of this.
7. "Skinner's behaviourism represents empty organism approach to understanding behaviour". Justify the statement.
8. Make a comparative study of the major viewpoints of hard behaviourists and soft behaviourists.
9. Discuss the major points of distinctions between early behaviourism and later behaviourism.

■

CHAPTER 12

GESTALT PSYCHOLOGY

CHAPTER PREVIEW

Gestalt psychology is a German school founded by Max Wertheimer and subsequently expanded by his colleagues, namely, Wolfgang Kohler and Kurt Koffka. The important developers of this school was Kurt Lewin, R.H. Wheeler, E. Brunswik and Roger Barker.

Like other system, the Gestalt psychology had strong antecedent forces that were instrumental in its emergence. The viewpoints of I. Kant, Wilhelm Wundt, John Stuart Mill, Franz Brentano, Carl Stumpf and the laboratory works done at Gottingen University were important such forces.

Wertheimer's study on the phi-phenomenon was highly impressive and important for this school. From this, the famous concept of part-whole psychology emerged. Kohler and Koffka by emphasizing upon insight learning added glamour to the school.

Gestalt psychology lodged its protest against various other systems like structuralism, associationism and behaviourism. Among the important contributions that have been included are the emphasis of Gestalt psychology upon part-whole psychology, principles of organization, field dynamics, phi-phenomena and isomorphism. Apart from its contribution in the field of perception Gestalt psychology has also made significant impact in the field of learning, thinking and memory.

Gestalt psychology not only contributed in a fragmented way but also as a system, its impact had been widely felt. As a system, it has made its stand clear regarding the subject-matter of psychology and methods of psychology, mind-body problem, principles of selection, principles of connection, etc.

Despite all these Gestalt psychology has been criticized. Its present status is that its influence is widely felt and being experimented.

In 1912, the same year that Watson gave a series of lectures at Columbia University and that ultimately led to the foundation of behaviourism in 1913, Max Wertheimer published a series of experiments on apparent movement. These experiments were conducted in collaboration with Wolfgang Kohler and Kurt Koffka. In fact, these experiments served the basis for foundation of what was called *Gestalt*

Psychology. Wertheimer was recognized as founder and Kohler and Koffka were recognized as *cofounder* of this new school. Although the term *Gestalt* had no literal translation in English, the words 'form', 'shape' or 'configuration' have been most frequently used as the nearest translation. This new school cleared away some of old problems of psychology and presented the importance of new problems. The problem of how various elements are organized into wholes was the central theme for Gestalt psychology. Initially, Gestalt psychologists concentrated in the field of perception but later, it broadened its area of study to the fields of learning, thinking and memory. As a consequence, by 1930s, the Gestalt psychology fully established itself as a completely developed system of psychology. Kurt Lewin, R. H. Wheeler, E. Brunswik and Roger Barker were the *developers* of Gestalt psychology.

ANTECEDENT FORCES

Like other systems of psychology, Gestalt psychology also had some antecedent forces. Some of the important antecedent forces may be discussed as under :

1. *Immanuel Kant*

We have already considered the contribution of I. Kant in chapter 3. Kant had insisted on the unity of perception. It meant that for Kant perception couldn't be analyzed into its divisible parts. This notion became the heart of the Gestalt psychology. Apart from this, Kant's nativism had also shown that our ability to perceive space and time as such was not wholly dependent upon learning or experience rather it was native or inborn. This notion also influenced the thinking of Gestalt psychologists who have deemphasized the role of learning in perception and have made it explicit that ways of organization in perception are quite natural or native.

2. *Wilhelm Wundt and John Stuart Mill*

Wundt developed the concept of creative synthesis which, in fact, recognized the difference between wholes and sum of their parts. This principle stated that two or more elements of consciousness might form a state, which was, of course, different from the mere sum of the component elements. This principle had already been anticipated by John Stuart Mill in his concept of 'mental chemistry' which also stated the same things. Thus both J.S. Mill and Wundt had recognized that new characteristics might emerge from the combination of elements into wholes. This view had a direct impact upon Gestalt psychologists who pointed out that perception of whole was not the sum of perception of its part. The whole had characteristics which differed from the characteristics of its parts.

3. *Franz Brentano and Carl Stumpf*

We have discussed the contributions of both Brentano and Stumpf in chapter 5. We have seen that both persons had anti-analytical attitude. They had, in fact, objected to the psychology of elemental content. They held the view that mind was not a passive receiver of our experiences and emphasized upon the act of perceiving or sensing rather than upon the analysis of various elements. This type of attitude had a direct bearing upon the modern Gestalt psychologists who were also inclined to study perception as a whole rather than upon studying it by dividing into different parts. For them, whole was not the sum of its parts.

4. *Ernst Mach (1838–1916) and Christian Von Ehrenfels* (1859–1932)

Mach was a physicist who came into the history of psychology by the back door (Marx & Cronan-Hillix, 1987). He pointed out the existence of two entirely new types of sensation—*sensations of space-form* as illustrated in the perception of triangle or any other kind of geometrical figure and *sensation of time-form dimension* as heard in a melody. He considered these space-form and time-form to be independent of their elements. For example, a triangle can be red or green, small or large but it still remains the quality of being a triangle. Similarly, a melody remains a melody irrespective of the key in which it is played. The importance of the concept of *form* was very crucial for the Gestalt psychology. Ehrenfels was basically a philosopher and shared with Mach's psychological notions of the new *elements* into a theory called *Gestalt qualitaten* or *form qualities*. He has pointed out that there are new qualities or elements in experience that go beyond those recognized in our sensations. For example, in melody there is a temporal pattern that is independent of the individual sensation tones which may be regarded as elements of which it was composed. The same may be said to be true one for space-form dimension. These new elements are present in our mind and don't exist in physical objects. This concept of *form-quality* became an important source of inspiration of Gestalt psychologists who integrated it into their own interpretation.

5. *Laboratory works at Gottingen University*

The various laboratory researches done at Gottingen were also major antecedent forces. G.E. Muller did several laboratory works there that resembled the Gestalt phenomenological approach. The other three young persons, almost exactly of the same age as Wertheimer, Kohler and Koffka, also supported the laboratory work of G.E. Muller. Those persons at Gottingen were E.R. Jaensch (1883–1940), David Katz (1884–1957) and Edgar Rubin (1886–1951). Jaensch had pointed out that in explaining the phenomenon of visual activity the large inter-acting systems had to be taken into account because the elementary atomistic approach would do nothing. Likewise, Katz was studying the perception of colour and in 1911 he published a monograph on colour. It presented a beautiful phenomenological explanation of three types of colour : surface colours, volumic colours and film colours. He *rejected* the explanation of these colours in terms of combination of sensations of colour with some other elements and favoured explanation in terms of conditions under which each type of colour could be observed. Rubin started work on the psychology of perception of figure and ground. He emphasized that in perception some parts of the total stimulus situation stood out and some part remained vague and indistinct one. The former was named as *figure* and the latter was named as *background*. He also pointed out several conditions in which perception of figure and ground could be *reversed*. The works of these three men were highly valued by Gestalt psychologists and soon, they incorporated them into their framework. These three men had started working and publishing their results of the phenomenological investigations in 1911 or 1912, the year that Wertheimer had founded the Gestalt psychology. Had these three men wished to make their results the basis of a school, then the *names of the founders* of the Gestalt psychology would have been Jaensch, Katz and Rubin. Definitely, these three men, however, may be regarded as pioneers of Gestalt psychology.

In this way we find that Gestalt psychology had its strong antecedent forces. It was founded by Wertheimer, Koffka and Kohler who were influenced by the works of several other persons.

THE FOUNDING OF GESTALT PSYCHOLOGY

The Gestalt psychology was founded by Max Wertheimer who did the initial experiments on apparent movement. Wolfgang Kohler and Kurt Koffka were the cofounders and who had also served as subjects in several experimentations by Wertheimer on apparent movement.

Max Wertheimer (1880–1943)

Wertheimer was born in Prague. He studied law there before coming to the field of psychology. He obtained his Ph. D. degree at Wurzberg University as a pupil of Kulpe.

Wertheimer became interested in the perception of movement. The problem before him was how to explain using sensations as elements in the perception of movement which basically arose from the perception of a series of stimuli that actually didn't move. The story goes that in 1910 he was travelling from Vienna to Germany in train for a holiday. He left his train at Frankfurt and stopped at a place to buy a toy stroboscope (Harper, Newman & Schab, 1985). Stroboscope is a kind of instrument which allows still pictures to be exposed alternatively in such a way that we perceive motion in pictures. With the help of this stroboscope he made several observations and finally concluded that what we perceive did not necessarily conform to what was really found in the environment. This idea was perhaps to be the starting point of Gestalt psychology.

Wertheimer conducted a series of experiments to provide a scientific explanation of the apparent movement. Kohler and Koffka, then about 23 and 24 acted as *subjects* in Wertheimer experiment. Later Dr. Klein-Koffka, wife of Koffka, also became his regular subject. In one of his initial experiments he presented two different vertical lines in separate places through the window of tachistoscope—one line was on the right side and another was on the left side. In each presentation the two lines were presented in an alternative manner and was separated by some interval of time. His findings revealed that if one second elapsed between the two exposures, subjects reported no movement and perceived one still vertical line on the left side and another still vertical line on the right side. This perception was exactly similar to the actual physical presentation. But when the exposure time was shortened, the subjects gradually reported not two lines but the single line moving from one point to another. At one-fifteenth of a second, the subjects clearly reported that one line was moving across the screen from left to right. But if the exposure intervals were further reduced, the subjects reported less apparent movement and at one-thirtieth of a second, subjects reported only two still lines and the perception of apparent movement was abolished. Wertheimer conducted similar other experiments and he invariably found that the perception of apparent movement occurred only when an appropriate interval of time was given between the two flashes of stimuli. If he reduced or increased that appropriate interval, the perception of movement in the either case disappeared. The results of all such experiments were published in 1912 and the illusion of the apparent movement came to be known as *phi-phenomenon*. Wertheimer considered this to be the most important phenomenon. He further said that in faster exposures the lines or figures appeared without movement. Why not movement in such situation ! Wertheimer's explanation was that in such situation movement really took place in brain.

The author wishes to make it clear at this point that such illusion of the apparent movement was in fact known prior to Wertheimer and had been served with some explanation, too. For example, Wundt had explained such illusion in terms of the movements of eyes. But Wertheimer's experiment ruled out the validity of this conclusion. The results of his experiments in which lines moved in opposite directions, could not be explained in terms of movements of eyes because both eyes can't move in two directions at once.

The discovery of phi-phenomenon was very important for Wertheimer and it had some implications for him. He pointed out that when subjects perceived the apparent movement in the visual stimuli, they were perceiving *whole* or Gestalt rather than the succession of isolates stimuli. The perception of this whole was primary and unanalyzable experience and was *not* the sum of its parts. Perceptual wholes emerged and they had their own characteristics that were obviously different from the characteristics of the parts. This became the most important principle of Gestalt psychology. For this explanation, it is obvious that Wertheimer lodged a strong protest to the analysis of psychological fact into simple elements. He claimed that through elementalistic analysis (as it was done by structuralists) the perceptual field or phenomenological field (in which perception takes place) would be destroyed.

Wertheimer died in 1943. His long promised volume *Productive Thinking* was published in 1945, two years after his death.

***Wolfgang Kohler* (1887–1967)**

Kohler was born in Estomia in 1887 but received his Ph. D. degree at Berlin with Stumpf in 1909. He had also studied physics with Max Planck and had become interested in acoustics. His doctoral dissertation was in the field of *psychoacoustics.* After receiving his doctoral degree Kohler went to Frankfurt where he came into contact with Wertheimer. In 1913 he left Frankfurt and Wertheimer to go to study apes on the island of the Tenerife. He was interned there during World War I but continued his researches. He experimented on chimpanzees and chickens to study their visual discrimination. Kohler concluded that these animals also perceived relations among stimuli. According to Kohler, perception of such relation was the indicator of intelligence of the animals and sudden perception of such relations was called by him as *insight.* The ape who perceived that two poles fitted together would make a long pole enough to reach the banana kept at a distance, showed insightful behaviour. Likewise, the ape who perceived that by putting boxes upon one another the distance to banana hanging from ceiling could be reduced and then, by standing upon them, he could get banana, was also the example of insightful behaviour Kohler pointed out that such insight facilitated learning. Kohler's book, *The Mentality of Apes*, gave a good account of these things.

Kohler came back to Germany in 1920 and succeeded Stumpf as professor at Berlin in 1922. Wertheimer had also came back to Berlin and the old association established at Frankfurt was revived. In 1921 Kohler in collaboration with Wertheimer and Koffka had started publishing a periodical *Psychologische Froschung* which was then the major organ of experimental researches and theories of movement. Kohler, Wertheimer and Koffka remained united and there was no dissensions and no diverse developments. However, they went on specializing in different aspects of psychology. For example, Kohler specialized in auditory perception whereas Wertheimer in psychology of thinking and judgement.

***Kurt Koffka* (1887–1941)**

Koffka was born in Berlin and took his Ph. D. Degree in 1909 at Berlin under the supervision of Stumpf. His doctoral dissertation was on rhythm. He came to Frankfurt in 1910 and started his association with Kohler and Wertheimer. In 1911 he was appointed *Dozent* at Giessen about 40 miles away from Frankfurt. Despite this distance, he kept his relations with Wertheimer and Kohler maintained. As stated above, three important figures, namely, Wertheimer, Koffka and Kohler founded a periodical *Psychologische Forschung* which became soon an important organ of the Gestalt school. This continued until 1938 when the Nazis suppressed it. Koffka stayed at Giessen until 1927. The importance of the 'new' psychology that Koffka, Wertheimer and Kohler had started in Germany, was soon recognized by Americans. Therefore, they were eager to get the summary of the new psychology from Germany. Consequently, Koffka was persuaded to write an article on this new movement for *Psychological Bulletin* published from America. Accordingly, in 1922 he wrote the article, *Perception : An Introduction to Gestalt-Theorie* which incorporated the results of many experiments conducted by these three giant figures on the Gestalt movement. In 1921 he also wrote his *Development Child Psychology* that was subsequently translated under the title *The Growth of the Mind*. The German edition of this book appeared in 1925 and the English editions in 1924 and 1928. Thus the book became popular both in Germany and America. In 1924 Koffka came to America and visited the Universities of Cornell and

Wisconsin. In 1927 he was appointed to chair the department of psychology at Smith College and remained there until his death in 1941. In 1935 he had also published his *Principles of Gestalt Psychology*, a very important book that was difficult for many psychologists to understand. Even without proper understanding, they have, however, used this book for reference.

PROTEST OF GESTALT PSYCHOLOGY AGAINST OTHER SYSTEMS

Gestalt psychology lodged strong protest against the schools or systems that preceded it as well as against those that were evolving at the same time. Its major objections against structuralism, associationism and behaviourism may be outlined as under :

1. *Objections against structuralism*

Structuralists were attacked by Gestalt psychologists on two grounds—*elementalism* and the *constancy hypothesis*. Structuralists had held that experience could be broken down into its elements. Gestalt psychology had strong belief in the uniqueness of perceptual wholes which were not the sum of their parts. It obviously meant that parts had their separate characteristics and wholes had their own separate characteristics. Therefore, perceptual wholes couldn't be explained or understood by analyzing them into parts. Gestaltists have claimed that in analyzing the experience into its elements, the structuralists have destroyed the basic characteristics of the experience. The *constancy hypothesis* states that there is one-to-one relationship between physical event and the psychological event. Such viewpoint had been obviously expressed by structuralists' *doctrine of psychophysical parallelism*. Several experimentations by Gestalt psychologists on optical illusion refuted the constancy hypothesis. Gestaltists have vividly shown that what we perceive is not the same as what remains physically present in the environment. In famous Muller-layer illusion the length of arrow-headed line is identical with the length of feather-headed line. But still we perceive the former to be shorter than the latter. Where is the constancy ?

2. *Objection against associationism*

Gestalt psychology also lodged protest against associationism as well as against persons like Thorndike who used various principles of association in explaining different psychological phenomena. The various bonds of association utilized by structuralists as well as Thorndike were referred to as *bundle hypothesis* by Wertheimer. The theme of bundle hypothesis was that the experience was a composition of elements (Heidbreder, 1961). The Gestalt psychologists conducted several researches that went against the bundle hypothesis. They pointed out that like elements, the bonds of connection were unreal and artificial. Since experience was molar (rather molecular) in nature, and consists of whole, it needed no principle of connection to lump its parts or elements together.

3. *Objection against behaviourism*

Gestalt psychology also objected against behaviourism and all those related systems that broke behaviour into simple and discrete stimulus-response units. This objection came true because from Gestalt psychologists the nature of behaviour was molar which did not need discrete stimulus-response units. They also lodged protest against behaviourism because it had rejected consciousness as the subject-matter of psychology. For Gestalt psychologists, psychology was the study of both consciousness and behaviour. Psychology studied consciousness or immediate experience but not in an analytical manner suggested by structuralists.

Apart from the above objections, Gestalt psychologists also objected to the use of physiology by other schools. Various schools had treated the nervous system as a series of connected neurological units that operate like a telephone system. Gestaltists presented a separate explanation in form of principle of *isomorphism*. This principle assumed a one-to-one relationship between what one actually perceived and what happened in the brain. The isomorphic principle incorporated a patterning of cohesive and restraining forces that presented a picture in the brain like a map of things that was received.

BASIC EXPERIMENTAL CONTRIBUTIONS OF GESTALT PSYCHOLOGY

Initially the Gestalt psychologists worked in the area of perception only. Later on, they expanded their field to include learning, thinking and memory. Accordingly, we shall examine their contributions in the four areas : perception, learning, thinking and memory.

1. *Perception*

The Gestalt psychology is well-known for its contribution in the field of perception. It would be neither wise nor feasible to attempt here to present a detailed description of its contributions that has resulted from Gestaltists' work done in about forty years. However, for convenience, the major work of the Gestalt psychologists may be presented under following five separate headings :

(i) *Part-whole psychology*

Gestalt psychologists have made it clear that there is a distinction between whole and its parts (as we experience them) although prior to them a Chinese sage Lao-Tse in 700 B.C. had expressed the view that sum of parts was different from the wholes (Hartmann, 1935 : 9). Thus perceptual wholes are more than the sum of its parts. Such wholes emerge and have their characteristics which are different from the characteristics of the parts. The whole as given in experience has two major characteristics. *First,* these perceptual wholes are unfilled wholes and not clusters of sensations. If we try to break whole, something new will emerge. It means the original characteristics of whole will be lost. *Second,* Such perceptual wholes are separate and distinct from background. Therefore, they are *segregated whole* and not simply holes.

Thus by emphasizing upon the unanalyzable character of the perceptual wholes, the Gestalt psychologists were digging the base of elementalism of structural psychology.

(ii) *Principles of organization*

Gestalt psychologists enunciated certain principles or laws that govern the organization of perceptual wholes. Wertheimer pointed out that these laws of organization were native and therefore, natural. Hence, they were also called as principles of *primitive organization.* Thus through these laws the Gestalt psychologists tried to de-emphasize the role of learning in perception. There were several such principles of which the important ones are as under :

(a) ***Principle of similarity :*** Those objects which are similar in their structure tend to be perceived as organized together into whole. In figure 11·1 we find one example of this. Here most people see triangle formed by dots with its apex at the top.

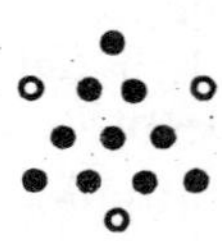

Figure 11·1

(b) ***Principle of proximity :*** Those objects which are close together either in time or space would tend to be organized together as we find in Figure 11·2. In this figure we see three pairs of vertical lines instead of six vertical lines.

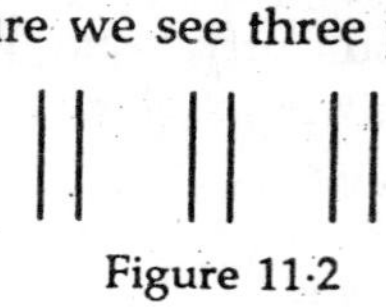

Figure 11·2

(c) ***Principle of continuity*** : Also known as principle of good continuation or principle of direction, it states that objects that have continuity with each other tend to be perceived as flowing in the same direction and therefore, they are perceived as a figure. In Figure 11·3 straight line and the wavy line are perceived as continuous even through one is intersected by other.

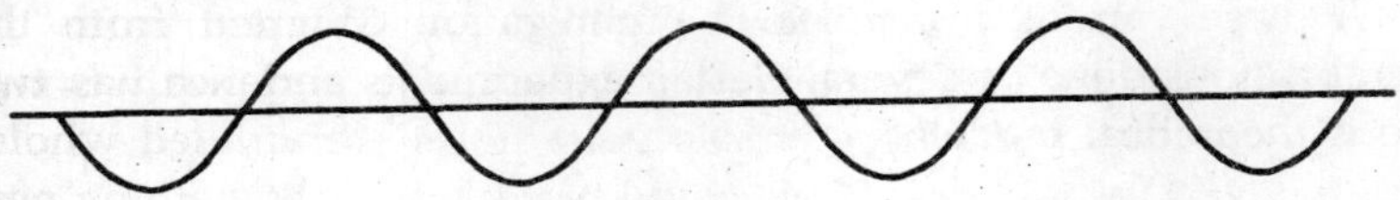

Figure 11·3

(d) ***Principle of objective set*** : If we see at a particular pattern of object and develop a mental set for it, it might be possible to continue to see that pattern even though the stimulus arrangements might be slightly changed. In Figure 11·4 as one continues to look from left (Where O's are grouped by proximity) to right where O's become more evenly spaced, it is possible to group them as one did in the first series.

OO OO OO OO OOOOOOOO

Figure 11·4

(e) ***Principle of pragnanz*** : Also known as principle of good form or good gestalt or principle of pregnancy, it states that we tend to assume the best possible forms of the objects even though physical objects may not be in developed and symmetrical form. For example, in Figure 11·5 we perceive the letter A and B in a clear form though they are written in distorted forms.

Figure 11·5

(f) ***Principle of closure*** : This is a special case of principle of good form. This principle states that when certain part of the perceptual object is left out, we have a tendency to fill the gap and perceive accordingly by making the Gestalt complete. For example, in Figure 11·6 we perceive it as a circle although by definition this is not a circle.

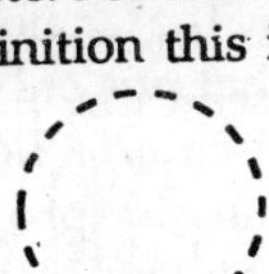

Figure 11·6

(g) ***Principle of figure and ground :*** This principle states that any perception tends to organize itself into a figure that stands out upon a certain background. One major characteristic of 'figure' is that it is distinct and outstanding. Background is comparatively vague and indistinct. In reversible figure, the figure and the ground tend to shift back and forth as one fixates his eyes on it.

All these various principles of organization emerged partly from generalizations done by several Gestalt experiments and partly from the various theoretical models.

(iii) *Object constancy*

From the various principles of organizations one basic generalization called phenomenon of perceptual constancy has emerged. This phenomenon indicates that perceived objects tend to remain constant in size even when they are viewed from varying distances. As we know, due to variations in distance, the resulting retinal images do change. For greater distance the retinal image becomes small and for shorter distance the retinal image becomes large. Despite these variations in the retinal images, the perceiver tends to perceive the object as remaining constant. This is called perceptual constancy and applies to every attribute of an object, namely, shape, brightness, size, colour, etc. A boy seen from 5 feet distance or from 15 feet distance will be perceived of the same size. This illustrates size constancy. A piece of coal kept in shadow and when kept in sun, will be perceived as coal although the level of reflection of brightness in sun is greater than the level of reflection of brightness in shadow. This is called brightness constancy. Gestalt psychologists have also revealed that perceptual constancy is affected by the information regarding changing conditions. If such knowledge is not given to the perceiver, the perceptual constancy is reduced to a greater extent.

(iv) *Field dynamics*

Since the Gestalt psychology is concerned with perceptual wholes, it naturally tends to explain field dynamics. For Gestaltists, a field is a dynamic whole or system in which changes in any one part affect the other parts (Boring 1950). The dynamic field of psychological experience is person and his environment with which he makes interaction. This interaction forms the basis of behaviour. Such field contains various interacting forces or vectors on the analogy of the forces in electrical field. Gestaltists made it clear that not only our perception but also our thinking seems to be organized within a field of such forces. In the field of perception such forces maintain proper balance, symmetry and stability in the configuration. The law of pragnanz applies well to this field. Kurt Lewin went a step further and developed a new theory based on these field concepts. We shall discuss Kurt Lewin's field theory in Chapter 15.

(v) *Phi-phenomenon and Isomorphism*

In Berlin in 1912 Max Wertheimer conducted a series of experiments on the perception of movement. In these experiments Kohler and Koffka had assisted him in several ways. In these experiments he observed that when the time interval between the two exposures of the same vertical line (second exposure a little right or left to the first exposure) was one-fifteenth of a second, the subject reported the line to be moving the right or left. This illusion of movement was named as *phi-phenomenon*. If the time interval increased or decreased, the illusion of the movement stood abolished.

Since the perceptual field of movement was not identical to what happened actually, how could this be explained ? In order to explain this, the Gestalt psychologists formulated the *principle of isomorphism*. According to this principle there exists one-to-one relationship between what one actually perceived and what happened in brain although the correspondence between the two may not exist in exact form. Therefore, the relationship between the two is topological and not topographical. Explaining phi-phenomenon with the help of this principle, Gestaltists assumed that there must be dynamic relation between two centres in brain stimulated by two flashes of light. This dynamic relation must be in such a manner that one area of brain influences the other area in a way similar to the flow of electricity across a poorly insulated gap.

In order to explain the principle of isomorphism in a still broader perspective, Woodworth (1948) used an analogy showing relationship between a map and the country it represents. Although the two are not the same but they bear the similarity in the sense that one can read the characteristics of the country from the map. The perceptual field and the physiological brain field demonstrate such direct relationship. To know what happens in the brain field, Gestaltists assumed that there were two types of forces in brain—*cohesive forces and restraining* forces. The cohesive forces refer to the tendency of the excitations of nerve impulses in the brain that attracted each other provided there remains nothing to interfere with. Restraining forces refer to those excitations that prevented the cohesive forces.

In support of the principle of isomorphism the Gestalt psychologists have presented some meagre and indirect experimental support. Kohler and Held (1949) conducted one experiment in which EEG waves were recorded from the visual area of the brain when a test object was moved through subjects' visual field. It was found that some changes did occur in the brain waves indicating the fact that there was some relationship between the perceptual field and the physiological brain field. Kohler and Wallach (1944) have tried to provide evidence through *satiation phenomenon* in brain. They pointed out that if we fixate our eyes on a certain object for some time, say for example, thirty-five seconds or more, the cortical or brain areas so stimulated become satiated. When we shift our attention to new object, the new object may tend to be perceived distorted. In one of their experiments subject fixated eyes on black squares for thirty-five seconds and thus the concerned brain areas were fully satiated. Later he shifted his fixation to white squares and this resulted in distortion of the white squares (probably smaller and also perceived as shifted from its original place). Likewise, in another experiment subject fixated at a covered line for some time and then shifted his fixation to straight line. It was found that the straight line appeared to be slightly curved. Such distortions in perception were named as *figural afteraffects*.

In this way we find that Gestaltists made significant and very broad contribution in the field of perception.

2. *Learning*

Gestalt psychologists applied his principles of perception into the field of learning. They pointed out that learning was nothing put the perceptual reorganization of the field. After learning has occurred, there occurs perceptual reorganization and the person sees the situation in new perspective. They also made it clear that learning occurs by insight. In learning situation the person is faced with a particular problem. He thinks of many possible solutions and sets up many tentative hypotheses. Once correct solution is reached, insight occurs and learning is also said to have occurred. Insight is understood as sudden shift in perceptual field (Marx and Cronan-Hillix, 1987). Since insight is sudden, learning is also sudden and not a gradual improvement with practice. Once the solution is learnt, the organism proceeds immediately to the solution on further trials without making any random behaviour. Gestaltists have cited four behavioural indices of insightful learning. They are : sudden transition from helplessness to mastery, quickness and smoothness in performance after grasping of principle, sound retention, and readiness with which the solution is transferred to similar problems involving the same principle.

In 1913 Kohler who was also director of the anthropoid station at Tenerife in Canary Island and was confined there due to World War I, conducted several experiments on dogs and chimpanzees. However, his experiment on Sultan, one of the most intelligent chimpanzees could become very famous. In one experiment on Sultan, he presented a joint stick problem for its solution. There were two bamboo sticks, neither of which was long enough to reach the banana kept outside the cage. However, the structure of these two sticks were such that they could be joined end on end by fitting one into the other. It was found that in the beginning Sultan tried to reach banana with the help of either of the two sticks but remained unsuccessful. Then Sultan started playing with these two sticks and during play both sticks happened to join them together by chance. Suddenly, he ran towards banana with the help of this longer stick and got the banana. The now-longer stick gave him insight suddenly and he solved the problem. On the following day, the animal solved the problem without any useless angling. Likewise, he conducted series of experiments and obtained more or less similar conclusion.

His final conclusion was that learning occurs by insight and insight was a sudden mastery of the problem and not a gradual improvement with practice. Both Kohler and Koffka rejected Thordinke's idea of trial-and-error learning although in Kohler's experiments there appeared to be a good deal of what may be called as trial-and-error before insight occurred. Both Kohler and Koffka pointed out that the apparatus used by Thorndike and other animal psychologists forced the learning organism to use trial-and-error. In more appropriate situation where nothing is kept concealed from the subject, trial-and-error has no significant role to play. Learning here occurs suddenly due to insight.

Gestalt psychologists also studied other aspects of insight such as *transposition*. It refers to learning a principle in one situation and applying the same to other situation. Hence, it was a case of *transfer*. For Gestaltists what is transferred is a 'whole' or 'Gestalt' and not the identical element between the two situations as it had been proposed by Thorndike. To demonstrate this, Kohler conducted one experiment in which chickens were trained to peck at the darker of the two gray surfaces. Pecking at the darker of two gray surfaces was followed by food but pecking at lighter surface was not followed by food. In about hundred trials chickens learnt to make the discrimination between the two gray surfaces. In the next step Kohler presented this original dark gray surface along with a still darker gray surface. It was found that animals acted according to the rules that had been learnt earlier. Now the animals pecked at the darker of these two surfaces (that is, on new surface) and not at the original dark surface which they had learnt. This conclusion obviously show that chickens had learnt to react to the whole situation and thus, a Gestalt had been formed and transferred to the second learning situation. They had learnt the basic principle, that is, to peck at the darker of the two gray surfaces and not at a particular surface. In nutshell, the chickens had learnt a pattern and not a specific response. Kohler named such learning as transposition which was a case of insight.

3. *Thinking*

The views of the Gestalt psychologists regarding learning were also applied to the field of problem solving and thinking. Wertheimer's book *Productive Thinking* presents a detailed study of the principles of productive thinking derived from the experiments conducted with the help of simple geometrical problems on young children. In fact, he applied the Gestalt principles of learning to creative thinking done by human beings. The ground for studying thinking by Gestaltists had been provided by Wurzburg school. He emphasized that thinking should be done in terms of wholes. In solving a problem or thinking one should take the whole or broad view of the situation and he should not be lost in details. One should not take any step blindly and procedure adapted should be from the whole to its parts. While solving a problem if errors are committed, they should be good errors (that is, errors leading to the probability of success) and not blind errors as done by Thorndike's cat. Wertheimer explicitly denied any application of trial-and-error in thinking. For him, Thinking was always goal-directed as well as insightful and it created new gestalts. Experimental studies conducted by Dunker (1945) and Maier (1930–1931) have made it clear that thinking is insightful and changes the structure of the perceptual field.

Wertheimer distinguished among three types of thinking—a, b and y. Type a thinking refers to the productive thinking which the individual is concerned with decisive issues relating to the structural problems and includes processes like grouping, reorganization and discovery of the important features. In such thinking the person tries to relate means with the ends or goals. Productive thinking is the best example of this type of thinking. Type y thinking refers to blind and trial-and-error type of thinking. Such thinking tends to eliminate type a thinking. Here if solution occurs, it occurs by chance. Such thinking should be avoided. Type b thinking was partly productive and partly mechanized and unproductive. One of the most important features of Wertheimer type a thinking or productive thinking is that it involves the process of *centering* and *recentering*. In the process of centering there is transition from a personal or subjective view to a detached view of the situation, viewing it objectively and as a whole. Recentering refers to taking a new and penetrating perspective. In fact, it provides a new angle or outlook from which the creative solution is reached.

Wertheimer has also undermined the importance of repetition in solving a problem. He was warned that continuous use of mechanical repetition may produce harmful effect by creating a habit of blindness and mechanical actions.

4. *Memory*

Gestalt psychologists have also applied the principles of perception to memory. At that time one common theory of memory was that when we perceive something and subsequently try to recall it, we get success in that because a trace of the same was left in the brain. When we don't get a success, we forget it. This happens because the 'trace' gradually wipes out. The Gestalt psychologists have tended to reject such theory although they have retained the concept of trace. They have emphasized that memory is a dynamic process in which traces undergo several types of progressive changes with lapse of time. Such progressive changes occur in accordance with the principles of perceptual organization. As an example, we can take the principle of pragnanz. Wulff (1922) conducted one study that nicely demonstrated that changes in memory traces took place in accordance with this principle of organization. In this experiment subjects were presented with simple irregular geometrical figures for five seconds only. Subsequently, they were asked to draw the figures that they had seen after a time interval of thirty seconds, twenty-four hours and one week. It was found that the subjects tended to sharpen the figure and made it appear in good Gestalt where they were vague. Likewise, there were some other experimental supports to such theory of memory. Gibson (1929), Bartlett (1932) and Allport & Postman(1947) have reported that subjects tend to sharpen the original materials and thus produce distortion in reproduction no doubt but these distortion occurs in the direction of good form. These experimental evidences clearly show that memory can be easily explained with the help of principle of perceptual organization.

Thus we see that Gestalt psychologists have made valuable contributions in the fields of perception, learning, thinking and memory. In fact, their contributions in the field of perception were the most important ones and in the remaining three areas there have been simply application and extension of the principles of perception.

GESTALT PSYCHOLOGY AS A SYSTEM

After examining the contributions of the Gestalt psychology in different areas, it is also essential to examine this as a system. Like other systems in psychology, Gestalt psychology was also no less important and has made important methatheoretical and mehodological contributions. As a system Gestalt psychology may be examined as under :

1. *Definition and methods of psychology*

Some earlier Gestaltists like Kohler, Koffka and Werthiemer pointed out that psychology was the study of immediate phenomenal experience which covered psychological functions like memory, thinking, perception, learning, etc. However, they began with studying perception and later extended to other areas of psychology. Later Gestaltists among whom Kurt Lewin is one important figure, pointed out that behaviour should also be included in purview of the subject-matter of psychology. These later Gestaltists tried to relate perception and behaviour by conducting several studies. The present position is that for Getaltists, psychology is the study of both immediate phenomenal experience as well as behaviour of the organism. Their methods were experimentation and introspection. However, his method of introspection was different from that used by the trained introspectionists of the structural psychology.

2. *Postulates*

Like behaviourism, Gestalt psychology had some basic postulates for explaining its viewpoint. Those postulates may be divided into *primary* and *secondary*. The primary postulate which is only one in number, is concerned with whole-part psychology. We have already considered this in detail. As stated earlier, they have pointed out that the whole is not the *sum* of its parts. Whole has characteristics distinct and different from the characteristics of the parts. The whole dominates its part and provides basic data for study. The secondary postulates are several in number. The principle of isomorphism, the principle of perceptual organization, the non-continuity view about learning and the principle of contemporaneity (that is related to the principle of isomorphism) are some of the basic secondary postulates. The noncontinuity viewpoint as emphasized by Gestalt psychology is contrasting with the continuity viewpoint emphasized by Thorndike or reinforcement theorist. According to Thorndike, each trial or reinforcement contributes to learning. But Gestalt psychologist have said that in learning sudden discontinuous ingradients which are associated with insight do occur.

The principle of isomorphism states that the present perceptual experience is solely explicable on the basis of the present brain physiology because there is one-to-one relationship between the two. The past is past and there is no sense in looking at back. The only importance of past is that it may affect the present condition. Brain injury of the past may affect the present physiology of brain but our perceptual experience will always be guided and controlled by this present physiology. Thus the principle of isomorphism in a way incorporates the principle of contemporaneity.

3. *Mind-body problem*

For Gestaltists, isomorphism was the real solution to the mind-body problem. It was definitely a parallelism but not a psychophysical parallelism of Wundt and Titchener who had assumed a one-to-one relationship between mental events and physical events. It may be said that for Gestaltists it was a *psyhocphysiological parallelism* because it assumed one-to-one relationship between perceived or mental field and the brain field. Besides these two fields, there is another field called physical field or geographical field which may not correspond to perceived or mental field as it happens in a case of various types of illusion.

4. *Nature of data*

Facts obtained from immediate, unanalyzed experience form the major data for Gestalt psychology. Gestalt psychologists called data based upon these experience as *given*. The 'given' was used most frequently in the study of perception. In accepting data based upon immediate unanalyzed experience they were very much like the structuralists. But they were at the same time different from the structuralists in the sense that they rejected the type of analysis provided by them (the structuralists).

Gestaltists also accepted behavioural data particularly in the fields of learning and problem solving. That way Gestaltists also accepted the psychology of behaviourism. On this point, it can be said that Gestaltists were more tolerant than the structuralists who were not ready to accept the basic tenets of behaviourism. Gestaltists differed from behaviourists in the sense that they wanted to study and relate behaviour with psychological fields and not simply with environmental factors.

5. *Principles of selection*

Gestaltists enunciated various principles of perceptual organization that obviously tried to explain how a particular form of the figure was organized or selected for perception. They pointed out that almost all parts of the field played some role in perception. Therefore, for them how were they organized, was more important than how were they selected. Why some parts of the field were perceived as figure and why some other part as background. Rubin, one of the major supporters of Gestaltistic principles, pointed out certain principles though which some parts of the perceptual whole were selected as figure and others were treated as a background. One such major principle was that those parts which were most distinct and clear, were selected to be perceived as figures and relatively vague and indistinct parts were selected to be perceived as background. Later, Gibson (1966) tended to specify some properties of the stimuli that made such selection more smooth.

6. *Principles of connection*

For Gestaltists, the problems of connection are not the same as we find for associationists and structuralists. We have seen that for structuralists, the elements of consciousness are connected through various laws of association. This was termed by Gestaltists as *bundle hypothesis* and they have rejected this hypothesis because for them the whole is not the sum of parts and therefore, it is meaningless to reconstruct the wholes by connecting the parts. Gestaltists have argued that if bundle hypothesis is taken to be true one, perception is nothing but simply the sum of simple and elementary perceptions. But really our perception can't be explained by connecting the various simple perceptions. They also made it clear that principles of perceptual organization were not principles of connection because they (principles) stated that a particular structure would emerge and not what elements would be connected to produce the structure, Needless to say, Gestalt psychologists, like other systems, emphasized upon the connection or relationship between antecedents and consequents of immediate experience and behaviour.

On the whole, we can say that the Gestalt psychology as a system was no less important than any other system. Its various postulates are still the primary source of inspiration to modern research and experimentations.

CRITICISMS OF GESTALT PSYCHOLOGY

Some pshycologists have criticized Gestalt psychology for its various omissions and commissions. Some of its major criticisms are as under :

1. According to Marx & Cronan-Hillix (1987), Gestalt psychology was too dependent upon theory and lacked sufficient evidences to support the theory. They further pointed out that the entire system of

Gestalt psychology had a nebulous character about it. For example, the concept of insight was only theoretically inferred not empirically defined.

2. Harrower (1932), one of Koffka's students, has agreed with critics in saying that Gestalt psychologists have failed to define their *key term*, that is, *organisation*. Critics state that this term has, no where, been defined empirically. Moreover, they also claim that the term should be distinguished from non-organization so that experimental studies must be pinpointedly be carried out on organization only. They further claim that if the term organization is left to be interpreted differently by different psychologists, how can perception be studied in a scientific way ?

3. Gestalt psychology has been charged to be mystical or metaphysical. Perhaps this criticism has been done due to the complexities of the Gestalt position. But this criticism is not cent per cent true. In fact, Gestalt psychology, like behaviourism, is a natural science and not a metaphysical science.

4. Gestalt psychology has also been criticized on the basis of physiological assumptions relating to isomorphism. Critics said that the isomorphic principle of map in the brain relating to what one perceived was a unique speculative explanation and any proof of it was only indirect. Such speculation decidedly cast doubt on the validity and acceptability of the experimental results.

5. Critics have also pointed out that Gestalt psychologists have conducted *poorly controlled, ill-designed, non-quantitative,* and *non-statistical experiments.* They have depended mostly upon introspection, a method that was hard to replicate. Not only this, critics have also charged them to provide subjects unnecessary cues in experimental situation that have affected their problem solving ability in some unknown way making the results biased one.

6. Sometimes it is said that Gestalt psychology was not new and its basic principles were in use since long. But this does not appear to be a valid criticism because every system was born not suddenly and it had its own antecedent forces. If this criticism is held to be valid one, it can be said that no system in psychology was new one.

Despite these criticisms, it can be said with full confidence that Gestalt psychology has made several positive contributions. Its researches and experimentations in the field of perception gave certainly a 'new look' to the theory of perception. The renewed interest of the psychologists of today in cognitive psychology is nothing but reflection of strong Gestaltists' influences. They were, in fact, intellectual forefathers of what is today known as cognitive psychology.

PRESENT STATUS OF GESTALT PSYCHOLOGY

Although Gestalt psychology remained the most active system only until 1930s, its impact is widely felt even today. Its opponents might not accept or admit this view but this is a reality. Its one of the founders, Wolfgang Kohler, died in 1967 and till that period it had a founder as a leader. The researches done by Gestalt psychology have actively influenced the modern viewpoints. In 1960s there occurred a resurgence of interest in the Gestalt approach to the psychology of learning. Asch *et. al.* (1960) has conducted researches that show how perceptual organization affects coherence of elements in memory. The recent viewpoint of human learning called *organizational view of memory* has a very close resemblance to the basic tenets of Gestalt psychology. Tulving & Donaldson (1972) and Anderson & Bower (1972) have conducted studies in which the role of perceptual factors in learning and memory has been examined and they have also contrasted the Gestaltistic view and structuralists' view on learning and memory. Likewise, the views of Gestalt psychology regarding thinking and problem solving are being incorporated by modern computer scientists on computer stimulation of human problem solving (Newell & Simon, 1972). Gestaltists' view specially concerning those of whole-part psychology has kept scientists interested because of several complexities involved therein. Modern computer scientists are evolving certain techniques and models to simplify those complexities.

Although Gestalt psychologists' emphasis on experimentation has not been much instrumental in achieving popularity of the system, they have certainly forced re-examination and revamping of the more mechanistic and analytical systems which are inclined now to incorporate many of the Gestaltistic findings into their respective systems.

In making final evaluation of the present status of Gestalt psychology it can be said that there has occurred transformation in the systematic Gestalt psychology. As a consequence of this, its good concepts and ideas still persist. Modern psychologists' renewed interest in cognitive psychology and their rejection of piecemeal analysis are nothing but the reflection of the impact of Gestalt psychologists. Bower & Hilgard (1981 : 325) have rightly commented on German Gestalt psychologists, "They were, in fact, the intellectual forefathers of much of what is today called cognitive psychology, which is now a dominant viewpoint in American experimental psychology."

CHAPTER HIGHLIGHTS

1. Gestalt psychology was founded by Max Wertheimer. Wolfgang Kohler and Kurt Koffka were the cofounders. All three persons were German. This school was fully established by 1930s. Like any other systems, this system had also some antecedent forces. The viewpoints of Immanuel Kant, Wilhelm Wundt, John Stuart Mill, Franz Brentano, Carl Stumpf, Ernst Mach and Christian Von Ehrenfels were most instrumental in laying the foundation of Gestalt psychology. Apart from all these persons, laboratory works done at Gottingen University were also very important antecedent forces for its birth.
2. Max Wertheimer conducted a series of experiments on apparent movement. In those experiments Kohler, Koffka and Klein-Koffka, wife of Koffka, had participated as subjects. He concluded that when an appropriate interval of time (one-fifteenth of a second) was given between the two flashes of stimuli, subjects perceived that one stimulus was moving across the screen from one point to another. This was called *phi-phenomenon.* Time interval shorter or longer than one-fifteenth of a second led to reduction and finally abolition of illusion of movement. The discovery of phi-phenomenon was the base for the foundation of Gestalt psychology because when subjects perceived the apparent movement in the visual stimuli, they were perceiving whole or Gestalt rather than succession of isolated stimuli. Kohler, a cofounder of Gestalt psychologists, is famous for his studies on chimpanzees at the island of Tenerife. He concluded that animals learnt by insight rather than by trial-and-error. Sudden perception of the correct relations among stimuli was called insight. Since this insight was sudden, learning was also sudden and not gradual. His book *The Mentality of Apes* presented a good account of experiments conducted on chimpanzees by him. Koffka, another cofounder of Gestalt psychology, became instrumental in popularizing this basic tenets of psychology in America by writing about this new movement in *Psychological Bulletin.* His article published in this journal presented the results of many experiments conducted by Kohler, Koffka and Wertheimer. The title of this article was : *Perception : An Introduction to Gestalt-theorie.*
3. It is said that Gestalt psychology established itself by lodging a strong protests against the dominant systems like structuralism associationism, behaviourism, etc., of the time. Gestaltists objected against structuralism by rejecting constancy hypothesis, elementalism and bundle hypothesis. They also objected against

associationism for showing its sympathy towards bundle hypothesis. Behaviorism was objected on the ground that it had outright rejected consciousness as the subject-matter of psychology.

4. Initially, Gestalt psychology contributed only in the field of perception. But later on, it expanded its programme to learning, thinking and memory. In the field of perception Gestalt psychologists' emphasis upon perceptual wholes, principles of perceptual organization and isomorphism was the most important ones. In the field of learning they, on the basis of their experimentations, made it clear that the organism learnt by insight and not by trial-and-error. Hence, learning was sudden rather than gradual. Wertheimer's work on productive thinking has been very crucial. He emphasized that in solving a problem or in thinking, one should take the whole or broad view of the situation and one should not be lost in details. Gestaltists have emphasized that memory is a dynamic process in which traces undergo several types of progressive changes with lapse of time. Such progressive changes occur in accordance with the principles of perceptual organization.
5. Gestalt psychology as a system was no less important. Its viewpoint regarding subject-matter of psychology, methods, postulates, mind-body problem, nature of data, principles of relation and principles of connection have proved much valuable to modern psychologists.
6. Gestalt psychology has also been criticized. Among several criticisms, three points of criticisms are worth summarizing. *First,* it has been said that Gestalt psychology was too dependent upon theory and lacked sufficient evidences to support the theory. *Second,* it has also been said that they had conducted poorly controlled, ill-designed, non-quantitative and non-statistical experiments. *Third,* its physiological speculations about the principles of isomorphism were unique explanation that lacked direct experimental support for its confirmation.
7. Despite the fact that gestalt psychology has passed its premier days, its impact on modern psychology is widely felt. The renewed interest in cognitive psychology widely confirms such impact. In this sense, they have been rightly called as intellectual forerunners of cognitive psychology.

REVIEW QUESTIONS

1. Assess the major antecedent forces that led to the emergence of Gestalt psychology.

2. Discuss the major points of protest of Gestalt psychology against structuralism, associationism and behaviourism.
3. Discuss the contributions of Gestalt psychology in the fields of perception, learning, thinking and memory.
4. Critically examine the role of Gestalt psychology as a system in psychology.
5. "Gestalt psychologists were the intellectual forerunners of cognitive psychology". Elucidate.
6. What is the fate of Gestalt psychology in modern days ? Examine the major points of criticisms directed against this psychology.

■

CHAPTER 13

PSYCHOANALYSIS

CHAPTER PREVIEW

Psychoanalysis is a school founded and developed by Sigmund Freud. This system grew in non-academic situation, which marks an important point of its distinction from other systems in psychology.

The development of psychoanalysis as a system had also some antecedent forces. The views expressed by Gottfried Leibnitz, Johann Herbart, Arthur Schopenhauer, Friedrich Nietzsche, Hermann Helmholtz, G.T. Fechner and Charles Darwin served as the major forces behind the emergence of this school.

As a school of psychology, psychoanalysis was concerned with seven major aspects : topographical structure of mind, structural model of mind, psychic energy and theory of instinct, anxiety and defence mechanism stages of psychosexual development and mind-body position. Of these, emphasis upon psychosexual development made him more popular among the psychologists.

Finally, psychoanalysis has been critized for various lapses and overemphasis upon sex.

Psychoanalysis is a school developed in a very different environment from other schools. Other schools have been developed by people who considered themselves as academic psychologists having their association with universities and various laboratory works done in those universities. These academic psychologists conducted experiments to verify their hypotheses and expand their theories, which was not the history of psychoanalysis. It developed in a medical and clinical tradition.

Psychoanalysis was founded by Sigmund Freud (1856-1939) who was a practising physician and Jew by birth. He used the term psychoanalysis in three senses. *First,* it was a method of treating mentally ill-people. *Second,* it was a theory of personality and *third,* it was a school or system of psychology. In the present chapter, we shall discuss psychoanalysis as only a system of psychology. In early years Freud was mainly interested in neurology and also conducted several experimentations but these had very little impact upon development of psychoanalysis. His later works, however, made psychoanalysis very popular and its influences on not only psychology but also other disciplines such as literature, sociology, anthropology, art and drama were felt. Due to its widespread influences, Freud was rated by American psychologists as the most eminent psychological theoretician of all time (Coan & Zogona, 1962).

BRIEF LIFE-SKETCH OF SIGMUND FREUD (1856-1939)

Freud was born on May 6, 1856 in the little town of Freiburg, Austria (now Pribor, Czechoslovakia). His father, Jacob was a poor wool merchant. His mother, Amalie was the third wife of Jacob (Ellenberger, 1970) and he (Freud) was the eldest of seven children. Jacob had also two grown sons from previous marriage. At the age of three, he (Freud) moved with his family to Leipzig and a year later to Vienna where he remained for nearly eighty years, that is, until 1938 when the Nazi invasion forced him to go to London. He remained in London until his death on September 23, 1939.

At this time anti-semitism was rampant in Vienna and therefore, for Jews only two professions were left open—medicine and law. Freud opted for the former. He entered the University of Vienna in 1873 and obtained his M.D. degree in 1881. He had some inclination toward neurology and during period (1873 to 1881), he came into contact with the famous neurologists of the time, Ernst Brucke. Freud had begun to work in the laboratory of Brucke. He published several articles on anatomy and neurology and also discovered the analgesic properties of cocaine. However, he could not recognized the application of cocaine for human anaesthesia. Soon, however, he gave up the position in Brucke's laboratory and started private practice. Although this private practice did not flourished, three important things happened, *First*, it became clear to him that as he was a Jew, there was little chance of advancement in research-academic environment that was rampant with anti-semitic feelings. *Second*, his practice and research efforts did not seem to produce much personal income. *Third*, he had fallen in love with Martha Bernays. But as it also stands today, married life requires money and Freud had very little money. Therefore, he decided to bear the resulting monetary expenditure by the opening practice as a neurologist. Finally, he married Martha and produced six children, one of whom, Anna Freud, became later a famous psychoanalyst.

Shortly before obtaining his M.D. degree in 1881, he had also became acquainted with Joseph Breuer, an eminent physician of Vienna and 14 years older than Freud. Breuer gave Freud not only advice and friendship but also money. The friendship lasted until 1895. In 1895 they jointly authored and published the famous paper *Studies in Hysteria*. This year is important because this marked the beginning of psychoanalysis as a system. In fact, this paper contained the germ for psychoanalysis. In this paper a case of hysteria of 21-year-old woman under the pseudoname of Anna O. had been published. Both Breuer and Freud and discussed this case in detail. They believed that hysteria was disease characterized by paralysis or the improper functioning of certain parts of the body. The real name of Anna O. was Bertha Pappenheim who later became so famous that Government of Germany issued a commemorative stamp in her memory as well as in recognition of his various work for women and children.

In 1885 Freud received a grant from the University of Vienna to study in Paris under a French physician Charcot. Freud learnt how to treat the patient of hysteria with the help of hypnosis. In fact, he was already interested in studying hypnosis and this interest was further augmented by Charcot. The treatment of hysteria through the technique of hypnosis had made Freud convinced of psychogenic origin of hysterical symptoms. Freud had spent only four months with Charcot at Paris.

After returning to Veinna from Paris, he resumed his old association with Breuer. He reported about what he learnt about hypnosis and hysteria, He had also learnt about male hysteria from Charcot and therefore, in a bid to make a major discovery, he presented a paper on male hysteria to the Viennese Society of Physicians. Freud was of view that people knew only about female hysteria because hysteria was such a disorder that was presumed to be caused by wandering womb. But his paper was not well-received by physicians because the disorder was already known to them. Freud and Breuer continued to use the technique of hypnosis in treating hysterial patients. But later on Freud abandoned this technique in favour of his new technique of *free association* which, in fact, evolved from Breuer's Cathartic method. Freud listed *four* reasons for giving up the method of hypnosis. *First,* hypnosis often led to strong sexual arousal in the patient. *Second,* he found himself not particularly gifted as a hypnotist. *Third,* the symptoms were removed only temporarily by the technique of hypnosis. *Finally,* not all patients could be deeply hypnotised to have suggestions full of impact upon them.

In 1896 Freud and Breuer developed a professional disaggrement. After being separated from Breuer, in 1887 he developed a strong friendship with Wilhelm Fliess, a Berlin physician. It is said that Freud's association with Fliess had a considerable impact upon the major concepts of psychoanalysis that he was formulating. Fliess offered many valuable constructive suggestions that improved his various concepts like wish-fulfillment, nature of dream, pleasure principle, primary and secondary processes and cathexis.

By the late 1890s his friendship with Fliess started cooling and eventually ruptured in 1903. Now he had begun to analyze his own dreams and conflicts. That way he started *self-analysis* that continued for the whole lifetime. However, self-analysis for him was most difficult during the late 1890s because he regarded himself to be his best patient (Ellenberger, 1970).

Perhaps the greatest heyday in Freud's career was his publication of the *Interpretation of dreams* in 1900, exactly two years death of his father. This book was an outgrowth of his self-analysis and contained several of his own dreams written under the fictitious names. In fact, this book created an international stir and brought a good recognition and name. This also attracted so many intellectuals among whom Alfred Adler, Otto Rank, Gustav Jung, Sandor Ferenczi were important ones. These persons were close associates of Freud but later rebelled. Misunderstanding and difficulties in personal interaction were the major causes of rebel. A few years later they left the orthodox Freudian camp to develop their own theories.

One obvious sign of international recognition of Freud was G. Stanley Hall's invitation to lecture on psychoanalysis at Clark University's twentieth anniversary celebration in 1909. Along with Freud, Jung, Brill, Jones and Ferenczi also went there. Besides Freud, Jung had also lectured. From the side of academic psychologists, E. B. Titchener, J.M. Cattell and William James were present at the time of lecture. But soon Freud returned because he, in reality, never liked America and attributed his bowel trouble to different types of American food.

Jung later went to America for further lectures on psychoanalysis. He wrote to Freud from America that most of the psychologists in America were ready to accept psychoanalysis except for his overemphasis upon sex. This remark widened the breach between Freud and Jung and by 1914, the break was complete and final. In 1911, Adler had already broken with Freud.

Despite the fact that his professional colleagues were snapping their ties with Freud, his recognition continued to grow. In the fateful year 1923 a cancer was detected in Freud's mouth. It is said that this cancer was connected to Freud's atypical habits of smoking twenty cigars per day. He underwent about 32 operations and bore almost constant pain for the remaining sixteen years of life.

In 1933 Hitler came to power and due to getting various types of ill-treatment, most of the German psychoanalysts ran to America. In 1933 the Nazis burnt the books of Freud in Berlin. Freud had also been persuaded to leave Austria but he did not. In 1938 the Nazis had taken Austria under their full command and Freud's home was surrounded by the Gestapo. Through the active cooperation of Ernest Jones and William Bullitt, American ambassador to France, Freud was allowed to leave Vienna for London. However, before leaving Vienna and receiving exist visa, he was force to sign a paper attesting respectful treatment he had received from the Gestapo.

In London he was well-received and was welcomed as hero. He was soon made a member of Royal society as Newton and Darwin had been before him. During the short period before his death, he completed his last book *Moses and Monotheism* which was of little psychological importance. Finally, he died in peace and honour on September 23, 1939 with apprehension that his four sisters left in Austria might have been killed by the Nazis.

ANTECEDENT FORCES OF PSYCHOANALYSIS

Like Titchener, Watson and Wertheimer, Freud did not invent his system named psychoanalysis without prior influences. Therefore, like other systems in psychology, psychoanalysis had also some antecedent forces which may be explained as under :

1. *Gottfried Leibnitz*

As we have already discussed, in the early part of the eighteenth century Leibnitz developed a new kind of theory about elements of reality. This was called Leibnitz's theory of monads. Monads were explained as a point of force or energy. They consisted of elements of both physical and mental reality. They did not interact with each other but had degree of clarity or consciousness—from most conscious to the unconscious or least clear. Leibnitz's this theory had two sound implications for Freudian psychoanalysis. *First,* from Leibnitz's concept of energy Freud derived inspiration for his concept of psychic energy that played role in his psychoanalysis. *Second,* Leibnitz's division between conscious and unconscious particularly his idea about degree of consciousness was a direct source of inspiration for Freudian concept of conscious, subconscious and unconscious.

2. *Johann Herbart*

Ernest Jones, Freud's biographer, clearly wrote that Freud was directly influenced by the work and writings of Herbart. About a century after Leibnitz, Herbart developed the concept of a threshold between consciousness and unconsciousness. He had pointed out that ideas existed both in consciousness and unconsciousness. If unconscious idea was compatible with ideas already residing in consciousness, it got entry into consciousness. If any two ideas in consciousness were incompatible, one of them might be forced into unconscious. Likewise, several ideas might join forces in unconscious and then, they might force their entry into consciousness. Thus we find that Herbart gave full recognition of the concept of unconscious though it was foretold by Leibnitz about a century before (Boring, 1950). Freud was directly influenced by Herbart's writings and he soon incorporated the idea of unconscious in his psychoanalytic system. Thus Freud was not the first to discover the unconscious and his only contribution was that he detailed the mode of operation of unconscious and listed its several characteristics (Ellenberger, 1970).

3. *Arthur Schopenhauer and Friedrich Nietzsche*

Schopenhauer (1788-1860) and Nietzsche (1844-1900) also influenced Freud's thinking about formulation of psychoanalysis. Sometimes Freud had acknowledged this and sometimes the impact of these two philosophers was indirectly implied in his writings. Schopenhauer also advocated the concept of unconscious that contained repulsive ideas whose entry into consciousness might cause disorganization of personality. From this, Freud evolved one of the basic concepts, that is, repression that later became the cornerstone of psychoanalysis. Freud also evolved the concept of sublimation from Schopenhauer's philosophy. Nietzsche emphasized upon aggressive nature of human beings. He had further pointed out that man was basically an animal and much of the basic animal nature remained in unconscious. When aggressive behaviour is repressed, it leads to various types of perversions. Freud was greatly indebted to these ideas of Nietzsche and he incorporated the concept of aggression in his famous doctrine of death instinct that later became very important concept in psychoanalysis.

4. *Helmholtz and Fechner*

Freud had received training under Ernst Brucke at Vienna Physiological Institute and Brucke himself was very much influenced by Helmholtz because he had joined the latter's camp along with Ludwig and Du Bois-Reymond. They wanted to prove that there were no forces or energies in living bodies which were not in non-living bodies. Helmholtz influenced Freud via Brucke. Helmholtz had also emphasized that there was no energy within the organism that went unaccounted for. From this, Freud later developed the notion that every human behaviour whether it is dream, fantasy, everyday common errors like slip of pen, slip of tongue, etc. was not automatic rather determined by some forces. This was called as *psychic determinism*. Helmholtz had also enunciated the concept of unconscious inference, which emphasized upon the fact that when we perceive something, our resulting perceptual experience contained such thing that was neither contributed by stimulus nor by the receptor but by our past experiences in unconscious way. This notion of Helmholtz helped Freud in understanding the significance of unconscious and importance of past experiences in determining the present behaviour. Freudian view that the seeds for adult personality were sowed during the first five years of life was readily influenced by this doctrine of unconscious inference of Helmholtz.

Ellenberger (1955) has pointed out that unlike Helmholtz, Freud's relation to Fechner was direct and hence, Fechner's influence upon Freud was direct, too. Freud had read Fechner's books and his topographical concept of mind (conscious, preconscious and unconscious) and mental energy were, to a greater extent, motivated by Fechner's work.

5. *Hughlings Jackson*

Jackson had developed an approach that is characterized by the combination of physiological and evolutionary outlook. He emphasized the fact that nervous system through various evolutionary development, came to achieve such a hierarchical structure in which higher structures became more complex than the lower structures. Subsequently, during the lifetime of a person appropriate neural connections among higher structures develop. In nervous diseases a process that is exactly the opposite of the process set up by evolutionary development comes into being. This he termed as dissolution. Freud developed the concept of regression from this concept of dissolution (Herrinstein & Boring, 1965).

6. *Charles Darwin*

Darwin's evolutionary principles had two main effects upon Freud. Darwin had presented the concept of natural selection. There were certain determinisms for the evolutionary theory. Freud later applied this determinism to the explanation of normal and neurotic behaviour of the person. Another influence from Darwin was his belief that human beings were similar to animals. Freud had emphasized upon animal nature of man and had also pointed out that many characteristics of lower animals were found in human beings. Instinct is one such example.

In this way we find that Freudian psychoanalysis did not fall upon the world like a bomb. It had its own historical background and antecedent forces.

FREUDIAN PSYCHOANALYSIS AS A SYSTEM

Due to differences between Freud and his rebels and developers, there is no single and coherent system of psychoanalysis as we find in case of structuralism, functionalism, behaviourism, Gestalt psychology etc. However, we shall keep our discussion limited to the major thrust of Freud in presenting this theme. As with these various systems, psychoanalysis as a system will be discussed under the following six major headings :

(1) *Definition of Psychology* :

Freud was more interested in developing a very systematic framework of psychoanalysis in which there was little direct scope for defining psychology in a simple and straight forward manner. If we pay attention to this framework of psychoanalysis, it will be obvious that psychoanalysis was such a discipline which began in the study of neurosis utilizing different techniques like free association, dream analysis, hypnosis, etc. and emphasized upon unconscious motivation. Since inception, it has broaden its methods of study to include laboratory experiments, testing techniques, anthropological studies and study of normal persons and cultures. Implicit in these writings and studied are some clues for indirect way of defining psychology (Rapaport, 1959). From this perspective, it can now be inferred that for Freud, psychology may be defined as the study of various types of behaviour both normal and abnormal, so that a better understanding of the unconscious level can be had for making a sound prediction and control of the person's behaviour.

(2) *Basic Postulates* :

Freudian psychoanalysis had certain assumptions or postulates about human behaviour. Some of the important postulates are as under :

(i) Unconscious is a very important part of human personality and plays a dominant role in determining human behaviour.

(ii) The psychic life is determined, that is, human behaviours, both rational and irrational, are not just happened rather determined by some motivations.

(iii) Different types of behavioural manifestations can be explained by a single underlying motivational concept. So, in Freudian psychoanalytic system the term motivational or dynamic is one of the most important explanatory concepts.

(iv) In determining present behaviour, past or the history of the person has been regarded as the most important.

(v) The basic drive is sex which is biological in nature. This primal energy is manifested through two kinds of instincts—life instinct and death instinct.

(vi) There is conflict between life instinct and death instinct.

(vii) The relationship between child and parents account for the neuroses.

(viii) The individual passes through the five stages of psychosexual development—oral, anal, phallic, latency and genital.

(ix) For explaining unconscious activities, the concepts of consciousness, subconsciousness and unconsciousness on the one hand and the concept of id, ego and super ego on the other hand are important.

(x) Various kinds of defence mechanisms or ego mechanisms under the control of ego protects the person from various types of psychological harm.

(xi) Dreams and various kinds of psychopathologies of every day life do represent the repressed sexual contents.

(3) ***Nature of Data :***

For Freudian psychoanalysis the basic data come from the therepeutic settings in which the patients gives a verbal report (a type of introspection) about his past events. There past events are inferred from the kind of data collected.

However, the therepeutic settings are not the only setting in which data for psychoanalysis have been obtained. Kardiner (1939), Mead (1950) and Malinowski (1950) have provided relevant data for psychoanalytic theory from primitive societies. Sometimes these data have provided support to the theory and sometimes they have provided grounds for modification of the theory. For example, data obtained from primitive societies have not supported the basic psychoanalytic notion that oedipal complex is an universal phenomenon. Data for psychoanalystic theory have also been provided from human subjects in laboratory or classroom situations (Hilgard, 1952; Silverman, 1976) and also from animal experiments (Sears, 1943; Fisher & Greenberg, 1977).

Some of these data have provided support to the theory whereas some of these data have discouraged the theory.

Freudian sources of data have been criticised. First, it is said that past events are not generally recalled well and they are subject to forgetting. As a consequence, from the present verbal reports of the patients, past can't be accurately assessed. This also casts doubt on relationship between the data and the theory of psychoanalysis which is genetic in nature. Second, it has been observed that what a patient states during therapy, is influenced by previous statement of the analyst. Such influence inclines the patients towards behaving in accordance with the expectations of theory. The overall result of this is that it becomes very difficult to gather objective and convincing data which may relate events of the therapy to the psychoanalytic theory.

(4) *Principles of connection :*

The problem of connection has not been as seriously taken by psychoanalysic theory as we find in case of those psychologists who are related to the academic psychology like Wundt, Titchener, Watson, etc. These academic psychologists have given due emphasis upon classic principles of connection such as upon the principles of contiguity, similarity and constrast (or opposition). All these principles relate to the experience of the individual as it has been made clear by various academic psychologists. In psychoanalytic theory those principles of connections have been considered important ones which relate to the motivational factors. In free association of Freud or words association of Jung, there may be similarity or opposition of motives or feelings. These associations enable the analysts to know why the free association of patients produced so many materials or informations which are important to the patient's major problems. These problems, infact, produce motives that, in turn, control the associations. In Freudian psychoanalysis some other complex principles like principles of distortion, displacement, condensation, etc. which tend to explain why certain manifest context arises from its latent content are also considered important. Psychoanalytic theory also recognizes some defence mechanisms of ego such as projection, rationalization and reaction function, which explain the connections between some other behaviours and their important motivational bases.

(5) *Principles of Selection :*

Psychoanalytic theory has also emphasized upon the various principles of selection which don't apply to the selection of stimuli in the environment. The theory regards motivation as the fundamental key to selection. In psychoanalysis the selection is exercised in the movement of materials or information into consciousness from preconsciousness and unconsciousness. In fact, the selection of any idea depends upon the dynamic balance between repressive forces and instinctive forces which do strive hard for the expression of the repressed materials. Through repression the person selectively keeps the materials removed out of consciousness and resistance act to keep out the emotion-laden materials. An analyst tries his best to redistribute the available libdial energy so that the repressive forces of the ego or super ego may be lessened as compared to the expressive forces. Sometimes the libido attached to the repressed ideas is so strong that it forces its our selection own expression in disguised form. For example, a repressed idea may be expressed to others through rationalisation towards objects or persons. The ego always tries to select appropriate repressed materials for such symbolic expression and in doing so, it also uses various principles of connection.

(6) ***Mind-body problem :***

Freud was not much concerned with this issue. However, he can be declared to be a psychophysical parallelist because he was of view that psychical processes can't occur in absence of psychological processes. He also pointed out the physiological processes start after the psycical processes. He may also be regarded as one ardent supporter of psychophysical interactionism (Lundin, 1985). This is because, for him, there is a constant interaction between three provinces of mind—id, ego and super ego as well as the other physical reality.

Thus we find that psychoanalysis as a system has its own distinctiveness. Its systematic features are gratefully accepted even by some unfriendly psychologists.

CONTRIBUTIONS OF FREUDIAN PSYCHOANALYSIS

Like the psychology of an academic psychologist, Freud's psychology never presented the look of systematic psychology. However, his concept and ideas were voluminous in nature and it is impossible to deal with his ideas and concepts in details here. A glimpse of the details of the work can be had from *The Standard Edition of the Works of Sigmund Freud*, 24 volumes that has been edited by J. Strachey (1955). However, Freud's systematic position can be presented under the following *seven* headings :

1. ***Topographical structure : Conscious, Preconscious and Unconscious***

Before developing his famous concept of id, ego and superego, he divided mind into two parts—*conscious,* and *unconscious.* The unconscious has two different levels—the *unconscious proper* and *preconscious.* Consciousness is defined as consisting of those mental elements that are in awareness at any given moment. Freud pointed out that only a small part of mental life is in consciousness. In famous "iceberg" analogy, the upper small portion of the ice represents consciousness. The preconscious consists of all those mental elements which are not conscious but can become readily available to consciousness with little effort. For this reason this is also sometimes called as *available memory.* The contents of preconscious comes from two sources. First source is conscious perception. What a person perceives remains in consciousness for a temporary period and subsequently, when our attention shifts to something else, it quickly goes into preconscious. The *second source* is the unconscious. Some ideas come to consciousness from unconsciousness via preconscious state in disguised forms such as dreams, slip of pen, slip of tongue, etc. Since such ideas quite easily slip out of consciousness, they are said to be in preconscious. In Freudian psychoanalytical system preconscious thus acts as a bridge between conscious and unconscious.

The unconscious is the most important part of the mind and in terms of 'iceberg' analogy, it is equivalent to that part of the ice that is submerged into the water. Obviously, then unconscious is the largest part of the mind. The unconscious consists of those mental elements that can't become conscious or which can do so with much difficulty. The unconscious ideas mostly relate to childhood experiences and sexual desires as well as conflicts. Freud was of view that unconscious processes play a very significant role in shaping our behaviour. Freud pointed out the unconscious ideas enter into consciousness in a disguised or distorted form. They are disguised in order to avoid the censor guarding the passage from the unconscious to the preconscious. For Freud, the unconscious ideas are the only explanation for meaning behind psychopathology of everyday life, dreams and various types of forgetting called repressions.

2. *Structural Model : Id, Ego and Superego*

Freud divided mind into three provinces—Id, ego and superego. Id refers to the biological elements of personality. It is such a mental agency that is inherited and fixed in the individual's constitution. Id impulses are unorganized and obey no rules and no laws. In fact, they are free from all inhibitions. Id acts like a spoiled child because it wants immediate gratification of its wishes and desires by reducing tensions.

This is called *pleasure principle*. Id has no contact with reality. Therefore, it is not changed by the experiences of person or by the passage of time. According to Freud, id employs two mechanisms for reducing tension. They are *reflex action* and *primary process*. In reflex action the id responds to the sources of tension automatically and thus immediately removes the tension. Coughing, blinking and sneezing are some of the examples. Primary process refers to a process in which person reduces tension by developing a mental image of an object that is previously associated with satisfaction of basic drives. In this process the person does not distinguish between real and unreal. An infant is purely guided by such primary processes in reducing tension.

As infant grows, the ego comes into being, evolving out of the id. It grows throughout the individual's lifetime. The ego of 'I' is that region of the mind which remains in contact with reality. It is governed by the *reality principle* which is a principle that enables the person to release gradually the id energy keeping in view the social restrictions and person's conscience. It allows satisfaction of instinctual gratification only when appropriate environmental conditions have arisen. Thus the basic purpose of reality principle is to maintain integrity of the individual. Since ego remains in contact with the external reality, it becomes the decision-making or the executive of personality. Since the ego is party conscious, partly subconscious and partly unconscious, it makes decision at each of the three levels. The ego basically serves two functions. *First,* it tries to reduce anxiety by preventing threatening impulses from coming into consciousness by means of *defence mechanisms*. *Second,* it tries to maintain communication between the id and the outside world. For serving this function nicely the ego preserves accurate observation and makes use of them at the appropriate places.

The superego or 'above–I' is the moral commander of personality. It grows out of the ego and like ego, it has no energy of its own. It is guided by the *idealistic principle*. It differs from the ego in the sense that it has no contact with world of reality and therefore, it is unrealistic in its demand for perfection. Freud divided superego into *two* subsystems—the *conscience* and the *ego-ideal*. Although Freud did not care to distinguish between these two subsystems, conscience results from experiences with punishment for behaviour whereas the ego-ideal develops as a result of reward given to child for his proper behaviour.

At last, Freud also made it clear that the divisions between these three provinces of mind were not sharp and defined. The development of three divisions varies widely in different persons. In some individuals the superego may dominate whereas in some individuals the id may dominate. In a normal healthy individual all these three provinces, namely, the id, the ego and the superego are well-integrated and work in harmony with every other.

3. *Psychic energy and theory of instincts*

Freud maintained that human beings are the complex energy systems. He assumed two types of energy—the *physiological energy* and the *psychic energy*. The physiological energy is derived from the food we consume and it is utilized for purposes like breathing, walking, running, writing, etc. The psychic energy is derived from the "neurophysiological states of excitation" (Hjelle & Ziegler, 1981) and is utilized in psychological activities like thinking. He further assumed that these two kinds of energy could be transformed into each other. The id was the mediating point between the psychic energy and the physiological energy. According to Freud, each person has a limited amount of psychic energy and the total amount of the psychic energy is expanded in those mental activities that attempt to reduce bodily excitation created by the various needs. The psychological or *mental* representations of these bodily excitations or need is called *instinct*. In other words, instinct is a wish (psychological representation) to fulfil a physiological need. For example, thirst instinct is derived from water deficit in the body cells and it is mentally represented as a wish for drinking water. Thus instinct indicates quantity of psychic energy and all instincts taken together constitute the total amount of energy available to the personality. In nutshell, an instinct is an internal drive that operates as a constant motivational force. Instinct originates from id but comes under the control of the ego.

Instincts have *four* major features—a *source*, an *aim*, an *object* and an *impetus*. Throughout life the source of an instinct is the bodily need it represents and its aim is to gratify the need. Both source and aim remain constant over time. The object of an instinct includes things that can satisfy the instinct. For example, food is object for hunger instinct. The impetus refers to strength or force of the instinct.

In his writings after 1920, Freud distinguished two categories of instincts—*the life instinct or eros* and the *death instinct or Thanatos*. The life instinct includes all those forces that maintain vital life processes and assure propagation of species. Of the various life instinct, sex instinct was singled out by Freud because this was the most important one in development of personality. The energy of the sex instinct is called *libido*. The term sex instinct was used by Freud in *broaden* sense to include not just the desire for and enjoyment of genital sexual pleasure but also pleasure derived from several bodily areas. The death instinct or thanatos or also known as *destructive instinct* includes all those forces that underline the manifestations of murder, suicide, aggression and cruelty. Such instincts are no less important in determining the individual's behaviour. Freud opines that there is an empirical basis of death instinct because there exists in all living organisms a tendency to reestablish the inanimate state out of which they have been formed. That is why Freud claimed, "The goal of all life is death." (Freud, 1920:38)

Right from the beginning, the life instinct and the death instinct constantly interact against each other and both to the reality principle. These two types of instincts may work together as we find in case of eating. Eating maintains life but also includes destructive acts like biting, chewing and swallowing. The life instinct may also neutralize death instinct. These two types of instincts may be in conflict with each other as we find in loving and hating the same object or person. Sometimes the death instinct may get the upper hand as we find when a person kills even his beloved one.

4. ***Anxiety and Defense mechanism***

Anxiety is another important variable in psychoanalytic system. Although Freud has not clearly defined anxiety, he emphasized that when the ego is threatened by danger, anxiety originates. Therefore, anxiety is understood as the emotional unpleasant state that is followed by a physical sensation, which signals the person against impending danger. He recognized three types of anxiety—*realistic anxiety, neurotic anxiety* and *moral anxiety*. A *realistic anxiety* or also known as *objective anxiety* is one in which there occurs emotional response to real threat or danger present in the environment. In other words, it results from the ego's dependence upon the external world. Neurotic anxiety is one in which there occurs emotional response or a threat to ego that the id impulses may breakthrough into consciousness. Thus it comes from the ego's dependence upon the id. Sometimes the superego gives threats to punish the go. This causes an emotional response called moral anxiety. Thus in moral anxiety ego's dependence upon superego is found. In such anxiety the superego responds with feelings of guilt, self-condemnation and shame. It is apparent from the foregoing discussion that both the neurotic anxiety and yhe moral anxiety have their points of origin within the person and are derived from the realistic anxiety.

Whatever may be the type of anxiety, the person wants to protect ego from the ensuing anxiety. For doing this, ego adopts some strategies which are called *defense mechanisms* or *ego defense mechanisms*. These mechanisms help the person in protecting ego from open expression of id impulses and opposing superego directive. There are varieties of defense mechanisms and all these mechanisms share two common characteristics. First, defense mechanisms operate at unconscious level, that is, they occur without awareness of the individual. Hence, they are self-deceptive. Second, they tend to make anxiety less intense and threatening because they tend to distort person's sense of reality. Following are the major defense mechanisms enlisted in Freudian psychoanalysis.

(i) ***Repression*** : It has been regarded by Freud as the most primary and important ego defense. Repression is a process that forces the unwanted feelings that are threatening to ego, into state of unconscious. A college girl may wishes to have a sex relationship with one of his classmates. Since that is a threatening wish, she may repress it into unconscious and may forget that she had ever wished so. Freud used hypnosis, free association and dream in unearthing such repressed impulses.

(ii) ***Reaction formation*** : It is a process in which ego defends itself through adopting a disguise form or having quite opposite form of the threatening impulses. Therefore, this mechanism operates at two levels. *First*, the forbidden impulses are repressed. *Second*, the opposite of the impulses is expressed on a conscious level. For example, a girl who really hates her mother may repress her this impulse because hating one's own mother is threatening to ego and therefore, causes anxiety. To avoid this, girl may develop the opposite impulse—love. Of course, this love towards the mother will be showy rather than genuine one. Still girl may keep herself free from such anxiety by deceiving herself.

(iii) ***Fixation*** : As we know, the psychical growth takes place through various stages of psychosexual development. When due to apprehension of some stress and anxiety at the next stage of psychosexual development, ego prefers to remain at the present stage, which is more comfortable, it results in what is called *fixation*. Thus fixation leads a person to remain fix on some old ways of life. He resists novelty because he apprehends danger behind such novelty. For example, even at the age 12, a child may suck his thumb and feel frightened in going anywhere without his parents. Fixation is similar to regression because a fixated behaviour is also rigid and infantile. However, regression is usually temporary whereas fixation is relatively permanent.

(iv) ***Projection*** : It is a mechanism by which the person finds in others those unacceptable feelings and impulses that actually reside in him. In other words, this is a process whereby the ego may get rid of unwanted and threatening impulses to an external object or person. A student who fails in examination easily attributes the reason of his failure to professor who did not taught him properly or to parents who did not give him money for purchasing books at the right time.

(v) ***Regression*** : It is a mechanism in which during the times of stress and anxiety, the person reverts back to earlier stage of psychosexual development or to some simpler mode of expression. Regression is very commonly seen in children and adults. A 5-year old child may regress to demanding a bottle when a baby brother or sister is born. A young woman after fighting with her husband may return to her parents' home only to allow her parents to 'baby' her and fulfil her every wish like that of a child.

(vi) ***Rationalization*** : This mechanism is based upon the old saying, "grapes are sour". Here the person tries to distort reality and protect his ego thereby making the irrational behaviour appear rational. For example, a male student who was not given any opportunity to enjoy by his girl classmate may console himself by saying that afterall she was not so beautiful and attractive.

(vii) ***Displacement*** : In this mechanism the person protests his ego by redirecting his impulses from threatening persons or situations to less threatening one. For example, a student after being chided by his father, may swears at his servant. Likewise, a child scolded by his father may hit his younger siblings. Sometimes hostile impulses turn not towards others but towards oneself. This is uncommon form of displacement and it often leads to depression and self-devaluation.

5. *Stages of Psychosexual development*

One of the basic assumptions of Freudian psychoanalysis is that at birth sex energy (libido) remains present and subsequently, it passes through a series of *psychosexual* stages. The term psychosexual emphasizes that the major factor underlying personality development is sexual instinct. According to Freud, between birth and the age 5 or 6, child passes through three stages of psychosexual development—*oral, anal* and *phallic*. These three stages are together called *infantile stage*. *Latency stage* is the fourth stage that lies between ages 6 or 7 and 11 or 12. During this stage, sexual impulses tend to be repressed and sublimated. The last stage is *genital stage*. The sudden bodily changes on the start of adolescence reactivate impulses that are coupled with interest in opposite sex. Each stage (except latency stage) is characterized by primary erogenous zone which refers to the regions of body that are sexually stimulating. Freud has regarded the first three stages of psychosexual development, that is, the period of first 5 or 6 years of life to be decisive for the formation of personality. A discussion of these five stages is presented below :

(i) ***Oral stage*** : The oral period extends from birth to second year of life. For Freud, sex remains present at birth and the infant gets pleasure out of sucking and taking food. This is called *oral erotic* period. When teeth appear, the child gains pleasure from biting. This is called *oral-sadistic*. The erogenous zone at this stage is obviously mouth. The basic feature of this stage is that the baby shows total dependency upon others for its care and fooding. Therefore, a person who is fixated at this stage, is too dependent, pessimistic and argumentative. Smoking cigarettes, biting a pencil, chewing gum are all examples of fixation at oral stage.

(ii) ***Anal stage*** : This period extends roughly from second year to third year of life. At this stage erogenous zone shifts from mouth to anal region. The child gets considerable pleasure from both retention and expulsion of feces. In anal expulsion the pleasure is gained through elimination. As adults, such people show orderliness, destructiveness or cruelty. In anal retention the pleasure is gained through retention of feces. As adults, such persons show traits like stinginess, stubbornness, punctuality, extreme messiness, etc.

(iii) ***Phallic stage*** : This stage covers period between about third and fifth or sixth year of life. At this stage the erogenous zone shifts from anal region to genitals. The children are often observed examining their sex organs, manipulating their sex organs and showing interest in matter relating to sex and birth. The male child recognizes his penis and touching it appears to him interesting. He also realizes that he is different from his little sister. The girl realizes that she does not possess the penis like his father or brother. This, according to Freud, leads to the feeling of *penis envy*. The dominant conflict of the phallic stage is

Oedipus complex in boys and *electra complex* in girls. Freud regarded these complexes as biologically rooted and as occurring in all human beings. By Oedipus complex is meant sexual attachment of son with mother. Similarly, by electra complex is meant sexual attachment of daughter with father. Along with oedipal complex there arises what is called *castration anxiety*, that is, the anxiety or fear that his father may castrate him. Such anxiety, in fact, helps a lot in resolving the Oedipus complex because the boy does not wish to lose his penis. The female counterpart of the castration anxiety is the *penis envy*. She hates mother who denied her with penis. She likes father who possessed the organ lacked. This is called *penis envy*. Some persons remained fixated at Oedipus complex or electra complex. Therefore, they never marry and maintain their attachment with the parents of the opposite sex.

(iv) ***Latency stage*** : This stage covers the age between 5 to 11 years approximately. At this stage the sexual urges and instincts are repressed. Boys prefer to mix with boys and girls prefer to mix with girls. Thus a kind of sex antagonism arises. The libido of the person is sublimated into intellectual interests and various types of athletics. Some psychologists have taken the view that since no new erogenous zone emerges in this period and the sexual urges remain dormant, this stage does not qualify for one of the stage of psychosexual stage.

(v) ***Genital stage*** : With the start of puberty, there occurs rearousal of sexual interest but this time interest is directed towards the opposite sex. The sex organs mature and the endocrine glands become active with the result that some secondary sex characteristics appear. Such changes result courtship and marriage. The genital period continues throughout the years of maturity but it never completely replaces the earlier four stages together called *pregenital stage*.

6. *Freud's Social Psychology*

Freud published *Totem and Taboo* in 1913 and showed his concern for social psychology. In this book he presented a psychoanalytic interpretation of primitive man and his religion. In ancient periods there might had been murder of father by son in the family. This type of family of the prehistoric time is known as *primal horde*. Consequently, some taboos were set up against such act or similar other act such as incest. From such taboos gradually evolved the systems of morality and religion. Of the three major provinces of mind, namely, id, ego and superego, the last one largely develops due to the dictates of social forces. In his another book *Group Psychology and the Analysis of the Ego* (first published in 1922) he has explained the formulation of group. For him, the emotional ties that develop among people are the major base of formation of group. Freud also presented the analysis of human conflicts in civilization. The major reason of such conflict was competition between man's basic instincts and the requirements of civilization. Since civilization put restrictions on persons' sexual instinct, there is bound to be conflict. Like sexual impulses, we are forced to suppress our aggressiveness. Such suppression helps in incorporating aggression into superego that has the capacity to punish the ego. The superego may punish ego by producing in it a feeling of guilt. Such guilt feeling, in turn, becomes necessary for control of aggression in civilization.

7. *Mind-body position*

Freud did not bother much for the mind-body issue. Jones (1953) has pointed out there are several instances due to which Freud may be said to have shown this concern for philosophical mind-body issue. His system may be placed into psychological parallelism because he expressed the view that psychical processes can't occur in absence of physiological processes and physiological processes come prior to the psychical processes. He may also be said to be as one supporter of psychophysical interactionism. (Lundin, 1985). This is because there is a constant interaction between the three provinces of mind—id, ego and superego as well as the outer physical reality.

In this way we find that Freudian psychoanalysis was a broad-based system having a much wider applicability.

CRITICISMS OF FREUDIAN PSYCHOANALYSIS

Freudian psychoanalysis has an important impact upon not only psychology but also upon other allied sciences. Still, there are many psychologists who have attacked Freud. Some of the major points of criticisms are as under :

1. *Non-verifiability of the data*

Critics have claimed that most of what psychoanalysis reports as its data have to taken on faith. As they further claim, Freud had developed his system mainly from his personal experiences. Other sources of his data were what was told to him in free association by the patients. Dreams were his another source. All these sources of data are such that they can't be replicated and therefore, can't be verified. A system based upon such data, therefore, can never be scientific.

2. *Overemphasis upon sex*

Critics have also said that Freudian psychoanalysis has over-emphasized sex. His idea that an infant shows sexual activities has been widely rediculed. The famous concepts of Oedipus complex, penis envy, castration anxiety and electra complex are overloaded with sex emphasis. Freud's claim that Oedipus complex is universal and sexual in nature has been challenged. Some cross-cultural evidences do suggest that Oedipus complex is neither universal nor sexual. In some societies this occurs as consequence of rivalry between the son and the father because of the latter dominant position in the family (Hjelle & Ziegler, 1981).

3. *Unscientific concepts*

There are some theoretical concepts in Freudian psychoanalysis whose existence can't be proved because they are unscientific as well as purely theoretical concepts. For example, the concepts of psychic energy and the superego are its examples. Like other forms of energy, we can't assess psychic energy. Likewise, it is very difficult to give proof for the existence of superego. Such concepts have made Freudian system as highly dubious.

4. *Skinner's Criticisms*

Skinner (1954) has criticized Freudian psychoanalysis for its lack of providing data for quantification. Freud talked much about ideas, memories, etc. but provided no means for measuring it. Skinner also said that Freud included several intervening variables like id, ego and superego in his system but through those variables he could not trace the original causes of behaviour. Although Freud favoured the explanation of behaviour in terms of early childhood experiences, these intervening variables contributed in no significant way in their understanding.

Despite these criticisms, the positive contributions of Freudian psychoanalysis should not be undermined. It opened up new areas of researches and investigations. It encouraged motivational researches and pointed to the importance of childhood experiences in determining personality. After getting a formal recognition by the American Psychological Association, it has became also a centre for active research of may clinical psychologists.

CHAPTER HIGHLIGHTS

1. Psychoanalysis was founded by Sigmund Freud, who was a practising physician and Jew by birth. Freud spent his whole life except the last year of his life in Vienna. In 1938 he was forced to leave Vienna and go to London where on September 23, 1939 he died.

2. Like any other system, psychoanalysis had some antecedent forces. Freud was readily influenced by the work of G. Leibnitz, J. Herbart, A. Schopenhauer, F. Nietzsche, H. Helmholtz, G. T. Fechner, H. Jackson and Charles Darwin. The writings of these persons had a considerable impact upon his formulation of psychoanalysis as a system.
3. There are some obvious systematic features of psychoanalysis. As a system, psychoanalysis has expressed its opinion on the six major issues—definition of psychology, basic postulates, nature of data, principles of connection, principles of selection and mind-body issue. Although opinions on these six points are not so obvious as we find in case of other systems of psychology developed in academic setting, they are vital for understanding the basic tenets of psychoanalysis.
4. Freudian psychoanalysis is sprang up in non-academic circle, that is, in the circle of medical and clinical traditions. This was a major point of distinction between psychoanalysis and the rest of the system. Freudian psychoanalysis had been presented in terms of seven different headings such as topographical structure (conscious, preconscious and unconscious), structural model (id, ego and superego), psychic energy and theories of instincts, anxiety and defence mechanisms, stage of psychosexual development, Freud's social psychology and mind-body problem. Of his various contributions the concepts of conscious, preconscious, unconscious, id, ego, superego have been very influential ones even today.
5. Freudian psychoanalysis despite wider popularity and scattered impact upon different sciences, has been criticized. Non-verifiability of data, overemphasis upon sex, unscientific concepts, etc. are among its major criticisms.

REVIEW QUESTIONS

1. Discuss the major antecedent forces that led to the emergence of Freudian psychoanalysis.
2. Examine critically the major contributions of Freud in the field of psychoanalysis.
3. 'A person is born with sex, lives in sex and finally dies in sex.' Justify the statement from the pointview of Freudian psychoanalysis.
4. "The goal of all life is death." Elucidate the statement in light of Freudian contributions.
5. Examine critically the systematic features of psychoanalysis.

■

CHAPTER 14

HEIRS TO FREUD

CHAPTER PREVIEW

Psychoanalysis as developed by Sigmund Freud attracted many persons who became associated with him but later broke with him to establish their own thoughts and ideas. Alfred Adler, Carl Jung, Otto Rank, and Sandor Ferenczi were four such rebels. Apart from these rebels. there were psychologists who were not directly associated with Freud's psychoanalysis but tried to improve upon it by giving emphasis upon social and cultural factors. They are called Neo-Freudians. Karen Horney, Erich Fromm, Harry Stack-Sullivan and Erik Erikson are the popular neo-Freudians.

Adler's contributions are associated with organ inferiority and compensation, striving for success or superiority, social interest, style of life, creative power, fictional finalism, and birth order. Difference between Adler and Freud has also been emphasized.

Jung's analytical psychology mainly stresses upon conscious and unconscious attitudes and functions, psychic energy and personality development. Attempt has also been made to distinguish between Freud and Jung.

Neo-Freudians like Horney, Fromm, Sullivan and Erikson have emphasized upon social and cultural forces that were outright rejected by Freud. Horney's concepts like basic anxiety, neurotic needs and neruotic trends, defence mechanism, have been very popular ones. Fromm's emphasis upon methods of escape, basic needs, personality types has also earned him much popularity. Sullivan has formulated developmental stages of personality and has also emphasized upon various modes of cognition like prototaxic, parataxic and syntaxic modes. Erikson is well-known for his developmental outlook to personality and his eight stages of development are definitely an improvement over Freudian five stages of psychosexual development. A comparative outlook between Freud and Erikson has also been presented. Finally, Erikson's system has also been criticized.

We have seen that psychoanalytic movement was set forth by Sigmund Freud. It became very popular among social scientists as well as psychiatrists. It had attracted a lot of persons who became associated with Freud but later broke with him to establish their own thoughts and ideas. Historians mention the name of four such persons. They are Alfred, Adler, Carl Gustav Jung, Otto Rank and Sandor Ferenczi. Of these the first two have been very important rebels. Apart from these rebels, there were also persons who were not directly associated with Freud but had been well-versed in psycho-analysis and tried to improve upon Freudian psychoanalysis by giving emphasis upon *culture and society* that play an important role in shaping the development of personality. They did not rebel against Freudian system but tried to make improvement upon the system. These persons have been popular as *social analysts* or *neo-Freudians.* Karen Horney, Erich Fromm, Harry Stack Sullivan and Erik Erikson are the popular *social analysts.*

The present chapter, therefore, covers the contributions of six persons—two important *rebels* and four *improvers.*

ALFRED ADLER'S INDIVIDUAL PSYCHOLOGY

Life Sketch

Alfred Adler (1870-1937) was the second of parents' six children. His father, Leopold, was a wealthy merchant. Adler was also a Jew and as a child he was weak and frail. He had also suffered rickets. At the age of five, he developed pneumonia and came very nearer to death. Adler'»s younger brother had died a year earlier. All these bitter childhood experiences specially related to health forced him to take a decision to be a doctor. Accordingly, he entered the University of Vienna from where he received his medical degree in 1895. He took his specialization in opthalmology but later changed to medical practice and ultimately to psychiatry. In 1902 Freud invited Adler to join him in formation of organization that became popular as the *Vienna Psychoanalytical Society.* This was the starting point of association of Adler to Freud. Adler was *not* a disciple of Freud nor did he consider himself as a psychoanalyst (Feist, 1985). However, he was much influenced by Freud's work. For the next several years Adler remain the charter member of the Vienna Psychoanalytic Society and became its president in 1910. However, he was not ready to accept Freud's heavy emphasis on sex in explanation of neurosis. Gradually, theoretical and personal differences between the two Viennese physicians (Alder and Freud) grew and in 1911 he resigned from his post of presidentship and left Freudian circle along with six other followers to form *Society for Free Psychoanalysis.* A year later its name was changed as *Society for Individual Psychology* (Ellenberger, 1970). The term *individual* here does not connotate individualism or self-centredness but it means that each person is unique and indivisible because of his unique style of life that gives unity (or indivisibility) to all behaviours. Gradually, Adler became popular and started taking interest in child psychology and participated actively in child guidance clinic and the public schools.

After several visits to United States, he finally decided to settle in this country in 1935. He settled in New York City where he became professor of medical psychology. He lectured widely in the United States and abroad. In 1937 he died probably of heart attack while on a lecture tour in Aberdeen, Scotland.

Adler's psychology

Adler's psychology had many distinguishing features. *First,* it was like a commonsense psychology that could be easily applied or understood. *Second,* his psychology was more optimistic. He always took a realistic attitude in explaining human personality. The entire psychology of Adler can be presented under the following *seven* headings :

1. *Organ Inferiority and Compensation*

In 1907 Alder published one of his most important papers named *The Study of Organ Inferiority and its Psychical Compensations.* In this paper Adler tried to explain that people having some kind of organ inferiority such as poor vision, poor hearing, etc. try to compensate for it by developing excellence in other fields. However, the important things is that what type of attitude the person has developed toward the self. He may try to compensate the loss or he may keep himself satisfied by having only defensive measures. In 1910 he extended his concept of inferiority and reported that inferiority feelings are innate and therefore, universal in nature. Such feeling is created in children due to being helpless and having weak structures. It is this feeling of inferiority that gives birth to the striving for superiority and that gives us 'upward drive' from 'below to above'. Thus it is the feeling of inferiority and not the defective organ that motivates us for making proper compensation. Adler has cited several cases of such compensation from history. For example, Demosthenes who was a stutterer, became a famous orator and Cunningham, with severely injured legs became a good runner. From Indian personalities example may be given of Surdas who was blind but became a famous poet.

Related to the concept of inferiority and compensations is the concept of *masculine protest.* By masculine protest he meant a striving to be strong and powerful as a compensation for feeling of being inferior and unmanly. To be masculine means to be superior and to be feminine means to be inferior. Later on, Adler replaced the concept of masculine protest by striving for superiority and the term masculine protest was kept reserved for only a restrictive use. It now referred to the protest woman expressed against their feminine role (Ansbacher and Ansbacher, 1956). Women, being weaker than men, wish for qualities and privileges regarded in our society as important and dominant such as strength, courage, sexual freedom, etc. As a consequence, they prefer to be lawyers, business executives, car drivers—roles usually played by men. Sometimes such women don't marry or don't want to have any children. This use of masculine protest is similar to be Freudian concept of penis envy. Modern women's lib movement in which women are striving for greater equality is nothing but the expression of masculine protest.

2. *Striving for success or superiority*

In 1908 Adler pointed out that aggression was the dynamic power behind all motivation. That way, he antedated Freud in postulating aggressive drive. Soon after, he changed the name of this drive and called it masculine protest. By 1912, he replaced the concept of masculine protest with the concept of striving for superiority because he thought that masculine protest did not explain human motivation in a satisfactory way. Later in Adler's writings this term was modified as striving for success or perfection. It refers to the basic urge to move towards getting perfection. This has many features as under :

(i) The striving for success is innate and remains present at birth. Therefore, it precedes the feelings of inferiority rather than springs from them.

(ii) Although the striving for success is innate and remains present at birth, it must be developed because at birth it exists in form of potentialities and not in from of actuality. It, therefore, continues throughout life.

(iii) The striving for success is not a confluence of motives rather is a single motive that shapes the other drives.

(iv) The striving for superiority is an universal drive found in both normal as well as neurotic individuals. However, the path adopted by these two types of people in arriving at goal differs. The neurotic persons adopt the path of exaggerated personal superiority whereas the mentally healthy people adopt the path of *social interest* or perfection for everyone.

3. *Social Interest*

The notions of social interest and striving for success are closely related. According to Adler, it is the social interest that motivates the person to strive for success in healthy way. When this lacks person's functioning becomes maladaptive. What is after all, meant by the concept of social interest ? Adler's original term is a German word *Gemeinshaftsgefuhl* from which social interest is an approximate translation. Social interest may be defined as an attitude of caring and concern for humanity in general as well as showing an empathy for others. It guides human behaviour throughout the life. Like striving for success, social interest is inborn no doubt but it also needs to be developed because at birth it remains present at potentiality in everyone. There are people who never develop social interest and among them, exaggerated personal superiority dominates. Neurotics, drunkards, criminals, sex preverts, prostitutes are some of the examples who lack social interest.

4. *Style of Life*

Adler claimed that the social interest of a person develops in accord with the persons' style of life. By style of life is meant a person's unique way of arriving at a particular goal as well as his self-concept, feelings towards others and attitude towards world. It is the product of several forces like heredity, environment, social interest, goal of success, etc. Adler considered style of life as one major governing force and in that sense, it is equivalent to Freudian concept of ego. However, style of life includes no forces like id and superego. It always refers to the whole personality plus the unique attitude that makes a person unique. Style of life is formed and established by the age of four or five and person's major actions revolve round that. Ordinarily, style of life does not change but it may change if the person clearly recognizes the errors or faults and deliberately changes the direction (Ansbacher & Ansbacher, 1956).

Adler proposed four general life style attitudes—the *ruling type* the *getting type*, the *avoiding type* and the *socially useful type*. The ruling type of people has dominating attitude towards others and has little social interest. The getting type of persons is interested in getting as many as possible from others. Such person is too much dependent upon others. Under extreme stressful situation, he may become neurotic. Such persons has little social interest and contributes little to society. The avoiding type of person is characterized by having attitude of general avoidance and withdrawal that is accompanied by little social interest. The socially useful type of person is one that does behaviour which is useful to society. Such person is active and has high social interest. He rightly recognizes three basic social problems, namely, neighborly love, sexual love and occupation and tries to solve any social problem in a way of cooperation and personal encourage that is most beneficial to society.

Adler also recognized *three faulty* style of life—the inferior style, the pampered style and the neglected style. Persons having inferior style of life suffer from some strong organ inferiority and remain unable to make adequate compensation. Such persons adopt escape or avoidance as the primary mode of their behaviour. Persons having pampered style are too self-centered and selfish and lack social interest. Persons having neglected style of life are much like pampered style of persons and they always consciously wish to be spoiled.

5. *Creative Power*

Creative power develops the style of life of a person to a greater extent. Adler was of view that each person possesses a freedom to create his own style of life and therefore, is solely responsible for who he is and how he behaves. Such creative power also contributes to the development of social interest and determines the method of striving for achieving a goal. It also determines cognitive abilities like perception, memory, dreams, fantasy, etc. For Adler, creative power is a dynamic concept because it implies free movement toward a goal.

6. *Fictional Finalism*

Adler was of view that people are motivated more by the subjective perception than by the external causes. On aspect of such subjective perception is fiction or expectation of the future. Our personality is more governed by such expectations rather then past. In fact Adler's ideas on *fictionalism* had originated with Hans Viahinger's book, *The Philosophy of 'as if'* published in 1911. Viahinger had postulated that fictions were such ideas that have no real existence but sitll influenced human behaviour *as if* they were a reality. This viewpoint of Viahinger, then, obviously suggests that we are motivated not only by what is real but also by what we believe to be real. For Adler, the important fiction is the final goal of success or superiority. Such fictional final goal is not an objective reality but it has a great significance because it brings unification in personality and makes human behaviour easily comprehensible. In reaching the final goal, we make many preliminary goals. These subgoals are often conscious but the connection between these goals and final goal remains in unconscious.Through fictional final goal, Adler has expressed his stand on teleology, that is, the fact that our future strivings tend to shape our present behaviour.

7. *Birth Order*

Adler is well-known for his viewpoints regarding impact of a child's birth order on the development of personality. He studied four types of birth order—the first-born, the second-born, the last-born and the lone child. The first-born child gets undivided attention and care from parents and then experiences a traumatic experiences of dethronement when a new baby is born. This creates a feeling of hostility and resentment in the first-born child towards younger brother or sister. This child has also overprotective tendencies and high anxiety. The second-born child starts his life in a better situation. Such child is highly competitive, cooperative and has wider social interest. His style of life constantly tries to prove that he is better than his older siblings. Thus the second-born child is achievement-oriented. It is also a matter of interest here that Adler was himself second-born. The position of the *last-born* is unique and he has a great risk of being a problem child. He has strong feelings of inferiority and lacks independence. However, he is highly motivated to surpass the older siblings. Hence, he is also achievement-oriented and competition minded. The *lone child* has no siblings to compete and hence, he has to compete with his parents. This child has an inflated self-concept and exaggerated sense of superiority. Such child is too dependent upon others and lacks the feeling of cooperation and social interest.

Thus, Adler's psychology, on the whole, was more optimistic and realistic and recognized the impact of social forces in shaping human behaviour.

Criticisms of Adler's Psychology

Adler's psychology has been criticized by several persons. Some of the major criticisms are as under :

(i) Like Freud, Adler has several untestable concepts in his system. His use of concept like creative power and fictional finalism are the examples. Critics claim that no meaningful conclusion can be drawn from such untestable concepts. Everything relating to that has to be taken on guess.

(ii) Most of the terms of individual psychology lack precise operational definitions. Terms like style of life, social interest, striving for superiority and creative power have no operational definitions. His term like creative power is highly illusory one.

(iii) Critics claim that his concept of birth order can't be definitively studied (Feist, 1985). Researches have failed to correlate personality traits with different birth order of persons. In fact, no consistent generalization regarding birth order and personality traits can be made because the second-born child may perceive the situation of his babyhood similar to that of the first-born and the last-born.

Despite these criticisms, Adlerian psychology, though not to the extent of Freudian psychology, has the power to organize and encompass different explanations of human behaviour into a meaningful framework.

DIFFERENCES BETWEEN FREUD AND ADLER

The basic differences between Freud's system and Adler's system may be outlined as under :

(i) Freud basically emphasized upon the biological nature of human beings. He tried to explain every aspect of human behaviour by giving such emphasis. Adler, on the other hand, emphasized upon social nature of man and considered social forces to be the important determinant of behaviour. He was, in fact, first of the social analysts to give such emphasis.

(ii) Freud was basically a determinist stressing the importance of past in shaping our present behaviour. Adler, on the other hand, was basically a teleologist empahsising upon future aims that determined present behaviour. Adler gave very little importance to early events and past experiences. The only examples of such importance is found in case of his recognition of birth order as one determinants of the traits of human personality.

(iii) Freud has overemphasized upon sex. For Freud, sex drive was the most important drive for human beings. Adler did not approve this emphasis and in his early writings he emphasized upon aggression and striving for power to be the major drive. Later, these concepts were replaced by striving for superiority and finally, by social interest.

(iv) For Freud unconscious was the most important aspect of mind because it was the most powerful determinants of our human behaviour. Adler emphasized more upon consciousness than upon unconscious processes. He simply stated that what was unconscious become conscious and then, it becomes important and appropriate for being called as one basic determinant of behaviour. Thus although Adler did not entirely reject unconscious process, he definitely undermined its importance.

(v) Adler's Individual psychology placed more emphasis upon uniqueness and indivisibility of the person. He considered personality as a whole and as unique system not to be divided into any subsystems. For him, each person created a unique style of life that bestows unity or indivisibility of all behaviours. Freud lacked such emphasis upon individual.

Thus we find that Adler's psychology is different from Freud's system though the former got much inspiration from the latter.

CARL JUNG'S ANALYTICAL PSYCHOLOGY

Life Sketch

Carl Jung (1875-1961) was born in a small village in Switzerland. His mother's family had long tradition of spiritualism and mysticism. His father was believer in the occultism and often reported to have some talk with dead including his first wife. Due to such family background, it seems natural that Jung had developed interest in spiritualism and in occult. As a child, Jung was very emotional as well as sensitive one. He was deeply attached with both his parents. He was a Christian but was not a church-goer.

Jung's initial choice was archaeology but later on he shifted to medicine. He completed his medical degree from Basel University in 1900. He joined Burgholtzli Mental Hospital in Zurich as a psychiatric assistant. The director of this hospital was Eugen Bleuler, a Swiss psychiatrist and authority on Schizophrenia. During 1902-3 he had also chance to study for six months in Paris under Pierre Janet, a successor to Charcot. After returning from Paris to Switzerland, he got married with Emma Rauschenbach, a young Swiss woman. Two years later he started teaching at the University of Zurich and also kept himself associated with duties at mental hospital. Under the directorship of Bleuler at the mental hospital, he began to study word association and also started writings on schizophrenia. It was through this writings that he made contact with Sigmund Freud. In 1909 he resigned from his post of psychiatric assistant at Burgholtzli because of some differences with Bleuler.

Freud's famous book *The Interpretation of Dreams* was published in 1900. Like Adler, he was deeply influenced by this book. He became a good defender of Freudian psychoanalysis and the correspondence between two persons started (McGurie, 1974). In 1907 Jung visited Vienna upon the invitation of Freud. Freud loved and respected him much. With backing of Freud, Jung was selected as the first president of International Psychoanalytic Association in 1911. This also arose some protests among Freud's Viennese colleagues. In 1909 Freud and Jung had gone together to America to deliver lectures at Clark University at the invitation of

G.S. Hall. Gradually personal as well as theoretical differences between Freud and Jung started emerging and as a consequence, in 1913 these two persons terminated their personal correspondence. The next year Jung resigned his presidency and shortly thereafter he withdrew his membership from International Psychoanalytic Association (Brome, 1978). The breaks was complete and these two men never saw each other again. He founded his own school called *analytical psychology*.

Subsequent years of Jung's life were not so important from the pointview of academic interest. In the years immediately following the break with Freud, he was surrounded by loneliness and self-analysis. After several years, he resumed his research works and writings. He travelled widely in developing his theory of personality and published his most influential books *Psychological Types* in which he discussed his religious beliefs, myths, etc., in detail. In recognition of these works he was awarded honorary degrees from several famous Universities like that of University of Harvard, Oxford and the University of Calcutta (Feist, 1985). In 1944 he became professor of medical psychology at the University of Basel but in 1945 he had to resign on ill-health ground. He died on June 6, 1961, in Zurich at the age of 86 years approximately.

Thus Jung lived long and his reputation was of world fame and extending beyond psychology.

Jung's Psychology : Analytical Psychology

Jung was the second of Freud's earlier associates to rebel and establish his own system called *analytical psychology*. In this system Jung accepted some of the concepts of Freud no doubt but he rejected several other concepts charging them to be overloaded with sex. The major contributions of Jungian analytical psychology may be outlined under the following *four* headings :

1. *Conscious and Unconscious*

Like Freud, Jung divided the structure of psyche into two parts—conscious and unconscious. Any psychic event that is sensed by ego is called conscious and any psychic event not sensed by ego is called unconscious. Thus, for Jung, ego is always identified with conscious aspect of psychic. It is different from self that is identified with both conscious and unconscious psychic. Thus, self is concerned with whole of the personality whereas ego is concerned only with conscious psyche.

Unconscious, as said above, is that aspect of the psyche which is not related to the ego. It contains all previously repressed conscious images as well as those psychic events that have never been conscious. For Jung, unconscious is more important and therefore, he emphasized unconscious even more than Freud (Jung, 1953). Unconscious is divided into two parts—personal unconscious and collective unconscious. *Personal unconscious* consists of repressed infantile memories, forgotten events or subliminally perceived experiences of a person. It is called personal because it varies from person to person and at the same time, is unique to the person concerned. The contents of personal unconscious are called *complexes.* He devised his famous *word association test* to uncover the such complexes particularly feeling-toned complexes. The nature of the contents of personal unconscious is such that some may be recalled readily, some are remembered with little difficulty and some can't be recalled at all. Obviously Jung's personal conscious differs a lot from Freudian concepts of unconscious.

Collective unconscious is the most important but controversial concept of Jung. It consists of primordial images that include memory traces not only from our human past but also from our prehuman and animal ancestry (Hall, Lindzey, Loehlin and Manosevitz, 1985). In fact, these images are the record of those experiences that have passed from one generation to other. Our distant ancestors' experiences with God, sun, earth, which are transmitted from one generation to another, are stored in collective unconscious. People's many types of myths, legends and religious beliefs are stored in collective unconscious which are revealed through various activities of the persons. It is also manifested through "big dream". The contents of collective unconscious consist of ancient and archaic images called *archetypes.* Like complexes, archetypes are affectively toned. But these two also differ from each other. Complexes are individualized and constitute the contents of personal unconscious whereas archetypes are generalized and constitute the contents of collective unconscious.

Jung recognized several types of archetypes. However, the most important types of archetypes that shape our personality and behaviour are : the *persona,* the *anima,* the *animus,* the *shadow* and the *self.* The persona is the mask that people exhibit before public. It reflects the way a person wishes to be perceived by others. Like Freud, Jung reported that all human beings are essentially *bisexual* and possess both a masculine and a feminine side. The feminine side of the male represents *anima* and the masculine side of the female represents the *animus.* Through these two types of archetypes Jung tried to focus upon the traditional views of what is masculine and what is feminine. The *shadow* archetype reflects the animal instincts that human beings have inherited through their evolutionary cycles. The *self* archetype is one which motivates the person towards the wholeness. It governs the process of individuation that is useful and creative aspect of the unconscious and is made productive and conscious.

2. *Attitude and Functions : Jung's psychological types*

Jung pointed out that there are two aspects of personality that function at both conscious and unconscious level. They are *attitudes,* that is, introversion and extraversion and the *functions,* that is, thinking, feeling, sensing and intuiting. A person having attitude of introversion tends to focus on inner and private world having very limited objective experiences. Such people are reserved, and self-centered. Likewise, a person having attitude of extraversion tends to focus on external activities, events and things. These people are active and outgoing. These two types of attitude oppose each other and while one tends to rule the personality, other remains repressed and unconscious. There are four functions—thinking, feeling, sensing and intuiting. Thinking is a function that seeks to connect ideas with each other so that a person may solve the problem and understand the world nicely. Thus it is an intellectual function. Feeling produces some subjective experience relating to pleasure, pain, love and anger. So it is an evaluative function. Sensing means providing sensation and perception of oneself and the world around the persons. Intuiting refers to the subliminal perception or unconscious perception. Since sensing and intuiting are not evaluative functions, they are called *non-rational function.*

One basic characteristic of these four functions is that normally one function is dominant and conscious, while the other three functions remain dormant and unconscious. Jung also stressed that everyone has his own unique pattern of attitudes and functions and on the basis of these two types of attitudes and four type of functions, he recognized eight basic psychological types—introversion-thinking, extraversion-thinking, introversion-feeling, extraversion-feeling, introversion-sensation, extraversion-sensation, introversion-intuition, extraversion-intuition.

3. *Psychic energy*

Like Freud, Jung postulated the concept of psychic energy that can't be destroyed. Out personality structure is charged with psychic energy. The nature of psychic energy is such that is can be repressed, displaced and sublimated. However it can never be destroyed. He postulated two principles that govern psychic energy—*principle of equivalence and principle of entropy.* The principle of equivalence (first law of thermodynamics) stated that energy may be transformed but not lost.

One common example of this principle is that of an adolescent boy deeply infatuated with his girl friend. In such situation the energy that he previously used in concentration on academic activities, is now being spent on his girl friend. After the infatuation is over, there occurs improvement in the academic performance. In this example, we find a mere change in energy first from academic activities to beloved and then from beloved to again academic activities. The principle of entropy (the second law of thermodynamics) states that when two bodies are kept together, the energy from higher charge tends to flow to one of the lower charge until they are equal. Applied to the personality structure, this principle states that there is a tendency toward a balance of energy charges among the various systems. This principle brings stability in functions and results in a certain kind of attitudes in the person. That is why this is also called as the *equalization of energy principle*. One example of the principle of entropy can be found in the opposing attitudes of introversion and extraversion. In the beginning these two attitudes may produce greater tension. If the two attitudes are relatively equal in strength, a new stable attitude somewhere near the midpoint will emerge and will become stabilized. If, however, our attitude is relatively unconscious, little tension will emerge.

4. *Personality development*

For Jung, personality development takes place through a series of stages that culminate in individuation. He divided those stages into four parts—childhood, youth, middle age and old age. He emphasized particularly upon the second half of the life which starts at middle age that begins at approximately age 35 for women and 40 for men. At this stage the person has sufficient opportunity to bring together the different aspects of personality that help in the fulfilment or actualization of the self. Thus he emphasized upon self-actualization that is one of the major goals of personality. However, impulse for neurotic reactions remains also present at that time and a person's direction of movement depends upon his ability to maintain balance between the poles of the various conflicting forces.

In explaining personality development Jung used two terms—*individuation* and *transcendent function*. The concept of individuation refers to the process of becoming an individual or whole person. It is responsible for analytic processes like distinguishing different aspects of personality. Transcendent function refers to going beyond ordinary development by bringing together all different parts of perso-nality in harmony. Thus transcedent function contains synthetic process like integrating unconscious with conscious materials and integrating the different aspects of personality into a meaningful whole. A sound development of personality involves both individuation and transcendent function.

Thus we find that like Freud, Jung also made significant contribution to psychology. His concept of self-actualization has been very much inspiring to later psychologists like Maslow, Allport and Murphy who have incorporated this in their own explanation of motivational basis of personality, Likewise, Jung's words association test has been considered by many psychologists to be one of the most valuable contributions to psychology. It has proved very useful in uncovering feeling-toned complexes, emotional conflicts as well as in detection of lie.

Criticisms of Jungs's Psychology

Jung's psychology has been criticized on the following grounds :

(i) Although some psychologists and followers of Jung have credited Jung to add a new dimension to personality, namely, collective unconscious, many psychologists have opined that the concept of collective unconscious has no heuristic value because it failed to generate the testable hypotheses.

(ii) Edward Glover (1950) has rejected Jungian concept of archetypes on the ground that they are highly subjective and can be explained only in terms of personal experiences. The validity of such concept has to be accepted more on faith than on empirical evidences. Jung has also accepted this criticism when he opines that archetypal statements are not rationally grounded and have nothing to do with the reasons.

(iii) Jung has also been criticized for ignoring theory totally and basing his viewpoints on comparative method which for him, is the only acceptable scientific method. To quote Jung (1946, p. 7), "Theories in psychology are the very devil.... No doubt theory is the best clock for lock of experience and ignorance but the consequences are depressing..."

(iv) It has also been said that Jung's writings are vague, contradictory and unsystematic. The writings of his later life very clearly revealed that he was no longer a psychologist rather a metaphysician.

Despite these criticisms, Jung's influence crossing psychology and psychiatry, reached history, art, literature and even music. In fact, the originality and audacity of Jung's thinking have very few parallels in the history of modern psychology.

DISTINCTION BETWEEN FREUD AND JUNG

There are some basic points of distinctions between Freud and Jung. The following are the major points of distinctions :

1. Like Freud, Jung accepted the concept of psychic energy. For Jung, the origin of psychic energy arises from different bodily processes that tend to form a basic drive for life. Obviously, Jung did not incorporate Freudian emphasis upon sex in psychic energy. For Freud, the origin of psychic energy was instinct particularly sex instinct.

2. Although both Freud and Jung explained the concept of unconscious Jung did it in a different tone. He considered unconscious to be racial and archaic. Freud, too, had hinted on the concept of racial unconscious in his famous concept of Oedipus complex but he could not develop it.

3. Freud was a determinist who emphasized upon past experiences to be the major factor in present behaviour. We have seen that Adler has rejected this explanation because he was a teleologist who held the future to be the major determinant of the present behaviour. Jung incorporated the viewpoints of both determinist as well as teleologist by emphasizing that a person's behaviour is guided both by his future goals as well as by his past experiences.

Thus like Adler, Jung also maintained independence from the orthodox Freudian psychoanalysis.

NEO-REUDIANS : HORNEY, FROMM, SULLIVAN AND ERIKSON

There is a group of psychologists who did not rebel like Adler and Jung against orthodox Freudian psychoanalysis but it tried to improve upon Freudian biological framework by giving emphasis upon social and cultural factors—factors totally ignored by Freud. This group of psychologists is called neo-Freudians. In this section we shall discuss the contributions of four popular neo-Freudians like Horney, Fromm, Sullivan and Erikson.

Karen Horney's Psychology

Life Sketch : Karen Horney (1885-1952) was born in Hamburg, Germany. She decided at the age of 12 to study medicine. She took her M. D. from the University of Berlin. She completed her medical training in 1913. She started her career as an orthodox Freudian and was psychoanalyzed by Karl Abraham, one of Freud's first followers. For several years he followed Freudian tradition at Berlin Psychoanalytic Institute. It was in 1923 that she challenged Freudian concepts in a research paper that dealt with the notion of penis envy. In 1932 she came to Unites States at the invitation of Franz Alexander who asked her to become his associate director at the Chicago Psychoanalytic Institute. Two years later she moved to New York City to join New York Psychoanalytic Institute. She soon became one vital part of the group of psychologists, anthropologists, sociologists, etc. The group comprises Harry Stack Sullivan, Margaret Mead, John Dollard, Abraham Maslow, Medard Boss, Ruth Benedict, etc. Her important books were : *The Neurotic Personality of our Time* (1937), *Our Inner conflicts* (1945) and *Self -Analysis* (1942), *Neurosis and Human Growth* (1950). She died in 1952 from cancer.

Horney's Contributions

Horney presented a new approach to psychology and at the same time she also maintained orthodox psychoanalytic thinking of Freud. She tried to explain the fundamentals of psycho-analysis by giving emphasis upon social and cultural forces. In 1923 she first challenged Freudian theory by attacking his concept of penis envy. However, rather than totally rejecting Freud like Jung and Adler, she preferred to work within his basic frame of references correcting what she considered to be fallacious in his formulations. Her major contributions may be enlisted as under :

1. ***Basic Anxiety***

The concept of basic anxiety is basic to Horney's psychology. She is of view that each normal and healthy person has some creative and positive potential. When he gets love and affection in the environment, he expresses those potentials and develops confidence in the self. On the other hand, if this basic potential is not fulfilled and expressed, *anxiety* results. *Basic anxiety* occurs in childhood when the child is allowed to feel helpless and isolated in the world that appears hostile and threatening. There are *there* components of basic anxiety. They are the feelings of helplessness, hostility and isolation. All these components grow out of devoid of genuine warmth and affection in home. When the child is neglected or rejected by parents or parents substitutes, he develops feeling of painful helplessness. He feels all above and tries to end isolation in vain. The natural outcome of such situation is hostility which predisposes him to anticipate harm from others and forces him to feel that any aggressive act on his part may cause him to be deserted. He is overloaded with the feeling of guilt that he represses which, in turn, leads to anxiety. Thus a cyclical process is set in. Horney called this as *vicious circle*. Thus the important reason of developing basic anxiety is such home environment in which parent-child relationship is characterized by the absence of genuine love and affection.

2. *Neurotic needs and Neurotic trends*

When the person is not able to solve most of the problems of his life and therefore, repeated failures occur, certain needs are developed. These needs have been termed by Horney as *neurotic needs* because they don't result in rational solutions. These needs, however, are such that they are experienced by both normal as well as neurotic people. Horney has further emphasized that neurosis is not the result of inner conflict between id, ego and superego but results from the conflict between a person and his environment. Thus she has shifted the major point in neurosis from within a person to outside factors. She has further emphasized that a neurotic person always tends to move in one of three possible directions—*moving toward people, moving against people* and *moving away from people.* Horney has called these directions as *neurotic trends.* In neurotic trend of moving towards people overcompliance is the primary feature and the persons tries to gain acceptance, affection and approval from others by complying with their desires. In neurotic trend of moving against people, aggressiveness and hostility are prime. In neurotic trend of moving away from people the person is unable to face others and tries to avoid them. The basic common denominator of these three neurotic trends is social maladjustment (Wolman, 1979).

Related to each of these three types of neurotic trends, three types of personality emerge as under :

(i) ***The complaint type*** : This type is related to *moving toward people.* Such persons ware too dependent and overvalued affection and approval from others.

(ii) ***The hostile type*** : This type is related to *moving against people.* The dominant features of such persons are that they become aggressive, suspicious, antisocial and hostile.

(iii) ***The detatched type*** : This type is related to *moving away from people.* Such persons are egocentric, aloof and withdrawn.

3. *Attempts at coping anxiety*

Horney pointed out that in order to cope with basic anxiety, a person resorts to several strategies. These strategies are of the following two types :

(i) ***The idealized self-image***

To reduce his basic anxiety a person develops an idealized self-image which refers to some fictitious and illusory picture of the self as possessing many unlimited and superlative qualities and powers. Therefore, the idealized self is unrealistic and exaggerated. In such case there occurs a big gap between the real self and the idealized self. Generally, there occurs a neurotic striving for fulfilling this idealized self. Such striving are compulsive, indiscriminate and insatiable. To support this idealized self-image, the persons develops what is called *pride system* in which the persons thinks himself to be the possessor of something such as strength or intelligence in such amount that no other person has.

(ii) *Defence mechanisms*

Horney recognized only two types of defence mechanisms that help persons in reducing their basic anxiety. They are—*rationalization* and *externalization.* Rationalization is used in Freudian sense by Horney with the only difference that it is used with the whole organism and is not related to specific instinctual components as Freud had assumed. Externalization is more or less equivalent to projection. In this defence mechanism the person attributes every motive or action to some external agents and not only to the undesirable and weaker ones. Thus the persons may not attribute their failures to others but they also attribute their successes to some agents in the environment. For example, a person may attribute his success in the examination to some teachers who had helped him a lot.

Thus we find that Horney by giving emphasis upon social and cultural factors, has tried to show that human behaviour is governed not only by biological and instinctual forces but also by environmental forces. Thus her approach to explain behaviour was holistic rather than instinctual (Kelman, 1971). She made it clear that a child is the product of both his heredity as well as environment. She only dismissed the importance of those factors that were overloaded with sex and were important for orthodox Freudian psychoanalysis.

Despite these achievements, some psychologists have been critical to Horney's position :

(i) Some psychologists have pointed out that in the history of psychoanalytical movement Horney was much less important figure as compared to Freud, Adler and Jung (Lundin, 1985).

(ii) Horney's approach to psychology may be considered as partial or incomplete. She mainly concentrated upon basic anxiety as well as upon neurotic needs and neurotic trends. She tried to explain even normal personality with the help of these concepts, which was an unscientific attempt.

Erich Fromm's Psychology

Life-Sketch : Erich Fromm (1900-1980) was born in Frankfurt in Germany and was trained there. He studied both psychology and sociology at Universities of Frankfurt and Munich. He obtained his Ph. D. degree from Heidelberg University. He also attended Psychoanalytic Institute at Berlin where he completed his training in psychoanalysis. He emigrated to United States in 1933. For many years in Unites States no academic institution gave him a formal place. Therefore, he spent his time in lecturing at different institutes and universities in America. For example, he lectured at the Chicago Psychoanalytic Institute and taught at the National Institute for Social Research at New York and at Columbia University. He served as faculty member of Bennington College from 1941 to 1950. In 1951 he became a professor at the University of Mexico and later became Director of the Mexican Psychoanalytic Institute. In 1976 he shifted with his third wife, Annis Freeman Fromm, to Switzerland where he died in 1980 at the age of 79. He authored several books. Some of his important books were : *Escape from Freedom* (1941), *Man for himself* (1947) and *The Sane Society* (1955).

Fromm's Contributions

Being a social analyst, Fromm was much concerned with social influences particularly his relationship to society. For Freud this relationship was constant but for Fromm this was constantly changing. In fact, in his approach to psychology he tried to combine the views of Freud and social theories and philosophy of Karl Marx (Hall, Lindzey, Loehlin and Manosevitz, 1985). Fromm's contributions to psychology may be enlisted under the following four heads :

1. *Escape from Freedom*

The first book of Erich Fromm was *Escape from Freedom* that was published in 1941. In this book he has accepted man as a social animal. As persons have developed from their biological past, they have gained greater independence. But in so doing, they have become more isolated and lonely. Therefore, freedom or independence became such a condition from which they wanted to escape. In modern society a person has gained independence no doubt but he is alone and insecure. Man has tried his best to escape from such helplessness and loneliness which have become somehow intolerable. To solve this problem, Fromm suggested formation of a society in which there was equality for every person and in which every person related to every other person in a meaningful and loving way.

2. *Methods of Escape*

Fromm pointed out that persons have chosen several methods of escape from their helplessness and loneliness arising out of feeling of independence. These methods are much similar to Freudian defence mechanisms. Important methods are *masochism, sadism, destruction* and *automation conformity*. In masochism the person tries to escape his feelings of helplessness and loneliness by showing much dependence upon others. In sadism, he tries to escape these feelings by showing a tendency to rule and exploit others. In destruction, as its name implies, the person escapes these feelings by destroying the world around him, In automation conformity the person blindly accepts the social order. By showing a strong conformity to what others expected of him, he is relieved of his sense of helplessness and loneliness.

3. *Basic needs*

As a person interacts with society, he develops some needs. Fromm has distinguished five such needs. They are *need for relatedness, need for transcendence, need for rootedness, need of identity and need for orientation.* Need for relatedness refers to a person's desire to create his relationship to others through a productive love involving mutual respect and understanding. Need for transcendence refers to man's inclination to rise above his animal nature so that he can creatively think something. Need for rootedness refers to need to belong to the active world so that he may also consider himself to be a meaningful organism. Need for identity refers to a person's desire to be unique and therefore, distinguished from the rest of the individuals. Need for orientation refers to getting such a frame of reference that he may develop a correct orientation towards self as well as towards others. Fromm insisted upon creating such a society in which every person may develop full sense of self and there is equality for all. Such society has been called by him as *humanistic communitarian socialism.*

4. *Personality types*

For Fromm, personality is the sum of both inherited and acquired characteristics. He made a distinction between *temperament* and *character*. Temperament refers to the mode of reaction that is inherited, constitutional and unchangeable. Character is different from temperament and is formed in life experiences through various kinds of social influences. Character is determined both by physical constitution and temperament as well as by social and cultural influences acting upon them. Character is relatively a permanent form in which two processes, namely, assimilation and socialization do play an important part. These two together are called orientation by Formm and form the "Core of character" (Wolman, 1979). The various *types* of personality arises from a person's attempt to assimilate his own character with social forces as well as to relate himself with society. Fromm distinguished among the following *five* types of persons each having a different character :

(i) ***The receptive character or type*** : Such type of person always, expects help from others. Such person is 'receiver' and not 'giver' of anything such as love, material possessions etc. Such persons becomes too anxious when his supply is cut off.

(ii) ***The hoarding character or type*** : Such people are selfish, pedantic and orderly. The outside world is perceived as threat and they feel secure only when they save and keep something.

(iii) ***The exploitative character or type*** : Such persons acquire something by force or cunningness. They also feel aggressive towards others.

(iv) ***The marketing character or type*** : For such persons success depends 'how well they can sell themselves'. They consider themselves a commodity which can be bought and sold like something in the market.

(v) ***The productive character or type*** : Such type of person is more desirable person in the society. For Fromm, such type of personality results from the combination of the previous four types but is always guided by genuine love, care, responsibility and creativity. The major characteristics of productive type of persons are his productive activity as well as devotion to the well-being of others.

On the whole, we find that Fromm tried to present an optimistic view of man by giving emphasis upon social and cultural factors encountered by persons in their lifetime.

Despite this Fromm's psychology has been criticized. It is said that Fromm's viewpoints were extremely idealistic and therefore, unrealistic. He also failed to provide empirical data in support of his viewpoints. Keeping these comments in view Fromm is more fit to be called as an *ethical philosopher* rather than a *psychologist*.

Harry Stack Sullivan's Psychology

Life-Sketch : Sullivan (1892-1949) was another important neo-Freudian who gave emphasis upon social and cultural forces in development of human behaviour. Unlike Horney and Fromm, he was born and trained in United States. He was born in New York State on

February 2, 1892. His early years were not happy because his father was a distant person and mother was semi-invalid. However, in classroom he was a superior student. He obtained his M. D. degree in 1917 and studied medicine at the Chicago College of Medicine and Surgery. In 1921 he got an appointment at St. Elizabeth Hospital in Washington. D. C. where he worked with mentally ill-people. These experiences were very much vital for the formulation of his theory of personality. Later, he moved to New York in 1931 for starting a private practice. He did this practice for nearly eight years and during this period, he came into contact with Karen Horney and Erich Fromm. In 1936 he again returned to Washington, D. C. Here he founded *Washington School of Psychiatry* and started a journal *Psychiatry*. He was editor of this journal during the rest of his life. Until his death in 1949, he was director of Washington School of Psychiatry. In 1947, he had published his book *Conceptions of Modern Psychiatry*. This was the only book published in his lifetime. The other famous book *The interpersonal Theory of Psychiatry* was published posthumously.

Sullivan's Contributions

Sullivan is perhaps such a neo-Freudian who entirely developed different conceptional principles. In fact, his theory was influenced more from non-psychoanalytical sources and therefore, he deviated farther from Freud. He dropped most of the important concepts of Freudian psychoanalysis such as libido, id, ego, superego, sex theory, etc. Despite these, there were enough elements that were taken from Freudian psychoanalysis and were incorporated in his system. For example, Sullivan adopted most of his concepts from Freud's dynamic psychology such as needs, tensions, anxiety, unconscious motivation, defence mechanism and dream interpretation. Like Freud, he also stressed the importance of several distinct periods in development of personality. In this sense, Sullivan was a true development theorist. The system that Sullivan represented is known as the *interpersonal theory* of psychiatry, which emphasizes that personality is "the relatively enduring pattern of recurrent interpersonal situations which characterize a human life" (Sullivan, 1953 : 11). Right from the day of birth, we make interaction with others. This interaction shapes our behaviour. Our personality is something that develops in the context of such interpersonal behaviour. His important contributions to psychology may, however, be explained under *three* headings—*dynamics of personality, enduring aspects of personality* and *developmental stage*. These are as under :

1. *Dynamics of personality*

For Sullivan human being is basically an energy system that seeks to reduced tension created by needs. Tension are divided into two parts—tensions created by needs and tensions created by anxiety. Tensions due to need potentialities call for integrating actions and tensions due to anxiety produce disintegrative behaviour. Satisfying the needs reduces the tension. If needs are not satisfied for longer period of time, it may lead to *apathy*. Anxiety is transmitted to an infant by its mother. When mother herself is anxious, she expresses these disturbances in voice, actions and look. Gradually, the child picks up these things and become anxious.

Sullivan has recognized three *levels* or *modes* of cognition. They are *prototaxic, parataxic* and *syntaxic, Prototaxic experiences* are the primitive experiences of an infant. Such experiences are undifferentiated, pre-symbolic. momentary, incapable of being conceptualized and therefore, non-communicable. Thus prototaxic experiences are the primary mode of cognition of the neonate. The *paratixic experiences* are prelogical, personal and communicated only in distorted from to others. Such experiences are more differentiated than prototaxic experiences. These experiences begin very early in infancy and continue to be a very important mode of experience in future lifetime. *Syntaxic experiences* are meaningful interpersonal communication. They are meaningfully communicated through language including words and gestures.

All these three modes of cognitions occur throughout the life. However, syntaxic experiences start dominating since the age of six.

2. ***Enduring aspects of personality***

Sullivan, in his system, has also emphasized upon several such aspects of personality that have stability over time. Important such aspects are : *dynamism, personification* and *self-system.*

The concept of dynamism is equivalent to the concept of trait. Dynamism may be understood as relatively consistent pattern of action that characterized the persons throughout the life (Sullivan, 1953). He divided dynamism into two classes—dynamism related to particular zone of the body and dynamism related to tension. The former class of dynamism tries to satisfy the basic needs of the persons such as need for hunger and thirst. The latter class of dynamism consists of three categories—disjunctive dynamism, isolating dynamism and conjunctive dynamism. *Disjunctive dynamism* includes destructive pattern of behaviour that is related to what is called malevolence which refers to a behaviour pattern that is characterized by the attitude that people are evil and harmful and this world is a bad place to live in. *Isolating dynamism* includes dynamism of lust which is a biological phenomenon and is produced by tensions either directly or indirectly related to genitals. It may involve homosexual or heterosexual behavioural patterns. *Conjunctive dynamism* includes beneficial behaviour pattern as we find in case of intimacy and self-system. Of these, the self-system is a very important dynamism,

The self-system is the most complex system that tries to protect person from anxiety by maintaining interpersonal security. Hence, the self-system is *anti-anxiety system* because it contains those dynamisms that tend to reduce anxiety. This self-system begins to develop out of interpersonal situation when the child is about $1^1/_2$ or 2 years old. Although the self-system tends to reduce anxiety, it also interferes with the ability to live constructively. Just how ? When a child has more experience with anxiety, his self-system becomes more inflated and separated from the rest of personality. Such self-system, in fact, prevents the person from taking a realistic view and objective judgment of the situation. This creates an interference in living constructively.

Personification is another important enduring aspect of personality. It refers to an image of self or of another. The image of personification is built out of experiences with anxiety or need satisfaction. Satisfying interpersonal relationship produces positive images and interpersonal relationship producing dissatisfaction and anxiety leads to negative images. Sullivan claimed that during infancy five elementary personifications are built. They are *bad-mother, good*-mother, *bad-me, good-me* and *not-me.* The bad-mother personification develops out of an infant's anxiety producing experiences with mother. The good-mother personification develops out of satisfying relationship of an infant with mother. The personifications of bad-me and good-me develop in a similar way with rewarding experiences of satisfying feeling and anxiety producing experiences growing out mother's anxiety or rejection respectively. The not-me personification develops out of very intense anxiety. Because of such painful experiences those things about self that are connected with them (painful experiences) is dissociated from the rest of the personality. In this way it can be said that the not-me personification represents the dissociated aspects of the self and is accompanied by dangerous emotion or *uncanny* (as Sullivan has called it).

3. *Developmental stages*

Sullivan has postulated seven stages or epochs of personality development. These stages are : infancy, childhood, juvenile era, pre-adolescence, early adolescence, late adolescence and childhood. He is of view that changes in personality can take place during any stage of development but they basically take place during transition from one stage to another. How does a child perceive others and how does he react with others are basic to the development of personality. In other words, interpersonal relationship is the basic thread that runs throughout the different stages of development of personality. His seven stages may be explained as under :

(i) *Infancy* : This period extends from birth to the development of articulate speech, usually about 18 to 24 months of age. At the time of birth, the infant is basically like an animal but becomes human through tenderness and affection received from mothering. At this stage the infant develops a dual personification of mother. She is perceived both as 'good-mother' and 'bad-mother'. She is perceived as 'good-mother' when she satisfies her baby needs. She is perceived as 'bad-mother' when she arouses anxiety in her. It is during this stage that the baby makes the transition from the prototaxic mode of cognition to parataxic mode of cognition.

(ii) *Childhood* : This stage begins from the development of articulate speech and learning and extends to the apperance of the need for peer relationship, that is, age of five or six. The development of language leads to fusion of different images or personifications development at infancy stage. For example, personification of 'good-mother' and 'bad-mother' are fused together into one image called 'mother'. This stage is a period of rapid acculturation because besides learning language, a child also learns cultural patterns like toilet training, eating habit, sex role expectancies. Two other basic learning processes which are dominant at this stage are *dramatizations* and *preoccupations.* Dramatizations refer to the efforts of child to act like father or mother or any other significant figures. Preoccupations refer to strategies by which a child avoids his anxiety by keeping himself engaged in some works that were early proved to be rewarding one.

(iii) *Juvenile era* : This stage begins from the age five or six and closes when a strong need for an intimate companion develops, that is, usually at the age of eight or nine. There are three basic characteristics of juvenile era. They are competition, compromise and cooperation. However, there are three negative developments in this period. They are learning of stereotypes, ostracism and disparagement. *Stereotypes* are the personifications that are handed down from one generation to another. *Ostracism* is forcible isolation which a child may experience if he falls in any outgroup. *Disparagement* refers to putting other people down and is usually learnt from parents who often speak about the people whom they hate and dislike.

(iv) ***Preadolescence*** : This stage marks the beginning from the appearance of need for intimacy until puberty. This stage is characterized by developing interest in one particular person of the same sex. In previous stage the interpersonal relationship were based upon personal need satisfaction but during this stage intimacy and love form the basis of friendships. The young person's such type of intimate companionship with the same sex has been called a *chum*. Sullivan maintained that without chum, the pre adolescents may suffer from a desperate loneliness which will be worse than anxiety, and which may further interfere in completing with the task of adolescence.

(v) ***Early adolescence*** : This stage starts with puberty and ends with the need for love with a person of opposite sex. At this stage the adolescent develops genital interest and *lustful* relationship. Most of the problems arising in this stage centre round three basic needs—security, intimacy (with someone of opposite sex) and sexual satisfaction. In fact, these three needs collide with each other and produce various kinds of stress and strain during this period of adolescence. Sullivan has regarded this stage as a turning point in personality development because the person either successfully solves the problems related to intimacy and lust and lead a stable future life or faces serious interpersonal difficulties in future life.

(vi) ***Late adolescence*** : This stage begins with stabilization of genital activities and ends with establishing a lasting love relationship in adulthood. During this stage the syntaxic mode of cognition dominates. The most important characteristics of late adolescence is the fusion of intimacy and lust. A final outcome of this stage is self-respect this is prerequisite for giving respect to others.

(vii) ***Maturity*** : Sullivan has little to say about adulthood or maturity because true maturity is beyond the scope of his system. He has pointed out that the significant achievement of each of the previous stage manifests in mature personality. There are several characteristics of a mature personality. Sullivan (1953 : 310) has rightly said that the mature people are "quite sympathetically understanding of the limitations, interests, possibilities, anxieties and so on of those among whom they move or with whom they deal."

On the whole we see that Sullivan has presented a fuller and a more systematic theory of personality and consequently, it has achieved wide acceptance among psychologists. Interpersonal relationship has been one of the basic principles of Sullivan's system.

His system has been criticized for incorporating some hypothetical constructs like personification, self-system, etc. But this does not appear to be a valid criticism in the sense that he has always used a more objective language in describing his system. His data were closely related to the observations of people making interaction with each other.

Erik Erikson's Psychology

Life-Sketch : Erikson (1902-1982) was born of Danish parents in Frankfurt in Germany. His parents took separation before his birth. At the age of 25, he began to teach in Vienna at a small progressive school for American children. At Vienna, Erikson met Freud and his family members. Soon, he joined Vienna Psychoanalytic Institute as a student and began a personal analysis with Anna Freud, Freud's daughter. He was one of the brilliant students of the Institute. He got himself trained in both adult and child psychoanalysis. With the rise and invasion of Hitler in 1930s, he came to the United States and became a naturalized citizen in 1936. In America he was given appointments at the Harvard Medical School and at Massachusetts General Hospital. He also became affiliated with Harvard psychological clinic and Judge Baker Guidance Centre. These clinics were the primary centres for treatment of emotionally disturbed children. At Harvard he also met genius like Margaret Mead, Ruth Benedict, Henry Hurry and Kurt Lewin who influenced his thinking to a very considerable extent. From Harvard University, he moved to the University of California at Berkeley and there, he wrote his first book *Childhood and Society* (1950). Later, he resigned from the University of California, and he moved to Austen Riggs Centre for Psychoanalytic Training and Research in Massachusetts. In 1960 he returned to Harvard University as professor of psychology and remained there until his retirement in 1970. It was during this second stay at Harvard that he established his famous course on "Human Life Cycle". His other important publications were : *Identity : Youth and Crisis* (1968) and *Gandhi's Truth* (1968). For the latter book he received Pulitzer Prize and National Book Award. In 1977 another book *Toy and Reason* was published and in 1978 his new book *Adulthood* was published. He died in 1982.

Erikson's Contributions

Erikson has broadened the structure of psychoanalysis of Freud. He has himself maintained that he has been faithful to Freud and his own concepts are in no way contradictory to Freud's original formulations. Erikson has emphasized upon ego rather than upon id and superego. He was of view that ego possesses the capacity to unify the experiences of man and his action in a meaningful and adaptive manner. Ego possesses creative qualities and tries to provide creative solutions to each new problem. He is of view that ego is determined not only by inner forces but by social and cultural influences. Many of the *ego qualities* that emerge in the different stages of development reflect in influence of these social and cultural factors.

Erikson has built his developmental stage on Freudian system. He accepts the Freudian oral, anal, phallic, latent and genital stages and has added three more stages—early adulthood, middle adulthood, and old age. Thus Erikson's was *eight-stage theory* of development. He believed in the principle of epigenesis, according to which "a new, living organism develops out of an initially undifferentiated entity that is somehow programmed to develop all the organisms' parts in sequence" (Hall, Lindzey, Loehlin and Manosevitz, 1985 : 76). Erikson pointed out some basic features of these developmental stage as under :

(i) Each stage has its own developmental characteristics and has a typical *crisis*. By crisis is meant a turning point in personality and is brought about by interaction of increasing physical maturity on the one hand and by demands placed upon him by parents, teachers, society, etc., on the other hand.

(ii) This crisis is normally resolved by the ego qualities of the concerned period.

(iii) All stages have both psychosexual as well as psychosocial aspects of growth and change. Of the two, Erikson, however, places more emphasis upon psychosocial component of development.

The eight stage of development which is the most fundamental contributions of Erikson, may be outlined as under :

1. *Infancy*

This is the first stage of psychosocial development and corresponds to Freudian oral stage that covers approximately first year of life. At this stage the baby keeps itself engaged in mainly eating, sleeping and eliminating under proper maternal care. When it is able to do all these things in a peaceful and relaxed way under maternal care, it leads to development of the first ego quality called a sense of *basic trust*. It is the mother's ability to give the baby a sense of familiarity, consistency, continuity and sameness of experiences that produce a sense of basic trust. But when maternal care is inadequate, rejecting and unreliable, this produces a crisis in form of *mistrust*. The child develops an attitude of suspicion, fear and threat towards others. Erikson maintained that a healthy growth of personality results not necessarily from sense of trust only but it results from a favourable ratio of trust over mistrust. When the baby is able to solve the trust-versus-mistrust conflict, the first psychosocial strength or virtue called *hope* emerges. By help of this virtue, the baby is able to perceive meaning in his existence. Gradually, the baby learns to focus on meaningful hope and gives up useless hope.

2. *Early childhood*

This is the second stage of psychosocial development and covers second and third year of life. It corresponds with Freudian anal stage. In comparison to the previous stage, the neuromuscular maturation, verbalization and sense of social discrimination of the child becomes more developed. As a consequence, he wants to explore and interact with his surroundings more independently. In fact, he feels pride in such exploration and manipulation. He often reports to the parents, "let me do it". Parents must allow them to do their task at their own. This leads to the development of what is called autonomy. However, autonomy does not mean unrestricted freedom rather the parents must maintain a reasonable but firm limits over child's activities being done independently. When parents themselves do what the children can do or when the parents expect that children are not capable of doing a particular work, it creates a feeling of shame and doubt in them. This may result in feeling of self-doubt, powerlessness and inaptitude. Too much shaming may force the child to rebel or may produce a lasting feeling of insecurity. When this crisis is resolved, it fosters a *will power* in the children.

3. *Play age*

This is the third stage of psychosocial development and it corresponds with Freudian phallic stage and extends from about age 4 to 5 or 6. This is the age where social environment of the child makes him more active and encourages him to win the approval of others by being productive and mastering new skills. The child tries to own new responsibility for himself. Thus ego quality of initiative emerges in the child. The danger of this stage is development of *guilt* in children. When parents are unwilling to allow the children to complete their tasks at their own or to assume additional responsibility, a sense of guilt develops. Those parents who resort to excessive use of verbal punishment or physical punishment in response to child's desire to love or to be loved by opposite sex parents, a sense of guilt arises. Thus Erikson in a way adapts Freudian concept of Oedipus complex and electra complex although his own interpretation is decidedly different and more social than that of Freud. When initiative versus guilt conflict is resolved properly, the virtue of *purpose* develops which is vital for subsequent development of personality. The virtue of purpose refers to the courage to pursue goals without having any fear, guilt or any sort of punishment.

4. *School age*

This is the fourth stage of psychosocial development and covers roughly about 6 to 11 years. This corresponds to Freudian latency period. According to Erikson (1963 : 260), this stage is "only a lull before the storm of puberty" and is "socially most decisive stage". At this stage the child learns to control his imagination and utilize it in learning the rudimentary skill of the cultures. At school children are taught the technology of their culture via formal education. When they are able to learn the various technologies of their culture, a sense of *industry* develops. The danger of this stage is that if the child fails to master the technology of the culture and has some doubts outer his skills in mastering tasks of school and home, a lost sense of *inferiority* or *incompetence* develops. Sometimes sense of inferiority also develops in children because they find that their sex, race, religion, etc. are inferior to those of others. A satisfactory resolution of industry versus inferiority conflict leads to the development of the virtue of *competence* which refers to "the exercise of dexterity and intelligence in the completion of tasks" (Erikson, 1964 : 124).

5. *Adolescence*

This is the fifth stage of psychosocial development which extends from 12 or 13 to 19 years . At this stage the adolescents try to consolidate various types of knowledge that they have gained and integrate them into a personal identity. They became aware of the fact that they have adequate strength to control their own destinies and try to establish themselves in the society. This is called *ego identity.* At this stage the child's body is flooded with genital puberty and his immediate future collides with too many conflicting choices. Among these choices, the most difficult choice is that of occupation (Erikson, 1968). Sometimes the adolescents fail to develop ego identity due to some social circumstances or unfortunate childhood experiences. This crisis is known as *identity crisis* or *identity confusion* or *role confusion* which refers to "an inability to select a career or pursue further education" (Hjelle & Ziegler, 1981 : 126-127). A satisfactory resolution of ego-identity versus identity confusion leads to the development of virtue of *fidelity* which refers to the person's ability to behave according to social mores, ethics and norms of society.

6. *Young Adulthood*

This is the sixth stage of psychosocial development and covers the period of roughly twenties. At this stage the young adults are genuinely ready to make social and heterosexual intimacy with another persons. Erikson has also made it clear that a true sense of *intimacy* develops only in those persons who have already developed a sense of personal identity, that is, a sense of who and what he or she is. The chief danger of this stage is development of sense of isolation. The persons may become self-absorbed or avoid interpersonal contacts that may commit him to intimacy and social involvement. Such persons, then, develop inability to enter into intimate personal relationship to others that ultimately leads to feelings of social *isolation* and emptiness. The healthy resolution of intimacy versus isolation crisis leads to the development of virtue of *love* which is expressed when a person demonstrates an attitude of respect, care and responsibility toward others.

7. *Middle Adulthood*

This is the seventh stage of psychosocial development that covers ages from about 30 to 60 or 65. This stage is marked by *generativity* which refers to a concern of a person regarding not only the welfare of the next generation but also for the future of the society in which the people of that generation will live. Thus generativity is concerned with older generation's attempt to establish and guide those persons who are going to replace them in near future. The sense of generativity is found not only in parents but also in those who have a strong sense of betterment for younger persons. When a person as Erikson has pointed out, fails to develop the sense for generativity, it risks to develop what is called *stagnation* which is defined as a stage of self-absorption in which the person cares for the satisfaction of his own personal needs. The satisfactory resolution of generativity versus stagnation leads to the development of virtue of *care* which refers to the need to look after others as well as to teach them. Teaching as well as proper care helps a lot in our cultural progress and its survival.

8. *Maturity*

This is the eighth and last stage of psychosocial development which in all cultures signals the onset of old age. The stage starts at about age of 65 and extends up to death. At this stage the ego quality of *integrity* appears. This is called *ego integrity* where the person glances back on his or her life, he tries to summate, integrate and evaluate his accomplishment, in correct perspective and reportedly states that "on the whole, I am satisfied". Erikson believes that it is only at this stage that true maturity and practical sense of wisdom spring up. The person also thinks that his death is near but he is no longer afraid of death because he perceives his existence through their offsprings. The danger of this stage is *despair.* While evaluating his ups and downs of his previous life, he risks to develop the sense of despair. He may sense that he has ruined his life and his life is series of unfulfilled opportunities and missed directions. However, when integrity versue despair crisis is resolved, that is, when integrity outweighs despair, one develops the virtue of *wisdom.* It is this wisdom that maintains and transmit the integrity of accumulated knowledge.

Erikson (1977) has further elaborated his psychososical stages of development in terms of *socio-cultural aspects* of development. He considered three socio-cultural phenomena such as *ritualization, ritual and ritualism.* These phenomena tend to add new dimension to the developmental stage and develop according to Erikson's epigenetic principle. Ritualization is a culturally pattern way of doing something in interaction with at least two persons. It has adaptive values for both persons (Erikson, 1966). Each stage is characterized by this ritualization. In adulthood this ritualization becomes the ritual which refers to an activity done by a community of adults for marking and important event of a recurring nature. In India we find that holy days like days of *Ramnavami, Durga Puja, Vasantpanchmi* and *Holi* are marked by special rites. When there occurs distortion in ritualization, it results in ritualism in which people become more concerned with their own achievements rather than with their relationship with others.

Psychologists, on the whole, prefer Erikson's system because he has given emphasis upon the psychosocial aspects of development rather than focusing upon psychosexual dynamics. Many psychoanalysts have praised Erikson for his sensible interpretations and acuteness of observations of human behaviour.

Criticisms of Erikson's System

Erikson's works has been criticized on the following *four* major grounds :

(i) Critics have pointed out that Erikson has watered down Freudian theory by emphasizing only upon ego and conscious mind. In a broader sense, he has sacrificed his other concepts like id, superego and unconscious mind. But in reality this is not a point of criticism rather a point of distinction from Freudian system.

(ii) Critics say that Erikson's most of the concepts are based upon personal observation and subjective data. It means his concepts lack experimental support.

(iii) Erikson has been charged to be too optimistic in explanation of human behavior. However, Erikson (1975) has denied this charge and has pointed out that in each psychosocial stage he has discussed about a crisis as well as negative ego equality like sense of mistrust, guilt, shame, identity confusion, inferiority, etc. How can he then be said to be *too* optimistic ?

(iv) Some psychologists point out that most of his ideas are purely theoretical and unverified (Lundin, 1985). His ideas about hope, purpose and will are examples.

Despite these criticisms, Erikson's system has been welcomed by many contemporary psychoanalytical theorists. His emphasis particularly upon problems of adolescents, adulthood, and aging has proved very valuable for modern behavioural and social scientists.

COMPARISON BETWEEN FREUD AND ERISKON

We have considered the contributions of both Freud and Erikson. There are some points of similarities and contrast between Freud and Erikson. The similarities are that both persons have explained development of personality in terms of some invariant stages. Both of them have considered stages of personality development as determined by past experiences. Erikson has also accepted the biological and sexual foundations of motivational and personal disposition of Freud. Despite these similarities, there are some points of distinction between Freud and Erikson. According to Maier (1965), the major points of distinction between Freud and Erikson are as under :

(i) Freud emphasized upon id, ego and superego to be the primary force in determining human behaviour and functioning. Erikson emphasized only upon ego and undermined the importance of id and superego in determining human behaviour. According to Erikson, ego represents, "man's capacity to unify his experience and his action in an adaptive manner." (Erikson, 1963 : 15). In fact, he has made ego the master rather than the slave of id and superego. Obviously, then, Erikson is a true *ego psychologist* who has regarded ego as an *autonomous structure* of personality.

(ii) Freud emphasized only upon the influence of parents on child's emerging personality. Erikson has broadened the scope by giving stress upon the psychohistorical setting in which social forces and value systems dominate and influences the emergence of personality of a child. Thus, for Erikson, development of personality of a child is governed not only by parental influences but by entire social forces and value systems.

(iii) Erikson's system includes eight stages of psychosocial development starting from infancy to maturity or old age. Thus he has included the whole life-span of the individual in development of ego. Freud mainly kept himself limited to the effects of early childhood experiences that never went beyond the genital stage. Erikson's system and Freud's system run almost parallel to the first five stages of life. Subsequently, Frikson goes beyond that covering the remaining span of life in three stages.

(iv) Freud and Erikson also differed on the nature and resolution of psychosexual conflicts. Freud wanted to show that the major abnormalities in adulthood were related to the childhood experience lying in the unconscious mind. Erikson wanted to emphasize upon *ego qualities* or *virtues* that emerge at different levels of psychosocial development. These ego qualities are important in resolving the psychosocial conflict called crisis by Erikson.

Thus we find that despite some similarities, Erikson and Freud differ from each other. It is these distinctions that have led Erikson to be called as *ego psychologist*, because through these distinctions he has mainly emphasized upon the dominant role of ego in guiding human behaviour.

DISTINCTIONS BETWEEN FREUDIAN AND NEO-FREUDIAN

We have examined Freudian system as well as neo-Freudian system in detail. A look at these two systems reveals that there are some points of distinctions between Freudian system and neo-Freudian systems.

First, Freud emphasized upon biological forces especially upon sex instinct to be the major determinant of human behaviour and functioning. Neo-Freudians, on the other hand, emphasized upon social and cultural forces to be the major determinant of human behaviour and functioning.

Second., Freud claimed his two major complexes, that is, oedipus complex and electra complex to be universal and to be due to sexual jealousy. Neo-Freudians like Sullivan, Fromm and Horney explained that these are neither universal nor loaded with sexual jealously. They have reported that there are many cultures in which the rivalry between son and father is based upon latter's dominant and influential position in the family (and not due to any type of sexual jealously).

Third, Freud recognized anxiety to be an ego function. When ego is threatened by id and/or superego, anxiety emerges. Neo-Freudians, in general, and Horney in particular have stated that anxiety, particularly basic anxiety is formed in childhood when a child is allowed to feel isolated and helpless in the world that seems full of threats and hostilities.

CHAPTER HIGHLIGHTS

1. Alfred Adler and Carl Gustav Jung have been the two most important rebels of Freudian Psychoanalysis. While rejecting overemphasis upon sex by Freud, Adler made significant contributions by way of formulating and recognizing concepts like organ inferiority and compensation, striving for success or superiority, social interest, style of life, creative power, fictional finalism, birth order. Despite these, his individual psychology has been criticized on three major grounds. His system also differed from that of Freudian system on five major grounds.
2. Carl Jung has been another important rebel of Freudian psychoanalysis. Like Adler, he also rejected Freudian overemphasis upon sex. Among his important contributions are conscious and unconscious, attitudes and functions, psychic energy and personality development. His analytical psychology, has also been criticized on four major grounds. Jung's psychology differed from that of Freud's psychology basically on three major grounds.
3. The contribution of four important neo-Freudians have been discussed. These persons are Horney, Fromm, Sullivan and Erikson. They did not rebel against Freudian psychoanalysis. However, they tried to improve upon Freud by including emphasis upon social and cultural factors. Horney is well-known for her some concepts like basic anxiety, neurotic trends, neurotic needs, idealized self-image, rationalization and externalization etc. Fromm is known for his book *Escape from Freedom* and explaining personality in terms of various types such as receptive type, exploitative type, marketing types and productive type. Sullivan's psychology has helped us a lot in understanding dynamics of personality as well as its different developmental stages. Erikson has been a very popular ego psychologist and has been such a neo-Freudian who while accepting

Freudian five stage of psychosexual development, has added three more stages providing a coverage to the explanation of personality development till maturity or old age. Throughout his eight stages of psychoscial development he emphasized upon certain *ego qualities* that have been considered as basic for the development of personality.

4. Freudian psychology differs from neo-Freudain psychology in at least three major respects.

REVIEW QUESTIONS

1. Assess the contributions of Alfred Adler to the development of psychology.
2. Evaluate the contributions of C. G. Jung in development of psychology.
3. What were the major points of distinctions among Freud, Adler and Jung towards their interpretation of various psychological concepts.
4. Evaluate the contributions of Karen Horney in the development of psychology. How did she make herself distinct from Freud.
5. Evaluate the contributions of Erich Fromm. How does his personality types differ from that of Freudian type ?
6. Discuss the major contributions of Harry Stack Sullivan. Does his various stage of personality differ from those of Erikson in a significant way ?
7. Make a comparative study of Freud and Erikson in development of personality.
8. Evaluate the contributions of Erik Erikson in the development of psychology.

■

CHAPTER 15

FIELD THEORY

CHAPTER PREVIEW

Field theory owes its origin in natural sciences like Physics, Chemistry and Mathematics and has been applied in psychology to explain various aspects of behaviour. Important field theorists are Kurt Lewin, E.C. Tolman and E. Brunswik. Field theorists, in general, argue that an organism is influenced by all those factors in the field that surrounds him.

Lewin's life space has been one of the important concepts through which behaviour has been explained. Apart from his topological psychology, his vector psychology and the concept of group dynamics have been lucidly presented. Finally, Lewin's system has been criticized.

Tolman's cognitive field theory has been no less important for psychology. His emphasis upon cognitive map, cathexes, field expectations, field cognitive modes, need system, behaviour space and belief-value matrix establishes his position as a cognitive field theorist.

Brunswik's field theory has also been emphasized. He is popular for his viewpoints regarding thing constancy or object constancy. His emphasis upon representative design is no less important for field theory.

Important constituents of physical sciences like physics, chemistry, mathematics have influenced the course of newer science like psychology by providing new look to its subject-matter. The field theories in physics have been important in exerting such influences. Physicists have utilized the concept of field in explanation of gravitational field, electromagnetic field, etc. Some psychologists have tried to adapt this notion of "field" in understanding of human behaviour. Gestalt psychologists may be set as an example of such psychologists. They have tried to show that human behaviour is determined by the psychophysical field consisting of an organized system of various stresses or strains similar to that of gravitational field or electromagnetic field. Field theory represents more or less an outgrowth of Gestalt psychology. Field theorists, in general, point out that an organism is influenced by all those factors in the field that surrounds him. There are several field theorists like Kurt Lewin, E.C. Tolman, E. Brunswik, R.G. Barker, R. H. Wheeler, J.R. Kantor, etc. The space does not permit to consider all of them.

However, the contributions of the first three field theorists would be considered in this chapter.

KURT LEWIN'S FIELD THEORY

Life-Sketch

Kurt Lewin (1890–1947) was born in Mogilno, Germany. He was second in the family of four children. When he was 15, his family moved from Mogilno to Berlin for properly educating the children. After completing his secondary education, he joined the University of Berlin as a student and studied psychology under Karl Stumpf, a well-known experimental psychologist. In 1914 he received his Ph. D. in psychology from Berlin University and then served in the German Army during World War I. During early years he was very closely associated with the Gestalt psychologists like Wertheimer and Kohler. From these Gestaltists, he had borrowed the concept of a field (Lundin, 1985). However, this was not the isomorphic brain field upon which Gestalt psychologists had emphasized rather an *environmental field* that contained one or more than one persons. Due to this direct relationship of Lewin with Gestalt psychology, some psychologists have considered him as one of the Gestalt psychologists. But this idea is not universally shared. Lewin had started his early studies on association and this marked a significant departure from the Gestaltistic ideas. After returning to Berlin from the German Army, he joined the faculty of the Psychological Institute and remained there for several years.

In early 1930s Lewin became visiting professor at Stanford University in United States. Then, he decided to settle in America. This decision had also been further substantiated due to Hitler coming to power. He joined Cornell University as a professor in 1933 and remained there till 1935. He, then, became a professor at the University of Iowa where with the help of his postdoctoral students, he pioneered in action research and group dynamics. In 1945 he moved to Massachussets Institute of Technology where he founded *Research Center for Group Dynamics* and became the first director. He remained director of this Institute until his untimely death in 1947 at the young age of 56. During his stay at United states, he had attracted a large number of students who later became prominent psychologists. As a person, he was friendly, democratic and stimulating.

Lewin's system

Lewin has been considered by many psychologists to be one of the brilliant figures among contemporary psychologists. Lewin considered his field theory to be a *topological psychology* and a *vectoral psychology*. In fact, he borrowed these two terms 'topology' and 'vector' from mathematics. As we know, topology is a form of geometry that investigates spatial properties of figures. However, as we shall examine his system, it will be clear that his analogy to topology is not strong rather is superficial. Therefore, his system can be understood even by those who don't possess the knowledge of topology. To explain his system fully, he also needed a concept of force and therefore, he borrowed the concept of vector from mathematics to describe the resolution of stresses or strains (forces) within the organism. Lewin's field system may be explained in terms of the following three major headings :

1. ***Lewin's topological psychology***

Lewin's topological psychology contains discussion of the person, the psychological environment, the differentiation of the person as well as the psychological environment, the life space and its various dimensions, etc. However, his major concepts of topological psychology can be explained in terms of the following headings :

(i) ***Life Space :*** Lewin started his system with the description and analysis of life space. The life space (L) consists of the person (P) and the psychological environment (E). (cf. Figure 14·1). Person is represented as an enclosed circle. Person is such entity which is differentiated from every thing else in the world and yet included within the world. As the Figure 14·1 suggests, person is

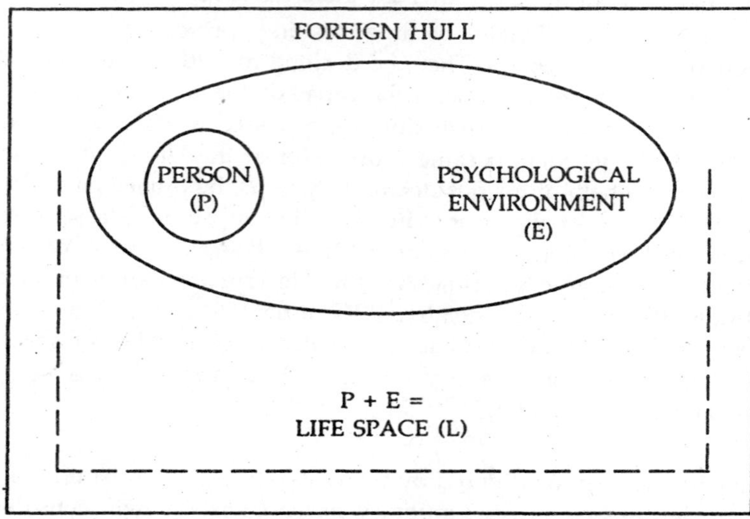

Figure 14·1

included within the life space but at the same time differentiated from the environment. Lewin has not only separated the person from the environment but has held that he (person) is differentiated from within. He has divided person into two major regions—*the perceptual-motor region* and *the inner-personal region*. The perceptual-motor region lies on the periphery of circle enclosing *P* and the inner-personal region is represented by central part of the circle. The inner-personal region is, therefore, completely surrounded by perceptual-motor region and consequently, it has no direct contact with the outside environment. The perceptual-motor region controls perceptual and motoric functions of the person. The inner-personal region controls the motivational functions. Thus, for Lewin, the person is heterogeneous and not homogeneous.

Psychological environment (E) is another important aspect of life space. As Figure 8 suggests, the psychological environment covers the area within the ellipse but outside the circle that contains P. Like person, Lewin divided the psychological environment into different regions. Some regions have permeable boundaries and some regions have impermeable boundaries. We can influence the others through permeable boundaries and through these boundaries, we can be influenced by others.

Lewin maintains that human behaviour is a function of both person and the psychological environment or taken together the life space. In terms of equation, he outlined

$$B = f\,(P, E)$$

or

$$B = f\,(L).$$

The external environment lying outside the person's life space is called *foreign hull*. The boundary between the foreign hull and the psychological environment is permeable and therefore, there is a two-way communication between the external world (foreign hull) and the psychological environment. This means that facts in the psychological environment can produce changes in the physical world and the events in the physical world can also influence the facts of psychological environment.

In nutshell, it can be said that the life space of a person includes himself and other people or objects as perceived by him. It also includes ideas. Lewin also maintained that the life space may be divided into regions which are separated by boundaries. Each region contains a *psychological fact* which need not be only observable thing but it may be a social event or intellectual event or something that is inferred only. The boundaries of the region of the life space has two dimensions such as *nearness-remoteness* and *firmness-weakness*. The notion regarding regions, boundaries and its dimensions may be explained through an example. Suppose a student wants to be an I.A.S. (Indian Administrative Service) Officer. For this, he will have to obtain a bachelor degree from any university, then he will have to compete first in preliminary examination, then in the main examination and finally in viva-voce examination conducted by Union Public Service Commission. Thus in this example the student is the P and goal is to become an I.A.S. Officer. In between these two extremes, there are four regions—obtaining a bachelor degree from University, competing in preliminary examination, competing in main examination, and competing in viva-voce examination. In this example competing in viva-voce examination is *near region* while obtaining the bachelor degree is a *remote region*. Competing in the main examination may be a difficult task and therefore, this region may be said to have firm boundary. However, competing in the preliminary examination may be comparatively easier and hence, this region may be said to have a weak boundary. How many regions can be in the life space ? It depends upon the number of facts that exists at any particular time.

How do various regions of life space influence each other ? When two regions or cells of life space and therefore, two facts of life space interact with each other, this produces an *event*. The various regions influence each other through what is called *communication* and *locomotion*. Communication is an event through which one cell or region of the life space communicates with the other. Locomotion refers to the physical or the psychological movement of the person from one region of the life space to another region. In fact, many locomotions done through psychological environment (that are interesting to the psychologists) are psychological in nature which involves changes in perceptual and attentional processes. The locomotion from one region to another takes place through a fixed pathway or space. This is called as *hodological space*. Lewin has pointed out that there are three principles that govern communication and locomotions of events. They are : the *principle of relatedness*, the *principle of concreteness* and the *principle of contemporaneity*. The principle of relatedness states that any event is caused by interaction of two or more related facts. The principle of concreteness states that only those facts that exist in the life space have some effects upon the organism. The principle of contemporaneity emphasizes that only the present facts can produce present behaviour. It means those facts that relate to early childhood cann't influence the present behaviour unless they have been in existence at present (Lewin, 1936). That way, Lewin also perceived the possibility of the impact of *time dimension* upon the life space. Although the actual events of the past or the potential events of the time to come cann't influence our present behaviour, he stressed that our present attitudes, thoughts and feelings about past and future (which are part of the present life space) may have considerable impact upon our present conduct. Thus the present life space must be taken as something containing a psychological past and a psychological future (Lewin, 1951). One of the most important contributions of Lewin's system within the life space framework is his conceptualization regarding conflict. He recognized three types of coflict that ultimately produces frustration in us. They are : *approach-approach conflict, avoidance-avoidance conflict and approach-avoidance conflict.* In approach-approach conflict the person (P) wishes to achieve two positive goals, only one of which can be achieved. An example will be the desire to attend two marriage parties at the same time. In avoidance-avoidance conflict the person is caught between the two. An example will be of a student who is forced to choose between two subjects which he equally dislikes. In approach-avoidance conflict the person is both attracted as well as repelled by the goals. For example, a person may be offered a job having handsome salary but its location may be in extremely backward area.

One *common misinterpretation* of life space should be avoided. Generally, it is understood that the life space is identical with the phenomenal world of the person. This is *not* the truth. The life space simply include those factors which influenced our behaviour and perception. Some of these factors may be unconscious, too. This phenomenal world may be close or may lie at distant from life space.

(ii) ***Levels of reality*** **:** According to Lewin (1936), there are levels of reality and unreality that applies to both the person as well as the psychological environment. Reality comprises actual locomotions and unreality comprises imaginary locomotions. A person may change his work or may join a new party. This illustrates Lewin's concept of reality. Likewise, a person may daydream to become the president of political party or a country. This illustrates Lewin's concept of unreality. There are various degrees or levels between these two extremes—the concept of reality and the concept of unreality. Planning or thinking lies somewhere at intermediate level between these two extremes. Lewin emphasized that as one moves from reality to unreality side, locomotion becomes easier. With growing maturation, the reality-unreality dimension also broadens and becomes more sharp and differentiated (Lewin, 1936).

2. *Lewin's Vector Psychology*

Lewin's Vector psychology consists of his dynamic concepts which are related to motivational aspects of human behaviour. These concepts are different from the topological concepts or structural concepts. These dynamic concepts tell us how a person is going to behave in situation. To understand behaviour fully, these motivational concepts must be taken into account. Lewin's major dynamic concepts are as under :

(i) *Energy :* Lewin considered person as a complex energy system. That energy which performs psychological work is called psychical energy. Psychical energy is created when the psychic system (or the person) wants to return to equilibrium after it has been thrown into the state of disequilibrium due to increase in tension in one part of the system relative to other part. When the system becomes successful in equalizing tension throughout the system, the output of the energy halts and the system returns to rest.

(ii) *Tension :* Tension is a state of person and refers to a state of disequilibrium or lack of balance between the forces of one inner-personal region or system and the other inner-personal region or system. It has *two* properties. The first property is that tension tends to become equalized. Suppose there is high tension in system X and low tension in system Y and Z. Then tension from X will flow to Y and Z until the tension in all the three systems becomes equalized. The psychological means by which tension tends to be equalized is known as a *process.* Thinking, remembering, perceiving or the like are some of the examples of the process. The second property of tension is that it tends to exert pressure on the boundary system in which it is contained. If boundary is weak and permeable, tension will easily flow to other systems. But if the boundary is firm and impermeable, the diffusion of tension will be hindered.

There were several experimental attempts to test the propositions relating to the tension system of Kurt Lewin. One of the well-known attempt was made by Zeigarnik (1927) in her dissertation research completed under his supervision. Her experiments were based on her two major assumptions. *First,* when a subject is given a task to perform, tension will be aroused. *Second,* if tension is not relieved as it occurs if the task remains incomplete, it would lead to *greater recall* of incompleted task. In her experiment, she gave 22 tasks to 138 subjects. The task included things like solving simple puzzles, modelling a figure from clay, etc. The subjects were allowed to complete some of the tasks but were prevented to complete certain other tasks on some false pretext. Later, she asked her subjects to recall the number of tasks on that they were working. It was found that the subjects recalled many more from incomplete tasks. The ratio of the recalled complete tasks to the recalled in completed tasks was 1 : 9. This became popular in psychology as *Zeigarnik effect.* Later on, other psychologists also found evidences for this effect (Alper, 1948; Deutsch, 1954). Ovsiankina (1928) later conducted another experimental test of the Lewinian tension system. She reported that the subjects voluntarily resumed the interrupted task than the completed task. Thus she also provided support to Zeigarnik effect.

(iii) ***Need :*** Need is either a physiological condition such as hunger or a psychological condition such as desire to become a wealthy person. It is this need that causes increase or decrease in tension of a system or region. Lewin also made it clear that only those needs that exist currently are important. He made distinction between needs and quasi-needs. Quasi-needs are nothing but the specific intentions which are shaped by social factors (Lewin, 1951). Need to take meal in a particular hotel is the example of quasi-need.

(iv) ***Valence :*** As we know, in Lewin's system there are various regions of the psychological environment. Every region has either a positive or a negative value. This value is the valence for the person. A region having positive valence contains such goal object that will reduce tension. For example, for a thirsty person a region that has water, will have positive valence. A region with negative valence contains a goal object that will increase tension. For example, for a girl who fears spider, that region which contains spider will have negative valence. Lewin has considered valences in quantitative terms, that is, they can be strong, moderate or weak.

These valences are related to the needs of the persons. For example, if a person is not hungry, food will nc 'onger have positive valence for him. Lewin has pointed out that our lite space may contain several regions having several valences at the same time. As a consequence of this, conflict arises. The approach-approach conflict, the avoidance-avoidance conflict and the approach-avoidance conflict can be explained by arousal of several valences at the same time. Lewin put forward a hypothesis that as the distance between a person and a goal object increases, the attractiveness of the valence or the effect of positive valence is decreased. Fajans (1933) experi-mentally confirmed this hypothesis. She took a group of children whose age range varied from one to six. She put very attractive toys (positive valence) at some distance (5 to 100 centimetres) from the children. It was found that as distance increased, the attractive toys failed to attract the child. Another hypothesis of Lewin with regard to valence is that a goal which is obstructed or towards which a person is not allowed to go, develops a stronger positive valence. This is like the popular saying that *grass on the other side of the river looks more greener.* Wright (1943) conducted several experiments to test this hypothesis. In one of his popular experi-ment he suspended two strings from a wall and a piece of stick candy was attached to the ends of both strings. One of the strings was little higher up so that it was not easily accessible. Another string was, however, easily accessible. Results revealed that there was a strong tendency among children to take candy from the less accessible string.

(v) ***Vector*** **:** Vector refers to those psychological forces that influence the person to the extent that he moves in a particular direction. It is represented by an arrow when related to the person (P). (See Figure 14-2).

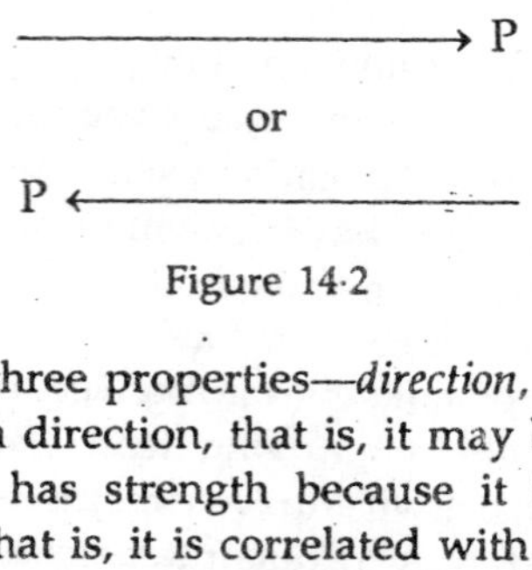

Figure 14-2

The vectors have three properties—*direction, strength* and a *point of contact.* A vector has a direction, that is, it may be toward or away the goal object. A vector has strength because it is correlated with the valence of the object, that is, it is correlated with attraction or repulsion of a valence. The longer the line of arrow, the greater is the strength of the vector. A vector has also a point of contact.

3. *Group Dynamics*

In his later years of life Lewin paid attention towards the problems of social psychology. He enunciated the concept of group dynamics which refers to the collective interactions such as power shifts, leader-ship, group formation, cohesiveness, discruptiveness, decision-making, etc. taking place within a group. In other words, it is a social process by which people interact face-to-face in group. He was of view that the group of the person and its environment constituted the social field. The major characteristic of social field is the relative position of the members of the group. Group behaviour is solely characterized by the dynamic interdependence of its members. The activities of each member of a group are the function of activities of other members. The group is influenced by both cohesive as well as disruptive forces. When the relations among members of a group are satisfying, cohesive forces result. But when relation among members of a group remains conflicting and when members have frequently hampered communications, the disruptive force emerge.

The concept of group dynamics opened avenues for important researches in the field of social psychology. During World War II Lewin (1943) conducted several researches that attempted to alter group decision-making. At the time of war there were shortage of certain food products such as meat. Therefore, the housewives (or 'gatekeepers' as Lewin called them) were encouraged to buy and make use of certain unpopular meats such as brains, kidneys, liver, heart and other animal organs not generally taken to be good food items. There were six groups of housewives. He used two methods of persuasion. The first three groups of housewives were persuaded by lecture method in which they were told about the nutritional values of these meats and how they could be tastily prepared. Three other groups of housewives were persuaded through group discussion method. In this method the members discussed about the pros and cons of eating, cooking, etc. of such meat substances. Later on the housewives from both groups were asked wheter or not they were using these meat substances. It was found in the result that only 3 per cent of the housewives persuaded through lecture method used such meat substances whereas 32 per cent of the housewives who were persuaded through group discussion method used these meat substances by changing their food habits. Similar results were obtained by Lewin (1958) in experiments that aimed at increasing the consumption of fresh and evaporated milk and encouraging habits of taking orange juice to infants. On the basis of these results, he concluded that in group discussion more forces were made available for changing behaviour of the persons. According to Lewin, the change in attitude through such group-decision procedures consists of three-step processes. In the first step the group attitude is 'unfreezed' because such attitude in fact, becomes a major force in resisting change in attitude. In the second step a new set of attitude is established and in the third step the new attitude is 'freezed' or consolidated.

Lewin's system has been *criticized* on the following grounds :

(i) Critics have said that Lewin's system is full of imaginary, untestable and unverifiable hypothetical constructs like vectors, tensions, energy systems, etc. They have never been experimentally tested. His various topological concepts failed to provide anything meaningful in true explanatory sense. They were only 'pictorial analogies and illustrative metaphors' (Broyler, 1936–37). According to London (1944), they were such pictures that added nothing to our psychological knowledge.

(ii) Lewin has misused the mathematical concepts. Various terms like force, valence, path, boundaries were taken from the context of physics, chemistry and mathematics and were wrongly applied to psychology (Hall & Lindzey, 1978). London (1944), likewise, has also criticized his topological concepts that were removed from geometry and misapplied to psychology.

(iii) Critics have also said that Lewin has failed to specify a clear-cut relation of the life space to the external environment (Brunswik, 1943; Cartwright, 1959; Leeper, 1943; Tolman, 1948). According to these psychologists, nowhere Lewin has explained how the external environment produces change in the life space or how the life space produces change in the external environment. Due to this reason, his system runs the risk of being trapped into the subjectivism.

(iv) Lewin did not take into account the past history of the individual (Garrett, 1939; Leeper, 1943). Lewin has denied this criticism. He has said that his principle of contemporaneity has been widely misunderstood and hence, this criticism has been labelled. He claimed that "nothing can be more mistaken" (Lewin, 1951 : 45). In fact, he stressed that the knowledge of past history is important in inferring about the present life space.

Despite these criticisms, Lewin's system has great heuristic value because it generated a tremendous amount of researches and experimentations in many areas of psychology. His viewpoints have very clearly shown that for understanding the vital aspects of human behaviour a system has to be multi-dimensional in scope. Heider (1959 : 119) has very nicely capsuled the importance of Lewin's system, "Lewin's basic notions ... have a wealth of implicit meaning which has not been exhausted and they are, therefore, still full of promise for further development."

TOLMAN'S COGNITIVE FIELD THEORY

We have already considered Edward Chace Tolman (1886-1959) as a behaviourist. In his early years of career Tolman was very much impressed by Watsonian behaviourism and considered it as a "relief" from traditional introspective psychology of Wundt and Titchner. However, he soon departed from Watsonian behaviourism. As he started developing his new ideas about psychology, he placed much emphasis upon cognition and showed a strong inclination towards field theory approach. As a consequence, in explaining his viewpoints about psychology he borrowed several concepts from Gestalt psychology as well as from Lewin's system. In view of this, he may legitimately be classified as an important field theorist.

Although it is not easy to separate Tolman as a behaviourist and Tolman as a field theorist, the use of certain concepts like cognitive map, cathexes, field expectancies, field cognition models, need system, behaviour space and belief-value matrix in explaining behaviour makes us realize that his contributions as a field theorist are distinct and independent. Tolman has stressed that the organism learns a cognitive map of the whole situation. The organism learns "what leads to what". In other words, the organism acquires the knowledge of the learning situation as a whole. It is at this juncture that the concept of field enters Tolman's psychology because the concept of cognitive map represents a kind of field in the brain of the organism that enables it to run from one place to another without showing any dependence of bodily movements. In "1949 version" of his system, Tolman announced six types of connections or relations that the organism can learn. Cathexis (Plural cathexes) was one of them. This is equivalent to Lewin's concept of valence. It refers to some acquired relationship between an object and the motivating condition. A person may learn a relationship between his thirst and a glass of water. Field expectancies are another important type of connection considered by him. These refer to the representations of environment through which latent learning is possible. Field cognition modes are another important type of learning which Tolman has emphasized. These are the higher-order functions that amounted to a readiness to develop new field expectancies through perceptual, memorial or inferential processes.

As a field theorist, Tolman was much influenced by Lewin. Much on the pattern of Lewinian system, Tolman accepted three important classes on intervening variables as under :

(i) ***The need system :*** This system is closely related to drive notion that can be physiological or psychological. This stand of Tolman is similar to Lewin. However, he does differ from Lewin in the sense that he does not emphasize anything like quasi-needs as done by Lewin.

(ii) ***The behaviour space :*** This concept is very intimately related to Lewinian concept of life space. Tolman has stated that behaviour space is the space in which locomotion, that is, the persons' movement takes place. Any object in the behaviour space might attract or repel the person.

(iii) ***The belief-value matrix :*** This refers to a kind of inferred state of motivation or some preference for attaining some positive goals or tendency for being repelled from some negative goals. This is much like Lewin's belief that objects have positive or negative valence.

Tolman has a vast number of experimental researches for supporting his stand as a cognitive field theorist. Experimental evidences provided by Tinklepaugh (1928) on reward expectancy phenomena, by Blodgett (1929) as well as by Tolman and Honzik (1930) on latent learning and by Lashley and Ball (1929) and Tolman *et al.* (1946, 1947) on place or goal learning have readily confirmed Tolman's position as field theorist. Since we have discussed these various source of experimentations in chapter 10, we will not repeat them here.

Making a fair evaluation of Tolman's position as a field theorist, we may say that Tolman's intervening variables deserve the same comment and criticisms as those of Lewinian concept. Like Lewin's concepts, any of these concepts can't be tested because they contain the element of subjectivism similar to the concepts of Gestalt psychologists and Lewin.

BRUNSWIK'S FIELD THEORY (OR PROBABILISTIC FUNCTIONALISM)

Life-Sketch

Egon Brunswik (1903–1955) was born in Hungary. His initial training was in the field of engineering but later on, he shifted to the field of psychology at the University of Vienna. Under Karl Buhler he conducted research in psychology and took his doctorate in 1927. After holding various academic appointments, a critical turning point came in his life during 1933-34. E.C. Tolman met Brunswik in Vienna and was much impressed with him. Subsequently, he received Rocke-feller Fellowship and mainly due to Tolman's initiativeness, he came to the Berkeley campus of University of California as a visiting lecturer and research fellow in psychology. In 1937, he returned to Berkeley as an assistant professor. He remained there till his death in 1955.

Brunswik's contributions

Psychologists agree that Brunswik's work is difficult to be categorized (Marx & Cronan-Hillix, 1987). When he came to United states, he worked a lot within the general framework of behaviourism although he was not a S–R theorist in the true sense. Keeping in view his most important work, that is, work in the field of *perceptual constancy* for which he is well-known in psychology, we can say that he was associated with Orthodox Gestalt psychology, although he has categorically denied any such specific relationship with Gestalt psychology. On the basis of his work, he can't be categorized as a field theorist in the sense Lewin was. However, he was a field theorist because of the following reasons :

(i) In his basic attempt to establish a system called probabilistic functionalism he considered the totality of various interacting forces or factors involved in determination of behaviour.

(ii) He gave emphasis upon *representative design* for experimentation in which all interacting factors involved in determination of behaviour could be studied.

His major contributions can be enlisted under the following two categories :

1. ***Brunswik's emphasis upon research based system***

Brunswik has conducted his well-known researches in the field of *thing constancy* or more specifically in the area of size constancy. In fact, researches conducted in the field of thing constancy were so important that E.C. Tolman was much attracted towards him. The most important conclusion drawn by Brunswik from researches done in thing constancy was that the subjects tend to make a compromise in the perceptual judgement between distal or real characteristics of the objects and the proximal or sensory characteristics of the objects. Generally, they tend to keep their perceptual judgement near the distal or real characteristics despite the various distorting conditions. Thus his perceptual experiences remain more or less constant despite the various sources of distortions. The index of the influence of distal or real characteristics upon perceptual experience is called *Brunswik ratio*. If this ratio is one (unity ratio), it indicates that constancy is perfect. This ratio may also be zero and in that it indicates that retinal stimulus (or proximal stimulus (or stimulus as being perceived) completely determines the perceptual experiences. Brunswik's thing constancy or perceptual constancy applies to size, shape, brightness etc. and in all cases it tells that our perceptual experiences remain more or less constant and independent of variables like angle of tilt, distance, amount of luminosity, etc., Later, Brunswik in collaboration with Tolman, demonstrated interest in the study of instrumental behaviour and in the study of perception. They jointly published a research paper (Tolman and Brunswik, 1935) in which they expressed their common ideas in the concept of what is popularly known as *vicarious function* that simply emphasized that cues or behaviours could be substituted for each other because they acted vicariously for each other. The commonality of ideas between Brunswik and Tolman was that former had shown that the persons use varying cues to come to the same conclusion regarding an object whereas the latter had shown that the organisms use the various behavioural means to come to the same goals or ends.

Brunswik (1939) also attacked the problem of *partial or intermittent reinforcement*. He stated that the all-or-none reward condition used frequently in learning situation was not the true representative of the real situation. Consequently, he conducted experiments on rats in T-shaped maze in such a way that he varied the proposition of reward to total trials to both ends of T-shaped maze. Results revealed that rats showed preferences that highly correlated with the degree of probability of reward in two ends or goals of such maze. In other words, rates demonstrated 'probability matching'. In this way, he initiated the study of *probability learning*.

Based upon above research programme Brunswik developed his system of *probabilistic functionalism*. He claimed that his system was probabilistic in the sense that the various goals in our environment were related only probabilistically to different cues and responses. His system was called functionalism because it was mainly concerned with "the degree of success or achievement in perception and instrumental behaviour' (Marx & Cronan-Hilix, 1987).

2. *Brunswik's emphasis upon representative design*

Burnswik (1956) emphasized upon representative design rather than upon systematic design in his long series of experimentations. He criticized the classical systematic design that is most frequently used by psychologists. He was of view that since these classical systematic design used a limited samples of variables, its results could no longer be representative of the natural behaviour of the subjects. He considered those experiments in which only one or two variables were included at a time as highly hopeless ones. Their results could *never* represents behaviours in natural environment. Obviously, then, Brunswik was giving hints towards the possibility of conducting experiments in multivariate analysis situations. Such experiments are very common today though they were rare in Brunswik's lifetime. He has also criticized the systematic design in which, he claimed, the variables are artificially manipulated. He recommended that in his representative design the correlational techniques should be used and they should replace the differential statistical techniques that are very much in vogue in the systematic design.

There are evidences to support the contention that Brunswik's analysis of the representative design that originated in the study of perception, has been successfully used (outside the experimental study of perception) in clinical psychology (Hammond, 1954, 1955). In the field of clincal psychology the systematic design has been frequently criticized in light of the basic requirements of the representative design. It is said that diagnostic test scores fail to sample adequately the relevant personality traits of the examinees, the range or number of the exminers as well as the various situational variables.

Brunswik has, however, been criticized on some grounds. *First* it has been suggested by critics that Brunswik has overvalued his representative design and has undervalued the orthodox systematic design. There are situations in which the systematic design may be more appropriate and scientific than representative design. This appears to be specially true in case of medical researches. *Second,* some critics have emphasized that Brunswik's methodology has not been very corroborative because it opposes researches on mediational mechanisms and it assumes non-universality in behavioural laws.

Despite some criticisms, we remember Brunswik for his important methodological contributions particularly in form of representative design as well as for his work in the field of perceptual constancies. He also championed the field of probability learning.

CHAPTER HIGHLIGHTS

1. Field theory represents more or less an outgrowth of Gestalt psychology. Field theorists, in general, point out that an organism is influenced by all those factors in the field that surrounds him. There are several field theorists of whom Lewin, Tolman and Brunswik are the most important ones.
2. Lewin's field theory is partly topological psychology and partly vectoral psychology. In his topological system he has emphasized upon the study of life space that includes person and psychological environment. He has divided the person into the inner-personal region and the perceptual-motor region. He has also divided psychological environment by dividing it into different regions.

Some of these regions have permeable boundaries and some of these have impermeable boundaries. Lewin considers that human behaviour is function of both the person and the psychological environment or taken together of life space. In this vectoral system, Lewin has emphasized upon several motivational concepts like energy, tension, need, valence and vector. All these motivational concepts attempt to answer why does a person behave in a particular manner in particular situation.

3. Tolman's cognitive field theory is another important theory that has been discussed. Tolman is both a field theorist as well as a purposive behaviourist. As a field theorist Tolman has stressed that the organism learns a cognitive map of the whole situation. In other words, the organism acquires the knowledge of the learning situation as a whole. Like Lewin, he also attempted to explain his system with the help of various kinds of intervening variables like the need system, the behaviours space and the belief-value matrix.
4. Brunswik's probabilistic functionalism is another important contribution in the region of the field theory. He has made notable contributions in the field of perceptual constancy and probability learning. His representative design as an alternative to systematic design has been very popular among psychologists. Keeping in view the nature of his work, he appears to be highly associated with the orthodox Gestalt psychology although he has himself denied the possibility of any such relationship.

REVIEW QUESTIONS

1. Examine the importance of Lewin's topographical psychology in studying human behaviour.
2. Examine critically the importance of Lewin's vectoral psychology in studying human behaviour.
3. Examine the contribution of E.C. Tolman as a field thorist.
4. "It is difficult to separate E.C. Tolman as a purposive behaviourist and as a field theorist." Comment.
5. Examine the role of Egon Brunswik's probabilistic functionalism in the study of perception and learning.
6. What do you mean by Egon Brunswik's representative design ? How does it differ from the popular systematic design.

■

CHAPTER 16

HORMIC PSYCHOLOGY AND DYNAMIC PSYCHOLOGY

CHAPTER PREVIEW

William McDougall developed the system of hormic psychology. He emphasized upon purposive behaviour which is spontaneous and continuous. He defined psychology as "the positive science of conduct of living creatures". His theory of instinct, a well-known theory in psychology, has also been emphasized. McDougall has considered these instincts as very important because they are the primary "movers" of our activities. Originally, he gave a list of twelve instincts but subsequently, the number was reduced to seven, each combined with a certain emotion. His concept of group mind has also been discussed.

William Woodworth's name is associated with dynamic psychology. Woodworth did not aim at establishing a formal system in psychology. He carried a psychology that was based upon motivation and drive. He also made it clear that S-O-R formula was a better formula than mere S-R formula for explaining the various aspects of behaviour.

Finally, a comparison between McDougall and Woodworth has also been presented.

William McDougall (1871-1938), the Englishman by birth, developed the system of hormic psychology. He borrowed the word 'hormic' from the Greek word 'horme' which meant an "urge". This urge has an obvious purpose. His contention was that an end or purpose drives us to do activities without our awareness although sometimes a vague kind of awareness is involved. This striving to achieve a purpose or end was the central theme for psychology to study. In the fifth edition of his famous book *Introduction to Social Psychology* published in 1912, he has outlined several characteristics of purposive behaviour. Some of those characteristics are as under :

1. Purposive behaviour is spontaneous. Seeing the purpose or end, such behaviour is automatically evoked. Seeing a cat (an end) a dog immediately attacks upon it.
2. Purposive behaviour, once started, continues for some time even after the goal stimulus has been removed. Even after the cat has

entered into a safe place, the dog continues to be in the mood of attack for sometime.

3. In purpose behaviour the duration of the activity varies. If the organism remains unable to reach his goal by doing a certain activity, he goes on making changes in his activity till he reaches the goal.
4. Purposive act terminates when the organism has reached the goal.
5. A goal-seeking behaviour improves with repetition. In other words, some elements of learning were involved in purposive behaviour although McDougall was not in much favour for emphasizing this factor.

BASIC FEATURES OF MCDOUGALL'S HORMIC PSYCHOLOGY

Life-Sketch

William McDougall (1871-1938) was an Englishman by birth who developed his systematic viewpoint about psychology when he left England for United States in 1920. He received his early medical training at Cambridge University and at the University of London. He had also some occasions to come in contact with G.E. Muller at Gottingen University. In between 1899 and 1900, he was also a member of Cambridge Anthropological Expedition to the Torres Stratis. On returning to England, he became a reader in University College, London where he also developed a small psychological laboratory. For the period of 1904-1920 he became "Wilde Reader in Mental philosophy" at Oxford University. He also served in British Medical Corps during World War I. Here he worked with patients having different type of mental disorders. These experiences led him to publish a book *Outline of Abnormal Psychology* in 1926. In 1920 he went to Harvard University in United States to fill the post which was once occupied by William James, a person for whom McDougall had maximum respect and admiration. He developed his system of hormic psychology in a scientific way in America but it can hardly be said that America accepted him. In 1927 he became the head of the department of psychology at Duke University where he remained until his death in 1938.

His major books were: *Physiology Psychology* (1905), *Body and Mind* (1911), *Outline of Abnormal Psychology* (1926), *Introduction to Social Psychology* (1908 and subsequent editions), *Psychology, the study of Behaviour* (1912), *Outline of Psychology* (1923). Out of these books, books on social psychology and abnormal psychology became very popular.

McDougall's System

McDougall's contribution to psychology may be systematized as under :

1. *Definition of Psychology*

In his first book *Physiological psychology* published in 1905, he defined psychology as "the positive science of conduct of living creatures." By conduct, he meant *behaviour* of the living creatures. In this way we find that Watson was not the first person to define psychology as the science of behaviour. Moreover, McDougall had also intended to emphasize that mental processes, in fact, produce activity or behaviour in the living organisms. Such mental processes should be studied by methods other than the method of introspection. These activities ultimately lead the person to some goal or end.

2. *Heredity : The Lamarckian experiment*

McDougall accepted the theory of Lamarck who had shown that there occurs hereditary transmission of acquired characteristics. In other words, the acquired characteristics of the organism are transmitted through genes from one generation to other. McDougall was opposed to the fact that human behaviour could be interpreted in terms of learning. To prove hereditary transmission of acquired characteristics, McDougall undertook a long-range experiment in 1920. In this experiment he trained twenty-four generations of rats. Rats were placed in tank with two exits—a brightly illuminated exit and a dimly illuminated exit. The former was incorrect path to escape whereas the latter was the correct path to escape. Accordingly, when the rats escaped by the brightly illuminated exit, they received electric shock. In each generation only half of the rats received training. The whole experiment continued through twenty-four generations for nearly ten years. In each generation the average number of errors committed by rats were calculated. McDougall presented in his last report that the rats in the untrained group (control group) made an average of 125 errors before they learnt to escape by the correct exit while those in the trained group (experimental group) made an average of only 25 errors in learning the same thing. On the basis of this results, McDougall found a very clear support for the validity of Lamarckian theory.

This study has, however, been criticized and some contrary evidences have also been reported. Major criticisms have been done regarding the experimental procedures and selective breeding techniques. His rats had died and were replaced. Due to these drawbacks William Sahakian (1975) had called McDougall's this experiment as an "abortive attempt". However, there had been some support to McDougall"s stand. For example, Kuo (1928) conducted experiments on cats and reported that it is heredity and not the environment that determines the behaviour. In recent days there has, however, been modest revival of the Lamarckian theory and the experimental findings of McDougall. Hence, we finally conclude that McDougall's emphasis upon heredity in determination of behaviour was not cent per cent wrong.

3. *Theory of Instincts*

McDougall had pointed out that the activities led the person to some goal or end. Such activities are known as *purposive activities* or *behaviour.* He has postulated that if these activities lead the person to a goal or end, there must be some kind of energy behind those activities. He termed this energy as *instinctive energy.* In this book *Introduction to Psychology* (1908), he outlined his most famous theory of instinct. He has defined instinct as inherited psychophysical dispositions which determine the person, "to perceive or to pay attention to objects of a certain class, to experience an emotional excitement... and to act in regard to it in a particular manner." (McDougall, 1908: 35). McDougall considered instincts as "release mechanism or just easily exploding containers of energy". Thus for him, instinct is the storage of potential energy that is liberated into appropriate channels when that is excited.

For McDougall, instinct is one of the vital forces that strives the organism towards some sort of goal. It has following three *aspects* or *functions :*

(i) ***Cognitive or perceptual aspect*** : This relates to our perceptual predisposition to notice some stimuli. For example, to perceive certain food odours when one is hungry constitutes the cognitive aspect of instinct.

(ii) ***Conative or motivational aspect*** : This relates to our ability to move towards the final goal. For example, having perceived certain food odours, we move towards taking that food.

(iii) ***Affective or emotional aspect*** : This is the central or main part of the instinct. It relates to the feeling involved in the instinct. For example, feeling of fear is involved in the escape mechanism.

All these three aspects of instinct make a complete mental act. McDougall has pointed out that the affective or the emotional aspect of instinct is inherited and therefore, no modification in it is possible through experience or learning. However, the perceptual and motivational aspects can be changed by experience or learning.

In 1908 McDougall listed twelve major instincts in the first edition of his famous book *Introduction to Social Psychology.* Subsequently he revised the list and in 1932 the list expanded to seventeen. By this time, he had substituted the term *propensity* for instinct because that term came into some considerable disfavour and criticism. However, his basic idea underlying the term propensity remained the same. The original list of twelve instincts include hunger, rejection of certain substances, escape, curiosity, fight or pugnacity, sex, maternal or paternal, gregariousness, self-assertion, self abasement (submission), acquisition and construction. Finally, the number of instinct was reduced to seven, each with a certain emotion. These seven instincts were recognized as primary instincts. This list is presented below :

Instinct	*Emotion*
Rejection	Disgust
Fight	Anger
Self-assertion	Elation, positive self-feeling
Curiosity	Wonder
Maternal (Paternal)	Tender emotion
Self-abasement	Subjection, negative self-feeling
Escape	fear.

The remaining five instincts listed originally, namely, sex, gregariousness, hunger, acquisition and construction did not seem to have any definite and identifiable emotion. By 1932, the original list of twelve instincts had been extended to seventeen, that is, five new instincts were included. They were: comfort, rest or sleep, migration, laughter, appeal or crying aloud for assistance.

McDougall considered these instincts to be very important. These instincts were considered highly important because directly or indirectly they were considered to be "prime movers of all activity"—and tend to determine "the ends of all activities and supply of driving power." (McDougall, 1908:44).

McDougall has also talked about a new kind of modification of the instincts. Such modification may take place through what is called combination of several instincts towards the same object. The resulting state is known as *sentiments*. For example, social sentiment may result from combination of love, self-assertion and tenderness. Likewise, a wife's love towards her husband may combine a sex instinct and a maternal instinct.

4. *Group Mind*

As we know, the most popular and important aspect of McDougall's hormic psychology was his theory of instinct. There were several criticisms of the theory of instinct. One important criticism done by behaviourists was that his instinct theory failed to explain the behaviour of people in group, crowd and in other aggregates. To answer this criticism McDougall developed the concept of group mind in his book *The Group Mind* (1920). McDougall (1020 : 15) defined group mind as under :

"It (group mind) consists of the same stuff as individual minds, its threads and parts lie within these minds but the parts in the several individual minds reciprocally imply and compliment one another and make up the system which consists wholly of them."

It is obvious that for McDougall the behaviour of people in any congregation is explained in terms of group mind that tends to operate above and beyond the individual minds of which that (group mind) comprises. Thus there is some interactive effects among the individuals who constituted the group. The question now arises is: what factor binds the individual minds together which ultimately result in group mind ? McDougall's answer to this question was the intensity of emotions involved. For example, let us take violent behaviour of a mob of students burning a government bus. In such mob emotions reached such a peak that can't be found in emotionality of anyone individual mind. All students participating in the mob are caught in such intense wave of emotionality that they loose their individuality.

McDougall's concept of group mind was, however, could not be as popular as that of his theory of instinct. Most of the psychologist considered his explanation of group mind as descriptive rather than explanatory.

5. *Mind-body problem*

McDougall was also much concerned with mind and body problem. For him, the seat of conscious mental activity was synapse. In 1911 he introduced the doctrine of soul. For him, the soul was nothing but a process or sum of definite capacities for psychophysical interaction. Later, he extended his doctrine of soul by formulating the doctrine of animism. According to the doctrine of animism even the inorganic matter seemed to have a bit of soul. Organic matter had, however, a greater degree of soul through the various stages of evolution. Later, as a chairman of the department of psychology at Duke University, he provided a strong support to J.B. Rhine's psychic researches that left a scar on the department of psychology for many years even after the death of William McDougall.

On the whole, we can say that McDougall stressed the importance of instincts and goal-seeking behaviour. He also developed a new social psychology. Despite this, he has been negatively evaluated by many psychologists. Today, with almost near complete decline of McDougall's psychology, the concept of instinct had been practically dropped from psychology. Some psychologists have said that McDougall's theories can't be experimentally tested. Modern social psychologists feel that man's social nature is not the product of his instincts rather of social and cultural environment. The most severe criticism of McDougall was done by J.B. Watson, the founder of behaviourism. He lodged a strong protest against McDougall's dualistic and anti-mechanistic concepts. It is said that with rise of behaviourism in America, McDougall's influence and popularity began to be lost rapidly. McDougall, however, was also critical of behaviourism. As he said, "I regard Dr. Watson as a good man gone wrong... a bold pioneer whose enthusiasm in the cause of reform in psychology has carried him too far... and landed him in ditch..." (McDougall, 1924 : 14).

WOODWORTH'S DYNAMIC PSYCHOLOGY

We have already considered Robert Sessions Woodworth (1869-1962) as a functional psychologist in chapter seven. Therefore, we shall not repeat here his biographical sketch made already in chapter seven.

Woodworth was a contemporary of William McDougall. We can also regard Woodworth as successor to McDougall in the sense that after McDougall he carried a psychology that was based upon motivation and drive. Woodworth himself said that he had no intention to establish a formal system in psychology. But, like McDougall, he was very much interested in the study of psychology of motivation. Perhaps, due to this emphasis, he characterized his psychology as *dynamic psychology*. He also published a book named *Dynamic Psychology* in 1917 and republished it in 1957. His viewpoints regarding the systematic position of dynamic psychology can be presented under the following major heads :

1. *Definition and subject-matter of psychology*

Woodworth defined psychology as science of both consciousness and behaviour. In this way, he tried to bring opposing viewpoints of structuralism and behaviourism into a harmony. He pointed out that to restrict oneself to the study of mere motor acts as behaviourists had done, would not yield a whole and complete account because such motor acts were directly related to the state of conscious experiences that immediately precede. Therefore, in order to get a complete understanding and account of organism, it was essential to study the conscious experiences coming prior to their overt manifestations. Accordingly, he suggested that the method of introspection should not be discarded from psychology but at the same time, he cautioned that this method should not be regarded as the *only* method of psychology. In fact, his intention was to point out that introspection should be included in psychology as one of the supplementary methods.

Woodworth was of view that the knowledge of stimulus response relationship was the primary base from which psychological studies grow. He preferred to start with *response* and then, in investigating its antecedent conditions rather than in the *control* of the response by various specific factors. There were several *antecedent causes* of response. Stimulus was simply one such cause or factor. Other factors were the structure of the organism, its physical energy, etc. In this way, he made it clear that stimulus-organism-response (S-O-R) is a better formula than simply stimulus-response (S-R). He has explained the relationship of S-O-R with the help of a loaded gun. As in a loaded gun the action (firing) depends not only upon pulling the trigger (stimulus) but also upon the structure of gun and upon the energy contained in bullet so also the response depends not only the stimulus but also upon the type of organism and its physical and psychological energy.

2. *Mechanism and Drive*

One basic question is : In what sense Woodworth was concerned with dynamics of behaviour ? The answer to this basic question was his distinction between mechanism and drive. Mechanism tends to explain *how* an activity is performed. Drive tends to explain why an activity is performed. At Columbia University, Woodworth was very much impressed by series of Thorndike's experiments on cats in the puzzle boxes. Applying his distinction between mechanism and drive, he pointed out that the cat's activities like biting, pushing, clawings, scratchings, etc., were the example of mechanism and hunger was the example of drive. But mechanism does not remain always separate from drive. The distinction between the two is not always absolute. A drive can be accepted as mechanism or as activities of nervous system facilitating a particular action and inhibiting other. For example, in swimming competition once the whistle sounds, the person is driven to drive and swim ahead. Mechanism also serves as a basis for drives. In other words, what started out to be a merely mechanism may became later on a drive for other activities. For example, a child who has learnt to read, write and comprehend the books will purchase book, attend library, ask parents to attend book fair, comprehending books taken on the function of its own drive. In this way Woodworth anticipated much ahead the famous concept of *functional autonomy* of motivation enunciated later by Gordon Allport. This concept of Allport more or less tells the same thing.

3. *Learning*

Learning was one of the central topics of Woodworth's Dynamic Psychology. He pointed out that activities like learning, memory, thinking etc., might also be evaluated in terms of mechanism. Learning, as a mechanism, needs a drive to start with but once started, it (learning) takes its own driving properties through practice. Thus in learning a particular S-O-R connection is established through practice or exercise. In establishing such connection both heredity and environment play an important role. All these have been nicely incorporated in his book *Experimental Psychology* published in 1939 and later revised by Harold Schlosberg in 1954. This book still happens to be one of major textbooks in psychology.

On the whole, it can be said that Woodworth very firmly established the role of motivation in psychology and this became an important source of inspiration to later learning theorists. With his emphasis upon O (organism), he inspired people to study the details of physiological psychology. His *Experimental Psychology* continues to be an unparallel textbook in psychology emphasizing this aspect of psychology. The latest revision of the book has been done by L. A. Riggs and J. W. Kling in 1984.

COMPARISON BETWEEN WOODWORTH AND McDOUGALL

There are some similarities and contrasts between Woodworth's system and McDougall's system. The basic point of similarity is that both persons based their systems upon a common core, that is, motivation. However, McDougall named it as *instinct* and Woodworth named it as *drive.* Another point of similarity is that both persons have regarded that human beings are borned with inborn gifts or activities. Besides these similarities, major points of *distinction* between Woodworth and McDougall are as under :

(i) For McDougall instinct does not take on its own motivational or driving force. Therefore, no concept of mechanism in Woodworth's sense can develop. Woodworth, on the other hand, has pointed out that drives may take on the properties of mechanism because they are less specific and don't possess specific built-in power of direction.

(ii) As stated above, both have agreed that human beings are born with some abilities or capacities. These capacities for McDougall, remain in dormant stage unless they are stimulated by some instinctual forces. For Woodworth, this is not necessarily the case. These inborn capacities can be taken at par with the drives themselves. Therefore, much like drives, they (capacities) have some native power for producing activities. In other words, such drive-like state can, after some time, became mechanisms having their own driving power for fulfilment.

Thus, despite some similarities, McDougall differs from Woodworth in some important way.

CHAPTER HIGHLIGHTS

1. William McDougall developed the system of hormic psychology. The central theme of hormic psychology is the goal or end drives the human beings for performing some activities without our awareness although sometimes a kind of vague awareness is involved. Such purposive behaviour is spontaneous and goal-directed.
2. McDougall defined psychology as the study of the conduct of living creatures. By conduct, he meant the behaviour of the living creatures. Thus even before Watson, psychology was defined as the study of behaviour. McDougall tried to explain behaviour in terms of heredity transmission through genes. He had accepted the theory of Lamark that emphasized upon hereditary transmission of acquired characteristics of the organism. He established a support for this theory by conducting experiments on rats through their twenty-four generations.
3. McDougall is well-known in psychology for his theory of instinct. For him, instincts is an inherited psychophysical disposition. It has three aspects or functions—cognitive aspect, cognitive aspect, and affective aspect. Of these three aspects, affective or emotional aspect is inherited and therefore, there can be no modification in it. However, cognitive and conative aspects can be changed by experience or learning. In 1908, McDougall had listed twelve major instincts which was later reduced to seven primary instincts each with a definite emotional accompaniment. McDougall had considered these instincts as the prime movers of our activities.

4. McDougall also developed the concept of group mind in order to meet the criticism regarding his instinct theory done by behaviourists. Group mind is something which operates above and beyond the individual minds of which that (group mind) comprises. The intensity of emotions involved in the congregation of people binds the individual minds together which ultimately results in group mind. He also took the issue of mind-body problem. For him, the seat of conscious mental activity is synapse or point of connections between neurons. In 1911 he introduced the doctrine of soul which was later extended and expanded by the doctrine of animism.
5. R. S. Woodworth formulated his dynamic psychology in 1917. He defined psychology as the science of both consciousness and behaviour. He replaced S-R formula with S-O-R formula and took the organism itself to be one of the major antecedent forces that produces the responses. He was deeply concerned with explaining the dynamics of behaviour. Therefore, he developed the concept of *mechanism* and *drive*. Mechanism tends to explain *how* an activity is performed and drive tends to explain *why* an activity is performed. The distinction between mechanism and drive is, however, not absolute.
6. There are some similarities between McDougall and Woodworth. Despite these similarities, there are some points of distinctions between these two persons.

REVIEW QUESTIONS

1. Assess the contributions of William McDougall ? Why does his theory of instinct sparke the behaviourists ?
2. Critically examine the contributions of R. S. Woodworth as a dynamic psychologist.
3. Make a comparative study of William McDougall and R. S. Woodworth with respect to their contributions made in the field of psychology.

■

CHAPTER 17

HUMANISTIC PSYCHOLOGY

CHAPTER PREVIEW

The humanistic psychology has been regarded as a third force in psychology, the first force being psychoanalysis and the second force being behaviourism. This movement (and not a system) started taking shape in early 1960s. Abraham Maslow's name is closely associated with this movement because he is regarded as spiritual father of humanism in America.

Humanistic psychology emphasizes person as a whole and explains behaviour in terms of the entire life history. Like other systems, it has some antecedent forces which were instrumental in its emergence. The psychology of William James, existential psychology and the early efforts towards humanism were among the primary forces.

Rogers who formulated self-theory is an important contributor to humanistic psychology. He emphasized upon three important constructs—organism, self and self-actualization.

Maslow's self-actualization theory has been another important innovation. He formulated the concept of need hierarchy in which five needs such as physiological needs, safety needs, love and belongingness need, esteem needs and self-actualization needs are arranged in order of prepotency. Self actualization, for him, is an umbrella need that covers seventeen metaneeds. Self-actualization means to reach the peak of one's potential so that one becomes a fully functioning person.

The term humanistic psychology was coined in 1962 by a group of psychologists under the leadership of Abraham Maslow who was mainly interested in providing an important theoretical alternative to *two* most influential forces or currents in psychology—psychoanalysis and behaviourism. Maslow called it as *third force of psychology*. It is a move-ment in psychology, that is a collection of number of lines and thoughts of different schools. It is never a system of single person or a group of persons.

Since 1950s the opponents of the two forces—psychoanalysis and behaviourism, were criticizing them. It was being said that behaviourism was too cold and lacking interest in real understanding of human beings. This movement considered man as a passive victim of the stimuli present in the environment. This movement also fails to recognize the person's growth, potentialities and self-actualization that distinguish him from laboratory animals like rats, pigeons, etc. Bugental (1967) has rightly said that behaviourism reduced the person "to a large white rat or a slower computer'.

Some psychologists also voiced against the basic tenets of psychoanalysis that considered man as the products of instincts and conflicts only. Criticizing psychoanalysis, Maslow argued that by focusing upon abnormal people alone how can psychoanalysis explain the behaviour of a normal and mentally healthy people ? It means a psychoanalyst can't explain the positive side of the person. Maslow (1954 : 234) has rightly commented. "The study of crippled, stutterer, immature and unhealthy specimens can yield only a cripple psychology and cripple philosophy".

The humanistic psychology has tried to present a radically different picture of human nature. According to Abraham Maslow, who is considered as *spiritual father of humanism* in America, human beings are considered basically good and worthy of respect and self-actualization. If the environmental conditions are favourable, persons will readily move towards realization of their underlying potentialities and abilities. Thus humanistic psychology by opposing the pessimism, conflict and despair of psychoanalysis on the one hand and "robot" view of human beings of behaviourism on the other hand, has tried to emphasize upon potential for healthy and creative growth of human beings.

BASIC TENETS OF HUMANISTIC PSYCHOLOGY

As it has been stated above, humanistic psychology is not a single organized theory or system. It is a movement which incorporates psychologists of different lines and thoughts. Therefore, all humanistic psychologists like all structuralists of functionalists, don't think exactly alike. However, there are some common threads that bind them together. Buhler (1971) who is considered as one of the important humanistic psychologists, has spelled out some of the basic tenets of humanistic psychology in her encouraging and clear style. Those tenets, with some modifications, are presented below :

1. *Person as an whole*

The person as an integrated, unique and organized whole is the main subject of humanistic psychology. The humanistic psychologists emphasize upon understanding rather than explaining human behaviour. Maslow has pointed out that psychologists, for a considerable period, have concentrated only upon minute analysis of behaviour neglecting the study of whole person which, in fact, can yield more valuable information.

2. *Emphasis upon entire life history*

The humanistic psychology is concerned with collecting knowledge of a person's entire life history. For understanding the person as an integrated whole, it is essential that the entire life history of the person is taken into account. Thus Buhler intended to include the study of entire life cycle for complete understanding of the person. In emphasizing upon such cycle he gave considerable importance to human existence and intention. By intention he meant the experiences of the person regarding his own identity.

3. *Self-actualization as life goals*

Humanistic psychology is not only concerned with satisfaction of biological needs and instincts but is also concerned with self-realization or self-actualization as the basic life goal. Maslow emphasized upon such goal to be highly motivating to persons.

4. *Person's inner nature*

As we know, Freud had considered man's nature as necessarily of evil character which, if left uncontrolled, would lead to destruction of others as well as to self. Contrary to this view of Freud, humanistic psychologists have pointed out man's nature is basically good. The evil and destructive forces in a person arises from a bad environment rather than from anything rotten within the person.

5. *Deemphasis upon animal's researches*

Humanistic psychologists have deemphasized upon animal researches. They have considered these animals researches as irrelevant because they ignore the basic characteristics of human beings such as ideals, values, art, humour, etc. Maslow and his supporters have pointed out that behaviourism had emphasized upon such animal researches too much. They further pointed out that behaviourism had "dehumanized" the persons who were nothing but simply a machine that consisted of chains of conditioned and unconditioned reflexes. Humanistic psychologists made distinction between human behaviour and animal behaviour and concentrated upon the former. For them, the study of animal behaviour gives no clue to understanding about the basic nature of human beings.

6. *Creative potentiality*

Humanistic psychologists have considered creativeness as a common characteristic to human nature. Maslow (1970) is of view that creativity is potentially present in all persons at birth. It becomes a universal human function that leads to different forms of self-expression.

Prior to Maslow, Adler had also stressed the idea of creative self but it remained for Maslow to emphasize upon it a scientific way.

7. *Emphasis upon psychological health*

Humanistic psychology criticized the orthodox Freudian psychoanalysis by branding it to be one-sided because it simply concentrated upon the abnormal part of human behaviour. Maslow has strongly emphasized that even the mental illness cannot be properly understood without understanding the mental health of the persons. If one studied only crippled and immature persons, it will produce only a "crippled" psychology. Therefore, he has strongly stressed upon the study of the self-actualizing and psychologically healthy persons as the primary care and base for understanding human behaviour.

It is obvious, therefore, that the humanistic psychology gives overall emphasis upon "healthy functioning of human beings", his "modes of living" and his "goals in life".

ANTECEDENT FORCES

Like any other movement in psychology, humanistic psychology has also its antecendent conditions and not that it suddenly sprang up in the writings of Abraham Maslow, Carl Rogers, etc. Its major antecedent forces may be outlined as under :

1. *The Psychology of William James*

William James demonstrated in his writings a strong concern for life's problems. In fact, his entire theory of pragmatism demonstrated his passionate concern for the various kinds of human problems and needs. In his famous book *Principles of Psychology,* he included a chapter on *self* which has influenced other self-theorists directly or indirectly to a greater extent. He had divided this self into four categories—*material self, social self, spiritual self* and *pure ego*. The material self comprises one's own possessions, body and friends. Social self comprises one's interactions with other persons. Spiritual self comprises one's potentialities and various mental functions. The pure ego was like the 'I' or self as knower. This last concept, that is, pure ego was the most important for modern self-theorists.

2. *Important self-theorists*

The emergence of humanistic psychology was to a greater extent influenced by the concept of self and by the various self theorists because such concept was the heart of humanistic psychology. Carl Rogers' self theory may be put as one such example. G.H. Mead (1934) published a book in which he highlighted the concept of self as an object of awareness rather than a series of functions of processes. He was of view that at birth the person has no self. As he matures, he learns to think and have certain attitudes and feelings towards himself and that way gradually the self emerges. In emergence of self he also recognized the importance of social forces. As a consequence of encounter with various social groups and forces, he may develop various types of self. Thus like William James, Mead also recognized the importance of different types of self. Snygg and Coombs (1949) have emphasized upon the phenomenal self as one immediate antecedent factor of the humanistic psychology.

3. ***Existential psychology***

Existential psychology has given strong influence upon the humanistic movement. Existential psychology is mainly concerned with a person's consciousness, his feelings, moods, as well as his various personal experiences as they relate to his existence in the world. Therefore, the basic aim of existential psychology is to understand his total existential reality. In so aiming it has influenced the humanistic psychology directly. Since the existential psychology and the humanistic psychology have much in common, the former has also been recognized as *third force* in psychology.

4. ***Early efforts towards humanism***

The emergence of humanistic psychology has also been influenced by early efforts of philanthropists towards human welfare. During the Renaissance and even before, there was a strong concern for those who were considered somehow less fortunate. These people demonstrated altruism and charity towards humanism. Such concern towards humanism influenced the thinking of several psychologists who later established the humanistic psychology.

In this way we find that there were several sources that provided inspiration to psychologists who ultimately established the humanistic psychology as movement in psychology.

ROGERS' SELF THEORY
OR
ROGERS' PERSON-CENTERED THEORY

Concepts related to self are central to humanistic theories. As we know, there are several such theories which, in general, focus upon subjective perception of self, the world and the self within the world. Of the various humanistic theories, two theories are very important and influential—Rogerss' self theory and Maslow's self-actualization theory.

Carl Rogers (1902–1987) was born in Illinois in 1902. In 1924 he graduated from the University of Wisconsin. Subsequently, he joined Union Theological Seminary in New York City. Then he went to Teacher's College at Columbia University from where he received his Ph. D. in 1931. He also taught at several universities including University of Chicago, University of Wisconsin and Ohio State University. Among his important publications were *Counselling and Psychotherapy* (1942) and *Client Centered Therapy* (1951).

Roger's self theory is based upon his experiences as a client centered psychotherapist or as a non-directive psychotherapist. His method of treatment is called client-centered therapy. In this method the patient (called client) makes interaction with the therapist in such a way that client gradually becomes aware of his conflict, wishes and forces. The role of therapist is passive in the sense that he never directly gives any advice but simply reflects the feelings of the client. Based upon such therapeutic influences, he developed his self theory which is also called as person-centered theory. This is a holistic theory and therefore, it can be outlined or divided only arbitrarily. However, the basic rubrics of the theory can be understood in terms of its fundamental constructs. The following *three* constructs are important in Roger's theory :

1. *Organism*

Ordinarily in psychology organism refers to biological being that responds to various stimuli in the environment. But Rogers has used this term in slightly different sense. For him, organism refers to totality of experiences going on within the whole individual at a particular moment. Thus organism is considered as a locus of all experiences varying from our own perception of events that occur within our body to our perception of events that occur in the external world.

2. *Self*

We have just seen that for Rogers organism has a direct reference to the totality of experiences. The totality of experiences constitutes both conscious and unconscious experiences. Such totality of experiences constitute *phenomenal field* or *perceptual field*. Thus the experiences of phenomenal field are inner experiences that "can never be known to another except through empathic inference and then can never be perfectly known". (Rogers, 1959 : 210). Although these experiences are inner experiences of the organism, the sources may either be external, internal or both.

From this perceptual field or totality of experiences, the self emerges. In infancy when a portion of phenomenal field becomes personalized and differentiated as "I" or "me" experiences, the self is said to have formed. For Rogers, the self is a fluid, changing gestalt and it may be either in awareness or out of awareness. With the development of self, the infant begins to understand good or bad as well as it tries to evaluate its experiences as positive or negative. For Rogers, this self is not a separate dimension of personality as is Freud's notion of ego or Jung's concept of self. For him, an individual does not possess a self rather self incorporates the whole organism, that is, what one really is on the organismic level. There are two subsystems of *self—self-concept* and *ideal self* (Rogers, 1959 : 200 – 203).

Self-concept consists of all those aspects of experiences which are perceived by the person in awareness. Such experiences may not sometimes be perceived accurately. Once the self-concept of the person is formed, change and further learning become difficult, if not impossible. Those experiences which are inconsistent with the self-concept are either distorted or denied by the individual. Self-concept is *different* from real self or organismic self. Self-concept is limited to only those experiences with which we are aware. But organismic self may also include those experiences which are beyond our awareness. For example, adrenal gland is the part of our organismic self but unless it malfunctions, that is overreacts or underreacts that causes concern, it is not likely to be the part of our self-concept.

Another subsystem of the self is the *ideal self* that consists of experiences relating to what one thinks one ought to be and would like to be. Therefore, it contains all those attributes or characteristics that one aspires to possess. Thus the concept of ideal self is basically equivalent to the concept of superego in Freudian theory. A wider gap between the ideal self and the perceived self indicates incongruence and psychologically unhealthy personality.

What is *relationship* between the self and the organism ? We have seen that the self emerges out of the experiences of organism. In a psychologically healthy person those experiences that constitute self are in line with the experiences of the organism. In case, these two are not in congruent with each other, anxiety results and the person becomes defensive. The two major defenses are *distortion* and *denial.* In distortion the person misinterprets an experience so that it fits well with some aspects of self-concept. In denial the expereince is not perceived in awareness. Of these two, distortion is more common than denial. If the amount of anxiety is high, persons' defenses do not work and his personality becomes disorganized. Under such condition of incongruence the person is given psychotherapy.

Rogers has also suggested that both the self-concept and the ideal self can be operationally measured with the help of Q-sort and content analysis.

3. *Self-actualization*

Self-actualization is a common concept shared by many humanistic psychologists. Both stalwarts of humanistic psychology, that is, Rogers and Maslow, share this common concept. Rogers assumed that every person has an inherent tendency to actualize his unique potential. He claimed that self-actualization is a growth force that is a part of person's heredity. This not only includes biological potentials but also involves a psychological growth and a moving towards maintaining and enhancing the organism. It has several characteristics. *First*, self-actualization gradually develops from simple to complex. As the person grows richer in his experiences, his self can be better actualized that ultimately allows for greater development of creativity. It means that such experiences make the person more creative. *Second*, self-actualization is a dynamic force. Persons who have adequate degree of self-actualization always keep moving forward. Such persons never like to stop at a particular point. They always have faith in fulfilling their self-potential in socially approved way. Rogers recognized two basic needs that are related to the self-actualization. They are need for positive regards of others and the need for *self-regard*. Both these needs are learnt during infancy when the infant is loved and cared by his mother.

Rogers' self theory has been criticized. It is said that his theory has ignored the unconscious which plays a very important role in controlling behaviour. Smith (1950) has pointed out that Rogers' theory is based upon a naive type of phenomenology. Despite some criticisms Rogers' emphasis upon self has encouraged a lot of researches and empirical findings. However, not all researches and findings are in his favour.

MASLOW'S SELF-ACTUALIZATION THEORY

Abraham Maslow (1908–1970) was born on April 1, 1908 in New York and took all his academic degree from this University of Wisconsin. He took his Ph. D. degree from this University in 1934. He taught at this University for short period. In 1935 he returned to New York to join as E.L. Thorndike's research assistant to Teacher's College, Columbia University. Later, he joined the faculty at Brooklyn College where he remained until 1951. From 1951 to 1969 Maslow taught at Brandies University in Waltham, Massachusetts. It was during this period (1951–1969) that he started writing extensively in various journals. It was also during these years that he emerged as the leading figure of the *third force* in psychology. His important publications were : *Motivation and Personality* (1970), *Toward a Psychology of Being* (1968) and *The Further Reaches of Human Nature* (1971).

Maslow has been considered as the spiritual father of the humanistic psychology. Like Rogers, he took the optimistic view about human nature. He believes that people have some inherent potentials and capacity for kindness, love, generosity, etc., which flourish if given a favourable social environment. But an unfavourable social environment leads to the repression of those potentials and capacities.

His self-actualization theory has been best explained in terms of the motivational processes. Maslow is of view that human motives are innate and they are arranged in the ascending hierarchy of potency or priority. Before we discuss his hierarchical view of motivation, it is essential to examine his basic assumptions about motivation :

(i) Maslow assumed a holistic approach to motivation. It means, for him, the whole individual and not his any single part or function, is motivated. If we attempt to isolate motive from the whole individual and study it, it will be inaccurate and misleading. For example, in sex motive not only the genitals are stimulated but also the brain, some endocrine glands, intestines, and thus the whole organism is motivated.

(ii) Organism is continually motivated by one need or the other. If one need of the person is satisfied, another need automatically arises and guides our behaviour. For example, if the hunger and thirst need (basic physiological needs) are satisfied, he will feel the need for security and protection.

(iii) Motivation is usually complex and the complexity of motivation is due to the unconscious elements of the drive. Thus Maslow also recognized the existence of unconscious motivation. Due to this recognition, he differs from Allport who mainly emphasized upon conscious motivation.

(iv) All people in different cultures may differ in *manner* in which people express their physiological needs like need for food, water, sex, etc. but these fundamental needs remain the same in all people.

(v) The various needs of the persons can be arranged in a hierarchy of potency or priority.

Maslow's theory of hierarchy of needs recognizes five needs in order of their prepotency—physiological needs, safety needs, love and belongingness need, esteem need, and self-actualization need. He separated these five needs. The lower level need consists of physiological needs and safety needs whereas the higher level need consists of love and belongingness need, esteem need and self-actualization need. The basic idea behind arranging these five needs into a hierarchy is that lower level needs must be satisfied before higher level needs becomes motivators of human behaviour. Thus lower level needs have a prepotency over the high level need because if they are not satisfied, the higher level needs will no longer emerge and the persons will return to unsatisfied lower level needs. These various needs may be discussed as under :

1. ***Physiological needs***

Physiological needs are the basic needs that include need for food, water, oxygen, temperature, sex, etc. These needs are most prepotent and if these needs are not satisfied, no other higher needs will originate. For example, if the person is strongly hunger, he will never think of safety, love and respect for self and others. There are *two* basic characteristics of physiological needs :

(i) Physiological needs have their recurrent nature. Hence, they are cyclic needs. They can be fully satisfied at a particular time but after a lapse of certain period of time, they again tend to reoccur. A person's need for hunger may be fully satisfied at a particular time by eating but after some time again that need may arise.

(ii) Another characteristic of physiological needs is that they can be wholly satisfied. This is not true in case of other higher needs.

2. ***Safety needs***

Safety needs include need for physical security, protection, stability, freedom from anxiety, danger and chaos. Safety needs arise when the physiological needs have been satisfied or relatively satisfied. Safety needs differ from the physiological needs in the sense that they can't be wholly satiated or satisfied. For a healthy adult persons safety needs are not important motivators. But for children these needs are great motivators. However, during emergency situations like war, accidents, fire, etc., safety needs become the prime source of motivators.

In developed countries like America, Russia, etc. both the physiological needs as well as the safety needs are not the prime motivators of behaviour because these lower level needs remain automatically satisfied to most people.

3. ***Love and belongingness needs***

Love and belongingness need become effective as motivators only when the above two needs have been satisfied or relatively satisfied. These needs include our urge for friendship, for belonging to a group, and for showing love and affection to our families. Need for having a partner such as wife or husband also come under this category. Maslow has pointed out that without the fulfillment of love needs the children as well as the adults can't grow into a developed personality having sound psychological health. Adults who are deprived of the satisfactions of these needs often become cynical and self-defeating in interpersonal relationship.

4. ***Esteem needs***

Esteem needs come into existence at the next level of hierarchy when the previous three types of needs have been fulfilled. These needs include *two* sets of need. The first set includes needs for strength, competence, self-confidence, independence mastery, etc. The second set includes needs for prestige, fame, dominance, dignity and appreciation. In fact, the second set of need is derived from the first set. Maslow (1970) has pointed out that satisfaction of self-esteem needs produces feelings like self-confidence, capability, strength, worth, etc. and thwarting of these needs lead to feelings of inferiority, helplessness, weakness, etc. Esteem needs of Maslow are similar to Alfred Adler's striving for superiority and Erik Erikson's need for mastery.

5. ***Need for self-actualization***

Self-actualization need is fulfilled only when the other needs at lower hierarchy are satisfied. Self-actualization refers to the desire for self-fulfillment, to realize one's all potentials, to become what one wishes and to be creative in true sense of the term (Maslow, 1970). In brief, to self-actualize means to reach the peak of one's potential so that he becomes a fully functioning person. In framing this concept Maslow (1970) has acknowledged his debt to Kurt Goldstein. In fact, need for self-actualization is an umbrella need that covers 17 *metaneeds* or *being values*. The various metaneeds have no hierarchy and are equally potent. Some examples of metaneeds are need for perfection, wholeness, richness, beauty, goodness, truth, etc.

The five needs of the above hierarchy are *conative needs* that is often called by Maslow as *basic needs*. Maslow also coined two terms—*deficient motives* or *deficiency motives* or *D motives* and *growth motives* or *B motives*. D motive includes the first four needs of motivational hierarchy and the B motive includes the self-actualization need or metaneeds.

Maslow also pointed out that only a small percentage of people (about 10 per cent) really become self-actualized. He has enlisted some important characteristics of self-actualizing persons as under :

(i) They have more efficient perception of reality. They have freedom from various kinds of prejudice and bias that ordinarily tend to distort reality.

(ii) They fully understand their self and they lack defensiveness, phoniness and self-defeating guilt.

(iii) They are not artificial nor conventional. Therefore, they have the trait of spontaneity, simplicity and naturalness.

(iv) They show strong interest in problems outside themselves. Most often they have a particular mission to accomplish.

(v) They have a stronger need for privacy and autonomy. They maintain proper detachment. In fact, they can be alone without being lonely. Such people depend more upon their own feelings for growth, etc.

(vi) They have a sense of continued freshness of appreciation. Such people are constantly aware of their good fortunes, friends and health.

(vii) They have more frequent peak experience which means a feeling of complete perfection or ecstasy.

Maslow has also made it clear that self-actualization is not an all-or-none process but rather a matter of degree. No human beings are perfectly self-actualized. Even the self-actualized persons may show frailty, inconsistencies, emotional outbrusts, etc.

Although Maslow's theory has been one the most provocative of the holistic or organismic theories, it has been a bit criticized on the ground that various theoretical concepts included in the theory overlap to a considerable extent. As a consequence of this, it becomes difficult to collect data in a scientific way independently from any one set of concepts.

CRITICISMS OF HUMANISTIC PSYCHOLOGY

Humanistic psychology has been criticized by several, psychologist particularly by behaviourists. Some of the major criticisms are as under :

1. Behaviourists like Skinner often have pointed out that the humanistic psychology is subjective and dualistic in nature. They have further argued that the viewpoints of humanistic psychology often lack empirical validity and their method favours that of introspection which is definitely a unscientific method. Humanistic psychologists have based their findings mainly on the introspective self-reports which are highly unreliable.

2. Some psychologists have felt that the humanistic psychologists have regressed psychology back to vigorous religion and Middle ages where anything must be taken on faith. These psychologists have tried to pull psychology back from the objective efforts of the experimental psychologists.

Despite these criticisms the contributions of humanistic psychologists are much valuable. They have given us a positive and optimistic theory and by emphasizing upon the fact that human nature is basically good, have opened vigorous possibilities for self-realization. Their view point that we are master of own fate rather than merely a product of environmental forces have been one of their major teachings to mankind.

CHAPTER HIGHLIGHTS

1. The term humanistic psychology was coined by a group of psychologists under the leadership of Abraham Maslow in 1962. This was also branded as *third force* in psychology, the remaining two forces being psychoanalysis and behaviourism. In psychology humanistic psychology grew as a movement rather than as a system. Its major emphasis is that human nature is basically good rather than evil as said by Freud and we all move towards realization of their underlying potentialities and abilities.
2. Basically, humanistic psychology tends to emphasize upon seven factors. They are : to study the person as a whole, to stress upon entire life history, to move towards self-actualization, to understand person's inner nature, to deemphasize upon animal's researches, to aim at studying creative potentiality and to emphasize upon psychological health.
3. Humanistic psychology did not grow suddenly. It had some antecedent forces. Those who influenced the emergence of humanistic psychology were William James and some other self-theorists. Apart from this, the existential psychology had also a direct impact upon the emergence of humanistic psychology.
4. There were two major humanistic psychologists whose viewpoints have been considered in this chapter. They are Rogers and Maslow. Rogers' self theory is based upon the clinical experiences of Rogers gained during his person-centered or client-centered therapy. His system has been explained under three headings like organism, self and self-actualization. His basic notion is that organism consists of a totality of experiences from which gradually self emerges. There are two subsystem of self—self-concept and ideal self. The greater the

difference between the self-concept and the ideal self, higher the incongruence and therefore, greater the disorganization in personality. He was also of view that every person has an inherent tendency to actualize his unique potential. This is called self-actualization which is a kind of growth force.

5. Abraham Maslow is well-known for his concept of hierarchical model of motivation. Assuming a holistic approach to motivation, he proposed that there are five basic needs of the persons that have been included in this hierarchical model. They are physiological needs, safety needs, love and belongingness need, esteem needs and need for self-actualization. Of these the last need, that is, self-actualization need lies at the top of the hierarchy where only some people (about 10%) reach. He has outlined several characteristics of self-actualizing person.
6. Humanistic psychology has also been criticized on the ground that it is subjective, dualistic and favours unscientific method like introspection.

REVIEW QUESTIONS

1. Discuss major antecedent forces that led to the growth of humanistic psychology.
2. Assess the contribution of Carl Rogers in development of humanistic psychology.
3. Evaluate the contributions of Abraham Maslow in development of humanistic psychology.
4. "Humanistic psychology has tried to bring psychology back to the prescientific stage." Do you agree with statement ? Give reasons.

■

CHAPTER 18

EXISTENTIAL PSYCHOLOGY

CHAPTER PREVIEW

Like humanistic psychology, the existential psychology is also a movement (and not a system) in psychology. It is also recognized as third force in psychology.

Existential psychology deals with person as such an individual who exists as being-in-the-world (Daesin). Basically, it aims at understanding of a person in his total existential reality. This movement in psychology had a strong antencedent forces. Persons like Soren Kierkegaard, Jean-Paul Sartre, Karl Jaspers, and Martin Heidegger were important forces whose viewpoints led to the emergence of existential psychology.

Ludwig Binswanger was one of the important existential psychologists who emphasized upon being-in-the-world (Daesin). Medard Boss emphasized upon different characteristics essential for human existence. Rollo May also emphasized upon the principle of Daesin or being-in-the-world. For him, there are three important modes of existence—the physical and the psychological needs, the social environment of the persons and the particular relationship with the inner nature.

Finally, existential psychology has been criticized. A comparative study of existential psychology and humanistic psychology has also been done.

As pointed out in the previous chapter, the existential psychology is highly related to humanistic psychology. Together these two psychologies constituted the *third force* in psychology. Like humanistic psychology, the existential psychology was a *movement* rather than a system in psychology.

Although the existential psychology developed in Europe, it gradually spread to America. It arose as a protest to behaviourism that had reduced the human beings to a machine made up of chains of conditioned and unconditioned reflexes. Existential psychologists have claimed that behaviourism has *dehumanized* the persons. They argued that the basic nature of the person is human and in a bid to be scientific and experimental, one should not forget about this basic nature.

BASIC TENETS OF EXISTENTIAL PSYCHOLOGY

Existential psychology has rejected the mechanistic view of the behaviouristic psychology and instead tries to view people as engaged in definite search for meaning. It appears to promise the restoration of meaning to life and tends to bring spiritual awakening and growth that may bring freedom from the conventional shackles of the society (Bugental, 1965). The major tenets of the existential psychology may be outlined as under :

1. Existential psychology deals with person as such an individual who exists as a being-in-the world.
2. The basic aim of the existential psychology is to understand a person in his total existential reality. It takes special interest in those problems which are unique to each individual. Thus it recognizes that every person has a unique personal life with various types of perceptions. It further emphasized that a man is unique not only from inner or personal life but he is also unique from all other species. He is a special creature with some endowments not found in other animals.
3. Existential psychology is basically concerned with a person's consciousness, his modes, emotions, feelings, thinking as well as his various experiences as they are related to the existence in the environment of other people. It always aims at understanding human nature as a whole.
4. There are some common elements that have been emphasized by different existential psychologists. They are : human values, meaning of life, man-to-man relationship, suffering, anxiety, conflict, and death.
5. Existential psychology states that since a person has freedom to choose, he is also responsible for his own existent. What he is and he will be, is the sole responsibility of the person himself. Thus the existential psychologists have rejected any kind of external determinism.
6. The major concerns of the existential psychologists have been areas like personality, psychotherapy and counseling.

ANTECEDENT FORCES

Existential psychology first developed in the existential philosophy of Europe and gradually spread to America. Existential philosophy is concerned with human beings and their unique problems of existence. The basic nation is that a person shares common conflicts and anxieties. He is aware of his own existence and the problems associated with it. Thus it gives emphasis upon the human side of the individual and his personal subjective experiences. In this way the existential philosophy is not a rationalistic nor a materialistic movement. Its beginnings date back in the viewpoints of nineteenth century Danish Philosopher, Soren Kierkegaard. Subsequently, as a European philosophical movement it grew in the philosophies of Martin Heidegger and Karl Jaspers in Germany and in the philosophies of Garbiel Marcel, Jean-Paul Sartre, Maurice Merlean-Ponty in France. These philosophers directly influenced the emergence of existential psychology. Hence, these acted as the immediate antecedent forces for the existential psychology. Some of these forces may be discussed as under :

1. *Soren Kierkegaard* (1813-1855)

Kierkegaard was a Danish philosopher. He holds the view that individuals have a lasting desire for eternity with God while at the same time they realize that their existence was temporal or very short. Moreover, they also recognize their various kinds of trivialities and weakness of their own existence. Despite this, they desire to gain. A conflict, therefore, arises between their recognition of temporal and finite existence and their desire for eternity. Such conflict may later produce various kinds of anxieties and fears.

2. *Jean-Paul Sartre* (1905-1980)

Sartre is a French philosopher. He put one basic question : What is the meaning of a person's existence ? Giving answer to this basic question, he pointed out that man and his existence has no real meaning in this world. He does not believe in God and in persons' thinking that man and his existence can be explained in terms of God. For him consciousness is the main reality although it is difficult to comprehend the origin and continuity of consciousness. In an existential style, he pointed out that man has freedom and choice. If somehow he tries to escape from this freedom and choice, there arises conflict, anxiety and fear.

3. *Karl Jaspers* (1883-1969)

Jaspers was a German philosopher. For him there were three primary modes of man's existence : *being-there, being oneself*, and *being-in-itself*. Being-there refers to the world of reality that a person comes to know through his own observations. Being-oneself refers to a man's ability to perceive his personal existence and to be aware of his own decisions and choices. Being-in-itself refers to the transcendent world. He pointed out that a person is in constant communication with the existence of other persons. This communication is a wide term which involves social relationship, altruistic behaviours, and dealing with the political systems. When person meaningfully communicates with others, he is said to have *existed*.

4. *Martin Heidegger* (1889-1976)

Heideggar was a German philosopher. He emphasized that of all animals, only human beings had consciousness of their own existence. Individual is aware of various dreads and threats of the world. He is also aware of the thought of the inescapable death that ultimately produces various kinds of fears and dread. He also adopts some convenitional ways to overcome these experiences of dread and fears. Thus, like Kierkegaard, he considers man in conflict. He had strong faith that a person's existence was neither of his making nor of his choice. Rather, it was something which was thrust upon him that would continue till death.

All these philosophers had a direct bearing upon the emergence of existential psychology as a movement. Apart from these philosophers, many others philosophers had more or less similar impact upon the existential psychology.

MAJOR CONTRIBUTIONS OF EXISTENTIAL PSYCHOLOGY

Existential psychology is not a clear-cut system. It is such a movement that incorporates the viewpoints of several persons of which popular names are Adrian van Kaam, Ludwig Binswanger, Medard Boss. and Rollo May. Before we consider their viewpoints separately, it is essential that the common thread that has kept different existential psychologists tied together, should be examined. The common thread is their viewpoints regarding the subject-matter and methods of psychology.

According to the existential psychologists, psychology is concerned with the study of nature of consciousness and the subjective reality. They are opposed to the traditional experimental psychology where independent variables are manipulated and the organism is studied under maximum control condition. They considered the technique of experimental psychologists as *push and pull* technique where the organism is not allowed to exercise his freedom and choice and is treated like a *robot*. For existential psychologists, the scientific method of analysis is not *experimental* rather *phenomenological* that gives emphasis upon description of the experienced state of consciousness. Spiegelberg (1960) pointed out that the phenomenological technique makes distinction between *intuiting, analyzing* and *describing*. Intuiting refers to intensive concentration on the phenomenon of one's consciousness. *Analyzing* refers to seeing the relationship among the various parts of consciousness. Describing refers to giving an account of consciousness in such a language that can be understood by others.

The major contributions to the development of existential psychology are as under :

***Ludwig Binswanger* (1881-1966)**

Binswanger was a Swiss exponent of existential psychology. He had also important influence upon American psychology. He got his basic training in medicine but applied his existential ideas to psychology. His important publication is *Being-in-the world. Selected papers by Ludwig Binswanger* (1963). He has also written three important chapters that appeared in Rollo May's edited book, *Existence* (1958).

Being-in-the world (Daesin) was considered to be the most important concept for existential psychology. Daesin means *to be there* : It means that as human beings a person has no existence apart from the world. In other words, there is no line which separates human beings and the objects in the world. It means there exists a oneness between persons and the objects in the world. Binswanger pointed out many modes of being-in-the world—*singular mode, dual mode and plural mode. A singular mode* is one in which a man lives only to himself as we find in case of a loner. A *dual mode* is one which two people have mutual interactions as we find in case of love. A *plural mode* is one in which person makes interactions with several people as we find in case of struggle, strife and any competitive effort. Apart from all these modes, a person also develops a *world design* which is nothing but a highly subjective and unique mode of being-in-the world. There are several mentally ill-people who somehow develop inadequate world design.

Being-in-the world consists of a threefold reality—physical, human environment and the persons himself. Physical reality includes surroundings of the person himself. Binswanger was also aware of the fact that the person was not concerned with his present surroundings but he also intended to go beyond-the-world. That way he was aware with the viewpoints of earlier existential philosophers who had made distinction between authentic existence and unauthentic existence. The former included realization of one's future possibilities and the latter included restriction on realization of such possibilities due to environment. A person has always freedom to choose between these two kinds of existence.

Binswanger had deemphasized upon determinism, materialism as well as upon positivism. The significant implication of rejecting determinism or cause-effect relationship was that he regarded a person as not the product of heredity nor of the environmental influences. For him, a person was left with a complete freedom of choice and therefore, he was solely responsible for what he would do or would not do. Although Binswanger rejected the heredity and environmental explanation for a person's existence, he stressed the concept of *becoming or growth*. He pointed out that an infant's mode of existence was different from an adult's mode of existence. Likewise, a neurotic's mode of existence was different from normal persons' mode of existence. Why ? This is because of the role of becoming or growth in human development. It means that the existence changes and there is always possibility for becoming something better. Those who refuse to become, remain fixed and static. Neurotic persons have such fixed or static mode. Binswanger's idea of becoming was later praised and shared by many existential psychologists.

***Medard Boss* (1903-1990)**

Boss was also a Swiss psychologist who received his degree in medicine. His important publications included *Psychoanalysis and Daesinanalysis* (1963) and *Existential Foundation of Medicine and Psychology* (1977). Rather than talking about different modes of existence and about being-in-the world, he prefers to emphasize upon the different characteristics inherent in human existence. He has called these characteristics as *essentials*. Some of these characteristics are as under :

1. ***Spatiality*** : It refers to the psychological closeness or distance that a persons develops towards others.
2. ***Temporality*** : This refers to having a time or not having a time for doing a creation thing.
3. ***Bodyhood*** : It refers to not only human physical body but also extends to our relations with objects, events and persons of the world.
4. ***Sharing*** : It refers to sharing the feelings with other people of the world.
5. ***Mood*** : It indicates that the way we perceive the world depends upon our moods at that movement. This is also known as *attunement*.

Like other existential psychologists, Boss emphasized upon *becoming*. He pointed out that human existence was a constant process of becoming something new. A man is free to choose an authentic or an inauthentic life. Since a man has such freedom, he is also considered capable of changing and growing. Of course, there are people who refused to become or grow. However, they can change the direction of their lives towards realization of their basic potentialities.

Boss also stressed that man was aware of his death. Since death is inevitable, a person is aware of the termination of his life. This has also been the major concern of the existential psychologists.

Boss was also interested in making analysis of dream. He rejected the symbolic analysis of dreams as made by Sigmund Freud. His notion was that dreams could be fully understood only by questioning the dreamer properly. There could be more than one meaning of dreams and they should not be regarded as disguises rather they tended to give a different expressions of modes of living. In his analysis of 823 dreams during psychotherapy, Boss pointed out that there was a parallel between changes in the contents of dreams as well as in improvement in the waking existence of the patients. In fact, during psychotherapy the patient moved from inauthentic existence to a more dependable authentic existence.

***Roll May* (1909 -)**

May was born in Ada, Ohio in 1909. He obtained his Ph. D. degree from Columbia University. He was one of the American supporters of the existential psychology whose chief exponents (Binswanger and Boss) were in Europe. His important publications were : *Man's search for himself* (1953), *Love and Will* (1969) and *Existential Psychology* (1969).

He is very close to his other colleagues in explaining the basic principles of the existential psychology. For example, like Binswanger, he emphasized upon the principle of *Daesin* or *being-in-the world*. According to him, there are *three* important modes of existence : the psychical and psychological modes, the social environment of the persons and the particular relationship with the inner nature. The notion of being-in-the world requires that the person must develop responsibility to choose his own freedom and must be accountable for his various activities done for fulfillment of benign-in-the-world.

May has also pointed out that a person has the realization of termination of his existence and this realization causes anxiety. If a persons remains unable to fulfill his basic potentials, it produced guilt. Thus May recognized two important emotions of a person—anxiety and guilt. Despite giving emphasis upon these emotions, he also stressed on the positive side by recognizing a person's capacity to *will*. This includes a person's active desire to select the best of different possibilities and to plan for actualization of his potentials. On the positive side, he also considered love of human beings which has four major components : sex, eros (to get associated with others whom one considers significant), philia (concern for other's welfare) and agape (a deep concern for affectionate relations to all).

Existential Neurosis

Since the existential psychologists like Binswanger, Boss and May were also concerned with giving therapy to the mentally ill-persons. They designated a new kind of neurosis called the *existential neurosis*. This term was first explained by Maddi (1967). Such neurosis has several symptoms. The patient shows withdrawal tendency and loss of self-identity. He lacks interest in his day-to-day activities. He fails to put faith in the truth. On affective side, he is bored and this boredom is accompanied by the occasional feelings of depression. On the whole, an existential neurotic finds no meaning in his life and he considers his life as dull and colourless. In general, existential neurosis results mainly from continued stress in life particularly at the time of social change.

Thus we find that existential psychology, on the whole, deals with the different aspects of the whole person and how he relates to those around him. It is also concerned with anxiety and conflict that results from human awareness regarding the termination of human existence and inability to choose between authentic existence and inauthentic existence.

CRITICISMS OF EXISTENTIAL PSYCHOLOGY

Existential psychology has been criticized on many grounds. Following are the major points of criticisms :

1. Some critics have said that the existential psychology has brought psychology back to philosophical speculations and theological conjectures. It lacks objective methods and principles. In absence of such objectivity, it is difficult to accept the basic tenets of the existential psychology specially in modern days of experimental science. Critics stress that with recognition of existentialism, psychology has completed its cycle—from the complete subjectivism of the Middle age through experimental and objective ps chology back to the subjective psychology.

2. Behaviorists and related experimental psychologists have frequently pointed out that the existential psychology is characterized by subjectivism, dualism and lack of objective referents. Moreover, its

methodology also resembles the classical method of introspection. As such, it is difficult to accept the existential psychology as representative of scientific psychology.

3. In a bid to explain human nature and inner states existential psychology has used obscure and vague language. It has used vague terminology that does not give a clear picture to the reader's mind.

Despite those criticisms, the existential psychology has contributed a lot and its concepts offer a new challenge to the present day experimental psychology.

COMPARISON BETWEEN EXISTENTIAL PSYCHOLOGY AND HUMANISTIC PSYCHOLOGY

As we know, both the existential psychology and the humanistic psychology are together called *third force* in psychology. The two psychologies are very similar to each other because they basically aim at explaining human nature by considering the whole organism. Following are the major points of similarities between the existential psychology and the humanistic psychology.

1. Both the existential psychology and the humanistic psychology emphasize upon the study of a person's inner structure, his experiences, images, feelings, cognitive abilities. Hence both emphasized upon subjectivism in psychology.
2. Both psychologies emphasize upon the common method, that is, phenomenological method in studying and analyzing the inner structure of the person.
3. Both psychologies emphasize upon "free will" of the person and consider each person as having complete freedom to choose his own style of life. It is this freedom that brings a sense of responsibility to own life in a creative way.
4. Both emphasize upon man's uniqueness and individuality. They consider that each person is different from other in approaching the objects and events of the world in his own unique way.
5. Both psychologies are concerned with treatment of mentally ill-persons. They believe that the personality disorganization arises when the persons develops incongruence in the perception of several objects. Such incongruence in the long run tends to disrupt human psychological growth.
6. Both are movements in psychology and not systems of psychology.

Despite these similarities, there are some points of *distinction* between the existential psychology and the humanistic psychology. Those major points of distinctions are as under :

1. The humanistic psychology emphasizes more upon the study of different types of needs including the need for self-actualization. The existential psychology, on the other hand, emphasizes more upon the study of being-in the world for studying human nature.
2. Humanistic psychology is more optimistic in explanation of human nature and his potentialities. It gives much emphasis upon the potentials for good in human beings. The existential psychology points a pessimistic picture in explaining human nature because in making such explanation it stresses upon fear, anxieties, sorrow, etc., which it considers a natural part of human existence. Thus the explanation of humanistic psychology is more similar to the explanation of Freudian explanation that was very pessimistic about human nature.
3. Two psychologies differ basically with respect to the interpretation of motivation. Humanistic psychology has emphasized more upon the process of self-actualization or self-fulfillment whereas existential psychology has emphasized more upon the spiritual motives or spiritual mission in our lives. It emphasizes that it is this spiritual mission that gives person his freedom, responsibility, dignity and superiority in his life.

Thus we find that the existential psychology, despite some similarities, is a slightly different movement from that of humanistic movement.

CHAPTER HIGHLIGHTS

1. Existential psychology, like humanistic psychology, has been included within *third force* in psychology. It developed in Europe but gradually spread to America. It mainly deals with the person as such an individual who exists as a being-in-the world. It basically aims at understanding of person in his total existential reality.
2. The emergence of existential psychology has some antecedent forces. It first developed in the existential philosophy of Europe and gradually spread to America. Subsequently, it also developed in the philosophies of Martin Heidegger and Karl Jaspers in Germany as well as in the philosophies of Gabriel Marcel, Jean-Paul Sartre, Maurice Merlean-Ponty in France.
3. Major contributors to the development of existential psychology have been Ludiwg Binswanger, Medard Boss and Rollo May. These

psychologists emphasized upon the study of the nature of consciousness. Their method of analysis was phenomenological. Their fundamental concept was being-in-the world (Daesin). They were also concerned with the phenomenon of existential neurosis which is characterized by withdrawal tendency and loss of self-identity and interest in day-to-day activities. Existential psychology has also been criticized on three major grounds.

4. Both the existential psychology and the humanistic psychology have some points of similarities and distinctions.

REVIEW QUESTIONS

1. Discuss the major antecedent forces that led to the emergence of the existential psychology.
2. Discuss the contributions of Ludwig Binswanger and Medard Boss as existential psychologists.
3. Present a comparative study of the existential psychology and the humanistic psychology.
4. Assess the contributions of Rollo May in development of the existential psychology.
5. Write short notes :—
   (a) Daesin
   (b) Existential neurosis.

■

CHAPTER 19

COGNITIVE PSYCHOLOGY

CHAPTER PREVIEW

Today psychologists have witnessed a rebirth of their interest in studying cognitive psychology which is considered as a revolt against the behaviourism. The cognitive psychologists are basically interested in studying what happens between the stimuli and the resulting behaviour. They assume certain cognitive or mental process intervene between the two.

Cognitive psychology has some antecedent forces. The view point of British empiricist, nativism, structuralism, cognitive behaviourism and Gestalt psychology served as an important forces that led to the emergence of cognitive psychology. There are three varieties or paradigms of cognitive psychology. They are : "new" structuralism man and machine (information processing model and computer) and the "new" mentalism. As "new" structuralist, Jean Piaget has contributed significantly. His theory of cognitive development has been presented in detail. Noam Chomsky's theory of grammar and his eye-catching criticisms of Skinner's theory of language have been incorporated in detail.

The use of various information processing models and computer have also strengthened the stand of cognitive psychology. The "new" mentalism tried to explain mental processes without making any reference to the principles of associations. Finally, the contributions of cognitive psychology have been criticized.

During the past three decades (that is, beginning of 1960s) there was been a rebirth of interest of psychologists in the cognitive approach. Cognition is a term which is used to define a very active field of inquiry in contemporary psychology. The word itself is quite old, probably first introduced by St. Thomas Acquinas (1225-1274). He had divided the study of behaviour into broad areas: one was labeled cognition refering to how we know the world and the other was labeled affect which refered to feelings and emotions. Today's definition of cognition is equally as broad as that of Acquires. Nowadays, Cognition is a broad term which includes mental processes like thinking, perceiving, imagining, attending, and the information processing by which the person acquires knowledge, solves a problem and makes future plan. The scientific study of cognition is called *cognitive psychology*. The cognitive psychologists are basically interested in one question : what happens between the stimuli and the resulting behaviour? They assume that there must be certain cognitive or mental processes intervening between the two.

Cognitive psychology is a revolt against behaviourism which it claims to be too narrow in its approach. Cognitive psychologists have pointed out that only simple human activities in terms of stimulus input and response output can be understood through behavioristic explanation. For understanding complex activities, it is essential to look for the different mental processes that go within the person. The cognitive psycho-logy basically represents an attempt to investigate all those mental processes in a manner different from that adopted by old-fashioned structuralists. A cognitive psychologist tries to be more objective and scientific in investigating those mental processes.

The viewpoints of cognitive psychology can also be understood when we pay attention to its analogy with the *modern computer* and compare this analogy to that of the analogy of behaviouristic or S-R psychology. The S-R psychology has an analogy with that of *telephone switchboard*. Like Switchboard, in brain the stimulus goes in and after a series of connec-tions and circuits in brain, the response comes out. The analogy for cognitive psychology is that of a *computer* or in most general sense can be called as *information-processing* model or system. Here incoming information is processed on several ways. In computer, information is selected, compared, combined with other information already there and then transformed, rearranged. The final response depends upon all these internal processes.

Today the cognitive psychology is not restricted to the study of thinking, perceiving and knowledge but has been successfully applied to all related areas of psychology (Mandler, 1985). Thus for cognitive psychologists, psychology is the study of *higher mental processes*.

ANTECEDENT FORCES

Cognitive psychology has been influenced by developments in different fields like language, computer science as well as by some earlier works in philosophy and psychology. Some of the major antecedent forces of the modern cognitive psychology may be discussed as under :

1. *British Empiricism*

British empiricists like John Locke, George Berkeley and David Hume have influenced the modern cognitive psychology to a greater extent. Locke in his famous book *Essay* has proposed an explanation regarding how we come to know about the world. He has also explained that all knowledge came from our experiences and our mind was capable of doing two major things : it received various experiences from the external world and subsequently, it reflected those experiences. This process of reflection included higher mental processes like thinking and reasoning. Subsequently, he had also explained how various experiences, through association, came to form complex ideas. Later on, George

Berkeley pointed out that experiences didn't come from external world but came from God and they existed in the minds of those who received them. About 50 years after Locke, David Hume said that our cognition or knowledge was made up of various experiences. He also emphasized upon the various law of association for explaining the complex thought processes. He held that the law of contiguity to be the fundamental law of association. For many modern cognitive psychologists, these law were fundamental for explaining the process of thinking and perception.

2. *Nativism*

As we know, nativism was a reaction against empiricism. It flourished under the leadership of Immanuel Kant who also believed in the existence of mind no doubt but differed from empiricists regarding its nature and functions. He emphasized that our mind was not influenced by prior experiences or learning rather it worked in native or inherent way. We clearly find the impact of this nativistic view of Kant on thinking of modern cognitive psychologists. For example, Noam Chomsky (1972), a modern cognitive psychologist, has vehemently emphasized that our knowledge of the grammar of language is innate and not only that the children's skills for language, to a greater extent, are also innate though that is also governed by experience and learning to some extent.

3. *Structuralism*

The development of cognitive psychology has been, to a greater extent, influenced by the viewpoints of structuralists, particularly by those of Wilhelm Wundt and E. B. Titchener. These psychologists had made it clear that the subject-matter of psychology was conscious experience. They also had shown that perception was the most correct way of knowing about the world. Modern cognitive psychologists have emphasized upon the study of perception and have considered it to be a very important mental function. These structuralists had emphasized that introspection was the best method of analyzing the conscious experience. Although modern cognitive psychologists have not accepted introspection in identical manner, they have emphasized that some scientific methods should be developed for analyzing the experiences of the persons.

4. *Cognitive Behaviourism*

As we know, Edward Tolman was one important cognitive behaviourist. He prefers to be called as a *purposive behaviourist*. Tolman introduced the concept of cognitive map which was the base for both animal learning and human learning. He had further emphasized the important role of expectations or signs or *What leads to What*. Gradually, on the basis of the confirmed expectancies, a cognitive map was set up in the mind of the animal. This cognitive map was manifested in terms of correctly learnt response. Thus for Tolman, a set of intervening variables like expectations, signs, cognitive map, etc. goes in between the input (stimulus) and the output (learnt behaviour). Modern cognitive psychologists, much on the pattern of Tolman's interpretation, have emphasized upon explaining what goes on between the input (environment) and the output (the resulting behaviour). Like Tolman, these cognitive psychologists have emphasized upon the intervening cognitions that ultimately lead to some kind of behaviour. Bandura (1977b) was another important cognitive behaviourist who by emphasizing upon self-reinforcement and cognition, had shaped the development of cognitive psychology in the right direction.

5. *Gestalt psychology*

The work of Gestalt psychologists was also important and inspiring for modern cognitive psychologists. Gestalt psychologists had made it clear that perception should be studied as whole. It should not be analyzed into parts because the whole was not the mere sum of its parts. It had its own characteristics different from the characteristics of parts. They explained the mental events by the laws of perceptual organization. Modern cognitive psychologists take perception of cognition and try to study it by explaining with the help of various principles.

Thus we find that the emergence of cognitive psychology was not sudden. It had its roots in the viewpoints expressed by major systems of psychology.

MAJOR CONTRIBUTIONS OF COGNITIVE PSYCHOLOGY

Cognitive psychologists in general, emphasize upon cognitions and intervening mental processes but they tend to differ in many respects among themselves. Just as there is *no one* humanistic or existential or behaviouristic psychology so also there is *no one* cognitive psychology. There are different types of cognitive psychology but they are tied together with a common thread of giving emphasis upon cognitions and intervening mental processes. Leahey (1980) has recognized three basic paradigms (or varieties) of cognitive psychology : *the "new" structuralism, man and machine* (information-processing model and computer) and *the "new" mentalism*. These three paradigms may be discussed as under :

1. *The "New" Structuralism*

The cognitive psychologists working under the banner "new structuralism" have nothing to do with Wundt and Titchener. They have worked with a new aim in a newer perspective. They simply emphasize upon the *relationship* of language and cognition. Two important psychologists have made their contributions in this field. They are : Jean Piaget who is famous for his studies of development of language and thought in children and Noam Chomsky who is well-known for his theory of language. The contributions of these two psychologists may be enumerated as under :

***Jean Piaget* (1896-1980)**

Piaget was a Swiss psychologist who was trained as a zoologist. But he began his work on cognitive development of children while he was working with intelligence tests in the laboratory of Alfred Binet. He was of view that the children tend to reason in a way different from that of adult. He divided the growth of cognitive development into four stages : *Sensorymotor, preoperational, concrete operational* and *formal operational*. He was of view that each stage is determined by age. A different type of intelligence tends to operate in each of these stages. Intelligence grows not only quantitatively but also qualitatively during these stages. For example, a six-year old child not only knows less than twelve-year old but also his thinking and reasoning processes are different.

Before we discuss Piaget's four stages of cognitive development, it is essential to examine his four major *assumptions* of this theory. Those assumptions may be enumerated as under :

(i) Hunan beings are innately programmed to resolve their uncertainty (called *adaptation*) and they also tend to develop various interrelated and coordinated *schemes* (called *organization*) Piaget uses the term scheme to include both the internal things such as mental images, ideas, etc., and external things such as motor responses and verbal behaviours. By the term adaptation he meant an innate tendency that accounts for various developmental changes taking place in the cognitive structure. By organization is meant an innate tendency that aims at interrelating various schemes. Results of effective organization is a stable cognitive structure.

(ii) Those events which vary from tl ose experienced in the past tend to produce cognitive disequilibrıum and motivates the person to equilibriate through the process of *assimilation* and *accommodation*. Assimilation and accommodation are the two learning mechanisms through which the principle of adaptation operates. Assimilation refers to the ability to deal with a new problem using previous or familiar strategies or schemes. Sometimes accommodation is found to be no longer effective in resolving the uncertainty. *Old* schemes don't work and we need *new* schemes. In accommodation we *change* our scheme or strategy so that we may understand and adapt to new information.

(iii) The process of equilibration depends not only upon the external environmental forces that interact with these present cognitive structures but also upon the internal changes like physical maturation, nervous system and sensory abilities.

(iv) The result of equilibration is the attainment of an advanced cognitive structures.

A discussion of the four stages of Piaget now may be presented as under :

(a) *Sensory-motor stage*

This stage extends from birth to first two years of life. This stage is divided into *six phase. First phase* is the phase of reflex activity which covers the period of first month. During this period the child shows little more than reflexive behaviour. The prominent reflexive response of the child during this phase is the sucking reflex. In *second* phase (1 to 4 months) the reflexive activities of the child become modified by experiences and coordinated with each other. For example, during this phase hand movements and eye movements become coordinated to a greater extent. In the *third phase* (4 to 8 months) the child begins to concentrate on manipulation of objects rather than focusing upon his own bodies. Besides, he can also intentionally repeat responses that produce some interesting results. As a matter of fact, the goal-directed activities tend to appear from this stage. In the *fourth* phase (8 to 12 months) the child begins to differentiate between means and goals. For example, if a toy is hidden, he will continue search for it by removing the obstacle. At this phase the child also starts imitating responses initiated by other people. In the *fifth* phase (12 to 18 months) the child becomes involved in active experimentation, variation and modification of behaviour. The curiosity motive is born and the child becomes interested in novelty. He becomes also interested in the properties of falling objects. In the *sixth* phase (18 months to 2 years) the child develops the ability to respond to even those objects that are not observable. This is called *object permanence.* Several studies have confirmed the emergence of object permanence observed by Piaget (Uzgiris & Hunt, 1975). Evidence of some degree of problem solving also appears. For example, a child may use a stick for pulling any object or toy.

(b) *Preoperational stage*

This is the second stage of cognitive development and extends from 2 to 7 years. Piaget has divided this stage into two parts—the *preconceptual* period (2 to 4 years) and the *intuitive* period (4 to 7 years). The intuitive period is also known as *conceptual* period. The major characteristics of preconceptual period is that here a child acquires what Piaget has called *signifiers.* By signifiers is meant that objects, images, words or thoughts stand for something. Piaget has recognized two classes of signifiers—*symbols* and *signs.* For Piaget symbols and signs are the tools of thought. A child acquires these signifiers, understands that these signifiers are different from the objects that they signify and also develops ability to use various signifiers in thought and actions. Piaget named these characteristics or cognition as *semiotic function.* Piaget also stressed that the development of semiotic function during preconceptual stage takes place through *imitation* and *play.* There are, however, two major *limitations* of preconceptaul thought—*animism* and *egocentrism.* In animism a child attributes life to inanimate objects like wind, cloud, fan, etc. In egocentrism the child has the faith that the objects of the environment are organized and created for him and are centered on him. He considers himself to be the most important object around which most of the things centre. Thus egocentrism simply reflects an inability to take the point of view of others.

In intuitive period the child's thinking and reasoning mature and as a consequence, he is able to do some mental processes like addition, subtraction, multiplication and division but he remains unable to understand the principles underlying those operations. Thus his thinking does not yet completely become logical. Hence, Piaget tells it to be *intuitives.* Thus for Piaget, intuitive thinking refers to the thinking that is not guided by a systematic logic but at the same time it is not an unintelligent behaviour. The children here tend to concentrate on the most noticeable or observable objects of things and therefore, remain unable to *conserve* identities in volume, number and mass. Children are also found to discover true relationship through trial-and-error but remain unable to think and reason in a flexible way that involves *reversibility.* It means their reasoning is characterized by irreversibility. They often show confusion between fantasy and reality and often take chance to test what is what.

(c) *Concrete operational stage*

This stage extends from 7 years to 11 years. This stage is characterized by development and use of operational thoughts. Operational thoughts are the logical reasoning and they are built upon the semiotic function of the preopertional stage. At this stage, children also demonstrate reversibility of thought processes and become decentered. They develop three important set of concepts—*conservation, relations* and *classification*. Children can solve problems that involve conservation of liquid, number, substance and weight. Their ability to solve problems in these areas also generalizes to several different situations. The ordinal problems involving relationship of greater then/ less than are solved by the children at this stage. Such ordinal problems involve tasks like seriation, multiple seriation and transitive inference. Problems relating to classification of objects into mutually exclusive categories or relating to multiple classification and class inclusion are also readily solved by the children at this stage.

Despite the fact that thinking at the concrete operational stage is highly complex and logical than that of preoportional stage, it has *two* limitations. One limitation is suggested by the term concrete itself. It means that the child in this stage can use his operational reasoning successfully only when it is applied to concrete things rather than to those that are abstract. Another limitation is that thinking in this stage is not much systematic. A child is no longer able to use all types of logically possible solutions to a problem.

(d) *Stage of formal operations*

This stage extends from the age of 11 to adulthood (Lundin, 1985). A person in this stage can think and reason hypothetically. New objects need not be physically present for deriving any meaning from them. The thinking of the person at this stage is systematic. Not only this, the person can also detect inconsistencies in beliefs. According to Piaget, this stage is most variable of all stages and is directly related to the level of education. That is the reason why such formal operations are low in those societies which are educationally backward or have non-industrialized cultures. All forms of sophisticated and conceptual analysis are involved in such formal operations.

Although Piaget theory of cognitive development has been a dominant theory, some psychologists have *criticized* this theory on the following grounds :

(i) Critics have pointed out that Piaget's methods of observation are too subjective. They sometimes requires such responses that are very difficult for young children to do. Thus Piaget's methods of assessing cognitive development particularly intelligence are said to be less dependable and objective than many traditional tests of intelligence.

(ii) Some psychologists have criticized Piaget's interpretation of children's failures on different tasks as reflecting lack of cognitive competence. Thus in Piaget's theory lack of response equals lack of cognitive competence. Gelman (1978, 1979) has shown that if the problems relating to conservation, relations and classifications are modified, then it is possible to obtain more appropriate and mature responses from children who failed on the traditional tasks. Some studies have also reported that the preschool children are not as egocentric in their thinking as Piaget had assumed. Piaget had probably based his conclusion regarding egocentricism in thinking of preschool children on their performance in "mountain problem".

(iii) According to Piaget cognitive growth within a stage is continuous but it is discontinuous and qualitatively distinct between stage. The latter assumption has been challenged by most of the psychologist. These psychologists state that children don't suddenly show the development of object permanence and conservation. Moreover, once children have developed the ability of conservation, they soon generalized it and use this ability in later stage. Therefore, Piaget's emphasis that difference in cognitive growth between one stage and another represent difference in quality rather than in quantity, does not appear to be warranted one.

(iv) Piaget has also been criticized for providing no precise specification of mechanism that tends to account for cognitive growth. Piaget has devoted time simply in *describing* rather than in explaining the various concepts and the ways or modes of reasoning that a child develops. For example, it is difficult to answer these questions from Piaget's theory : what role do the sensory stimulations' play in development of ability for conservation and object permanence ? What should be the level of formal education for developing formal operations ? etc.

Despite these criticisms, Piaget theory has been very important. Psychologists using methods more rigorous than those of Piaget have confirmed Piaget's viewpoints.

Noam Chomsky

Chomsky is a linguist who first caught the attention of psychologists when he did a critical review of Skinner's book *Verbal behaviour* (Chomsky, 1959) and later in similar critical review of Skinner's *Beyond freedom and dignity* (Chomsky, 1971). He has attacked Skinner theory of operant conditioning as applied to verbal behaviour or language. Before we explain Chomsky's viewpoints, it is essential to explain briefly Skinner's theory of language.

As we know language is a verbal form of communication that uses sounds in some combinations to communicate meaning. However, language is not necessary for communication. The basic elements of language are simple sounds (phonemes) with some meanings (morphemes). In addition, prosody (intonation and inflection) and syntax that govern word combinations are also important elements. According to Brown (1973) the defining characteristics of language are *meaningful displacement* (in the sense that it permits the representation of objects and events that are not immediate) and *productiveness* (in the sense that language allows us to create or generate meanings).

Skinner (1957) has proposed a theory of verbal behaviour that insists upon complete divorce of mentalistic notions like ideas, meanings and grammatical rules and tries to relate the aquisition of language to the laws of operant conditioning. The central idea of Skinner's theory is that the children learn language in just the same way they learn to do all other behaviour. They imitate the linguistic behaviour of adults and if they are able to do so correctly, adults reinforce or reward them by telling 'correct' or by positively praising them. However, if they do mistake in correctly imitating the linguistic behaviour, adults withhold the reinforcement and sometimes also provide verbal punishment by telling, "No, you are absolutely wrong." As consequence of this *imitation and correction* processes, the children gradually learn how to speak. This *imitation-and-correction model* is also known as *learning theory approach* to language development. Thus using Skinner's terminology it can be said that children tend to learn labels (*tacts*) and demands (*mands*) due to being reinforced for suing the right labels or for requesting the right things. Some experimental evidences are available to support Skinner's theory. Rheingold, Gewirtz and Ross (1959) have demonstrated that vocalizations (crying, cooing and fussing) in three-month old babies can be increased by providing adequate social reinforcements. Likewise, Routh (1969) has demonstrated that the probability of occurrence of a particular sound can be increased or decreased through reinforcement.

Although Skinner's theory is very simple and straightforward, Chomsky has criticized this theory and has provided his own psycholinguistic theory of language development. Let us first discuss Chomsky's criticisms :

(i) According to Chomsky, Skinner has simply relied upon the multitude of stimulus-response relations for explanation of linguistic behaviour of a person. But this is not enough. That way he has ignored the role of internal strucutre of organism in developing the language. Chomsky is of view that all human beings have a built-in predisposition to learn language, a predisposition with which many psychologists agree (Lenneberg, 1969). This built-in predisposition reflects the innate neurological mechanisms that facilitate child's acquisition of language. Skinner did never think about these innate neurological mechanisms.

(ii) Chomsky has questioned the validity and objectivity of the basic terms included by Skinner to explain linguistic behaviour. These terms are : stimulus, response, reinforcement and response strength. According to him, Skinner has failed to define the terms like stimulus and response in objective way and hence, his explanation of linguistic behaviour in terms of stimulus and response can't be objective and dependable one. Recent evidences, likewise, have indicated that reinforcement does not work as response-strengthening event as claimed by Skinner rather it works only as an informational events. (Dulany, 1968; Estes, 1969). Moreover, any particular event may be assigned a positive reinforcing value or negative reinforcing value depending upon the instruction or information given to the subjects. Thus Skinner has failed in explaining even these basic concepts.

(iii) Chomsky has pointed out that Skinner has attempted to extrapolate his concepts from restricted 'rat-in-a-Skinner box' situation to explain human verbal behaviour. He has further argued that what might be adequate for a rat or pigeon is wholly inadequate for explaining human speech. He has claimed that if Skinner's extrapolations are interpreted literally for explaining human speech, they became totally false and when they are interpreted in a vague and Skinner's metaphorical way, they become an ambiguous and poor substitute for our day-to-day usages.

(iv) Chomsky and his colleagues (Bever, 1968; Bever *et al.*, 1968) have pointed out that any theory of language that deals only with observable or surface features of utterances can't provide a scientific and illuminating explanation of our linguistic behaviour. Skinner's theory is one such theory that touches only the surface features and never cares to reveal grammatical "deep structure" of utterances. As such his theory cannot be a meaningful and widely applicable theory of language development.

Apart from these criticisms by Chomsky, Skinner's theory of language development has also been criticized by others as under :

(v) Skinner has postulated that our linguistic habits were determined by environmental or reinforcing conditions. Critics say that there occurs a wide variability in the environmental or reinforcing conditions from child to child in any society or culture. If language development is governed by these environmental or reinforcing conditions, there should occur wider variability in language development in different children. But this is not the reality. Despite variations in opportunities for training and environmental or reinforcing conditions, language development among children of different cultures and social classes follow a relatively standardized universal pattern. Lenneberg's study (1969) provided a strong support to this effect. He took two groups of infants—six born of both deaf parents and six born of both hearing parents. The home environment of children having both deaf parents was such that there was less sound from other sources like TV, radio, taperecorder, etc. On the other hand, the home environment of the hearing parents was enriched with these sources of sound. Thus the children having both deaf parents and "deficient" home environment has experienced little in the way of normal speech sound from them as compared to the children having both hearing parents and "enriched" home environment. Results revealed that these sharp environmental differences made no difference in these two groups in their vocalizations. Such study casts doubt over Skinner's claim regarding development of our linguistic behaviour on the basic of environmental facts.

(vi) Critics have said that the children often learn to say things that cannot be regarded as *imitations* of adults' speech because adult never say with that spirit. There are so many two-word sentences in our language which are often spoken by children but never uttered by adults. Such observation also goes against Skinner's theory.

(vii) Reality is that parents don't tend to correct the speech of a child as learning theorists have, in general, contended. If we pay attention to parent-child interaction, it will be obvious that parents show more concern with comprehending *what* the child intends to say rather then with *how* it is being said. In such situation the child should not have developed a meaningful framework for language development. But this is not the reality.

(viii) If imitation and reinforcement would have been the only factors in learning a language, then the children should have learnt only those sentences that were imitated and were properly reinforced. But this is not the reality. Both children and adults alike continually learn new and original sentences in their lives. This shows that Skinner's position was inherently weak.

All these criticisms of Skinner's theory of language development force us to look for an alternative theory of language development. Here we shall consider Chomsky's theory of language development. In fact, Chomsky was partly responsible for the rise of cognitive psychology to its peak of prominence (Bower & Hilgard, 1981). His theory of language development proved a boon for cognitive psychologists who set out to borrow whatever they could and apply them to psychological correlates of language development.

Chomsky's major contribution to cognitive psychology was his theory of grammar. He developed a psycholinguistic theory of language development having a biological base (Lefrancois, 1983). According to him, all human beings have a built-in-pre-disposition to learn grammar. This viewpoint was strongly supported by Lenneberg (1969) who has considered that the ability to learn language is species-specific and largely innate. Chomsky has assumed some innate neurological mechanisms-like stage that facilitate child's acquisition of syntax. These mechanisms are called as *language acquisition device* (LAD) or an acquisition model (AM). Thus all children are equipped with certain biological potentials that make them possible to learn any language to which they are exposed. For Chomsky, competence in language development rests upon the knowledge of the complex system of *rules* and such competence is *innate*. Perhaps due to this, a growing child acquires language very rapidly. When the children learn a complex system of rules rather than just several strings of words, such system allows them to generate infinite number of new sentences and develop language skills very rapidly. In his theory Chomsky has focused mainly upon the *productive* aspect of language, that is on how persons are able to produce a completely new sentence. For him this aspect of language is directly based upon a person's ability to use different syntactic rules. Chomsky has divided these rules into *two* classes—rules relating to *surface structure* and rules relating to *deep structure*. The surface stricture (of a sentence) refers to its different component parts such as nouns, adjectives, verbs, etc., and plays an important role in determining verbal expression. The *meaning* of the sentence is determined by the deep structure. The surface structure and the deep structure are not identical. For Chomsky, the major problem in understanding a language is to derive deep structure from the surface structure of the sentence. This is done through what he called as knowledge of *phrase-structure* and *transformational rules*. These two together are called *transformational grammar*. Phrase-structure refers to the types and functions of words that constitute phrase. For example, *The Indian* is a noun phrase that consist of an article (the) and a noun (Indian). Transformational rules are those rules that transform the structure of phrases or combine the structure of phrases to make a meaningful sentence. Therefore, such rules help in understanding meaningful units of language.

Despite the fact that Chomsky's theory of language development is more acceptable and provides a challenging alternative to that of Skinner's theory of language development, some basic questions remain unanswered. Critics have pointed out that from Chomsky's theory it is not clear what the innate competence or ability of child's mind is and how does it operate in *producing* various linguistic behaviour ? Not only this, Chomsky's theory also fails to answer how does a child learn his native language ?

2. *Man and Machine (Information Processing and the computer)*

This is the second paradigm of cognitive psychology. After World War II the world witnessed a massive programme of computerization. Psychologists have been able to draw many *analogies* between function of a computer and a person's cognitive abilities. Prior to the development of such analogies, psychologists were only concerned with stimulus-response connections and never bothered for what happens in between the two.

Like a computer, some stimuli (input) are given to the person who, in turn, processes those information somewhere inside and then, on that basis, he constructs a particular response (output). Thus psychologists today have taken man as machine particularly as computer. This idea has given birth to a particular model or theory to study mental processes—*information-processing model*.

Before describing this model, a few words about what a model is. A model is an attempt to explain something unknown in terms of already known principles. A model is always subject to change depending upon new technological development in the concerned field. Information-processing model attempts to explain cognition (the unknown) in terms of the principles of operation of computers (known). Howard Atken developed the first computer in 1944 (Lundin, 1985) and since then the use of computers gave psychologists a new way of thinking over cognitive abilities. A computer receives information, detects and analyzes it, stores it for future use, searches, locates and retrieves information and finally makes decisions and solves problems. This is much clear from Figure 18·1. Of course, for doing all these functions, the computers must be properly *programmed*, that is, they must be told about *when* and *how* to do all these things. However, a human being with central nervous system (spinal cord and brain) is more flexible information processor than even the most sophisticated computer.

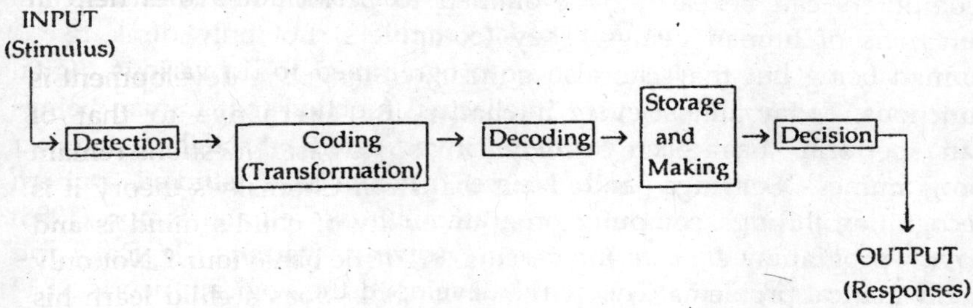

Figure 18·1

What benefits information processing and computer have given to cognitive psychology. It is said that information processing models based upon computer designs have generated considerable research and many new insights into the nature of memory, perception and thought processes, which have further been utilized by the cognitive psychologists to broaden its field. Memory is the basic component of human information processing and researches conducted by cognitive psychologists have revealed that memory never functions simply as a dynamic system of storage and retrieval strategies but also influences other aspects of information processing like decision-making, problem solving, etc. This view has encouraged the analytical view of memory. Memory has been divided into three subsystems—sensory memory, short-term memory and long-term memory. A sensory memory is said to reside in each sensory system for the briefest period of time (usually in milliseconds). After this information goes to the next stage where it is stored for a longer but still brief period (say for example, 10 seconds, 30 seconds, etc.). This stage or system is called as short-term memory (STM). Here information is also coded in a form that is definitely different from the stage of sensory memory. At last, due to rehearsal or sufficient attention, some information is transferred from the short-term memory to the long-term memory where information is held for any indefinite period of time. Experimental evidences have indicated that those items of information which are processed at 'deeper' level, are remembered well even at longer period of time. These researches have also shown that there are limitations at every stage of memory in handling the information.

Information processing models have also given birth to the concept of *artificial intelligence* which is very important in study of the problem solving behaviour, concept learning and perception. By artificial intelligence is meant the intellectual capabilities of computers. Computers can be easily programmed to perform many intellectual functions of human beings. They (computers) not only think like a human being but they can also be programmed to do various digital functions. Today almost every intellectual function that human beings can perform has been widely investigated through computer programmes. Selfridge and Neisser (1960) have studied pattern recognition through computer programming. Newell and Simon (1956) have programmed computers in solving various logical and mathematical problems. They have developed the Logical Theorist (LT) as one application of artificial intelligence. LT works like human brain and strategies are used for solving a problem. The general idea involved in LT has proven a boon for cognitive psychologists in understanding human problem solving behaviour. Solving any complex human problem incorporates logical thinking rather than trial-and-error or blind searching. Later, by combining several computer programmes, including LT, Newell, Shaw and Simon (1960) developed the "General Problem Solver" (GPS), a programme that could easily simulate the solution of a variety of human problems.

Thus these various computer programmes that utilize information processing approach have provided meaningful clues to the cognitive psychologists in understanding the detail functioning of human mind.

3. *The "new" mentalism*

According to Leahey, this group of psychologists consists of those who could not be placed in the first two groups. The major characteristic of this group of psychologists is its emphasis upon explaining mental processes without the help of the principles of association. In fact the genesis of such viewpoint lies in the work of Wurzburg School of psychology, which after studying the process of thinking came to the conclusion that thinking occurs even in absence of images. Such viewpoint of the school came to the known as *imageless thought*. They had pointed out that since there occurred no images in thinking, there was no question of getting them associated. They also claimed that association of ideas no longer explained the process of thinking—a viewpoint that was obviously against the major tenets of introspectionism. The eventual basic description of Wurzburg school was that the task which was given to the subject itself produced a mental set that directed his thinking.

The major claim of this group of cognitive psychologists that mental processes can be explained without resorting to the principles of association has been experimentally supported. Barclay (1973) has indicated that it is the instruction that influences how a subject repeats a sentence of words presented to them. Likewise, Schweller, Brewar and Dahl (1976) have reported that the subjects tend to paraphrase a sentence depending upon the context in which that is given. Likewise, Bransford and Franks (1971) have shown that people can form a meaningful representation from completely different ideas. For example, from the given words like *teacher, book, class* a meaningful sentence like *The teacher gave book in class* can be formed. Johnson, Doll, Bransford and Lapinski (1974) have pointed out that when the vague sentences without any context were given to the subjects, they had difficulty in subsequent recall. But when the appropriate context was provided, the recall improved significantly. All these studies show that the cognitive psychology can explain memory and thinking by using some non-associative principles in a better way.

Apart from these, there are cognitive psychologists who believe that our behaviour is controlled not only by environmental factors as the traditional behaviourists would argue but also by internal factors. As a consequence, intermediary mental events also control our behaviour. The cognitive psychologists holding this viewpoint are known as *cognitive behaviourists.* Bandura has been one of the chief proponents of this viewpoint. He is well-known for his emphasis upon *observational learning or modeling* and he has stressed upon the importance of cognitive processes in such observational learning. His major contention is that a person not only learns by doing but also by watching and simulating others.

In this way we find that the cognitive psychologists have made important contributions in exploring areas like problem-solving, thinking and memory. They have also not been hesitant in stressing the role of mental processes in explaining behaviour of the persons.

CRITICISMS OF COGNITIVE PSYCHOLOGY

Cognitive psychology has been vehemently attacked by behaviourists. As we know, cognitive psychologists had criticized behaviourism so also the behaviourists criticized them by giving suitable reply. In this famous article entitled 'Why I am not a Cognitive Psycholoist ?' Skinner (1977) has outlined some of the major criticisms as under :

(i) Skinner has been much critical of the emphasis of cognitive psychology upon internal mental states or processes. According to him, since these mental states can't be observed, they help us in simply making an inferential settlement regarding the cause and effect relationship between behaviour and these various mental events.

(ii) Skinner has also made it clear that the use of the term like *mind, will* or *thought* by cognitive psychologists are nothing but simple reflection of behaviour. Behavior can be overt or covert. These terms reflect the covert aspect of behaviour. Therefore, the cognitive psychology does not seem to have any independent status.

(iii) Skinner also pointed out that the whole field of information processing can be explained simply as changes in the control exercised by the environment. Behaviour is always the function of environmental control and we don't get any evidence to the effect that it is controlled by mental events.

Despite these criticisms, the cognitive psychology has an important effect upon modern psychology. Their contributions in the field of language development, memory, thinking and perception are considered as highly valuable for today psychology.

CHAPTER HIGHLIGHTS

1. The scientific study of cognition is called cognitive psychology. Cognition is a broad term that includes mental processes like thinking, perceiving, imagining, attending and information processing by which the persons acquires knowledge, solves a problem and makes future plan. The cognitive psychology is a revolt against behaviourism. It attempts at investigating mental processes in objective and scientific way.

2. Cognitive psychology has not been born suddenly rather some antecedent forces were active in giving birth to the cognitive psychology. The viewpoints expressed by the British empiricists, nativists, structuralists, Gestalt psychologists, and cognitive behaviorists like Tolman and Bandura had significant impact upon emergence of cognitive psychology.
3. Leahey (1980) has recognized three major paradigms of cognitive psychology. They are : the 'new' structuralism; man and machine (the information processing model and computer) and the 'new' mentalism. Piaget and Chomsky contributed a lot as new structualists. Piaget is well-known for his theory of cognitive development and Chomsky by formulating the theory of grammar and making severe attack on the theory of language development of Skinner, has given a right direction to cognitive psychology. Information-processing model and complete programme have also given cognitive psychologists an important idea about functioning of human mind and its various processes. The cognitive psychologists under the head 'new' mentalism tried to explain the various mental processes without the help of the principles of association. Bandura, by giving emphasis upon self-reinforcement and various other cognitive processes, has shown that the cognitive psychologists can easily explore various mental events such as memory and thinking by using some unassociative principles in a better way.

REVIEW QUESTIONS

1. Discuss the major antecedent forces that led to the emergence of cognitive psychology.
2. Discuss the contributions of Jean Piaget in development of cognitive psychology.
3. "Noam Chomsky was partly responsible for rise of cognitive psychology". Elucidate the statement.
4. Do information processing models provide a base of development of cognitive psychology ? Give arguments in favour of your answer.
5. How does cognitive psychology differ from classical structuralism ? Illustrate you answer with suitable examples.
6. Discuss the major paradigms of cognitive psychology. Which of these paradigms proved most influential for modern psychology ?

■

CHAPTER 20

PSYCHOLOGY : TODAY AND TOMORROW

CHAPTER PREVIEW

Psychology today and tomorrow has been examined. Modern psychology has outgrown the various schools. Those schools are no longer alived today but their impact is still felt. Modern trend is toward specialization. As a consequence we have today experimentel psychology, abnormal psychology, developmental psychology, clinical psychology, organizational psychology, etc. as an independent branch of psychology. Modern psychology has also been influenced by information theory borrowed from the field of engineering as well as by computers. Various information-processing models have been formulated to account for various aspects of behaviours. Computers have influenced almost all areas of psychology.

Psychology, in the next centuries to come, would very likely to be absorbed by those disciplines from which it came : philosophy, physics and biology. The growth of interdisciplinary approach in psychology is the basis for such possibility. The cross-cultural psychology and the indigenous psychology also have much influence upon future trend of psychology. However, only time will reveal accurately what psychology will be.

PSYCHOLOGY TODAY

Psychology today stands fragmented as it was in the beginning. In this respect we can say that the history has repeated itself with some minor modifications. The era of schools of psychology declined around 1940 or so and since then, psychologists did not find it profitable to divide the fields of psychology in the way done by various schools. The basic question is : why did psychologists drop the systems or schools in psychology ? There were two reasons for decline of schools in psychology. First, with advancement of psychology and gradual emphasis upon its experimental nature, a vast number of researches started pouring into the general fund of knowledge from almost all sides. As a consequence, it became difficult for any school or system to incorporate such a vast area. *Second,* the different areas and their expanding nature attracted psychologists to break the affiliation and cross the boundary set up by anyone system or school. The growing realization was that if they remain tied with the major focal theme of the school, they would no longer justify their stand particularly in growing and expanding fields of psychology. Therefore, these psychologists also did not like to remain within the clutches of a school.

Although the various schools have declined and they no longer exist today, they still have influence on the contemporary research. Their impact upon modern psychology is evident from the following description.

Although the structuralism met its natural death long back, we have a clear impact of its basic principles. The famous Swiss developmental psychologist, Jean Piaget, has developed his theory of cognitive development that basically emphasizes upon the fact that the structure of human mind changes with advancement in age. The various principles of association that were developed by structuralists for the explanation of the formation of complex mental events out of simpler mental events, also played an important role in formulating various theories of learning.

Functionalism in United States developed partly as a reaction to structuralism and it basically emphasized upon the functional significance of mind or upon the functions of mental processes and structures. This school produced a significant legacy in its emphasis upon learning as the most important adaptive process of human beings.

The impact of psychoanalysis is widely felt. Its emphasis upon unconscious forces is still persuasive. The principles outlined by this school still form the important basis of a widely used psychotherapeutic technique. In the field of clinical psychology and personality theory its impact is also widely felt.

Behaviourism and Gestalt psychology have produced the greatest impact upon modern psychology although there are a few psychologists who identify themselves as behaviourists or Gestaltists in true sense. The behaviourists' emphasis upon the importance of learned responses is a key principle for modern psychologists. Likewise, Gestalt psychologists' emphasis upon the organizational process against analytical process has important bearings upon many aspects of modern psychology.

Despite all these, the schools of psychology have disappeared and today the organization of the fields of psychology lies along a different lines, that is, towards *specialization*. Today psychologists don't identify themselves by schools but by areas of interest. Modern psychologists today prefer to be called as social psychologists or developmental psychologists, or cognitive or experimental psychologists (perception, memory, language, thinking, information-processing, etc.) or personality psychologists or animal-learning psychologists and so on. Besides these, psychologists are doing specialization in clinical psychology, organizational psychology, occupational or industrial psychology, as well as in psychobiology. The specialization movement has became so strong that psychologists working in one area know little about the other area. The trend is though unfortunate but there appears to be a very little alternative.

Apart from the trend towards specialization, modern psychology has witnessed the considerable impact from outside fields. Of these fields, the *information theory* borrowed from the engineering and the *computers* have been the two major source of influence.

Information theory was borrowed from engineering in the late 1940s and it has had an important impact upon psychology since 1950s to the present. Information theory allowed a vigorous quantification of the concepts which were only poorly assessed previously. Such theory has served many useful purposes in psychology. Today psychologists conceptualize human cognitive processes mainly in terms of the information flowing through the system. As a consequence of various researches being done in different fields, human beings are considered to possess a truly phenomenal information-processing system though with a limited capacity.

Computers have influenced almost all areas of psychology. A computer is used in a variety of ways such as analyzing data, controlling experiments and stimulating the ways human beings process the various kinds of information. Some areas of psychology have been benefitted much from the use of computers. Computers do various functions that bear marked similarity to human learning, remembering and thinking. Apart from this, in the study of some psychological problems, computer programmes have nicely served as a *theoretical model* that tends to explain how the human mind operates.

With the onset of cognitive revolution, very important efforts were made in disclosing the information processing functions of human mind. Today when computer science and information technology have advanced, new scientific tools such as functonal magnetic resonance imaging (*f*MRI) and positron emission tomography (PET) are extensively used in brain researches. These new tools have raised the hope of finding new mechanism for relation between human behaviour and brain functions. In fact, a new age in psychological sciences may grow out of the collaboration between the cognitive psychology and neuroscience. In applied areas, the psychology is gaining popularity day by day by contributing much to the welfare of the people at large.

Modern psychology can be seen to be divided into two major camps : One camp tries to study human beings as a functoning organism and the other camp tries to study human beings as an active social person. Biological psychologists or neuropsychologists belong to the first camp. The second camp includes those psychologists who study behaviour as a function of socio-cultural systems. Thus the second camp consists of humane psychologists like clinical psychologists, social psychologists, counselling psychologists and several other psychologists who are concerned with the social nature of human beings.

Biological psychologists incorporate both human beings as well as animal beings as a scientific way to explore human psychology and experimentation is taken as a valid method of study. They have their own established methodology and standard to assess research results. If this part of psychology really succeeds in separating itself from the rest and gains its independence, then biological psychologists would really be developing their part of psychology into a *paradigmatic science* (Kuhn, 1962).

Psychologists of the second camp try to look at the purposive behaviour of human beings and also try to develop their potentialities. Survey, observations, social experiments and the like are utilized as their methodologies. In fact, psychologists of this camp are no doubt loosely organized but they contribute more widely to the practical needs of society than the neuropsychologists.

PSYCHOLOGY TOMORROW

No psychologist is a prophet like that reported in Old Testament. Hence, it is difficult to tell precisely what psychology will be in future. However, as morning shows the day, the present reflects the future. Psychology is breaking and it needs person like Isaac Newton (a renowned physicist) to synthesize its various principles. It is rapidly moving to be an interdisciplinary science. In the centuries to come, psychology may be absorbed by those disciplines from which it originally came : philosophy, physics and biology. We have physiological psychology and animal psychology (related to biology), human engineering (related to some of the basic principles of physics) and also philosophical psychology. In fact, there appears to be psychology of just about many things : economics, history, music, literature, politics, religion.

Now at the start of 21st century, there is a strong preference for cross-cultural psychology and indigenous psychology which, in fact, have challenged the validity of Euro-American psychology or more commonly called *mainstream psychology*. Today psychologists intend not to concentrate on the development taking place in one particular region of the world rather they take into account the observations made in the various parts of the world. In other wards. they admit that cross-cultural researches are very important to the development of psychology. Due to the active process of globalization and rapid information exchanges in the new century, the people are expected to be close in space as well as in time and no parts can be fully independent from other parts of the world. In such situation the cross-cultural studies become all the more important. Psychologists now need not be guided by the theories of mainstream psychology and they can develop their own theories for making significant contribution to the different fields of psychology. However, cross-cultural psychology as well as indigenous psychology can join their forces with mainstream psychology to offer more powerful theories. Thus psychology is marching towards becoming truly international and intercultural. The day it achieved this goal, cross-cultural psychology will be redundant and psychology will become a perfect discipline for understanding many aspects of human behaviour and mental processes.

CHAPTER HIGHLIGHTS

1. Today psychology has outgrown the various schools or systems although the different schools like structuralism, functionalism, behaviourism, psychoanalysis and Gestalt psychology have disappeared, their impact is felt to some extent. Modern psychology has been unduly influenced by information theory borrowed from the field of engineering as well as by computers.
2. Psychology, in the next a few centuries to come, may be absorbed by those disciplines from which it originally came : philosophy, physics and biology. The growth of interdisciplinary approach in psychology is the major basis for such possibility. The cry for cross-cultural psychology and indigenous psychology has also challenged the dominance of mainstream psychology. However, only time will reveal accurately what psychology will be.

REVIEW QUESTIONS

1. "Modern psychology has outlived schools." Elucidate.
2. "In future psychology seems to be absorbed by its parent disciplines." Do you agree with the statement.
3. Examine the impact of cross-cutltural psychology and indigenous psychology upon mainstream psychology.

■

CHAPTER 21

AN OVERVIEW OF PSYCHOLOGY IN INDIA

CHAPTER PREVIEW

In India psychology is known since ancient times. Hence, Indian psychology has been explained by dividing the developments in two periods—ancient times and modern times.

Psychology in ancient India started from the period of Rigveda and Upanishads. A beautiful glimpse of Indian psychology is found in Bhagavat Geeta. There we have a lucid discussions about the different aspects of personality like self (atman), mind (manas), senses (indriyas) and intelligence (budhi). Ancient Indian psychology also emphasizes upon controlling mind (manas) and senses (indriyas). This system is called Yoga System and has been also incorporated in what is called Abhidhamma in Pali language of Gautama Buddha's day (536–438 B.C.). In Sanskrit, it is called Abhidharma.

Indian psychology in modern times is different from ancient time and has been shaped on Western models. Today Indian psychologists have been most active in fields like clinical psychology, the psychology of personality, social psychology, industrial psychology, experimental psychology, military psychology, educational psychology, physiological psychology and comparative psychology, etc. In all these branches they are doing research works by adopting the techniques and methods discovered by Western psychology. Of course, there are some psychologists who are taking pains for discovering original techniques and methods and they take more pride in using these things in their research works.

The field of psychology is dominated by American books and American psychologists. To a lesser extent, it is also influenced by British and Russian psychologists as well as by psychologists of other countries. Books written by these foreign authors seldom make mention of the work of Indian psychologists. But this does not mean that there is no psychology in India. Indian psychologists are also doing active researches in different fields although due to various types of hurdles they may not be so organized and their various works may not be so systematically published as we find in case of those of American, British and Russian psychologists.

An overview of psychology in India can be presented by dividing the entire developments in ancient times and modern times.

PSYCHOLOGY IN INDIA DURING ANCIENT TIMES

Psychology in ancient India was completely different from today's psychology. Like in other countries, psychology in ancient India was governed by various philosophical as well as religious thoughts. If we trace the history of Indian psychology, we, to agreement of most people, will start from the periods of *Rigveda* and *Upanishads* or *Vedanta*. In these periods we get a lot of concepts that are of psychological importance. We get a good discussion regarding different aspects of personality—self (*atman*), mind (*manas*), senses (*indriyas*) and intelligence (*budhi*). In upanishads personality has been conceived as a synthesis of matter (*anna*), life (*prana*) and mind (*manas*) . Psychology in these periods was a practical psychology dealing with various principles to discipline our own minds and hearts. A beautiful glimpse of those principles can be had in *Bhagavat Geeta*.

In ancient psychology of India *Vedanta, Buddhism, Bhagavad-Gita* and *Yoga* have much to contribute. According to Vedanta, mind has been explained as one internal organ (*antahkarana*). It also emphasizes upon transformation and modification of mind. This is done through *Yoga*. When mind is controlled and attains a sense of full consciousness, it is called as *atman. Atman is of two types—jivatman* and *paramatman*. Jivatman is the realization of self-consciousness and therefore, it represents the initial stage of realization. In Indian philosophical literature Jivatman is equivalent to the modern term 'personality'. (Vrinte, 1995) As we go deeper and deeper, we develop a true sense of consciousness and it is called *paramatman.* Jivataman is said to include modern concept of empirical ego which includes cognitive processes of the self and paramatman is said to be equivalent to the modern concept of pure ego which is overall consciousness that has integrative forces and constitutes personality as we know it today.

Ancient Indian psychology has emphasized more upon those principles that help on controlling mind (*manas*) and senses (*indriyas*). This system is called Yoga System and has also been incorporated in what is called *Abhidhamma* in Pali language of Gutama Buddha's day (536-438 B.C.) In Sanskrit, it is called as *Abhidharma*. In India two most famous codifers of the psychological views of the Hindu schools of Yoga were *Pantajali* and *Shankara*. In India in true sense Abhidhamma developed fifteen centuries ago although it was already born in the teachings of Gautama Buddha in the fifth century B. C. It contains psychological principles describing the personality or self around which the workings of mind are analyzed. In *Abhidhamma* what appears to be self is nothing but the sum total of thoughts, desires, memories, sensations and so on. These various constituents of the sum total get continuity through a common thread called *bhava* (feeling). It is bhava which connects one moment of consciousness to that which follows. Abhidhamma also makes distinction between two types of mental factors—*Kusula* mental factors or pure wholesome and healthy mental factors and *akusula* mental factors or impure, unhealthy and unwholesome factors. One example of healthy factor is insight (*panna*) and one example of unhealthy factor is delusion (*moha*). In addition to these kusula and akusula mental factors, there are seven neutral factors present in every mental state. They are : apperception (*phassa*), perception (*Sanna*), volition (*centana*), feeling (*Vedanta*), spontaneous attention (*manasikara*), one pointedness (*ekaggata*) and psychic energy (*jivitindriya*).

Ancient Indian psychology also recognizes three types of *gunas* or material substance that makes the different traits and temperament of personality. Those *gunas* are of three types—*purity or essence (sattva gunas), intertia (tamas gunas)* and *energy (rajas gunas). Sattva gunas* cover traits like mental illumination, happiness, harmony, mental purity, etc. *Tamas gunas* cover emotional traits like mental disillumination, inactivity, depression, aggression dullness, etc. *Rajas gunasa* include traits like dynamism, activity, dominance, etc. All these three types of gunas remain present in all individuals in different degrees. Preponderance of any of these gunas produces a certain type of personality.

The person dominated by *tamas gunas* is likely to develop a personality which is susceptible to delusion and confusion. This type is specifically characterized by inattention, lack of understanding and indolence. Such person has neither the energy or zest of the person dominated by *rajasa* nor the enlightment of the person in whom *sattava* is dominant.

The person who is dominated by *rajasa* is full of unrest attachment to the object of desire, helpful and greedy. He is guided by impulses and emotion. His action generally leads to various kinds of grief and pain because his ability may not help him in achieving what he intends to achieve. This may create intense hostility for others with whom he works.

The person dominated by *sattava guna* is characterized by clamity of vision and intelligence. Such person is free from lust, anger and greed. His behaviours are guided not by personal gain at the cost of others but by *lokasamgraha*, that is, by well-being of the entire society. Such person is gentle, silent and full of self-control. He tries to fulfill his obligations without expecting reward in turn. He is characterized by *sadbhava* a sense of reality and by *sadhubhava*, a sense of morality and goodness. On the whole, desires and emotions of such persons are under his full control.

As said above, Patanjali is the traditional founder of Yoga system. For Patanjali, Yoga does not mean spiritual union of the individual soul with universal soul rather is meant a spiritual effect to attain perfection through various types of controls such as the control of the body, senses, and mind and through correct discrimination between *Purusa* and *Prakrti*. Yoga is very intimately allied to *Sankhya* which means knowledge. For all practical purposes, Yoga and Sankhya are treated as the theoretical and practical sides of the same system. Yoga believes in God as the highest self which is distinct from other selves. Pantanjali yoga is also known as *Raja yoga*. Here, Yoga is understood as the cessation of the modifications of *Chitta* and this cessation is through meditation or concentration which is also called as Yoga samadhi. Chitta means three internal organs of Sankhya, that is, *buddhi* (intellect), *ahankara* (ego) and *manas* (mind). Thus chitta is same as *antahkarna*. The cessation of the modifications of chitta through meditation is called as yoga. It is the return of Purusa to its original state of perfection.

The modifications of Chitta are of five kinds :

(i) right cognition *(pramana)* (ii) wrong cognition *(viparyaya)* (iii) verbal cognition or imagination *(vikalpa)* (iv) absence of cognition or sleep *(nidra)* and memory *(smriti)*. Right cognition is of three types perception *(pratyaksa)*, inference *(anumana)*, and verbal testimony *(shabda)*. Perception or pratyaksa is said to occur when the chitta through sense organs comes into contact with external object or with internal mental state. Inference is said to occur when chitta cognizes the generic nature of objects or things. Viparyaya is positively wrong knowledge as we perceive a rope as a snake. Vikalpa is verbal cognition. Nidra is called absence of cognition yet it is mental modification because after sleep the person is found to say that he knows nothing. Smriti is true recollection of previous associations through impressions left behind. The cessation of these modifications of chitta through mediation is the aim of yoga.

There are five levels of mental life *(chittabhumi)*—*ksipta* (restless), *mudha* (torpid), *viksipta* (distraction), *ekagra* (concentration) and *Nirudha* (restricted). Differences in these levels occur due to predominance of the different gunas. The lowest level is ksipta where mind is restless due to the excess of rajas guna. In mudha, the mind is dominated by tamas and tends towards ignorance, sleep and lethargy. Likewise, in viksipta, the sattva guna predominates but sometimes rajas also asserts its influence. In ekagra the mind is entirely dominated by sattva and other two gunas like rajas and tamas are subdued. In nirudha, which is the highest level, the mental modifications are arrested though their underlying impressions remain. It is said that only the last two levels are conducive to yogic life whereas the first three are not at all.

Yoga system believes in the principles that a sound mind needs a sound body. Therefore, it advocated control over the body, the senses and the mind. Sensual attachment and passions distracts mind and body both. So they must be conquered. For this, Pantanjali yoga gives us *Eight fold path of Discipline* called *Astanga yoga* which can be briefly discussed as under:

(1) Yama. It means restraints and includes five vows of janism : *Ahimsa* or non-violence including bodily or mental injury; *Satya* or truthfulness in all dealings of life; *Asteya* or non-stealing of anything in life such as, money, material, idea, speech, etc.; *Brahmacharya* or celibacy which means refraining from sexual activities directly or indirectly; *Aparigraha* or non-possession, that is, keeping one's requirements to the bare minimum.

(2) Niyama. It means observances. It is self-culture. Patanjali has prescribed five *niyamas : Shaucha* (cleanliness of body and mind), *Santosha* (contentment) *tapas* (austerity with regard to food, exercise, rest and recreation), *Suadhyaya* (interactive study) and *Ishvara Pranidhana* (devotion to God).

(3) Asana. It means steady and comfortable postures which are physical help to meditation. In fact, this disciplines body.

(4) Pranayama. It refers to the control of breath and deals with regulation of inhalation, retention and exhalation of breath. It is very helpful in concentration of mind.

(5) Pratyahara. It is a process of retraining the senses to go to outward objects. Senses are checked through this so that they must go to the internal goal.

(6) Dharana. It is fixation of mind as the object of meditation.

(7) Dhyana. It is meditation and consists in the undisturbed flow of thought round the object of meditation.

(8) Samadhi. It means deep meditation or concentration. This is the

final step in yoga and here mind is completely observed in the object of meditation. In fact, it is the highest means to realize the cessation of mental modifications which is the end.

Samadhi is of two types : *Samprajnata* or conscious and *asamprajnata* or supraconscious. In the samprajnata consciousness the object of meditation persists whereas in the latter it is transcended. In fact, the former is *Ekagra* whereas the latter is *Niruddha.* In the former, that is, samprajnata, the mind remains concentrated on the objects of meditation. This state is said to be of four kinds:

(a) Sovitarka. Here Chitta is concentrated on a gross object of mediation such as the tip of nose
(b) Sauichara : Here Chitta is concentrated on subtler object of mediation like the tannatras.
(c) Sananda. Here chitta is concentrated on a still subtler object of meditation which produces joy
(d) Sasmita. Here chitta is concentrated on the ego-subtance with which the self is generally identified.

Asamprajnata Smadhi is the state of supra-conscious concentration where the person who is mediatating and the object of meditation are completely fused together and there is not even consciousness of the object of meditation. In fact, it is the highest form of yoga where no new mental modification occur. It is a state of perfect mystic ecstasy which is both difficult to attain and describe. Even those who attain it cann't retain it longer. Immediately or after very short time, body is broken down and the person obtains complete liberation.

It is further recommended that unless one follows and practices all of them together in an integrated way, one will not be able to derive the full benefit from Yoga. The first two are related to social and personal behaviour of the person, third and the fourth are, in fact, yogic exercises and the last four are the stages of meditation.

In recent past one of the persons who made maximum contributions for spreading the message of universal harmony through yoga was Swami Vivekananda. The main themes of his lectures delivered in USA and UK was based on the Bhagavad Gita and Patanjali Yoga Sutra.

Bhagawad Gita also contributed a lot to the field of ancient Indian Psychology. Bhagawad Gita literally means 'the Lord's song' that is, philosophical discourse given by Lord Krishna to persuade the reluctant Arjuna to fight the battle against Kaurvas. Gita has been called as 'Gospel of Humanity' because it deals with metaphysics, religion and ethics. Mahatma Gandhi has called Gita as 'universal mother whose door is ever open to anyone who knocks.' The fundamental metaphysical teaching of Gita is that the soul or self is indestructible *(avinashi)*, eternal *(nitya)*, unborn *(aja)*, all-pervasive *(sarva-gata)*, undiminishing *(avyaya)*, immovable *(achintya)* and immutable *(avikarya)*. The body is born and dies but soul is neither born nor dies. The soul or self assumes a new body when its old body is worn out. The body, five cognitive organs, five motor organs, minds *(manas)*, intellect *(buddhi)* and egoism are composed of three gunas like purity or essence *(settva)*, energy *(rajas)* and inertia *(tamas)* which are effects of *prakrti*. But the self or soul is devoid of gunas.

The Gita presents a unique synthesis of Action, Devotion and Knowledge. Human beings are the complex of intellect, will and emotion. Intellect has given rise to the philosophy of knowledge, emotion to the philosophy of devotion and will to these philosophy of action. Modern psychology teaches us that the three aspects of mind are distinguishable only theoretically but not in reality. The teachings of Gita are also in line with this view and these three ultimately stand synthesized and this synthesis is called 'yoga' which means union of the individual with Absolute (or God). It means balance of mind *(Samatva)* and means higher perspective of action which comes through detachment *(Karmasu Kaushalam)*. Thus this meaning of yoga is different from its meaning in Yoga philosophy where by yoga is meant cessation of modification of chitta.

Keeping in view Knowledge, Action and Devotion, in Gita mention has been made of *Jnana yoga, Karma yoga* and *Bhakti yoga*. Jnana yoga is essentially and predominantly the path of knowledge. Here the individual attains great height by means of his intellectual activity. Having obtained knowledge, one soon embraces peace. In fact, there is nothing purer than knowledge. Karma yoga means performing one's duties in form of service to the people very sincerely and to the best of abilities without expecting anything in return. Krama yoga is possible only when the jnana yoga is attained. The constituent gunas of *Prakrti*, that is, *Sattva, Rajas* and *Tamas* necessarily give rise to actions. The ideal of this yoga is not negation of action but performance of actions in a detatched spirit. Actions are our sphere and fruits are not our concerns. We should never be attatched to the fruits of actions and at the same time we should never be passive or inactive. Thus it has been rightly said that the Gita teaching stands not for *renunciation of action but for renunciation in action*. In Bhakti yoga one carries on his duties with great humility and devotion and tries to surrender himself wholly to the God. This disintersted service is not possible without knowledge. Hence, Bhakti yoga can be performed only by a true Jnani. The devotee is here confident of the guarantee given by the Lord—"Never does my devotee perish." Here absolute dependence and utter faith in God are very necessary. The love of God is the supreme love and every other form of it is an imperfect manifestation of this supreme love. Out of the four types of devotees—the suffering *(arta)*, the seeker for truth *(jijnasu)* the self-interested *(artharthi)* and the wise *(jnani)*, the last one is considered as the best one.

Thus concluding the whole discussion of psychology made available by Gita, it can be said that *Jnana* is the most importat thing, being the very essence of reality. *Karma* and *Bhakti* are only manifestation of Jnana. Without *Jnana*, liberation is impossible and so is detachment or renunciation in action and so is disinterested devotion to God. The Lord has to give knowledge to his devotees so that they have access to Him. There is nothing purer than knowledge.

Buddhism also has much to contribute to psychology. Buddhism which originated in India and later spread to China and Japan, presented a systematic elaboration on the nature of the soul and its relation to material world. The term 'Buddha' is a general term meaning one who is enlightened or awakened. It applied to the founder of Buddhism known as Sakyamuni whose personal name was Siddhartha (560-480 BC). The teachings of Buddha were oral and were recorded by his disciples much later. Buddha was primarily an ethical teacher and a social reformer. He repeatedly told his disciples: *"Two things only do I teach—misery and cessation of misery"* Human existence is full of misery and pain. Our urgent and immediate duty, therefore, is to get rid of misery and pains.

A few months after Buddha's death, the first Buddhist council was held at Rajagrha to establish the Canon of the *Vinaya*, the Displine of the order. After about a century, there arose a violent controversy regarding some of the provisions of *Vinaya* and also divided Buddhists into *Sthaviranvadins* and *Mahasanghikas*. The second Buddhist council was held at Vaishali for expunging the ten controversial positions of Vinaya. The third Buddhis council was summoned by Ashoka, the Great at Patliputra in which about more than one thousand monks participated. Its object was to prepare a canon of Doctrine of Elders (Sthaviravada). The fourth Buddhist council was held in the first or second contry AD under king Kaniska to reconsider and compile the tenets of Sarvastivada School.

The present Pali Canon was probably complied by the third Buddhist council summoned by Ashoka, the great. The Pali Canon is called *Tipitaka* or the three Baskets. The first basket is called as *Vinaya-*

Pitaka that deals with the discipline of order. The second Basket is *Sutta-Pitaka* and is compilation of the utterances of the Master himself and consists of five collections called *Nikayas : Digha, Majjhima, Anguttara, Samyutta* and *Khuddaka*. The third Basket is called *Abhidhamma-pitaka* which deals with various types of philosophical and psychological discussions and is in seven parts. *Dhamma-Sangani* which is the short summary of discussion about the states of consciousness is the first book in the Abhidhamma Pitaka and and it is agreed that this book was complied towards the fourth century B.C.

The above viewpoints represent the *Hinayana* sect which was complied long after the death of Buddha. Same Buddhists were not happy with these viewpoints and felt that they did not represent the realing teaching of Buddha and contained many horrible misinterpretations of the teaching of Buddha. They called themselves *Mahayanis* and had a separate literature in Sanskrit.

Buddha's teaching may be said to be three-fold: *the Four Noble Truths, the Noble Eightfold path* and the *Doctrine of Dependent origination*. The Four Noble Truths (arya satya) are:

(i) There is suffering (duhkha). Human existence is full of pain and misery. None can deny. All beings, humans and animals, are caught up in *Sansara,* a cycle of rebirth that each living thing lives through a series of lives which occurs through various forms both in this world and the future world.

(ii) There is cause of suffering (duhkha-Samudaya). Everything has a cause. In facts nothing comes out of nothing—*ex nihilo nihil fit*. Suffering being a fact, must have a cause. Karma is the moral quality of actions done in past lives that determines the happines or suffering experienced thereafter.

(iii) There is cessation of sufferings (duhkha-nirodha). Since everything arises depending upon some causes and conditions, therefore, if these causes and conditions are removed, the effect also ceases. Thus the chain of suffering can cease and this is called as *Nirvana* by the Buddhists who conceived of it as a cessation of rebirth, an escape from *Sansara*.

(iv) There is a way leading to this cessation of suffering (dukha-nirodha-gamini-pratipat). There are ethical and spiritual paths through which misery can be removed and liberation can be attained. Thus by adopting these paths, cessation of rebirth can be attained. These paths are called the *Noble Eight fold path.*

The Noble Eight fold path consists of eight steps which are right faith *(Samyog drsti)*, right resolve *(sankalpa)*, right speech *(vak)*, right action *(karmanta)*, right living *(ajiva)*, right effort *(vyayama)*, right thought *(smrti)* and right concentration *(samadhi)*. Connected to these eight-fold paths, there are eight kinds of forbidden behaviours from which one must abstain to escape rebirth. They are killing, stealing, exaggeration in speech, adultery and lust, drinking, retiring on luxurious bedding, fancy dressing, enjoying song and dance and eating inappropriate food. These disciplinary practices when combined with training in meditation and concentration, lead to an ultimate state of *Moksha* which means spritiual release or liberation.

The doctrine of dependent origination *(Pratityasamutpada)* is the foundation of all the teachings of Buddha. It is contained in the the Second Noble truth which gives us the cause of suffering and in the Third noble truth which shows the cessation of suffering. Suffering is Sansara and cessation of suffering is Nirvana. This doctrine tells us that in the empirical world dominated by intellect every thing is relative, dependent and subject to birth and death and further, impermanent. The causal formula is : Depending upon cause, the effect arises. Since every object of thought is necessarily relative, it is neither absolutely real nor absolutely unreal. It hangs between reality and nothingness. In fact, it is like the appearance of *Vedantic Avidya* or *Maya*. It is in this sense that Buddha calls their doctrine the Middle path or *Madhyama Partipat* which avoids both eternalism and nihilsm.

Later some Buddhists emphasize upon yoga practice which is a method of self-cultivation of gaining release from the bondage of Karma and rebirth. It helps person in making concentration without distracting mind. This is basically done through breath and posture control.

Zen Buddhism is the sectarian movement of Buddhists religion that originated in China and flourished in the 7th century and spread to India and Japan. The original meaning of Zen was 'quiet meditation' but later on, the term also included wisdom. Today its objective is `enlightenment' In fact, it stresses the practice of meditation as the means to elightenment or non-conceptual conprehension *(satori)*. The means by which a practitioner realizes enlightment are following three:

(a) Zalen. This includes vaning types of exercises to regulate bodily posture, breathing and mind.

(b) Koan. It includes intellectual exercises of mediationg on question that logic can never answer such as How does one look before meeting one's father and mother ? Concentration on the meaning of the Koan frees the mind of several other concerns until only the Koan remains. Later on, Koan also vanishes, leaving only the mind as a blurless mirror.

(c) Sānshi-Mompo. It is a type of counselling of zen monks by their masters and it includes suggestions, explanations, contradictions, guides, force, etc:.

The aim of zen meditation is to create alert emptiness in which mind is like a mirror, simply reflecting what impinges upon it from the external world. If zen really transforms the mind into a mirror that reflects thought and stimulation, one might then predict that EEG studies of zen practictioners would reveal patterns characteristic of active concentration and show failure to habituate to some repetitive stimuli. Both of these predictions have been experimentally validated (Yamoaka, 1968; Kasamatsu & Hirai, 1966).

In fact, it is Zen Buddhist which had great impact on modern psychotheapy practices. Many Eastern psychotherapies today have their obvious roots in Zen Buddhistm and Yoga practices. Some of the examples are the *Chinese Qi Gong and Japanese Morita therapy.* The happy news is that in' recent years zen practices have also spread to western culture.

PSYCHOLOGY IN MODERN TIMES

With the intiatives of Sir Ashutosh Mukherjee, the then vice-chancellor of Calcutta University the Psychology of the western origin was first introduced as a subject in Philosphy department of Calcutta University and Sir Brojendra Nath Seal, a professor of Mental and Moral philosophy, drafted the very first syllabus for experimental psychology. He also established a small psychological laboratory in 1905. But some how this laboratory could not yield the desired result. After eleven years the first department of Experimental psychology was established in 1916 at Calcutta University. Prof. Narendra Nath Sengupta chaired this department. He had previliged to receive training at Harvard University under Huge Munsterberg, a student of Wilhelm Wundt.

Prof. N. N. Sengupta had a doctorate in Philosophy on *'anti-intellectualism* from Harvard University. He had also received training with Robert yerks and E. B. Holt. He had also visited the psychological laboratory at Cornell University. He along with Radha Kamal Mukherjee published the famous book *Introduction of Social Psychology* in 1928. In fact, in 1929 he moved to Lucknow University. One of his famous students, there, was H. S. Asthama.

Deb (2002) while presenting an account of the early developments of Calcutta University, pointed out that the Wundtian traidtion contributed one-third (16) of the total number of research papers (49) during the period of 1926-31 *Indian Psychological Association,* (IPA) was established in 1924 and Psychology was admitted to *Indian Science Congress* in 1925 and the same year IPA started publication of *Indian Journal of Psychology* in 1926. Later on, Prof.

Girindra Shekhar Bose succeeded Prof. Sengupta. Prof. Bose was very closely associated with Sigmund Freud. In 1922 he founded Indian Psychoanalytic Society which was affliated to the *International Psychoanlvtic Society in 1924.*

Prof. Bose was the first D. Sc. in Psychology at Calcutta in 1922 on the work of repression. He published a famous book entitled *Concept of Repression* in 1921. The book pleased Sigmund Freud so much so that he said, "the first book on psychoanalytic subject which comes to us from... India displays so good a knowledge of psychoanalysis, so deep an insight into its difficulties and so much of deep going of original thought. "(Deb, 2002) Prof. Bose remained as Chairman of the Department from 1929 to 1940. After Bose, Prof. S. C. Mitra was the next university professor who had Ph. D. from Leipzig University in 1926 on monocular and binocular perception of brightness. Still another notable professor was S. C. Sinha who had a Ph. D. from Graz University, Austria on the psychological appeal of Hindu region.

At Calcutta University the department of Experiment Psychology was rechristened in 1938 as the Department of Psychology. In 1943 Applied Psychology wing was started and a certificate course in Applied psychology was started in 1945. This year was a remarkable year in the history of Indian Psychology because eminent psychlogists like Jung, Myers and Spearman had been invited to the science congress. Jung was also awarded honoured degree by Calcutta University. M. V. Gopal Swami who had been trained under the guidance of Spearman at London University, headed the department at Mysore. He had also set up an animal laboratory for the researches. In 1924 Mysore University established the department of psychology which was followed by creation of department of psychology in Lucknow University. In 1946 Patna University started two separate full-fledged department of psychology–department of Experimental psychology and department of Applied psychology. The department of applied psychology was instituted at Institute of Psychological Researches and Service with the dual purpose of providing teaching in applied psychology and providing guidance and couselling to those who needed. Prof. H. P. Maiti of Calcutta University joined as its first Director. During visit of Prof. Gardner Murphy in 1950 as the UNESCO Consultant to Government of India on 'Social Tensions', this institute was selected as one of the research centers under the regional direction of Late Prof. H. P. Maiti. Subsequently, eminent psychologists like Late Prof. Durganand Sinha, Late Dr. A. K. P. Sinha and Late Dr. B. Deserved as the Director of the Institute. The author has also privilege to be the Director of this Institute twice. One of its Director, Late Prof. D. Sinha, also served as Director of A. N. Sinha Institute of Social Studies, a well-known institute for making unique contributions to the development of not only psychology but to other selected behavioural sciences.

Although the movement of psychology that grew under the influence of Structuralism with focus on the study of sensation, perception, psychophysics and reaction time was influential, many Indian psychologists had keen interest in the indigenous knowledge system. For example, at Baneras Hindu University, Prof. B. L. Areya worked on *Yoga Vashistha* and at Lucknow, Asthana worked on the *Samkhya theory of Personality*. Likewise, at Delhi Indira Sen (1943, 1946, 1951) focussed on the integral psychology of Shri Aurbindo. Prof. E. G. Parameshwaran worked on *triguna theory* at Osmania. At Ahmedabad Prof. P. H. Prabhu (1954) worked on *Indian Social Psychology*. Prof. B. Krishan (1974) worked on *Indian typological* concents of personality.

Today there are a large number of teaching and research institutions which are offering wide range of courses in psychology. However, it is not exactly known how many colleges and universities offers course in psychology and how many psychologists are actively engaged in their profession Although no data are available on this account, there are more than 15,000 psychologists in India who are said to be professionally active (Jain, 2005). The teaching activities in India have followed a generic framework with Master's degree in psychology or applied psychology with sufficient degree of overlapping in orientation and coverage. Only recently some departments have started special programmes in clinical psychology (SNDT, Mumbai), Cognitive Psychology (Allahabad) and Counselling Psychology (Banglore and Andhra university) Some departments have started diploma programmes in guidance, counselling and Human Resource development (HRD). For example, Departments of Psychology, Patna University had started Postgraduate Diploma in Human Research Development in 2003 and full-hedged M. A. in Criminology in 2007. Likewise, Institute of Psychological Researches and Service, Patna University is successfully impating teaching in Postgratuate Diploma in Clinical psychology since 1995.

At present there are four professional organizations of Indian psychologists : *The Indian Psychological Association* (IPA) established in 1925; the *Indian Academy of Applied Psychology* (IAAP) established in 1966; the *Indian Association of Clinical Psychology* (IACP) established in 1968 and the *National Academy of Psychology* (NAOP) established in 1987. At present India is represented by NAOP at the *International union of Psychological Sciences* (IUPS). ICCR Publishes the *Indian Psychological Abstracts and Reviews* since 1990 which documents brief summary of works published in Various important Indian Journals.

Now-a-days there are as many as forty university departments of psychology is India. Most of these departments offer instructions in psychology at graduate and post-graduate levels. Some research works either in form of various research projects sponsored by bodies like University Grants Commission, Indian Council of Social Science Researches, etc., or in from of doctoral dissertations leading to Ph. D. degrees are being conducted in these various departments of psychology. Indian Psychologists are running some journals in which they published their research works. Some of the important journals are : *Psychological Studies, Indian Journal of Applied Psychology, Indian Journal of Industrial Relations, Indian Journal of Experimental Psychology, Indian Psychological Review, Journal of Applied Psychology, Journal of Foundation for Organizational Research, Journal of Psychological Researches, Bombay Psychologist, Abhigyan, Psycho-lingua, Indian Journal of Psychometry and Education.* Indian psychologists also make contributions in foreign journals.

In India the most unfortunate thing is that its general environment is not well conducive for carrying psychological researches. People have little realization about the psychological problems and hence, they seldom think that psychological researches will be of any help in solving their problems. But now the picture has started changing. With rapid growth of education, industrialization and realization about the importance of psychological researches by various institutions and people in general, psychology in India seems to be picking up its lost glory. The Government of India has set-up body like Indian Council of Social Science Research (ICSSR) which gives proper encouragement to not only psychological researches but researches being conducted in the entire field of social science. More recently, the Government of India has set-up *Institute of Banking Personnel Selection* at Bombay, in which a large number of psychologists have been employed and they by carrying out various psychological researches, help the Government in personnel selection and placement. Fortunately, the author was also associated with this institute as one of the Chief Test Administrators.

In India psychological researches are also done in some para-educational institutions and psychological research centers. Some of these institutes and centers are : the National Council of Educational Research and Training (NCERT), the Tata Institute of Social Sciences, the Indian Institute of Mass Communication, Directorate of Psychological Researches, National Institute of Health Administration and Education (NIHAE), National Institute of Family Planning, All India Institute of Public Health and Hygiene, National Institute of Community Development, A. N. Sinha Institute of Social Studies, Institute of Management etc. Some of psychologists employed in these institutions have been trained in countries like America and Britain and some have been trained on Indian soil. The contributions of these psychologists have been so vital that their recognition has been formally made by Government by giving them suitable awards.

According to a publication of ICSSR on doctorates in Social Sciences in

India, up to 1969 approximately 250 persons had received their doctorate in psychology from the various Indian Universities (ICSSR*, 1971). Today the actual number of persons who received such doctorate degree might have been increased several times than the cited figure. There are also some professional organizations of psychologists in India. At the national level there is the *Indian Psychological Association.* It publishes its official journal named *Indian Journal of Psychology* that is the oldest Journal in India. There are also *Indian Association of Clinical Psychologists, Indian Academy of Applied Psychology, Madras Psychological Society, Bihar Psychological Association* (almost non-functional now), *Mysore Psychological Society,* etc. Apart from all these, there is a section of Psychology and Educational Sciences in Indian Science Congress Association which meets annually for almost a week in January. In this section scientific papers are read and symposia are held.

For presenting a broad picture of growth of researches done in psychology in India, ICSSR presents critical reviews and reflect some major changes and shifts in Indian Psychological researches. It published a first *Survey of Research in Psychology* in 1971. This survey, edited by Prof. S. K. Mitra, covered the period of 1950-69. According to this survey total number of publications in this period was 2,981. The number of actual published papers and various publications by Indian psychologists ending the present year are definitely more than this figure. A formal survey, however, is awaited. Taking research publications as standard measure, we find that of the total publications referred to in the reviews during 1950-70, four areas contributed 64 per cent-Clinical Psychology (19%), Psychology of Personality (17%), Social Psychology (16%) and Experimental Psychology (12%). Six others areas contributed only 36 per cent-Industrial Psychology (11%). Educational Psychology (6%), Methodology and Research Technology (6%), Military Psychology (6%), Developmental Psychology (4%) and Physiological and Compara-tive Psychology (2%). From this analysis, it appears that modern psychology in India has five major fields where Indian psychologists are most active-Clinical Psychology, Psychology of Personality, Social Psychology, Experimental psychology and Industrial Psychology. A brief description of the nature of researches done in these various areas is as under :

1. *Clinical Psychology*

Prof. B. Krishnan reviewed this area. According to his review, Calcutta University was the first University that started an applied section in Psychology department in 1938 with the purposes of developing psychological testing and rendering help to the students in selecting their courses and vocations. Calcutta University was also first in imparting

* ICSSR (1971) Doctoral Students in Social Sciences, 1969, ICSSR, New Delhi, Vol. 2.

training to younger people in psychoanalysis as a method of psychotherapy. Prof. Girindra Shekar Bose founded the Indian Psychoanalytical Society in 1922. This Society started at the Lumbini Park Mental Hospital in Calcutta in 1940. According to UGC report* (1968) there were 19 Universities that offered a course in clinical psychology at Master level as one of the optional papers. Today there are several more Universities that offer such facilities. In India there are three major clinical centers that provide training to clinical psychologists with facility of supervised practicum or internship. They are : National Institute of Mental Health and Neurosciences (NIMHANS), Bangalore; Central Institute of Psychiatry Kanke, Ranchi; and Mental Hospital, Lumbini Park, Calcutta, The Clinical Psychologists in India have organized an All India Association of their own and its first convention was held in October, 1969 at NIMHAMS in Bangalore. According to Prof. B. Krishnan, Indian Psychologists have mainly conducted their researches in fields like psychopathology covering all the mental disorders including mental retardation, psychodiagnosis, counselling, guidance and psychotherapy. These psychologists have also devoted time in either constructing or adapting diagnostic instruments and techniques, which have been used successfully by them.

2. *Psychology of Personality*

Prof. T. E. Shanmugam, after making a careful review, presented a report for the work done in this area. Researches in this field have grown considerably in India. But this is not peculiar to India rather it has been an international trend. Indian psychologists have mainly concentrated in developing assessment techniques and in studying about self-concepts, motivation, delinquency, criminality and abnormal personality. In these studies, however, there have been uncritical acceptance of Western models. Indian concepts of personality have not received due attention. He also noted that there had been much emphasis upon translating a western questionnaire into a language of the country. Fortunately, this trend has now been minimized. In the field of personality studies, achievement motivation, on the pattern of McClelland's study, have been very prolific. Commenting upon such view Prof. Shanmugam has stated that studies on achievement motivation have certainly meaning in countries like America where these exists a higher level of need satisfaction. But in countries like India where people are struggling at a lower levels of need (using Maslow's terminology), studies of affiliation and/or security motive would have been more meaningful. For him, in almost all researches done in the fields of personality there was no evidence of underlying theory. Such studies often stand aloof and without any obvious direction and goal. Wherever a

* Psychology in Indian Universities : Report of the Review Committee of University Grants Commision, New Delhi, 1968

particular instrument has been used, no rationale for selecting the instrument has been shown. Keeping all these in view, it can be said that Indian approaches to the fields of personality are 'eclectic'.

3. *Social Psychology*

Prof. R.N. Rath had reviewed this area. According to his report there are eight areas of social psychology in which Indian psychologists have contributed a lot. They are : cultural and social processes, attitudes and opinions, group and interpersonal processes, communication, aesthetics, sexual behaviour, smoking, drug and alcohol use. He reported that there were 527 published papers till 1970. Today this number stands considerably increased. About 50 per cent of the published papers were in the field of cultural and social processes. The field of theory and methodological development stood comparatively neglected. The areas that demanded immediate attention are social change, social tensions, social problems like unemployment and poverty, student unrest, etc. Some of the Indian social psychologists were most active in these areas. For example, Late Dr. Amar Kumar Singh (Ranchi University) and Retired Prof. Dr. J.B.P. Sinha have widened some of these areas by their valuable scientific contributions.

4. *Experimental Psychology*

Prof. V.K. Kothurkar had reviewed the work done by Indian psychologists in the area of experimental. psychology. According to his review till 1970, there were 288 published papers. There were nine areas of experimental psychologist in which Indian psychologists had contributed a lot. There were : psychophysics, sensory processes, perception-attention, reaction time, work-fatigue, physiology of behaviour including animal behaviour, learning-memory, thinking and problem-solving, and psycholinguistic. Most of the researches done in these fields were based on western models. In fact this is a discouraging trend and the exclusive dependence upon western leadership is likely to harm our own enterprise. It is also disheartening to note that many of the leaders of Indian psychologists are not working in this field. Some young people are, however, active and making contributions. They have kept the field alive. They are now using more sophisticated design of the experiment as well as developed instruments and materials. However, the fields that required more immediate attention were learning theory, verbal behaviour, perception and information theory, etc.

5. *Industrial Psychology*

Late Prof. Durganand Sinha had reviewed this field and has tried to present an overview of researches done in the field of industrial psychology since the founding of the first department of psychology in country in 1915. He reviewed 533 published studies as well as a few unpublished studies. His analysis revealed that out of 533 published studies only 25, that is, about 4 per cent studies were conducted in pre- independence era. The remaining 508 studies (about 96%) were conducted in post-independence era. He divided all these studies in eleven subfields-vocational choice and guidance, selection and placement, training, task and work analysis, performance and job satisfaction, management and organization, special environment, advertising and consumer psychology, engineering psychology, driving and safety, surveys and general studies. From the analysis presented above, it is obvious that the growth of Industrial psychology in India is of recent phenomenon. After properly scrutinizing all the 533 researches, he came to the conclusion that about 145 (that is, 28.7%) researches were non-empirical in nature. They consisted of purely theoretical discussions over the issues. Moreover, the scrutiny also indicated that most of the Indian industrial psychologists were depended upon the west for the problems, methods and techniques that have been used. Most of these studies have been repetitive. Rarely some efforts has been made to show inventiveness and originality in the research work. This has been rather an unfortunate trend. Fortunately, this trend is changing in recent years. The establishment of different institutes of management, technology, and various research organizations like ATIRA (Ahmedabad Textile Industry Research Association), SITRA (South Indian Textile Research Association) and Shri Ram center for Industrial Relations as well as the gradually increasing contact between the academic psychologists and industry have provided a big change in the general outlook.

6. *Educational Psychology*

Prof. M.B. Buch had reviewed this field with sole aim of providing a synoptic view of the status of research in educational psychology. As we know, the first department of psychology was established in 1916 in the university of Calcutta. But the first college of education had been established in Madras about more than 100 years ago. In India teaching of educational psychology began in colleges of education. But being an applied branch of psychology, educational psychology did not attain a status of merits in education. In the department of psychology, it also failed to get due recognition. According to Dr. B. Kuppuswamy, Chairman of a Review Committee on Psychology appointed by UGC in 1961, educational psychology was included as one of the compulsory papers at M.A. level only in Calcutta University. But in recent days the picture stands entirely changed. Now almost all the university departments of psychology have included educational psychology as one of the papers at M.A. level. Prof. M. B. Buch has presented the review by dividing the area of educational psychology into eight subfields– attitude and adjustment, testing, physical education, special education, educational and career guidance, personnel, school learning and achievement and teaching methods. His review included works done at doctoral level, post-doctoral levels, books, and research papers published in journals, brochures, and bulletin. His review indicated that there were bulk of studies relating to the attitudes of students towards school activities, attitudes of teachers towards their profession, adjustment of students but there were very few studies relating to achievement as it affected by ability, school, personality, motivation, etc. There were hardly any study relating to programmed learning and impact of television. But in recent years such studies have been found to be reported.

7. *Methodology and Research Technology*

This field was reviewed by Prof. S.K. Mitra. According to him, the area of methodology and research technology covers several subfields like models, mathematics and statistics, factor analysis, computer programming, testing, construction and validation of instruments, experimentation and observation. His review indicated that not much work in the area of methodology and research technology has been done by Indian psychologists. They have mainly concentrated in the fields like test construction, validation and factor analysis, and they have shown little enthusiasm in methods. According to his review, historically the research work in the field of test development started in India at about the same time it started in England and America. But its progress remained retarded. In the beginning the test development work was mainly devoted to the development of individual scales of intelligence. Rice was the first person who standardized the Binet test in Hindustani. This was followed by Kamat in Marathi and Kannada as well as by Shukla in Gujarati. Group test of intelligence was first developed by Mahalanobis and this was followed by Sohan Lal, Jalota, Mohsin, Desai and Joshi. Much work on the development of similar tests were done in the various University departments of psychology and teacher training colleges, but they were not systematically reported. Among the various tests developed, the interest inventories attracted very little attention of Indian psychologists. In the area of aptitude, Varma made the first attempt to construct a battery of differential aptitude tests. Indian adaptation of DAT has also been done by Bhatt and Ojha. Weschler Intelligence Scale for Children (WISC) and Weschler Adult Intelligence Scale (WAIS) have also been adopted in various Indian languages. In the field of factor analysis the first attempt was made by G. Pal in 1948. He used the technique of factor analysis for analyzing a set of tests. Research paper relating to this was presented in Indian Science Congress held that year. In the field of methods the first paper was on questionnaire method prepared by P. Ram in 1939. He had raised the methodological issues of reliability and validity in this paper. Later on, several works in the field of methods were reported. For example, Shanker (1964) devised a simplified method of scoring a social distance scale. Ray (1965) compared the three different methods of item scoring. Das (1959) published a paper in which she presented a rapid and reliable method for estimating percentile scores of examination marks and test scores. Kundu (1961) presented a paper in which he compared three different methods of computing tetrachoric correlation. Prof. S.K. Mitra has cautioned that although in these various Indian studies the sampling has improved, but there is still preponderance of incidental sampling rather than probability sampling. This is to be checked. Likewise, in the field of item analysis, indices of item difficulty and item discrimination have been frequently calculated but the use of item statistics in improving distractors of the multiple-choice items have been ignored. National Psychological Corporation, Agra under the directorship of Dr. Mahesh Bhargava is publishing the various psychological tests being developed by Indian psychologists.

8. *Military Psychology*

The work in this area of psychology has been reviewed by Prof. A.K.P. Sinha. According to his report, research in military psychology in India started very late. In 1943, a small cell was created in the Ministry of Defence, to find out ways for selecting officers for Indian Armed Forces. After independence, the work of this cell was expanded and reorganized. Accordingly, the cell was designated as Psychological Research Wing. This wing developed some tests which proved very helpful in defence selection. Encouraged by this success, its activities were expanded and it was named as the Directorate of Psychological Research in 1962. According to Prof. A.K.P. Siriha, the works in the field of military psychology in India are very limited. They are mainly limited to development of some tests (for use with defence personnels) like intelligence tests, personality tests, aptitude tests, interview techniques, group testing, sociometric technique, etc. as well as to training of defence personnel, displays and controls engineering psychology, driving and safety, etc. Dr. D.P. Sen Mazumdar was also actively engaged in conducting researches in these fields.

9. *Developmental Psychology*

This area was reviewed by Prof. E.G. Parameswaran. According to him, Indian psychologists have entered in this field very late. After making a careful review of the works done in this area by Indian psychologists, he came to the conclusion that more than 60 percent of the studies were in some selected fields like intelligence, emotionality, adjustment and personality. The other areas of developmental psychology like physical development, learning and parent-child relationship, etc. have been comparatively neglected. Methods employed by Indian psychologists in studying the various areas of developmental psychology were mostly cross-sectional. Only two studies were longitudinal-Gupta (1945) and Verma et al. (1969). The sampling procedures in most of these studies were incidental. Random sampling or stratified sampling was used only in six studies. Four of the studies, namely, Gupta (1945), Nawaratna (1939), Fathak (1966) and Verma et al. (1969) were conducted on single subjects. The only one study, that is, developmental Norms Project of NCERT was conducted on national-wide sampling.

10. *Physiological and Comparative Psychology*

Prof. M.M. Sinha had reviewed the work done in this area by Indian psychologist. According to his review, Indian psychologists have not been much conscious about making contributions in these fields. Among the fields of animal psychology or comparative psychology areas like natural observation, early experiences, motivation and emotion, conditioning, discrimination, avoidance escape, reinforcement schedules, punishment and extinction, sensory processes, social and sexual behaviour have been their active areas. As one example of studies in the field of natural observation the study conducted by Singh & Manocha (1966) may be cited. They were interested in examining the reactions of rhesus monkeys and langurs in some novel situations through vocalizations. Both qualitative and quantitative differences were found between these two classes of monkeys-rhesus monkeys were found to express greater number of fearful responses than langurs. Also, langurs were found to be more manipulative, active and less fearful than rhesus monkeys. The fields of physiological psychology in which Indian psychologists have been most active are brain lesions, brain stimulation, electrical activities, sensory physiology, biochemistry, cardiovascular processes, environmental stress, nutrition, psycho-pharmacology, etc. In some of these fields, Prof. S.N. Sinha, has also made valuable contributions. As one example, we can cite one study by Sinha and Sharma (1970) on the comparative effects of Beta-carotene and Vitamin 'A' on the learning of short-term retention of light-dark discrimination among rats in the four phases. There were two experimental groups of rats-Group A and B. Their findings revealed that with initial administration of Beta-carotene and Vitamin 'A' in Group A and B respectively, there existed a clear difference. The brightness discrimination scores were significantly higher in Group B than in Group A.

The second survey of research in psychology has also been late published. This second survey of research in psychology in India was edited by Late Prof. Udai Pareek (1980, 1981). It covered the works done by Indian psychologists during 1971-1976 and it adopted basically a thematic and cross-disciplinary approach. It consisted of two parts-Part I (1980) and Part II

(1981). Part I covered only six areas like psychological theory and research methods, culture and personality, developmental processes, cognitive processes (including attention, perception, learning, remembering and forgetting, thinking, problem-solving and creativity) deviance and pathology and counselling and therapy. Part II emphasized upon the fields like communication and influence processes and behaviour and environmental psychology. The second survey basically showed that various significant developments took place in psychological researches in India with greater emphasis upon the above- mentioned areas. Prof. Udai Pareek (1981), in his editorial comment, had expressed a great faith in psychology as having strong potential for developing various strategies to contribute to the solution of various social problems of India. He commented that psychology is *"standing at the crossroads today"*.

The third survey of research in Psychology in India has also been published by ICSSR (1988). It covers the researches done in period 1977 to 1986 (Middle of 1986). It has been edited by Prof. Janak Pandey (1988) and the survey has been published in three volumes, entitled *Psychology in India : The State-of-Art* Volume I is named as *Personality and Mental Processes* which consists of six chapters. The first chapter is on *Psychological assessment*, which focuses on the present and future trend in the field of psychological assessment. In this chapter Prof. S. S. Kulkarni and Prof. B. N. Puhan, authors, have given special emphasis upon undertaking problem-oriented rather than tool-oriented researches. The *second* chapter is on current trends in *Development psychology* and has been authored by Prof. T. S. Sraswathi and Prof. Ranjan Dutta. These authors have given emphasis upon studying important areas of child's development like cognitive development, language development, physical development and personality. The study of the socially disadvantaged children and their implication for social policy has also been emphasized. The *third* chapter is on *Personality* which has been prepared by Prof. H. S. Asthana. Prof. Asthana has emphasized upon the need for studying the individual in a broader framework, that is, in the context of the totality of his existence. He has also given stress upon the role of social institutions, socialization and culture in development of personality. The *fourth* chapter is on *Stress and anxiety* which has been authored by Prof. Sagar Sharma. He has highlighted theoretical, methodological and conceptual issues that are related to stress and anxiety. The *fifth* chapter is on *Perceptual and cognitive processes* prepared by Prof. K. D. Broota. He has raised issues related to the cross-cultural studies in cognitive functioning and has highlighted the analysis of the development of perceptual and cognitive skills. He also emphasized upon the study of sensory deprivation. The *sixth* chapter is on *Higher mental processes* which has been prepared by Prof. L. B. Tripathi. He has highlighted a critical approach to the researches made in the field of memory, thinking, creativity, and learning. He has also explained the neurophysiological bases of these various higher mental processes.

Volume II of 'The Psychology in India' entitled as *Basic and Applied Social Psychology* consists of again six chapters. The *first* chapter is on *Attitude and social cognition*, which has been prepared by Prof. R. Singh. He has highlighted the researches done in the field of attitudes, attribution, judgment, decision and impression formation. The *second* chapter is on *Social influence processes*. This chapter has been authored by Prof. J. Pandey. He has very nicely made a critical review of researches done in the field of altruism, interpersonal attraction and manipulative social behaviours like ingratiation and machiavellianism. Prof. R. C. Tripathi has authored the *third* chapter entitled *Applied social psychology*. He has reviewed researches done in the field of family planning and fertility behaviour, health behaviour, poverty, deprivation and the social disadvantage. The *fourth* chapter entitled *intergroup relations and social tensions* was authored by Prof. A. K. Singh. The author has made a critical review of the researches done in the field of prejudice, attitudes and stereotypes. On the basis of his review he has pointed out that a final resolution on prejudice, discrimination and hostilities must be done by bringing changes in the larger socio-economic and political contexts because they are basically rooted in these contexts. The *fifth* chapter entitled *Dynamics of rural development* was prepared by Prof. B. C. Muthayya. He has emphasized upon the researches done in the field of rural development particularly upon the rural leadership, disadvantaged groups and people's participation in various development programmes. The chapter also raises issues related to attitudes, motivation and perceptual style of the rural people. The *sixth* chapter entitled the *Social psychology of education* was written by Prof. K. C. Panda. In this chapter he has reviewed researches conducted in different fields of educational psychology and has raised various issues related to the psychological problems of scheduled castes, scheduled tribes and socially disavantaged children, social factors in academic achievement, the school as a social system and as a socializing agent, personality and motivational characteristics of* pupils, problems of dropouts and stagnation and education as a broad instrument of social change, etc.

Volume III of 'The Psychology in India' entitled as *Organizational Behaviour and Mental Health* comprises five chapters. The *first* chapter is on *Job attitudes* prepared by Prof. R. Padaki. This chapter reviews researches done in various fields related to job attitude such as job satisfaction, motivation, job involvement, job commitment, etc. Various determinants of job attitudes such as demographic determiniants, personality determinanants, organizational determinants are discussed. The cross-cultural comparison, methodological and other issues related to job attitudes have also been discussed. The *second* chapter is on *Organizational effectiveness* prepared by Prof. P. N. Khandwalla. He has reviewed researches done on the implications of the effectiveness of organization in Indian developmental context. He has also presented a model of organizational effectiveness. The chapter also summarises findings relating to determiniants and consequences of organizational effectiveness and also proposes several hypotheses that have attracted the attention of psychologists to do further researches. The *third* chapter is on *Mental health* authored by Prof. K. Sathyavathi. The author reviews the researches related to the various attitudes and belief of people about mental health problems. The chapter also assesses the importance of counselling, guidance and yoga for the different areas of mental health. Major issues related to the community and mental health have also been reviewed. The *fourth* chapter is on *Mental illness and treatment* written by Prof. S. K. Verma. Prof. Verma has nicely summarizes the various views related to the definitions and classification of mental illness and discusses the importance of the various socio-cultural factors in diagnosis, classification, causation and treatment of the different types of mental illness. The *fifth* chapter is on *Psychology in India* and presents the emerging trend in psychological researches in India. This chapter was authored by Prof. J. Pandey.

In this way we find that the eminent Indian psychologists through these three volumes (of The Psychology in India) have tried to present, review and make a careful assessment of Indian psychological researches by dividing them into seventeen major areas. A critical review of all these seventeen major areas reflect among other things, one basic point- Indian psychologists are now competent enough to develop their own models and theories and they are now showing a strong concern over their applications to the solution of various problems being faced by Indian society. Now the time is gone for blaming Indian psychologists for doing repetitive researches and conducting researches on .borrowed models of West. Thus "some creative directions" have emerged in Indian psychological researches (Pandey, 1988) and now the psychology is not strictly "standing at the crossroads today" as Pareek (1981) had commented.

The *fourth survey* of psychological research in India has been released by ICSSR (2001) and was published by Sage, New Delhi in 2001. The fourth survey covers researches done by Indian psychologists in various fields for the period 1983-92. It has also been edited by Prof. Janak Pandey and has been named *Psychology in India Revisited*. The fourth survey has been organised in three volumes. The first volume has been entitled as *Physiological foundation and Human cognition*, the second volume has been entitled as *Personality and Health psychology* and the third volume has been entitled as *Applied social and organizational psychology*. The first volume consists of six chapters. The first chapter is simply an introduction to the first volume, which briefly summarizes the nature and scope of various chapters in the first volume. It has been written by J. Pandey, Professor of psychology and presently the vice-chancellor, Central university of Bihar, Patna. The second chapter is on *Animal behaviour* written by Mewa singh, Professor of psychology, University of Mysore and the third chapter is on *Physiological Foundations of Behaviour* by Manas K. Mandal, Associate Professor of Psychology IIT, Kharagpur. Both animal behaviour and physiological phychology have been the less researched area in India. However, at some centres excellent examples of research in these areas have been reported. On such example is the research conducted in the animal laboratory established by Professor Saroj K. Mishra at the centre of Advanced study in Psychology, Utkal University, Bhubaneswar. Manas K. Mandal has beautifully presented the reasearches under four subsections, namely, neurophysiology of behaviour, neuropsychology, neurochemistry of behaviour and psychopharmacology. The fourth chapter is on *Perceptual learning and memory processes* written by Ramesh C. Mishra. Professor of Psychology, Banaras Hindu university, Varanasi; and it has been vividly shown that Indian psychologists have actively engaged in research on perception, learning and memory during the last one decade and have generated useful information. Researches in pictorial perception and cognitive style have been very impressive whereas interest in topics like selective attention, depth perception, time perception, colour perception and perceptual defence have been very limited. In the field memory STM and LTM have been the choice area of research. Studies of motor memory has added a new attraction among Indian psychologists. In the field of learning, there has been greater focus upon the determinants of learning rather than on the process of learning in which emphasis upon perceptual-cognitive skills has been given. The fifth chapter is on *Intelligence and Cognitive process* writeen by J. P. Das and Komilla Thapa. Prof. J. P. Das is Professor of Educational psychology and former Director of the Developmental disabilities centre, University of Alberta, Canada and Komilla Thapa is the senior lecturer at the centre for Advanced study, Dept of Psychology Allahabad university. They have briefly reviewed the researches done in these areas and have presented them under the rubrics of information processing approach, multiple intelligence, the triarchic theory of intelligence, views from neurophysiology and PASS theory that broadly defines intellegence as cognitive processes constituting Planning, Attention-Arousal and Simultaneous and Successive Information processing. The sixth chapter is on *Language behaviour and Processes* written by A. K. Mohanty who is Professor of psychology at the centre of Advanced study in psychology, Utkal university, Bhubneswar. He has presented the researches done by Indian psychologists under subsection like language acquisition and processes, major trends in acquisition research, reading and text processing and biligualisim in a multilingual society.

The second volume of the fourth survey entitiled *Personality and Health psychology* consists of seven chapters. The first chapter written by prof. J. Pandey, is simply an introduction to volume two which briefly introduces the different chapters included in this volume. The second chapter is on *Consciousness studies : A Survey of Perceptives and Research* written by K. Ramkrishna Rao, Professor of psychology, Andhra university. He has reviewed both Indian and Western perpectives of consicousness which provides a better and comprehensive understanding of the subject. The third chapter is on *Child and Adolescent Development Research* written by Baljit Kaur, Shailaja Menon and Rajani Konantambigi. Baljit Kaur is Reader in the Deptt. of Human development and Family studies at MS university. Baroda; Shilaja Menon is also associated with the Department of Human development and Family studies and Rajani Konantambigi is Reader at Tata Institute of Social Sciences, Mumbai. There authors have tried to focus on the effects of the environment, personality and social factors on the development of children. The authors have proposed multidisciplinary research approach that explicates interactive process through which biology and culture tend to pave the way for individual needs (Pandey, 2001). These authors have also advocated a context-time relationship for a better study of children and students. The fourth chapter is on *Personality, Self and Life Events* written by R. K. Naidu, Professor of psychology, Allahabad University. He has reviewed researches done in these fields by dividing them under two sections-section one is personality and section two is life events stress. He has also covered certain aspects of state of psychology as a profession in India. The fifth chapter is : *On the Periphery : The psychology of Gender* written by Shalini Barat, Reader at the Tata Institute of Social sciences, Mumbai. This chapter presents an interdisciplinary discussion on gender issues and has mainly emphasized that women's issues yet remain out of central focus in psychology in India. The sixth chapter is on *Health Psychology* written by A. K. Dalai, Professor of psychology at University of Allahabad. He has reviewed the researches in this field that relates to both traditional health beliefs and practices as well as modern health practices including community health care, yoga and mediation. The seventh, chapter is on *Mental Health, Illness and Therapy* written by Malavika Kapur, Additional Professor of clinical psychology as the National Institute of Mental Health and Neurosciences (NIMHANS), Banglore. She has reviewed the Indian researches in these fields from developmental perspectives and has concluded that researches on children, adolescents, adults and aged persons have been generally modelled after the theoretical and methodological paradigms of western studies and have failed to make significant contributions to Indian context. Not only that, her review has also cautioned that future research needs to be culturally sensitive and indigenous rather than being influenced by western conceptulizations of mental health and ill health.

The third volume of the fourth survey entitled *Applied Social and Organisation Psychology* consists of eight chapters. One chapter entitled *'Attitudes, social cognition and justice* has been prepared by Lila Krishnan who has tried to highlight the major contribution in these areas by Indian psychologists from a theoretical and cultural viewpoints. Another chapter is on social values written by Jyoti Verma. She has argued in this chapter through evidences that both individualistic as well as traditional collectivist Indian values can coexist. Another chapter is on *Psychological dimensions of poverty and deprivation* written by G. Mishra and K. N. Tripathi. The authors have tried to highlight various dimensions of poverty and poors in a very comprehensive way. Another chapter is on *An intergroup persepective on Ethnic Minority Identity* written by Nimmi Hutnik. He has reviewed the major theoretical approaches to the concerned issue. Still another chapter is on *Environment and Behaviour* written by Uday Jain and M. N. Passane. These authors have explored recent trends, problems and related methodological issues in the environmental psychology. In another chapter on *'Motivation, Leadership and Human performance'* written by R. N. Kanungo and Sasi Mishra various important issues using a conceptual framework and theoretical perspectives have been raised. The last chapter of this volume in on *Emerging Trends* which examines the strengths and weaknesses of the displine as well as changes and shift in the contents of research as we are entering into the 21st century.

Recently, the fifth survey was undertaken by the Advisory Committee with Prof. Girishwar Misra as the chief editor of the ICSSR. The committee decided to cover major trends in research during a decade covering the span of 1993-2003. The present survey (fifth survey) entitled *Psychology in India* published in 2009, was made more comprehensive covering many new themes such as indigenous psychology, psychoanalytic studies, methodology, motivation and affective processes, psychology of disabled people and gero psychology. The various chapters of fifth survey are organized in *four* volumes described briefly as under.

The first volume entitled as *Basic Psychological Processes and Human development* has six chapters. The first chapter written by Raghubir Singh Pirta is on *'Biological and Ecological Bases of behaviour* and covers all the major work done in the area of biological and environmental processes responsible for determining psychological phenomena. The second chapter is on *Human Development: Contexts and Process* and it has been written by Neerja Sharma and Nandita Chaudhary. Th third chapter is on *'Language and Communication'* and has been written by Prakash Padakannaya. The fourth chapter is on *'Cognitive Processes'* prepared by Anupam Nath Tripathi and Nandita Babu. The fifth chapter entitled *'Affective and Motivational Process'* has been prepared by Adesh Agrawal. The sixth chapter is on *'Trends in Personality Research : An overview'* and has been prepared by J. M. Jerath and Anjum Sibia.

The second volume has been subtitled as *'Social and Organizational Processes'* and has again six chapters. The first two chapters relate to social-psychological process, that is, *Understanding the social world : Issues and challenges* by Purnima Singh and *'Social Psychological Perspective on Self and Identity'* by Arvind Kumar Mishra, A. Bimol Akoijam and Girishwar Misra. The next two chapter relate to organizatial behaviour, that is, *'Individual and Group-level Process in Organizations'* by Arvind Kumar Sinha and *'Culture, Institutions and Organizations in India'* written by Rajen Kumar Gupta and Abinash Panda. The fifth chapter is on *'Dynamics of Schooling'* prepared by Ashok Kumar Shrivastava. This chapter emphasizes upon psychological aspects of school education. The sixth chapter is on *'Psychology and Societal Development'* prepared by Rekha Singhal and P. S. N. Tiwari. This last chapter emphasizes upon the society level processes.

The third volume subtitled as *Clinical and Health psychology* has also six chapters. The first chapter is on *'Clinical Psychology'* prepared by Prabal K. Chattopadhyay. Here author has tried to describe latest trend in the study of various disorders and has given focus on the problems and prospects in the field of clinical psychology. The second chapter is on *'Psychology of Disabled People'* prepared by Anita Ghai. The third chapter is on *'Geropsychology'* and has been written by P. V. Ramamurti and D. Jamuna. The fourth chapter is on *'Health Psychology : Progress and Challenges'* and it has been prepared by Sagar Sharma and Girishwar Mishra. The fifth chapter is on *'Psychological Interventions : From Theory to Practice'* and it has been prepared by Kiran Rao. The sixth chapter is on *'Psychological Interventions for Community Development'* and its has been prepared by Ajit K. Dalai.

The fourth volume subtitled as *Theoretical and Methodological Developments* has also six chapters. The first chapter is on *'Landscaping a Perspective : India and the Psychoanalytic vista'* and has been prepared by Honey Oberai Vahali. In fact, here author has tried to provide a comparehensive analysis of the important psychoanalytic combinations and writings emerging from India. The Second chapter is on *'Qualitative methods in Psychology'* written by Anand Prakash and third chapter is on *'Issues of Gender in Psychology : Traversing from sex differences to Quality of woman's lives'* and has been written by U. Vindhya. This chapter exclusively deals with conerns of gender in psychological research in India. The fourth chapter is on *'Quantitative methods in Psychology'* and has been prepared by Damodar Suar and Biranchi N. Puhen. The fifth chapter is on *'Indian Indigenous concepts and Perspectives : 'Development and Future Possibilities'* and it has been written by S. K. Kiran Kumar. The sixth and last chapter is on *'Psychology in India : Retrospect and Prospect'* and has been prepared by Girishwar Misra and Manasi kumar. This chapter focuses on some critical perspectives on the developments in theory, research and practice in psychology in India.

Despite all these, our dependence upon west has not entirely ended. Still for valuahble books and journals we have to look towards west. If we really want to improve psychology and make it free from dependence on west, the various academic departments and Institutes must be encouraged to develop good books and publish journals containing authentic Indian researches and examples. For this, the moral responsibility also lies with the Government to make these institutions financially strong enough to run various projects for writing books, conducting research and publishing journals.

We finally stop with a hope that the psychology in India appears to have a bright future partly due to its expanding role being played in Indian society and partly due to the realization about its significance by mass.

CHAPTER HIGHLITHS

1. Psychology in India has been roughly divided into two parts—*Psychology during ancient times* and *Psychology during modern lines.* In ancient time glimpse of psychological thoughts are found in *Rigveda* and *Upnishads.* In ancient psychology of India, Vedanta and Yoga have also much to contribute. In Vedanta mind has been explained as one internal organ. It also emphasizes upon transformation and modification of mind. This is done through yoga. Yoga system has also been incorporated in what is called *Abidhamma* in Pàli language of Gautama Budha's day (536-438 B.C.). In Sanskrit it is called as *Abhidarms.* Ancient Indian psychology also recognizes three types of *gunas* or mental substance that makes different traits and temperament of personality. Those gunas are of three types—*Sattava gunas, Tamas gunas* and *Rajas gunas.*
2. Psychology in modern times in India is of recent origin. In India developments in the field of psychlogy is mainly limited to academic circles. The first Indian psychological laboratory was established in the University of Calcutta in 1916, about thirty-five years later since Wilhelm Wundt had established his first psychological laboratory at the University of Leipzig in Germany. Indian Psychologists have formed different associations and publish different journals in which their psychological researches and findings are reported. Various institutions established by Government provide necessary help and work environment. ICSSR, UGC, NCERT are among these prominent institutions. ICSSR published a *Survey Resarch in Psychology* in 1971 and it covered the period of 1950-69. According to this survey there were five major fields in which Indian psychologists were most active *Clinical Psychology, Psychology of personaltiy, Social Psychlogyr Experimental psychology and Industrial psychology.* There are also other fields in

which Indian psychlogists have shown interest. *The second survey of research* in psychology in India has also been published. This survey has been edited by Late Prof. Udai Pareek. It covers the work done by Indian psychologists during 1971-76 and basically it adopted a thematic approach. In his editiorial comment, Udai Pareek had commented that psychology in India is "standing at the crossroads today." The third survey of research in psychlogy in India has been published by ICSSR (1988). It covers the researches done in period 1977 to 1986 (middle of 1986). It has been edited by Prof. Janak Pandey (1988) and survey has been pubslihed in three volumes. Volume I is named as *Personality and Mental process,* Volume II is named as *Basic and Applied psychology* and Volume III is named as *Organizational Behaviour and Mental Health.* In all these three volumes selected areas have been reviewed. Keeping in view the researches in various fields in India Prof. Janak Pandey has made an intelligent observation, which states that psychology in India today is not standing at 'crossroads'. The fourth survey of research in psychology in India has been published by ICSSR (2001). It has again been edited by Prof. Jank Pandey and has been named as *Psychology in India Revisited.* It has been published in three volumes. The first volume entitled *Physiological foundation and human cognition* has six chapters; the second volume entitled *Personality and Health Psychology* has seven chapters and the third volume entitled *Applied Social and Organizational Psychology* has eight chapters.

3. The fifth survey of research in psychlogy in India has been published by ICSSR (2009). It has been edited by Prof. Girishwar Misra. It covers the researches done in India during the span of 1993-2003. It has been published in four volumes, each volume having six chapters. The first volume has been subtitled as *Basic Psychological Processes and Human Development,* the second volume as *'Social and organizational Processes'* the third volume as *'Clinical and Health Psychology'* and the fourth volume as *'Theoretical and Methodological Developments.'*

REVIEW QUESTIONS

1. Present and overall view of Ancient Indian Psychology.
2. Present an overall view of modern Indian Psychology.
3. Do you think that psychology in India has reached a take off stage ?
4. "Psychology in India is not standing at the crossroads today." Comment. Discuss the present day emerging trend in Indian psychological researches.

■

CHAPTER 22

INTERNATIONAL PSYCHOLOGY

CHAPTER PREVIEW

Psychology is international in serval respect including its history, active presence and aspirations. Psychology studies human nature and behaviour and views of ancient Greek philosophers, ancient Chinese philosophers and ancient Indian thinkers have great impact. In modern time psychology is said to be systematically and experimentally emerged in Germany with the efforts of University of Leipzig in 1879. From there, psychology is said to spread over other countries including Britain, France, Russia, India, China and in others.

To promote the growth of psychology the psychological associations at national level were formed in different countries. The first such national psychological association was American Psychological Association formed in 1892. For further promoting the growth of psychology at the international level, the International Congress of Psychology was started and it held its first meeting in 1889 in Paris. At its eleventh meeting in Stokhlom, International Union of Psychological Science (IUPSYS) was formed with eleven national organizations as its charter members. Many national and regional organizations are affiliated to it. The distribution of psychologists and psychological organizations is not even all over the world. Today there has been revolt against the domination of Western psychology or Mainstream psychology and this domination is clearly reflected in the emphasis being given by modern psychologists upon cross-cultural psychology and indigenous psychology.

Psychology has a short history but long past. Psychology is the science of behaviour and the reference to the human mind and how it may operate and translate into overt behaviour can be traced back to specimen of written history and philosophical speculations dating centuries BC. If we pay a closer look on the development of psychology around world, it will be obvious that psychology is international in several respects including its history, active presence and aspirations. In different countries the development of psychology has been determined in part by the cultural backgrounds of the concerned countries and in part by their political and economic histories. To promote the development of psychology at international level, the *International Union of Psychological Science* (IUPSYS) was founded as a sequel to various international conferences of psychology, the first such conference was held in Paris in 1889, ten years after Wilhelm Wundt had established the first psychological laboratory at the University of Leipzig. In fact, international psychological organization work hard to promoted the development of psychology through their various meetings, publications and international cooperation and exchange of scholars.

VIEWS OF ANCIENT GREEK PHILOSOPHERS

A systematic study of human nature and behaviour occured only two to three thousand years ago by ancient philosophers both in west and east. Philosophers in Greece, China and India developed various theories about human mind, nature and behaviour at about the same time, that is, 300 BC to 500 BC. Among these philosophers, Greek Philosophers like Plato and Aristotle and their contemporary in China, that is, Confucius and Mencius and the great Indian teacher Lord Buddha were the most important ones.

The Greek philosphers were considered as the first and foremost scholars to study human mind and nature in a systematic way. Most of these early great philosphers searched for the primary elements from which everything was ordinarly made. For example, Thales (624-547 BC) held that the element was water; Democritus (460-370 BC) and Empedocles (554-495 BC) formulated the theory of four primary elements : *earth, water, fire and air*.

As we know from Chapter 2, Plato (437-347 BC) adovocated a dualism that divided human being into a body that was material and a mind (soul) that contained a pure knowledge. Plato was of view that all knowledge is innate and can be known only through introspection that is through reminiscence of the experience the soul had before entering the body. He also believed that the soul is immortal and had a rational component.

Aristotle (384-322 BC) was a student of Plato and in fact, was the first philosopher who studied many such topics which, later on, became the most important parts of psychology. He was of view that all living things possess a soul and it was the soul which was the primary source of energy. To Aristotle, there were three kinds of soul; the *vegetative soul* also called as *nutritive soul*, the *sensitive soul* and *rational soul*. The vegetative soul is possessed by the plants; the sensitive soul is possessed by animals who acquire knowledge about the environment through five senses; sight, hearing, taste, touch and smell. The rational soul is possessed only by humans and does functions like reasoning and thinking in addition to doing all the functioning of the other two souls. Aristotle also held the view that everything in the nature had a purpose, that is, they were teleologically determined.

If we look at the views of these ancient Greek philosphers minutely, it will be obvious that the Greek concept of psyche or soul is different from the modern concept of mind. For these Greek philosphers, all living things including plants and lower animals have a soul. They laid emphasis upon the distinction between what is alive and what is not alive. But modern psychologists, on the other hand, laid much emphasis upon the distinction between what possesses mind and what does not. Since material objects and also plants don't possess mind, these are out of realm of the study of psychology. Hence, today there is no psychology of inanimate objects.

ANCIENT CHINESE PHILOSOPHERS

The great chinese thinkers Confucius (551-479 BC) and his successors Mencius (372-289 BC) and Xun Zi (298-239 BC) had a profound effect on the development of Chinese philosophy. A very important feature of ancient Chinese philosophy relating to psychology was discussion about human nature and how it was shaped by education.

Confucious had opined that human habits are different but human nature is similar. He further pointed out that at birth all human beings are equal and considered all individual differences to be the result of training and environmental influences. Human beings constantly try to improve themselves and in this direction, education plays a central role. They are inherently capable of achieving the higher level through learning and self-improvement. In this regard, human interactions are guided and controlled by a specific value system called *Li* (convention or propriety). Persons who have mastered *Li* become sages and rulers and ultimately provide models of behaviour for other people to follow. Confucious also talked about moral development and said that when people acquired *Ren* (benevolence), they are said to reach at the highest level of moral development. In fact, confucian ideological philosophy consists of ethical principles which guide people in achieving the ideal states of ethical and moral standards to live in the society. Even to this date, the behaviour of Chinese more or less conforms to the ideology of Confucius. Although Confucius did write about his teachings in a scattered way, his disciples collected those teachings and complied them in a book entitled *The Analects*.

Confucius's successor was Menicus who opined that human beings are born with good nature. By following bad examples, they become bad but by following good examples, they become still more refined and better. Xun Zi, another important Chinese thinker, had proposed that human nature is malevolent and human behaviour must be corrected in the right direction rather is should be left to run its own course. Human nature involves the interaction between nature and nurture and this tends to mould the human personality. In Chinese philosophy, in understanding human nature and its importance in understanding personality, the role of education has been much emphasized. The views of these Chinese thinkers have been the major tenets of Chinese philosophy for more than two thousand years and also forerunner of modern Chinese educational psychology.

ANCIENT INDIAN PSYCHOLOGY

A glimpse of ancient Indian psychology can be had from chapter 21.

RISE OF MODERN PSYCHOLOGY IN DIFFERENT COUNTRIES OF THE WORLD

Wilhelm Wundt founded the first psychological laboratory at the University of Leipzig in 1879 with a few rooms and some equipment and apparatus for psychological experimentation. However, in 1875, that is, four years earlier William James had also set up a room for psychological experimentation at Harvard University. But history acknowledged Wundt as the founder of modern experimental psychology and Leipzig was recognized as *'Mecca of the psychology'*. Here Wundt not only conducted some experiments but also trained many persons who become important presonalities in subsequent history of psychology. Prominent men who were trained under the guidance of Wundt were Email Kraeplin, Oswald Kulpe, Ernst Meumann and Hugo Munsterberg from Germany itself; G. S. Hall, James Mckeen Cattell, Fank Angell, Gorge Ladd from America and Englishman E. B. Titchener who become leader of the first generation of American psychology and founded the famous school of psychology called *Structuralism*. George I. Chelpanov and Nikolay N. Lange were from Russia; Ernst Durr from Switzerland; Matataro Matsumoto from Japan; Cai Yuanpei from China and Alfred Lehman from Denmark (Jing, 2000). In 1886 Alfred Lehman had established the first psychlogical laboratory in Copenhangen (Koppe, 1987). V. M. Bekhterev founded the first psychological laboratory in 1885 at Kazan. In 1912 the first Russian Psychological Institute was opened in Mascow under the directiorship of George I. Chelpanov. Prominent Russian psychologists like Vygotsky, Luria and Leontiev all successfully worked at this institute (Brunshlinskii, 1995).

In Japan the first psychological laboratory was established in 1900 by Yujiro Motora (1859-1912). Amane Nishi (1829-1897), after returning from Germany, coined the Japanese term *Shinvigaku* for Psychology which is well-established in Japan today. Matataro Matsumoto (1865-1943) was a student of Wundt and became the first chairperson of the department of psychology at the University of Tokyo in 1918 (Azuma & Imada, 1994). With the support of Cai Yuanpai, a chinese student at Leipzig, Chen Daqui in China established the first psychological laboratory in 1917 (Yang, 1998). Another Chinese psychologist, that is, Zhang Yaoxiang, who was a student at Columbia University in 1916, founded the Chinese Psychological society in 1921. In India the first psychological laboratory was established in 1915, 36 years after Wundt's laboratory, by N. N. Sen Gupta, a student under Munsterberg at Harvard University (Sinha, 1987).

PSYCHOLOGY IN BRITAIN AND FRANCE

Britain and France slowly follwed Germany and United States in development of psychology since 1879. At the turn of the 20th century, in Britain the philosophical psychology and the evolutionary psychology established by Charles Darwin had a lasting effect upon psychology. Later on Darwin's counsin Francis Galton studied individual differences which was further developed by Karl Pearson who developed the technique of Coefficient of correlation that later become one of the statistical tools in the field of psychological studies. In 1897, James Sully in University college in London and W. H. Rivers in Cambridge established first psychological laboratories in the United Kingdom. In 1906 Charles Spearman also studied measurement of intelligence in the London laboratory. As a sequel to these studies, the technique of factor analysis was developed. In 1936 a psychological laboratory was established. Thus we see that early British psychology developed along the line of psychometric rather than following the trend of Wundtian psychology.

Comparatively, Frnace had little to contribute to psychology. In this country the early psychology ran the course of clinical psychology. The French physician Jean Charot by way of studying hypnotism and hysteria showed the beginnings trend. Later on, Theodule Ribot and P. Janet propounded a psychology that was based upon the treatment of mental diseases. At college de France in 1887 Robot became the first chairman of the department of experimental and comparative psychlogy. In 1889 the Government of France set up the first psychological laboratory under Henri Beaunis who was later on succeeded by Alfred Binet. P. Janet had organised French Psychlogical society in 1901. Thus psychlogy in France, as a whole, did develop only in the field of clinical psychology.

DEVELOPMENT OF PSYCHOLOGY IN UNDIVIDED SOVIET RUSSIA

In 1917 Russian Revolution took place and this shaped the development of psychology in Russia in a way quite different from Wundtian tradition and European philosophical thinking. After world War II not only all republics of Soviet Union but eastern European countries as well as China, Cuba, Vietnam tried to develop what is called as Marxist psychlogy after thinkings of Karl Marx (1818-1883). Marxist psychology held that social existence determines social consciousness, that is, the mind of human being is determined by the social position held by the person in the social environment. He also held that material production is the major force of social development and the production relations, which meant that all people are involved in class struggle that brings about revolution to promote social progress, are important in the process of social development. Besides this, viewpoints of V.I. Lenin who was the founder of Russian communist party, were also taken into consideration for the new emerging Soviet psychology. Lenin held the view that the consciousness is the function of brain and in fact, it is a reflection of the objective world. In soviet Psychology this was called as the theory of reflection.

After Russian Revolution, Valdimirm M. Bekhterev established the Institute of Brain Research in St. Petersburg and generated new concepts like 'Objective psychology' and 'Reflexology'. In 1921-23, Konstantin N. Kornilov and Petrovich Blonsky first tried to introduce dialectical materialism into psychology. Later on, Marxist psychlogy was improved and expanded so that it clearly included the principles of determinism, reflective nature of mind, integration of consciousness and social historical development of mind. During this period major contributions were made in the field of educational psychology and psychoneurology. The neutrological studies of Alexander Leuria and cultural-historial theory of Lev Vygotstay were considered important. Later in 1942, Rubenstein organized a department of Psychology in Mascow University. In 1945 he set up the first psychological laboratory in the Institute of Philosophy in the Soviet Academy of sciences, now known as Institute of Psychology of Russian Academy of Sciences since 1971.

Another major event that was fruitful for psychology is Soviet Russia was the recommendation of joint conference of Soviet Academy of Sciences and Soviet Academy of Medical Sciences held in 1950. The recommendation stressed to improve Psychology on the line of theory of I.P. Pavlov, a Russian physiologist, who was awarded Nobel Prize in 1904 for his work on the physiology of digestion system. In China also this recommendation had an impact and psychology was started being reformed on that pattern. In Soviet Union now, it was realized that the psychological functions were much the product of higher nervous activity. Pavlov's theory of two signal systems provided base for the scientifc study of language. The first signal system was the conditioned response to the sensory stimuli and the second signal system was an abstraction process resulting in symbolic language activity. Soviet psychologists and philosophers reacted against the American cognitive revlution in form of computer simulation of cognitive processes started in 1950s as simply vulgar materialism and also made comments on the impossibility of artifical intelligence (Simon, 1991). But on the other hand, Simon and Jing (1988) tried to explain the fact that dialectical materialism by soviet psychology could be compatible with the American cognitive psychology.

After world war II, principles of Marxist psychology became the state policy for many communist contries like Soviet Union, Cuba, Czechoslovakia and China. Now Psychology started introducing many new branches. After dissolution of Soviet Union in 1991, Marxist Psychology's stand in most of the eastern European countries deteriorated although in China still its principles have considerable impact.

ESTABLISHMENT OF PSYCHOLOGICAL ASSOCIATION AROUND THE WORLD

The Psychological Associations in various countries were formed by the development of psychology at the national level. These national associations were formed for the sole purpose of giving new dimensions to the researches being conducted for the over all development in both established and new emerging branches of psychlogy. Table 22.1 presents a yearwise description of National psychological association established in different countries.

Table 22.1 : Yearwise presentation of National Psychological Assocation established in different countries.

Year	Countries where National Psychological Associations were established
1892	United States of America
1901	United Kingdom
1901	France
1904	Germany
1908	Agrentina
1910	Italy
1921	China
1925	India
1926	Japan
1928	Hungary
1934	Norway
1939	Canada
1943	Switzerland
1945	Australia
1945	Brazil
1946	Netherlands
1946	Korea
1947	Denmark
1947	Belgium
1948	Poland
1948	Egypt
1949	South Africa
1950	Yugoslavia
1951	Mexico

1952	Spain
1952	Finland
1953	Austria
1953	Uruguay
1954	Iceland
1954	Peru
1955	Swedan
1955	Columbia
1956	Turkey
1957	Venezuela
1957	Soviet Union
1958	Czechoslovakia
1958	Israel
1960	Indonesia
1962	Philippines
1963	Greece
1968	Hongkong (China)
1968	Iran
1968	Pakistan
1969	Bulgaria
1971	Zimbabwe
1975	Donimican Republic
1975	Paraguay
1975	Ireland
1979	Singapore
1981	Nicaragua

If we carefully analyze Table 22.1, the following points will be highlighted.

(i) The first national psychological association in the world was found in United States of America.

(ii) Between 1879 when Wilhelm Wundt founded the first psychological laboratory in the world and 1981, only 13 National psychological associations were established before the start of world war II.

(iii) By the end of 1950s most industrialised countries had a National psychlogical association.

(iv) In Latin America, Africa and third world countries National psychological association was established after world war II.

(v) National psychological associations were established in some of the leading industrialized nations before world war I.

BIRTH OF INTERNATIONAL ORGANIZATION OF PSYCHOLOGY

As we know, the first psychological laboratory was founded by Wilhelm Wundt in 1879 at Leipzig University in Germany, and the modern psychology is said to have started since then. Psychologists were not satisfied wholly with the start of the their experimental science formally. They were in need of an international forum for their exchange of ideas and disccussion. As a consequence, the first international congress of Psychology took place in Paris in 1889, eactly ten years after Wundt's first psychological laboratory was established and even two years earlier than the establishement of Amnerican psychological Association in 1892. Subsequently, international conferences of psychology have taken place every three to four years with gaps caused by the two world wars. For example, the second international congress of psychlogy was held in London in 1892, third in Munich in 1896. In this way the eleventh International congress took place in Paris in 1937. The most important congress was the *thirteenth* International congress of Psychology which take place in Stockholm in 1951 after second world war and it was in this congress that *International Union of Psychological Science* (IUPSYS) was formed with eleven national organizations as charter members. Since 1951 these congresses have been organized by IUPSYS and sicne 1972 the international congresses are taking place every four years. In 1980 the international congress of psychlogy was held at Leipzig, in 1984 at Aeapulco, in 1988 in Sydney, in 1992 at Brussels and in 1996 at Montreal. In each of these congress about 4000 participants attended the congress. The 27th congress was held in 2000 at Stockholm and the 28th International congress was held at Beijing in 2004.

IUPSYS, up to mid 1999, has 66 national members which are national associations of scientific psychlogy (Rosenzweig et al., 2000). As per statute of IUPSYS, each country where the scientific psychology has flourished can have only one such national assocation or organization admitted to IUPSYS. A number of organizations are also affiliated with IUPSYS. The conditions of affiliation are that such organization must have individuals rather than national organizations as members and it must be regional or global in its character. Some of the important such affiliated organizations are : *International society of Comparative Psychology, International Society for the study of Behaviour Development* (ISSBD), *International Association for cross-cultural Psychology* (IACCP), *International Council of psychologists* (ICP), *International Association for Applied Psychology* (IAAP), *Inter-American Society of Psychology* (SIP), *Association de Psychologie Scientifique de Langue Francaise* (APSLF), *European Association of Experimental Social Psychology, European Association of Personality Psychology, European Association of Psychological Assessment and International Neuro Psychological society.*

The major task of these affiliates of IUPSYS is to convene meetings for every two or four year for wider expansion and growth of psychology. In fact, these affiliates include many major international and regional organization of psychological science in the world. Apart from this, for promoting meeting and exchanges, there are many displinary, interdisciplinary and regional organization of psychology. *The Eurpoean Federation of Professional Psychologists Association* (EFPPA) is one such organization which was established in 1981. It has at present 25 European countries as its member and it basically aims at reducing differences among European contries regarding standards of training and various professional practices adopted by psychologists. In cooperation with IUPSYS, EFPPA also organizes the biennial European congress of psychology. There are also some.regional groups like *Asian Association of Social Psychology, Pan-Arb Psychology Association, Afro-Asian Psychological Association, Asia-Oceania Psychological Association* which promotes exchanges and meetings for the growth of psychology.

DISTRIBUTION OF PSYCHOLOGISTS AT INTERNATIONAL LEVEL

Some attempts at the international level have been made to prepare the total number of psychologists in the world and their approximate distribution in terms of sex, fields, population density, etc., Reality is that the total number of psychologists in the world is rapidily increasing in last a few decades. Rosenzwig (1982) has shown that till 1980, the total number was 260,000. According to 1991 IUPSYS survey, it rose to almost double that is, 500,000 and it is expected to exceed one million in near future. In making these etsimates, all these were included who were considered to be qualified to call themselves psycholostists in each country.

Sexton and Hogan (1992) counted ratio of female to male psychologists in the main regions of the world. Their findings revealed that in South American and Caribbean countries 70% of all psychologists are women, in European countries 53% of all psychologists are women and in Asian countries only 25% are women although in some of Asian countries percentage of women is higher than this. In United States of America percentage of women earning doctorate degree had risen to 58%. By 1990, the ratio of women to men obtaining doctorates in USA was lowest in fields like experimental psychology (0.52) and industrial/organizational psychology (0.75). However, this ratio of women to man was higher in are a like educational psychology (2.38), development psychology (2.36), school psychology (1.89), social psychology (1.74), counselling psychlogy (1.52) and clinical psychology (1.42).

According to American Psychological Association (1995) percentage of psychologists working in different specialities is unequal. For example, of the total psychologists, 44% work as clinical psychologists, 11% as counselling psychologist, 4% as industrial/organizational psychologist, 4% as a school psychologist, 3% each as developmenal psychologist and educational psychologist, 2.5 as social psychologist, 17.5 as generalist and 7% in other basic research areas. This percentage clearly show that clinical psychologists make up the largest percentage of members of the American Psychological Association. Accordingly, clinical psychology is the *largest* preferred area or speciality.

Psychologists are also distributed very unequally in the world. According to IUPSYS survey done in 1991, the number of psychologists per million population was 550 in eleven industrialized countries outside the Eastern Europe, 83 per million in four countries of Eastern Europe, 191 per million in 14 developing countries and 2.4 per million in China. Not only this, the number of psychlogists engaged in research showed still more greater inequality of distribution, that is, 23 per million in 15 industralized countries and only 4.2 per million in 15 developing countries. Making a comprative study of the numerical strength of psychologists with number of physicians and neuroscientists, Rosenzweig (1992) pointed out that the total number of psychologists was about one-twelfth the number of physicians in the world but about twenty times the number of neuroscientists.

DISTRIBUTION OF PSYCHOLOGICAL ORGANIZATIONS AT INTERNATIONAL LEVEL

Psychologists have formed different associations and organizations. Some of these organizations are regional whereas some are national and international. Apart from these, some organizations are for specialized fields of psychology. The first national psychological organization was that of American Psychlogical Association formed in 1892. International Union of Psychological Science (IUPSYS) was formed with eleven national organizations as charater members. IUPSYS traces its history back to the first international congress of psychology held in Paris in 1886. Till mid 1999, 66 national organizations belong to IUPSYS and more are joining every year. In fact IUPSYS is the main body that promotes cooperation and exchange among psychologists across nations. Apart from these national and international organizations, there are some regional organizations of psychologists, which help in the work of IUPSYS. Inter American society of Psychology (SIP) and Association de Psychologie scientifique de Langue Francaise (APSLF) are the examples of regional organizations. Among the international associations with individual memberships, the largest is the International Association for Applied psychology (IAAP) from 94 countries and which is affliated to IUPSYS and was founded in 1920. IAAP has 14 divisions such as *organizational psychology, environmental psychology, sports psychology, health psychology, clinical and community psychology economic psychology, political psychology, applied cognitive psychlogy, psychological assessement and evaluation, psychology and national development, educational, instructional and school psychology, applied geronotology, psychology and Law as well as traffic and transportation psychology*. Besides IAAP, ten other organizations are affiliated to IUPSYS. American Psychological Association is the largest national psychological organization with full time individual members of about 87,000 till 1999.

These various organizations of psychology keep their members up-to-date in day-today advances, publish scientific and professional journals and also strive for various types of legislation to improve the standards of research and professional tasks.

COMMON CHARACTERTISCS IN DEVELOPMENT OF PSYCHOLOGY

If we pay attention to the development of psychology in the different countries and regions, it will be obvious that psychlogy originated under different circumstances in different countries. Despite these intercountry and interregion differences, there are some shared characteristics in the develop-ment of psychology. These shared characteristics can be focused as under.

(i) In almost each country the development of psychology is historically linked with the philosophical, ethical and cultural background. For example, in western countries the development of psychology is influenced by its roots in European or American philosophy and some branches of natural sciences like biology, physics and physiology. That is why, the early pioneers of western psychology were either philosophers or scientists (like physicist and physiologists) turned psychologists like Wilhelm Wundt, William James, Ernst H. Weber, Gustav Fechner. In Eastern countries like India, China and Japan the development of modern psychology although originated from west, is deeply influenced by ideology of Buddhism, Yoga philosophy, Vedanta and Confucianism. Today with wider exchange of views between East and West, it is hoped that there will be more commonalities than differences in the study of behaviour and mental process.

(ii) Psychology is both science and profession. In fact, psychology first developed as a basic scientific approach mainly answering questions about behaviour and mental process. Subsquently, it extended to applied fields such as health, industrial and societal problems. Which of these two parts of this developmental trend is stronger depends upon the national investment in sciences and in effectiveness of psychology in solving problems relating to applied fields such health, industrial and educational In advanced countries there is trend towards greater investment for basic research in psychology.

(iii) Developments in psychology as science of human behaviour and mental process transcends both natural science and social science. This two-sided nature of psychology as a science spinning across social and natural sciences is one of the important characteristics of psychology as a science and profession. Studying behaviour and mental process as a joint function of organismic and social factors define the unique characterstic of psychology that has attracted the attention of wide range of scientists throughout the world. The two-sided nature of psychology also makes it more vulnerable to social and political crises. In such situation, social science particularly psychology has to suffer a lot because of infringment of academic freedom. History bears evidence that during the Stalin period in 1930s and in Germany in 1930s when political and social crises recurred, many psychologists had to emigrate to America. During Chinese revolution in 1960s, psychology was almost in a suspended position for a decade. For the research psychologists this is a good topic of investigation as to under what circumstances such crisis in psychology occurs and what can be their consequences for development of psychology of a whole.

Thus the development of psychology has some commonalities despite their different social and philosophical outlooks provided by the framework of the different countries.

CROSS-CULTURAL PSYCHOLOGY

As we know, modern scientifc psychlogy was first developed in Germany and United States of America and became the mainforce of psychology called *mainstream psychology*. Today what goes on in the name of psychology is nothing but mainly theories and ideas developed in the United States. Teaching in other countries was based on the western text books and the researches got not only inspiration from western researches but were largely imitiative and replications of the western studies.

Many psychologists today have expressed their view that in order to study human behaviour from a wider perspective, the study of bahaviour must include observations made in different cultures of the countries and not only in a few industrialized countries. They have also reasonably questioned the validity of the generalizability of the principles of mainsteram psychology to different cultures of the world. For example, description of mental functioning in American laboratory may not equally apply to the people of other countries. Many standardized psychological tests develped in United States mainly on the basis of subjects of middle socio-economic status or class cannot fair well when applied to subjects of other countries or culture. Apart from this noncultural approach, the mainestream psychology also disregards researches done in other countries. This has a serious repercussion on healthy growth of psychology.

Keeping in view the above limitations of the mainstream psychlogy, a need for such psychology arose which can make a comparative study within and between cultures. Cross-cultural psychology is the psychology that fulfills this need. Cross-cultural psychology is broadly the study of culture's effects on human behaviour (Jing, 2000). More specifically, however, it is the scientific study of members of various cultural groups with identifyable experiences that lead to some predictable and significant similarities and differences in behaviour (Brislin, 1987). Thus in cross-cultural psychology a comparative study of various cultures is made so that the influence of various cultural factors on human development can be discerned. The special feature of cross-cultural psychology is that the individual variation is held constant while variation in the culture is the subject of the study (Whiting, 1968; Kline, 1977). Cross-cultural psychology thus broadly tries to isolate and study these culture-specific factors which are of help in understanding and explaining human behaviour (Sinha, 1981).

Basically, there are two approaches or goals of cross-cultural research—*emic approach* and *etic approach*. The emic approach to cross-cultural research studies the behaviour of a particular culture in terms of those things which are given importance and are only valued by the persons of that culture. This approach believes that a better understanding of a culture is gained by using indigenous tools rather than by a foreign tools or tools used in other cultures. The etic approach, on the other hand, tries to make a comparative study of the behaviour of persons in one culture to the behaviours of the persons in other cultures. This approach tries to establish valid principles for different cultures and tries to provide such theoretical frameworks which are useful in comparing human behaviour in various cultures (Berry, 1984), The best cross-cultural research is one that *combines* both these approahes, that is, first emic studies should be carried out in order to know position within a culture and for a making a comparative study, then etic approach should be followed (Jing, 2000).

During the last 30 years, some psychlogists in Asia have tried to establish what is called *indigenous psychology* by allowing the native psychologists to study their own problems because they are much familiar with their culture than forgein psychologists. Supporters of indigeneous psychology have also questioned the validity of the applicability of Euro-American Psychlogical studies to the third world countries. In Taiwan China Yang (1993) not only led this movement but also proposed a *Sinolized psychology* or indigenous psychology of chinese people that included psychologists from mainland, Taiwan and Hongkong China. In mainland China, Pan (1987) proposed a psychology with chinese characteristics and that psychology should be guided by Marxism which can solve problems of chinese society. Recently, there have been some calls for indigenization in psychology from other countries also (Azuma & Imada, 1994). In fact, this cry for indigenization in psychology is a revolt against western domination and a search to restore the true identity of the people of the land (Sinha, 1994).

PSYCHOLOGY IN CROSS-DI$PLINARY INTERACTION

Psychology like any other discipline, has derived its existence and identity not only from the features specific to it but also from the several topics that is shared with other disciplines. For example, psychology for its existence makes interaction with biology and life sciences, human and social sciences and recently to also engineering sciences. It has also maintained its contact with discipline like philosophy from which it originally emerged and then, with also psychiatry. These interactions with other disciplines have resulted in what is called *interdisciplinary exchange.* Such intedisciplinary exchange has been more common for the last several decades. The interaction between psychlogy and other discipline usually takes place at three levels :

(a) Pluridisciplinary research

(b) Interdisciplinary research

(c) Transdisciplinary research

In pluridisciplinary research several disciplines provide their respective points of views on the problem being investigated. This approach is so named because a plurality of methods is implemented to attack the problem under investation at different levels of anlysis. In such research, however, no attempt is made to implement the form of joint involvement or degree of its reciprocity or whether the joint venture serves common objectives.

In interdisciplinary research the various disciplines investigating the problem not only share the resources and methodologies but an attempt is made to show cooperation to solve the problem. Here underlying assumption is that of a common enterprise in which a stronger integration and convergence on the part of the disciplines for solving the problems is the main demand. Every discipline, however, maintains its separate identity in the joint venture.

In transdisciplinary approach attemp t is made to investigate whether or not the joint efforts of the different disciplines reflect a new broader approach for further investigation. The very assumption here is that the work done in the interdisciplinary research may force the partners to cross boundaries between the disciplines so that a new domain that encompass several disciplines may came into being. In such situation a common language which is going beyond the individual discipline, is also required for the new sciences to be founded.

Of these three levels of interaction, pluridisciplinary approach is considered best and is seen as a sort of *metamethod* that is to be used to answer research question that cann't be answered by a single discipline. However, here scientists don't completely rule our cooperation in doing such research. There are many such areas of psychology where need for such pluridisciplinarity is urgently needed. Thus psychological sicence by making various types of interactions goes beyond the establishment of scientific knowledge in itself. In fact, it takes part in providing such a broader concert in which human beings interact with their environment from many angles.

CHAPTER HIGHLIGHTS

1. Psychology has a short history but long past. If we pay attention to its past, we shall definitely find the views of ancient Greek philosophers are very important and providing seeds for development of psychology. Among such ancient Greek philosophers, the views of Plato and Aristotle were very important. Aristotle's view that all living things possess a soul and it was soul which was the primary source of energy inspired many subsequent philosopher turned psychologists in shaping the subject-matter of psychology.
2. The emergence of modern psychology at the international level has also been influenced by the views of ancient Chinese philosophers like Confucius and Mencius and Xun Zi. These Chinese philosophers had very relevant discussion about human nature and the way it was shaped by education. Confucius' claim that human habits are different but human nautre is similar helped many cognitive pshychologists to concentrate and study well many secrets of human nature.
3. Ancient Indian psychology had also germinal impact upon the development of psychology at international level. In ancient psychology of India *Vedanta, Buddhism, Bhagvat Gita* and *Yoga School* had much to contribute.
4. Wilhelm Wundt founded the first psychological laboratory at the University of Leipzig in 1879 and Leipzig was recognised as *Mecca of Psychology*. Here Wundt not only conducted some experients but also trained many persons who become important personalities in subsequent history of psychology throughout the world. Prominent persons who were trained under the guidance of Wilhelm Wundt were Emil Kraeplin, Oswald Kuple, Ernst Meumann and Hugo Munsterberg from Germany itself, G. S. Hall, J. M. Cattell, Frank angell, George Ladd from America and Englishman E. B. Titchner who founded the

famous school of psychology called Structualism, George I. Chelponon and Nikolay N. Lange from Russia, Ernst Durr from Switzerland, Matataro Matsumoto from Japan; Cai Yunpei from China and Alfred Lehman from Denmark.

5. In Britain the development of psychology was influenced by the principles of the philosophical psychology and the evolutionary psychology established by Charles Darwin. Other important persons to influence the development were Francis Galton, James Sully, Charles Sperman. France had little to contribute to psychology. Alfred Binet and Jean Charcot worked mainly in the field of psychlogical testing and clinical psychology.
6. Development of Psychology in undivided Russia was mainly influenced by the major principles of Marxist psychology. Pavlov, Kornilov and Blonsky were the major contributors to the development of psychology.
7. In various conuntries psychological associations were formed to promote the development of psychology at national level. The first such national assication was formed in United States of America in 1892. It was American Psychological Association founded by G. S. Hall. By the end of 1950s, most industrialised countries had a national psychological association.
8. Psychologists also need an international forum for their exchange of ideas and discussion. As a consequence, the first international congress of psychology took place in Paris in 1889. Subsequently, international conferences of psychology have taken place every three to four years with gaps caused by the two world wars. The most important congress was the thirteenth international congress of psychology which took place in Stockholm in 1951 after second world war and it was in this congress that *International Union of Psychological Science* (IUPSYS) was formed with elevent national organisations as charter members. Since 1972 the international congresses are taking place every four years. The 27th congress was held in 200 at Stockholm.
9. Distribution of Psychologists at international level is not even. The findings by Sextan and Hogan (1992) have reveled that in South American and Caribbean countries 70% of all psychologists are women, in European countries 53% of all psychologists are women and in Asian countries only 25% are women although in some of Asian countries percentage of women is higher than this. According to American Psychological Association (1995) the percentage of psychologists working in different specialities is also unequal.
10. Distribution of Psychological organizations at international level has its own specialities. Some of these organizations are regional whereas

some are national and international. IUPSYS was formed with eleven national organizations as charter members. Apart from this, there are some regional organizations of psychologists which help in the work of IUPSYS. Inter American Society of Psychology (SIP) and Association de Psychologie Scientifique de Langue Francaise (APSLF) are the examples of regional organizations. Among the international assotiations with individual memberships, the largest is the *International Association for Applied Psychology* (IAAP) from 94 countries and which is affiliated fo IUPSYS and was founded in 1920. IAAP has 14 divisions.

11. Psychology originated under different circumstances in different countries. Despite these intercountry and interregion differences, there are some shared characteristics in the development of psychology.
12. Many psycholosists today have expressed their view that in order to study human behaviour from a wider perspective the study of behaviour must include observations made in different cultures of the contries and not only in a few industralized countries. Cross-cultural psychology through two of its approaches, namely, emic approach and etic approach fulfills this need.
13. Psychology for maintaining its existence and at the same time expanding its scope makes interaction with other disciplines. The interaction between psychology and other discipline usually takes place at three levels : *pluridisciplinary research, interdisciplinary research* and *transdisciplinary research.*

REVIEW QUESTIONS

1. Discuss the contributions of ancient psychologies of the world towards the emergence of modern psychology.
2. Present an account of the emergence of modern psychology in different countries of the world.
3. Review the history of establishment of psychological associations around the world.
4. Trace the history of various international organizations of psychology. How far they have succeeded in promoting the growth of psychology at international level.
5. Present an account of distribution of psychologists and psychological organizations at international level.
6. Cross-cultural psychology and indigenous psychology are basically revolt against mainstream psychology. Comment.
7. How far psychology has succeeded in making cross-disciplinary interaction more useful ?

■

GLOSSARY

GLOSSARY

Absolute threshold : The smallest amount of a stimulus that can be detected 50 percent of the time.

Accomodation : In Piaget's theory of cognitive development modification of existing mental framework for explaining any new information.

Act Psychology : A system of psychology developed by Brentano and emphasizes upon mental processes rather than contents of consciousness.

Adaptation : In Piaget's theory of cognitive development building mental representation of the situation by making interaction with it.

Adaptive behaviour : A unit of behaviour emphasized by Harvey Carr which involves three phases—(i) a stimulus (ii) a sensory situation and (iii) a response that alters the situation to satisfy the motivating conditions.

Afterimage : The lingering sensation commonly reported in visual stimulation after removal of stimulation.

All-or-none principle : A principle which dictates that a neuron responds completely or not at all.

Anal stage : A period in Freud's theory of phychosexual development that mainly emphasizes upon interest or pleasure in anal region.

Analytic Psychology : Carl Jung's system of psychoanalysis, a system which came into being after formal separation of Jung from Freud.

Anecdotal method : A method that depends upon the use of casually observed events as scientific data.

Anima : According to Jung, the archetype representing feminine side of male.

Animus : In Jung's theory the archetype representing the masculine side of females.

Apperception : A clear and vivid perception of things, events or situation.

Approach-approach conflict : In Lewin's theory a conflict that occurs when the person tries to reach two goals, only one of which can be obtained at a time.

Approach-avoidance conflict : In Lewin's theory a conflict that occurs when the same goal has both positive and negative valance for the person.

Archetype : According to Jung inherited images in collective unconscious that determine our perception of the environment.

Associationism : A system in psychology which emphasizes that mental complexity can be produced through learned connections between simple sensations and ideas.

Avoidance-Avoidance conflict : In Lewin's theory a conflict that occurs when a person in required to choose between two undesirable goals.

Artificial intelligence : Capacity of the computers to demonstrate performance that could be described as intelligence if produced by human beings.

Assimilation : In Piaget's theory a tendency of the person to understand new information in terms of existing mental works.

Basic Anxiety : In Harvey's theory the feeling of a child being isolated and helpless in a potentially hostile world.

Behaviourism : A system of psychology founded by Watson and which emphasizes that all psychological functions can be explained in terms of stimulus and response.

Behaviour Space : Similar to Lewin's concept of life space, a totality of factors that affect the behaviour of a given individual.

Belief-value Matrix : Hierarchy of learned expectations concerning the different objects and their role in relation to behaviour.

Birth trauma : A concept propounded by Otto Rank that emphasizes the emotional experience of the new born ending its prenatal life.

Biopsychology : A branch of psychology that concerns with how biological processes affect important behaviour and cognitions.

Brunswik ratio : A ratio that emphasizes the relationship between real or physical to sensory representations of an object, indicating the extent to which physical attributes determine any given perception.

Bundle hypothesis : A hypothesis which emphasizes that a complex perception is a group of simple perceptions.

Catharsis : A psychoanalytic principle of emotional release.

Cognition : A general mental activity associated with thought, knowledge, perception, memory etc.

Cognitive development : Changes in cognitive abilities and functioning as individuals grow order.

Cognitive maps : A mental representation of the spatial location of different objects in the environment.

Collective Unconscious : In Jung's theory, a part of unconscious shared by all human beings.

Complex : A debiliting belief held by an individual despite contradictory objective evidence.

Conditioned reflex : A response that is produced by a mental stimulus after being paired presented with an initially effective stimulus.

Connectionism : A school of psychology that explain all or most behaviour in terms of stimulus-response connection.

Consciousness : A state of awareness with one's own mental condition.

Construct : A concept representing relationship between objects or events.

Context theory of meaning : The fact that the meaning of anything results from the context in which it occurs in consciousness.

Contiguity : A principle that emphasizes upon nearness in time and/or space.

Continuity : A principle of learning that emphasizes upon small, smooth and regular changes step by step.

Creative synthesis : A principle that lay emphasis upon the fact that new characteristics generally emerge from the combination of elements into wholes.

Cybernatics : Study of communication and control mechanism. Control is typically achieved by feedback information about the behaviour done.

Darwinism : Principle of organic evolution enunciated by Charles Darwin in 1859.

Death Instinct : Desire of the person to return to an inorganic state.

Defence mechanism : Mechanisms or techniques adopted by ego to keep unacceptable materials or thinking out of consciousness so that anxiety can be kept at minimum.

Determining tendency : A tendency to behave in specific way.

Determinism : The view that all events are explicable in terms of antecedent factors or cause-and-effect manner.

Difference threshold : The minimum amount by which two stimuli must differ in order to be just noticeably different.

Double-aspect view : A metaphysical position in which both mind and body are held to be function of one underlying reality.

Drive : A concept used by Hull to refer to the subjective feelings associated with needs.

Dynamic : The motivational forces underlying behaviour.

Eclecticism : The selection of what seems to be best from various system or theories.

Ego : In Freudian system that part of the personality which is concerned with reality and which thinks, feels and decides.

Ego-defence mechanism : Unconscious process adopted by ego to protest itself from various kinds of anxiety and threatening situation.

Empirical : Refers to facts and sensory experience.

Empricism : A school which emphasizes that all knowledge originates in experience; Also a methodology that emphasizes data and gives little emphasis on theoretical inference.

Environment : A totality of stimuli or events that impinges the organism.

Environmentalism : The principle which dictates that environmental factors are the major determinants of behaviour.

Equivalence belief : A concept enunciated by Tolman to indicate a state of an organism due to which it behaves towards the subgoals as if thing were goals.

Erogenous Zones : Zones or region of the body which are especially sensitive to manipulation.

Ethology : A branch of zoology which studies animal behaviour through observation in actual field situation.

Existential Psychology : A school of personality theories who lay emphasis upon individuals self-understanding. Also the name applies to the structuralism an important school of psychology founded by Titchener because it treated elements of consciousness as existent.

Expectancy : In Tolman's theory anticipation of a particular relationship between stimulus and response.

Extrasensory Perception (ESP) : Perceptions that are not based upon input from our sensory receptors. Telepathy and Clairvoyance are included under this category.

Factor Analysis : A statistical technique based on correlation and which is used to extract the underlying factor or factors, that account for the observed relationship between scores.

Field-cognition modes : In Tolman's theory a combination of thinking, perceiving and remembering of the organism that helps in knowing specific characteristic of the environment.

Field expectation : In Tolman's theory a kind of expectation on the part of the organism that a particular response to a particular stimulus or cue will lead to a particular consequence.

Field Theory : A theory that apply to fields of force as an explanation of psychological events.

Figure-ground relationship : Person's tendency to divide the perceptual world into two distinct types–clear and distinction part usually called figure and relatively vauge and indistinct part usually called background against which figure stands out.

Fixation : In psychoanalytic theory persistence of immature behaviour or thinking accompanied by a lack of normal development.

Fixed-Interval Schedule : A schedule of reinforcement in which a fixed interval of time must elapse before a response is reinforced.

Fixed-ratio schedule : A schedule of reinforcement in which reinforcement is given only after a fixed number of reinforcements have occurred.

Free association : An important procedure in psychoanalysis in which individuals spontaneously report all thoughts, even trivial ones, to the therapist.

Fully functioning persons : In Roger's theory a psychologically healthy person who enjoy life to the utmost in realistic way.

Functional autonomy : A concept enunciated by Allport in which the person maintains a behaviour by motives other than the ones originally responsible for the occurrence of that behaviour.

Functional Fixedness : The tendency to think about the objects only as they have been used in past.

Functionalism : A school of psychology that emphasizes upon the func-tion or utility of behaviour in making adaptation to the environment.

Genital stage : A final stage in psychosexual development in which the individual desires to have sexual relationship with members of opposite sex.

Grestalt Psychology : A system of psychology that emphasizes upon the phenomenological study of molar stimulus and response units, that is, upon the tendency to perceive sensory patterns as well-organized wholes rather than as separate and isolated parts.

Goal gradient : An important concept in Hull's theory emphasizing the gradual increment in response strength that occurs as a result of nearness to goal.

Habit : A learnt response to a stimulus or situation.

Habit family hierarchy : A hierarchy in which total set of responses occurring in a given stimulus situation are arranged according to their strength.

Habit strength : An intervening variable in Hull's theory that states that learning is a function of number of reinforcements given after the occurrence of the response.

Heredity : Biologically inherited characteristics of the organism.

Heirarchy of needs : A concept in Maslow's theory that states that human needs exist in a certain hierarchy so that higher-level needs are not satisfied till the lower level needs are satisfied.

Hodological space : A concept in Lewin's theory which emphasizes upon vectors to represent dynamic psychological factors.

Homeostasis : A state of physiological balance within the body of the organism.

Hypnosis : An altered state of consciousness in which individuals appear to be highly susceptible to the suggestions given by others and in which they sometimes behave as if in a state of trance.

Hypothesis : A tentative answer to a research question.

Hypothetical construct : A construct whose meaning really goes beyond the relationship between stimulus and response.

Hypothelico-deductive method : A method which starts with a few general postulates from which testable theorems and carollaries are derived by rigorous deductions and subsequently, the derivations are tested empirically.

Id : In psychoanalytic theory the portion of personality which is concerned with immediate satisfaction of primitive needs.

Idiographic approach : A approach of personality that makes detailed analysis of one individual and of the dimensions relevant to that individual's personality.

Imageless thought : Mental processes that denote that images are not formed in introspective analysis.

Individual Psychology : The school of psychology developed by Alfred Adler.

Information-Processing approach : An approach to study human memory which emphasizes encoding, storage and retrieval of information.

Inferiority complex : The feeling that a person has as a result of real or imagined deficiency.

Instinct : A innate but complex and stereotyped made of behaviour.

Interactionism : A metaphysical proposition in which mind and body are supported to be two different and independent entities making interaction with each other.

Intervening variable : A variable which abstracts the relationship between stimulus and response, with no meaning beyond this relationship.

Introspection : A method of study which relies upon the subjective report of the subject.

Isomorphism : A concept in Gestalt's theory which assumes one-to-one relationship between brain fields and experience.

IQ : A numerical value obtained by dividing mental age by chronological age and multiplying the same by 100.

Just Noticeable Difference (jnd) : The amount of minimum change in stimulus necessary for a individual to notice a difference in its intensity.

Kinesthetic : Relating to the sense of body movement or position.

Latent learning : A concept much emphasized by Tolman and is a learning which is not yet reflected in performance.

Learning set : An increased ability to solve problems of similar nature. Such set is acquired through experience with solving a large number of similar problems.

Libido : According to Freud the psychic energy that underlies all mental activities.

Life style : The overall pattern of behaviours that determine the health and quality of life.

Life Instinct : The desire of the person to maintain his life constructively.

Longitudinal Research : A kind of research in which the same set of individuals are studied across relatively long periods of time.

Long-term memory (LTM) : A memory system that keeps large amount of information over long periods of time. Also known as secondary Memory (SM).

Masculine Protest : A concept enunciated by Adler and which indicates the desire of both males and females to overcome feminity.

Materialism : A metaphysical position in which a single physical reality is assumed underlying all events.

Means-end readiness : As emphasized by Tolman, a stage of readiness that leads to the acquisition of certain expectancies more readily than others.

Mechanistic explanation : An explanation of phenomena in terms of known or presumed mechinelike functions.

Mental chemistry : A doctrine that the simple ideas mix to form new ideas and lose their individual identity.

Mental Mechanics : The doctrine that explicitly states that any complex idea is no more than the sum of the simple ideas from which it is formed

Methodological (Behaviourism) : The view that for studying behaviour strictly objective techniques are required. Also known as **empirical behaviourism.**

Methodological objectivism : A proposition which emphasizes upon the use of such techniques which are open to verification by another observer.

Methodological Subjectism : A proposition which emphasizes upon the use of techniques not open to verification by another observer.

Mind-body problem : A problem or puzzle created by the apparent concomitant operation of mind (or mental function) and body (or physical functions) and it also includes the question of how their relationship may best be understood and described.

Monism : A position in which only one basic reality, that is, either mind or body is said to be in existence.

Movement-produced stimuli : A concept emphasized by Guthrie and it indicates stimuli originating in the movements of organism.

Nativism : A doctrine that emphasizes upon the role of hereditary factor rather than upon environmental factor in development of behaviour.

Naturalism : The view that natural phenomena can be wholly interpreted by principles found by the studies of those natural phenomena without the help of any other external theories.

Naturalistic observation : Observation or study of the phenomena made in its natural state independent of any external or experimental inteference.

Nature-Nurture Controversy : A debate concerning the extent to which various aspects of behaviour are determined by genetic factors (nature) or environmental or experimental factors (nurture).

Neobehaviourism : New version of early Watsonian behaviourism.

Neo-Freudians : A group of theorists who accepted basic portions of Freud's theory that rejected or modified some other portions.

Neurotic trend : A concept enunciated by Horney in which the person adopts a particular approach in an attempt to avoid conflict and find security.

Nonsense Syllable : A meaningless item of three letters of which two consonants are separated by a vowel so that its sequence becomes CVC. It was developed by famous German psychologist Herman Ebbinghuns.

Objective tests : Inventories or questionnaires used to assess different aspects or dimensions of personality.

Object Permanance : A basic understanding among children that any object continue to exist even when it has passed off from the view.

Observational learning : A process of learning in which the person acquires knowledge by observing the behaviour of others.

Oedipus Complex : In Freud's theory a crisis of psychosexual development in which male child has sexual attraction for mother and hatred for father.

Operant behaviour : A response or behaviour for which their is no known eliciting stimulus and has a definite effect upon the environment.

Operant conditioning : Conditioning of operant response by establishing a contingency between a response and its consequence.

Oral stage : A stage of psychosexual development during which the pleasure is derived from activities of mouth only.

Organismic : Relating to any study which stresses the study of behaviour of the whole organism rather than its parts.

Orienting Reaction : A attentional response towards a novel stimuli. It mainly includes perceptual, physiological and postural responses towards stimuli.

Paradigm : An inclusive framework of methods, concepts and assumptions within which a scientific enterprise is usually possible to carry out.

Parapsychology : A relatively new branch of psychology that studies the psychological aspects of supernatural phenomena.

Preoperational stage : A stage in Piaget's theory of cognitive development during which children become capable of mental representations of the external world.

Principle of Parsimony : A simple principle that of the two hypotheses the simpler one should be accepted but at the same time it does not exclude the possibility of accepting the complex one if data so required.

Partial Reinforcement : A schedule of reinforcement in which reinforcement is presented intermittently after occurrence of the correct response.

Penis envy : A psychoanalytic concept showing a repressed desire of a female child to possess a penis like her brother.

Peripheralism : A kind of psychological phenomena that emphasizes the role of muscular action and similar events rather than upon the functioning of central nervous system.

Persona : In Jung's theory an important archetype that represents a human being's social self.

Personal Equation : A sort of correction for individual differences in reaction time denoted by astronomers in noting the movement of stellar transists.

Phallic stage : A stage in psychosexual development in which pleasure is centered in the genital region.

Phenomenology : A kind of observation in which experiential data are accepted without any attempt to analyse it.

Phi-phenomenon : A name given by Wertheimer to the perception of apparent motion produced by stationary stimulus.

Phrenology : A concept emphasized by Gall which demonstrates that the mental characteristics can be understood by examining the contours of the skull.

Physiology : A science that emphasizes the functions of various organ systems of the body.

Pleasure Principle : A principle in Freudian theory on which id operates and according to which immediate pleasure is the primary motivation for behaviour.

Pluralism : A philosophical position relating to mind-body problem in which several different processes are assumed.

Positivism : Any method designed to produce positive knowledge.

Postulate : A theoretical proposition within a given logical framework and which is tested indirectly through its empirical implications.

Pragmatics : Study of relationship between different signs and their users.

Pragmatism : A philosophical proposition telling that which is useful is true.

Precouscious : In psychoanalytic theory that portion of mind which consists of materials not presently conscious but can be easily recalled if needed.

Primary Process : A process whose aim is immediate instinctual satisfaction.

Probabilistic Functionalism : A position held by Brunswik that both the correctness of perception and the effectiveness of action are only probable. An organism's task simply reflects adaptive and functional relationship between distal stimuli and distal effects of responses.

Proximal reactions : A peripheral motor response of the organism without taking its consequences on the environment in account.

Psychoanalysis : Three meanings—(i) A school of psychology founded by Sigmund Freud (ii) a method of psychotherapy and (iii) a theory of personality.

Psychogenesis : Origin and development of mind and behaviour.

Psychophysical Parallelism : A metaphysical position in which mind and body are treated as independent but correlated entities.

Psychophysics : Scientific study of interaction between stimuli and sensation.

Psychotheraphy : A psychological technique for curing or treating a mental patient.

Purposivism : A doctrine which emphasizes that behaviour is directed towards some goal rather than it is purely mechanical one.

Puzzle box : A box invented originally by Thorndike and which prevents an organism from reaching a goal until a certain kind of behaviour is done.

Qualitative : Attribute that can be distinguished or identified as different in kind or quality.

Quantification : A process of establishing relationship between objects of empirical study and numbers.

Quantitativism : A doctrine that emphasizes on measured knowledge.

Reaction potential : A concept that indicates degree of strength of a habit or association between stimulus and response.

Reaction time : Time elapsing between presentation of stimulus and the reaction make by organism towards it.

Reality Principle : A principle in which ego operates in such a way that the external consequences of behaviour are considered important in regulating the expression of id impulses.

Reciproal determinism : The doctrine that the internal determinants of behaviour, the external determinant of behaviour and behaviour itself all influence one another in a complex and reciprocal fashion.

Reconditioning : In classical conditioning the recovery of a conditioned response to the pairing conditioned-unconditioned stimulus following extinction.

Reductionism : The view that the complex phenomena should be under-stood through its reduction or analysis into simpler components.

Reflex : An involuntary and stereotyped response of organs of the body towards the stimulus.

Reflex arc : A simplest functional unit of the nervous system consisting of a reception, synapse and an effector.

Reflexology : A school of psychology enunciated by Bekhterev and which holds that reflexes and combination of reflexes are the major basis of all human behaviour.

Representative Design : A concept emphasized by Brunswik and is basically an experimental approach which allows several variables to change together in a randon but known fashion and that way better represents the effects of existing combination of variables.

Repression : A defense mechanism in which unpleasant thoughts or feelings from consciousness are removed to unconscious.

Respondent behaviour : A response which is elicited by a specific stimulus.

Retinal disparity : A binocular visual depth cue that results from the slight difference between the two retinal images.

Restrospection : Refers to a sort of introspection of a past event.

Salivary conditioning : A process of conditioning in which salivary response becomes attached to some mental stimulus.

Schedule of reinforcement : Rules proposed by Skinner determining when and how reinforcements will be delivered during experiment.

Schemes : A cognitive framework representing a person's knowledge about different aspects of the environment.

School : A group of persons having more or less similar view to a particular issue, with varying degree of spatial and temporal contiguity.

Secondary Process : A deliberate and conscious activity of the ego guided by external reality.

Self : It has been used in at least three basic sense (i) a construct developed by persons to account for the integrity and continuity of their experiences. (ii) a general name for a set of phychological processes including different evaluatic and attitudinal functions, of an individual and his relationship to the world (iii) a general picture of an individual's post behaviour and experiences as he perceives it.

Self-actualization : A stage where individual reaches its maximal potential.

Self-awareness : Increased awareness of oneself as a social object.

Self-concept : All kinds of beliefs and information that an individual have about their own characteristics and themselves.

Self-esteem : The extent to which the persons have positive or negative feelings about their own worth and themselves.

Semantics : Study of relationship of signs to objects.

Semiotics : Study of uses of signs and symbols including three components, namely, syntactics, semantics and pragmatics.

Sensory adaptation : Reduced sensitivity to unchanging stimuli over time.

Sensory isolation : Removal of almost all stimulation for an individual for a specified period of time.

Shaping : A technique used to produce a desired pattern of response by selectively reinforcing responses that approximate it.

Sign learning : A concept in Tolman's theory that emphasizes learning of the relationship between signs, that is, what leads to what.

Sign significate : In Tolman's theory any object which gives rise to the expectany that a particular response will lead to a particular goal.

Skinner Box : A box or chamber containing a device which the organism can manipulate to produce some reinforcement.

S-O-R : Stimulus-organism-response.

Stimulus Error : A Titchener's term which dictates that the subject is paying attention to the stimulus rather than to the characteristics of sensation being produced by that stimulus.

S-R Psychology : Stimulus-Response psychology whose basic framework depends upon stimulus and the responses made toward this.

Structuralism : A system of psychology by Wundt and Titchener and that emphasizes the view that consciousness can be analyzed into elements through the method of introspection.

Subjectivism : A doctrine that forces person to base his belief on own perception and thinking.

Super ego : In Freud's theory the portion of personality which represent the conscious.

Supernaturalism : A doctrine which emphasizes that natural phenomena can be completely interpreted by making some assumption about principles.

System : Sets of ideas or suggestion about how to construct a psychology.

Systematic design : A classical methodology of an experimental research that utilizes vigorous control of variables.

Tabula rasa : A proposition which states that mind at birth is blank and later, experience writes something on it.

Teleology : A doctrine that explains behaviour in terms of its ultimate utilities, although evidence does not support that there are actually determining factors.

Tension System : In Lewin's theory a motivational factor in which some particular act gains directive influence in behaviour until dissipated.

Theorem : A statement derived from postulate.

Third Force : Name given to humanistic psychology envisioned by Maslow.

Topology : Geometry of spatial relationship; used in Lewin's theory as a model for representation of behaviour functions.

Transference : In Freud's theory shifting of emotion and feeling (positive or negative) from an object or person to the psychoanalyst during psychotherapeutic session.

Tropism : A forced moment which directly results from certain kind of stimulation.

Type A Behaviour : A cluster or traits such as aggressiveness, competitiveness, hostility and urgency.

Unconditional Positive Regard : In Roger's theory telling others that they will be respected regardless of what they say or do.

Unconscious : Refers to that portion of mind which consists of activities with which the person is not aware.

Unconscious inference : An important concept envisioned by Helmholtz and refers to drawing of a conclusion in absence of any reasoning process with which one is aware.

Unconscious mentalism : A doctrine that clearly states the importance of mental activities that occur outside the conscious awareness.

Utilitarianism : A doctrine that emhasizes upon seeking knowledge for applying it to the solution of some practical problems.

Valence : Attractiveness of an object; it can be either positive or negative.

Vector : In Lewin's theory a directional force assumed to underlie any behavioural relationship.

Vicarious function : In Tolman's theory substituting one means for another for achieving a particular result.

Vitalism : A philosophical doctrine which stresses that life cann't be fully explained in terms of physiochemical principles.

Weber's law : A law which states that just noticeable difference (jnd) for any intensity of a stimulus is a constant function of the intensity of that original stimulus.

Weber-Fechner law : A modified Weber's law presented by Fechner and which states that the intensity of a sensation is proportional to the logarithm of stimulus intensity.

Ziegarnik effect : The doctrine that uncompleted tasks are better recalled than completed task.

Zeitgeist : Refers to the spirit of the times.

■

REFERENCES

REFERENCES

A

ANDERSON, J. R. & BOWER, G. H. (1972). Recognition and retrieval processes in free recall. *Psychological Review, 79*, 97-123.

ANGELL, J. R. (1913). Bahaviour as a category of Psychology. *Psychological Review*, 20, 255-70.

ANSBACHER, H. L. & ANSBACHER, R. R. (EDS.) (1956). *The Individual psychology of Alfred Adler.* New York : Basic Book.

ALLPRT, G. W. & POSTMAN, L. (1947). *The Psychology of Rumor.* New York: L Henry Holt and Co.

ALPER, T. G. (1948). Memory for completed and incompleted task as a function of personality : Correlation between experimental and personality data. *Journal of Personality, 17*, 104-37.

ARNOLD, W. J. (1947). Simple reaction chains and their integration : Homogeneous chaining with terminal reinforcement. *Journal of Comparative and Physiological Psychology*, 40, 349-63.

ASCH, S. E., HAY, J. & DIAMOND, R. M. (1900). Perceptual organization in serial rote learning. *American Journal of Psychology*, 73, 177-198.

AZUMA H. & IMADA, H. (1994) Origins and development of Psychology in Japan: Interaction between western science and the Japanese cultural heritage. *International Journal of Psychology*, 29, 707-715.

B

BEAR, D.M. (1962). Laboratory Control of thumbsucking by the withdrawal of reinforcement. *Journal of the experimental analysis of behaviour*, 5, 525-26.

BANDURA, A. (1977A). *Social-Learning Theory.* Englewood Cliffs, N. J. : Prentice Hall.

BANDURA, A. (1977B). Self-efficiency : Toward a Unifying theory of behaviour change. *Psychological Review*, 84, 191-215.

BANDURA, A. (1978). The Self-system in reciprocal determinism. *American Psychologist*, 33, 344-358.

BANDURA A., ROSS, D., & ROSS S. A. (1964). Vicarious Reinforcement and Imitative Learning in W. A. Stoats, (ed.), *Human Learning.* New York : Holt, Rinehart and Winston.

BARCLAY, J. R. (1973). The role of comprehension in remembering sentences *Cognitive Psychology*, 4, 229-54.

BARTLETT, F. C. (1932). *Remembering : Experimental and Social Study.* London: Cambridge University Press.

BECKER, R. J. (1959). Outstanding contributors to Psychology. *American Psychologist,* 14, 297-298.

BERGMANN, G. (1956). The contribution of John B. Watson. *Psychological Review,* 63, 265-276.

BERRY, J. W. (1984) Toward a universal psychology of cognitive competence. *International Journal of Psychology,* 6, 193-197.

BEVER, T. G. (1968). Associations to stimulus-response theories of language. In T. R. Dixon and D. K. Horton, (eds.) *Verbal behaviour and general behaviour theory.* Englewood Cliffs, N. J. Prentice Hall.

BEVER, T. G., FODOR, J. A. & GARRETT, M. (1968). A formal limitation of associationism. In T. R. Dixon and D. L. Horton, (eds.) *Verbal behaviour and general behaviour theory.* Englewood Cliffs, N. J. : Prentice-Hall.

BHUMENTHAL, A. L. (1980). Wilhelm Wundt—Problems of interpretation. In W. G. Brigmann and R. D. Tweney (eds.), *Wundt Studies,* Toronto : C. J. Hogrefe.

BLODGETT, H. C. (1929). The effect of the introduction of reward upon the maze performance of'rats. California University. *Psychology,* 4, 113-34.

BORING, E. G. (1950). *A History of experimental Psychology,* New York : Appleton-Century-Crofts.

BOWER, G. H. & HILGARD, E. R. (1981). *Theories of Learning.* Englewood Cliffs : Prentice-Hall International.

BRANFORD, J. D. & FRANKS, J. J. (1971). The Abstraction of Linguistic Ideas. *Cognitive Psychology,* 2, 331-50.

BRIDGES, K. (1932). Emotional development in early infancy. *Child Development,* 3,324-341.

BRINGMANN, W. (1979) WUNDT'S LAB : "humble ... but functioning." (letter to editior) APA Monitor (Sept./Oct.) : 13

BRISLIN, R. W. (1987) CROSS-CULTURAL PSYCHOLOGY. IN R. J. CORSINI (ED.) *Concise Encyclopedia of psychology.* New York: Wiley.

BROLYER, C. R. (1936-37). Review of Lewin's Principles of topological psychology. *Character and Personality,* 5, 251-258.

BROME, V. (1978). *Jung.* New York : Athieneum.

BROWN, R. (1973). *A first language : The early stages.* Cambridge, Mass : Harvard University Press.

BRUNSWIK, E. (1939). Probability as a determiner of rat behaviour. *Journal of Experimental Psychology,* 25, 175-197.

BRUNSWIK, E. (1943). Organismic achievement and environmental probability : *Psychological Review,* 50, 255-272.

BRUNSWIK, E. (1956). *Perception and the representative design of Psychological experiments.* Berkeley : University of, California Press.

BRUSHLINSKY, A. (1995) Man as an object of investigation. *Herald of the Russion Academy of Sciences,* 65, 425-431.

BUGENTAL, J. F. T. (1965). *The search for authenticity : An existential-analytic approach to psychotherapy.* New York : Holt, Rinehart and Winston.

BUGEUTAL, J. (1967). *Challenges of a Humanistic Psychology.* New York : McGraw Hill Book Co.

BUHLER, C. (1971). Basic theoretical concepts in Humanistic Psychology. *American Psychologist.* Vol. 26, 378-386.

C

CARTWRIGHT, D. (1959). Lewinian theory as a contemporary systematic framework. In S. Koch (ed.) *Psychology : A Study of Science.* (Vol. 2) New York : McGraw Hill.

CHOMSKY, N. (1959). *Review of Skinner's Verbal Behaviour Language,* 35 : 26-58.

CHOMSKY, N. (1971). The case against B. F. Skinner. N. Y. Reviewed Books (Dec. 30, 1971). pp. 18-24. Also published as "Psychology and Ideology", *Cognitioin,* 1972, 1 : 11-46.

CHOMSKY, N. (1972). *Language and Mind. New York :* Harcourt Brace Jovanorich.

COAN, R. W. (1979). *Psychologists : Personal and Theoretical pathways.* New York : Irvington.

COAN, R. W. & ZAGONA, S. V. (1962). Contemporary ratings of psychological theorists. *Psychological Record,* 12, 315-322.

COHEN, D. (1979). *J. W. Watson : The founder of behaviourism.* London : Routledge and Kegan Paul.

D

DAS, R. S. (1959). A rapid and reliable method for estimating percentile scores of examination marks and psychometric test scores. *Psychological Studies,* 4(7), 50-58. g

DEB, M. (2002) *Blooming of Psychology in India at Calcutta University Psychology department.* Calcutta : Psychology Research Academy

DEUTSCH, M. (1954). Field theory in Social Psychology. In G. Lindzey (ed.) *Handbook of Social Psychology* Reading, M. A.: Addition-Wesley, pp. 181-222.

DULANY, D. E. (1968). Awareness, rules and prepositional controll : A confrontation with S-R behaviour theory. In T. R. Dixon and D. L. Horton, (eds.) *Verbal behaviour and general behaviour theory.* Englewood Cliffs, N. J. : Prentice Hall.

DUNCKER, K. (1945). On Problem Solving (Trans, by L. S. Lews) *Psychological Monographs.* 58, 270.

E

ELLENBERGER, H. F. (1965). Fechner and Freud. *Bulletin of Menninger Clinic, 20,* 201-214.

ELLENBERGER, H. F. (1970). *The discovery of the unconscious.* New York : Basic Books.

ERIKSON, E. H. (1963). *Childhood and Society.* (2nd ed.) New York : W. W. Norton.

ERIKSON, E. H. (1964). *Insight and Responsibility.* New York : W. W. Norton.

ERIKSON, E. H. (1966). Ontogeny of ritualization, In R. M. Loewenstein, L. M., Newman, M. Schur, and A. J. Solmit (eds.), *Psychoanalysis—A general psychology : Essays in honour of Heinz Hartmann.* New York : International University Press.

ERIKSON, E. H. (1968). *Identity : Youth and Crisis.* New York W. W. Norton.

ERIKSON, E. H. (1977). *Toys and reasons.* New York : W. W. Norton.

ESTES, W. K. & SKINNER, B. F. (1941). Some Quantitative properties of Anxiety. *Journal of Experimental Psychology,* 29, 390-400.

ESTES, W. K. (1969). Odtline of a theory of punishment. In B. A. Campbell and R. S. Church, (eds.), *Punishment and aversive behaviour.* New York: Appleton-Century-Crofts.

F

FISHER, S. & GREENBERG, R. P. (1977) Stomach symptons and up-down metaphors and gradients. *Psychosomatic Medicine,* 39, 93-101.

FAJANS, S. (1933). Erfolg, Ausdauer and Aktivitat beim sangling and kileinkind. *Psychologische Forschung,* 17,268-305.

FEARING, F. (1930). *Reflex action : A study in the history of physiological psychology.* Baltimore : Williams and Wilkins.

FEIST, J. (1985). *Theories of Personality,* New York : Holt, Rinehart and Winston.

FERSTER, C. B. & SKINNER, B. F. (1957). *Schedules of Reinforcement.* New York : Appleton-Century-Crofts.

FISHER S. & GREENBERG, R. P. (1977) Stomach Symptoms and up-down metaphors and gradients. *Psychosomatic Medicine,* 39, 93-101.

FREUD, S. (1920). *Beyond the pleasure principle.* Standard Edition, Vol. 18.

FUCHS, A. H. & KAWASH, G. F. (1974). Prescriptive dimensions of five schools of psychology. *Journal of the History of the Behaviour Sciences,* 10, 352-366.

G

GARRETT, H. E. (1939). Lewin's topological psychology : —Anevaluation. *Psychological Review,* 46, 517-524.

GATES, A. I. (1942). Conriectionism : Present concepts and interpretations. *Yearbook of National Society of the Study of Education,* 41, Part II, 141-164.

GEIS, G. L,, STEBBINS, W. C. AND LUNDIN, R. W. (1965). *Reflexes and Conditioned reflexes : A basic systems program.* New York : Appleton-Century-Crofts.

GIBSON, J. (1929). Reproduction of visually Perceived forms. *Journal of Epxerimental Psychology,* 2, 1039.

GIBSON, J. J. (1966). *The Senses Considered as Perceptual Systems.* Boston : Houghton Mifflin.

GELMAN, R. (1978). Cognitive Development. *Annual Review of Psychology,* 29, 297-332.

GELMAN. R. (1979). Preschool Thought. *American Psychologist,* 24, 900- 905.

GREENSPOON, J. (1955). The reinforcing effect of two spoken sounds on the frequency of two responses. *American Journal of Psychology,* 68, 409-416.

GUPTA. J. C. D. (1945). A Psychological study of a two year old. *Indian Journal of Psychology,* 20 (1-4), 77-85.

GUTHRIE, E. R. & HORTON, C. P. (1946). *Cats in Puzzle Box.* New York : Henry Holt and Company.

H

HALL, C. & LINDZEY, G. (1978). *Theories of Personality,* New York : John Wiley and Sons.

HALL, C.S., LINDZEY, G., LOEHLIN, J. C. & MANOSEVITZ, M. (1985). *Introduction to Theories of Personality.* New York : John Wiley and Sons.

HAMMOND, K. R. (1954) : Representative vs. Systematic design in clinical Psychology. *Psychological Bulletin,* 51, 150-159.

HAMMOND, K. R. (1955). Probabilistic functioning and the clinical method. *Psychological Review,* 62, 255-262.

HARPER, R. S., NEWMAN, E. B. & SCHAB, F.R. (1985). Garbriele Grafin Von Wartensleben and birth of Gestalt psychologist. *Journal of the History of the Behavioural Sciences,* 21, 118-123.

HARROWER, M.R. (1932). Organization in higher mental process. *Psychologische Forschung,* 17, 56-120.

HARTMANN, G. W. (1935). *Gestalt Psychology.* New York : Ronald Press.

HEIDBREDER, E. (1961). *Sewi Psychologies.* New York: Appleton-Century-Crofits..

HEIDER, F. (1959). On Lewin's methods and theory. *Psychological Issues,* 1 (3), 123.

HENLE, M. (1957). Some Problems of eclectism. *Psychological Review,* 64, 296-305.

HENLE, M. (1974). E.B. Titchener and the case of the missing element, *Journal of History of the Behavioural Sciences,* 10, 227- 2- 7

HERRNSTEIN, R.J. & BORING E.G. (EDS.). (1965). *A Source book in the history of psychology.* Cambridge, M.A. : Harvard University Press.

HILGARD, E. R. (1952) Experimental approaches to psychoanalysis. In E. Pumpian-Mindlin (Ed.) *Psychoanalysis as science.* Stanford, C. A. : Stanford University Preess, pp 3-45

HJELLE, L.A. & ZIEGLER, D.J. (1981), *Personality Theories.* Tokyo : McGraw-Hill International Book Company.

HILLGARD, E. R. & BOWER, G.H. (1975). *Theories of Learning.* Englewood Cliffs, N. J. : Prentice-Hall.

HILL, W.F. (1980). *Learning.* London : Methuen and Co. Ltd.

HILLIX, W.A. & BROYLES, J.W. (1980). The family trees of American Psychologists. In W.G. Brigmann and R.D. Tweney (eds.), *Wundt Studies.* Toronto : C.J. Hogrefe.

HOLLAND, J.G. & SKINNER, B.F. (1971). *The analysis of behaviour : A program for self- instruction.* New York : McGraw-Hill.

HONZIK, C.H. & TOLMAN, E.C. (1936). The Perception of Spatial Relations by the Rat, a Type of response not easily explained by conditioning. *Journal of Comparative Psychology,* 22,287-318.

HOUSTON, J.P. (1976). *Fundamentals of Learning.* New York : Academic Press.

HOVLAND, C.I. (1937). The generalization of conditioned responses IV. The effects of varying amounts of reinforcement upon the degree of generalization of conditioned responses. *Journal of Experimental Psychology,* 21, 261-276.

HULL, C.L, (1933). Differential Habituation to Internal stimuli in the Albino Rat. *Journal of Comparative Psychology,* 16, 255-73.

HULL, C.L. (1934A). The concept of habit family hierarchy in maze learning. *Psychological Review,* 41,33-54.

HULL, C.L. (1934B). Tha rat's speed of locomotion gradient in the approach to food. *Journal of Comparative Psychology,* 17,398-422.

HULL, C.L. (1952). *A behaviour System.* New Haven, C.T. : Yale University Press.

HUNTER, W.S. (1924). The Problem of consciousness. *Psychological Review,* 21,1-31.

J

JAIN, UDAY (2005) Towards understanding faith in science of Social Psychology. *Psychological Studies, 48,* 23-27.

JACOBSON, E. (1932). Electrophysiology of Mental Activities. *American Journal of Psychology, 44,* 677-94.

JACOBSON, E. (1979) I was there (letter to editor) *APA Monitor* (Sept./Oct.) 13

JAMES, W. (1890). Principles of Psychology, Vol. I. New York : Henry Holt.

JING, Q. (2000) International psychology. In K. Pawlik & M.R. Rosenzweig (eds) *International Hardbook of Psychology.* London. Sage.

JOHNSON, M.K., DOLL, T.J., BRANSFORD, J.D. & LAPINSKI, R.H. (1974). Context effects in Sentence memory. *Journal of Experimental Psychology*, 103, 338-60.

JONES, E. (1953). *The life and work of Sigmund Freud.* Vol. 1-3, New York: Basic Books.

JUNG, C.G. (1946). Psychic conflicts in a child. *In the Development of Personality Collected Works*, Vol. 17, Princeton, N.J. : Princeton University Press.

JUNG, C.G. (1953). *The Psychology of Unconscious.* In Collected Works. Vol. 7. Princeton University Press.

K

KALISH, H.T. (1969), Stimulus generalization. In M.H. Marx (Id.) *Learning Processes.* New York : MacMillan, 205-298.

KANTOR, J.R. (1970). An analysis of the Experimental anaysis of behaviour. *Journal of the Experimental Analysis of Behaviour,* 13, 101-108.

KARDINOR, A (1939) *The individual and his societies.* New York : Columbia University Press.

KASAMATSU, A. & HIRAI, T. (1966) An EEG study on the Zen Meditation. *Folia Psyckiatria Neurologica Japanica,* 20, 315-36

KELLER, F. S. (1937) *The definition of Psychology,* Newyork : Appleton Centur- Crotts.

KELMAN, H. (1971). *Helping people : Karen Honey's psychoanalytic approach.* New York : Science House.

KLINE, P. (1977) Cross- cultural studies and Frendian theory. In Neil warren (Ed.) *Studies in cross-cultural psychology* vol. I. Academic press.

KOCH, S. (1959). (ED). *General systematic formulations in Psychology : A Study of a Science :* New York : McGraw-Hill Book Co.

KOHLER, W. (1947). *Gestalt Psychology : An introduction to the new concepts in modern psychology.* New York : Liverright.

KOHLER, W. & HELD, R. (1949). The cortical correlates of pattern vision. *Science,* Vol. 110, p. 414-19.

KOHLER, W. & WALLACH, H. (1944). Figural Aftereffects : An investigation of Visual Processes. *Proceedings of American Philosophical Society,* 88, p. 269-357.

KOPPE, S. (1987) DENMARK. IN A.R. GILLEN & C. K. GILGEN (EDS). *International Hondbook of psychology.* New York: Greenwood Press.

KRECH, D. (1962). Cortical Localization of function. In L. Postman (ed.) *Psychology in the making.* New York : Knopf, 31-32.

KRISHNAM, B. (Ed.) (1974) *Studies in Psychology.* Mysore : Mysore University.

KUNDU, R. (1961). Computation of Tetrachoric correlation : A comparison of three methods. *Journal of Psychological Researches,* 5, 116-119.

KUO, Z.Y. (1928). The fundamental error of the concept of purpose and trial-and-error fallacy. *Psychological Review,* 35, 414-433.

L

LASHLHY, K.S. (1923). The behaviouristic interpretation of consciousness, *Psychological Review*, 30, 329-353.

LASHLEY, K.S. & BALL, J. (1922). Spinal conduction and Kinesthetic Sensitivity in maze habit, *Journal of Comparative Psychology*, 9, 71-105.

LASHLEY, K., CHOW, K.W. & SEMMES, J. (1951). An Examination of the Electrical Field theory of Cerebral Integration. *Psychological Review*, 58, 123-36.

LEAHEY, T.A. (1980). *A History of Psycyhology.* Englewood Cliffs, N. J. : Prentice Hall.

LEEPER, R. (1935). The Role of motiviation in learning : A Study of the phenomenon of Differential Motivational Control of the Utilization of Habits. *Journal of Genetic Psychology*, 46, 3-40.

LEEPER, R.W. 1943). Lewin' topological and Vector psychology : A digest and critique university of oregon. *Published Study of Psychology*, Vol. 1.

LEFRANCOIS, G.R. (1983). *Psychology.* California : Wadsworth Publishing Co.

LENNEBERG, E.H. (1969). On explaining language. *Science*, 164, 635^3.

LEWIN, K. (1936). *A dynamic theory of Personality.* New York : McGraw-Hill.

LEWIN, K. (1943). Forces behind food habits and methods of change. *Bulletin of the National Research Council*, 108, 35-65.

LEWIN, K. (1951). *Field theory in Social Science : Selected theoretical papers* (D. CartWright, ed.) New York : Harper and Row.

LEWIN, K. (1958). Group decision and Social change. In E. Macoby, T. M. Newcomb and E.L. Hartley (eds.) *Readings in Social Psychology* (3rd ed.), New York : Holt, Rinehart and Winston INC. 197-211.

LICHTENSTEIN, P.E. (1967). Psychological Systems : Their nature and Function. *Psychological Record*, 17, 221-40.

LONDON, I.D. (1944), Psychologists' misuse of the auxiliary concepts of Physics and Mathematics. *Psychological Review*, 51,226-291.

LUNDIN. R.W. (1985). *Theories and Systems of Psychology.* Toronto : D. C. Heath and Company.

M

MAIER, H. (1965). *Three theories of child development : The Contributions of Erik H. Erikson, Jean Piaget and Robert R. Sears and their applications.* New York : Harper and Row.

MAIER, N.R.F. (1930). Reasoning in Humans : I. On direction. *Journal of Comparative psychology*, 10, 115-143.

MAIER, N.R.F. (1931). Reasoning in Humans : II. The solution of a Problem and its appearance in consciousness. *Journal of Comparative Psychology*, 12, 181-194.

MADD, S. (1967). The Existential Neurosis. *Journal of Abnormal Psychology*, vol. 72, pp. 311-325.

MALINOWSKI, B. (1950) *Argonauts of the Western Pacific* New York : Dutton

MANDLER, G.C. 1985). *Cognitive Psychology : An Essay in Cognitive Science.* Hillsdale, N.J. : Erlbaum.

MARX, M.H. & HILLIX, W.A. (1963). *Systems and Theories in Psychology,* New York : McGraw-Hill Book Co.

MARX, M.H. & CRONAN-HILLIX, W.A. (1987). *Systems and theories in Psychology.* New York : McGraw-Hill Book Co.

MASLOW, A. (1954). *Motivation and Personality.* New York : Harper and Bros.

MASLOW, A. (1970). *Motivation and Personality.* New York : Harper and Row.

MAX, L.W. (1937). Action-Current Responses in the Deaf during Awakening, Kinesthetic, Imagery and Abstract Thinking. *Journal of Comparative Psychology,* 24, 301-44.

McDOUGALL, W. (1908). *An Introduction to Social Psychology.* London : Matheun and Co.

McDOUGALL, W. (1920). *The Group Mind.* New York : Patnam.

McDOUGALL, W. (1924). *Fundamentals of Psychology.* Psychology 5, 13-32.

MCGEOCH, A. (1933). The Formal Criteria of a Systematic Psychology. *Psychological Review,* 40, 1, 11.

MCGURIE, W. (ED.) (1974). *The Freud/Jung letters : the Correspondence between Sigmund Freud and C.G. Jung,* Princeton, N.J. : Princeton.

MEAD, G.H. (1934). *Mind, Self and Society,* Chicago : University of Chicago Press.

MEAD. M. (1950) *Coming of age in Samoa* Garden City, New York : Doubleday

MULLER, C.G. & SCHOENFELD, W.N. (1954), "Edwin R. Guthrie" in W.K. Estes. et al. *Modern Learning Theory.* New York : Appleton-Century-Crofts.

MURPHY, G. (1949). *Historical Introduction to Modern Psychology.* New York: Harcourt, Brace and World.

N

NAGARATHNA, B. (1939). A Study of anger in children. *Indian Journal of Psychology,* 14 (4), 189-198.

NEWELL, A. & SIMON, H.A. (1956). The Logic Theory. Machine. *Transactions on Information Theory,* Vol. 2, pp. 61-79.

NEWELL, A. SHAW, J.C. & SIMON, H.A. (1960). Report on a General Problem-Solving Program for the computer. *Proceedings of the International Conference on Information Processing.* (UNESCO, 1960), pp. 256-64.

NEWELL, A. & SIMON, H.A. (1972). The simulation of human thought. In W. Dennis et al. (eds.) *Current trends in psychological theory.* Pittsburgh: University of Pittsburg Press, 152-179.

O

OVSIANKINA, M. (1928). Die Wiedraufnahme unterbrochener Handlungen. *Psychologische Forschung*. 11, 302-379.

P

PANDEY, J. (ED.) (1988). *Psychology in India*. New Delhi : Sage Publications India Pvt. Ltd.

PAN, S. (1987) *Selected psychological papers of Pan Shu*. Jiangsu: Jiangsu Educational Publishers.

PANDEY, J. (ED.) (2001) *Psychology in India Revisited*, (Three volumes), New Delhi : sage

PAREEK, U. (ED.) (1980). *A Survey of Research in Psychology*, 1971-76, Part I, Bombay : Popular Prakashan.

PAREEK, U. (ED.) (1981). *A Survey of Research in Psychology*, 1971-76, Part II, Bombay : Popular Prakashan.

PATHAK, P. (1966). Behaviour Patterns of infants under testing. *Psychological Studies*, 11 (2), 115-123.

PRABHU, P. H. (1954) *Hindu Social Organization : A study in social-psychological and idealogical foundations* Bombay : Popular Book Depot.

R

RAY, A. B. (1965). Comparison of two different methods of item-analysis. *Psychological studies*. 10 (1), 66-69.

RAPAPORT, D. (1959) The structure of psychoanalytic theory : A systematizing attempt. In S. Koch (Ed.) *Psychology : A study of Science*. Vol. 3. *Formulations of the person and the social context*. New York : McGraw-Hill, pp. 55-83.

RHEINGOLD, H.L., GEWIRTZ, J.L. & ROSS, H.W. (1959). Social conditioning of vocalizations in the infant. *Journal of Comparative and physiological psychology*, 52, 68-73.

RICHARDS, R.J. (1980), Wundt's early theories of unconscious influence and cognitive evolution in their relation to Darwinian biopsychology. In W.G. Brigmann and R.D. Tweney (eds.) *Wundt Studies*. Toronto : Hogrefe.

ROGERS, C.R. (1959). A theory of therapy, personality and interpersonal relationship as developed in the client-centered framework. In S. Koch, *Psychology : A Study of Behaviour*, vol. 3. New York : McGraw-Hill Book Co.

ROSENZWIG, M. R. (1982) Trends in development and status of psychology. An international perspective. *International Journal of Psychology*, 17, 117-140.

ROSENZWIG, M. R. (1992) Resources for psychological science around the world. In M. R. Rosenzwig (Ed.) *International Psychological Science: Progress Problems and Prospects*. Washington, D. C.: American Psychological Association.

ROSENZWIG, M. R., HOLTZMAN, W. H,, SABORIN, M,, & BELANGER, D. (2000) *History of the International Union of Psychological Science (IUPSYS) Hove,* England : Psychology press.

ROSS, D.G. (1972). *Stanley Hall : The Psychologist as a prophet.* Cihcago : University of Chicago Press.

ROUTH, D.K. (1969). Conditioning of vocal response differentiation in infants. *Journal of Development Psychology,* 1, 219-26.

S

SAHAKIAN, W. (1975). *History and Systems of Psychology.* New York : Halsted Press, a division of John Wiley and Sons.

SCHULTZ, D. P. (1969) *A History of Modern Psychology,* New York : Academic Press.

SCHWELLER, D,, BREWER, W.F. & DAHL, D. (1976). Memory for illocutionary Forces and Pre-illocutionary effects of certain utterances. *Journal of Verbal learning and verbal behaviour,* 15, 325-37.

SELFRIDGE, O.G. & NEISEER, U. (1960). Pattern recognition by machine. Scientific American, 203, 60-68.

SEN, INDIRA (1943) The integration of personality. *Indian Journal of Psychology,* 7, 11-40

SEN, INDIRA (1946) The urge for wholeness. *Indian Journal of Psychology,* 21, 1-32

SEN, INDIRA (1951) The standpoint of Indian Psychology. *Indian Journal of Psychology,* 26, 81-90

SEARS, R.RT(1943) *Survey of objective studies of psychoanalytic concepts.* New York : Social Science Research Council.

SEXTON, V. S. & HOGAN, J. (EDS.) (1992) *International Psychology,* Views from around the world (2nd ed.) Lincoln : University of Nebraska Press.

SHANKAR, P. (1964). A simple method of scoring a Social Distance Scale. *Journal of Psychological Reserches,* 8 (1), 7-12.

SILVERMAN, L. H. (1976) Psychoanalytic theory : "The reports of my death are greatly exaggerated." *American Psychologist,* 9, 179-193.

SIMONS, H. A. & JING, Q. C. (1988) Recognizing thinking and learning as information processes. *Psikhologiskii Ruannal,* 9, 33-46.

SIMONS, H. A. (1991) *Models of My life* USA : Basic Books

SINHA, D. (1981) Non-western perspectives in psychology: Why, what and whiter? *Journal of Indian Psychology,* 3, 1-9.

SINHA, D. (1987) India. In A. R. Gilgen & C. K. Gilgen (Eds.) *International Handbook of Psychology,* Newyork: Greenwood Press.

SINGH, S. D. & MANOCHA, S.N. (1966). Reactions of Rhesus monkeys and the langur in novel situation. *Primates,* 4, 259-262.

SINHA, S.N. & SHARMA, K.L. (1970). Effects of Beta-carotene on light-dark discrimination in rats. *Proceedings of the 57th Session of the Indian Science Congress,* III, 593.

SKINNER, B.F. (1938). *The behaviour of Organisms : An experimental Analysis* New York : Appleton-Century Company.

SKINNER, B.F. (1954). Ctitique of Psychoanalytic Concepts and Theories. *Scientific Montly,* 79, 300-305.

SKINNER B.F. (1957). *Verbal Behaviour.* New York : Appleton-Century-Crofts.

SKINNER, B.F. (1971). *Beyond Freedom and Dignity.* New York : Alfred A. Knopf.

SKINNER, B.F. (1977). Why 1 am not a cognitive psychologist. *Beahviourism,* 5,1-10.

SNUGG, D. & COOMBS, A.W. (1949). *Individual Beahviour.* New York : Harper and Row.

SMITH, M.B. (1950). The phenomenological approach in personality theory : Some critical remarks. *Journal of Abnormal and Social Psychology,* 45, 516-522.

SPENCE, K.W. (1951). Theoretical Interpretations of Learning in S.S. Stevens (ed.), *Handbook of Experimental Psychology,* Wiley.

SPIEGELBERG, H. (1960). *The phenomenological Movement : A Theoretical Introduction :* Haag : Hyhof.

STARCHEY, J. (ED.) (1955). *The Standard Edition of the Complete Work of Sigmund Freud.* London : Hogarth Press.

STEVENS, S. S. (1934). The attributes of Tone. *Proceedings of the National Academy of Science,* 20, 457-59.

SULLIVAN, H. S. (19&) : *The interpersonal Theory of Psychiatry.* New York: W.W. Norton.

T

TERRACE, H.S. (1966). Stimulus Control. In W.K. Honing (ed.) *Operant behaviour : Areas of research and application.* New York : Appleton-Century-Crfots.

THORNDIKE, E.L. (1933). An experimental study of rewards. *Teachers College Contributions to Education,* No. 580.

THORNDIKE, E.L. (1949). *Selected Writings from a Connectionists' Psychology.* New York : Appleton-Century-Crofts.

TINKER, M.A. (1980). Wundt's doctorate students and their theses 1875-1920. In W.G. Brigmann and R.D. Tweney (eds.) *Wundt Studies.* Toronto : C.J. Hogrefe.

TINKLEPAUGH. O.H. (1928). An Experimental Study of Representative Factors in Monkeys. *Journal of Comparative Psychology,* 8, 197-236.

TOLMAN, E.C. (1932). *Purposive Behaviour in Animals and Men.* New York: Appleton-Century Company.

TOLMAN, E.C. (1948). "Kurt Lewin, 1980-1947". *Psychological Review,* 55, 1-4.

TOLMAN, E.C. & BRUNSWIK, E. (1935). The organism and the causal texture of the environment. *Psychological Review*, 42, 43-77.

TOLMAN, E.C. AND HONZIK. C.H. (1930). Introduction and Removal of a Reward and Maze Performance in Rats. *University of California Publications in Psychology*. 4, 257-75.

TOLMAN, E.C., RITCHIE, B.F. & KALISH, D. (1946). Studies in Spatial learning : II. Place Learning versus Response learning. *Journal of Experimental Psychology*, 36, 221-29.

TOLMAN, E.C., RITCHIE, B.F. & KALISH, D. (1947). Studies in Spatial learning : A. Response learning versus place learning by the non-correction methods. *Journal of Experimental Psychology*, 37, 285-92.

TULVING, E. & DONALDSON, W. (1962). (eds.). *Organization of Memory*. New York : Academic Press.

U

UZGIRIS, I.C. & HUNT, J. MCV. (1975). *Assessment in infancy : Ordinal Scales of Psychological development*. Urbana, IL : University of Illinois Press.

V

VALENTINE, W.L. & WIGGINS, D.D. (1949). *Experimental Foundations of General Psychology*. New York : Rinehart and Co.

VAN HOORN, W. &VERHAVE, T. (1980). Wundt's Changing conceptions of a general and theoretical psychology. In W.G. Bringmann and R.D. Tweney (eds). *Wundt Studies*. Toronto : C.J. Hogrefe.

VERMA, A., POFFENBERGER, T., PATHAK, P., SHAH, T.M. & SHAH H.B. (1969). Motor and Mental growth of Baroda Babies. *Research report No. 3 Department of Child Development*, M.S. University, Baroda.

VOEKS, V.W. (1954) Acquisition of S.R. Connections : A Test of Hull's and Guthrie's Theories. *Journal of Experimental Psychology*, 47, 437-47.

VRINTE, J. (1995) *The concept of Personality in Shri Aurbindo's Integral Yoga Psychology and A. Maslow's Humanistic / Transactional Psychology. New Delhi: M. M. Publishers Ltd.*

W

WATSON, R.I. (1967). Psychology : A perspective science. *Amercian Psychologist*, 22, 435-443.

WATSON, R.I. (1978). *The Great Psycholgists* : Philadelphia : J.B. Lippincott.

WHITING, J. W. M. (1968) Methods and problems in Cross-cultural research. In G. Lindzey & E. Aronson (Eds.) *The Handbook of social Psychology*, vol. II Massachusetts : Addison wesley Publishing co. Ltd.

WEIGELR, R.G. & GOTTFURCHT, J.W. (1972). Faculty genealogies: A stimulus for student involvement in history and systems. *Amercian Psychologist, 27,* 981-983.

WEYER, E.M. (1921). Comment in B.T. Baldwin (ed.). In Memory of Whilhem Wundt. *Psychological Review,* 28, 153-188.

WOLMAN, B.B. (1960). *Contemporary Theories and Systems in Psychology.* New York : Haper and Bros.

WOLMAN, B.B. (1979). *Contemporary Theories and Systems in Psychology.* New York : Harper and row.

WOODWORTH, R.S. (1948). *Contemporary Schools of Psychology.* New York : Ronald Press.

WRIGHT, H.F. (1943). The effect of Barriers on the strength of motivation. *In Child Behaviour and Development,* R. G. Brker, J.S. Koumin and H.F. Wright, (eds.) New York : McGraw-Hill Book Co.

WULFF, F. (1922). Uber die veranderung von verstellungen. In C.E. Osgood's book *Method and Theory in Experimental psychology* (1953). Oxford University Press.

Y

YAMAOKA, T. (1968) Psychological study of mental self-control. In Y. Akishige (Ed.) *Psychological studies in Zen.* Eukuoka, Japa; Kyushu university.

YANG, K.S. (1993) Why we are constructing indigenous psychology of Chinese people. In K. S. Yang (Ed.) *Indigenous psychological research in Chinese societies.* Taibei: Gui Guan Book co.

Z

ZEIGARNIK, B. (1927). Das Gehalten erledigter and uncrledigter Handlugen. *Psychologische Forschung,* 9-1-85 (Trans, and Cond. as "On finished and unfinished tasks" in W.D. Ellis (ed.) (1938). *A Source book of Gestalt Psychology.* New York : Harcourt, Brace andWorld, pp. 300-314.

INDEX

NAME INDEX

Adler, A., 307–314
Alper, I.G., 349
Allport, G.W., 275
Anderson, J.R., 280
Angell, J., 150
Angell, J.R., 150-152, 207
Ansbacher, H.L., 310
Ansbacher, R.R., 310
Aristotle, 20–22,
Arnold, W.J., 226
Asch, S.E., 280
Asthana, H.S., 431
Augustine, St., 27, 28
Azuma, H., 451

Baer, D.M., 277
Bain, A., 47-50, 197
Ball, J., 354
Bandura, A., 251–255, 398
Barclay, S.R.I., 411
Bartlett, F.C., 275
Becker, R.J., 130
Bell,S.C. 65
Bekhterev, U.M., 175, 204
Berkeley, G., 34-36, 197
Berry, J.W., 461
Bever, T.G., 405
Bergmann, G., 242
Binswanger, L., 388
Blodgett, H.C., 354
Boring, E.G., 48-49, 75, 78, 96-97, 103, 122, 136, 205, 270
Bose, G.S., 421, 424
Boss, M, 389
Bower, G.H., 156, 222, 280, 407
Bransford, J.D., 411
Broyler, C.R., 352
Brentano, F., 101–103, 261
Brewer, W.P., 473
Bridges, K., 225
Bringmann, W., 129
Brislin, R.W., 461
Broca, P., 71
Brome, V., 357
Broota, K.D., 431
Brown, R., 404
Brown, T., 43-44, 187
Brunswik, E., 352, 354–357
Brunshlinsky, A., 450
Buch, M.B., 426
Buddha, G., 419
Bugental, J., 371, 385
Buhler, C., 371
Buhler, K., 109

Cabanis, P., 210
Carr, H.A., 152-157
Cartwright, D., 352
Cattell, J.M., 138-142
Chomsky, N., 234, 237, 403–408
Coan, R.W., 285
Cohen, D., 193
Comte, A., 210–11
Confucius, 449, 450

Darwin, C., 81–83, 290
Dahl, D., 411
Das, R.S., 428
De, B., 421
Democritus, 17
Descartes, R., 27–29
Deutsch, M., 349
Dewey, J., 149
Doll, T. I., 411

Donaldson, W., 280
Donders, F.C., 74, 76
Douglas, S., 35, 37
Dulany, D.F., 405
Dunker, K., 274
Dutta, R., 495

Ebbinghaus, H., 171–173, 189
Ehrenfels, C.V., 261
Ellenberger, H.F., 328, 331, 332
Epicurus, 23
Erikson, E., 332–339
Estes, W.K., 233, 405

Fajans, S., 350
Fearing, F., 192
Fechner, G.T., 61-64
Ferster, C.B., 231
Feist, J., 349, 355, 358
Fisher, S., 292
Flourens, F., 60
Franks, J.J., 411
Freud, S., 284–288, 298
Fromm, E., 324–326
Fuchs, A.H., 7

Gall, F.J., 69
Galton, S.F., 83-85, 147
Galvani, L, 68
Carrett, H.E., 352
Gates, A.I., 203
Gibson, J.J. , 375
Geis, G.L., 266
Gelman, R., 403
Gewritz, J.L., 404
Gibson, J.J. 275
Glover, E., 363
Greenberg, R.P., 292
Greenspoon, J., 233
Gupta, J.C.D., 423
Guthrie, E.R., 216–220,

Hall, G.S., 352
Hall, M., 72
Hammond, K.R. 357
Harrower, M.R., 279
Hartley, D. , 39-41
Hartmann, G.W., 306
Heidbreder, E., 161, 230, 207
Heidgger, M., 387
Heider, F., 352
Held, R., 311
Helmholtz, H.V., 75
Henle, M., 161
Herbart, J.F., 52-54, 49–51, 330
Heraclitus, 17
Hering, E., 80
Herrinstein, R.J., 333
Hilgard, E.R., 156, 222, 280, 292, 407
Hill, W.F., 253
Hillix, W.A., 50, 130, 154, 174, 182, 212, 246, 261, 272, 278, 355, 356
Hippocrates, 18
Hirai, T., 429
Hjelle, L.A. 304
Hobbes, T., 32, 187
Hogan, J., 457
Holland J.G., 266
Holt, E.B. 209–210
Honzik, C.M., 245, 354
Horney, L., 320–323
Horten, C.P., 245
Houston, J.A., 253
Hovland, C.I., 226

Hull, C.L, 220–227, 243
Humboldt, A., 68
Hume, D., 37–38
Hunt, J.M., 400
Hunter, W.S., 209, 234

Imada, H., 451

Jackson, H., 290
Jacobson, E., 129
Jaensch, E.R., 262
James, W., 128-136, 147
Jaspers, K., 386
Jing, Q., 450, 453, 461
Johnson, MK., 411
Jones, E., 303,
Johsi, M.C., 493'
Jung, C. 314–319

Kalish, H.T., 238
Kant, I., 51-52, 260
Kardiner, A., 292
Knator, J.R., 246–251
Katz, D., 262
Kasamatsu, A.
Kawash, G.E., 7
Kelman, H., 323
Keller, F. S., 20
Khandwalla, P.N., 432
Kierkeggaard, S., 386
Kline, P., 461
Koch, S., 227
Koffka, K., 265–266, 273
Koppe, S., 450
Kohler, W., 264–265, 272,
Kothurkar, V.N., 425
Krishnan, B., 424
Krech, D., 238
Kulpe, O., 106–107
Kundu, R., 428
Kuppuswamy, B., 427

Lapinski, R.H., 411
Lashley, K., 210, 354
Leahey, T.A., 398, 413
Leeper, R. 243
Leeper,R.W., 352
Lefrancois, G.R., 407
Leibnitz, G., 29–30, 288
Lenneberg, E.H., 405–407
Lewin, K., 343–352, 349, 351
Lichtenstein, P.E., 5
Lindzey, G., 352
Locke, J., 33-34,
Lochlin, J.C., 359
Loeb, J. 191
London, I.D., 352
Lotze, H., 55
Lundin R.W., 294, 409

Mach, E., 261
McGeoch, A., 2, 7
Maier, H., 274
Maddi, S., 449
Mc Gurie, W. 314
Magendie,F., 65
Maier, H., 338
Maiti, H.P., 485
Mandler, G.C., 396
Manocha, S.N., 429
Manosevitz, M., 359
Marbe, K., 107
Marx, M.H., 50, 130, 154, 174, 182, 212, 246, 261, 272, 278, 355
Maslow, A., 371–372, 377–381
May, R., 390

Mazumdar, D.P.S., 429
McDougall, W., 359–365, 367–368
McGeoch, A., 2, 7, 8
Meed, G.H., 373,
Mead, M., 292
Megendie, F., 65
Mettric, J., 210
Mill, J., 44–45, 187
Mill, J.S., 46–47, 187, 260
Mitra, S.K., 427, 428
Mohsin, S.M., 428
Morgan, C.L., 190
Muller, J., 66–68
Muller, G. E., 104-105
Murphy, G., 101
Muthayya, B.C., 432

Nawaratna, B., 429
Neisser, U., 410
Neitzsche, F., 289
Newell, A., 410

Ovsiankina, M., 349

Padaki, R., 498
Pan, S., 462
Panda, K.C., 432
Pandey, J., 430
Parameshwaran, E.G., 429
Pareek, U., 429–30
Pathak, P., 429
Pavlov, I.P., 173, 191–93
Piaget, J., 399
Plato, 19–29, 169,
Pythagorus, 17
Postman, L., 275

Rapaport, D., 291
Rath, R.N., 425
Ray, A.B., 428
Reid, T., 41–42
Rheingold,H.L., 404
Rogers, C., 375–377
Ronaldo, L., 70
Romanes, G.J., 211
Rosenzwig, M. R., 457
Ross, D.G., 137
Ross, D., 254
Ross, S.A., 254
Ross, H.W., 404
Routh, D.K., 404
Rubin, E., 298

Sahakian, W., 361
Saraswath, T., 431
Sartre, J.P., 386
Satyavathi, K., 432
Sexton, V. S., 457
Schweller, D., 473
Schopenhauer, A., 289
Schultz, D. P., 101
Sechenov, I.M., 192
Sears, R.R., 292
Selfridege, O.G., 410
Shanker, P., 428
Shanmugam, T.E. 424
Sharma, K.L, 430
Shaw, J.C., 410
Silverman, L.H., 292
Simon, H.A., 410, 453
Singh, A.K., 425, 431
Singh, R., 497
Singh, S. D., 429
Sinha, A.K.P., 421, 428–249
Sinha, D., 421, 426, 451, 461

Sinha, J.B.P., 425
Sinha, M.M., 429
Sinha, S.N., 430
Skinner, B.R., 227–236, 404, 412
Smith, M.B., 377
Socrates, 18–19
Spence, K.W., 239
Spencer, H., 50, 187
Spiegelberg, H., 387
Spinoza, B., 23
Spurzheim, 69
Stevens, S.S., 125
Stobbins, W.C., 266
Strachey, J., 333
Stumpf, C.I, 103, 297
Sullivan, H.S., 326–332
Stewart, D., 42
Strachey, J. 294

Thales, 17
Terrace, H.S., 238
Thomas, St., 17, 18
Thorndike, E.L, 157, 176-181, 215
Tinker, M.A. 98
Tinklepaugh, O.H., 244, 354
Titchener, E.B., 114-121
Tolman, E.C., 238–246, 352–354
Tripathi, L.B., 431
Tripathi, R.C., 431
Tulving, E., 280

Uzgivis, I.C., 400

Valentine, W.L., 249
Verma, A., 429
Verma, S.K., 429, 432
Vocks, V.W., 245
Volta,A., 68
Vrinte. J., 419

Wallach, H., 272
Watson, J.B., 188, 193–205
Watson, R.I., 7
Watt, H., 108
Weber, E.H., 59-61
Weiss, A.P., 208
Wertheimer, M., 262–264
Wiggins, D.D., 249
Whiting, J. W. M., 461
Wolman, B.B., 322
Wundt, W., 90–97, 123-125, 260
Woodworth, R.S., 148, 158-59, 205, 271, 365–368
Wolman, B.B., 212, 240
Wright, H.F., 400
Wulff, F., 275
Xun Zi, 449, 450

Yamaoka, T.
Yang, K.S., 451, 462
Yerkes, R.M., 213
Young T., 76

Zeno, 23
Zeigarnik, B. 384
Ziegler, D.J., 304
Zogona, S.V., 285

SUBJECT INDEX

Absolute personal equation, 74
Act Pscyhology, 101
Adler Psychology, 308–312
    Criticisms of, 312–313
Analytical Psychology, 315
Artifical intelligence, 410
Apperception, 54, 96–97
Association :
    conditions of, 45
    doctrine of, 46, 49
    laws of, 22, 34–35, 38, 40–41
    principles of, 95
Associationism, 2, 39, 169
Aufgabe, 108
Available Memory, 295

Basic anxiety, 365
Behaviour space, 354
Behaviourism :
    antecedents of early, 188–193
    criticisms of Watsonian, 205
    secondary features of, 200–202
Bell–Magendie law, 65
Brith order, 312
Bundle hypothesis, 278

Cognition, modes of 328
Cognitive behaviourism, 327
Cognitive development, stages of, 400–402
Cognitive Psychology :
    antecdent forces of, 396
    criticisms of, 412
Collective unconscious, 316
Constancy hypothesis, 266
Context theory of meaning, 120
Creative Power, 311
Creative synthesis, 95
Cross-cultural psychology, 460

Daesin, 388
Deductive behaviourism, 229
Defence mechanism, 299–300, 323
Descriptive behaviourism, 229
Determining tendency, 108
Determinism, 12
Docile behaviour, 241
Dualistic systems, 8,40
Dynamism, 328

Ebbinghaus curve, 172
Elementalism, 183, 266
Emic approach, 461
Empiricism, 32, 78
Empty organism appraoch, 229
Equipotentiality, principle of, 211
Erikson's developmental stages, 333–337
Etic approach, 461
Evolution :
    theory of, 81–83
Evolutionary associationism, 50
Existential neurosis, 391
Existential psychology :
    antecedents forces of, 385
    basic tennets of, 384
    criticisms of, 391
External reinforcement, 254

Fictional finalism, 311
Field dynamics, 270

Figural aftereffects, 272
Fromm's personality types, 325–326
Functionalism :
antecedents of, 146–148
criticisms of, 160–161
fate of, 163–164

Gestalt Psychology :
antecedent forces of, 260
criticisms of, 278–290
founding of, 262–266
present status of, 280
protest of, 266
Goal gradient hypothesis, 226
Group dynamics, 350
Group Mind, 364

Habit strength, 224
Humanistic Psychology :
antecedents forces of, 373
basic tenets of, 371
criticisms of, 381

Idea :
association of, 34, 38
impression and, 37–38
meaning of, 37
Identity hypothesis, 64
Indigenous Psychology, 462
Individual difference variables, 241
Imageless thought, 107
Inductive behaviourism, 229
Information-processing model, 410
Intelligence, types of, 181
Interdisciplinary research, 462, 463
International Psychology, 447
International Union of Psychological Science (IUPSYS), 456
Instinct, 297, 362–363
Interbehavioursim, 247–251
Interference theory, 106
Isomorphism, 267, 271

Jung's Psychology, criticism of, 319

Language acquisition device (LAD)., 407
Last response, principle of, 217
Learning, laws of, 178–179
Leipzig laboratory, work of, 97
Libido, 297
Life-space, 344–345

Marxist Psychology, 452
Mainstream Psychology, 460
Maintenance variables, 241
Mass action, principle of, 211
Meaning :
theory of, 36
Mental Act, 102
Mental Chemistry, 46, 171
Mental chronometry, 74
Mental mechanics, 172
Metaphysical position, 20
Methods of breaking habits,219
Mind-body problems, 8, 31, 97, 121, 154, 199, 277, 294
Modelling, 253–254
Modern Psychology :
father of, 27
Molar analysis, 10
Molecular analysis, 10
Monadology, 29
Monism, 31
Motor conditioning, 176

Nativism, 9, 51–55
Naturalism, 16
Nervous circle, 66–67
Neurotic needs, 322
Neurotic trends, 322
New mentalism, 410
New structuralism, 399

Object constancy, 270
Objective Psychology, 452
Objectivism, 11
Organ inferiority, 308

Parallelism, 30
Part-whole psychology, 268
Perceptual organization, principles of 268–270
Personal equation, 73–74
Phi-phenomenon, 263, 271
Phrenology, 69
Pluridisciplinary research, 462
Pragmatism, 129
Primary memory, 134
Probablistic Functionalism, 354–357
Psychoanalysis :
    antecedents forces of, 288
Psychological doubleaspectism, 31
Psychological objectivism, 189
Psychophysical methods, 63, 141
Psychosexual development, stages of, 300–302
Purposive behaviourism, 239–246

Reaction time, 74, 140
Reflex action, 72–73
Reflexology, 452

School :
    meaning of , 2
    of psychology, 2–4
Saving method, 172
Schedule of reinforcement, 231
Secondary Memory, 134
Self, 133, 375
Self-actualization, 380
Self-esteem, 380
Self-observation, 95
Self-produced reinforcement, 254
Self-system, 329
Shaping, 233
Single-trial learning, 216–17
Social interest, 309
Space perception :
    theory of, 35–36
Stimulus error, 118
Stimulus-response connection, 177–78
Stream of consciousness, 134–136
Striving for superiority, 309
Structural model, 295–297
Structural Psychology, 115
Structuralism :
    criticisms of, 122
    fate of, 125
    subject-matter of, 116
Style of life, 310
Subjective idealism, 35
Subjectivism, 11
Sullivan's Developmental stages, 329–332
Superstitious beahviour, 233
System :
    criteria for evaluation, 7–9
    function of, 6–7
    meaning of, 1–2

Tabula rasa, 33, 180
Teleology, 12
Theory :
    meaning of, 4
    prerequisites of, 4–5
Topographical structure, 294–295
Transdisciplinary research, 462, 463
Transposition, 273
Tridimensional theory, 94
Tropism, 241
Two-point threshold, 60
Type R conditioning, 229–30
Type S conditioning, 229–30

Unconscious inference, 78–79

Vector Psychology, 397
Verbal report, method of, 137
Vicarious reinforcement, 254

Watson's environmentalism, 201–202
Weber's law, 61
Will :
    doctrine of, 49
Word associations, 99, 111
Wundt's systematic Psychology, 93
Wurzburg School, 106

Zeigarnik effect, 349